Connie L. Kaplan
146 W. 28th
NYC 10001

Clinical Psychopathology

The Psychiatric Foundations of Medicine

GEORGE U. BALIS, M.D.
Editor in Chief

LEON WURMSER, M.D.
ELLEN McDANIEL, M.D.
Editors

ROBERT G. GRENELL, Ph.D.
Consulting Editor

BUTTERWORTH PUBLISHERS INC.
Boston   London

THE BUTTERWORTH GROUP

United States
   Butterworth (Publishers) Inc.
   19 Cummings Park
   Woburn, MA 01801

England
   Butterworth & Co.
   (Publishers) Ltd.
   88 Kingsway
   London WC2B 6AB

Australia
   Butterworth Pty Ltd.
   586 Pacific Highway
   Chatswood, NSW 2067

Canada
   Butterworth & Co. (Canada) Ltd.
   2265 Midland Avenue
   Scarborough, Ontario M1P 4S1

New Zealand
   T & W Young Building
   77–85 Customhouse Quay
   CPO Box 472
   Wellington 1

South Africa
   Butterworth & Co. (South Africa)
      (Pty) Ltd.
   152–154 Gale Street
   Durban

Cataloging in Publication Data:

Library of Congress Cataloging in Publication Data
Main entry under title:

Clinical psychopathology.

   (The Psychiatric foundations of medicine ; v. 4)
   Includes bibliographies and index.
   1. Psychology, Pathological--Addresses, essays,
lectures. I. Balis, George U. II. Series.
RC458.C52   616.8'9'07   78-14417
ISBN 0-409-95100-5

Contributors

Mary Joan Albright, Ph.D.
Assistant Professor
Institute of Psychiatry and Human
    Behavior
University of Maryland
    Medical School
Baltimore, Maryland

José D. Arana, M.D.
Clinical Associate Professor
Institute of Psychiatry and Human
    Behavior
University of Maryland
Medical School
Baltimore, Maryland

George U. Balis, M.D.
Professor of Psychiatry
Director
Undergraduate Psychiatric Education
Institute of Psychiatry and Human
    Behavior
University of Maryland
Medical School
Baltimore, Maryland

Willem G. A. Bosma, M.D.
Associate Professor of Psychiatry
Director

Alcohol and Drug Abuse Program
Institute of Psychiatry and Human
    Behavior
University of Maryland
Medical School
Baltimore, Maryland

Gerald L. Brown, M.D.
Medical Officer
Adult Psychiatry Branch
National Institute of Mental Health
National Institutes of Health
Bethesda, Maryland

William E. Bunney, Jr., M.D.
Chief
Adult Psychiatry Branch
National Institute of Mental Health
National Institutes of Health
Bethesda, Maryland

Lloyd Eckhardt, M.D.
Assistant Professor
Department of Psychiatry
University of Colorado
Medical School
Denver, Colorado

Daniel J. Freedenburg III, M.D.
Assistant Professor

Institute of Psychiatry and Human
    Behavior
University of Maryland
Medical School
Baltimore, Maryland

George E. Gallahorn, M.D.
Clinical Associate Professor
Clinical Director
Walter P. Carter Center
Institute of Psychiatry and Human
    Behavior
University of Maryland
Medical School
Baltimore, Maryland

Kurt Glaser, M.D.
Associate Professor
Department of Psychiatry
Department of Pediatrics
University of Maryland
Medical School
Baltimore, Maryland

Ghislaine D. Godenne, M.D.
Professor of Psychology
Associate Professor of Psychiatry
Associate Professor of Pediatrics
Johns Hopkins University
Clinical Associate Professor
Institute of Psychiatry and Human
    Behavior
University of Maryland
Medical School
Baltimore, Maryland

Robert Goshen, M.D.
Clinical Assistant Professor
Institute of Psychiatry and Human
    Behavior
University of Maryland
Medical School
Baltimore, Maryland

Virginia Huffer, M.D.
Professor of Psychiatry
Director
Liaison Service

Institute of Psychiatry and Human
    Behavior
University of Maryland
Medical School
Baltimore, Maryland

Eleanor M. Jantz, Ph.D.
Assistant Professor
Institute of Psychiatry and Human
    Behavior
University of Maryland
Medical School
Baltimore, Maryland

Andreas Laddis, M.D.
Madison, Wisconsin

John R. Lion, M.D.
Professor of Psychiatry
Director, Violence Clinic
Institute of Psychiatry and Human
    Behavior
University of Maryland
Medical School
Baltimore, Maryland

Ellen McDaniel, M.D.
Associate Professor of Psychiatry
Director
Adult Ambulatory Services
Institute of Psychiatry and Human
    Behavior
University of Maryland
Medical School
Baltimore, Maryland

Manoel W. Penna, M.D.
Assistant Professor of Psychiatry
Institute of Psychiatry and Human
    Behavior
University of Maryland
Medical School
Baltimore, Maryland

Dane Prugh, M.D.
Professor
Child Psychiatry
University of Colorado

School of Medicine
Denver, Colorado

Anne C. Redmond, M.D.
Assistant Professor of Psychiatry
Director
Brief Psychotherapy Clinic
Institute of Psychiatry and Human
   Behavior
University of Maryland
Medical School
Baltimore, Maryland

Constantine J. Sakles, M.D.
Associate Professor of Psychiatry
Director, Adult Inpatient Services
Institute of Psychiatry and Human
   Behavior
University of Maryland
Medical School
Baltimore, Maryland

Jon A. Shaw, M.D., LTC, MC
Chief
Child and Adolescent Service
Walter Reed Army Medical Center
Washington, D.C.

Bernard Shochet, M.D.
Associate Professor
Institute of Psychiatry and Human
   Behavior
University of Maryland
Medical School
Baltimore, Maryland

Ülku Ülgür, M.D.
Clinical Assistant Professor
Division of Child and Adolescent
   Psychiatry
Institute of Psychiatry and Human
   Behavior
University of Maryland
Medical School
Baltimore, Maryland

Leon Wurmser, M.D.
Professor of Psychiatry
Director
Alcoholism and Drug Abuse Program
University of Maryland
Medical School
Baltimore, Maryland

Contents

Preface

The Psychiatric Foundations of Medicine is a modern textbook of psychiatry written specifically for medical students and physicians. In its comprehensive scope, it contains the contributions of all the disciplines that are relevant to the behavioral, psychological, social, and humanistic aspects of medicine, as well as the contributions of clinical psychiatry that constitute an integral part of the healing art and science of medicine.

The necessity for creating this textbook emerged from our recognition of the lack of a comprehensive textbook of psychiatry that is exclusively oriented toward meeting the educational needs of medical students and the continuing educational requirements of physicians. In spite of the plethora of established as well as newly introduced textbooks of psychiatry, there is no such book that meets these demands. This awareness if based on our extensive experience in the field of undergraduate psychiatric education and is shared by many of our colleagues in other medical schools of this country.

Psychiatric education in the medical schools of this country is in the midst of rapid change, which represents not only intrinsic adaptations of medical education to new developments in the field of psychiatry but also outside influences of emergent social conditions and government policies. In searching for a definition of the educational emphasis and scope in our changing psychiatric curricula, we are experiencing a compelling need for anticipating the future in a precipitiously evolving field that offers few constancies as directional guidelines. In formulating educational goals, departments of psychiatry are influenced by the changing milieu of medical education, the emerging new societal demands of health care services, and the challenge of the unmet needs in medicine. Thus, the pressing community expectations for community-oriented systems of continuous and comprehensive health care and for new roles and patterns of medical practice have necessitated drastic reorganization of medical curricula. Furthermore, with the ever-expanding boundaries of the field of psychiatry and the recent progress in the behavioral and social sciences, medical educators are becoming increasingly aware of the need for adjusting the medical curriculum to current and anticipated shifts in orientation. Contributions of the behavioral and social sciences and clinical psychiatry relevant to the practice of medicine must be appraised and communicated in the curricula.

It is the general consensus among medical educators in the United States that the overall goal of undergraduate psychiatric education is to assist students in developing an understanding of and an appreciation for the application of behavioral and psychiatric principles in patient care and health maintenance. More specifically, the curriculum aims to assist the student to (1) acquire a foundation of knowledge regarding the psychological, sociological, and humanistic aspects of the practice of medicine based on the study of the behavioral and social sciences and clinical psychiatry; (2) master basic interpersonal skills relevant to the management and treatment of patients with medical or emotional illness, or both; (3) emulate attitudes and values which enhance the professional roles and practices that physicians have toward their patients and their community. These goals have served as the general guidelines in determining the scope and depth of this textbook.

The basic philosophies and organizing principles for this textbook reflect the current trends in medical education and the recent developments in the field of psychiatry, with an emphasis on the emerging themes that characterize the evolving status of the practice of medicine in this country. However, the major principles for organizing its content defines a comprehensive scope of subject matter, as determined by the recommendations of the American National Board of Medical Examiners, the trends in the curricular reorganization of our medical schools, and the prevailing philosophies of American medical educators. Drawing from our experience in developing a model behavioral-social science and psychiatry undergraduate program at the University of Maryland Medical School, we have been particularly influenced by the philosophy that medical students should be able to receive a preparation in this field as thorough as that which they receive in other major medical disciplines. However, the thoroughness of this preparation does not imply the training of a minispecialist in psychiatry but the broad education of a physician in a field that permeates every aspect of medical practice. In this regard, we have attempted to construct an educational series that allows the student to grow intellectually and professionally through critical understanding and scientific insight rather than through the acquisition of technical knowledge of facts and theories.

We have further followed an unfolding sequence of organization, which is unique for a textbook of psychiatry, and which parallels the progression of a standard medical curriculum in behavioral-social science and psychiatry. We have included numerous topics and issues, which to our knowledge have never appeared in a textbook of psychiatry, in an effort to emphasize aspects of the field relevant to the practice of the non-psychiatrist physician—aspects significant to a holistic view of man* in health and illness. In view of the great diversity and fluidity of theories in this field, we have been guided by a pluralistic approach that tends to emphasize common grounds and unifying principles without neglecting to give adequate representation to the contributions of every major discipline and school of thought. Special effort was made to choose topics that cut across disciplines or particular theories in order to present a comprehensive, integrated, multidisciplinary, and holistic view of human behavior.

The textbook has been organized into six volumes in an evolving sequence, fitting the structural development of a standard curriculum. Each volume presents a progression of concepts that will enable the student to develop the various components of competence as he progresses in medical school through an exposure to unfolding intellectual stimulations, clinical experiences, and appropriate contexts of professional socialization.

Volume 1, *Dimensions of Behavior*, provides the general background of the field and lays the foundations of the origins of behavior. The volume is divided into six parts. Parts I and II are introductory and present the historical development of psychological thinking in medicine and the evolving status of psychiatry in the contemporary scene, with an emphasis on the need for a new medical model. They further attempt to sketch a general conceptualization of human behavior that transcends the disciplinary boundaries of biological and psychosocial sciences, through an introduction into the philosophical and epistemological approaches to studying man and his behavior. By including an introduction into the general systems theory of biosystems, it is hoped that the student interested in the holistic understanding of man will recognize and appreciate the usefulness of a unifying paradigm that bridges the fragmented conceptualization of the multidimensional phenomena that pertain to the

---

* As a convenience of style we use the word man and the term mankind, as well as the pronoun he, to refer to human beings without distinction to gender.

life sciences. Part III deals with the longitudinal dimension of the evolutionary organization of behavior, including the phylogenetic organization of the central nervous system, the adaptation and evolution of behavior, as well as extrapolations from ethological and laboratory animal studies relevant to the understanding of human behavior. Parts IV through VI deal with the longitudinal dimension of the developmental organization of behavior. After the presentation of the biological foundations of development, including the ontogenesis of the central nervous system and the genetic determinants of behavior, part V reviews the various theories of personality development, including cognitive, motivational, psychoanalytic, and psychosocial theories. Part VI presents the developmental stages of man, from infancy to adulthood.

Volume 2, *The Behavioral and Social Sciences and the Practice of Medicine,* consists of seven parts. Parts I and II deal with the cross-sectional dimensions of the infraorganismic, organismic, and supraorganismic organization of behavior, which constitute the scope of the behavioral and social sciences. Included are the biological substrates of behavior, emotions, cognitive functions, and psychodynamic views of personality, as well as communicational, interpersonal, social, and cultural aspects of behaviors, including family and social organizations. A general systems theory approach to understanding behavior is given as a means of providing a measure of unification of these diverse disciplinary fields. Parts III through VII present the contributions of behavioral and social science to the practice of medicine. Part III deals with the various facets of the doctor-patient relationship, with special emphasis on the contractual, psychodynamic, interpersonal, and placebogenic aspects of this interaction. Part IV focuses on patient interviewing, and includes a review of research in this area, as well as basic principles of medical and psychiatric interviewing. Part V presents issues concerning patient care within the context of social institutions, governmental policies and regulations, and other social aspects of the organization and delivery of health services, with an emphasis on meeting mental health needs. Part VI deals with aspects of the physician in relation to society, with a focus on values and ethics in medicine, professional accountability and peer review, and the emotional health of physicians and medical students. Finally, Part VII deals with general topics on the psychology of women, psychohistory, and creativity.

Volume 3, *Basic Psychopathology,* introduces the student into the area of the abnormal biology of behavior, at the level of the fundamental concepts of mental illness and deviancy, experimental psychopathology, various pathogenetic mechanisms, basic phenomenology, and organizing principles of psychiatric nosology. Specifically, after an introduction to the range of normality and pathology and conceptual models of disordered behavior, Part II focuses on experimental psychopathology, including maternal deprivation and other developmental deprivation studies, drug-induced model psychoses, and animal models of addictive behavior. Parts III and IV present the pathogenesis of disordered behavior, including genetic, neurochemical, neuropathological, and psychophysiological mechanisms, as well as psychodynamic, sociocultural, and communicational determinants of the pathogenesis of the various types of psychopathology. Part V deals with the community aspects of psychopathology, including topics related to psychiatric epidemiology, preventive psychiatry, social and community psychiatry, and forensic psychiatry. Part VI discusses the phenomenology and taxonomy of psychopathology, including the phenomenology of disordered behavior, symptoms and syndromes of disordered behavior, and a discussion of nomenclature in psychiatry.

Volume 4, *Clinical Psychopathology*, deals with the various nosological categories of adult and child psychiatry. In organizing this volume on psychiatric nosology, we followed the *Standard Nomenclature* of the *Diagnostic and Statistical Manual-II (DSM-II)*, which currently represents the accepted system of the American Psychiatric Association. In anticipation, however, of *DSM-III*, which is presently undergoing field tests in this country, we have attempted to incorporate elements of this new nosological system into the discussion of the various psychiatric disorders.

Volume 4 is organized into six parts. Part I includes chapters on behavior disorders associated with epilepsy, acute brain syndromes, chronic brain syndromes, and mental retardation; part II, the psychotic disorders, including schizophrenic psychosis, paranoid psychoses, and affective psychoses; part III, the various psychoneurotic disorders; part IV, personality disorders and addictive disorders; part V, psychophysiological disorders, sexual dysfunctions, sexual disorders, and stress-related disturbances; and part VI, the psychiatric disorders of childhood and adolescence.

Volume 5, *Psychiatric Clinical Skills in Medical Practice*, includes the major diagnostic and treatment approaches of psychiatry and related disciplines, with an emphasis on those methods which can be mastered to some degree by nonpsychiatric physicians. Thus, students are provided with enough information to understand and appreciate the specialized diagnostic and therapeutic procedures of psychiatry and with details of these methods which are relevant to medical practitioners in enhancing their competence. Part I deals with basic diagnostic approaches, including mental status examination, differential diagnosis, psychodynamic formulation, and prognostication of psychiatric disorders. Part II is devoted to special diagnostic methods: psychological testing, assessment of family and social milieu, and laboratory diagnostic procedures. Part III deals with the various specialized treatment methods, including pharmacotherapy, somatic therapies, psychotherapies, (individual, group, and family), behavior modification and aversive therapies, and hospital and milieu therapy. Part IV deals with selected therapeutic approaches relevant to medical practice, e.g., use of psychotropic drugs in medical practice, the drug management of childhood and adolescent psychiatric disorders, crisis intervention and supportive techniques in patient management, brief psychotherapy in medical practice, child psychotherapy, the use of hypnosis in medical practice, social work counseling in medical practice, as well as the role and utilization of psychiatric consultant, clinical psychologist, and social worker.

Volume 6, *Psychiatric Problems in Medical Practice*, encompasses selected psychiatric aspects of medical practice, with the inclusion of parts dealing with (a) diagnostic problems of special interest to the physician, e.g., the nature of pain — psychogenic pain, episodic behavior disorders, traumatic neurosis, severe psychic trauma, and psychogenic death, eating disturbances, disturbances of sleep and wakefulness, and postpartum reactions; (2) clinical problems of medical practice requiring special management, e.g., management of issues of normal sexuality, management of the hospitalized patient, the dying patient and his family, the suicidal patient, the violent patient, the chronically ill patient, the geriatric patient, and the alcoholic patient and his family; and (3) clinical areas of child psychiatry of special interest to the pediatrician, family practitioner, and generalist physician, e.g., psychiatric evaluation of the child, common problems of the preschool-age and school-age child, hyperkinetic child, diagnosis and management of the battered child and his family, management of the mentally retarded child and his family, management of the handicapped child, problems and management of the hospitalized child, and child advocacy.

From the point of view of a standard medical curriculum, the first two volumes cover subject matter taught in the first year of medical school; the third and fourth volumes match the scope of the second year curriculum; and the fifth and sixth volumes are designed to meet the requirements of the clinical years of medical education that include the psychiatric clerkship and clinical electives, with an emphasis on the psychiatric aspects of medical practice.

The textbook is multi-authored, along the tradition of many other classical textbooks in medicine. This was felt to be the only approach for the writing of a textbook of the scope and authoritativeness envisioned by the editors. The majority of contributors are members of the faculty of the Institute of Psychiatry and Human Behavior of the University of Maryland Medical School. All of them are actively involved in teaching medical students and residents and are acknowledged experts in their fields. A significant portion of the chapters has been contributed by members of the faculty of other departments and schools of the University of Maryland. Finally, for selected chapters we have sought out contributions from other authors in various educational institutions of this country.

We believe that this work will prove useful to medical students and physicians, as well as other students interested in the study of behavioral and social science and psychiatry.

A successful textbook is viewed as an evolving product that has the potential to improve its shortcomings. In this regard, the appraisal of this work by our colleagues will be most valuable to us.

We wish to express our gratitude to all the authors who have contributed to this textbook. Their enthusiastic response has been an invaluable source of support and encouragement to us during the four years of editorial effort.

We are indebted to many of our colleagues for their support, and wish especially to express our gratitude to Dr. James Mackie for his invaluable editorial assistance in this undertaking. Our thanks are also due to Ms. Joyce Taylor and her staff for their editorial help in seeing the book through press.

We wish to express our gratitude to Mrs. Betty Sima for her managerial and coordinating work and for her immense patience in bearing with us during the many changes and revisions.

We would also like to express our appreciation to the staff of our publishers, Butterworth Publishers Inc. for their cooperation and assistance.

G. U. Balis, M. D.
Editor in Chief

Introduction

Clinical psychopathology involves the study, diagnosis, treatment, and prevention of the various nosological categories of adult and child psychiatry. It represents the central focus of clinical psychiatry, which is one of the medical specialties. On the other hand, basic psychopathology involves a cross-sectional approach to the study of the phenomena and underlying mechanisms of psychopathology in general. It encompasses many basic disciplines, including biological, behavioral, and social sciences.

Clinical psychopathology is founded on a taxonomic system of nosology that categorizes pathology into clinical entities, described as syndromes and diseases. These categories have characteristic sets of signs and symptoms and predictable course, but with unknown, presumed, and in some instances known etiology and pathogenesis. Some of them represent operational definitions of pathology, based on pragmatic grounds rather than on clinical or scientific evidence.

These various diagnostic categories are classified into larger groups on the basis of criteria which are generally descriptive, with the exception of organic brain syndromes of known etiology. They include the following major categories: organic brain syndromes, psychoses, neuroses, adjustment reactions, personality disorders, and psychophysiological disorders. None of these groupings are clearly differentiated from each other, with borderlands existing not only between schizophrenia and neuroses and between affective psychoses and neuroses but also between personality disorders and other major groups. In the light of accumulating evidence, affective disorders (traditionally subsumed under psychoses and neuroses) are emerging as a separate group of major clinical significance. Behavior disorders associated with substance abuse are also receiving increasing attention and recognition, although there is still much controversy about psychiatry's role in these types of pathology.

The psychiatric system of nosology in this country — the *Diagnostic and Statistical Manual II* (DSM-II) — is currently in the process of change, following in parallel the concurrent revision of the International Diagnostic System 8 (IDS-8). The organizational design of this volume is essentially based on the Standard Nomenclature of the DSM II, which will continue to represent the accepted system of the American Psychiatric Association until the year 1980. In anticipation, however, of the DSM-III, which is presently undergoing field tests and further revisions before its final approval, an effort was made to present elements of this new system wherever it appeared to be appropriate.

It is well documented that a large number of patients with psychiatric disorders — predominantly neurotic, psychophysiological, and affective disorders — are seen in the daily practice of physicians not specialized in psychiatry. An adequate knowledge of these disorders is as much part of the required background in medical practice as the major somatic disciplines. In particular, primary care physicians turn more and more toward acquiring the necessary skills for the diagnosis and management of such patients, including the attainment of a modicum of psychotherapeutic expertise.

The purpose of this volume is not to provide the reader with detailed and comprehensive textbook knowledge of clinical psychiatry, but to emphasize those aspects which are most relevant to general medical practice.

Part I includes chapters dealing with behavior disorders associated with epilepsy, acute brain syndromes, chronic brain syndromes, and mental retardation. Clearly the diagnosis and management of organic psychopathology are of major importance to all physicians.

Part II deals with psychotic disorders, including chapters on schizophrenic psychosis, paranoid psychoses, and affective psychoses. In the light of the impact of psychopharmacology on the treatment of psychoses, the growing relevance of heredity, and the recent neurobiological findings associated with these disorders, it has become more and more likely that biological factors represent the major cause of these psychoses.

Part III includes chapters dealing with the psychoneurotic disorders. For the explanation of these disorders, the concept of inner conflict has, since Freud's discoveries, become pivotal. Symptoms are viewed as representing a compromise solution between wish and repudiation (drive and defense).

Part IV includes personality disorders and addictive disorders. Personality disorders represent a field which is particularly in flux and is characterized by more controversy than solid knowledge. There has recently been an enormous upsurge of interest in borderline and narcissistic psychopathology. It appears, though, that much well established knowledge is submerged under this vogue. Real gains concern the detailed study of narcissism as part of everyone's psychodynamics and especially of all psychopathology. Disorders associated with substance abuse have become the focus of intensive investigation and represent a major concern in contemporary medicine.

Part V includes chapters on psychophysiological disorders, sexual dysfunctions, sexual disorders, and stress-related disturbances. These areas are of major relevance to medical practice.

Finally, part VI contains seven chapters dealing with the psychiatric disorders of childhood and adolescence. The interaction between ongoing development and pathogenic impact of various noxae (psychogenic, social, and somatogenic) brings about an often rapidly changing and atypical picture of psychopathology, if compared with that in adults.

It is good to keep in mind that not all inner suffering is pathological, but that psychic pain and anguish are major motives for the never ending process of emotional maturation, as stressed by the Greek tragedians. In particular Aeschylus reiterated: "Through suffering insight." Given psychotherapeutic and social support, this maxim even holds true for neurotic and psychotic terror and grief.

G. U. Balis, M.D.
L. Wurmser, M.D.
E. McDaniel, M.D.

I
Organic Psychiatric Disorders

1

Behavior Disorders Associated with Epilepsy

George U. Balis, M.D.

Epilepsy represents a category of disorders that stands at the borderline between neurology and psychiatry. The study of the phenomenology and pathogenesis of these disorders offers a unique opportunity to understand psychopathology from a holistic point of view that allows the integration of the dichotomous aspects of mind and body. The rich psychopathology that characterizes the clinical picture of epileptic disorders encompasses the full range of psychiatric disorders and needs to be understood in both neurophysiologic and psychodynamic terms in order to diagnose it correctly and provide the patient with proper management.

Epileptic disorders represent basically psychopathological phenomena, manifested as disturbances involving some aspect of behavior and conscious experience or both. Therefore, the commonly used reference psychic aspects of epileptic seizures is inappropriate and tends to perpetuate the mind-body dichotomy in medical thinking.

It is common to divide the various psychopathological manifestations of epilepsy into ictal, postictal, and interictal, a distinction which lacks internal consistency and which is often based on inadequate differentiating criteria. While the term *ictal* defines a set of phenomena on the basis of pathogenetic mechanisms, the terms *postictal* and *interictal* define a set of phenomena on the basis of their temporal sequence in relation to the ictal phenomena. The term ictal refers to those disturbances which are associated with excessive and uncontrollable neuronal discharges and which are commonly described as epileptic or seizural. The term fails to take into consideration the contribution of psychological mechanisms to the development of the ictus, especially with regard to its precipitation and psychological elaboration.

On the other hand, the term *postictal* describes those phenomena which follow immediately after the cessation of an ictal episode and represent the consequence of the electrical storm that occurred in the brain during the seizure. The diagnosis of the postictal character of these disturbances may often be missed, either because one failed to witness the preceding seizural episode or because the seizure was not typical enough in order to be correctly diagnosed. It is often difficult to differentiate postictal pathology (i.e., postconvulsive twilight states) from certain ictal episodes of temporal lobe epilepsy (i.e., ictal twilight states). Postictal episodes may also be misdiagnosed as being of ictal or psychogenic (functional) etiology.

Also, the term *interictal* is vague, and at times misleading. It literally means everything that may occur in between ictal episodes. The time span defined by the term is usually so long and the phenomena that may occur during it are so diverse that the term has limited usefulness for the clinician. This term also presupposes the establishment of a diagnosis of ictal episodes as points of reference that delimit the range of interictal disturbances, which are considered, by definition, as nonictal. In many instances involving complex behavioral seizures, however, these reference points cannot be easily established. Furthermore, the term fails to define the nature of the phenomena that belong to this category; it only presupposes that all interictal disturbances are nonepileptic (nonictal). However, even this criterion requires a diagnostic effectiveness, which has been proven, in clinical practice, to be unattainable. For example, there are various episodic behavioral disturbances which, although generally considered as nonictal, may indeed have an ictal origin.

It becomes apparent that, in any discussion of these disorders, it is necessary that one view their phenomenology as being part of what would be appropriate to call a spectrum of neuropsychological dysfunction, which is due to several underlying pathogenetic mechanisms.

From a clinical point of view epileptic manifestations in the form of a seizural episode represent only part of the total range of the clinical expression of the spectrum and are singled out because of their dramatic character and their disruptive effect on the ongoing life experience of the patient. For example, in the case of focal epilepsy, such as temporal lobe seizures (i.e., psychomotor attacks), the seizural episode constitutes only a component of the total clinical picture of the disorder. During the interictal period the patient may demonstrate various other disturbances or deficits resulting from the presence of either the structural lesion in the temporal lobe (organic) or from the patient's psychological response to the disease (psychogenic) and, in some instances, from subictal discharges that fail to develop into a typical seizure (epileptic). Thus, the patient may show distractibility, limited attention span, irritability, deficit in the retention of recent memories, explosive aggressiveness, hyposexuality, obsessional or paranoid personality traits, and, in some cases, florid psychosis, personality deterioration, and dementia. Most of these so-called interictal manifestations lack the paroxysmal character of the seizural episode.

From a pathogenetic point of view the underlying mechanisms that are responsible for the diverse manifestations of this spectrum can be differentiated into (1) ictal, (2) organic, and (3) psychogenic.

1. *The ictal mechanisms* involve massive uncontrollable electrical discharges at the neuronal level and are responsible for the seizural episode. The reversible nature of both the epileptic attack (ictus) and its underlying pathophysiological process points to the fact that the seizural episode represents an actue brain syndrome. Even in the case of focal epilepsy in which there is localized irreversible tissue damage (i.e., scar), the pathophysiological process of uncontrollable neuronal discharges is "triggered" but not caused by the focal lesion.

2. *The organic mechanisms* involve the presence of reversible or irreversible damage of the neuronal tissue and are primarily responsible for some of the interictal manifestations of epilepsy, especially of the so-called focal or acquired epilepsies. It is possible to classify the various interictal disturbances associated with the organic mechanisms as follows: *elliptic disturbances*, which are due to permanent loss or impairment of a central nervous system function secondary to an irreversible destruction of cortical neuronal elements (i.e., memory impairment in a chronic brain syndrome accompanied by seizural disorders); *ecliptic disturbances*, due to a temporary loss or impairment of a function secondary to reversible neuronal damage (i.e., clouding of consciousness in an acute brain syndrome associated with convulsive disorders); *release disturbances*, due to disinhibition of more primitive functions subserved by subordinate subcortical areas following the destruction of an inhibitory circuit (i.e., elicitation of Babinski reflex); and *compensatory disturbances*, due to the taking over of a lost function by another area of the brain and resulting in a modified or less effective function (i.e., the assumption of certain functions by the nondominant hemisphere following damage to the dominant one).

3. *The psychogenic mechanisms* represent the patient's psychological responses (defensive-adaptive processes) to the impairment or loss or

modification of a particular central nervous system (CNS) function in his effort for reparative adaptation (i.e., "organic orderliness," restriction of environmental situations that might provoke a catastrophic reaction, and so forth). They are primarily responsible for certain interictal manifestations of epilepsy, and especially those pertaining to the so-called epileptic personality. It should be noted, however, that the various psychopathological manifestations of the spectrum of neuropsychological dysfunction are generally determined by more than one of the above-mentioned pathogenetic mechanisms. As a matter of fact, in many instances all three mechanisms may be contributing, to a variable degree, to the psychopathology of the various disturbances that characterize the ictal, postictal, and interictal periods in the life of the epileptic patient.

The following discussion deals with the various behavioral disorders associated with epilepsy, with an emphasis on the psychosocial and psychodynamic contributions to the psychopathology of these disorders.

ICTAL PSYCHOPATHOLOGY

Phenomenology of Seizures

The ictal psychopathology, which is the result of uncontrollable electrical neuronal discharges, represents diagnostically the most characteristic symptomatology of the epileptic state in its manifestations as a seizural episode.

Phenomenologically, the seizural episode is a circumscribed event or a series of events with a more or less stereotyped profile and limited variability, and it consists of a characteristic sequence of behaviors which are delimited by a precipitous onset and outset. In general, these paroxysmal behavioral events occur spontaneously or without significant environmental interaction. They lack adaptive value and goal-directedness and are beyond volitional (conscious) control or unconscious motivating processes. They are recurrent and self-limiting, representing parenthetical events in the life flow of the individual. The behavioral manifestations that characterize the seizure consist of a broad range of phenomena, including simple motoric disturbances (i.e., convulsions or jerky movements) or more integrated behavioral events of variable complexity (i.e., psychomotor automatisms, twilight states); alterations in conscious awareness, perceptual, affective, and cognitive experiences; and autonomic manifestations.

Electroencephalographically, the most common feature during a seizure is greatly increased voltage, or hypersynchrony, which is thought to be due to the progressive recruitment of massive dendritic potentials.

The polymorphism that characterizes seizural phenomena makes it very difficult to classify them into a coherent system of taxonomy. From a descriptive point of view seizures have been distinguished into several symptom-complexes (syndromes) including grand mal (major seizures), petit mal (minor seizures), psychomotor seizures, myoclonic seizures, partial seizures (motor, sensory), and other less common forms.

The most significant unifying characteristic of all the seizural syndromes is the observation that they represent a paroxysmal and transitory disturbance which develops and ceases precipitously and exhibits a conspicuous tendency to recurrence. It appears that the sine qua non characteristic of seizural phenomena is their paroxysmal occurrence, a term that refers to the time gradient of abrupt onset and termination. The duration of the episode, although a less critical variable, is also a significant criterion. The usual duration ranges from a few seconds to several minutes, but in some seizural syndromes (i.e., twilight psychomotor attacks) it may extend into hours and rarely, days or weeks.

Another characteristic of the seizural symptom-complex is its tendency to recurrence, a fact which suggests the presence of an underlying off-and-on mechanism. It appears that this mechanism's off-and-on pattern is determined not only by the intrinsic nature of the pathophysiological process of ictal discharges but also by various other conditions, both physiological and psychological.

Most clinicians emphasize the impairment or complete obliteration of conscious awareness during the episode — and the subsequent amnesia of the events surrounding the episode — as one of the most significant, although not pathognomonic, characteristics of the seizure. Alterations of consciousness and dysmnesic symptoms, although very common characteristics of the clinical profile of most epileptic seizures, do not represent a universal concomitant of these phenomena. On the other hand, such changes also occur in nonepileptic syndromes, such as acute brain syndromes (deliria) and hysterical dissociative states, as well as in postictal syndromes. In delirium, which is the commonest clinical expression of acute brain syndromes, the nonepileptic, transient, and episodic phenomena associated with it are usually of relatively slower onset and outset, of longer duration, generally nonrecurrent, and with a characteristic off- and on-pattern of clinical course, described as fluctuating. The electroencephalogram (EEG) usually shows diffusely generalized slow wave activity. [39] The seizural episode represents pathophysiologically a form of acute brain syndrome, expressing transient and reversible pathology of disturbed neuronal activity. In dissociative states, such as fugues, the alterations of consciousness and subsequent amnesia of the episode are psychodynamically motivated, and therefore they can be understood within the context of intrapersonal and interpersonal dynamics. The presence of a normal electroencephalogram will further assist in identifying the nonepileptic nature of these conditions.

Postictal syndromes, although representing sequelae of epileptic seizures, differ clinically and pathophysiologically from the ictal episode. The occurrence of a postictal phase following an epileptic seizure is also used as evidence to demonstrate the epileptic nature of the attack.

The presence of auras (sensory, motor, psychic, autonomic) occurring independently or preceding an ictal episode, further contributes to the diagnostic identification of the ictal nature of an attack. Auras characterize focal epilepsies and have, therefore, considerable localizing value.

The therapeutic response to antiepileptic drugs, on a trial basis, is often used by clinicians as an empirical criterion for the diagnosis of the epileptic nature of atypical syndromes of an episodic character. This inferential criterion has a reasonable degree of diagnostic validity, especially when positive results are obtained, but most importantly, it is of undisputed clinical usefulness. A trial treatment with antiepileptic drugs, however, in order to be of any value, must extend over several weeks with concomitant measurements of serum drug levels and preferably be compared with a placebo trial.

Other clinical criteria indirectly contributing to the diagnosis of the ictal nature of an attack include a history of brain injury, the presence of organic or neurological deficit, and a family history of epilepsy. A history of established or presumptive brain injury (i.e., head trauma with loss of consciousness, anoxia, CNS infections, poisonings, stroke, perinatal pathology, febrile convulsions during childhood, and so forth) would be suggestive of an organic brain syndrome (chronic) which might serve as the triggering cause for focal epileptic seizures. The presence of some central neurological deficit would also be suggestive of an organic (focal or diffuse) form of epilepsy. Nevertheless, the use of the so-called soft neurological signs as a criterion for demonstrating brain injury (organicity) requires a careful evaluation of this presumptive evidence. Organic deficit may exist independently of epilepsy and vice versa. On the other hand, a family history of epilepsy would be suggestive of the presence of a genetically determined epileptic predisposition (or diathesis), which is contributory not only to the centrencephalic forms of epilepsy (idiopathic, essential) but also to acquired or focal epilepsies. The latter forms may present a combination of heredity and acquisitional factors, in which the additional genetic element has been conceived as "threshold genes" [27–30,136,145–147].

Finally, the absence of psychodynamic factors of conscious (malingering) or unconscious (hysterical) motivation, as well as the ego-dystonic character of the episode, further contribute to the identification of the ictal nature of an attack. Nevertheless, one may also observe psychogenic contributions to the precipitation of seizures.

Electroencephalography represents the most important laboratory method for the diagnosis of epileptic disorders [66,79–81]. However, a normal EEG does not in itself rule out epilepsy. Conversely, an abnormal EEG is not in itself diagnostic of epilepsy, unless it is associated with the clinical manifestations of the disease. In conclusion, it appears that there are no clinical symptoms pathognomonic of epileptic phenomena. Although various forms of epilepsy have discrete profiles, they all share in various combinations the general phenomenological characteristics mentioned in this review.

Psychogenic Contributions to Seizure Precipitation

For purposes of discussion, the emotional precipitation of seizures is distinguished from the motivational precipitation of seizures.

With respect to the emotional precipitation of seizures, it is a well-established observation that various internal and external influences, impinging upon the "steady state" of dynamic fluctuations of excitatory and inhibitory processes of the brain, may serve in epileptic patients as seizure-precipitating factors. Such influences include various drugs (i.e., chlorpromazine, diazepam, tricyclics), changes in the acid-base balance, hypoglycemia, the waking-sleeping (circadian) cycle (i.e., matutinal versus nocturnal seizures), arousal (dyshormia), as well as specific afferent-sensory mechanisms and emotional excitement which may act as triggering factors in eliciting a seizure. The elicitation of seizures by sensory stimuli is commonly referred to as reflex epilepsy and can be associated with visual (photogenic), auditory (audiogenic, musicogenic), olfactory, or cutaneous stimuli. Photogenically induced attacks are the commonest and are usually associated with staring at a flickering light or watching television [23,73,74,120,144,167].

Analogous to reflex epilepsy is the well-documented phenomenon of the psychogenic precipitation of epileptic seizures by various emotions [6,22,138,149,190,199,200,207]. There is evidence suggesting that sensory stimuli, especially visual, are more likely to precipitate in centrencephalic epileptics a generalized grand mal or petit mal seizure (photosensitive epileptics). On the other hand, temporal lobe psychomotor epileptics are more likely to experience a seizure in response to auditory stimuli and to the arousal of emotions [31,87,149,177,207,231].

In a systematic study of various precipitants of epileptic attacks, Servit and associates [190] concluded that conflicting situations or emotions appear to be by far the most important factors, operating in about one-quarter of the patients. Reexperiencing emotionally charged memories appeared to be a frequent factor in triggering seizures. Mignone and associates [149] estimated that 53 percent of their epileptic patients presented evidence of an emotional precipitation of seizures. Similarly, Small and associates [200] in a study involving forty-four epileptics, found 27 percent of them showing activation of the EEG during psychogenic stress. This emotional activation of seizure discharges was reported to be significantly associated with focal epilepsy and with a psychiatric diagnosis of schizophrenia or schizoid personality disorder. Stressful interviews, designed to provoke various emotional responses (i.e., anger, fear, sorrow, pleasure), were used by Stevens [207] to precipitate epileptiform EEG abnormalities in epileptic patients. Three-quarters of the psychomotor epileptics reacted with abnormal EEG responses, as compared to one-third of the patients with undifferentiated grand mal seizures. Similarly, Barker [6] has presented some data regarding the appearance of bursts of abnormal waves in epileptics under stress, while communicating significant life problems and conflictual thoughts. He concluded that such EEG abnormalities occur with stress-induced disruptions of integrative mechanisms such as problem-solving; these are often preceded by arousal and alerting patterns which indicate sudden intensification of integrative effort. Nonspecific emotional arousal or psychological stress seems to be the most likely factor in this mechanism.

It appears that specific affects (i.e., anger, fear), specific emotional conflicts [87], or specific ideational content (memories, thoughts) may also serve in some cases as seizure-precipitating factors. Epstein [41] suggests that it is when the intrapsychic conflict reaches its highest pitch that seizures occur. In a patient with reflex epilepsy associated with a fetish for safety pins, reported by Mitchell, Falconer, and Hill [156], seizures were specifically triggered whenever the patient looked at a bright, shiny pin. They were accompanied by a pleasurable sensation described as "thought satisfaction" and as "better than intercourse." This patient had a left anterior temporal lobe epileptic focus. An anterior temporal lobectomy on the left side cured both in seizures and the fetishism. Because these episodes seem motivated in character and meaningful, the clinician may be misled to a diagnosis of hysteria or hysteroepilepsy [40,41,58,99,226]. Psychotherapy has been found to be effective in reducing or eliminating uncontrollable seizures in patients who are emotionally disturbed as a result of intrapsychic or interpersonal conflict, by removing emotional factors as triggering circumstances [41].

Motivated behavior as a determinant of the precipitation of seizures is not an uncommon occurrence. Epileptic patients, especially children, after they become cognizant of the phenomenon of reflex epilepsy or psychologically induced seizures, may deliberately induce seizures as a pattern of behavior of adaptive value to them. Self-induced seizures may be associated with various motivational dynamics (conscious or unconscious), which can be classified as follows: effort to obtain relief from mounting tension, irritability, depression, and other prodromal dysphoric feelings preceding a seizure, especially when the seizure is not forthcoming; manipulation of the social environment by exploiting the secondary gains of having a seizure (i.e., attention-seeking, guilt-evoking); means of self-inflicted punishment to alleviate guilt; means of experiencing pleasurable sensations; and consciously or unconsciously motivated obliteration of a painful conscious awareness or threat of awareness of overwhelming anxiety, guilt, or threat of loss of control, in the face of a intrapsychic or interpersonal conflict. In the case of unconsciously motivated seizure induction, loss of painful awareness serves to provide primary gain and assumes the role of a quasi–ego-defense mechanism.

Techniques for self-induced seizures in photogenic epilepsy consist of hand-waving — which is the commonest — staring at the television screen, eye-blinking, or simply looking at a bright light [3,25,180].

In a review of twenty-one patients who induced seizures deliberately, Andermann et al. [3] found that these patients were younger (five to eighteen years) and had difficulties in school and home life. Induction of seizures in these patients persisted in spite of punishment and appeared to be motivated by pleasure-seeking, attention-getting, and evoking guilt in others. Whitty and Oxon [228] explained self-induced seizures on the basis of pleasure linked to a reduction of cortical activity. Another hypothesis was that loss of consciousness might be a biological protection against intense unpleasant stimuli. In two cases, reported by Hutchison [110] self-stimulation was clearly associated with pleasure. Another patient, reported by Ehret and Schneider [38], induced petit mal attacks by moving his finger back and forth in front of the sun in order to obtain sexual arousal and then to masturbate. Clement [25] reported two young women with generalized seizures (centrencephalic) and with a long history of self-induced seizures by staring at illuminated windows or at television screens. Both patients described a vague feeling of inability to resist this compulsion. The seizures were almost always induced in situations of guilt, frustration, or both, and were followed by a feeling of tension-relief associated with an escape from a painful reality. Both showed a narcissistic character disorder with a very low self-esteem and had a family history of major psychiatric disturbance in the mother, as well as disturbed early object relations. Control of unacceptable instinctual urges accomplished through an impaired consciousness, such as is characteristic of petit mal epilepsy, was also exemplified by cases reported by Bartemeir [7] and Barker. [5] It is thought, however, that the precipitation of grand mal seizures serves as the most effective means of relieving the prodromal dysphoria, of manipulating the environment to evoke supportive responses, or of obliterating consciousness in the face of conflictual situations [157].

Vicissitudes of Psychological Processes during Seizures

This section deals with the psychopathology of seizural episodes and describes the defensive, adaptive, motivational, and other behavioral aspects of the ictal episode in terms of the vicissitudes of the psychological processes that result from ictal discharges. The discussion is limited to the centrencephalic and temporal lobe seizures.

CENTRENCEPHALIC SEIZURES

Centrencephalic seizures, also known as idiopathic or common generalized seizures, include the classical petit mal absence, the nonprogressive myoclonus, and the primarily generalized grand mal seizure. Briefly, *classical petit mal* consists of momentary episodes of loss of conscious awareness, during which the patient appears to suddenly interrupt his ongoing activities and to stare (absence). The patient is generally amnesic of the episode; however, some patients may show variable degrees of impairment with regard to awareness, response capacity, and postseizural amnesia of the event. The attack may be accompanied by minor motor phenomena including eye opening, eyelid myoclonus, myoclonus of the face, minor loss of postural tone, and at times, automatic movements involving primarily the perioral area and the hands. The attacks are not preceded by auras and are not followed by postictal confusion. The seizures begin after the third year of life, and characteristically during young age, and are not associated with brain damage or retardation. A large percentage of these children will also exhibit generalized convulsive seizures (grand mal) at some time in life. The so-called akinetic petit mal that was once thought to constitute the concept of the petit mal triad has been reclassified among the petit mal variants, with the designation of Lennox-Gastaut syndrome. The syndrome is due to diffuse brain damage.

The occurrence of petit mal status (or, spike and wave stupor) may be intermittent or continuous, lasting for hours or days; during the episode the patient shows extreme psychomotor retardation, in which he appears to be dull and confused, with variable degrees of awareness.

The *nonprogressive myoclonus,* which may be associated with petit mal, is another variety of idiopathic epilepsy, consisting of bilateral myoclonic movements, single or repetitive, occurring frequently in relation to the drowsy state of approaching sleep, or in relation to arousal from sleep.

The *primarily generalized grand mal seizures* are matutinal in occurrence and consist of tonic-clonic motor manifestations accompanied by loss of consciousness. The seizures are not preceded by an aura. Loss of consciousness is the initial sign; the patient falls on the ground and after a short tonic generalized contraction of muscles, he shows clonic movements involving both upper and lower extremities. During this stage, the patient may lose sphincter control and suffer injuries from tongue biting. The duration of the attack is two to five minutes. This is followed by a variable postictal period, characterized by successive stages of coma, stupor, confusion, and drowsiness or sleep, spanning a total duration of thirty to sixty minutes, from onset to full recovery. There is amnesia of the events surrounding the attack and the earlier stages of the postictal period. These idiopathic grand mal seizures must be differentiated from *secondarily generalized seizures.* The latter are symptomatic to focal epilepsy, tend to have a nocturnal character of occurrence, and to be preceded by an aura; the grand mal simply indicates the generalization of an orginally focal epileptic event.

The most significant aspect of centrencephalic seizures is the obliteration of consciousness (dyssyneidetic disturbances). The dyssyneidetic disturbance of impairment or loss of consciousness, which is associated with centrencephalic seizures, must be differentiated from the dynmnesic disturbance which characterizes the psychomotor temporal lobe seizures. Both conditions are associated with an amnesia of the episode. In the latter condition, however, the patient is capable of experiencing, although he is unable to maintain a mnemonic record of the experience.

It is obvious that in a grand mal seizure, which consists of elementary motoric movements (convulsions) and complete obliteration of the integrative process (eclipse of consciousness), the manifest psychopathology lacks any behavioral or psychological organization, and therefore, it is void of adaptive-defensive functions. The manifestations of the seizure express only a neurological pattern of discharging neurons. In spite of this observation, psychoanalytic theorizing has resulted in the formulation of various psychodynamic interpretations of the motivational and symbolic meaning of the grand mal attack. Freud, in his essay "Dostoevsky and Patricide" [62], has viewed the epileptic attack as expressing a conflict between murderous aggressive criminal impulses on the one hand and attempts to control these impulses through punishment on the other, resulting in sadomasochistic behavior. Most analysts have followed

Freud's formulation. For instance, Berg [12] has viewed the grand mal attack as representing a fusion of murderous rage and guilt. On the other hand, the grand mal seizure was described by Abraham [1] as an extragenital orgasm or orgastic equivalent, following Reich's [179] conception of the convulsion as an orgastic equivalent that satisfied unconscious needs of a predominantly narcissistic character.

Such ludicrous interpretations are widely quoted and go unchallenged. They are based on promiscuous generalizations which attempt to identify psychodynamic meaning in grand mal seizures through an extrapolation from the psychodynamic understanding of interictal psychopathology of individual cases, in which the alleged symbolic meaning of the seizure might have been a post facto elaboration. The patient, however, may view his seizures as a welcome punishment, satisfying his sadomasochistic needs, in the same way that he could view his infliction by any other disease. The organization of the grand mal seizure lacks motivational dynamics, expressing a neuronal pattern of organization at the simplest level. In petit mal absences, the momentary loss of conscious awareness is associated with lack of any drive component, and therefore this seizure is considered to be void of any defensive-adaptive significance. Although the occurrence of grand mal, and to a much lesser extent petit mal, may result in relief of tension from mounting dysphoric feelings or drives, the latter is accomplished through the preempting of the drive at the level of its neurophysiological substrate. Generally, centrencephalic grand mal seizures do not involve the activation of the drive systems (temporolimbic), and therefore, lack motivational aspects. They literally obliterate any form of purposeful behavior or introspected experience through the elimination of consciousness and preemption of drives.

TEMPOROLIMBIC SEIZURES

Seizural episodes associated with ictal discharges within the temporolimbic structures are complex and polymorphous. They are differentiated into auras and psychomotor attacks. *Temporal auras* often precede a psychomotor attack or may occur as isolated symptoms, in which case they are regarded as minor focal seizures. They represent momentary episodes, characterized by perceptual, apperceptive, affective, ideational, or autonomic disturbances, occurring in clear consciousness but with varying capacity for the recall of their content, and perceived by the patient as ego-alien experiences. *Psychomotor attacks* represent extended focal seizures involving wider areas within the circuitry of the temporolimbic system. They generally occur under conditions of altered consciousness of variable severity, resulting in partial or complete amnesia of the events surrounding the seizure. They are distinguished clinically into psychomotor automatisms and twilight states (fugues and furors), both of which may progress into a secondarily generalized seizure (grand mal). *Psychomotor automatisms* last from a few seconds to several minutes, and are characterized by automatic movements, fragments of behavior or more complex behavioral sequences, which appear to be either purposeless (coordinated or uncoordinated) or purposeful (coordinated or uncoordinated) of variable adaptive value and goal-directedness. *Twilight states* represent more complex and florid psychomotor attacks, usually lasting five to ten minutes and in some instances much longer. During the attack, the patient appears to be in a dreamlike state, wandering around aimlessly in a state of altered awareness and impaired cognitive capacity, and with a varying degree of responsiveness to environmental stimuli which is generally inappropriate and maladaptive. Twilight states may be also characterized by psychomotor retardation, episodes of affective excitement, and intense emotional responses (i.e., panic, rage, aggressiveness), or vivid hallucinatory experiences. After recovery, there follows a brief period of postictal confusion or cognitive sluggishness.

Psychomotor seizures frequently incorporate, in varying degrees, elements of consciousness and motivational dynamics, as determined by the activation of primary drives and the emergence of their derivative drives. Although ego and superego operations are largely suspended during the episode, they may still be evident, in varying degrees, as expressed in the use of primitive defenses representing attempts at resolution of conflict in the face of "activated" drives, as well as in the use of behavioral responses of varying complexity representing attempts at adaptation to concurrent environmental contingencies. Therefore, the defensive-adaptive aspects of the seizure, which express rudimentary ego-superego functions, may contribute significantly to the behavioral and psychological patterns of organization of the psychopathology of the seizure. Foster and Liske, commenting on the role of environmental contributions to temporal lobe seizures, concluded: "Environmental clues play a role in the content of psychomotor seizures, in at least some patients. The most important role of environmental clues is the prevention of injury" [58:305]. In a study of two temporal lobe epileptics, treated with psychotherapy, Epstein and Ervin [41] found that the content of psychomotor attacks reflected psychodynamic conflicts and that it changed during the course of psychotherapy. They concluded that seizures were possibly of adaptive value.

The above-described seizural syndromes represent reversible episodes of disordered behavior which involve a complex contribution from both neuropathological and psychopathological processes. Therefore, they must be understood at the psychological as well as the neuronal level of organization of behavior. In spite of our still limited understanding of the functional significance of the temporolimbic systems, there exists sufficient evidence to allow certain generalizations about the major contributions of these systems to the ictal psychopathology of temporal lobe epilepsy and the behavioral disturbances that have been reported to be associated with temporolimbic dysfunction [11,68,71,103,106,159,160,175,218,219,227].

On the basis of available evidence, one can postulate that the temporal lobe (and its connections) is intimately associated with a number of integrative and modulatory functions, which may be classified into the following three major categories: (1) mnemonic functions (ictal disturbances of these functions are described as dysmnesic), (2) perceptive/apperceptive functions (ictal disturbances of these functions are described as oneiroid), (3) Motivational/affective functions (ictal disturbances of these functions are described as dyshormic). Each of these disturbances contributes variably to the clinical syndromes described as temporal auras and psychomotor attacks (automatisms and twilight states).

1. Mnemonic functions and dysmnesic disturbances. There is significant clinical and experimental evidence supporting the observation that structures within the limbic system and their connections forming circuits with other areas of the brain play an important role in the registration (encoding), retention, and retrieval (recall) phases of memory processes, More specifically, the hippocampus, the medial diencephalic structures, and connecting projections have been shown to represent a major information-processing system with regard to functions subserving memory. One must distinguish between short-term memory and long-term memory. Short-term memory appears to involve protein synthesis–independent-memory storage processes, thought by some to be subserved by reverberating electrical circuits, whose temporal parameter appears to span a period of a few seconds, or perhaps, somewhat longer. These are labile processes which can be easily disturbed by seizural discharges and other noxious interferences. Such noxious interferences may compromise all phases of short-term memory processes (registration, retention, retrieval) as well as their transition to long-term memory processes (consolidation). On the other hand, long-term memory appears to involve protein synthesis–dependent memory-storage processes, which are resistant to reversible pathophysiological processes, such as seizural discharges.

Vulnerability of memories to destruction may be due to imperfect initial encoding, loss of information while in store (in either the labile or consolidated phase), impaired ability to retrieve, or a combination of these factors. Irreversible (structural) destruction of the hippocampal regions bilaterally results in the so-called amnesic syndrome (i.e., Korsakoff's syndrome). The memory deficits in the amnesic syndrome, as reported for patients with presumptive bilateral hippocampal damage, do not seem to be an impairment in the transition of memories from the immediate span of attention to short-term memory, since attention mechanisms and processes for short-term memory appear to be intact. Instead, they seem to be indicative of a disturbance related to the conversion of new information to long-term storage. The patients remember experiences as long as they are maintained within the focus of attention but quickly forget them when their attention is diverted. This suggests that they have an intact short-term memory; the deficit could arise in the transition to long storage or from difficulty in the retrieval of long-term storage information.

Reversible (pathophysiological) interferences with the memory processes of the same regions result in the so-called dysmnesic syndrome. In the dysmnesic syndrome, which is associated with ictal discharges affecting the hippocampal regions and their connections, memory deficits involve only the processes of short-term memory and its transition to long-term storage. Dysmnesic disturbances that commonly accompany psychomotor seizures consist of a loss or impairment of the mnemonic record of the currently experienced reality during the seizure, as well as immediately before the seizure (retrograde effect), and for a short period after the seizure (postictal effect). The dysmnesic disturbances are particularly characteristic of the psychomotor automatisms. Although the patient in the automatic state does not seem to be unconscious, nevertheless he appears to be confused and move aimlessly. According to Penfield and Roberts [170], the basic defect appears to be an inability to record present experience, that is, a loss of the capacity to make a record of the current stream of consciousness. The confusion is due to an interference with experiential recording before the phase of experiential interpretation (apperception). The hippocampal structures represent low threshold areas, vulnerable to injury and prone to seizure discharges. Depending on the intensity of interference by hippocampal ictal discharges, the deficit may be of variable degree. Thus interference with the encoding process (registration) would result in no experience, that is, loss of continuity of the informational input from the current environment and a loss of the cognitive-affective experience occupying the stream of consciousness. Interference with the phase of labile retention would result in variable degrees of impairment or loss of the experience. Interference with recall mechanisms would result in loss of the ability to retrieve stored information from past experiences and, therefore, in failure to interpret the experience and attach meaning to it (apperceptive disturbance). Interference with the transition from short-term storage to long-term storage would result in the loss of the experiential input during the seizure.

This mnemonic deficit may be further compounded by a clouding of consciousness when the discharge spreads to involve centrencephalic centers, thus resulting in a gross disorganization of psychological experience and behavior that is proportionate to the degree of the impairment of consciousness. As a consequence, awareness, orientation, attention, concentration, memory, and other cognitive functions become impaired during the spread of the seizure (dyssyneidetic disturbance). Similarly, the defensive-adaptive operations of the ego suffer disorganization, which is proportionate to the dysmnesic and dyssyneidetic disturbances. In the absence of motivational arousal during such seizure, the patient would show purposeless and uncoordinated behavior patterns, occurring in a state of altered consciousness. One must differentiate ictal dysmnesic states from hysterical dissociative states (fugues).

2. Perceptive/apperceptive functions and oneiroid disturbances. The temporal cortex processes exteroceptive information input mediated by distance receptors (visual, auditory, olfactory) and is vitally important in the integration of all perceptions, whether exteroceptive or interoceptive. One aspect of these integrative functions is the apperceptive process by which present experiences are compared against past ones and are interpreted, so that they acquire personal meaning in the here-and-now as well as relevance to the individual's past and future. It appears that hippocampal mechanisms must be involved in this apperceptive process, since this process requires the retrieval of past experiences to be compared with new ones. Furthermore, cortical input must also be involved in this process.

Seizural discharges within the temporolimbic structures may result in perceptual disturbances in the form of hallucinations, apperceptive disturbances in the form of illusory experiences, or both. Penfield and Roberts [170] describe the perceptual responses (hallucinatory) to stimulation of the temporal cortex as experiential and the apperceptive responses (illusory) as interpretive.

Perceptual disturbances associated with temporolimbic seizures constitute the ictal hallucinatory syndrome, which involves hallucinations from the visual, auditory, olfactory, gustatory, or vestibular sensory modalities. These hallucinatory experiences are generally ego-alien and are experienced and recalled as long as memory processes are not compromised by the ictal discharges, but they may suffer interpretive distortions when they are associated with an interference with the apperceptive process.

Apperceptive disturbances associated with temporolimbic seizures constitute the ictal illusory syndrome, which may involve the following distortions: (1) apperceptive disturbances in the visual sphere, which are clinically manifested as distortions of space, size, and distance — i.e., micropsias (Lilliputian illusions or hallucinations), macropsias, fluctuating boundaries in object configuration, and distorted spatial planes; (2) apperceptive disturbances in the auditory sphere, which are manifested as distortions of sounds and voices, perceived as hollow, whispering, distant or extremely loud; (3) distortions of body image, which are perceived in the form of depersonalization experiences, feelings of floating or detachment, and so forth; (4) distortions in the way current reality is experienced vis-à-vis past experiences, which result in qualitative experiential changes — described as derealization, déjà vu or déjà vécu (familiarity feelings), jamais vu or jamais vécu (unfamiliarity feelings) — reflecting distortions of past-present relationships; (5) distortions of temporal perception, which are frequently experienced "as if" everything stopped or occurred in rhythm, representing temporal disintegration; and (6) cognitive interpretive distortions, which may be experienced as sudden paranoid ideas.

These ictal hallucinatory and illusory experiences constitute what has been referred to as oneiroid disturbances. They are experienced as dream-like occurrences, having a novel quality, often described as bizarre, grotesque, or indescribable. They may occur clinically in the form of perceptual-illusory auras or as part of complex twilight states.

In temporolimbic seizures associated with qualitative alterations of conscious experience and other aural perceptual distortions (depersonalization, derealization, déjà vu, hallucinations, illusions, and so forth), the psychic changes often present a striking similarity with the so-called psychedelic experiences induced by hallucinogenic drugs, such as lysergic acid diethylamide (LSD). Both states may become associated with distortions of body image and altered perceptions of the subject's relationship to his body and its parts, as well as distortions of three-dimensional space. In the psychedelic experience body boundaries may become fluid or fused with the surroundings; objects may change in size and shape with pulsating contours; spatial planes become distorted, collapsed, or telescoped; faces of people appear twisted in a caricaturistic or frightening way; and voices become hollow, distant, whispering, or unbearably loud. Illusory and hallucinatory experiences may be vivid, acquiring a quality of compelling immediacy. Similar experiences occur during temporal lobe ictal auras. In this state of derealization and depersonalization, induced by either LSD or a temporal lobe ictus, the subject may experience a peculiar awareness of apartness, which may account for the reported feelings of extreme loneliness, or a feeling of double consciousness, in which there is a splitting of the self into a passive, detached, and observing monitor — the "spectator ego" — and an experiencing self. [60] Subjects may show the whole spectrum of affective responses, ranging from depression, despair, or panic to exhilaration, ecstasy, and euphoria.

The oneiroid disturbances that often accompany the ictal episodes of temporal lobe epilepsy are generally ego-dystonic, simulating a state of primary process experiencing of the self and the world and in which the ego remains intact, monitoring the experience as a participant observer (spectator ego). The breaking through of a primary process thinking into conscious awareness, in the presence of an intact organization of secondary process thinking, seems to distinguish the oneiroid state from the schizophrenic state.

3. Motivational/affective functions and dyshormic disturbances. Neurophysiological evidence has established that systems associated with the limbic-hypothalamic axis are intimately connected with the integration and modulation of the motivational and affective dimensions of behavior. These dimensions pertain to major effector CNS functions (variously described as connative, innate, instinctual, or drive behaviors), affective phenomena (commonly referred to as emotions), and autonomic responses accompanying these behaviors.

It may be postulated that instinctual or drive behaviors contribute to the maintenance of the individual and the species through an innate "programming" of the nervous system, that is, through phylogenetically "learned" behaviors that proved to be of adaptive value to the species. It may be further postulated, from an evolutionary point of view, that innately determined behaviors evolved as a means of supplementing or replacing earlier and much simpler reflex behavior, in response to increased adaptational demands for preprogrammed behavioral responses to environmental cues that could serve the survival needs of the naïve newborn organism. In contrast to reflex behavior, innate behavior has a motivational dimension and is more complex and more sustained. The motivational dimension of drive behavior has both energizing and directional aspects; that is, it builds a potential to discharge in action and gives an "aim" through which the instinctual goals are realized. Intimately related to this motivational function is the introspected experience referred to as affect (such as fear, anger, sadness). One may postulate that the various affective responses evolved phylogenetically in the mammalian organisms from the adaptational need to reinforce, prolong, and intensify corresponding behavioral responses, which are of major significance for the survival of the organism (alimentation, mating, fight, flight, attachment). Thus, affect has evolved as an auxilliary function to behavioral responses elicited by either drives or environmental stimuli, in the sense that they reinforce and sustain effector responses. The emergence of affect has added an extension to the temporal and intensity parameters of stimulus-response behaviors, as well as an energizing and directional effect to behavior in general. Innately determined drive and affective behavior in man is characterized by an enormous plasticity and versatility, modified by the greater capacity of the human brain to be "reprogrammed" by new information (learning), by symbolic language, by hindsight and foresight, and by reasoning.

The innately programmed and experientially reprogrammed drive behaviors modulated by the limbic system can be classified, for purposes of the present discussion, into five major drive systems: alimentary (feeding), mating (sexual), attachment (object relationships), flight (avoidance), and fight (aggressive). Using an ethological approach, drive behavior may be further differentiated into appetitive (exploratory) and consummatory. In temporolimbic seizures, the activation of any of these drive systems will result in ictal phenomena, characterized by dyshormic disturbances. These dyshormic disturbances constitute what is termed the drive dyscontrol syndrome, which often characterizes the psychopathology of temporolimbic episodes, such as complex psychomotor attacks and temporal auras.

Defensive-adaptive ego mechanisms may exert modifying influences on the ictally aroused drives during a psychomotor attack. The extent to which psychological mechanisms may influence various drives activated by the temporolimbic ictal discharges depends on a number of concomitantly occurring phenomena, including the associated presence of dysmnesic and dyssyneidetic disturbances, the presence of oneiroid disturbances, the type of drives elicited by the epileptic discharge (for example, aggressive, sexual) the intensity of these drives, the ongoing motivational state of the individual prior to the seizure, and the internalized controls of the individual to the extent that they are preserved during the seizure. These internalized controls are determined by the defensive and adaptive patterns that are characteristic of the individual's personality in handling conflicts associated with the gratification of various drives.

Within this conceptual framework, the dysfunctional manifestations of behavior which are associated with ictally induced interferences with the modulation of drives are described as dyshormic disturbances. The various dyshormic disturbances can be classified into the following categories: alimentary, sexual, attachment, avoidance, and aggressive.

Alimentary dyshormic disturbances: Dysfunctional manifestations of an ictal origin that involve feeding behavior are commonly seen in simple psychomotor automatisms and in the more complex twilight states. These manifestations express components of the feeding drive and can be easily identified as pertaining to appetitive or consummatory acts, or both. Their occurrence is generally associated with the concomitant presence of dysmnesic disturbances and may be preceded by oneiroid disturbances as well. Exploratory manifestations characteristic of appetitive behavior in general may include automatic searching movements, orienting movements of the head and eyes, and vocalization, all suggesting orienting or exploratory behavior. Alimentary appetitive movements of sniffing, tasting, and autonomic symptoms of increased salivation are not uncommon in these attacks. On the other hand, consummatory manifestations are commonly expressed in the form of involuntary movements of lips and tongue, mastication, swallowing, licking, lip smacking, which are all related to alimentary behavior. Hallucinations of smell or taste may be present. The activation of the alimentary drive is generally conflict free, and therefore it does not necessitate the alerting and mobilization of ego defense mechanisms. It should be noted that hyperphagia has been reported to accompany ventral hypothalamic neoplasms [178]. It is also of interest that some cases of compulsive eating were found to respond to dilantin treatment [85].

Sexual dyshormic disturbances: Dyshormic phenomena of an overt or suggestive sexual nature may accompany the auras or psychomotor attacks of temporal lobe epilepsy. A number of studies have reported disturbed sexual behavior in epileptics, especially in patients with psychomotor epilepsy and temporal lobe disease [9,13–15,32,35,42,57,61,69,96,109, 123,188,214,220,223]. The paroxysmal arousal of sexual drives and the precipitation of sexual behavior may be of ictal origin and may constitute part of the content of a psychomotor seizure. In the simple automatisms, appetitive manifestations of the sexual drive may include involuntary undressing, automaticlike movements of exhibiting one's genitals, and similar rudiments of sexually appetitive behavior, while in more complex psychomotor attacks (twilight states), the patient may manifest more coordinated and goal-directed sexual behavior of an appetitive nature, such as seductive postures, fondling movements, petting, and sexually inviting gestures. Consummatory manifestations of a sexual nature may occur in complex psychomotor attacks and may range from copulatory movements to violent rape. Such sexual dyshormic disturbances are generally accompanied by dysmnesic symptoms. In general, the expression of consummatory behavior during ictal episodes assumes a much more violent or forceful character than that of appetitive sexual behavior.

Heath [98] has reported that septal stimulation by implanted electrodes in a patient with narcolepsy resulted in the awareness of sexual feelings, as if building up to an orgasm which he could never attain. This led the patient to push the button frequently in an effort to reach the orgastic climax. Heath [96] also found that during orgasm spike and large slow-wave activity along with superimposed fast activity occurred in the septal region and in the median forebrain bundle, following implanted electrode stimulation; also acetylcholine stimulation in the same region produced intense feelings of orgastic pleasure.

Delgado [35] has reported the occurrence of sexual excitement following stimulation of the deep areas of the temporal lobe. Sem Jacobson [188] has reported on two cases in which stimulation of the posterior part of the frontal lobe resulted in sensation similar to a sexual pleasure. Stimulation of the ventrolateral thalamic region has been found by Bechterewa [9] to evoke pleasurable sensations and orgasm. Flor-Henry [57] has suggested that orgasm is lateralized to the right (nondominant) hemisphere.

There have been only a few clinical cases of temporal lobe epilepsy with an orgasmic component reported in the literature. Erickson [42] reported a female epileptic patient with a prolonged aura consisting of nocturnal episodes during which she would feel "hot all over" and then experience depression and an orgasm, a condition that led her to seek multiple sexual contacts. The attacks progressively became associated with episodes of laughing and crying and with myoclonic jerking of her left leg. After surgery, she was found to have a vascular tumor of the flax, which was compressing the paracentral lobule and cingulum of the right hemisphere. Both sexual attacks and epileptic seizures disappeared after surgery. Four cases of temporal lobe epilepsy and episodic hypersexuality with an orgasmic aura, reported by Van Reeth [220], were found to have an epileptogenic focus in the right temporal lobe. More recently, Warneke [223] reported on a thoroughly investigated case of a thirty-one-year-old man with temporal lobe epilepsy with, probably, multiple foci of origin on the right side. This patient presented different types of attacks of a nocturnal occurrence, which included attacks of panic and suicidal depression as well as orgasmiclike sensations, which spread across his face from right to left and were followed by muscle twitching, which extended into the left side of the neck and left arm. The EEG showed a generalized slow-wave dysrhythmia most prominent on the right frontotemporal regions. Response of these attacks to anticonvulsant medication was dramatic. Several other authors have reported on ictal phenomena consisting of sexual dyshormic disturbances including paroxysmal feelings of sexual excitement, [13], episodes of fetishism, transvestitism, and exhibitionism [57,109,123,156], and verbally as well as behaviorally expressed coital activity preceded by genital sexual stimulation. [32,59]. Kilarsky, Freund, Macheck, and Polak [123] reported a significant association of all sexual deviations with temporal lobe lesions which were present before the first year of life.

Defensive-adaptive processes may be operant during the seizure in varying degrees, depending on the presence and extent of dysmnesic and dyssyneidetic impairment, intensity of the ictal arousal of the drive, preexisting intrapsychic conflicts in the sexual area, and type of psychological mechanisms used to resolve such conflicts. It is reasonable to assume that the greater the dyssyneidetic impairment (clouding of consciousness) and the greater the arousal of the sexual drive, the less effective the secondary process of defensive-adaptive operations and the more primitive the behavior will be.

Attachment dyshormic disturbances: We view attachment behavior as a primary drive that governs interpersonal bonds and object attachments in general. The phenotypic expression of this drive becomes established after the sixth month of life in humans through the interaction of the infant with a mothering object and is manifested in subsequent years in many derivative forms, as attachment to security objects, shelter, love objects, and attachment to self (self-esteem). In the early years of life attachment behavior guarantees the survival of the newborn, and in later years it establishes interpersonal bonds.

The drive characteristics of attachment behavior are similar to those of hunger-thirst drive: They are activated by privation, which in the attachment drive takes the form of separation, detachment, or loss of the object of attachment (love object). The appetitive phase of the drive, which is elicited by a privation of the object of attachment (real, imagined, or threatened), consists of a behavioral response commonly referred to as a depressive reaction or grief (conservation-withdrawal syndrome). Depressive symptoms, therefore, constitute pathological components of the appetitive phase of the attachment drive, representing a dyshormic disturbance. The consummatory phase of the drive is reunion with the object of attachment and is accompanied by a behavioral response characterized by excitement, hyperactivity, elation, and euphoric feelings. The manic reaction is viewed as pathological consummatory behavior of the attachment drive, representing a vicarious reunion (in vacuum).

Affective symptoms of depression appearing during the course of temporal lobe seizures (psychic attacks) are very common. There have been several reports on ictal depressions [4,15,36,45,49,54,76,89,108, 140,208,224,225,229,232,233]. Acute feelings of despair and depression during the attack may be accompanied by suicidal impulses; in a typical attack these symptoms last for a few minutes at most. Auras of premonition of death, end of the world, and other catastrophic expectations have also been reported. A marked feature of the twilight state is psychomotor retardation.

In general, patients with temporal lobe EEG abnormalities, with or without the presence of seizures, frequently experience short-lived episodes of mood swings, often with concomitant anxiety, occurring with normal consciousness, that are not ordinarily thought to be ictal [44]. It is well known that the epileptic is liable to sudden variations of mood, independent of seizures, often resembling manic-depressive swings. Characteristically, the epileptic mood is of extreme sudden onset and builds up to the full extent within a few hours; during this period suicidal ideation is very common; the episode passes off in a few hours, but may last for a few days [44]. Asano [4] has suggested an atypical manic-depressive psychosis with an epileptoid mechanism.

Various investigators have attempted to establish criteria that differentiate ictal from nonictal depression. The paroxysmal character of the episode (acute onset and equally acute remission, lasting for relatively short periods, and very often associated with intense anxiety) point to an ictal mechanism. On the other hand, feelings of inferiority and guilt are relatively milder when compared with nonictal depressions [232,233]. The presence of dynmnesic and oneiroid symptoms, as well as EEG abnormalities localized in the temporal regions would further contribute to their differentiation from nonictal depressions. Of the forty-four patients with brief paroxysmal depressions reported by Macrae [140], thirty-seven had abnormal EEGs, and twenty-nine of the thirty-seven had focal abnormalities limited to the temporal area. In a group of 388 patients with symptomatic epilepsy reported by Weil [225], 7 percent of the total group and 28 percent of the temporal lobe group had ictal emotions. Feelings of fear and depression were frequently reported, and both were invariably associated with various visceral sensations, feelings of unreality, déjà vu, and paranoid ideation. Weil [225] suggested that ictal fear is of shorter duration and is associated with localized lesions of the temporal cortex, while ictal depression is of longer duration and associated with lesions involving the hippocampal-amygdaloid temporal complex. It is of interest that in several cases with fear and depression, there occurred episodes of explosive rage. The ictal depressive episodes reported by Weil [225] were found to be refractory to psychotherapy but frequently responded favorably to anticonvulsant drugs. In Slater's study [192] of sixty-nine cases of epileptic patients with psychotic (schizophrenialike) reactions, thirty-eight (55 percent) had episodic depressions, which were short-lived but very severe and often accompanied by suicidal attempts. Twelve patients reported euphoria. Ictal feelings of pleasure and elation are generally rare in temporal lobe seizures. It is well established that stimulation of the temporolimbic structures and symptoms associated with temporal lobe epilepsy are invariably unpleasant (depression, irritability, anger, foul odors, fear), with the exception of occasional pleasurable feelings (elation, sexual feelings), elicited especially with stimulation of the septal region. Although pleasurable feelings of an ictal nature are rare [33,229], manic swings are not uncommon.

It is not clear whether environmental factors can precipitate ictal depressive episodes. Psychogenic contribution to the precipitation of ictal depression should be considered as a likely mechanism. The reported masochistic and self-punishment quality in the behavior of patients with temporal lobe seizures, reflecting a regression to the pregenital phase of development, may stem from their repeated exposure to dysphoric feelings which are characteristic of limbic stimulation. This regression may enhance their proclivity to respond to a seizure discharge with an ictal episode of a depressive nature; stated differently, psychogenic factors may exert a "priming" influence on the elicitation of the appetitive phase of the attachment drive (depressive response), and in some instances they may serve as releasing stimuli.

Avoidance (flight-fear) dyshormic disturbances: Paroxysmal attacks of fear, terror, or anxiety very often accompany temporal lobe seizures and constitute an aura [140] or are part of a twilight psychomotor seizure. Attacks of panic very often interrupt the psychomotor retardation which is commonly observed in twilight states; in these cases, panic may represent a direct result of ictal discharges or may be a response to frightening hallucinations and to feelings of strangeness that characterize a twilight state. Flight responses to fear in the form of frantic escape (consummatory behavior) may occur during the attack. Attacks of fear are of shorter duration than episodes of depression, and according to Weil [225], tend to be associated with lesions localized in the temporal cortex. Attacks of fear and phobic symptoms accompanied by depersonalization have been reported to be associated with temporal lobe epilepsy [92,185]. It is likely that ictal attacks of anxiety and fear may become conditioned to concurrent environmental situations and secondarily result in the phobic avoidance of the latter situations. The frequent occurrence of paroxysmal autonomic manifestations in temporal lobe epilepsy, namely those associated with a sympathetic discharge, may represent the visceral components of flight responses and may occur without the affective component of fear (dissociation of visceral and affective components of flight responses).

Aggressive (fight-anger) dyshormic disturbances: Paroxysmal outbursts of irritability, anger, aggressive impulses, and rage, are reported to be frequent ictal manifestations of temporal lobe epilepsy, occurring in clear consciousness or with varying degrees of amnesia of the episode. Aggressive acts of a consummatory nature may also occur during ictal twilight states and may range from episodes of violent destructive behavior to attack and even homicide [47,49,70,90,91,121,141,157,165,181,213,217,222].

Ictal aggressive behavior must be differentiated from aggressive behavior occurring during postictal twilight states. Gastaut and Miletto [70] have reported that half of their patients suffering from temporal lobe epilepsy manifested paroxysmal outbursts of rage. Similarly, in a study by Falconer, Hill, Meyer, and Wilson [47], 38 percent of temporal lobe epileptics showed aggressive outbursts, presumed to be of an ictal origin; these outbursts appeared to be incongruous to the life-styles of these patients (out of character). Another 14 percent of the total group had milder but more or less persistent aggressiveness, often associated with a paranoid attitude. In a group of fifty institutionalized epileptics studied by Roger and Dongier [183], it was found that 84 percent of those showing aggressive episodes had EEG abnormalities suggestive of a mesial temporal epileptogenic focus. The proposed syndrome of mesial temporal sclerosis is thought to be characterized primarily by ictal episodes of rage [167,217].

Recurrent episodes of aggressive or violent behavior, occurring under circumstances of minimal or no provocation in subjects who are not known to suffer from epileptic seizures are thought by some investigators to represent ictal phenomena. This so-called episodic behavior dyscontrol syndrome needs to be differentiated from conditions associated with an aggressive or explosive personality.

POSTICTAL PSYCHOPATHOLOGY

Following a grand mal seizure (primarily or secondarily generalized) or a focal seizure (i.e., psychomotor attack), there follows at the close of the seizure a postictal or "postconvulsive" syndrome, usually characterized by symptoms of apathy, sleep, and confusion. In some cases, especially in chronic and severely deteriorated epileptics with grand mal, the postictal syndrome may begin or be followed by a period of delirious excitement lasting for several minutes or hours, and in some instances for days or weeks. This deliriouslike state may consist, at times, of dramatic outbursts of agitation associated with paranoid ideation, delusions, and hallucinations and may lead to repetitive acts of extremely violent aggression, and occasionally murder. The aggressive acts committed during such prolonged postictal syndromes are characteristically violent and brutal, as compared to aggressive acts committed during a psychomotor attack; in the latter cases, the aggressive acts are slow and clumsy and usually ineffective; the patient may swing wildly and miss [161]. During this so-called postconvulsive delirium, the patient shows altered consciousness, appears to be confused and disoriented, and presents complete amnesia or spotty recollection of the events surrounding the confusional period, thus suggesting a diffuse impairment of those central mechanisms underlying discriminative consciousness [44]. Throughout this period, the EEG shows diffuse symmetrical slow-wave activity or a rather ill-defined low-voltage activity, with no categorical abnormalities and with notable absence of spikes. This electroencephalographic phenomenon is reminiscent of Landlot's forced normalization, which is reported to occur during the psychotic episodes of temporal lobe epilepsy [129]. The underlying pathogenetic mechanism of these postictal states remains obscure. It has been variously attributed to a partial postictal recovery with persistent breakdown of higher cortical systems of inhibitory function [162], to a state of "exhaustion" following a period of excessive discharge, to a refractiveness of neurons resulting in a disturbed balance between excitatory and inhibitory systems, or to subcortical circumscribed excessive neuronal discharges [157].

It is likely that the postictal syndrome represents basically a state of excessive neuronal inhibition that develops in reaction to the massive excitation produced by an epileptic discharge, rather than an expression of the breakdown of inhibitory functions or of subcortical excessive discharges. A similar mechanism may account for the psychotic episodes that are reported to occur in patients with temporal lobe epilepsy. It is reasonable to postulate that it is the massive reactive inhibition, particularly in the limbic and diencephalic areas, in response to a progressively augmenting excitatory (ictal) process, that seems to be associated with the more or less prolonged psychotic episodes in temporal lobe epileptics, rather than the commonly postulated subcortical epileptic discharges. Therefore, one may postulate that the psychotic manifestations of the postconvulsive syndrome (postictal delirium or twilight states) and those of the so-called temporal lobe psychosis (schizophreniform) have a common underlying mechanism, characterized by a massive reactive neuronal inhibition. The differences in the clinical manifestations between the two syndromes — predominantly confusional in the postconvulsive, while predominantly schizophreniform in the temporal lobe epilepsy — may be due to the differential involvement of two different systems, the centrencephalic and limbic respectively. The reported disappearance of categorical abnormalities, such as spikes during the postconvulsive deliria, and the comparable phenomenon of forced normalization that occurs during the psychotic episodes of temporal lobe epilepsy may be due to the same common mechanism of reactive inhibition. It is also likely that the disappearance of the seizural EEG abnormalities in both conditions is the result of the development of generalized slow-wave activity which in milder forms may be limited only in subcortical structures (picked up by subcortical electrodes), while in more severe forms it spreads in the cortical areas, where it can be picked up electroencephalographically.

The psychopathology of postictal psychotic episodes reflects a mixture of inhibitory processes (obliteration of conscious awareness and recall, apathy, lethargy, stupor, sleep) and phenomena secondary to the inhibition of inhibitory circuits modulating emotional behavior (inhibition of inhibitions). The latter are clinically manifested as excitement, emotional arousal, drive dyscontrol, furor states, or violent and sexually aggressive acts. Environmental (perceptual) contribution to the postictal psychopathology would appear to depend on the degree of the preservation of the higher discriminative functions during the episode, that is, on the capacity of the patient to process information and comprehend the meaning of it within the context of the occurrence of the attack. Although gross discrimination appears to be present in most cases, higher level of discrimination of cortical origin is generally lacking. Therefore, the patient's responsiveness to external stimuli, as well as to the internal arousal of various drives and emotional experiences, would be under a diminished inhibitory control or an impaired secondary process. It would appear that the greater the impairment of the discriminative ego functions and the greater the arousal of aggressive or sexual drives, the less effective the secondary process of defensive-adaptive operations and reality testing. The registration of the experiential events during the episode is variably impaired, and therefore, their subsequent recall varies from complete amnesia to spotty recollection of the events surrounding the episode.

INTERICTAL PSYCHOPATHOLOGY

The psychopathology defined by the term *interictal* includes a broad range of behavioral disturbances which can be classified into characterological, neurotic, psychotic, psychophysiological, and organic. The etiology and underlying pathogenetic mechanisms of these disturbances appear to be uncertain and controversial. Although this psychopathology is, to a large extent, of psychogenic (functional) origin, there is very little doubt that ictal, organic, and perhaps constitutional factors contribute variably to it. With the present understanding of the nature of these disturbances, it is not possible to define precisely their pathogenetic determinants, and therefore, they will be discussed on the basis of a descriptive classification. It is clinically useful to divide them into episodic and nonepisodic.

Episodic Psychopathology

These behavioral disturbances, although lacking the paroxysmal character of seizure, appear, nevertheless, to have an episodic occurrence and a clinical profile which resembles that of ictal phenomena. In spite of the existing controversy over their etiology and pathogenesis, it is very likely that they represent ictal disorders manifested by atypical syndromes. Some of them may be of a postictal origin. When these episodic disturbances occur in patients who are known to suffer from epileptic seizures, they are generally diagnosed as constituting a component of the epileptic disorder. On the other hand, when they occur in patients who do not present a history of epileptic seizures, they pose a difficult diagnostic problem. These episodic disturbances related to epilepsy can be classified into episodic mood changes, episodic (acute) psychoses, and episodic behavior dyscontrol.

EPISODIC MOOD CHANGES
The depressive symptoms that very often occur during the course of temporal lobe seizures have already been discussed. The ictal character of

these paroxysmal depressive episodes cannot be easily established. They usually precede a seizure as an aural phenomenon or accompany a psychomotor seizure. They may also occur independently of seizures, in the form of paroxysmal episodes lasting for a few seconds or minutes, and are associated with electroencephalographic seizural discharges.

In addition, epileptic patients are very frequently subject to variations of mood (depression, elation, euphoria, ecstasy, suspiciousness, irritability, hostility), whose ictal etiology cannot be adequately defined.

A number of epileptic patients often experience mounting irritability, tension, anxiety, and depression, in spite of the fact that their seizures are well controlled under medication. These symptoms invariably subside after the patient experiences a seizure of the grand mal type. Patients often recognize this effect and learn to skip medication in order to induce a seizure for relief. Reducing the dosage of the anticonvulsant medication, thus allowing the patient to have an occasional fit, or inducing an artificial seizure may serve as an effective means of eliminating these symptoms. It is of interest that these prodromal preictal mood changes are seldom accompanied by EEG abnormalities [194]. Furthermore, the occurrence of a petit mal attack, unlike that of a grand mal one, seldom has any effect on these mood changes [194]. This correlates with the common observation that depressed patients receiving electroconvulsive therapy respond therapeutically only to grand mal seizures but not to minor ones. It is not known whether these prodromallike mood changes are due to repetitive subictal electrical discharges or to some other mechanism characteristic of functional affective disorders.

Mood changes (depression, irritability, and more rarely elation), which may follow the occurrence of a seizure for some days, are usually associated with EEG dysrhythmia [194], presumptively of a postictal etiology. This postictal psychopathology may be due, however, to some other mechanism.

Interictal mood swings, simulating manic-depressive episodes, are characterized by sudden onset, progress to a fully developed affective syndrome in the course of a few hours, and terminate precipitously after a period lasting from a few hours to a few days. The paroxysmal character of these mood changes is suggestive of an underlying ictal mechanism.

In Dongier's [36] review of a collaborative study involving 516 epileptic patients, it was reported that these patients had experienced a total of 536 psychotic episodes, occurring between seizures and including both schizophreniclike and affective psychoses, as well as combined syndromes. More specifically, it was found that 45 percent of the temporal lobe epileptics and 24 percent of the centrencephalic epileptics showed depressive psychosis. Furthermore, 65 percent of the temporal epileptics and 46 percent of the centrencephalic epileptics showed disturbed affective reactions during the psychotic episodes. It is generally agreed that patients with temporal lobe epilepsy are particularly prone to experiencing affective disturbances, and particularly irritability and depression. Brief episodes of depressive or manic behavior which occur recurrently with a paroxysmal character in subjects who are not known to suffer from epileptic seizures may have an ictal etiology.

EPISODIC (ACUTE) PSYCHOSES

In addition to the manic-depressive manifestations discussed in the preceding section, epileptic patients are reported to develop confusional (delirioid) and twilightlike interictal episodes, as well as schizophreniclike psychoses. In general, the majority of these psychotic episodes occur in patients with temporal lobe epilepsy. In Dongier's collaborative study [36], 44 percent of patients with interictal psychotic episodes suffered from psychomotor epilepsy. This morbidity rate is quite high in view of the fact that the general incidence of psychomotor epilepsy in the total epileptic population is 15 to 20 percent. According to a study by Bruens [21], based on EEG criteria, only 16 percent of the epileptic patients with psychotic episodes did not have temporal lobe epilepsy. As to the laterality of temporal lobe foci and the type of psychosis, it appears that the epileptic involvement of the dominant temporal lobe is more likely to be associated with schizophreniclike psychosis, whereas the involvement of the nondominant temporal lobe is more likely to be associated with manic-depressive changes [53]. On the other hand, confusional-delirioid episodes are presumed to be more common in centrencephalic epileptics rather than in temporal lobe epileptics [36,54].

Confusional-delirioid psychoses constitute two-thirds of the psychotic episodes occurring in centrencephalic epileptics [36]. In general, these episodes are relatively brief in duration (several hours) and are always followed by complete recovery. These episodes never evolve into a chronic condition. Their self-limiting character points up to an underlying reversible pathophysiological disturbance involving, most likely, the centrencephalic system. In Dongier's study [36], centrencephalic epileptics showed, during the psychotic episode, EEG modifications in the direction of a diffuse slow dysrhythmia or with spike and wave discharges that sometimes developed into an EEG pattern typical of petit mal status. It was extremely rare to observe normalized or unmodified EEGs during these episodes. It is of interest that these episodes often began with a seizure and only rarely ended with one. According to Dongier [36], these cases represent prolonged postictal states. It appears, however, that some of these cases might be of ictal origin.

Schizophreniclike psychoses and their association with epilepsy, studied in early reports [83,88,125], first raised the question whether the former was a true schizophrenia of functional origin, a symptomatic schizophreniform psychosis secondary to epilepsy, or a schizophrenialike psychogenic reaction to epileptic personality changes. Numerous subsequent studies have given further support to the observation that temporal lobe epileptics are particularly prone to developing schizoid personality traits, and in some instances, schizophrenic-type psychoses of a paranoid character [8,21,36,53–56,67,78,97,98,101,102,128–133,137,176,182,191,193,205, 209,214,226].

From a diagnostic point of view, it is important to distinguish between acute and chronic schizophreniform psychoses associated with epilepsy, since they differ in terms of course of illness and perhaps treatment response. The acute psychotic episodes are of an episodic character, and therefore, suggestive of an ictal mechanism.

In comparing the acute psychotic episodes of psychomotor (temporal lobe) epileptics with those of the centrencephalic epileptics, Dongier [36] found several significant differences. The psychotic episodes of patients with psychomotor epilepsy lasted longer (days or weeks), and they were rarely preceded by a grand mal seizure but often ended in one; also, there was marked paranoid ideation and other symptoms characteristic of schizophrenia which usually occurred in clear consciousness. Clouding of consciousness (confusion) was an infrequent finding. These episodes were usually accompanied by disturbances of affect, such as mood swings, and especially by depression, which was commonly mixed with anxiety. During these episodes, the EEG rhythms were either normal or desynchronized with disappearance of pathological rhythms (forced normalization). In occasional cases, there was reinforcement of focal epileptic discharges in the temporal region without modification of background rhythms. On the other hand, slow-wave dysrhythmia was rare, and spike-wave discharge patterns were never present. The phenomenon of *forced normalization* of EEG abnormalities in psychomotor epileptics during an acute psychotic episode has been reported by several investigators [36,53,128]. This reported inverse relationship between the occurrence of seizures and psychotic episodes may lead to a seesawlike phenomenon, in which predominantly epileptic manifestations alternate with a preponderance of the psychosis, with the latter often occurring following drug control of the seizures. The seesaw relationship of the two clinical syndromes (epileptic, psychotic) is also reflected in the EEG, which may change rather abruptly from severe epileptic discharges accompanying seizural episodes to complete normalization, with the swing toward a transient seizure-free activated psychosis. According to Landolt [128,130], these psychotic episodes that are accompanied by forced normalization represent the actual mania epileptica; patients show a severe excitement, associated with hallucinatory and other psychotic symptoms, and very often disorientation and amnesia. The latter symptoms of apparent sensorial impairment are thought by Landolt to be the result of an abnormal heightening of perception (engrossment), rather than the result of clouding of consciousness. Psychotic episodes without forced normalization of the EEG are described by Landolt as psychotic (twilight) states of an organic nature.

Several investigators have pointed out that temporal lobe epileptics may characteristically show acute psychotic episodes with prominent schizophrenialike features and little or no EEG abnormality to suggest a relation to epilepsy, and these patients often are misdiagnosed as schizophrenic [43,44,157]. Monroe [157] has emphasized the frequent absence of EEG abnormalities in patients with episodic behavioral disorders manifesting psychotic reactions (episodic reactions), and who, on repeated EEG recordings, especially activated ones, may show categorical EEG abnormalities, usually characteristic of temporal lobe epilepsy. These patients are presumed to have deep-seated subcortical discharging focuses, which may not become manifest in routine EEG recordings.

Schizophreniform psychoses occurring in temporal lobe epileptics may progress to a chronic psychosis. These chronic paranoid and schizophrenialike psychoses are clearly distinguished from the acute forms. The latter are episodic, of short duration, and self-limiting. The classical study by Slater, Beard, and Glithero [191], which involved sixty-nine epileptics with chronic psychosis, showed that in 80 percent of these cases there was evidence of temporal lobe epilepsy. This study revealed that most of these patients had developed a chronic schizophrenic psychosis with paranoid and hallucinatory symptomatology undistinguishable from schizophrenia. The prepsychotic personality of these patients fell within the normal range. A high proportion, 40 percent, of these patients had a past history of having experienced conditions liable to cause a brain lesion (i.e., birth trauma, closed head injuries, middle ear infections, encephalitis, etc.). There was no increased incidence of schizophrenia in the relatives of these patients; on the other hand, the incidence of epilepsy in these relatives was somewhat higher than expected. The psychopathology observed in these patients commonly included delusional ideas typically seen in schizophrenic patients; feelings of passivity of external influence and control; and hallucinations, usually auditory, which occurred in clear consciousness in 75 percent of the cases. Repetitive stereotyped ritualistic behavior and mannerisms of a catatonic character were fairly common; affective disturbances of a violent, depressive, or ecstatic nature also occurred, either insidiously or after a series of psychomotor seizures; in addition, signs of slight organic impairment could also be elicited, including mild expressive aphasia, learning difficulties, some impairment of recent memory, as well as circumstantiality, perseveration, and concreteness of thinking processes. However, affective responses were often warm and well preserved and were accompanied by a retention of the capacity to establish good emotional rapport. A follow-up study carried out at a mean interval of eight years after the onset of the psychosis showed a tendency towards remission of the psychosis but also a tendency to evolve into chronic organic brain syndrome, commonly seen in chronic deteriorated epileptics [194]. Finally, it is worthy to note that the occurrence of psychosis in these patients was not found to be related to the severity of epilepsy, the number of seizures sustained, the quantity of the drugs consumed, or the degree of control of attacks by drugs.

The etiology and pathogenesis of both the chronic and acute schizophreniform psychoses that have been reported to occur primarily in patients with temporal lobe epilepsy remain obscure. In the continuing controversy over the nature of their underlying mechanisms, various hypotheses have been proposed, spanning the range of both psychological and neurophysiological theorizing. For instance, Pond [176] has suggested a psychogenic hypothesis which is based on the assumption that repeatedly experienced ictal twilight attacks and auras, which are similar to the psychotic experiences of the schizophrenic, may become organized into delusional interpretations and result in confusion of reality and autistic thinking. Some of the chronic paranoid-schizophreniform syndromes seen in temporal lobe epileptics may indeed represent an adaptive-defensive psychological response which may emerge as a consequence of repeated ictal derealization and hallucinatory and other psychoticlike experiences, and which may further become incorporated into a delusional system representing the patient's attempts to give a quasi-logical interpretation of these experiences (psychotic insight). More specifically, it can be hypothesized that in epileptic patients with a limited integration of ego organization, this emergent psychosis (paranoid-schizophreniform syndrome) may represent an adaptive-defensive response on the part of the patient to integrate the intrusive ego-alien ictal experiences into his psychic economy.

For instance, in the presence of ictal derealization, reality takes a new dimension in which familiar things acquire a new quality, the newness or novel character of which may give rise to feelings of unfamiliarity or strangeness, or may become portentous with mystical, religious, or supernatural overtones; such repeated experiences may be so compelling that they may become elaborated into delusional ideas (psychotic insight), such as possessing extrasensory perception (ESP), prophetic powers, or a capacity to read one's mind, or having divine revelations. Depersonalization phenomena may give rise to feelings of "transparency," expressed as loss of boundaries, people reading one's mind, and so forth. On the other hand, hallucinatory experiences, which are originally ego-dystonic, may be interpreted in a delusional manner and become incorporated into the patient's psychic organization. Olfactory hallucinations, which are usually of an objectional nature, may become such a compelling experience that the patient may develop ideas of reference or paranoid ideas about his body emanating unpleasant odors, and very often with sexual implications; i.e., a woman may imagine that she has a vaginal discharge of foul odor and may be consumed with her preoccupation to eliminate the odor through the use of repeated baths and deodorants; she may further develop ideas of reference, imagining that people avoid her, talk about her or laugh at her because of her "odor." Auditory hallucinations may be interpreted by the patient to mean that he is receiving messages through ESP or some supernatural power. Auras of forced ideas may be experienced as the passivity phenomena of schizophrenia, and the patient may come to believe that others put thoughts in his mind. Finally, the experience of the florid symptoms of repeated twilight states could further contribute to an impairment in reality testing and in a "schizophrenic way" of viewing the world and himself. Thus the temporal lobe epileptic with a poorly integrated personality may end up organizing his ictally experienced psychoticlike disturbances into his psychic economy, as a psychological response to adaptation. Nevertheless, it needs to be pointed out that psychogenic hypotheses are not sufficient to account for all the psychotic syndromes associated with temporal lobe epilepsy.

Several investigators have attributed certain of these psychotic episodes to an ictal mechanism, especially those which are acute, paroxysmal, and episodic in nature [37,43,49,116,187,210]. It has been suggested that the presence of a continuous aura [187] secondary to long latency effects [210], a status epilepticus of the limbic system [37,164], or "reverberating" limbic discharges [116] may account for the longer duration of these episodes. This concept of subictal states has been invented to account for a wide spectrum of episodic behavioral disturbances, including the psychotic syndromes under consideration. It is likely that some of these psychotic episodes may be due to an ictal mechanism, that is, directly produced by excessive neuronal discharges.

Alternative hypotheses suggesting a dysfunctional or disorderly neuronal state within the temporolimbic system have been offered as an explanation for the underlying mechanism responsible for these schizophreniform paranoid psychoses. Of special interest is Symonds' [214] hypothesis, which emphasizes the epileptic process as a continuous one, in which seizures and EEG abnormalities represent epiphenomena on a background disorder, the latter considered as the proximate cause of the psychosis.

Similarly, Landolt [130,131] hypothesizes that the occurrence of a psychotic state in temporal lobe epileptics is not directly related to ictal discharges; such discharges can continue recurring for years without producing any psychological disturbance. He further postulates that the psychosis represents a response on the part of normal brain tissues to functional disturbances, manifested probably as nonspecific EEG abnormalities, in areas of the brain connected with the local epileptogenic lesion. The nature of this adaptive response of the brain to the local disturbance takes the form of forced normalization. Landolt suggests that the phenomenon of forced normalization may apply not only to epileptic psychosis but also to schizophrenia. The view that both schizophrenia and temporal lobe epileptic psychoses are associated with disturbances within the temporolimbic system is shared by other investigators [209]. I have earlier argued that at least some of the acute schizophreniform psychoses in temporal lobe epileptics may be due to excessive neuronal inhibition within areas of the temporolimbic structures resulting, as a compensatory response, from the unsteady state produced by subictal discharges.

EPISODIC BEHAVIOR DYSCONTROL SYNDROME

Recurrent episodes of violent or aggressive behavior, unprovoked or minimally provoked, have been reported to occur in epileptic patients, especially those suffering from temporal lobe epilepsy. Similar episodic disturbances occurring in patients who have no history of epilepsy are thought by some investigators to have an ictal origin. The nosological concept of episodic dyscontrol syndrome defines seizurelike outbursts of violent behavior, often associated with clouding of consciousness and amnesia of the episode, and followed by symptoms suggestive of postictal depression [141,157]. The syndrome has been attributed to some underlying brain dysfunction, presumed to be ictal or subictal, based on the presence of EEG abnormalities, soft neurological signs, frequent histories of previous head injuries, and childhood seizure disorders (i.e., febrile convulsions). According to Mark and Ervin [142], the syndrome represents a focal disorder of the limbic system, representing an ictal phenomenon characteristic of limbic pathology but without the traditional psychomotor attack of temporal lobe epilepsy. Monroe [157] maintains that the episodic dyscontrol syndrome is not exclusive of limbic pathology. There have been several reports linking violent behavior with limbic-hypothalamic involvement. Hypothalamic lesions, especially those that present a bilateral involvement (expanding tumors, diffuse destruction of hypothalamic nuclei from pressure) have been demonstrated postmortem in patients showing outbursts of rage and violent behavior [118,178]. The association of violence with limbic system pathology has raised the issue of a specific localization for the expression of violent behavior in man [141,213]. Many electroencephalographic studies have attempted to correlate violent or aggressive behavior with temporal lobe abnormalities [102, 104,105,107,163,183,186,203,230]. Most of these studies were conducted on prisoners, often charged with murder and known psychopaths. In one study of murderers [203], it was found that the amount of EEG abnormality correlated with the degree of unpredictability of the crime. In another study [186], 65 percent of thirty-two criminally insane murderers showed EEG abnormalities, as compared to a 15 percent incidence in control subjects. Several other studies [49,77,90,91,122], however, have failed to confirm the above reported high incidence of EEG abnormalities in prisoners and murderers. Similarly, several other studies [31,181] have failed to substantiate the reported high incidence of aggressive or violent behavior in temporal lobe epileptic patients. Various explanations have been given to account for these controversial findings [157,222].

Nonepisodic Psychopathology

Nonepisodic psychopathology, as compared to paroxysmal and episodic disturbances, is generally viewed as nonictal in origin. Its development is attributed primarily to functional (psychogenic) and organic factors, which are considered to be nonspecific, and therefore, nonepileptic in nature. Although it is generally acknowledge that ictal mechanisms contribute very little to the pathogenesis of these disturbances — perhaps, with few exceptions — there exists a great deal of controversy about the contributing effect of an underlying specific pathogenetic process, characteristic of epilepsy as a disease entity, which may account for some of this pathology, especially with regard to the postulated existence of a so-called epileptic personality. Constitutional and genetic factors that determine the so-called epileptic diathesis appear to be basic to this concept. For purposes of this discussion, nonepisodic psychopathology is classified into psychophysiological disturbances, and psychological disturbances.

PSYCHOPHYSIOLOGICAL DISTURBANCES

Various nonepisodic psychophysiological disturbances have been reported to occur at a higher incidence rate among epileptics, and especially among those suffering from temporal lobe epilepsy.

Hypochondriacal complaints, expressing an excessive preoccupation with body functions and concern about personal health, have been found to be frequent in patients with psychomotor epilepsy [113,116,135,180]. It is not known whether these hypochondriacal symptoms are of a primary psychogenic origin or secondary to repetitive experiences of subictal temporolimbic seizures and somatosensory-autonomic auras. Autonomic symptoms have been reported to be frequent among temporal lobe epileptics [134].

Differences in *sleep patterns* have been reported to exist between centrencephalic and temporal lobe epileptics. According to Jovanovic [116], centrencephalic epileptics show a considerable sleep deficit which provokes grand mal seizures on awakening (matutinal attacks). These patients have difficulty in falling asleep and complain of a restless and superficial sleep which is unrefreshing. In contrast, temporal lobe epileptics, who experience primarily nocturnal seizures, show a sleep surplus. These patients go to bed early, fall asleep rapidly and peacefully, have a deep and refreshing sleep, and rise immediately on waking in the morning. Furthermore, centrencephalic epileptics feel sluggish and tired in the morning and are alert and lively in the afternoon and evening, while temporal lobe epileptics show the reverse pattern.

Sexual dysfunctions have been found to be frequently associated with temporal lobe epilepsy. Hyposexuality is an especially common finding in these patients and is characterized by loss of sexual interest as well as potency. In spite of claims that the hyposexuality of these patients is due to the sedative effect of anticonvulsant drugs, it appears that there is considerable evidence to support a specific etiology for this deficit [15,65,68,69,216].

Gestaut [65] was the first to report the characteristic hyposexuality, and this was later confirmed by Taylor [216] in a series of one hundred patients, and by Blumer [14]. In Taylor's cases, hyposexuality (defined as frequency of intercourse of less than once a month) was present in two-thirds of the patients. Taylor also found that perverse sexuality was frequent, but heterosexual hypersexuality was rare. He attributed such abnormalities to temporal lobe dysfunction, and secondarily to psychosocial factors.

This global sexual unresponsiveness has been contrasted with the states of hypersexuality reported in nonepileptic patients with destructive processes of the temporal lobe, such as temporal lobe tumors, and in monkeys that have undergone bilateral temporal lobectomy (Klüver-Bucy syndrome). It is postulated that irritative epileptogenic involvement of the temporal lobe in epileptic patients may account for the reported hyposexuality. The nature of this irritative process, however, remains obscure. It can be pointed out that paroxysmal ictal discharges in temporal lobe epileptics may produce sexual excitement of both appetitive and consummatory nature [13,14,32,59]. The nonepisodic character of this hyposexual state is suggestive of an underlying continuous process, probably due to reactive neuronal inhibition in limbic-hypothalamic neuronal circuits associated with the modulation of sexual drives. This postulated reactive inhibition is presumed to be secondary to an unstable "steady state" within the temporolimbic system which results from the presence of the epileptogenic process. The hyposexual state of these patients appears to be reversible, since it can be greatly improved following temporal lobectomy or with successful control of seizures by antiepileptic drugs [15]. Episodes of fetishism, transvestism, and exhibitionism reported to occur in temporal lobe epileptic patients may be of ictal or nonictal origin [109].

PSYCHOLOGICAL DISTURBANCES

The issue of psychological disturbances of a nonparoxysmal and nonepisodic character, observed during the interictal functioning of epileptics, has been the focus of continuing controversy among various investigators. Central to this controversy is the concept of the so-called *epileptic personality*, that is, a characteristic personality constellation whose organizational dynamics reflect either the specificity of an underlying epileptic process or the uniqueness of epilepsy as a disease entity in determining fixed characterological traits and patterns of behavior. Those who view the epileptic personality as being innately determined (primary) postulate hereditary factors associated with constitutional doctrines (constitutional somatotypes), or genetic factors (biological predisposition to epilepsy), or both. On the other hand, those who consider this personality as being acquired or secondary postulate psychological factors associated with the subject's reaction to the disease (reparative defensive-adaptive processes in reaction to the dysfunctional aspects of the disease) and/or somatic factors associated with underlying structural lesions (organic deficit), toxic effects of antiepileptic drugs (CNS-depressant effects), or ictal mechanisms (subictal dysrhythmia). The majority of authors appear to reject the notion that the epileptic personality is determined by hereditary factors. A number of other investigators have challenged the existence of a specific epileptic personality in noninstitutionalized epileptics, while others have maintained that epileptics do not differ significantly in the incidence or severity of reported psychopathology from other patients suffering from chronic disease.

The most prominent features of the personality of epileptic patients were first described by the nineteenth-century authors Falret [48] and Feré [50], and include explosive irritability, instability of mood, egocentricity (self-centeredness), mistrust, hypersensitivity, and religious and hypochondriacal preoccupations. In addition, subsequent authors have emphasized perseveration in thought, speech and affect (viscosity), inflexibility and lack of adaptability and creativity, mental and reactive slowness, unmodulated affect, fixity of opinions (dogmatism), stubbornness, circumstantiality (adhesiveness), meticulous attention to detail, rigid emotional attitudes, unresponsiveness to external factors, emotional poverty, and general "constriction" of personality, as well as pedantry, unusual verbosity, excessive pride, self-righteousness, and religiosity. Other features that have been emphasized by various authors include dysphoric mood with marked irritability, impulsivity, aggressiveness on slight provocation, explosions of affect, and in some of them, antisocial traits.

The concept of the epileptic personality has been debated for more than a century. In spite of the continuing controversy there has been a significant amount of literature pointing up the fact that epileptics, as a group, show a high incidence of psychopathology, both characterological and symptomatic (neurotic, psychotic). Earlier authors attempted to support the view that there exists a specific epileptic personality, which is constitutionally determined [51,52,54,111,127,128,142,204,205,212]. Although most of the authors have rejected a constitutional origin, there has been significant support of the concept of the relative specificity of this personality. There have been very few comparative studies in this area. Piotrowski [171,172], using criteria of Rorschach test performance, identified a list of fourteen response signs which significantly differentiated between epilepsy and neurosis. On the basis of these signs he was able to correctly diagnose 80 percent of the epileptics and concluded that there exists an epileptic personality. Another comparative study [173], between epileptics, neurotics, and chronic nonepileptic patients, similarly suggested that at least part of the personality deviation of the epileptics may not represent the reaction of the patient to the disease. Various other authors have emphasized the concept that the epileptic personality represents the expression of nonspecific determinants, including organic factors, effect of antiepileptic drugs, and psychological reaction to the disease [34,93,94,95,171,184,234]. Other studies by Gibbs and associates [75,76], Gastaut [72], Bingley [13], and others have supported the view that the psychopathology that characterizes the epileptic personality is encountered only in the temporal lobe epileptic. More recent studies have confirmed the view that epileptics, as a group, show a high incidence of psychiatric disorders but have suggested that the observed psychopathology encompasses the whole spectrum of disturbances. These studies have also failed to find differences in the incidence of psychiatric disorders among the various forms of epilepsy and especially between psychomotor and nonpsychomotor epileptics, including idiopathic (centrencephalic) epilepsy [52,143,148,149,154,155,196–198,200,207,211,221]. In the studies by Small and associates [196–198,200], it was found that both psychomotor and nonpsychomotor epileptics show a prevalence of certain personality traits which include rigidity, schizoid characteristics, passive-aggressive features, and impulsivity. Using criteria based on the MMPI scales, Meir and French [148] and Mignone, Donnelly, and Sadowsky [149] found that the entire group of epileptics was significantly different from a control group, with a preponderance of schizoaffective and depressive features, with the schizophrenia scores being the most significant.

The reported psychopathology of the epileptic personality will be presented on the basis of several categories, representing characterological or symptomatic dimensions secondary to different etiology. These dimensions are (1) perseveration-explosivity; (2) hereditary-constitutional-organic-reactive; and (3) centrencephalic-temporal-psychomotor.

1. *Perseveration (viscosity)-explosivity (impulsivity) traits:* It appears that most of the traits which are presumed to be characteristic of the so-called epileptic personality cluster around two basic dimensions: perseveration (viscosity) and explosivity (impulsivity). *Perseveration* is the fundamental personality trait, according to most authors. Terms used by various investigators to describe this trait include "glischroid" [151–153] "enechetic" [142,204,205], "viscous," "adhesive" [127], or "ixoid" [212]. The trait of perseveration or viscosity defines a slow, persevering, tenacious or "sticky" quality of behavioral expression, which is thought to account for the derivative traits of circumstantiality in speech, retardation, emotional poverty, rigid emotional attitudes, tenaciously adhered opinions and beliefs, inflexibility, limited repertoire of behavioral responses, impaired adaptability and creativity, and in general, "constriction" of personality. It appears, however, that this cluster of traits describes, by and large, obsessive-compulsive personality characteristics. Most of the early constitutionalist authors [127,141,151–153,204,205,212] maintained that perseveration is most marked in patients with idiopathic epilepsy. More recent studies, however, indicate that the viscous traits characterize only the personality of patients with temporal lobe psychomotor epilepsy [13,72,75,76].

Explosivity, a second basic trait, which appears to be the polar opposite of viscosity, has been reported by most of the authors [127,142,151–153,204,205]. Explosivity describes an episodically and paroxysmally occurring behavioral expression, especially with regard to aggressive, hostile, or violent behavior. This trait is thought to account for the reported characteristics of explosive irritability, aggressiveness, impulsivity, lability of mood, and proneness to outbursts of anger and violent behavior. The concept of episodicity seems to define a parameter of this trait.

The issue of whether explosivity is a primary or secondary trait appears to be a matter of dispute. For some investigators [127,151–153] it represents the polar opposite of perseveration, both constituting a single primary bipolar trait and consequently occurring in the same subject. Thus, the same patient may show at different times viscous retardation or explosivity. For other investigators [142,204,205], explosivity is not related to viscosity but rather involves a special type of patient (i.e., temporal lobe epileptic) or implies the presence of cerebral lesions (organicity), and therefore, it is viewed as secondary and occurring independently of perseveration.

Psychoanalytic theorizing about the psychodynamic aspects of the epileptic personality began with generalizations emphasizing its psychogenic conception in terms of a character neurosis that develops in a narcissistic type of individual dominated by conflicts over sadomasochistic or latent homosexual impulses. Thus, according to Stekel [206], the epileptic personality develops on the basis of anxiety and guilt involving aggressive homicidal impulses. Clark [24] proposed that "the epileptic personality is deeply rooted in narcissism which results in an only slightly repressed homosexuality" [24]. Freud [62] advanced similar ideas in his study of Dostoevsky. More recent psychoanalytic formulations of the epileptic personality are based on conceptualizations of ego psychology, postulating a primary impairment of the integrative capacity of the ego, which is thought to reflect an underlying impairment of the integrative capacity of the cerebrum due to a lowered threshold excitation, and which results in difficulties in the area of impulse control. According to Bellack [10], the impaired impulse control, which is secondary to an ego defect, may either manifest itself directly as impulsivity and explosiveness of behavior or, indirectly, in its defensive form, as reaction formation, which results in the development of a constricted and inhibited personality characterized by obsessive-compulsive traits. Thus, one is likely to find characterological features associated with impulsivity as well as excessive inhibition. Therefore, according to this psychoanalytic approach, the so-called trait of perseveration or viscosity is secondary to the so-called trait of explosivity or impulsivity.

The latter trait is considered to be possibly due to subthreshold abnormal brain potentials.

2. *Hereditary-constitutional-organic-reactive traits:* Various studies have attempted to define different dimensions in the epileptic personality in terms of hereditary-constitutional traits, organic traits, and reactive traits.

Hereditary-constitutional traits (primary) have been postulated by a number of authors, on the basis of evidence that a genetically determined predisposition to epilepsy exists. The genetic factor appears to be a recessive or dominant autosomal gene of irregular penetrance, the expression of which varies with age. It is considered to be a contributing factor in almost all epilepsies and is a necessary and sufficient factor in idiopathic (common generalized) epilepsy [27–30, 136, 139, 145–147].

Several studies involving the presumed hereditary aspect of the epileptic personality have attempted to correlate specific personality traits with constitutional types of body structure (somatotypes). The most frequently encountered somatotype in individuals with the characteristic epileptic personality (enechetic, viscous) is an athletic habitus [51, 52, 54, 100, 111, 127, 128, 204, 205, 208]. Thus, Minkowska [51, 52, 54] found that the glischroid types, who, according to her, are characterized by a bipolar trait (viscous retardation and impulsivity), present a constitution similar to the athletic habitus. Similarly, Kretschmer [127] and his school of thought [111] found that the bipolarity of tenacity and explosiveness correlates with an athletic constitution. Kretschmer concluded that there exists a relationship between the viscous character traits of the athletic type and the enechetic character traits of the epileptic type, the latter representing a pathological reinforcement of the traits of the former. On the other hand, Mauz [141] found that the enechetic constitution is predominantly characterized by a dysplastic habitus, with more than half of the idiopathic epileptics showing this type. Other studies, however, have correlated the epileptic personality with an athletic habitus [100, 208]. Jovanović and Shafer [117] attempted to define somatomorphic differences between centrencephalic (idiopathic) and temporal lobe (temporocephalic) epileptics. They found the centrencephalic group to be most commonly asthenic, leptosome, or athletic-leptosome types, and the temporocephalic group to be predominantly athletic, dysplastic, and pycnic types. Most of the studies in this area are methodologically unacceptable, and their findings are often conflicting. Evidently, if there exists a relationship between constitutional body structure and epileptic personality, it must be a complex one [34].

Organic traits describe characterological features which have been found to occur frequently in brain damaged patients and which are commonly referred to as soft neurological signs. A number of studies have supported the view that some of the characterological traits reported in the epileptic personality represent either nonspecific manifestations of underlying cerebral lesions or cerebral dysfunction. A comparison between the psychopathological changes observed in organic brain syndromes (i.e., temporal lobe syndrome) and those reported in epileptic patients, especially in those with a symptomatic form of epilepsy, such as with an involvement of the temporal lobe, reveals significant similarities. Thus, patients with post traumatic brain syndrome show lability of affect, irritability, impulsivity, loss of creativity, concrete thinking, distractibility and limited attention span, egocentricity, perseveration and circumstantiality, organic orderliness, diminished spontaneity in thought, depressed mood changes, a tendency to paranoid suspicion, and frequent intolerance of alcohol [86]. Furthermore, organic syndromes involving the temporal lobe are associated with emotional instability, irritability, aggressive behavior with occasional outbursts and acts of violence of an explosive character (impulse dyscontrol), and frequent hypochondriacal preoccupations. Also, patients with bilateral temporal lobe involvement show hyposexuality and recent memory deficit. All these traits have also been reported in epileptic patients, and especially in those with symptomatic epilepsy [72, 155].

A number of studies have supported the view that organic traits are present in all forms of epilepsy, including the idiopathic one. Most of these studies have used criteria based on Rorschach test performance [34, 93–95,151,184,234]. Studies comparing idiopathic and symptomatic epileptics with nonepileptic organic patients [184,234] on Rorschach test performance show that the personality of epileptics represents a combination of organic and reactional neurotic traits. However, patients with symptomatic epilepsy show a much more serious organic impairment, approaching that of patients with brain damage to the degree that the lesions are diffuse [93–95] Zimmermann, Burgemeister, and Putnam [234] found that the intellectual level of epileptics differs according to type, in the following decreasing order: idiopathic petit mal, idiopathic petit mal with grand mal, idiopathic grand mal, traumatic epilepsy, other symptomatic epilepsy. It is of interest that even idiopathic petit mal patients with a normal IQ showed Rorschach responses suggestive of organicity. The observed performance characteristics of epileptic patients pointed to a loss of creative power, a relatively unfavorable relationship between capacity and aspiration, and a poverty of inner life. Other findings included emotional instability, egocentricity, impulsive approach to human problems, and a lower degree of conformity to social norms. Similarly, in a Rorschach study involving fifty epileptic patients, Delay and associates [34] provided further evidence to support the view that the organic dimension in the epileptic personality includes traits which are found to be those of the personality of organic patients in general, and therefore, not specific of epilepsy. According to Delay and associates, they consist of reduction of creative intellectual productivity and of the quality of this productivity and reduction of imaginative capacity leading to ideational perseveration. They also concluded that these traits are independent of etiology and localization and are related to a small degree of intellectual deterioration, which occurs even in idiopathic epileptics. A more recent study by Mises, Sarcella, and Soul [155] also reported that epileptics in general show impairment in the cognitive area which includes poor attention; perseveration; short memory; concrete thinking; and difficulty in abstraction, synthesis, and conceptualization. Cognitive difficulties consisting of irrelevant detail, integration difficulty, and concreteness, were also reported by Ferguson and associates [52], on the basis of cartoon interpretations. Nevertheless, Gastaut and associates [72] found characteristic personality deviations suggestive of organicity only in temporal lobe psychomotor epileptics, which occurred independently of intellectual level and included perseveration, retardation in reaction time, a flat, blunted affect, and bradyphrenia. Idiopathic epileptics were found to show only overemotionality and a few neurotic traits attributed to the patient's reaction to the disease.

It is important to recognize the fact that the so-called organic traits or soft neurologic signs, which are suggestive of an underlying brain dysfunction characteristic of organic brain syndromes, do not represent the expression of a single pathogenetic mechanism but the result of several mechanisms, acting alone or in combination. The following examples illustrate this point. (1) Some of these organic traits or symptoms may represent impairment or loss of function due to an irreversible structural neuronal damage and therefore, are associated with a permanent deficit in the function(s) subserved by these neurons (elliptic phenomena); for example, deficit in recent memory secondary to diffuse brain damage or lesions localized in the hippocampal region of the temporal lobe. (2) Some traits may represent impairment or loss of function due to reversible pathophysiological changes associated with the effect of ictal mechanisms or the effect of drugs (ecliptic phenomena); for example, subictal electrical discharges or other mechanisms associated with the dysfunctional state of the epileptic brain appear to account for the functional deficit involving the inhibition of sexuality in temporal lobe epileptics or the momentary obliteration of consciousness of the petit mal epileptic children, which results in poor concentration and learning difficulties. (3) Some traits may represent an exaggerated expression of a CNS function due to direct stimulation of specific cerebral regions by subictal neuronal discharges (excitatory phenomena); for example, explosive behavior, irritability. (4) Some traits may be due to a reversible (functional) or irreversible (structural) disinhibition of more primitive functions subserved by subordinate areas of the brain following the temporary blocking or permanent destruction of an inhibitory circuit (release phenomena); for example, affective lability, overemotionality. (5) some traits may represent impaired integration at the neuronal level due to a reversible or irreversible interference with integrative CNS mechanisms and which is reflected in the integration of ego processes (disintegrative phenomena); for example, diminished creativity, difficulty in abstraction. (6) Some traits may represent modified or less effective functions as a result of the taking over of a lost function by another area of the brain (compensatory phenomena); for example, in a lateralized damage of the dominant hemisphere, one may presumably observe an impairment of linguistic and higher discriminative cognitive processes, with maintenance and possibly enhancement of nonverbal perceptual analysis involving visuospatial skills. (7) Some traits may represent a psychological reaction to the loss, impairment, modification, or enhancement of CNS functions, resulting from the above mechanisms.

Most of the so-called organic traits appear to be the result of adaptive-defensive ego processes, in an effort to maintain the steady state of the functioning personality in the face of cognitive deficit or affective dyscontrol. They will be discussed together with the reactive traits associated with patient's psychological reaction to having epilepsy. The diverse etiology of the above mechanisms emphasizes the point that soft neurological signs may be reversible or irreversible and may respond deferentially to pharmacological treatment or psychosocial therapies, depending on the nature of the underlying mechanism.

Reactive traits in the epileptic personality constitute the most important category. As a matter of fact, the majority of authors consider the epileptic personality as a reaction to the dysfunctional state produced by the epileptic disorder. These reactive traits can be classified into *intrapersonal*, associated with the intrapsychic reaction to the underlying dysfunctional CNS state; and *interpersonal*, associated with the psychological reaction to the interpersonal dysfunctional dynamics of having the disease.

The intrapersonal reactive traits can be further subclassified into organic and nonorganic, depending on whether or not they resemble the reactive traits which characterize organic brain syndromes. This distinction has only clinical or descriptive value, since all intrapersonal reactive traits share a common pathogenetic mechanism; that is, a psychological reaction to the underlying CNS dysfunction. Among those traits which have an organic implication are perseveration, circumstantiality, organic orderliness, and in general, traits attributed to the so-called viscous or enechetic personality, all of which have adaptive value for the patient in coping with the primary dysfunctional CNS state. Other intrapersonal reactive traits include various obsessive-compulsive and paranoid traits, expressing the use of reaction-formation and projection, respectively, as major defenses against the threat of loss of impulse control.

The interpersonal reactive traits are developmentally significant in that they are formed as a result of the attitudes of the epileptic child and those of his parents, especially with regard to situations involving parental overprotection, guilt, or rejection, and the child's conflict over independence, mastery, and self-control. Feelings of passivity, dependency, insecurity, and helplessness develop in the epileptic patient in reaction to the embarrassing instances of loss of control with regard to motor apparatus, sphyncter, or emotion, as well as in reaction to the discontinuity of experience during seizures. Similar traits have also been reported in patients with chronic diseases, especially when they begin from childhood.

On the basis of a Rorschach study involving fifty epileptics and an extensive review of the literature, Delay and associates [34] provided evidence to support the view that there are two basic dimensions in the epileptic personality: an organic dimension and a coartative-extratensive dimension. According to Delay and associates, the latter dimension, which is superimposed on the basic organic component, is of bipolar nature, is related to the degree of social adaptation of the subject, and varies as a function of etiology and localization. One pole of this dimension is characterized by a production of an extratensive experience type on Rorschach test performance while the opposite pole is characterized by a production of coartative experience type. Delay and associates found that the extratensive subjects make a poor social adaptation and show evident explosivity and impulsivity, sometimes of a serious nature. On the other hand, the coartative subjects make a good social adaptation and do not show personality disturbances. They further postulated that coartation can be considered as an adaptive type of reaction on the part of the epileptic to his disease: He attempts to achieve adjustment by a constriction of his personality. Alternatively, coartation can relate to the particular localization of the cerebral processes determining the epileptic condition. In contrast, extratensiveness in epileptics represents poor social adaptation and appears to be related to a specific organic process.

3. *Centrencephalic versus temporal epileptic personality disturbances:* A significant number of studies involving comparisons between centrencephalic (idiopathic) and temporal lobe psychomotor epileptics have provided respectable evidence that these two groups differ in personality and amount of psychopathology, with the temporal psychomotor epileptics appearing to be the most disturbed group [13,44,72,76,82,112–114,134, 135,149,189,215]. This evidence conflicts with that reported by a number of other investigators, who have failed to find significant differences between these two groups. Considerable evidence in support of the latter position has been provided by Stevens and associates[208,210].

In an early study involving 300 temporal lobe epileptics, Gibbs and associates [82] reported that 40 percent of these patients showed psychopathological disturbances covering a broad range of abnormalities. In a subsequent study, Gibbs [82] found that personality disturbances are chiefly encountered in epileptics with an anterior temporal lobe involvement. Gastaut and associates [72] found that temporal lobe epileptics show distinctive behavior disorders, while idiopathic epileptics are free of any significant psychopathology. Other authors have reported distinctive personality profiles differentiating the idiopathic from the temporal lobe epileptic.

A specific *centrencephalic epileptic personality* profile has been described by several European investigators. Jovanović [116,117], quoting studies by Leder [134,135,], Janz [113], Tellenbach [215], and others, describes the centrencephalic epileptic in terms of an extrovert, unstable, rather impulsive, and emotionally reactive type of personality, with a hysterical proclivity and a tendency to use excessive denial as his major defense against anxiety. They are emotionally labile, infantile, and irascible

[215]; they have strong emotions, with brief fits of temper, but they are easy to pacify and tend to react with infantile envy or spite [113,132,133,215]; they have a tendency to act spontaneously and socially and to be subject to passive momentary impulses and affections and always express themselves emotionally with labile variations of mood [134,135]. Gastaut has also found them to show overemotionality [72]. In their instability, they are suggestible and easily deceived, lacking tenacity and resoluteness. They are also found to be arrogant with heightened imagination and often showing strongly ambivalent behavior. Janz [113] elaborates on the indecisiveness that pervades these patients' everyday life both when faced with ethical, erotic, or religious conflicts, as portrayed by Dostoevsky. In contrast to the rigorously repressed psychomotor epileptic, the idiopathic shows weak repression. In his excessive use of denial as a major defense against threatening or conflictful situations, he persistently emphasizes the bright side, the good and the hopeful, and perceives menacing experiences as just the opposite. In his exaggerated optimism, he behaves as if he is able to solve all his problems and as if he is free from feelings of guilt, fear, or conflict [116]. According to Kraepelin [124], this group also includes subjects with psychopathic behavior.

With regard to behavior disorders, although a number of studies have supported the view that centrencephalic epileptics are generally free from serious psychiatric disturbances, many other studies have reported a high incidence of psychopathology in all epileptics, including the centrencephalic ones. Some authors have found characteristic disturbances in this group involving cognitive functions. Thus, Mirsky and associates [154] reported that centrencephalic epileptics perform poorly on tests measuring sustained concentration and attentiveness. There was a suggestion that failure in performance probably correlated more with subcortical midline paroxysms. Those patients showing focal epilepsy, particularly temporal lobe focus, did not show this deficiency. Similarly, Kimura [119], using letters randomly presented that had to be sorted alphabetically, found the ordering time to be slower for patients with centrencephalic epilepsy than for patients with focal epilepsy. Kimura attributed this impairment to an attentional disturbance, possibly involving a dysfunction of the reticular formation and the more rostral nonspecific thalamic nuclei.

The *temporal lobe epileptic personality*, has been described by a number of authors as constituting what is commonly known as the epileptic personality. This includes both the retarded, enechetic, or viscous type and the explosive, aggressive, or irritable type. In accordance with the findings of Gastaut [72] and Bingley [13], the most commonly encountered type of personality in temporal lobe epilepsy is the viscous type, which is also felt to characterize the schizoid personality and the frank schizophrenic. Perseveration and circumstantiality are prominent characteristics of this type. Gastaut further described them as obsequious, sensitive, and frequently showing perverse character traits, obsessive ideas, and morbid religiosity. More recent studies by Leder [134,135], Janz [113], and others, quoted by Jovanović [116], have described these patients as conscientious, hard-working, and reliable, as well as dogmatic, obstinate, pedantic, and overbearing, with a tendency to be introspective and with an appearance of solidarity and social stability. On the basis of Rorschach studies, these authors have further described them as apathetic, parsimonious, lacking spontaneous emotional involvement in their life events, and giving the impression of being immovable and difficult to communicate with in conversation. Their experiential orientation lacks fantasy and social concern and is primarily centered around bodily processes with a characteristic hypochondriacal preoccupation, which has been confirmed by several other investigators [130]. These patients score high on perseveration and low in originality. According to Janz [113], the dominant form of defense in overcoming conflict is probably found among the anancastic (obsessive-compulsive) defense mechanisms, and especially reaction formation. The exaggerated solitude, pedantry, humility, and pronounced sense of justice often reported in these patients have been interpreted as the result of reaction formation. Similarly, the enechetic personality changes have been regarded as a protection against an increased tendency to hostility and aggression [20]. The anal characteristics of these patients (cleanliness, economy, orderliness, resistance) have been elaborated by Braütigam [20]. In their social relationships, these patients seek physical closeness and intimacy, which is often manifested as obtrusiveness or as attachment to family and home, or hypersocial behavior. These characteristics have been similarly interpreted as representing a reaction formation because of fear of hostile opposition [20]. These patients are also prone to an excessive use of projection as a defense against hostile, sadistic impulses and run the increased risk of developing paranoid traits and delusional conditions, which have been reported to occur at a higher incidence among them. Schizoid personality traits have also been frequently reported among these patients.

Another less frequently encountered type, according to Gastaut [65,70] and others is the aggressive-explosive type, characterized by impulse dyscontrol. This type shows irritability, aggressiveness, impulsivity, emotional instability, and explosiveness, with a proneness to sudden changes in mood and violent rage reactions. Impulse dyscontrol behavior has been attributed to temporal lobe dysfunction and is thought by some to be the result of ictal mechanisms [43,46,141,157]. Falconer [46] has shown that interictal aggressive behavior can be eliminated by unilateral temporal lobectomy in more than 50 percent of the patients suffering from temporal lobe dysfunction secondary to mesial temporal sclerosis.

Many clinicians feel that patients with temporal lobe disease, including psychomotor epilepsy, show an unusually high incidence of psychiatric disturbances, especially labile affect and mood swings; some of them develop acute and chronic schizophreniform psychoses. Ervin and associates [43] in a study involving the personality characteristics of patients with electroencephalographic temporal lobe spike foci, found that the patients with the most persistently severe psychiatric disturbances, on both clinical evaluation and psychological testing, were those with psychomotor seizures, especially of the complex or psychical variety.

Gastaut [72] found characteristic personality deviations suggestive of organicity only in the temporal psychomotor epileptics. They were reported to occur independently of intellectual level and to include perseveration, retardation in reaction time, blunted affect, and bradyphrenia. However, Stevens [210] has reported higher scores in full scale IQ in temporal lobe epileptics, as compared to patients with generalized (idiopathic) epilepsy. On the other hand, Glowinski [84] in a study involving thirty unilateral temporal lobe and thirty centrencephalic epileptic patients, concluded, on the basis of testings with the Wechsler Memory Scale, that recent memory is more impaired in the temporal lobe patients. These patients showed particular difficulty in integrating and memorizing meaningful verbal material, which were attributed to subictal discharges interfering with registration and consolidation of new information.

It appears that there are differences in the type of behavior disorders depending on the lateralization of the epileptogenic focus. Aggressive behavior in temporal lobe epileptics has been linked with dominant hemisphere involvement and hence with speech and memory impairment [189]. Similarly, the epileptic involvement of the dominant temporal lobe is more likely to be associated with schizophreniclike psychosis, whereas the involvement of the nondominant temporal lobe is more likely to be associated with manic-depressive disturbances [54,56]. A number of studies have provided evidence suggesting the existence of functional hemispheric specialization concerning several functions. These studies involve patients with lateralized lesions [150,168,169,195], and with commissurotomies [16–18,201,202], as well as experimental situations involving lateralized hemispheric stimulation by intracarotid sodium amytal injections [108,170], independent or dichotic perceptual hemispheric stimulation [26], and electroencephalographic studies [64,158]. Currently available evidence indicates that, in righthanded individuals, the left hemisphere (dominant) is specialized not only for verbal information processing (language) but also plays a more significant role in response initiation. It is also specialized for higher discriminative cognitive processes involving a more analytic and sequential approach. On the other hand, the right (nondominant) hemisphere is more holistic and global with specialization in nonverbal perceptual analysis involving visuospatial skills (apprehension and processing of spatial patterns, relations, and information), as well as in the processing of affective stimuli (depression-euphoria). It is, therefore, very likely that lateralized or bilateral epileptic involvement of the temporal lobes may be associated with different types of cognitive deficit, characterological traits, and psychopathology.

CONCLUSION

Epilepsy is a chronic illness with superimposed acute episodes of seizures. Although seizures represent the most dramatic symptom of this illness, one must keep in mind that they constitute only a portion of the symptomatic range of the disturbances associated with it. When classical seizures are part of the symptomatic picture, it is easy for the clinician to suspect the presence of epilepsy and, therefore, proceed with the proper clinical and laboratory evaluation of the patient that would lead to the establishment of its diagnosis. However, epilepsy may manifest itself with nonseizural symptomatology or with atypical seizural episodes, in which case its diagnosis is frequently missed.

The whole spectrum of neuropsychological dysfunction that characterizes epilepsy has been presented in terms of a continuum of psychopathological disturbances rather than in terms of pathology that is compartmentalized into psychiatric and nonpsychiatric. In classifying the epileptic psychopathology, for purposes of discussion, into ictal, postictal, and interictal, as well as into seizural, episodic, and nonepisodic, it is necessary to emphasize the point that these terms do not always define what they imply and, therefore, they can be misleading. An effort was made to present this spectrum as being clustered into various psychosyndromes, whose complex pathogenesis involves varying contributions from ictal, organic, and psychogenic mechanisms.

The clinician must become fully familiar with the rich and polymorphous psychopathology of epilepsy in order to be able to diagnose it correctly. Furthermore, in order to provide proper management of the epileptic patient, the physician must have a thorough understanding of the various underlying pathogenetic processes of the illness and within the limitations of our present knowledge be able to appreciate their varying contribution to the dysfunctional state of the patient. It is through such a holistic approach that the physician can avoid the pitfall of attempting to diagnose and treat a symptom rather than a diseased person.

REFERENCES

1   Abraham, K. "Hysterical dream states," 1910. In *Selected papers on psychoanalysis*. New York: Basic Books, 1953.
2   Ajuriaguerra, J. de. La mentalité épileptique. *Rev. Psychol. Appl.* 3:192–208, 1953.
3   Andermann, K., Berman, S., Cooke, P. M., Dickson, J., Gastaut, H., et al. Self-induced epilepsy. *Arch. Neurol.* 6:49–65, 1962.
4   Asano, N. "Clinic-genetic study of manic-depressive psychosis." In *Clinical genetics in psychiatry*, ed. H. Mitsuda, Tokyo: Igaku-Shoin, 1967.
5   Barker, W. Studies on epilepsy: The petit mal attack as response within the CNS to distress in organism-environment integration. *Psychosom. Med.* 10:73, 1948.
6   Barker, W., and Barker, S. Experimental production of human convulsive brain potentials by stress-induced effects upon neural integrative functions: Dynamics of the convulsive reaction to stress. *Assoc. Res. Nerv. Dis. Proc.* 29:90, 1950.
7   Bartemeir, L. H. Concerning the psychogenesis of convulsive disorders. *Psychoanal. Q.* 12:336, 1943.
8   Bartlet, J. E. A. Chronic psychosis following epilepsy. *Am. J. Psychiatry* 114:338, 1957.
9   Bechterewa, N. P. "Human response to brain stimulation." In *Brain control*, ed. E. S. Valenstein, New York: Wiley Interscience, 1973.
10   Bellack, L. *The Rorschach and the epileptic personality*, trans. R. Benton and A. Benton, pp. 25–27. Communication quoted by Delay, J. et al. New York: Logos Press, 1958.
11   Bennett, A. B. Mental disorders associated with temporal lobe epilepsy. *Dis. Nerv. Syst.* 26:280–284, 1965.
12   Berg, C. Clinical notes on a case diagnosed as epilepsy. *Br. J. Med. Psychol.* 19:9, 1941.
13   Bingley, T. *Mental symptoms in temporal lobe epilepsy and temporal lobe gliomas.* Munksgaard: Copenhagen, 1958.
14   Blumer, D. Hypersexual episodes in temporal lobe epilepsy. *Amer. J. Psychiatry* 126:1099–1106, 1970.
15   Blumer, D., and Walker, A. E. Sexual behavior in temporal lobe epilepsy. *Arch. Neurol.* 16:37–43, 1967.
16   Bogen, J. E. The other side of the brain. I. Dysgraphia and dyscopia following cerebral commissurotomy. *Bull. Los Angeles Neurol. Soc.* 34:73–105, 1969.
17   Bogen, J. E. The other side of the brain. II. An oppositional mind. *Bull. Los Angeles Neurol. Soc.* 34:135–162, 1969.
18   Bogen, J. E., and Bogen, G. M. The other side of the brain. III. The corpus callosum and creative activity. *Bull. Los Angeles Neurol. Soc.* 34:191–220, 1969.
19   Brunn, R. von, and Brunn, W. L. von. Die Epilepsie im Rorschach'schen Formdeutversuch. *Arch. Psychiatr. Z. Neurol.* 184:545–578, 1950.
20   Bräutigam, W. Zur epileptischen Wesensveränderung. *Psyche* 5:523, 1951.
21   Bruens, J. H. Psychoses in epilepsy. *Psychiatr. Neurol. Neurochir.* 74:175–192, 1971.

22   Chafetz, M. E., and Schwab, R. S. Psychological factors involved in bizarre seizures. *Psychosom. Med.* 21:96, 1959.

23   Charlton, M. H., and Hoefer, P. F. A. Television and epilepsy. *Arch. Neurol.* 11:239–247, 1964.

24   Clark, L. P. A personality study of the epileptic constitution. *Am. J. Med. Sci.* 148:729–738, 1914.

25   Clement, P., Andermann, F., and Dongier, M. Self-induced television epilepsy. *Can. Psychiatr. Assoc. J.* 21(3):163–167, 1976.

26   Cohen, B. D., Berent, S., and Silverman, A. J. Field-dependence and lateralization of function in the human brain. *Arch. Gen. Psychiatry* 28:165–167, 1973.

27   Conrad, K. Erbanlage und Epilepsie: Untersuchungen an einer Serie von 253 Zwillingspaaren. *Z. Neurol.* 153:271–326, 1935.

28   Conrad, K. Erbanlage und Epilepsie. II. Ein Beitrag zur Zwillingskasuistik: die konkordanten Eineiigen. *Z. Neurol.* 155:254–297, 1936.

29   Conrad, K. Erbanlage und Epilepsie. III. Ein Beitrag zur Zwillingskasuistik: die diskordanten Eineiigen. *Z. Neurol.* 155:509–542, 1936.

30   Conrad, K. Erbanlage und Epilepsie. IV. Ergebnisse einer Nachkommenschaftuntersuchung in Epileptikern. *Z. Neurol.* 159:521–581, 1937.

31   Currie, S., Heathfield, K. W. G., Henson, R. A., and Scott, D. F. Clinical course and prognosis of temporal lobe epilepsy: A survey of 666 patients. *Brain* 94:173–190, 1971.

32   Currier, D., Suess, J. F., and Andy, O. J. Psychomotor sexual seizures. *Trans. Am. Neurol. Assoc.* 94:178–182, 1969.

33   Daly, D. Ictal effect. *Am. J. Psychiatry* 115:97–108, 1958.

34   Delay, J., Pichot, P., Lempériére, T., and Perse, J. *The Rorschach and the epileptic personality*, trans. R. Benton and A. Benton. New York: Logos Press, 1958.

35   Delgado, J. M. R. Permanent implantation of multilead electrodes in the brain. *J. Biol. Med.* 24:351–358, 1952.

36   Dongier, S. Statistical study of clinical and electroencephalographic manifestations of 536 episodes occurring in 516 epileptics between seizures. *Epilepsia* 1:117–142, 1959–1960.

37   Dreyer, R. Zur Trago des Status Epilepticus mit Psychomotorischen Aufallen: Ein Bertrag zum Temporalen Status Epilepticus and zur Atypischen Dammerzustanden und Verstimmungen. *Nervenarzt* 36:121–223, 1965.

38   Ehret, R., and Schneider, E. Photogene Epilepsie mit Suchtartiger Selbstauslösung Kleiner Anfalle und Wiederholten Sexualdelikten. *Arch. Psychiatr.* 202:74–94, 1961.

39   Engel, G. L., and Romano, J. Delirium, a syndrome of cerebral insufficiency. *J. Chronic Dis.* 9:260, 1959.

40   Epstein, A. W. Recurrent dreams (their relationship to temporal lobe seizures). *AMA Arch. Gen. Psychiatry* 10:25, 1964.

41   Epstein, A. W., and Ervin, F. Psychodynamic significance of seizure content in psychomotor epilepsy. *Psychosom. Med.* 18:43, 1956.

42   Erickson, T. C. Erotomania as an expression of cortical epileptiform discharge. *Arch. Neurol. Psychiatry* 53:226, 1945.

43   Ervin, F., Epstein, A. W., and King, H. E. Behavior of epileptic and nonepileptic patients with "temporal spikes." *AMA Arch. Neurol. Psychiatry* 74:488–497, 1955.

44   Ervin, F. R. "Brain disorders IV: Associated with convulsions (epilepsy)." In *Comprehensive textbook of psychiatry*, eds. A. F. Freedman and H. I. Kaplan, pp. 795–816. Baltimore: Williams and Wilkins, 1972.

45   Falconer, M. A. Some functions of the temporal lobe with special regard to affective behavior in epileptic seizures. *J. Psychosom. Res.* 9:25–28, 1965.

46   Falconer, M. A. Reversibility by temporal lobe resection of the behavioral abnormalities of temporal lobe epilepsy. *N. Engl. J. Med.* 389:451–455, 1973.

47   Falconer, M. A., Hill, D., Meyer, A., and Wilson, J. L. "Clinical, radiological, and EEG correlations with pathological changes in temporal lobe epilepsy and their significance in surgical treatment." In *Temporal lobe epilepsy*, eds. M. Baldwin and P. Bailey, pp. 396–410. Springfield, Ill.: Thomas, 1958.

48   Falret, J. De l'état mental des épileptiques. Arch. *Gén. Méd.* 16:661–679, 1861.

49   Fenton, G. W., and Edwin, E. L. Homicide, temporal lobe epilepsy, and depression: A case report. *Br. J. Psychiatry* 111:304–306, 1965.

50   Feré, C. *Les épilepsies et les épileptiques.* Paris: Alcan, 1890; trans. P. Ebers. Leipzig: Engelmann, 1896.

51   Ferguson, S. M., Rayport, M., Gardner, R., et al. Similarities in mental content of psychotic states, spontaneous seizures, dreams, and responses to electrical brain stimulation in patients with temporal lobe epilepsy. *Psychosom. Med.* 31:479–498, 1969.

52   Ferguson, S. M., Schwartz, M. L., and Rayport, M. Perception of humor in patients with temporal lobe epilepsy. *Arch. Gen Psychiatry* 21:363–367, 1969.

53   Flor-Henry, P. Psychosis and temporal lobe epilepsy: A controlled investigation. *Epilepsia* 10:363–395, 1969.

54   Flor-Henry, P. Schizophrenialike reactions and affective psychoses associated with temporal lobe epilepsy: Etiological factors. *Am J. Psychiatry* 126:400–404, 1969.

55   Flor-Henry, P. Psychosis, neurosis, and epilepsy. *Br. J. Psychiatry* 124:144–150, 1974.

56   Flor-Henry, P. "Generalized seizures, limbic seizures, and psychosis." In *Recent advances in clinical psychiatry*, vol. 2, ed. K. Granville-Grossman, pp. 281–284. London: Churchill-Livingston, 1976.

57   Flor-Henry, P. "Temporal lobe epilepsy and sexual deviation." In *Recent advances in clinical psychiatry*, vol. 2, ed. K. Granville-Grossman, pp. 248–287. London: Churchill-Livingston, 1976.

58   Foster, F. M., and Liske, E. Role of environmental clues in temporal lobe epilepsy. *Neurology* 13:301–305, 1963.

59   Freed, L. F. A Case of temporal lobe epilepsy with some unusual features. *S. Afr. Med. J.* 41:343–347, 1967.

60   Freedman, D. X. On the use and abuse of LSD. *Arch. Gen. Psychiatry* 18:330–347, 1968.

61   Freeman, F. R., and Nevis, A. H. Temporal lobe sexual seizures. *Neurology* 19:87–90, 1969.

62   Freud, S. "Dostoevsky and patricide," 1928. In *Standard edition*, vol. 21, ed. J. Strachey. London: Hogarth Press, 1961.

63   Galin, D. Implication for psychiatry of left and right cerebral specialization. *Arch. Gen. Psychiatry* 31:572–583, 1974.

64   Galin, D., and Ornstein, R. Lateral specialization of cognitive mode: An EEG Study. *Psychophysiology* 9:412–418, 1972.

65   Gastaut, H. So-called psychomotor and temporal epilepsy: A critical study. *Epilepsia* 2:59–99, 1953.

66   Gastaut, H. *The epilepsies: Their electroclinical correlates.* Springfield, Ill.: Thomas, 1954.

67   Gastaut, H. Etude électroclinique des épisodes psychotiques survenant en dehors des crises cliniques chez les épileptiques. *Rev. Neurol.* 95:588–594, 1956.

68   Gastaut, H. Apropos des symptômes cliniques rencontrés chez les épileptiques psychomoteurs dans l'intervalle de leurs crises. In *Bases physiologiques et aspects cliniques de l'épilepsie*, ed. T. Alajouanine, pp. 139–162. Paris: Masson, 1958.

69   Gastaut, H., and Collomb, H. Etude du comportement sexuel chez les épileptiques psychomoteurs. *Ann. Méd. Psychol.* 112:657–696, 1954.

70   Gastaut, H., and Miletto, G. Interprétation physiopathogenique des symptômes de la rage furieuse. *Rev. Neurol.* 12:5–25, 1955.

71   Gastaut, H., Morin, C., and Lesèvre, N. Etude du comportement des épileptiques psychomoteurs dans l'intervalle de leurs crises. *Ann. Méd. Psychol.* 1:1–27, 1955.

72   Gastaut, H., Roger, J., and Lesevre, N. Différenciation psychologique des épileptiques en fonction des formes électrocliniques de leur maladie. *Rev. Psychol. Appl.* 3:237–249, 1953.

73   Gastaut, H., Regis, H., Bostem, F., and Beaussart, M. Etude électroencephalographique de trente-cinq sujets ayant présentés des crises épileptiques déclenchées par la télévision. *Rev. Neurol.* 102:533–534, 1960.

74   Gastaut, H., Regis, H., Bostem, J., and Beaussart, M. A propos des crises survenant au cours des spectacles télévisés et de leur mécanisme. *Presse Méd.* 69:1581–1583, 1961.

75   Gibbs, E. L., Gibbs, F. A., and Fuster, B. Psychomotor epilepsy: A review. *Arch. Neurol. Psychiatry* 60:331–339, 1948.

76   Gibbs, F. A. Ictal and nonictal psychiatric disorders in temporal lobe epilepsy. *J. Nerv. Ment. Dis.* 113:522–528, 1951.

77   Gibbs, F. A., Bagshi, B. K., and Bloomberg, W. Electroencephalographic study of criminals. *Am. J. Psychiatry* 102:294, 1945.

78   Gibbs, F. A., and Gibbs, E. L. The likeness of the cortical dysrhythmias of schizophrenia and psychomotor epilepsy. *Am. J. Psychiatry* 95:225, 1938.

79   Gibbs, F. A., and Gibbs, E. L. *Atlas of electroencephalography*, vol. 1. Reading, Mass.: Addison-Wesley, 1951a.

80   Gibbs, F. A., and Gibbs, E. L. *Atlas of electroencephalography*, vol. 2, 2nd ed. Reading, Mass.: Addison-Wesley, 1951b.

81   Gibbs, F. A., and Gibbs, E. L. *Atlas of electroencephalography*, vol. 3, 2nd ed. Reading, Mass.: Addison-Wesley, 1964.

82 Gibbs, F. A., Gibbs, E. L., and Fuster, B. Types of paroxysmal syndromes. *Arch. Neurol. Psychiatry* 60:4, 1948.

83 Glaus, A. On the combination of schizophrenia and epilepsy. *Z. ges. Neurol. Psychiatry* 135:450, 1931.

84 Glowinski, H. Cognitive deficit in temporal lobe epilepsy: An investigation of memory functioning. *J. Nerv. Ment. Dis.* 157:120–137, 1973.

85 Green, R. S., and Rau, J. H. Treatment of compulsive eating disturbances with anticonvulsant medication. *Am. J. Psychiatry* 131:428–432, 1974.

86 Goldstein, K. *After effects of brain injuries in war: Their evolution and treatment.* New York: Grune, 1942.

87 Groethuysen, G. C., Robinson, D. B., Maylett, C. H., et al. Depth electrographic recording of a seizure during a structural interview. *Psychosom. Med.* 19:353–362, 1957.

88 Gruhle, H. W. On the psychoses of epilepsy. *Z. ges. Neurol. Psychiatr.* 28:148, 1936.

89 Gunn, J. Affective and suicidal symptoms in epileptic prisoners. *Psychol. Med.* 3:108–114, 1973.

90 Gunn, J., and Bonn, J. Criminality and violence in epileptic prisoners. *Br. J. Psychiatry* 118:337–343, 1971.

91 Gunn, J., and Fenton, G. Epilepsy, automatism, and crime. *Lancet* 1:1173–1176, 1971.

92 Harper, M., and Roth, M. Temporal lobe epilepsy and the phobic anxiety-depersonalization syndrome. I. A comprehensive study. *Compr. Psychiatry* 3:129–151, 1962.

93 Harrower-Erickson, M. R. Personality changes accompanying cerebral lesions. II. Rorschach study of patients with focal epilepsy. *Arch. Neurol. Psychiatry* 43:1081–1107, 1940.

94 Harrower-Erickson, M. R. Personality studies in focal epilepsy. *Bull. Can. Psychol. Assoc.* 19–21, 1941.

95 Harrower-Erickson, M. R. "Psychological studies in patients with epileptic seizures." In *Epilepsy and cerebral localization,* eds. W. Penfield and T. C. Erickson. Springfield, Ill.: Thomas, 1941.

96 Heath, R. Pleasure and brain activity in man. *J. Nerv. Ment. Dis.* 154,1:3–18, 1972.

97 Heath, R. G. Common characteristics of epilepsy and schizophrenia: Clinical observation and depth electrode studies. *Am. J. Psychiatry* 118:1013–1026, 1962.

98 Heath, R. G. "Closing remarks with commentary on depth electroencephalography in epilepsy and schizophrenia." In *EEG and behavior,* ed. G. H. Glaser. New York: Basic Books, 1963.

99 Hendrick, I. Psychoanalytic observations on the aura of two cases with convulsions. *Psychosom. Med.* 2:43; 1940.

100 Hildegund, C. Vergleichende Untersuchungen mit dem Rorschachschen Formdeutversuch zwischen gesunden Athletiker und genuiner Epileptiker mit athletischer Konstitution. *Arch. Psychiat. Z. Neurol.* 183:302—327, 1940.

101 Hill, D. The relationship between epilepsy and schizophrenia: EEG studies. *Folia Psychiatr. Cong.* No. 51:95, 1948.

102 Hill, D. EEG in episodic psychotic and psychopathic behavior. *Electroencephalogr. Clin. Neurophysiol.* 4:419, 1952.

103 Hill, D. Clinical associations of electroencephalographic foci in the temporal lobe. *Arch. Neurol. Psychiatry* 96:379–381, 1953.

104 Hill, D., and Parr, G. *Electroencephalography.* Ludgate Hill: McDonald, 1950.

105 Hill, D., and Pond, D. Reflections on one hundred capital cases submitted to encephalography. *J. Ment. Sci.* 98:23, 1952.

106 Hill, D., Pond, D. A., Mitchell, W., and Falconer, M. A. Personality changes following temporal lobectomy for epilepsy. *J. Ment. Sci.* 103:18, 1957.

107 Hill, D., and Watterson, D. Electroencephalographic studies of psychopathic personalities. *J. Neurol. Psychiatry* 5:47, 1942.

108 Hommes, O. R., and Panhuysen, L. H. H. M. Depression and cerebral dominance. *Psychiatr. Neurol. Neurochir.* 74:259–270, 1971.

109 Hooshmand, H., and Brawley, B. W. Temporal lobe seizures and exhibitionism. *Neurology* 19:1119–1126, 1969.

110 Hutchinson, J. H. Photogenic epilepsy induced by the patient. *Lancet* 274:243–245, 1958.

111 Janz, D. Klinische und experimentelle Untersuchungen über Konstitution und Krampfbereitschaft bei Epileptikern. *Arch. Psychiatr. Nervenkr.* 112:136–220, 1940.

112 Janz, D. "Differentialtypologie der idiopathischen Epilepsien." In *Psychopathologie Heute.* Thieme: Stuttgart, 1962.

113 Janz, D. Zur Abgrenzung verschiedener Psychosyndrome bei Epilepsie. *Hippokrates* 39:402, 1968.

114 Janz, D. Anfalls-Syndrome: Psychiatrie der Gegenwart, Forschung und Praxis. *Kilnische Psychiatrie,* vol. 2, eds. K. P. Kisker, J.-E. Meyer, M. Müller, and E. Strömgren, pp. 565–630. Berlin: Springer-Verlag, 1972.

115 Johnson, J. Sexual impotence and the limbic system. *Br. J. Psychiatry* 111:300–303, 1965.

116 Jovanić, U. J. *Psychomotor epilepsy.* Springfield, Ill.: Thomas, 1974.

117 Jovanić, U.J., and Schafer, E. R. Elektroencephalogramm and Klinik der Schlafepileptiker unter Berücksichtingung des Schlafes vor und nach der Behandlung. *Nervenzarzt* 37:290, 1966.

118 Killerfer, F. A., and Stern, W. E. Chronic effects of hypothalamic injury: Report of a case of near total hypothalamic destruction resulting from removal of a craniopharyngioma. *Arch. Neurol.* 22:419, 1970.

119 Kimura, D. Cognitive deficit related to seizure pattern in centrencephalic epilepsy. *J. Neurol. Neurosurg. Psychiatry* 27:291–295, 1964.

120 Klapetek, J. Photogenic epileptic seizures provoked by television. *Neurophysiology* 11:809, 1959.

121 Klighan, D., and Goldberg, D. A. Temporal lobe epilepsy and aggression. *J. Nerv. Ment. Dis.* 160:324–341, 1975.

122 Knott, J. R., Lara, R. T., Peters, J. F., and Robinson, M. D. "EEG findings in seventy-three persons accused of murder." In *Behavior and brain electrical activity,* N. Burch and H. I. Altshuler, pp. 549–550. New York: Plenum Press, 1970.

123 Kolarsky, A., Freund, K., Machek, J., and Polak, O. Male sexual deviation:

Association with early temporal lobe damage. *Arch. Gen. Psychiatry* 17:735–743, 1967.

124   Kraepelin, E. *Das epileptische Irresein: Lehrbuch der Psychiatrie*, vol. 3, pt. 2. Leipzig: Barth, 1913.

125   Krapf, E. Epilepsie und Schizophrenie. *Arch. Psychiatr. Nervenkr.* 83:547, 1928.

126   Kretschmer, E. *Körperbau und Charakter*, XX Aufl. Berlin: Julius Springer, 1921.

127   Kretschmer, E., and Enke, W. *Die Persönlichkeit der Athletiker.* Leipzig: Thieme, 1936.

128   Landolt, H. Über verstimmungen, Dämmerzustände und schizophrene Zustandsbilder bei Epilepsie. *Arch. Neurol. Psychiatr.* 76:313, 1955.

129   Landolt, H. L'Électroencéphalographie dans les psychoses épileptiques et les épisodes schizophréniques. *Rev. Neurol.* 95:595, 1956.

130   Landolt, H. *Die Temporallappenepilepsie und ihre Psychopathologie.* Basel: Karger 1960.

131   Landolt, H. Die Temporallappenepilepsie und ihre Psychopathologie. *Bibl. Psychiatr. Neurol.* 112:7–173, 1960.

132   Landolt, H. Psychische Storungen bei Epilepsie. *Dtsch. Med. Wochenschr.* 79:446, 1962.

133   Landolt, H. Über einige Korrelationen zwischen Elektroencephalogramm und normalen und pathologischen psychischen Vorgängen. *Schweiz Med. Wochenschr.* 93:107, 1963.

134   Leder, A. *Zur Testpsychologischen Abgrenzung und Bestimmung der Autwachepilepsie vom Pyknolepsie-Typ.* Diss. Zurich, 1966.

135   Leder, A. Zur Psychopathologie der Schlaf — und Aufwachepilepsie. *Nervenarzt* 38:434, 1967.

136   Lennox, W. G. The genetics of epilepsy. Am. J. Psychiatry 103:457–462, 1947.

137   Lohrenz, J. G., Levy, L., and Davis, J. F. Schizophrenia or epilepsy? A problem in differential diagnosis. *Compr. Psychiatry* 3:54–62, 1962.

138   London, N., Richter, P., and Bliss, B. E. Temporal lobe (psychomotor) epilepsy. *Psychosom. Med.* 18:427, 1956.

139   Luxenburger, H. Psychiatrisch-neurologische Zwillingspathologie. *Zentralbl. Neurol* 56:145–80, 1930.

140   Macrae, D. On the nature of fear with reference to its occurrence in epilepsy. *J. Nerv. Ment. Dis.* 120:385, 1954.

141   Mark, V. V., and Ervin, F. R. *Violence and the brain.* New York: Harper and Row, 1970.

142   Mauz, F. Zur Frage des epileptischen Charakters. *Zentralbl. Neurol.* 45:833–835, 1927.

143   Matthews, C. G., and Klove, I. I. MMPI performance in major motor, psychomotor, and mixed Seizure: Classifications of known and unknown etiology. *Epilepsia* 9:43–53, 1968.

144   Maudsley, C. Epilepsy and television. *Lancet* 1:190–191, 1961.

145   Metrakos, J. D., and Metrakos, K. Genetics of convulsive disorders: Introduction to problems, methods, and baselines. *Neurology* 10:288–240, 1960.

146 Metrakos, J. D., and Metrakos, K. Genetics of convulsive disorders. II. Genetics and electroencephalographic studies in centrencephalic epilepsy. *Neurology* 11:474–483, 1961.

147 Metrakos, J. D., and Metrakos, K. Genetic factors in epilepsy. In *Epilepsy*, ed. E. Niedermeyer, pp. 71–86 Basel: Karger, 1970.

148 Meier, M. J., and French, L. A. Changes in MMPI scale scores and in index of psychopathology following unilateral temporal lobectomy for epilepsy. *Epilepsia* 6:263–274, 1965.

149 Mignone, R. J., Donnelly, E. F., and Sadowsky, D. Psychological and neurological comparisons of psychomotor and nonpsychomotor epileptic patients. *Epilepsia* 11:345–359, 1970.

150 Milner, B. "Hemispheric specialization: Scope and limits." In *The neurosciences: Third study program*, ed. F. O. Schmitt and F. G. Worden. Cambridge, Mass.: MIT Press, 1974.

151 Minkowska, F. Recherches généalogiques et problèmes touchant aux caractères, en particulier à celui de l'épileptoidie. *Ann. Méd. Psychol.* 81:149–170, 1923.

152 Minkowska, F. Le problème de la constitution examiné à la lumière des recherches généalogiques et son rôle théorique et pratique. *Evolut. Psychiatry*, 2:185–216, 1927.

153 Minkowska, F. "Heredity of epilepsy and Schizophrenia. *Arch. Klaus-Stift, Vererb.-Forsch.* 12:33, 1937.

154 Mirsky, A. F., Primac, D. W., Marsan, C. A., Rosvold, E. H., and Stevens, J. R. A comparison of the psychological test performance of patients with focal and nonfocal epilepsy. *Exp. neurol.* 2:75–89, 1960.

155 Mises, R., Sarcella, M., Soul, L. Troubles observés chez les enfants épileptiques en dehors des crises: Discussion. *Rev. Neuropsychiatr. Infant.* 18:523–530, 1970.

156 Mitchell, W., Falconer, M., and Hill, D. Epilepsy with fetishism relieved by temporal lobectomy. *Lancet* 2:626–630, 1954.

157 Monroe, R. R. *Episodic behavior disorders.* Cambridge, Mass.: Harvard University Press, 1970.

158 Morgan, A. H., McDonald, P. J., and McDonald, H. Differences in bilateral alpha activity as a function of experimental task, with a note on lateral eye movements and hypnotizability. *Neuropsychologia* 9:459–469, 1971.

159 Morrell, F. Interseizure disturbances in focal epilepsy. *Neurology* 6:327, 1956.

160 Mulder, D. W., and Daly, D. Psychiatric symptoms associated with lesions of temporal lobe. *JAMA* 150:173, 1952.

161 Niedermeyer, E. *The generalized epilepsies.* Springfield, Ill.: Thomas, 1972.

162 Niedermeyer, E. *Compendium of the epilepsies.* Springfield, Ill.: Thomas, 1974.

163 Okasha, A., Sadek, A., and Moneim, S. A. Psychosocial and electroencephalographic studies of egyptian murderers. *Br. J. Psychiatry* 126:34–40, 1975.

164 Oller-Damella, L. Crises epileptiques psychiques de longue durée. *Rev. Neuropsychiatr. Infant.* 18:547–557, 1970.

165 Ounsted, J. Aggression and epilepsy: Rage in children with temporal lobe epilepsy. *J. Psychosom. Res.* 13:237–242, 1969.

166   Paillas, J. A., and Subirana. Le lobe temporal en O.N.O. *Rev. Otoneurooph-tal.* 22:123–92, 1950.

167   Pallis, C., and Louis, S. Epilepsy and television. *Lancet* 1:188–190, 1961.

168   Parsons, O. A. Human neuropsychology: The new phrenology. *J. Operat. Psychiatry* (1):47–56, 1977.

169   Parsons, O. A., Vega, A., and Burn, J. Different psychological effects of lateralized brain damage. *J. Cons. Clin. Psychol.* 33:551–557, 1969.

170   Penfield, W., and Roberts, L. *Speech and brain mechanisms.* Princeton, N.J.: Princeton, University Press, 1959.

171   Piotrowski, Z. The Rorschach inkblot method in organic disturbances of the central nervous system. *J. Nerv. Ment. Dis.* 86:525–537, 1937.

172   Piotrowski, Z. "The personality of the epileptic." In *Epilepsy,* eds. P. H. Hoch and R. P. Knight. New York: Grune and Stratton, 1947.

173   Pompilo, P. T. "The personality of epileptics as indicated by the Rorschach test: A comparison with neurotic subjects." Master's thesis, Catholic University, 1951.

174   Pond, D. A. Psychiatric aspects of epilepsy. *J. Indian Med. Prof.* 3:1141, 1957.

175   Pond, D. A., and Didwell, B. H. A survey of epilepsy in fourteen general practices. II. Social and psychological aspects. *Epilepsia* 1:285, 1960.

176   Pond, D. A. The schizophreniclike psychoses of epilepsy. Discussion. *Proc. R. Soc. Med.* 55:316, 1962.

177   Pond, D. A. The influence of psychophysiological factors on epilepsy. *J. Psychosom. Res.* 9:15–20, 1965.

178   Reeves, A. G., and Plum, F. Hyperphagia, rage, and dementia accompanying a ventral hypothalamic neoplasm. *Arch. Neurol.* 20:616, 1969.

179   Reich, W. Ueber den epileptischen Anfall. *Int. Z. Psychoanal.* 17:263, 1931.

180   Robertson, E. Photogenic epilepsy: Self-precipitated attacks. *Brain* 77:232–251, 1954.

181   Rodin, E. A. Psychomotor epilepsy and aggressive behavior. *Arch. Gen. Psychiatry* 28:210, 1973.

182   Rodin, E. A., DeJong, R. N., Waggoner, R. W., and Bagehi, B. K. Relationship between certain forms of psychomotor epilepsy and "schizophrenia." *Arch. Neurol. Psychiatry* 77:449–463, 1957.

183   Roger, A., and Dongier, M. Corrélations électrocliniques chez 50 épileptiques internés. *Rev. Neurol.* 83:593–596, 1950.

184   Ross, W. D. The contribution of the Rorschach method to clinical diagnosis. *J. Ment. Sci.* 87:333–48, 1941.

185   Roth, M, and Harper, M. Temporal lobe epilepsy and the phobic anxiety-depersonalization syndrome. *Compr. Psychiatry* 3(4), 1962.

186   Sayed, Z. A., Lewis, S. A., and Britain, R. P. An electroencephalographic and psychiatric study of thirty-two insane murderers. *Electroencephalogr. Clin. Neurophysiol.* 27:335, 1969.

187   Scott, J. S., and Masland, R. I. Occurrence of continuous symptoms in epileptic patients. *Neurology* 3:297–304, 1953.

188   Sem Jacobson, C. "Depth recording and electrical stimulation in the human brain." In *Electrical studies on the unanesthetized brain,* ed. D. A. O'Doherty, pp. 275–290. New York: Paul B. Holber, 1960.

189 Serafetidides, E. A. Psychiatric aspects of temporal lobe epilepsy. In *Epilepsy*, ed. E. Niedermeyer, pp. 155–169. Basel: Karger, 1970.

190 Servit, Z., Machek, J., and Stercova, A. Reflex influences in the pathogenesis of epilepsy in the light of clinical statistics. *Epilepsia* 3:315–322, 1962.

191 Slater, E. The schizophreniclike psychoses of epilepsy. *Int. J. Psychiatry* 1:6, 1965.

192 Slater, E., Beard, A. W., and Glithero, E. The schizophrenialike psychoses of epilepsy. *Br. J. Psychiatry* 109:95, 1963.

193 Slater, E., and Moran, P. A. P. The schizophreniclike psychoses of epilepsy: Relation between ages of onset. *Br. J. Psychiatry* 115:599–660, 1969.

194 Slater, E., and Roth, M. *Clinical Psychiatry*, 3rd ed. London: Bailliere, Tindall, and Cassell, 1974.

195 Smith, A. Verbal and nonverbal test performance of patients with acute lateralized brain lesions (tumors). *J. Nerv. Ment. Dis.* 14:517–523, 1968.

196 Small, J. G., Milstein, V., and Stevens, J. R. Are psychomotor epileptics different?: A controlled study. *Arch. Neurol.* 7:187–194, 1962.

197 Small, J. G., and Small, I. F. A controlled study of mental disorders associated with epilepsy. *Rec. Adv. Biol. Psychiatry* 9:171–181, 1966.

198 Small, J. G., Small, I. F., Hayden, R. N. Further psychiatric investigation of patients with temporal and nontemporal lobe epilepsy. *Am. J. Psychiatry* 123:303–310, 1966.

199 Small, J. G., Stevens, J. R., and Milstein, V. Electroclinical correlates of emotional activation. *J. Nerv. Ment. Dis.* 138:146, 1961.

200 Small, J. G., Stevens, J. R., and Milstein, V. Electroclinical correlates of emotional activation of the EEG. *J. Nerv. Ment. Dis.* 138:146–155, 1964.

201 Sperry, E. W. Hemispheric deconnection and unity in conscious awareness. *Amer. Psychol.* 23:723–733, 1968.

202 Sperry, R. "Lateral specialization in the surgically separated hemispheres." In *The neurosciences: Third study program,* F. O. Schmitt and F. G. Worden. Cambridge, Mass. M.I.T. Press, 1974.

203 Stafford-Clark, D., and Taylor, F. H. Clinical and EEG studies of prisoners charged with murder. *J. Neurol. Neurosurg. Psychiatry* 12:325, 1949.

204 Stauder, K. H. Epilepsie und Schläfenlappen. *Arch. Psychiatr. Nervenkr.* 104:181–212, 1935.

205 Stauder, K. H. *Konstitution und Wesensveränderung der Epileptiker.* Leipzig: Thieme, 1938.

206 Stekel, W. Die psychische Behandlung der Epilepsie. *Centralbl. Psychoanal.* Vol. 1, 1911.

207 Stevens, J. R. Emotional activation of the electroencephalogram in patients with convulsive disorders. *J. Nerv. Ment. Dis.* 128:339–351, 1959.

208 Stevens, J. R. Psychiatric implications of psychomotor epilepsy. *Arch. Gen. Psychiatry* 14:461–471, 1966.

209 Stevens, J. R. An anatomy of schizophrenia? *Arch. Gen. Psychiatry* 29:117–189, 1973.

210 Stevens, J. R., Ervin, F., and Panchoco, P. Deep temporal stimulation in man: Long latency, long lasting psychological changes. *Arch. Neurol.* 21:157–169, 1969.

211 Stevens, J. R., Milstein, V., and Goldstein, S. Psychometric test performance in relation to the psychopathology of epilepsy. *Arch. Gen. Psychiatry* 26:532–538, 1959.

212 Strömgren, E. Om den ixothyme Psyke. *Hospitalstid* 79:637–648, 1936.

213 Sweet, W. H., Ervin, F., and Mark, V. H. "The relationship of violent behavior to focal cerebral disease." In *Aggressive behavior*, ed. S. Grattini and E. B. Sigg, pp. 336–352. New York: Wiley Interscience Division, 1969.

214 Symonds, C. P. The schizophreniclike psychoses of epilepsy. Discussion. *Proc. R. Soc. Med.* 55:311, 1962.

215 Tellenbach, H. Epilepsie als Anfallsleiden und als Psychose. *Nervenarzt* 36:190, 1965.

216 Taylor, D. Sexual behavior and temporal lobe epilepsy. *Arch. Neurol.* 21:510–516, 1969.

217 Taylor, D. C. Aggression and epilepsy. *J. Psychosom. Res.* 13:229–236, 1969.

218 Taylor, D. C. Mental state and temporal lobe epilepsy: A correlative account of 100 patients treated surgically. *Epilepsia* 13:727–765, 1972.

219 Treffert, D. A. The psychiatric patient with an EEG temporal lobe focus. *Am. J. Psychiatry*, 120:765, 1964.

220 Van Reeth, P. C., Dierkens, J., and Luminent, D. L'hypersexualité dans l'épilepsie et les tumeurs du lobe temporal. *Acta Neurol. Belg.* 2:194–218, 1958.

221 Vislie, H., and Henrikson, G. F., "Psychic disturbances in epilepsy." in *Lectures in epilepsy*, ed. A. M. Lorentz de Haas, pp. 29–90. Amsterdam: Elsevier, 1958.

222 Walter, R. D. "Violence and aggression: ed. The state of the art." In *Behavior and brain electrical activity*, eds. N. Burch and H. I. Altshuler pp. 541–548. New York: Plenum Press, 1975.

223 Warneke, L. B. A case of temporal lobe epilepsy with an orgasmic component. *Can. Psychiatr. Assoc. H.* 21 (5):319–324, 1976.

224 Weil, A. A. Depressive reaction associated with temporal lobe uncinate seizures. *J. Nerv. Ment. Dis.* 121:505–510, 1955.

225 Weil, A. A. Ictal emotions occurring in temporal lobe dysfunction. *Arch. Neurol.* 1:87, 1959.

226 Weinstein, E. Relationship among seizures — psychoses and personality factors. *Am. J. Psychiatry* 116:124, 1959.

227 Whitten, T. Psychical seizures. *Am. J. Psychiatry* 126:560–565, 1969.

228 Whitty, C. W. M., and Oxon, D. M. Photic and self-induced epilepsy. *Lancet* 1:1207–1208, 1969.

229 Williams, D. The structure of emotions reflected in epileptic experiences. *Brain* 79:29–67, 1956.

230 Williams, D. Neural factors related to habitual aggression. *Brain* 92:503, 1969.

231 Winnik, H. Z., Assael, M. I., and Weiss, A. A. Psychiatric symptomatology and temporal lobe epilepsy. *Isr. Ann. Psychiatry* 4:99–104, 1968.

232 Yamada, T. "A clinicoelectroencephalographic study of ictal depression." In *Clinical genetics in psychiatry*. ed. H. Mitsuda. Tokyo: Igaku-Shoin, 1967.

233 Yamada, T., et al. A clinicoelectroencephalographic study of ictal depression. *Bull. Osaka Med. Sch.* 6:117, 1960.

234 Zimmerman, F. T., Burgemeister, B. B., and Putnam, T. J. Intellectual and emotional makeup of the epileptic. *Arch. Neurol. Psychiatry* 65:545–556, 1951.

2

Acute Brain Syndromes

Constantine J. Sakles, M.D., and
George U. Balis, M.D.

CLASSIFICATION, DEFINITION, AND TERMINOLOGY

Any classification system involves the process of taking complex phenomena, breaking them down, and sorting them into categories or groups according to certain criteria. A basic step in the classification of mental disorders has been to divide clinical phenomena into two main groups based on the criterion of the presence or absence of impaired brain tissue function. Mental disorders which are caused by or associated with impairment of brain tissue are called *organic brain syndromes*, whereas mental conditions not attributable to physical conditions are labeled *functional disorders*.

This basic division into organic brain syndromes and functional disorders has an unfortunate, unintended but erroneous implication that functional disorders are independent of brain function. This is not so; it is assumed in modern psychiatry that all psychological processes, both healthy and pathological, depend ultimately on brain function. Simply, it is clinically useful to distinguish two major classes of mental disorders: those for which an identifiable brain disorder is a necessary condition and those which can be adequately accounted for by the application of psychodynamics, psychological, and social concepts. This necessary dichotomy is at least in part a reflection of ignorance. There is growing evidence that many mental conditions classified as functional disorders, such as schizophrenia and manic-depressive psychosis, have organic determinants.

An organic brain syndrome is a clinical diagnosis based primarily on the patient's mental status and is usually found in patients with recognizable medical and neurological disorders which directly or indirectly affect brain structure and function. Although the condition can be present with a variety of nonspecific psychiatric symptoms such as delusions, hallucinations, depression, or obsessions, the diagnosis rests on the finding of impaired cognitive function, especially clouding of consciousness (acute brain syndrome) and impairment of recent memory (chronic brain syndrome).

Using solely the criterion of reversibility, organic brain syndromes are further subdivided into acute and chronic brain syndromes. The designation *acute brain syndrome* means that the condition is thought to be reversible and has nothing to do with its onset or course. The term *chronic brain syndrome* refers to an irreversible mental condition. Both the acute and chronic brain syndrome can occur with or without psychotic manifestations; and this finding can be included in the diagnosis (for example, acute brain syndrome, nonpsychotic; or acute brain syndrome with psychosis). Patients are described as psychotic when their mental functioning is sufficiently impaired to interfere grossly with their capacity to meet ordinary demands of life.

Nosology, which is the classification of disease entities, must be open to revision when more useful and reliable classes and categories can be devised. Thus, in the *Diagnostic and Statistical Manual of Mental Disorders* (DSM-I), prepared by the American Psychiatric Association (APA) and published in 1952 [1], organic brain syndromes were classified as either acute or chronic. The DSM-II [2], published in 1968, does not use the designation acute or chronic but divides all brain syndromes into psychotic or nonpsychotic groups. Apparently this was done in order to convey the severity of functional impairment within the formal diagnosis.

The DSM-III [3], which is to be introduced in the spring of 1979, uses neither the nomenclature of acute versus chronic nor psychotic versus non-psychotic. Using the medical concept of syndrome and strict criterial features, the authors of DSM-III cover the entire range of mental conditions due directly to brain pathology by devising seven distinct diagnostic categories, an atypical category, and a miscellaneous category as follows;

1. *Dementia:* Essential features of *dementia* are a decrement in the intellectual functioning occurring after brain maturation of sufficient severity to interfere with occupational or social performance or both. The cogni-

tive deficit always involves memory and usually there is also marked evidence of impairment associated with thinking, learning new skills, problem solving, and judgment. There are often also personality changes or impairment and impulse dyscontrol.

2. *Delirium:* The essential feature of *delirium* is relatively rapid onset of disorganization of higher mental processes caused by a disturbance of brain metabolism. The disturbance is primarily manifested by some degree of impairment of information processing (cognitive functions) and especially of consciousness. There is evidence of impaired or abnormal awareness, attention, perception, memory, and thinking. In addition, there is increased or decreased psychomotor activity, sleep disturbance, or both. The clinical features fluctuate rapidly.

3. *Amnestic syndrome:* The essential feature is a clinical picture predominated by the inability to retain memory for events longer than several minutes after they happen. Immediate memory is not impaired. The difficulty appears to be an impairment of the individual's ability to consolidate recent information into permanent memory stores (i.e., retention, which is not required for immediate memory). For example, in the mental status examination, the individual may have no difficulty with digital recall but will be unable to remember three objects which were shown to him fifteen minutes earlier.

4. *Hallucinosis:* The essential feature of *hallucinosis* is a clinical picture predominated by recurrent or persistent hallucinations occurring in a state of full wakefulness, alertness, and correct orientation in the presence of specific organic factors that are judged to be etiologically related to the hallucinations. The diagnosis of hallucinosis is not made when hallucinations are part of the more pervasive clinical syndromes such as in delirium, dementia, organic delusional syndrome, or organic affective syndrome.

5. *Organic delusional syndrome:* The essential feature is a clinical picture not meeting the criteria for an hallucinosis, delirium, dementia, or organic affective syndrome in which delusions are the predominant symptoms and there is a history of a specific organic factor judged to be etiologically related to the disturbance.

6. *Organic affective syndrome:* The essential feature of an *organic affective syndrome* is a clinical picture not meeting the criteria for an hallucinosis, delirium, dementia, or organic delusional syndrome in which the predominant symptoms closely resemble those seen in either the depressive or manic affective disorders but occur in the presence of a specific organic factor judged to be etiologically related to the disturbance (i.e., reserpine-induced psychotic depression).

7. *Organic personality disturbance:* The essential feature is a clinical picture in which the predominant disturbance is a change in personality

style or traits in the presence or concurrence of a brain disorder which is judged to be etiologically related to the disturbance. There is often impaired control of emotions or impulses and impaired social judgment manifested by unconcern about the consequence of this disinhibited behavior. Ability to initiate or complete complex goal-direct behavior, or both, may be diminished. Suspiciousness or paranoid sensitivity may be exhibited.

8. *Other or mixed organic brain syndrome:* This is a residual category reserved for syndromes which do not meet the criteria for any of the other organic brain syndromes and in which there is a maladaptive change during the wakening state associated with the specific organic factor judged to be etiologically related to the disturbance. An example would be the neurasthenic picture associated with early Addison's disease.

9. *Unspecific organic brain syndrome:* Unspecified Organic Brain Syndrome label is a category reserved for syndromes which do not meet the criteria for any of the other organic brain syndromes but in which there is an unidentified or multiplicity of organic factors.

In addition to the above free-standing diagnoses, which properly should also include a medical etiological diagnosis, there is another group of diagnostic categories where the above diagnoses are specifically related to substance abuse, including both drug intoxication and withdrawal, and in which the organic brain syndrome is directly related to substance abuse.

In the DSM-III classification [3] delirium, dementia, amnestic syndrome, hallucinosis, and organic delusional syndrome are roughly equivalent to the concept of organic psychotic disorders of DSM-II. Delirium and conditions associated with intoxication by chemical substance are roughly equivalent to the concept of an acute brain syndrome, whereas dementia, amnestic syndrome, and organic personality syndrome are often equivalent to the concept of chronic brain syndrome (see chapter 3).

Delirium is a common clinical syndrome which must be familiar to the student as well as the practicing clinician. Delirium is a subtype of acute brain syndrome in which, in addition to the pathognomonic finding of a reduction in the level of consciousness or a fluctuating consciousness, there is impairment of memory and orientation, reduced ability to maintain attention and, in general, disturbances in cognition. Delirium is assumed to result from a general "cerebral insufficiency" [7] associated with febrile, metabolic, and/or toxic conditions. Most often the course of the delirium parallels that of the underlying medical problem: The delirium usually subsides as the medical condition resolves. Although delirium is a type of acute brain syndrome, all acute brain syndromes are not delirium.

PATHOPHYSIOLOGY

Even though there are a great many etiological agents or causes of acute brain syndrome, the clinical features of impaired cognitive function and fluctuating consciousness is remarkably constant. The severity of the condition is highly variable, as is the assortment of secondary symptoms, but the cardinal symptoms of cognitive impairment associated with clouding of consciousness is constant.

The syndrome is attributed to presumably temporary or reversible damage of neuronal tissue. Regardless of the etiological cause, the widespread neuronal damage leads to generalized cerebral insufficiency. The phenomena of cerebral insufficiency can be demonstrated with the electroencephalogram (EEG) which shows generalized slowing. The degree of slowing of EEG correlates well with the degree of decrement in the level of consciousness [7]. It is the impairment of neuronal functions rather than the nature of the noxious process that is responsible for the characteristic clinical picture [7,9].

CLINICAL FEATURES

An acute brain syndrome is nearly always associated with medical, surgical, neurological disorders, or drug intoxications. This association is so common that any unexplained acute brain syndrome should alert the physician to the likelihood that such a medical disorder exist or is developing. The onset of an acute brain syndrome is highly variable: It may occur suddenly, abruptly, and dramatically, or it can progress over a few days or weeks with the patient's mental condition fluctuating and growing progressively delirious. In delirium, the levels of consciousness may fluctuate strikingly from day to day and even from hour to hour. Some patients will show a nocturnal pattern, with the most severe manifestations occurring at night. The nocturnal aggravation is attributed to a decrease in the sensory and interpersonal input to the patient.

Despite the highly variable clinical picture, the findings which are constant and pathognomonic are disorientation and impairment of recent memory, occurring in a state of clouded consciousness (impaired awareness).

Disorientation may relate to time, place, and person. Disorientation to time is the earliest and most common, and disorientation to person is the last to be impaired in an acute brain syndrome. Patients who have been sick or hospitalized for a long time sometimes make minor errors in

orientation and these should not receive undue emphasis. The other clinical finding is impairment of recent memory, in which the patient is unable
to recall the name of his physician or the last time he saw him; he cannot
recall what he had for breakfast or when his family last visited.

The behavioral and pyschological manifestations of organic brain
syndromes can be divided pathogenetically into primary disturbances and
secondary disturbances. The *primary disturbances* are due to neuronal injury or destruction and are characteristic only of organic brain syndromes.
The secondary disturbances are shared both by the organic and functional
mental disorders.

Besides the disorientation and impairment of recent memory, the
primary disturbance is also reflected in the patient's altered level of awareness and intellectual impairment. In more slowly developing conditions,
the symptoms are often mild and transient, but they tend to reoccur and
worsen. Impairment of levels of consciousness and attention span are
among the earliest indications of an acute brain syndrome. The patient is
likely to be aware that something is wrong and verbalizes his distress. As
the level of his consciousness becomes more affected, the patient may
seem to be in a haze and his responses slow and dull. Other faculties of
thinking become affected usually to the same degree. Intellectual functions, including the ability to think abstractly and perform arithmetical
calculations, are eroded. It becomes harder and harder for the patient to
orient himself as to time and location, and his memory faults him. An individual who cannot integrate past with present experiences or make decisions which are based on these experiences becomes helpless and frightened [4]. When there is clouding of consciousness, delirium is the likely
diagnosis. Five clinical types of delirium are distinguished [10]: quiet and
torpid, blandly confused, anxious and panicky, hallucinating, and mutter-
ing and inhoherent patients.

The secondary symptoms are shaped by the patient's personality as
he attempts to deal pyschologically with the cognitive deficit, the confrontation of illness, and its attendant mental and physical stress, result from
the interplay of various psychosocial factors, such as the patient's personality, patterns of ego defense, the psychosocial setting of the illness, the
nature of support from the family and interpersonal environment, and finally the characteristics of the culture in which the patient is raised.

The secondary symptoms of the acute brain syndrome are often the
same as many of the primary symptoms of the functional disorder. Secondary symptoms include mental phenomena, such as delusions, misin-
terpretations, panicky feelings; as well as behavioral changes, such as
motor restlessness. A large part of the patient's behavior is determined by
his efforts to avoid the painful effects of anxiety and his inability to cope
with cognitive demands. For instance, the patient may resort to the use of

psychological defenses, such as denial and projection, if they are characteristic of his personality. The similarity between the secondary symptoms of the acute brain syndrome and the symptoms of functional disorders suggest some very fundamental connection between the two and a human universality in coping with massive anxiety or stress. Secondary symptoms can offer some psychodynamic understanding of the patient's psychological response to stress and often provide a guide for psychiatric treatment which must accompany the medical treatment of the underlying disorder. For example, if a secondary symptom suggests that helplessness is of key dynamic significance to the patient, then the physician cannot only give verbal reassurance about this issue but also structure the patient's care so as to minimize the patient's feeling of helplessness and aid him in maintaining a sense of autonomy. Secondary symptoms are viewed as being reparative, restitutive, or protective in nature. They help the patient to ward off painful insight, anxiety, or depression [4].

When a patient is exposed to environmental demands of performance that exceed his cognitive capacity he may decompensate further and respond with anxiety, depression, agitation, irritability, anger, or even psychotic symptoms. When brain impairment is moderately severe, illusions, which are the misidentification of real objects, are common. Hallucinatory phenomena may also occur. Typically these hallucinatory experiences are visual, vivid, and frightening; the hallucinated experiences may be described in great detail by the patient. These hallucinations are more common in persons withdrawing from drugs or alcohol or during other toxic states. An acute brain syndrome should be suspected if the patient describes seeing insects, such as spiders, ants, or cockroaches, or animals, such as rats or snakes, or flashes of colored lights. Auditory hallucinations particularly in the form of very distinct sounds, such as bells or footsteps, may also occur.

Finally, individuals with organic brain syndromes demonstrate disturbances of affect. It is not clear whether this is a primary or secondary disturbance. In any case, their emotions may be highly variable and strong affective responses may be elicited by modest stimuli. Indifference or apathy to important events may also occur.

A thirty-five-year-old black male was admitted to the medical service of a Veterans Administration Hospital for the treatment of pneumonitis He was admitted with a temperature of 103°, and the diagnosis was made by both X-ray and physical examination.

A few days after admission, a request was made for an emergency psychiatric consultation because the patient had "become schizophrenic" and was delusional and hallucinating.

On psychiatric examination, the patient appeared acutely ill; he was moderately agitated, restless, fidgeted with the bed clothes, and at times waved his arms in the air. The patient was fearful, confused, and seemed to have difficulty in maintaining his attention. He also demonstrated fluctuating degrees of alertness and was easily distracted. He would start to answer a question and then drift off in some other subject or stop talking. At one point, he asked the examiner if he were there selling cigarettes.

He could give his name but could not understand that he was in a hospital: First he said he was in a bakery and, later on said he was in a bank. He gave the year as 1964 instead of 1977 and gave the wrong month, day, and date. He appeared to be hallucinating and when this was asked about, he replied that he was not sure but he could see at the periphery of his vision an angel that was there to watch over him. He was certain that the angel was there to protect him but on the other hand he could not be sure that maybe somebody or something was there with intent of harming him.

Of course, in this case the diagnosis of schizophrenia is wrong. The patient was suffering from an acute brain syndrome resulting from his pneumonitis.

The diagnosis is supported by the presence of an underlying physical condition, in this case, pneumonitis. The term acute is applicable because it is assumed that the mental symptoms and underlying brain pathology are reversible and will subside as the toxic effects of the pneumonia subside. The diagnosis of acute brain syndrome (delirium) rests on the presence of disorientation and impairment of recent memory, fluctuating sensorium, and difficulty in maintaining attention and mental awareness.

DIAGNOSIS AND DIFFERENTIAL DIAGNOSIS

An acute brain syndrome should be suspected in any medical or surgical patient who has an altered state of consciousness even if this is simple disorientation. The diagnosis should also be raised in any mental patient who suddenly develops evidence of cognitive impairment. In equivocal cases, Kahn and associates [8] found that ten simple questions were as reliable in detecting an acute brain syndrome as a longer psychiatric interview.

The questions are

1 What is the name of this place?
2 Where is it located (address)?

3   What is today's date?
4   What is the month now?
5   What is the year now?
6   How old are you?
7   When were you born (month)?
8   When were you born (year)?
9   Who is the president of the United States?
10 Who was the president before him?

The degree of impaired performance revealed by these questions correlates strongly with the severity of organic brain disease.

Other psychiatric conditions should be ruled out. The patient's anxiety during an acute brain syndrome may suggest anxiety neurosis; low mood and apathy of an acute brain syndrome may suggest an affective disorder; and hallucinations and delusions suggest schizophrenia. The crucial question in each case is whether the patient exhibits definite disorientation as well as impairment of awareness, confusion, recent memory impairment, and other cognitive difficulties. If a patient with an established functional psychiatric illness develops disorientation or memory impairment, one should suspect that something else has developed: a drug reaction or medical or neurological illness.

It is most important to distinguish acute organic brain syndromes from other psychiatric conditions because the former demands early etiological diagnosis and immediate specialized treatment. Schizophrenic patients are frequently reported as being confused, meaning that they are incoherent, due to their thought disorder. The term confusion is non-discriminating and should be avoided. Schizophrenic patients are distinguished by clear orientation and ability to retain and recall past events, demonstrating an intact memory. In acute schizophrenic excitement, or in cases in which the patient has been heavily sedated, the diagnosis may be difficult. However, brief periods of repeated observation usually lead to clarification. Depressive psychoses with retardation of thought may be confused with organic syndromes; however, they are not associated with disturbances of awareness, orientation, and memory. In patients with hysterical amnesia, the memory defects are either too gross or spotty or with great clarity in certain areas. Amnesia for personal identity is not found in delirium. In all functional psychosis and neuroses, the electroencephalogram will not show the slowing of frequency as it often does in acute brain syndromes.

Excited delirium must be differentiated from the manic phase of a manic-depressive psychosis, acute schizophrenia, catatonia schizophrenia, acute homosexual panic, and a rage reaction in a sociopathic personality. Sometimes side effects of the phenothiazine can cause excitement and delirium.

ETIOLOGICAL DIAGNOSIS

Once the diagnosis of delirium or acute brain syndrome has been established, it is extremely important to search for the etiological factors responsible for its development. It is well to remember that more than one cause may be involved in etiology. Laboratory and clinical findings will vary in accordance with the etiological factors. The physician should first consider the most common causes, such as drugs, especially atropine, anticholinergic agents, sedatives, bromides, and cortisone; focal and systemic infections; and withdrawal reactions to alcohol. In the elderly, pneumonia, urinary infections, dehydration, cardiac decompensation, and sensitivity to drugs — especially barbiturates, sedatives, and tranquilizers — are common causes of delirium. Elderly patients also tend to develop nocturnal delirium while they are lucid during the day [4].

Postoperative delirium may be due to conditions associated with electrolyte imbalance; dehydration; cerebral anoxia, secondary to respiratory impairment or cardiac failure; infections; and idiosyncrasies to drugs. The possibility of delirium tremens (DTs) should always be investigated in any delirious patient suspected of heavy drinking. In young adults and adolescents, acute brain syndrome and delirious states are commonly due to drug abuse such as phencyclidine intoxication and adverse reactions to illicit hallucinogenic drugs. In the younger age group, delirious states may be associated with the use of nutmeg, carbon tetrachloride inhalation, and glue sniffing.

TREATMENT

The treatment of the acute brain syndrome can be categorized as symptomatic-supportive and etiological; the former is directed towards the alleviation of symptoms. The latter is directed towards the specific correction of the underlying causes. A patient with acute brain syndrome should be treated in the general hospital unless he is highly disturbed or suicidal, in which case he should be moved to the psychiatric unit.

Preferably the patient should be placed in a single room which is quiet and fairly well lighted and one in which environmental stimuli are less subject to distortion or misinterpretation. A close family member or a special nurse should be in attendance continuously to supervise and comfort the patient. Acute brain syndrome patients, especially those who are delirious, require frequent reassurance regarding their psychotic experiences. Explanations about any change in the environment, about the intention of the physician and nursing staff must be provided repeatedly. Ideally, physical restraints are avoided. However, when applied, their judicious use requires attention to the patient's safety from accidents and suicide as well as concern for the patient's comfort and freedom of movement [4].

For the alleviation of the acute symptoms of delirium, especially hyperactivity, excitement, and panic, appropriate sedation is necessary. In general, phenothiazines, sedatives, and minor tranquilizers are used only sparingly in the management of delirium. These drugs affect the central nervous system and can aggravate or act in an unpredictable manner in a central nervous system which is already compromised. Barbiturates should be avoided because of their tendency to depress vital brain functions. The most useful drugs are small doses of neuroleptics, for example, 25 to 50 mg of Chlorpromazine (Thorazine) or moderate doses of the minor tranquilizers such as 10 to 25 mg of chlordiazepoxide (Librium) or 5 to 10 mg of diazepam (Valium). Much larger doses may be required in the presence of agitation. Standing orders for the use of these drugs, with acute brain syndrome or delirious patients is dangerous. Each dose should be given on STAT basis after careful evaluation of the patient's condition and response to previous dose [4].

Etiological treatment depends upon the identification of the underlying causes and the prompt institution of specific therapy which will reduce morbidity and may prevent the irreversible sequalae of chronic brain syndrome.

SPECIFIC CONDITIONS ASSOCIATED WITH ACUTE BRAIN SYNDROME OR DELIRIUM

Infectious Diseases

Meningococcal and tuberculous meningitis, various encephalitides (epidemic encephalitis, Sydenham's chorea, measles, pertussis, malignant tertian malaria, trypanosomiasis), and brain abscesses are common examples of intercranial infections. Although the brain damage caused by these infections may be reversible, it not infrequently becomes permanent and results in chronic brain syndrome.

Concomitant with the introduction of antibiotics, chemotherapy, and preventive inoculation, incidence of delirium due to systemic infections has decreased markedly. However, infections should always be ruled out before seeking other causes since they remain a fairly common cause of acute brain syndrome. Pneumonia, influenza, typhus, septicemia, rheumatic fever, erysipelas, infectious mononucleosis, bacillary dysentery, and cholera are most commonly implicated.

Metabolic Disturbances

Delirious acute brain syndrome can occur as a consequence of certain *metabolic* conditions including uremia, hepatic coma, hypoglycemia, and electolyte imbalance (i.e., depletion of potassium, sodium, and calcium), can result in delirious acute brain syndrome. Hypercapnia, diabetic acidosis, and anoxia (cardiac, respiratory, anemic, cerebrovascular) can cause an acute brain syndrome.

Endocrine Disturbances

Behavior changes typical of hyperthyroidism consist of irritability, restlessness, emotional lability, anxiety, increased sensitivity to noises and startle responses, fatigue, and excitability. Psychotic pictures may occur in the form of manic-depressive psychosis, schizophreniform reactions, or delirium. The mental symptoms occurring in myxedema (hypothyroidism) include psychomotor retardation characterized by slowing down and dulling of mental processes, sluggishness, lethargy, forgetfulness, irritability, and paranoid trends. Psychotic reactions associated with myxedema show paranoid characteristics, i.e., persecutory delusions and hallucinations. Deliriumlike confusional episodes may also occur. In Cushing's syndrome, depression, retarded or agitated, is the most common symptom. The clinical picture may also include panic reactions, asthenia, and hypochondriacal delusions or hallucinations and paranoid ideas mixed with affective symptoms.

The administration of cortisone and adrenocorticotropic hormone (ACTH) is usually associated with symptoms of euphoria and less commonly with feelings of derealization and depersonalization, depression, and frontal paresthesias. These drugs may also precipitate severe psychotic reactions, predominantly agitated depressions, as well as schizophreniclike paranoid syndromes and at times frank mania.

The psychiatric disturbances seen in Addison's disease are similar to those in Cushing's syndrome, i.e., they are schizoaffective. Other conditions in which endocrine imbalance is associated with psychiatric disturbances are acromegaly and Simmonds' pituitary cachexia.

Nutritional Disturbances

Delirious states, as well as other psychotic reactions of an affective or schizophreniform nature, are seen in several nutritional deficiencies, such as Wernicke's encephalopathy (primarily thiamine deficiency), pellagra (primarily nicotinic acid deficiency), pernicious anemia (defect in absorption of vitamin B_{12},), and starvation.

In the fully developed picture of Wernicke's encephalopathy a confused state accompanies the neurologic manifestations of opthalmoplegia, ataxia, and symptoms of polyneuritis. Upon recovery from the acute symptoms, this clinical picture is commonly followed by that of Korsakoff's syndrome.

Mental symptoms accompanying the dermatological, gastrointestinal, and neurological manifestations of pellagra include depressive and neurasthenic syndromes which may progress to delirium or subacute delirious states. The symptoms characteristically are intermittent.

Toxic Disturbances

Toxic psychoses secondary to drugs, poisons, intoxicants, and other chemical substances are common and may be associated with one of the following patterns of drug action: (1) drug idiosyncrasy, (2) acute intoxication, (3) chronic intoxication, (4) drug withdrawal, and (5) specific psychotomimetic action. [4].

Drug Idiosyncrasy

Transitory delirious states may develop in certain predisposed individuals after the administration of a single therapeutic dose of a drug which normally does not produce psychotomimetic effects. Such idiosyncratic psychotic reactions to drugs are seen especially in the elderly are also common in children and younger adults. They usually occur several days after the beginning of drug therapy and, rarely, a few hours after the first dose. They are characterized primarily by confusion and disorientation and, in some instances, by excitement accompanied by illusions and hallucinations. Drugs commonly responsible for such reactions are barbiturates; the nonbarbiturate sedatives glutethimide, ethinamate, ethchlorvynol, and methyprylon; chloral hydrate and paraldehyde; minor tranquilizers (especially diazepam); major tranquilizers (chlorpromazine, thioridazine); atropine and belladonna derivatives; antiparkinson drugs; cocaine; lidocaine; and others. Discontinuation of the drug results in complete recovery within one to two days. This type of toxic psychosis can be compared with the so-called pathological intoxication from alcohol [4]. Some of the paradoxical reactions to phenothiazine derivatives have been attributed to psychological factors rather than drug toxicity. These reactions may occur when the experienced pharmacological effect of the drug is psycholog-ically threatening to the patient or when it interferes with important ego functions and defense mechanisms [4].

The behavioral change observed in *acute intoxications* are caused by the administration of one or several large toxic doses of a drug in a rela-tively short period of time. Typical examples of this type of reaction are the acute intoxications due to alcohol and barbiturates. Acute barbiturate intoxication is most frequently the result of a suicidal attempt or of an ac-cidental overdose, especially in young people abusing these drugs. The symptoms depend on the amount of drug consumed and consist of drow-siness, ataxia, asynergia, dysarthria, and, in more serious forms, confu-sion and sleep deepening into coma. An example of acute intoxication from stimulant drugs is the abuse of amphetamines by young people who use large and repeated doses of methamphetamine intravenously. Acute intoxications from poisons result from chemicals such as carbon monox-ide, carbon tetrachloride, and cyanide compounds. Acute carbon monox-ide poisoning results in loss of consciousness. Following recovery from the comatose state, patients may immediately develop delirium or show a variable lucid period after which they may show apathy or indifference, and in more serious cases confusion, Korsakoff-like syndromes, and deterioration.

Conversely, *chronic intoxication* may result from the prolonged use of large intoxicating doses of drugs. Bromide psychosis is the most typical example of toxic psychosis secondary to chronic intoxication. The toxic ef-fect of bromide is closely related to their level of concentration in the blood, a fact which makes the laboratory test for serum bromides an im-portant aid in diagnosis. Blood bromide concentrations of more than 150 mg/100 ml are suggestive of bromism and usually are associated with a toxic psychosis, which may be manifested as simple intoxication, de-lirium, hallucinosis, or transitory schizophrenia. Treatment is directed toward promoting the excretion of the drug through the administration of large quantities of fluid, diuretics, and sodium chloride or ammonium chloride. For persistent psychotic symptoms, electroconvulsive therapy has been recommended [4].

The recent introduction of lithium carbonate as a highly effective agent in the treatment and prevention of manic-depressive psychosis is expected to result in an increased number of cases of lithium poisoning. Toxic symptoms appear when serum lithium concentration exceeds 2 mEq/liter (measured by flame photometry) and consist of severe and protracted clouding of consciousness and profound lethargy. This con-dition may also be accompanied by dehydration, coarse tremors or muscle twitches, and convulsions. Prodomal symptoms include sluggishness, drowsiness, anorexia, diarrhea, and vomiting. Treatment is mainly supportive and is directed toward the correction and prevention of complications [4].

Regular intake of large doses of barbiturate sedatives leads to the development of tolerance and physiological dependence and, hence, to chronic intoxication marked by increased emotional lability, dysarthria, ataxia, nystagmus, sluggishness, and frequently by persistent hypomanic excitement with periods of irritability. The electroencephalogram usually shows increased fast beta rhythm activity. Abrupt withdrawal of the drug results in the development of an abstinence syndrome characterized by grand mal seizures and delirium. Nonbarbiturate sedatives and minor tranquilizers (especially meprobamate) present similar clinical pictures of chronic intoxication and withdrawal reactions. [4]1

Excessive intake of amphetamines and similar stimulant drugs, have become a serious problem in recent years, especially among young people. The problem was compounded in the past by the promiscuous use of these drugs for the purpose of weight reduction. With regular consumption, tolerance to the drug develops and is accompanied by insomnia, anorexia, and increased tension, leading to the use of barbiturates for sedation. These drugs do not produce psysiological dependence, and therefore their abrupt discontinuation does not result in withdrawal reactions. The chronic use of amphetamines may result in the development of a serious psychosis which usually mimics the paranoid type of schizophrenia. Delirious states may also occur. The amphetamine-induced paranoid psychosis may be acute and short-lived or chronic and resistant to treatment. There is some indication that chronic amphetamine intoxication may produce irreversible brain damage. The illicit use of these drugs is usually associated with the use of marijuana, and lysergic acid diethylamide (LSD) [4,5].

The active constituent of marijuana or hashish is tetrahydrocannabinol. Cigarettes made of marijuana ("pot" or "grass") are smoked for their exhilarating or euphorizing effect. Chronic use of marijuana does not seem to produce tolerance and does not result in physiological dependence. Abrupt withdrawal of the drug is not followed by an abstinence syndrome. In small amounts it acts as a mild sedative and euphoriant, somewhat like alcohol. In sufficiently large doses it produce feelings of depersonalization, visual and temporal distortions, and hallucinations, without impairment of consciousness. The marijuana effect differs from the LSD experience in that it has a depressant-sedative component, whereas LSD causes heightening of awareness and wakefulness. Although there have been only a few cases of marijuana-induced psychosis in the United States, hashish has long been regarded as an important cause of psychosis in Eastern countries. There has been, however, considerable concern regarding the development of the "amotivational syndrome" which involves serious personality changes resulting from chronic marijuana use. Personality changes characterizing this syndrome include apathy, loss of effectiveness, inward turning and passivity, loss of drive for achievement, diminished capacity to carry out long-term plans, greater introversion, and tendency toward magical thinking. There is no adequate evidence to support a causative relationship between the amotivational syndrome and chronic marijuana use [4,5].

Known on the streets as PCP, angel dust, or flakes, Phencyclidine has become an alarming public health problem. It can be inhaled, smoked when sprinkled on parsley or marijuana, swallowed, or injected. It has marked sympathomimetic effects such as tachycardia, hypertension, and increased deep reflexes. Phencyclidine also induces cholinergic activity, such as sweating, flushing, drooling, and pupillary constriction. It can cause cerebellar signs which include dizziness, ataxia, dysarthria, and nystagmus.

The dramatic psychological effects of phencyclidine have been attributed to a defect in the integration of incoming sensory stimuli and has been compared to the effects of prolonged sensory deprivation. And inability to process sensory information gives rise to seconday deficits including a loss of reality testing ability, dissolution of ego boundaries, and intellectual and emotional disorganization.

With large doses, coma occurs and major convulsions are a possibility. Deaths related to phencyclidine use have been reported. Causes of death may be from status epilepticus, cardiac or respiratory arrest, or a hypertensive crisis with the rupture of a cerebral blood vessel.

In low doses (1–5 mg) phencyclidine produces the usual disinhibiting effects associated with psychoactive drugs. A buoyant euphoria is commonly described which sometimes is associated with a feeling of numbness. Behavior may be looser and there is characteristically emotional lability. With higher, doses, such as 5–15 mg, a toxic psychosis may result which appears as an excited and confused intoxication. Body distortions are a common finding. Pain and touch perception is reduced. The ability to communicate is severely impaired. Disorientation to time, place, and even person may be noted. Either the person moves around listlessly or is quiet and withdrawn.

With doses greater than 10 mg, a clinical picture can emerge which resembles various acute schizophrenic syndromes. Sometimes these states are difficult to differentiate from schizophrenia. They may last anywhere from a few days to several months.

The schizophreniclike toxic state can present as stuporous catatonia, excited catatonia, or paranoid schizophrenia. In the stuporous catatonia, there is mutism, grimacing, repetitive movements, posturing, and even waxy flexibility. In the excited catatonia, there is a psychomotor agitation, incoherent and abundant speech, and often unpredictable destructive behavior. Catatonic excitement is a dangerous condition because of possible destructive behavior against self or others. Another danger is the severe exhaustion which can develop over a brief period of time and can lead to death. Sometime phencyclidine psychosis will mimic paranoid schizophrenia and present with auditory hallucinations, ideas of reference, suspiciousness, and grandiosity.

Repetitive or chronic use of phencyclidine can result in a persistent impairment of mental functioning apparently on an organic basis. After chronic use, even without recent use of the drug, the patient can demonstrate memory gaps, some disorientation, and a great deal of difficulty with speech, such as blocking or the inability to retrieve the proper word. During the drug-free intervals, impulse control may be loosened and the patient is easily aroused to assaultiveness or uncontrolled belligerence. Unusual car accidents and criminal acts may occur.

Phencyclidine can be detected in urine qualitatively and quantitatively by commercial or hospital laboratories. High-dose intake is associated with a leukocytosis and an elevated creative phosphokinase (CPK). The presence of hypertension and tachycardia along with some of the aforementiond psychiatric symptoms should raise the suspicion of phencyclidine ingestion. Similar symptoms, however, may also occur with amphetamines and cocaine poisoning. Normally, the history of PCP intake will be readily provided by the patient or accompanying person. However, they may speak of THC or provide a slang name for PCP that is locally popular [6].

TREATMENT

Because of the unusual clinical picture, it is best to withhold drug therapy if the patient is not hyperactive. A quiet, nonstimulating environment may be all that is needed. Diazepam, 10 mg intramuscularly and repeated as necessary, will help control muscle spasms and restlessness. Vital signs require frequent recording in case cardiorespiratory intervention becomes necessary. Diphenylhydantoin (Dilantin) may be considered as a prophylactic against convulsions. Antihypertensive therapy is rarely required.

The containment of overactivity and aggressiveness is a serious problem. The major tranquilizers have had variable success in containing behavioral dyscontrol due to PCP. There is some indication that these drugs potentiate PCP, therefore, they should be used cautiously during the acute phase. They should be provided for treatment of prolonged psychotic reactions. Control of hyperactivity with paraldehyde or parenteral barbiturates can be considered [6].

DRUG WITHDRAWAL OR WITHDRAWAL PSYCHOSIS

In cases of drug dependence of the barbiturate-type, the abstinence syndrome which develops after drastic reduction or abrupt withdrawal of the drug consists of grand mal seizures and delirium. Drug dependence of the barbiturate type results from the chronic administration of excessive doses of a barbiturate or an agent with barbituratelike effects. The latter includes the nonbarbiturate sedatives ethchlorvynol (Placidyl), glutethimide (Doriden), methyprylon (Noludar), ethinamate (Valmid) — the minor tranquilizers — chlordiazepoxide (Librium), diazepam (Valium), oxazepam (Serax), and meprobamate (Miltown Equanil) — and paraldehyde, chloral hydrate, and dextropropoxyphene (Darvone). Alcohol should also be included among these drugs because the withdrawal phenomena of alcohol addiction (convulsions and delirium tremens) resemble those of the drug dependence of the barbiturate type. Apparently any depressant of the central nervous system may produce this type of abstinence syndrome, with the exception of major tranquilizers (phenothiazines, thioxanthenes, reserpine, and butyrophenones) and bromides. Bromides do not produce withdrawal reactions probably because of their slow elimination [4].

The clinical picture of the barbiturate abstinence syndrome, as it develops on abrupt withdrawal of a short-acting barbiturate after chronic use of daily doses of 0.8 to 2.2 g, consists of two categories of symptoms: (1) minor abstinence phenomena: apprehension, muscular weakness, tremors, postural faintness, anorexia, and twitches, which are observable within twenty-four hours after the discontinuation of the medication; and (2) major abstinence phenomena: grand mal seizures and delirium which develops between the second and eighth postwithdrawal day. The delirium develops in 60 percent of the cases and is characterized by disorientation, restlessness, hallucinations, and delusions. The occurrence of hyperpyrexia is an ominous sign. A Korsakoff-like syndrome, hallucinosis, and acute panic states may occur in milder cases. The treatment consists of stabilization of the patient on a short-acting barbiturate, i.e., pentobarbital followed two or three days later by a gradual withdrawal of the drug at a rate not exceeding 0.1 g a day. Diphenylhydantoin and phenothiazines are not effective in preventing withdrawal seizures.

Withdrawal reactions from nonbarbiturate sedatives and minor tranquilizers (especially meprobamate) closely resemble those of barbiturates. Their treatment is based on the pentrobarbital substitution method, although at least theoretically any drug of this group can be used as a substitute.

Psychotomimetic drugs, or hallucinogens [5] — popularly called psychedelic (mind revealing) drugs — embrace a number of compounds with varying chemical structure which produce markedly similar effects of a psychoticlike nature. The widespread use of these drugs by high school and college students has aroused great public and professional concern. The psychedelic drugs, especially LSD, or "acid," have become an integral part of the hippie subculture and seem to provide those who use them ("acid heads") with a social ritual within a cult, a focus for the expression of feelings of frustration, anger, and rebelliousness, and a means for escape from reality and for the satisfaction of a need for novel experiences and stimulations, usually of a mystical or transcendental nature. The nature of the psychedelic experience is influenced greatly by the *set*, the subject's psychological expectations of what a drug will do to him in relation to his personality, and the *setting*, the total environment, in which the drug is taken.

The psychological effects of a typical hallucinogen, such as LSD or mescaline, consist of marked perceptual distortions, pseudohallucinations and hallucinations, feelings of depersonalization and derealization, feelings of enhanced awareness of the self and of the universe (cosmic identification), alterations in mood, emergence of unconscious material characteristic of the primary process thinking, and impairment of intellectual processes. Repeated administration of LSD results in the rapid development of tolerance; however, there is no development of physical dependence on LSD. Evidence suggesting that the use of LSD results in chromosomal damage has been reported but is inadequate to support any general cause-and-effect relationship [5].

The use of hallucinogens carries the danger of serious adverse psychological reactions, a fact which was not sufficiently recognized in the early literature. These reactions may be classified into the following categories:

1   Acute dysphoric experiences, popularly known as "bad trips." These experiences develop while the subject is under the influence of the drug (a period of eight to twelve hours) and may occasionally persist for twenty-four hours to forty-eight hours. Their occurrence depends largely on the setting in which the drug is taken, especially when the trip takes place in an unstructured, nonsupportive environment. They are characterized by panic, frightening experiences, and hallucinations, and in some instances, by acute paranoid reactions and impulsive acts of violence or suicide. The treatment of these reactions consists in the intramuscular administration of large doses of chlorpromazine and the initiation of supportive measures.

2   Prolonged adverse reactions, which may occur after a single dose, but more commonly after multiple exposures, and which may persist for several months or longer. They include schizophrenic or schizophreniform reactions (usually in predisposed

individuals of an unstable personality), anxiety and depressive reactions, and very frequently a condition of intermittent hallucinosis known as flashbacks. The hallucinosis is seen in subjects who have had multiple LSD exposures and is characterized by the intermittent recurrence of spontaneous visual hallucinations which are similar to those experienced under the influence of the drug [5].

Acute Trauma

Acute trauma includes those reactions which develop immediately after an injury to the head produced by some external force or after neurosurgery. The traumatic reactions include: (1) acute delirious cases following trauma to the brain; (2) amnesic episodes, usually with limited retrograde and anterograde amnesia; (3) posttraumatic conditions or prolonged changes produced by head trauma; (4) defect conditions such as aphasia, asymbolia, or deterioration, with or without seizures as a late result of trauma; and (5) terminal deterioration due to progressive alterations of the injured parts of the brain, with or without arteriosclerosis.

Circulatory Disturbance

This type of reaction includes patients who show confusion, disorientation, and at times vague paranoid phenomena as a result of faulty circulation. These syndromes are most commonly due to cardiac decompensation and are always accompanied by other evidence or circulatory failure. In some instances this syndrome appears in cases of endocarditis with emboli which may lodge in the brain, producing transitory periods of confusion.

Alcohol Intoxication

These acute syndromes may occur in patients who are included under the general category of chronic alcoholism or alcohol addiction, or they may occur in persons who have been on a single isolated prolonged alcoholic bout. Symptoms are the result of the direct effect of alcohol on the brain.

Alcoholic Psychoses

Not all individuals develop a psychosis as a result of their drinking. It appears that the nutritional and physical status is important in producing the psychiatric reaction, and that the latter will be colored by the general personality pattern of the alcoholic patient. Alcoholic psychoses include the following syndromes.

1. *Pathological intoxication* is an acute mental disturbance due to varying amounts of alcohol, usually small, manifesting over a short period of time excitement or furor with confusion and hallucinations followed by amnesia of the episode. Persons showing this type of reaction usually are basically quite unstable and make a borderline adjustment when sober.

2. *Delirium tremens* reaction often begins acutely and is characterized by motor restlessness, distractability, hallucinations (particularly visual), illusions, great apprehension, and tremors. As the disease progresses the motor and mental activity becomes greatly increased. Tremors of the tongue and fingers are severe. The patient is sleepless and has fever, rapid pulse, low blood pressure, and loss of weight. There is albumin in the urine. In favorable cases the delirium terminates abruptly in a few days. Delirium tremens is often inadequately treated. Previously, it was thought that the alcoholic was dehydrated. Research has demonstrated in many cases overhydration and electrolyte imbalance. Vitamins, particularly the B-complex group, is essential in the proper management of all alcohol associated conditions.

3. *Acute hallucinosis* is characterized by hallucinations of hearing, with marked apprehension and fear, and fairly well-organized delusions of persecution. In contrast to the other forms of toxic psychoses, the sensorium is relatively clear in acute alcoholic hallucinosis. The absence of confusion, disorientation, and retention defects is the principle difference from other forms of delirious reaction. It cannot be easily differentiated from paranoid schizophrenia. The major difference from schizophrenia is that it does not persist longer than two weeks.

4. The patients marked by *acute paranoid reaction* are suspicious, have systematized persecutory delusions, and frequently misinterpret environmental events as having special application to themselves. These patients are distinguished from those who have hallucinosis by the absence of hallucinatory experience. The sensorium in these reactions is also clear.

REFERENCES

1   American Psychiatric Association. *Diagnostic and statistical manual of mental disorders*, DSM-I. Washington, D.C.: American Psychiatric Association, 1952.
2   American Psychiatric Association. *Diagnostic and statistical manual of mental disorders*, DSM-II. Washington, D.C.: American Psychiatric Association, 1968.

3   American Psychiatric Association. *Diagnostic and statistical manual of mental disorders,* (DSM-III.) Draft. Washington, D.C.: American Psychiatric Association, 1977.

4   Balis, G. "Delirium and other states of altered consciousness." In *Tice's practice of medicine.* vol. 10, chap. 39. Hagerstown, Md.: Harper and Row, 1970.

5   Balis, G. "The use of psychotomimetic and related consciousness-altering drugs." In *American handbook of psychiatry,* vol. 3, ed. S. Arieti, pp. 404–445. New York: Basic Books, 1974.

6   Cohen, S. Angel dust: The pervasive psychedelic. *Drug Abuse Alcohol Newsl. Vista Hill Found.* 5(7):1976.

7   Engel, G. Delirium: A syndrome of cerebral insufficiency. *J. Chronic Dis.* 9 (3), 1959.

8   Kahn, R. L., Golfarb, A. I., Pollack, M., and Peck, A. Brief objective measures for the determination of mental status in the aged. *Am. J. Psychiatry* 117:326, 1960.

9   Lipowski, Z. J. Delirium, clouding of consciousness, and confusion. *J. Nerv. Ment. Dis.* 145 (3), 1967.

10   Rosenbaum, C. P., and Beebe, J. E. *Psychiatric treatment: Crisis, clinic, consultation.* New York: McGraw-Hill, 1975.

RECOMMENDED READINGS

•   Friedman, A. M., Kaplan, H. I. and Sadock, B. J. *Comprehensive textbook of psychiatry.* Baltimore: Williams and Wilkins, 1972.

•   Noyes, L., and Kolb, A. *Modern clinical psychiatry,* vol. 6. Philadelphia: Saunders, 1963.

•   Stevenson, I. *The psychiatric examination.* Boston: Little, Brown, 1969.

•   Warner-Johnson, C., Snibbe, J., and Evans, L. *Basic psychopathology.* New York: Spectrum, 1975.

•   Woodruff, R., Goodwin, D., and Guze, S. *Psychiatric diagnosis.* New York: Oxford University Press, 1974.

3

Chronic Brain Syndromes

Manoel W. Penna, M.D., and
Andreas Laddis, M.D.

Organic brain syndromes are disorders characterized pathophysiologically by disturbances in brain function attributed to biological factors and clinically expressed through impairment in memory, orientation, intellectual functions, and judgment, as well as by lability and shallowness of affect. The addition of the term chronic substantially alters this concept by introducing the somber feature of irreversibility into these conditions.

Although many of the disorders which are clinically designated as chronic brain syndromes are indeed an expression of permanent dysfunction of the brain, this is not universally true. In order to avoid a semantic, if not a clinical difficulty, with serious prognostic and therapeutic implications, the concept needs further clarification and three basic considerations are in order.

1. The primary reason to group the clinical entities to be described under the heading of chronic brain syndromes is a historical one. These disorders have been recognized and described as characteristic clinical syndromes having in common the fact that their underlying etiology was presumed to be a specific, albeit often unknown, organic interference with brain function.

2. As knowledge has increased by the acquisition of additional clinical or laboratory data, many of those specific factors have been identified

leading to the breakdown of some of these syndromes into separate etio-pathogenic categories.

3. Some of the specific causes thus identified are actually either potentially treatable or indicate management strategies which may significantly alter the course of the pathological process involved. Therefore, the diagnosis of a chronic brain syndrome does not always carry the connotation of irreversibility. A cogent example can be seen in a recent review where Wells [15] summarizes three clinical studies involving 222 patients with symptoms and signs of dementia. A search for a more specific etiological factor, revealed that 51 percent of this group suffered from cerebral atrophy of unknown cause, most likely Alzheimer's disease. On the other hand, 15 percent presented disorders which were potentially correctable and required definitive treatment of depression, drug toxicity, normal-pressure hydrocephalus, benign intracranial masses, mania, thyroid diseases, pernicious anemia, epilepsy, and hepatic failure. A third group comprising 20 to 25 percent of the patients had conditions which were basically noncorrectable but required some form of intervention, including multiple infarct dementia with hypertension, malignant brain tumor, alcoholism, normal-pressure hydrocephalus, neurosyphilis, and Huntington's chorea.

These conditions, not withstanding, physicians are still confronted daily by patients presenting a clinical picture where a preliminary diagnosis of chronic brain syndrome becomes necessary before searching for a more specific etiology. Discussion is essentially limited to those conditions which are usually irreversible. It is important to remember that more than one syndrome may be present in the same patient as is often the case with dementia and delirium.

SYMPTOM FORMATION

In essence there are two broad categories of symptoms present in chronic brain syndromes: primary symptoms, represented by the cognitive abnormalities brought about by the brain dysfunction, and secondary symptoms, which reflect the patient's overall reaction to the manifest impairment. Or, to express it in another way, the deficits and abnormalities resulting from the interference with brain function lead to different clinical expressions, depending on the balance between the overall organismic resources and the environmental demands to be met. In practice, a clear-cut distinction between these two general groups of symptoms is not always possible.

The premorbid personality of the patient is an important variable in the determination of these specific symptoms. In general, personality traits associated with flexibility facilitate adaptation, whereas more rigid personality organizations make the patient more vulnerable. The obsessive-compulsive person may become fearful of losing control and react with mounting anxiety and depression; he may become even more rigid and try to compensate for his deficits by increasing the orderliness and predictability of his environment, reacting with irritation to novelties and surprise. Others will show less impulse control, especially of the sexual and aggressive drives. The aggressive person may become even more so, displaying increased irritability and anger and at times reaching the point of physical attacks upon others. The suspicious person may further increase the use of projection and develop a paranoid style of dealing with others, if not frank delusions. Other patients may withdraw from more demanding situations and even reach total apathy.

Emotional responses vary from depression to euphoria with various degrees of anxiety and shame. Denial of the deficit is not an uncommon feature. Goldstein [5] described the catastrophic reaction characterized by a wave of panic when an impaired function is challenged by a particular task.

The family's pattern of organization and its capacity to understand the patient's impairments; deal successfully with various feelings of sorrow, humiliation, and shame; and still provide the emotional support necessary to insure the patient's feelings of security; as well the financial resources available, are among a variety of social and economic variables that significantly influence the overall clinical picture.

The environmental and situational factors are not less important. The patient becomes more sensitive to changes in this environment, and, as emphasized by Verwoerdt [16] may decompensate because of change, both in sensory input and in output. Changes of input are represented by sensory overload, brought about by the experience of being hospitalized, or by sensory underload, due to sensory deprivation or isolation, lifelong character traits (as the ones present in a schizoid individual), or change elicited by new psychopathological developments, as in severe depression. Changes in output are exemplified by increased demands on social and occupational performance.

CLINICAL SYNDROMES

The symptomatology of chronic brain syndromes is comprised of those general clinical manifestations resulting from diffuse interference with brain function in isolation or in combination with symptoms and signs expressive of localized or focal lesion. Consistent with the clarification of the third edition of the American Psychiatric Association's (APA) *Diagnostic and Statistical Manual of Mental Disorders* (DSM-III) [1], reviewed in chapter 2, the organic brain syndromes can be subsumed under three major syndromes: dementia, the amnestic syndrome, and the organic personality syndrome.

Dementia

The essential clinical characteristic of dementia is an impairment of cognitive functioning to a degree that significantly affect occupational or social performance, or both. Memory loss is the most outstanding manifestation, but other intellectual functions are also deficient. The capacity for new learning is obviously impaired in correspondence with the memory deficit. Usually present are difficulties with abstract thinking and problem solving, as well as impaired judgment.

Secondary symptoms may include a variety of disorders of thinking, perception, and motor behavior according to the interplay of factors previously mentioned. Affective change, especially lability and shallowness of affect, are common features. Personality change, either as accentuation of preexisting traits or as a change in previous patterns, are equally common.

The onset may be sudden or insidious, and the course varies, depending on etiology. Thus, the condition may remain stable or progress in a steady or step-wise fashion. The etiology is most varied and includes senile and presenile pathological change in brain tissue, repeated infarcts, chemicals (such as alcohol and carbon monoxide), trauma, anoxia, infections like syphilis, encephalitis, neoplasms, metabolic and endocrinologic disorders, normal-pressure hydrocephalus, and neurodegenerative disease. Although most dementias are irreversible, an identical clinical syndrome may be a manifestation of depression in old age or other potentially treatable disorders, including abscesses and tumors, subdural hematoma, drug intoxication, normal-pressure hydrocephalus, hypothyroidism, and nutritional deficiencies.

Amnestic Syndrome

This syndrome [8,9] is characterized clinically by the development of anterograde amnesia. The impairment is mostly limited to retention. Immediate recall and remote memory are preserved, but the latter may show some deficits. Patients are usually unaware of their memory impairment and show a tendancy to fill memory gaps with confabulations, although this is not always present.

Other intellectual functions are relatively well preserved, but many patients show some degree of disorientation and difficulty with abstract thinking. Personality changes, when present, most often are represented by irritability and loss of motivation and emotional responsiveness.

The amnestic syndrome is thought to be associated with damage to the diencephalon and mesial temporal lobe due to a variety of causes including encephalitis, trauma, anoxia, chemicals, and more commonly, alcohol. It may be reversible and be followed by partial or total recovery. If it persists for three years, the condition is irreversible.

Organic Personality Syndrome

This syndrome is clinically differentiated from dementia by the fact that the decrease in the level of intellectual functioning is not as severe, and the alteration in brain function is expressed primarily through personality change. Many patients exhibit poor impulse control, impaired judgment, and affective lability. They may show a loss of initiative and motivation and become apathetic or show marked impulsivity. The final picture will depend on the cerebral localization of the lesion and on the social and psychological factors which shape the secondary symptoms.

Focal Syndromes

The organic process responsible for the development of the chronic brain syndrome may preferentially affect a specific area of the cortex leading to the creation of syndromes of relative distinction. They are briefly reviewed here according to the brain region affected, but more detailed information can be found in appropriate sources [7,8]. For the sake of brevity, the dominant hemisphere is referred to as left, while the nondominant one will be called right.

OCCIPITAL REGION

Lesion of the primary visual areas causes various anoptic defects. If, the secondary zones are involved, the patient shows an inability to synthesize the elements of perception into a visual whole; he is able to recognize or draw on request but only a series of fragments of the whole field. Some degree of anosognosia is more frequently seen with lesions of the nondominant hemisphere.

TEMPORAL REGION

Lesions in the primary auditory areas produce an increase in the threshold of auditory sensations in the opposite ear. If the secondary zones are damaged, the ability to discriminate sound complexes is impaired: sequential oncs (like speech and melody), when the dominant hemisphere is involved, and simultaneous ones (like chords and timbre), with involvement of the opposite sides.

Lesions of the superior left temporal lobe lead to sensory aphasia, i.e., a disturbance of speech perception. If the lesion is lower and deeper into the temporal lobe, the patient cannot memorize and repeat audioverbal material, particularly if presented rapidly. Further posteriorly, it interferes with the ability to match the perception of an object with its name; the patient cannot draw what he is told but only what he is shown.

The medial zones of the temporal lobes are related to aspects of alertness, memory, and higher consciousness. Lesions of the hippocampus, the mammillary bodies, and their interconnections produce various degrees of a specific memory disturbance characterized by the inability to exclude new stimuli in order to elaborate on and store recent information; this disorder is at the core of the amnestic syndrome.

If the lesion involves temporal frontal connections in the cingulate gyrus and around the septum, personality change with mutism, flat affect, or disinhibition of emotions can be observed. More sterotyped and impulsive emotional outbursts are related to lesions which disturb the coordination between limbic formations (amygdala, septal area) and the hypothalamus.

Irritative foci of the temporal lobes can cause a variety of symptoms associated with temporal lobe epilepsy.

PARIETAL REGION
Lesions of the tertiary zones cause loss of the function of spacial synthesis. The patient cannot tell right from left, find his direction in real space, or on a map, or manipulate materials in space. Left hemisphere lesions, in particular, extend the deficit to abstract relationships based on ordering into space, i.e., relations among generations of people, direction of action between two agents, and mathematical relationships and operations. Lesions in the right tertiary parietal zones effect mainly operations in real space and identification of individual objects in their uniqueness, for example, one's own face or belongings. Right-sided lesions in this area may result in anosognosia, which is associated with the notion of body image.

Lesions of the primary somesthetic zones cause decrease of sensation and also loss of kinesthetic information for the regulation of voluntary movements. If the secondary zones are affected there is an inability to synthesize stimuli into whole structures (astereognosis) and an impairment in the refinement of voluntary movements in space; the latter is more apparent in word articulation, but if the lesion is in the left lower secondary zones, the mistakes may be transferred to writing [7].

FRONTAL REGION

Disintegration of voluntary motor organization in time is the distinctive result of a lesion in the premotor (secondary motor) areas. Speed and smoothness of movement are lost. Motor perseveration is introduced. If the inferior part of the left zone is involved, similar patterns in speech create motor aphasia. Damage of the primary motor area causes paresis.

More detailed discussion of the tertiary zones of the frontal lobes (prefrontal areas) is warranted. Their lateral aspect is linked with motor programs, and local damage causes disturbances translated in an apparent disconnection between thought and praxis, affecting movements in general, or in speech. Pathology of the mediobasal aspect of the prefrontal areas disturbs the state of cortical activity; attention and thought cannot be initiated voluntarily or be induced by verbal instruction of others. With a lesion in the basal orbital part of the mediobasal complex related to the amygdala and the limbic system, emotional disinhibition and disruption of previous personality patterns predominate. Damage to the medial part of the complex, which borders on the limbic system causes wandering of attention, possibly resulting in a dreamy state. It should be noted that the programs for intellectual operations are potentially intact with mediobasal lesions.

In cases of massive frontal lesions, the patient suffers a pervasive loss of motivation and problem-solving activity. He remembers well and can imitate solutions presented to him by others but tends to perseverate with one fragment of the solution and may be distracted by irrelevant stimuli. This disorder of programs can be manifest in all goal-directed activity, whether the task involves getting a spoon from the drawer in order to eat, doing serial sevens, or searching the memory for the correct choice among several alternatives.

ETIOPATHOLOGICALLY DEFINED SYNDROMES

Senile and Presenile Dementias

These terms describe a variety of disorders having in common the presence of certain anatomopathological findings that occur in association with aging. They are characterized pathologically by the presence of senile plaques and neurofibrillary tangles in several parts of the brain. Although similar findings are not uncommon in the brain of old persons who showed none of the symptoms of this condition, they are not as widespread as in afflicted individuals.

Senile dementia was thought to be associated with anatomical change in brain tissue that accompanied the aging process and was diagnosed in patients over sixty-five years of age. When a similar condition develops prior to that time, sometimes as early as in the fourth decade of life, it was referred to as presenile dementia. There is now general agreement that these conditions are indistinguishable. However, some confusion remains in the nomenclature reflected in the use of the terms presenile dementia or Alzheimer's disease and senile dementia or senile dementia Alzheimer's type. This confusion is compounded by the lack of clarity as to which disorders are actually included in this category. An example is Jacob-Creutzfeldt disease, traditionally described as a form of presenile dementia and more recently determined to be associated with a slow-growing virus [4].

Even the assumed causal relationship between structural change in the brain and the clinical manifestation of symptoms of dementia has been the subject of debate. Such association was questioned by observations like the ones reported by Corsellis [3], who found on autopsy, that 20 percent of the patients diagnosed as having senile psychosis had little or no senile plaque formation, whereas 90 percent of those with the diagnosis of a functional psychosis had moderate to severe plaque formation. More refined techniques have recently provided information that is strongly in support of the existence of an association between morphological change in the brain and the clinical development of dementia [3].

The clinical manifestations start insidiously, often with forgetfulness and subtle personality change but progress steadily and irreversibly to profound memory and cognitive impairment. Progressive loss of problem-solving ability, judgment, impulse and emotional control, abstract thinking, and constructional ability are common findings.

Identification of the underlying condition has already been emphasized because an indistinguishable picture may be produced by a variety of conditions which can be successfully treated.

Repeated Infarct Dementia

The diagnosis of chronic brain syndrome associated with cerebral arteriosclerosis has been largely replaced on contemporary use by the term repeated or multiple infarct dementia because the latter is less restrictive and better describes the underlying pathophysiology. The frequency of this early diagnosis resulted from the assumption that most cases of dementia were the product of arteriosclerotic change in the vascular system of the brain. Such a hypothesis has not been substantiated by more recent studies. For example, the postmortem examination of a series of fifty patients who had shown clinical manifestations of dementia, revealed that 50 percent of them were suffering from Alzheimer's disease, while arteriosclerosis was definitely implicated in only 12 percent of the total [12].

The general clinical manifestations of this condition are similar to the previously described Alzheimer's disease. However, it shows three fundamental distinctions which are basic to establish the diagnosis: sudden, rather than insidious onset; a step-wise rather than a steadily progressive course; and the presence of focal neurological symptoms or signs as common findings.

Korsakoff's Syndrome

This amnestic syndrome originally described by Korsakoff, is nonspecific etiologically in the sense that it is due to vitamin deficiency most frequently met in alcohol abusers. The patient shows relatively good immediate recall but impaired selective recall of stored memories (especially recent) and usually preservation of the already acquired intelligence fund. New learning is characteristically impaired. There is sometimes a degree of retrograde amnesia. The memory of less abstract, e.g., sensory motor traces, tends to be better preserved. Recall is aided by semantic cues. Even when a trace is recalled, it is often experienced as unfamiliar, disconnected from the rest of the person's life experience. The patient may try to fill in the gaps with confabulations. More generalized deterioration sets in over many years of alcohol abuse with atrophy of the cortex mainly frontally, leading to an alcoholic dementia.

Infections

Syphilitic brain syndromes, are infrequent today. Meningovascular syphilis can produce various and inconsistent mental symptoms with alterations of alertness, intellectual performance, and focal cortical dysfunction, often of sudden onset. General paresis develops in about 5 percent of syphilitics with central nervous system involvement ten to fifteen years after the primary stage. Of people primarily infected, men and whites are more prone to develop general paresis than women and blacks. Pathologically, there is cortical atrophy, initially mainly frontal with ventricular dilation, inflammatory reaction of the meninges and the ependyma, and characteristic microscopic change in the parenchyma. Clinically, a severe deterioration of personality and social performance is seen, often after years of insidious deterioration. There may also be secondary characteristics of expansive euphoria, paranoia, or depression, with suicidal impulsivity. Motionless faces and slurred monotonous speech, with articulatory substitutions and perseverations — similarly reflected in handwriting, convulsions, and apoplexylike symptoms — are common developments. Neurological signs, as in tabes dorsalis, appear variably. The index of activity in the cerebral spinal fluid is the elevated white cell count, elevated protein (mainly globulin), and positive serology, in that order. It remits spontaneously in 10 percent of the cases. If untreated, it leads to severe dementia, general cachexia, and death in a few years.

Other infections of the brain can cause widespread involvement of the meninges and the parenchyma or focally create an abscess. They can cause various degrees of dementia with impairment of abstract operations, labile affect, and mental distractability. The lesions are mostly the result of inflammation of the parenchyma or failure of small vessels and capillaries. Meningitis spreads in the cerebral surface and some viral and protozoal (toxoplasma, plasmodium, trypanosoma) agents infiltrate deeper formations.

The herpes simplex virus sometimes selectively affects one or two lobes. There is some indication that some viruses (herpes simplex, measles, rabies) may have a predilection for the limbic formations, causing emotional tension and outbursts. The measles virus has been identified as the agent responsible for the development of subacute sclerosing panencephalitis [2]. A papovavirus seems to be the cause of progressive multifocal leukoenphalopathy in patients with malignancies or chronic infections of the reticuloendothelial system. Of considerable interest was the demonstration that Jacob-Creutzfeldt disease can be transmitted experimentally [4] and is associated with a filterable particle. This has raised the possibility of other chronic brain diseases of unknown etiology also being associated with slow-growing viruses.

Neoplasms

Neoplasms and other space-occupying lesions produce dementia symptoms through: (1) an increase in intracranial pressure with alteration of alertness and, if long-standing through atrophic changes; (2) focal effects; (3) organismic reaction to the defect; and (4) episodic irritative events.

The correlation between the rate of change in intracranial pressure and mental change is a controversial one. Slow-growing tumors (notably meningiomas) around the frontal lobes often present with psychiatric symptoms of insidious onset without neurological events. Such tumors are usually underdiagnosed, particularly if a coincidental mental disorder diverts attention from the organic symptoms. On the other hand, fast-growing tumors like gliomas, particularly infiltrating glioblastomas, may predominately cause a psychosis with the neurological findings often thought to be of psychological origin. Part of the initial picture is due to delirium. The psychosis can have a pervasive affective quality or a schizophrenic flavor. In either case, an episodic quality may be identified, suggesting an organic basis for such focally evoked syndromes imitating manic-depressive illness and schizophrenia, the latter, in particular, with temporal lobe tumors. The patient experiences the psychosis as ego alien, being able to maintain a sense of self as existing outside the psychosis.

The specific deficits, e.g., aphasia, often exaggerate or mask mental symptoms, particularly intellectual status. Primary psychiatric symptoms occur more frequently with mass lesions of the frontal and temporal lobes, corpus callosum, and the core of the brain. Slowly evolving mental symptoms of no localizing value are most likely to be memory defects, disorders in the intensity and quality of affect, and intellectual decline, in that order of appearance. Subdural hematomas and abscesses, besides other possible symptoms of trauma or infection, present a similar picture. There is a tendency for more drowsiness or irritability and convulsions, particularly with an abscess, and some fluctuation of symptoms with an early subdural. Concomitant epilepsy, general paresis, alcoholism, or senility blur the detection of subdural hematomas.

Neurodegenerative disease

There is a group of hereditary-degenerative diseases which can cause a variety of psychiatric symptoms and lead to dementia. Huntington's chorea, is the best studied entity. It is hereditary, with autosomal dominant transmission and complete penetrance. As a result of the magnitude of the hereditary risk, one encounters frequent reactive emotional disorders in affected, or even as yet unaffected members of the family. However, some personality change may be an inherent part of the degenerative process. The basic quality is an excess of emotional tone with disinhibition of activity leading to violence. A delusional hallucinatory state or an affective psychosis may develop. Any group of manifestations — dementia, choreic movements, suicidal depression, or personality change — may long precede the others.

Twenty percent of the cases of Wilson's disease may start with psychiatric symptoms, which may take the form of any common or bizarre syndrome. Mental and neurological symptoms are attributed to excessive deposit of copper in the brain and are largely reversible with penicillamine treatment.

Neurological Syndromes

There is a miscellaneous group of neurological syndromes which may be accompanied by psychiatric symptoms. A well-known example is normal-pressure hydrocephalus, which is manifested clinically by the triad of gait disturbance, incontinence (usually urinary), and dementia in the absence of increased cerebral spinal fluid pressure. The extent of its role as a cause of dementia is not well established at this point, although it seems that this condition is less frequent than it was initially assumed. Its diagnostic importance however lies in the fact that neurosurgical shunting is, in many cases, an effective measure in arresting the progress of the condition.

Paralysis agitans is another syndrome which has been associated with the development of psychiatric symptoms consisting basically of personality change, variable impairment of intellectual functions, and dementia. The latter manifestation may acquire new clinical significance in view of the recent report [11] that one-third of patients with Parkinson's disease develop dementia in the course of a six-year treatment with L-dopa.

Trauma

In addition to subdural hematomas and their psychiatric manifestations, and acute deliria, head injury also leads to a chronic brain syndrome. The direct expression of the structural damage can be an insidious loss of psychological agility across functions, as in the case of the boxer who is punch-drunk or measurable dementia with larger lesions. Deterioration after a period of stabilization of function suggests such complications. Epilepsy is added to the picture in 50 percent of injuries with penetration of the dura. Sometimes the syndrome is more circumscribed, such as a defect in cognition or Korsakoff's syndrome.

There are approximately 300,000 head injuries each year in the United States from traffic accidents alone of severity greater than simple concussion — implying contusion, laceration, hemorrhage, and cerebral edema. Most frequently they involve the frontal and temporal lobes. Those who develop a chronic syndrome (arbitrarily defined as one persisting for at least one to two years) often do not show a specific deficit or global impairment of cortical function that can be measured. Rather, what sets in is a vaguely defined state with a tendency to mild catastrophic reactions. The patient is irritable, tires easily, has unstable attention, and complains of poor sleep. Selective recall of recent memory is difficult and initiative lessened. Children are noted to show a sudden change of pattern, e.g., from shyness to disinhibited activity or vice versa. The severity of this syndrome tends to correlate with the duration of the posttraumatic loss of consciousness, less so with the presence of a skull fracture or focal deficits of function, and even more inconsistently with the anatomical extent of the injury.

The question of how much of this reaction constitutes a secondary emotional arousal due to a realistic appraisal or symbolic interpretation (conscious or unconscious) of the injury can be answered only indirectly. Indicators are the site and extent of structural damage and the patient's premorbid personality. Overall sluggishness, symptoms not modified by suggestion or environmental changes, headaches induced by change of posture or fatigue, and, of course, positive neurological, laboratory, and psychiatric findings indicate a strong organic component. The differential investigation must exclude other organic pathology which is often overlooked because of the dramatic evidence of injury. There is slim evidence that head trauma can accelerate arteriosclerosis of the brain or dormant general paresis.

Biochemical

Bochemical derangement leading to chronic brain impairment can be caused by hormonal change, intoxication by exogenous or endogenous poisons, or nutritional deficiencies. Such a derangement can damage the brain diffusely and gradually. Mixed with episodes of reversible delirious manifestations, there is usually a decline of intellectual functions, slow enough to allow for the development of a productive psychosis with delusional and hallucinatory elaborations and suicidal depression.

It is doubtful that excess of steroids and adrenocorticotrophic hormone (ACTH) can cause an irreversible syndrome. Chronic mental change should be attributed to the disease being treated, e.g., lupus, or to compounding events, e.g., hypertension or azotemia, rather than steroids. Whether Addison's disease can have chronic sequelae and how these may be related to electrolyte or carbohydrate disturbances or to intervening convulsive disorders is also controversial. Another ambiguous case in the steroid-sexual hormone circuit is that of Klinefelter's syndrome, in which, a mild intellectual defect and maladaptive pattern in adolescence seems to be irreversible and may be associated with a basic chromosomal or a secondary hormonal defect.

The thyroid seems to play an important role in brain metabolism, but an irreversible syndrome has been recognized only for its congenital hypofunction with mental retardation or later dementia with depressive and paranoid elements. Idiopathic hypoparathyroidism seems to be the only parathormone dysfunction that causes some degree of chronic impairment, mainly intellectual. Hyperglycemia from insular tumors or any other cause, if persistent, can cause diffuse brain damage as can diabetes through repeated severe ketotic poisoning. Mental deterioration can perhaps occur irreversibly also with chronic uremia.

Pellagra is caused by a deficiency of a vitamin of the B-complex and its characteristic clinical triad consists of diarrhea, dermatitis, and dementia. Early symptoms have a neurasthenic quality; later, all types of psychotic symptoms with affect or thought disorder develop, along with intellectual deterioration, which becomes irreversible in advanced cases. Deficiencies of B_{12} and folic acid independently have also been associated with dementia.

Toxic

Various metals can cause chronic brain damage, usually after long industrial exposure. Impairment of memory seems again to be the least disputed permanent defect in the case of mercury and lead, associated with depressive or confabulatory behavior. Some describe a general paresislike psychosis from lead. The maturational failure of the central nervous system in children with pica is well established. Magnesium can cause release of emotional and motor sterotypes from volitional control in a few patients, but its chonicity is not fully asserted.

Finally, severe carbon monoxide poisoning can leave sequelae, such as loss of initiative and a Korsakoff-like syndrome which may persist as long as two to three years, after which time one should consider these effects permanent. There is also evidence that mild prolonged industrial exposure may be responsible for subtle central nervous system damage.

EVALUATION AND DIAGNOSIS

The diagnosis of the patient suspected of having a chronic brain syndrome needs to be conducted with the aim at arriving, not only at a general diagnosis — for example, dementia — but also at the elucidation of the more specific underlying condition. That this is possible is well documented in studies such as the one .reported by Seltzer and Sherwin [10] who were able to place all but three of eighty randomly selected patients, who had received a diagnosis of chronic brain syndrome, into a more specific diagnostic category. The practical implication of such requirement is reflected in the fact that several of these conditions were potentially treatable disorders.

A good medical and psychiatric history followed by a careful neurological and psychiatric examination is a basic necessity. During the mental status examination, special emphasis should be placed on asking the appropriate questions and testing the psychological functions which are usually impaired by organic brain dysfunction. The psychiatrist's training in general allows only for a general detection of abnormalities in the medical and neurological fields; when indicated he should not hesitate to seek the assistance of more specialized colleagues.

A large number of ancillary laboratory procedures can be useful in elucidating the specific type of disorder. However, there is no justification for their indiscriminate use. Wells [14] has suggested the following procedures for a basic workup: urinalysis, chest x ray, blood studies (including a complete blood count, serological tests for syphilis, a standard metabolic screening battery, serum thyroxine by column, and vitamin B_{12} and folate levels) and computerized axial tomography. Depending on the abnormalities detected, more specific lines of laboratory investigation would be indicated. Two additional procedures are especially useful: electroencephalography and psychological testing.

The electroencephalogram in organic brain syndrome may show diffuse slow activity which correlates with the severity of the clinical picture [16]. In some instances, it shows focal disturbances, which are invaluable guides for the localization of lesions, especially under circumstances calling for surgical intervention.

Psychological tests are an extension of the initial clinical examination [6]. They can provide baseline scores for later comparisons, aid early detection of subclinical dysfunction, identify dysfunction affecting specific tasks, and help to differentiate between organic and functional disturbances of performance.

TREATMENT

In many instances the pathological process underlying the chronic brain syndrome requires specific medical and surgical treatment. In addition, the patient may need symptomatic treatment and a variety of psychosocial and rehabilitative measures useful in dealing with the patient's impairment and with his own and his family's reaction to it and in preventing regression.

Antipsychotic drugs are usually effective in controlling the psychotic manifestations of the organic brain syndrome, as in the functional psychosis. The dosage is usually lower, but a greater need for individualized regimens and a greater chance for paradoxical effects or side effects is anticipated with brain damaged patients. The benzodiazepines are of significant value in the more anxious or impulsive patients. With exceptions, depressive reactions to brain damage respond naturally to rehabilitative care and socialization; when antidepressants are indicated, supervision is needed for their use, since most brain damaged individuals are likely to have limitations in their judgment.

Forensic judgments, such as those concerning civil commitment, competence to manage a specific affair, criminal responsibility, require a combination of clinical skills and familiarity with the patient's life and support system.

With a little imagination, a variety of common-sense substitutes for lost functions can be devised in the management of these patients. Calendars and clocks to help with orientation, a night lamp to increase perceptual clarity, a writing pad for a weak memory, a numbered sequence of instructions for frontal lobe "apathy," or an orderly household for special disorientation gives security and dignity to the patient.

Between home and institution a combination of individualized personal care with elaborate rehabilitation techniques should be pursued as an ideal. Unfortunately, personal care is becoming harder to achieve in the community and has always been the exception in institutions. Rehabilitative techniques are becoming more sophisticated in terms of equipment and trained personnel for physiotherapy, vocational reeducation, speech therapy, adjustment of prostheses, and so forth, but, they are limited to specialized centers.

Psychotherapeutic guidance and support are necessary to help the patient to deal with, and compensate for, his losses in function. Certain defenses, such as denial of illness, need to be respected. Family counseling is often essential to decrease the level of suffering, to deal with the feelings of humiliation or shame, and to insure that the environment will provide the support and the stability that a patient with chronic brain syndrome so urgently needs.

REFERENCES

1 American Psychiatric Association. *Diagnostic and statistical manual of mental disorders*, (DSM-III). Draft. Washington, D.C.: American Psychiatric Association, 1977.

2 Brody, J. A., and Detels, R. Subacute sclerosing panencephalitis: A zoonosis following aberrant measles. *Lancet* 2:500–501, 1970.

3 Corsellis, J. A. N. *Mental Illness and the aging brain*. London: Oxford University Press, 1962.

4 Gibbs, C. J., Jr., et al. Creutzfeldt-Jacob disease (spongiform encephalopathy): Transmission to the chimpanzee. *Science* 161:388–389, 1968.

5 Goldstein, K. *The organism*. New York: American Book, 1939.

6 Lezak, M.D. *Neuropsychological assessment*. New York: Oxford University Press, 1976.

7 Luria, A. R. *The working brain*. New York: Basic Books, 1973.

8 Mayer-Gross, W., Slater, E., and Proth, M. *Clinical psychiatry*. London: Cassell, 1960.

9   Redlich, F. C., and Freedman, D. X. *The theory and practice of psychiatry.* New York: Basic Books, 1966.

10 Seltzer, B., and Sherwin, I. Organic brain syndromes: An empirical study and critical review. *Am. J. Psychiatry* 135:13–21, 1978.

11 Sweet, R. D., et al. Mental symptoms in Parkinson's disease during chronic treatment with levodopa. *Neurology* 26:305–310, 1976.

12 Tomlinson, B. E., Blessed, G., and Proth, M. Observations on the brains of demented old people. *J. Neurol. Sci.* 11:205–242, 1970.

13 Tomlinson, B. E. "The pathology of dementia." In *Dementia*, ed. C. E. Wells. Philadelphia: Davis, 1977.

14 Wells, C. E., ed. *Dementia*. Philadelphia: Davis, 1977.

15 Wells, C. E. Chronic brain disease: An overview. *Am. J. Psychiatry* 135:1–12, 1978.

16 Verwoerdt, A. *Clinical geropsychiatry*. Baltimore: Williams and Wilkins, 1976.

4

Mental Retardation

Kurt Glaser, M.D.

The practicing physician cannot avoid contact with the field of mental retardation, even if he does not treat the retarded per se. His involvement
may be in a variety of roles: He may be called upon to help in the differential diagnosis; to assess the ability and mental health of a retardate; to treat
physical, psychiatric, or behavior problems in a retarded child or adult; to
provide counseling and guidance to parents, siblings, and teachers; to advise on school and vocational training; or to assist in the vocational and
social adjustment of the adult.

Seemingly unrelated to mental retardation, however, the psychiatrist, in his professional work in individual, group, and family therapy or
in marital counseling, will have contact with individuals and families who
have a retarded relative. Without a thorough understanding of the psychosocial, economic, and day-to-day impact such a person can have upon
the family as a whole or upon an individual, the psychiatrist is ill
equipped to treat a patient who has difficulties in coping with such a life
situation.

DEFINITION

According to the second edition of the *Mental Disorders* (DSM-II) "mental
retardation refers to subnormal general intellectual functioning which

originates during the developmental period and is associated with impairment of either learning and social adjustment or maturation, or both" [1:14].

Mental retardation is not a disease entity but a condition of impaired intellectual functioning caused by a variety of developmental aberrations or diseases which interfere with normal growth during any phase of prenatal or postnatal development, up to about eighteen years of age.

The terms mental retardation and mental deficiency are usually used interchangeably. Most would agree that in order to apply the term mental retardation the degree of subnormality must be sufficient to interfere with adaptive behavior in the society where the individual lives and must be of a permanent nature. For practical purposes of classification specific IQ levels are usually agreed upon.

Mental retardation is believed to affect about 3 percent of the population, with 2.5 percent in the mild and moderate categories and 0.5 percent in the severe and profound group. The former is mostly due to familial or cultural influences, or both. Deprivation almost always plays a role and may be due to environmental factors or to sensory or neurological deficits which interfere with learning. Familial retardation occurs primarily in the lower socioeconomic educational group. Severe retardation is generally the product of recognizable organic factors and its distribution is fairly even in all population classes. Even in this group, however, the lower socioeconomic population may show a higher incidence due to greater exposure to risk factors and to delayed and less consistent treatment (for example, meningitis, phenylketonuria (PKU), trauma).

MENTAL RETARDATION VERSUS OTHER HANDICAPPING CONDITIONS

Mental retardation is a permanent handicap which does not necessarily shorten life expectancy and which produces life-long dependency to varying degrees. It interferes seriously with functioning in a society which requires increasing need for adaptation to progressively more complicated work and life-styles. In a society which places high value on independence and initiative of the individual, the person who lacks these qualifications will rate low.

A concurrent visible physical defect or a telltale appearance or facial expression will make social, school, and work adaptation more difficult. The absence of any physical signs, on the other hand, may also contribute to maladjustment, as the uninitiated observer will find it difficult to explain, excuse, or accept the defective functioning.

Mental retardation carried a stigma upon the retardate and his family. The human characteristic of viewing with suspicion and fear any deviation from the norm may lead to avoidance, isolation, humiliation and at times teasing and taunting. It is a common assumption that a person deviant in one characteristic (intellectual ability) may also be deviant in other areas of functioning (sexual deviancy, delinquency, violence, etc.). Some parents may be concerned that their child may learn bad habits from a retardate, learn to act dumb, or be mistreated by older retarded children who may like to associate with younger children because of lesser competition. Mothers often forbid their children to play with retardates, and neighbors may oppose the establishment of a group home residence in their community.

The entire family may be shunned by neighbors and relatives. Some of the reasons may have a rational basis: The retardate may be wandering about, seemingly without purpose, but likely in search of social contact or to satisfy his curiosity; in the process he may invade the privacy of his neighbors. The presence of a retardate may interfere with the normal social intercourse of families. Other reasons for ostracism may be superstitions: For instance, a family with a retardate may be perceived as being punished for immoral or unethical behavior in past generations. People are apt to look for and interpret almost any characteristic of normal family members of retardates as signs of deviancy.

Physical handicaps, especially if visible, are more easily understood and accepted. They usually evoke pity, a desire to help, often oversolicitousness, but they do not have the mystical character of mental disorders in the normal looking individual.

Mental retardation is usually not recognized or accepted by the patient himself. He is therefore less apt to understand why there are things he cannot do and activities from which he is excluded. Physical handicaps such as blindness, deafness, or orthopedic or neurological disorders cannot be as readily denied. This does not imply that persons with these handicaps do not at times use denial as an inappropriate defense or develop other coping difficulties. The child or adult who is unable to comprehend or accept his intellectual limitation is apt to show anger and hostility and possibly aggressiveness toward those who reject or exclude him.

Finally, genetic implications in many cases of mental retardation pose problems in terms of marriage and procreation, not only for the retardate himself but also in terms of possible future offspring for his parents and siblings. Modern diagnostic procedures (chemical analyses, chromosomal studies) have done much to clarify these issues and allow for genetic counseling on a scientific basis, such as providing reliable statistical data with regard to the likelihood of mental retardation in offspring of other family members.

The psychological sequelae of genetic implications for present and future generations can often be severe. Parents may feel guilty or accuse each other of being the transmitters of damaged genes. Siblings may feel hostile toward their parents and often condemn the retarded brother or sister, since they may have been unaware of the presence of defective genes until his or her birth. Their actual behavior or hidden wishes again produce guilt which in turn leads to hostility toward those upon whom the cause for the guilt is projected.

DIAGNOSIS AND DIFFERENTIAL DIAGNOSIS

Several conditions can mimic the above defined syndrome and must be excluded in order to arrive at a diagnosis of mental retardation, provide appropriate treatment and management, and supply prognostic information: infantile autism [7:115,149], childhood schizophrenia or adult forms of schizophrenia (in the relatively rare situations where a diagnosis of mental retardation has to be considered in an adult person not previously so diagnosed), organic brain dysfunction, and speech-language-learning disabilities (including aphasia) in the presence of normal intellectual endowment. Organic conditions such as undiscovered visual and hearing deficits and physical debilitation due to illness or nutritional deficiencies must also be considered.

In the absence of positive, identifiable signs and symptoms of any of the above conditions, the diagnosis is established by the fact that there is a permanent and significant deficit of the intellectual capacity, with or without identifiable cause. The terms primary or secondary mental retardation have been used to differentiate those cases where a definite cause could be established for the condition of mental retardation (secondary), from those where mental retardation is the only abnormal manifestation (primary). To meet the definition of mental retardation, the mental deficit must be such that even after removal of the cause, the mental deficit remains.

A child whose intellectual functioning is impaired by a visual or auditory handicap and whose IQ test results improve significantly after the correction of the sensory impairment is not considered retarded. However, if the sensory deprivation is severe and long lasting, the developmental dwarfing may not be reversible and the child would be considered retarded.

A person suffering from acute schizophrenia would be intellectually impaired during the acute phase of the illness. Psychological tests during such acute illness would show results in the "retarded" range. However, after recession of the schizophrenic process the individual would emerge with normal intellectual functioning. This is not a case of mental retardation.

A differential diagnostic difficulty arises when a schizophrenic reaction is superimposed upon mental retardation, especially if this was not clearly diagnosed earlier. Recovery from the schizophrenic reaction would then constitute only that and not a cure of the underlying mental retardation. A careful and detailed developmental history obtained from a reliable relative and documented by past school or medical records can be invaluable. The therapeutic approach and prognostic assessment in such a situation must take into account that the person's capacity to benefit or make use of psychotherapeutic intervention will be limited by his reduced intellectual capacity (ability to comprehend, to verbalize, to gain insight, and to think abstractly). After recovery from the schizophrenic bout, he will continue to be a mentally handicapped person.

Verbal and physical acting-out, rage reactions, or withdrawal by a retarded person, who may be frustrated by his inability to communicate effectively or to comprehend the situation around him or to tolerate stress, are often interpreted as psychotic reactions. Tranquilizing medication may be indicated and helpful in such cases, whereas attempts at insight therapy may be ineffective and stressful for both the patient and the therapist. Admission to a psychiatric facility often compounds the issue, as the patient finds it difficult to adjust to the situation. His noncompliance with rules and directions is often interpreted as part of the psychotic process, when in reality it is the result of his inability to comprehend due to intellectual limitation. Further demands and criticism tend to increase the stress and aggravate the behavior. Temporary admission to a mental retardation facility which is equipped to deal with the behavioral difficulties and has a structure and program geared toward the mentally retarded may be more successful. The patient will find peers on a similar functioning level and staff whose mode of communication is on his level of comprehension.

Chromosomal aberrations such as Down's syndrome, or mongolism, usually occur with significant reduction of intellectual ability. Neither the chromosomal aberration nor the concurrent mental retardation are corrigible. This does not preclude that education and training approaches cannot influence — positively or negatively — the development of the child's intellectual and emotional functioning within the limitations of his innate ability. Thus a child diagnosed early and benefiting from appropriate education and training approaches may reach his functioning potential and acquire adaptive behavior which will allow him to lead a less dependent life than a child who has been deprived of exposure to stimulating influences commensurate with his ability.

On the other hand, mental retardation due to certain metabolic aberrations, such as phenylketonuria, seem to be at least in part the result of noxious influences which continue to have their effect after birth, as metabolic products caused by enzymatic deficiencies accumulate. This type of mental retardation can be prevented at least to some extent by the early introduction of a dietary regime which will reduce the accumulation of metabolites in noxious amounts. Early diagnostic screening for metabolic aberrations or hormonal deficiencies (hypothyroidism) is therefore indicated and has been legislated for some conditions in some states. To what degree the organism has been damaged by the deficiency in utero or to what extent mental retardation may be part of the total entity has not been established. But it seems that even in those cases which are diagnosed and treated early, the intellectual functioning is below that of the normal siblings.

Minimal brain dysfunction, visual and auditory defects, and learning-language disabilities may not only mimic intellectual limitation but may actually produce it through deprivation of sensory and intellectual input. It is believed at present that once such deprivation has lasted for a prolonged period of time during the early developmental years, the intellectual deficit may be permanent or at least not remediable by current methods.

The above examples serve to illustrate why early diagnostic clarification is important for the therapeutic, educational, and/or preventive process.

PHENOMENOLOGY AND ASSESSMENT

After the condition of mental retardation is established or suspected, there remains the task of a comprehensive assessment of the individual and his environment. This would include the degree of intellectual limitation, concurrent handicapping physical and psychological conditions, and the individual's psychological and behavioral characteristics. But the assessment would not be complete unless it also takes into consideration the nature of his immediate and nearby surroundings (family and subculture) and the available resources for education, training, employment, and residential care at various levels of sheltering.

The Mentally Retarded Person

The objective of an assessment of assets and liabilities is to provide guidance for the treatment, management, education, training, or vocational preparation for the child and long-range prognostic guidance to the family or assisting agencies.

INTELLIGENCE

On the assumption that intelligence is normally distributed in the population, DSM-II uses the following classification, with "the range of intelligence subsumed under each classification (corresponding) to one standard deviation" [1:14]:

Borderline mental retardation	IQ 68–83
Mild mental retardation	IQ 52–67
Moderate mental retardation	IQ 36–51
Severe mental retardation	IQ 20–35
Profound mental retardation	IQ under 20

Educational systems usually adapt and simplify the categories to facilitate grouping. They consider the mildly retarded (IQ 50–70) as educable, the moderately retarded (IQ 30–50) as trainable, and those with an IQ below 30 as severely and profoundly retarded.

This classification implies that in the highest group modified methods of standard educational approaches are applicable. Such children can usually absorb academic material up to about the fourth-grade level, provided that no other handicapping conditions exist and that appropriate educational methods are used. In the second group, training in survival skills, self-care skills, and limited social adjustment are more reachable goals than formal education. In children with IQs below 30 training usually has to be limited to self-care skills or the simplest domestic or mechanical chores. The above classification also implies that below the level of a 30 IQ the child is not the responsibility of the educational system, and above an IQ of 70 the child does not need special facilities or methods of education. This view is currently being challenged.

NEUROMUSCULAR FUNCTIONING

Various degrees of neurological impairment, ranging from mild small muscle or visual motor coordination difficulties to gross cerebral palsy, may require orthopedic or neurological intervention and specialized training approaches. Such handicaps may affect the ultimate selection of training for vocational goals. Physical strength, body size, and coordination may be determining factors in whether an individual with marked intellectual limitations will be able to be at least partially self-supporting through physical labor.

VISUAL AND AUDITORY HANDICAPS

These handicaps may be partially corrigible, provided the individual's comprehension and behavior are such that devices can be tolerated and adaptive behavior learned.

SPEECH AND LANGUAGE IMPAIRMENTS

Speech and language impairments, which occur in about one-third of all mentally retarded, are often decisive factors in social adjustment and may interfere with occupational placement and functioning. Again the degree of intellectual deficit and psychosocial adjustment (comprehension, cooperation, motivation) will determine the applicability of special therapeutic and educational methods.

PHYSICAL APPEARANCE

Visible physical abnormalities and unusual facial expressions may present difficulties in social adjustment and must be taken into consideration for social and vocational planning. Children with such visible defects may require special counseling to help them cope with the almost unavoidable teasing, shunning, and pitying they will experience. Parents and the immediate environment, such as relatives or teachers, may need guidance in helping the child cope and avoiding overprotection as well as overexposure. Denial and overcompensation, which may be operative in child and parents, often lead to the selection of careers where external appearance is almost a prerequisite (salesperson, restaurant personnel, receptionist). Future disappointments are preventable through objective assessment and professional guidance.

Normal appearance in a retarded small child usually facilitates care for the mother, since she can take her child on errands, walks, or visits without exposure to stares, questions, and expressions of pity. During the school years the normal appearance may be deceiving to peers and teachers who may react with surprise and criticism when the normal looking child displays his abnormality in language, school performance, and social intercourse.

ASSESSMENT AND IMPLICATIONS OF BEHAVIOR

At various age levels assessment and implications of behavior present the greatest challenge to the psychiatrist, pediatrician, and all those specialists concerned with the care of the retarded and his family-psychologist, social worker, teacher, nurse, physical and occupational therapist, vocational counselor, and so forth. The placid, compliant, quiet child or adult presents different problems from the aggressive, negativistic, hyperactive person.

During the first two years of life, developmental landmarks may be reached with various degrees of delay or may never be reached (e.g., the profoundly retarded child who never develops speech). Most of the earliest milestones measure gross motor behavior rather than intellectual development and may be reached at average age levels in the mildly retarded child (e.g., head raising, turning, reaching, transferring between hands, sitting, crawling). If delayed, they are probably secondary to lack of motivation. This can be caused by environmental deprivation or as a result of the child's intellectual deficit. For instance, the child's turning and raising of the head, crawling, sitting, and other behaviors are a result of his interest in his surroundings and desire to explore. With diminished interest due to lack of curiosity, the stimulus for these activities is lacking. A delayed social smiling response is probably a more specific indicator for an intellectual developmental lag, provided there is no neglect or mistreatment. Delayed receptive and expressive language development is a later, significant indicator of mental retardation if deafness, aphasia, or neurological deficit and environmental deprivation can be ruled out.

Hyperkinesis is not infrequent in the retarded child. Before the walking stage it may not constitute a management problem, whereas at a later age it may be detrimental to the family and dangerous to the child. Similar to brain damage in the child with average intellect [6], hyperkinesis is considered to be the result of neurological damage. It manifests itself primarily in purposeless mobility (innerdrivenness) and may respond, paradoxically, to stimulant medication. It must be differentiated from overactivity caused by frustration and anxiety which may respond to tranquilizers or sedatives.

The prominent characteristics of the retardate under four years of age are his delayed speech and comprehension. He is unable to learn the customary games for this age group; he does not handle toys appropriately, since he does not understand their purpose; he may show apathy (giving up) or anger (whining, crying, hitting, biting) because of his inability to communicate or derive pleasure from activities or satisfaction from maternal approval. Aggressiveness toward peers may first be noted at this age level for the above reasons. Parents who up to then had not noticed or had denied and rationalized any developmental delays begin to show more active concern by searching for answers and often consulting a multitude of professionals.

At school age the above characteristics may become even more marked, as structured demands for behavior and performance are made by the school and standards are applied to measure performance and ability. Distractability may be added to the symptoms, even without evidence of organicity, based on lack of comprehension and thus lack of interest in the task at hand. Wandering about the classroom, disturbing other children, generally disruptive behavior, and seemingly unprovoked aggressiveness make continuation in the standard classroom setting intolerable.

It now becomes evident that the child has difficulties following directions and learning new tasks, such as reading or learning the rules of a game. He fails to comprehend their meaning and purpose. He has acquired some knowledge by rote memory but cannot apply it. He may have learned the use of a toy or tool or the technique of reading by sounding out each letter, but he cannot generalize and cannot apply the knowledge to a similar but not identical situation. He finds it difficult to follow directions if the instructions are not in simplest terms, require the application of prior knowledge, or contain too many items. In evaluating these characteristics, the experience and skill of the examiner are most important. A child may be able to follow several directives given singly and in sequence: "Go to the shelf — good; now pick up the red book — good; put it on the desk — good; now open it to page 12 — good." But he may not be able to follow a single compound directive: "pick up the red book from the shelf, put it on the desk, and open it to page 12." He may pick up the book and not know what to do with it, or put it on the floor, or be totally unable to carry out the directive. A request like "open the red book to page 12" may be even more confusing because it requires independent decision and action to take it from the shelf and place it on the desk.

Parents and often sympathetic but inexperienced examiners will misinterpret the child's abilities. The fact that he can follow all of the above directions, if given singly, is not equivalent to the ability to follow a compound directive or draw upon previous experience to complete a task.

The ability to understand abstract concepts develops in the normal child at about ten to twelve years of age. In the retardate it may never be acquired, even in adulthood.

Adolescence brings new problems of adaptation. This is the phase during which preparation for adult life begins to take place: moves toward independence, toward work and vocational choice, and toward sociosexual adaptation. Physical sexual maturation may not be delayed, but the comprehension of society's rules, values, moral concepts, control of drives, and implications for others are apt to be delayed or deficient, depending on the degree of mental retardation. With the awakening of undifferentiated sex drives, homosexual approaches and inappropriate heterosexual behavior are common.

Preparation for independent living and the choice of educational and vocational direction in the broadest sense present special problems for the mildly retarded person who is unaware of his limitations or uses strong defenses of denial. During this period the development of an appropriate self-image is most important for future adjustment [7:78–79]. Frequent disappointments, frustrations, criticisms, and the experience of younger siblings and peers proceeding at a more rapid rate can produce a low self-concept, underestimation of actual ability, discouragement, depression, and paranoid ideation. Such a person is unable to reach his potential and is apt to experience some adjustment difficulties.

Confusion about capability may also lead to an inflated self-image, and this is often overlooked by professionals. In the desire to be supportive, false encouragement to reach for goals beyond the retardate's ability is common. But an inflated self-image is not an appropriate self-image [3]. It leads to attempts to achieve goals which are unreachable, with disappointment and discouragement contributing to the stress of frustration. Under such stressful situations depression, suicidal tendencies, paranoid ideation, and psychotic thought disorganization have been observed. These symptoms may persist into adulthood, often leading to repeated hospitalizations or permanent institutionalization.

Most mildly retarded adults can lead a well-adjusted life if offered noncompetitive work and opportunities for recreational activities and social contacts on their level of functioning. These are most difficult to achieve, and social isolation with all its consequences and lack of occupational opportunities may lead to a decline in abilities and general deterioration of functioning. Adjustment difficulties are often compounded by declining support by aging parents and siblings who wish to lead their own lives unencumbered by the retarded relative.

The Family and Surroundings

Meaningful assessment of the retardate cannot occur in a vacuum but must include the level of functioning, attitudes, and resources of his family and the community. Two retarded persons with similar characteristics will have different needs for services and show different modes of adaptation if one is to live in an accepting, resourceful family in a rural setting, and the other in a competitive, individualistic family in an industrialized urban environment.

The mildly retarded child of parents who are themselves functioning on a borderline, low educational level may not be too different from the remainder of the family and the neighborhood in which he is apt to live. He may be well accepted socially and can find his place educationally and vocationally. The situation may be quite different for a child functioning on a borderline (70–80 IQ) or even average intellectual level (90–110 IQ), with siblings and parents of high intellectual abilities and high educational expectations, living among people with similar backgrounds. The adaptation and functioning of such children would present problems not too different from those with serious degrees of retardation. They may well be considered relatively retarded, even though they function technically within the normal range. In such cases professionals of all disciplines face a special challenge in management.

An attitudinal assessment of the family members must be part of the evaluation. Degrees of rejection and guilt in the parents may determine whether the child can be reared in the home or should be removed. Although current thinking in general places a high value on the child remaining with his biological family, severe rejection may make such a choice undesirable. Some parents are aware of their rejecting feelings and able to verbalize them and seek assistance in finding other resources for the child. Others will deny such sentiments to themselves and others. Such parental attitude may then manifest itself in child abuse and neglect in the extreme case or, more subtly, in accident proneness of the child, emotional and intellectual deprivation, or smothering overprotectiveness.

Early recognition of such family pathology is essential if the child is to be spared permanent damage. The skilled observer must first determine if the situation is likely to improve with counseling or if the feelings are so deep-rooted that the child is served best by being removed. Removal may be to a foster home, which imitates "natural" family settings most closely; a group home; or an institution, depending on the degree and nature of the handicap and the available resources. Such placement must not necessarily be permanent, as attitudes, resources, as well as the needs of the retardate change over the years.

The attitude toward the handicapped child is not the only factor in the environmental assessment process. The emotional and marital stability of the parents as well as their economic resources often play a determining factor in deciding whether the biological family is the best place to rear the child. The professional must consider these parental resources in relation to the degree of mental and physical handicap of the child and reassess them periodically as the child's growth and physical and emotional needs change with age. A severely physically handicapped retarded child may be manageable by his mother until his weight makes care without assistance impossible. A hyperactive baby and small child may be difficult to care for but present an unmanageable burden as he grows up.

Siblings must be considered not only for their effect upon the retarded child but also for the effect of the retarded child upon them. Parents are often misguided by "client-oriented" professionals: To sacrifice the opportunity for healthy and productive lives of parents and their normal children for the sake of the retarded offspring "because the home is the best place for him" may be guidance of questionable soundness. When separation is finally forced by circumstances, the guilt feelings and emotional strain experienced over years may have caused irreparable damage to parents and normal siblings [4,5].

The presence of another adult living with the family (grandparent, aunt, or uncle) can be a resource which not only makes child care in his own home feasible but may provide valuable occupation and meaning for the adult.

Personal and economic resources of the family change during the life cycle and periodic reassessment is necessary.

METHODS OF ASSESSMENT

Since mental retardation often occurs in families with known and unknown hereditary factors, historical information can be of considerable diagnostic assistance. A careful history of the intellectual functioning, school level reached, occupational and social adjustment of siblings, parents, siblings of parents and their children, grandparents on both sides, and siblings of grandparents (aunts, uncles, and cousins of parents) can be highly revealing. With the stigma attached to mental retardation, a relative will rarely be designated as "retarded" but rather described in camouflaging terms such as: He had to drop out of school; he never really held a job; he worked for a relative as a helper in an unskilled occupation; he was sort of odd; they put him in an institution because both parents had to work. At times it is possible to check on factual information through school records or hospital transcripts.

The child's developmental milestones should be carefully elicited and compared with norms. Here again it is most helpful if factual information, such as pediatric records or baby books kept by parents, are available. Possible early deviant development or later "slowness" due to learning disabilities, emotional trauma, or intercurrent illnesses or injuries should be elicited and may have therapeutic and prognostic significance. It is advisable to assist the parents in recalling the child's early development by asking for comparisons with siblings, cousins, or neighbors.

Unawareness or denial are common among parents of mentally retarded children during their early years, especially in the mildly retarded child without physical handicaps. But after complete denial — "All was well until he started school" — it is not unusual to obtain the information that the child did not raise his head; sit, stand, or walk; smile, or talk as early as a cousin of the same age.

This method of nonthreatening, detailed questioning about the early history is also a helpful tool in assisting the parents to gain awareness and learn to accept the delayed development as they describe their child to the examiner. The parents' question, after giving all the points on how their child was always slower than his cousin — "But you don't think he is retarded?" — is often the first time they dared to pronounce the word or face the issue with a straight question.

The approach to a child whose normal development has been arrested or slowed after certain significant emotional events (birth of a sibling, entrance in school, parental conflict and separation, illness or death of a significant family member) would be different from the methods used in a child whose development has been abnormally slow from birth and who may or may not have been affected by specific events. A psychotherapeutic approach with a developmentally retarded child to correct the putative emotional deviations may not only be ineffective but damaging to him and his parents. Expectations may go beyond his capabilities, thus leading to frustration, disappointment, and disapproval. Parental guilt for the inevitable implications of faulty child-rearing practices may have detrimental effects on the child-parent relationship.

ETIOLOGY AND PREVENTION

Etiology and prevention of mental retardation fall mostly into the sphere of the primary care physician (family physician, pediatrician, internist) or the researcher. However, the psychiatrist needs a basic appreciation when acting as therapist to parents or siblings of retarded children or when treating retarded children or consulting with schools, institutions, or other professionals. The various etiological categories are therefore only listed or described briefly in this chapter, and the reader is referred to the appropriate texts in the special fields [2]. The specialist in genetic counseling, who may very well be a psychiatrist, must, of course, have a thorough knowledge of the genetic implications, statistical data, and preventive methods.

Prenatal factors include metabolic aberrations, hormonal factors, chromosomal abnormalities, Rh incompatibility, placental or uterine malformations, maternal malnutrition, influence of drugs, and intrauterine damage due to other factors. Perinatal factors include anoxia, physical trauma, and prematurity. Postnatal factors include trauma (head injury), continued effects of metabolic disorders, infections (meningitis, encephalitis), deprivation. Some of the prenatal factors exert their greatest influence shortly after birth. Thus, if discovered at birth or soon thereafter, there is opportunity for prevention. For instance, in certain metabolic disorders retardation may be partially or completely prevented by early dietary management; hormonal deficiencies (hypothyroidism) require early thyroid replacement therapy.

The discovery of a chromosomal aberration in an offspring (e.g., Down's syndrome) allows for genetic counseling of the parents with regard to future children. Intrauterine studies (amniocentesis) may lead to a prenatal diagnosis of mongolism and the option for abortion. The rather recent developments in this field still need much clarification, especially with regard to ethical, legal, and religious questions. A careful, truly multidisciplinary approach is indicated.

Sensory, emotional, and psychoeducational deprivation of the preschooler can have lasting dwarfing effects on his intellectual and emotional development. Education of young women, especially teenagers, not only in prenatal care, appropriate management of the birth, and dietary and medical management of the child after birth, but also in child-rearing skills and mothering are essential if the effects of deprivation and emotional maladjustment of the child are to be reduced or prevented. The ability of the young mother to respond positively to her child is greatly influenced by economic factors. At times the professional must first address himself to these through proper referral before any psychoeducational correction can take place.

Inherited and environmental factors are difficult to separate completely. The IQ is normally distributed in the population along the Gaussian frequency distribution curve. One can therefore expect that a certain percentage of the population falls sufficiently below the level of average intellectual functioning to be considered retarded when compared with the general population. Assortative mating and assortative migration toward lower economic population centers are likely to result in accumulations of subaverage families whose children, without any other reason for retardation and of similar intellect as their parents and siblings, fall on the lower side of the Gaussian curve. In such an environment mental retardation is then not sufficiently deviant and therefore may not be discovered until standard measurements are applied, for instance, at school entrance and later in competition in the labor market.

The below-average functioning of these children may be the result of genetic endowment (innate intellectual ability) or environmental deprivation due to child-rearing practices, inadequate intellectual stimulation, and limited economic resources. Available psychological tests measure only current functioning and do not differentiate between the child with intellectual limitation due to presumably unalterable low intellectual endowment and the child with low functioning due to experiential deficiencies. The latter is assumed to be corrigible, at least up to a certain age. Attempts at designing culture-fair tests, which would differentiate between these two groups, have so far not been successful.

Since it must be assumed that some of the parents in this marginally functioning group are themselves the product of environmental deprivation during their childhood, one can further assume that some of the children are born with higher intellectual endowment than their parents' functioning may indicate. With this recognition, local and national efforts are being made to reduce the environmental deprivation during early preschool years so that the child with normal or above-average IQ would have the opportunity to develop in accordance with his innate potential. It is thus hoped that the self-perpetuating course of low intellectual functioning in successive generations of certain population subgroups may be broken through early stimulation in such facilities as day care centers and early education projects, such as Head Start.

REFERENCES

1   American Psychiatric Association. *Diagnostic and statistical manual of mental disorders*, DSM-II. Washington, D.C.: American Psychiatric Association, 1968.

2   Bergsma, D., ed. *Birth defects: Atlas and compendium*. Baltimore: Williams and Wilkins, 1973.

3   Edgerton, R. B. *The cloak of competence: Stigma in the lives of the mentally retarded*. Berkeley, Calif.: University of California Press, 1967.

4   Farber, B. *Effects of a severely mentally retarded child on family integration*. Monographs of the Society for Research in Child Development, vol. 24, no. 2, serial no. 71, 1959.

5   Farber, B. *Family organization and crisis: Maintenance of integration in family with a severely mentally retarded child*. Monographs of the Society for Research in Child Development, vol. 25, no. 1, serial no. 75, 1960.

6   Glaser, K. *Learning difficulties: Causes and psychological implications: A guide for professionals*. Springfield, Ill.: Thomas, 1974.

7   Menolascino, F. J., ed. *Psychiatric approaches to mental retardation*. New York: Basic Books, 1970.

RECOMMENDED READINGS

•   Richmond, J., Tarjan, G., and Mendelsohn, R., eds. *Handbook on mental retardation*, 2nd ed. Chicago: American Medical Association, 1974.

II
Psychotic Disorders

5

Schizophrenic Psychoses

José D. Arana, M.D.

The existence of psychoses as mental disturbances was acknowledged early in the history of psychiatry. The schizophrenic psychoses, however, were not defined as such until the end of the last century, when Morel in France, following the leads signaled by Pinel and Esquirol, introduced the term *dementia praecox* for one of his patients. Later, other clinical pictures like catatonia (Kahlbaum) and hebephrenia (Hecker) were described. But it was not until Kraepelin's work in 1896 that these and other syndromes were construed as a single clinical entity with various forms of presentation but a common, dim prognosis. A few years thereafter, Bleuler described the hierarchical connections between the various levels of schizophrenic psychopathology. He recognized the primary symptoms corresponding to the basic disturbance and, as reactions to them, the secondary symptoms. The latter were seen as impregnated with crucial psychodynamic meaning. Subsequently, a multitude of prominent clinicians and researchers approached the study of schizophrenia in an attempt to understand better its etiology, universality, clinical characteristics, and other factors.

The concept of schizophrenia has evolved to the point where evidence regarding its genetic roots and the role of environmental factors is available. Differences pertaining to diagnostic styles and diagnostic criteria have become a primary research task, for all discrepancies on the etiology and treatment of schizophrenia will not be surmounted until universally validated, specific symptoms are identified. Until such time, the diagnosis is widely based on Bleuler's characterizations and on Schneider's first-rank symptoms.

Schizophrenia is by no means a distinct, well-established, and easily recognizable nosographic group. It has, notwithstanding, survived vigorous objections that questioned its existence, and it remains the most frequent and devastating of the psychoses.

ETIOLOGY

The discussion of schizophrenia, practically since its conception as an illness, has focused on two major areas: diagnostic criteria and etiological factors. On the origin of schizophrenia, the current consensus is twofold: On the one hand, it is acknowledged that no clearly causal explanations have been presented. On the other hand, substantial evidence suggests the presence of multiple factors involved in the manifestation of the condition. A brief review of the findings in the areas of genetics, family environment, sociocultural influences, and biochemical hypotheses follows.

Inheritability of Schizophrenia

When schizophrenia was first described as an illness, or a group of mental illnesses, there was little doubt regarding its inheritability. Subsequently, an arduous search for such genetic foundation has taken various directions.

Several approaches have been utilized to determine the existence of heritable factors in schizophrenia and the modes of transmission of such factors. Research on twins and adoption studies, as well as studies of risk rates for the general population and for relatives of schizophrenics, have resulted in evidence for a genetic basis for schizophrenia.

TWIN STUDIES

A general conclusion reached by most authors is that the concordance rate for schizophrenia is higher for monozygotic than for dizygotic twins. This has been the case even when the twins were reared apart (which eliminates the possibility of excessive identification with the twin who became ill first). Moreover, twins always show a higher incidence of schizophrenia as compared with the general population. Aside from the general controversy over diagnostic practices applied to these studies, the need for age-correction methods has also been noted. That is, the discordant twin may become ill after the research is completed, more so if during the research period he had not reached the upper age limit for manifestation of the illness. However, age-correction methods, if necessary at all, still yield the same result. The criticisms regarding the reliability of serological techniques for determination of zygosity do not seem applicable to the more recent studies. These findings are a cornerstone in the determination of schizophrenia as a heritable disorder.

ADOPTION STUDIES

Rearing by a schizophrenic parent does not necessarily lead to the development of schizophrenia. On the other hand, follow-up studies of foster-reared children separated from their schizophrenic mother found more schizophrenia and other psychopathology such as sociopathy and neurosis among them than among those of normal mothers. Another series of studies have shown that the biological relatives of the schizophrenic adoptees present a greater percentage of schizophrenia and schizophrenia-related disorders than the control group. The concept of schizophrenia spectrum disorder has been supported by adoption studies, thus defining a variety of manifestations of the disease. However, more precision is needed in establishing just what nosographic pictures belong to the spectrum.

MORBIDITY RISK FOR RELATIVES OF SCHIZOPHRENICS

Children who have a schizophrenic parent have an approximate 10 to 14 percent risk of becoming ill. When both parents are schizophrenic, the risk increases to about 40 percent. The general population has a relatively low risk (0.85 percent) when compared with the substantial risk found for first-degree relatives. The degree of blood relationship seems to determine the morbidity risk for the illness, so that the closer the familial relationship, the higher the possibility of being affected by schizophrenia.

The possible genetic relationship between manic-depressive illness and schizophrenia has also been postulated, but no definitive conclusions have been reached.

Moreover, evidence is being gathered suggesting that true schizophrenia may be genetically different from acute schizophrenia, atypical schizophrenia, and all schizophreniform psychoses. The classical subtypes (hebephrenic, paranoid, simple, catatonic) do not seem genetically bundled, although more cases of schizophrenia appear to be present in the families of nonparanoid patients.

MODE OF TRANSMISSION

Although the mode of inheritance of schizophrenia is not known, there are some theories regarding its mode of genetic transmission. Of these, there are three which have received ample support from clinical research: the genetic heterogeneity, the monogenic, and the polygenic theories.

The *genetic heterogeneity theory* postulates a multiplicity of genes, each causing a distinct and clinically recognizable form of schizophrenia. According to the *monogenic theory*, there is one specific gene responsible for the transmission of the disease. Consequently, a dominant gene with reduced penetrance, a recessive gene, or a combination of both will be responsible for determining the manifestation of schizophrenia. The *polygenic theory* suggests that a combination of many genes of equal or diverse effect is necessary for a constitutional predisposition to schizophrenia. According to this model, the disease is precipitated by environmental factors operating on such genetic liability.

PARENTS OF SCHIZOPHRENIC PATIENTS

The characteristics of the family environment in which the schizophrenic grew up have been widely studied during recent years. The methods utilized in those studies include clinical interviews, psychological tests, questionnaires, and group behavior scales. Two main areas have been focused on: the characteristics of the interaction between parents and child and, in particular, the abnormalities of communication and speech prevailing in such interactions. A deviant transactional experience is assumed to be linked with the learning of faulty communication patterns, with inauthentic and defective roles, and, ultimately, with the development of schizophrenia. With few exceptions, family research studies need better controlled trials before generalizations can be made. Moreover, they have not demonstrated a *causal* relationship between abnormality of interaction in the family and the development of schizophrenia. The value of such studies resides in the ratification of the role played by interpersonal factors in the manifestation of the condition.

Several hypotheses advanced by family researchers will be briefly presented.

The *schizophrenic mother* theory categorizes the mother of the schizophrenic patient as dominant, overprotective, and hostile. She unconsciously prolongs her child's overdependence on her while displaying a cold and rejecting attitude toward him. Recent studies have found that this type of mothering is not exclusively seen in relation to schizophrenia and that the frustration and despair derived from rearing abnormal children seems to contribute to the overprotectiveness and ambivalence found in their mothers.

The *double-bind theory* postulates that the patient is affected by the parental messages most significant to him, which are incompatible at different levels of communication (e.g., saying one thing and meaning or doing another). This kind of message renders the patient helpless, confused, and forced to split his response and his attitudes. However, double-bind situations have been identified in other conditions as well and are not always present in relation to schizophrenia.

As to the *parental disharmony* hypothesis, a recent review of the literature finds that "there is a consistent finding that parents of schizophrenics show more marital disharmony than normals as indicated by open or tacit conflict, expressed hostility, opposition of spontaneously expressed attitudes and difficulty reaching agreement." With few exceptions, these findings "pertain to chronic schizophrenics or schizophrenics with a poor premorbid personality" [8:99].

According to the *transmission of irrationality* theory, certain distorted relationships between parents can account for the manifestation of schizophrenia in the family. When parents are engaged in open conflict (emotional divorce), a marital schism develops. When one of the parents performs inadequately in his role while the other takes over an abnormally dominant and possessive role, a marital skew is formed [10]. Schismatic parents are mostly found in relation to female schizophrenics and skewed marriages in relation to male schizophrenic patients, where fathers accept a passive role. The family research approach has not demonstrated that distorted family relationships are specific for schizophrenia and is generally criticized for the lack of control studies and strict diagnostic criteria.

The *pseudomutuality and amorphous and fragmented thinking* approach has resulted from carefully designed studies. The families of schizophrenic patients were found to be lacking in true mutuality and reciprocity in their interactions but strove to disguise such patterns of interaction. Wynne and Singer [17] have also recognized three types of thought disorder among schizophrenics (amorphous, fragmented, and mixed). Interpreting blindly psychological tests administered to the patient's parents, the authors have been able to predict the type of thought disorder that would be present in the patient. In other words, it would seem that disordered parental thinking communication is "transmitted" to the schizophrenic children. More studies using larger samples are needed.

Certain *transactional modes* occurring in the families of schizophrenics are viewed as pathogenic, particularly when they are inappropriately timed, mixed, or excessive. Stierlin [58] defines three major modes: binding, delegating, and expelling. In binding, there is an overprotection that encourages a loyal dependency in the child. In the delegating mode, certain "missions" are covertly assigned to the child for him to live out parental conflicts (i.e., the child is expected to achieve the beauty and vitality wished by the parents, or the child is expected to destroy one parent out of loyalty to the other). In expelling, the parents act toward extruding the child out of the family system.

Sociocultural Influences

Almost all studies indicate that the lower the socioeconomic class, the higher the prevalence of schizophrenia. It also appears that disorganized, disintegrated (rather than merely poor) communities show the highest prevalence of schizophrenia. Patients of low socioeconomic status tend also to remain hospitalized longer with a consequent impairment of their rehabilitation capability. Whether schizophrenic patients drift downward and contribute to the creation of society's disorganization or whether they are the necessary product of prolonged exposure to social and cultural malaise and marginality are hypotheses that remain to be tested.

A similar incidence of schizophrenia in different countries has been found in international studies. Symptom patterns, symptom content, and course of illness, as well as prognosis, vary according to environmental circumstances and prevalent social norms.

It has been suggested that "cultural exclusion" (which may engender withdrawal, hostility, and suspiciousness) and defective symbol and concept learning — secondary to low socioeconomic status and social changes — may theoretically be related to psychosis development. It has not been possible to discern, except at a high level of abstraction, those sociocultural elements that may have an etiological correlation to the development of schizophrenia. If social communication is effective, a sense of belonging develops, which may prevent the displacement to marginal positions and thereby the appearance of deviant behavior.

In addition to the unveiling of inequalities in the distribution of schizophrenia, these studies have focused upon the abnormal relationship and communication between the schizophrenic patient and his parents. It is not known whether the impact on the patient's identity of such deviating relationships plays an etiological role or whether such abnormal influences during the patient's development bring about manifestations of an illness for which both the patients and his parents have a predisposition.

Biochemical Studies

A vast number of researchers have attempted to elucidate the biochemical basis for schizophrenia. New techniques and elaborate methods are currently being tried in order to control the nonrelevant variables (such as the medication or the diet received by the patient) which seem to have interfered with earlier results. Various theories have attributed the disease to faulty metabolism of the biogenic amines, carbohydrates, vitamins, hormones, and so forth.

TRANSMETHYLATION HYPOTHESIS

It has been established that some methylated products of the biological amines are hallucinogenics or psychotomimetic compounds. For example, the O-methylation of tryptamine results in dimenthyltryptamine, a psychotomimetic compound. The possibility exists that methylated metabolites might be abnormally accumulated in schizophrenia. When large doses of methionine are administered to schizophrenic patients and normals, the former experience an exacerbation of the psychosis, whereas the latter do not become psychotic. Simultaneously, an increase in the excretion of dimethyltryptamine occurs which is thought to add to the already elevated levels of this product in the patients. Another methylated product of the biogenic amine dopamine, 3,4-DMPEA, has been found by some researchers to be excreted in the urine of many schizophrenics and to have a mescalinelike effect. A pink spot in the paper chromatograph of the urine of schizophrenics was attributed to 3,4-DMPEA, yet it has not been found to be a component of the pink spot. This substance has also been found in tea and has been identified among normals. Another methylated derivative, bufotenine, has been found exclusively in the urine of schizophrenics. The transmethylation hypothesis remains controversial due to methodological shortcomings; however, it has generated an even more disputed issue: the use of large doses of nicotinic acid in the treatment of schizophrenia. Most of the available reports fail to confirm the original hope that so-called megavitamin therapy would competitively divert the biological transmethylation process away from the production of psychotomimetic substances.

DOPAMINE HYPOTHESIS

Several observations have prompted the hypothesis that a relative overactivity of dopamine neurons may be related to the pathogenesis of schizophrenia. When an antipsychotic drug is used, dopaminergic receptors are blocked. The more blocking the action, the more effective that drug is. Conversely, drugs like amphetamines that potentiate dopamine activity at its receptors (releasing dopamine from nerve terminals) may produce a clinical picture indistinguishable from schizophrenia.

One suggestive line of research has resulted from two related observations: While neuroleptic drugs block dopamine activity, prolactin secretion is inhibited by dopamine. In fact, prolactin levels are elevated after administration of neuroleptics. This has provided additional support to the dopamine hypothesis.

Some mechanisms through which dopamine may produce the various schizophrenic symptoms have been postulated. The dopaminergic systems of the brain (i.e., the mesolimbic system) are said to be related to certain schizophrenic clinical features like auditory hallucinations or motor disorders, because of the known relation of such areas with psychological functions. Others think that the dopaminergic hyperactivity is probably secondary to some other basic core defect which could be of a varied neurochemical nature.

Other important abnormal findings include the isolation of alpha-2-globulin in the serum of schizophrenic patients (which reportedly induces schizophreniclike symptoms in normals), abnormalities in the carbohydrate metabolism (i.e., blood lactate and pyruvate increase abnormally when glucose is administered to schizophrenics), a diminished response in the decrease of glucose and a prolonged hypoglycemia when insulin is administered, and elevated levels of 17-hydroxy-corticosteroids during acute phases only. The schizophrenic's insensitivity to histamine and the seemingly genetically reduced levels of monoamine oxidase (MAO) in the platelets of schizophrenic patients are other developments in the biochemistry of schizophrenia. No conclusive results are available as yet, however.

Epidemiology

The results of epidemiological studies are generally assessed in terms of two parameters: the diagnostic definition employed and the characteristics of the population investigated. One important consideration to keep in mind about epidemiological studies is that, for the most part, they are based on adolescents or adult patients after their behavior has resulted in the diagnosis of schizophrenia. At that point most patients have usually suffered from the disease for a long time.

Most studies indicate an irregular distribution among the social classes, so that schizophrenia appears to flourish under conditions of social pressure and constraining life circumstances. Schizophrenia in particular, and not other functional psychoses, seems related to a series of social factors for its formation and manifestation. In this respect, it has been suggested that the usual statistical methods may be too superficial to detect the rather deep impact that the social environment has on the personality.

The incidence of schizophrenia is higher than the average incidence for hereditary diseases, which suggests the participation of other etiological factors for its manifestation in addition to inheritance. Most studies indicate that the incidence rate for schizophrenia lies somewhere between 0.30 to and 1.2 per 100, between the ages of fifteen and forty-five. The risk of developing schizophrenia during a lifetime (expectancy) is about 1 percent for the general population and increases considerably with consanguinity.

First admission rates are higher in the United States than in European countries, a phenomenon which has been ascribed to differences in diagnostic styles. Some studies have shown that certain populations immigrating to the United States have greater incidence rates than the non-immigrant populations of their native countries. Rosenthal [56], has found that individuals who do *not* have a biological schizophrenic parent constitute most of the immigrants. In the United States nonwhites are more likely to be affected by schizophrenia. Inner-city populations show comparatively higher rates of schizophrenia than populations of suburban areas. Schizophrenics tend to migrate to isolated areas. In turn, social isolation seems to be related to high incidence of schizophrenia. Unskilled workers show higher incidence of schizophrenia, which might be a late manifestation based on earlier maladjustments and failures in school life. Schizophrenic patients, particularly males, tend to remain single more frequently than the general population. Low fertility rates for schizophrenics have been recognized. In particular, it appears that single schizophrenic males have fewer children than other single men. One study shows that schizophrenics with normal or high IQs have more children than schizophrenics with low IQs.

In summary, it would appear that race, socioeconomic class, social mobility, geographic location, occupation, and fertility among schizophrenics are factors related to the incidence of schizophrenia. The epidemiological studies on schizophrenia are, however, far from definitive.

BEHAVIORAL ANTECEDENTS

It is difficult to isolate etiological variables once the patient has already become symptomatic and exposed to various treatments. The identification of behavior precursors of schizophrenia can illuminate areas for early, preventive intervention. It is hoped that the research on the behavioral antecedents of schizophrenia will eventually lead to a reduction of the incidence of this disease.

Prospective and retrospective studies have revealed some behaviors and life events which seem to occur more frequently in children who later become schizophrenic. They include disorders in the cognitive, emotional, social, and autonomic functions and deviant transactional experiences in the patient's family. For example, high-risk children appear to be more frequently involved in school disturbances; their academic and verbal test performance is lower; they display both reluctance and difficulties in developing relationships with their peers; they possess high autonomic excitability. Children of schizophrenics have significantly more chance of developing the illness than the general population. Moreover, some have observed that, as compared to controls, the mothers of high-risk children were exposed to more emotional stress during pregancy and that the mothers had more mental illness before pregnancy or became ill in immediate connection with the birth of the subjects. At times early maternal separation is found prior to the development of psychosis. In addition, schizophrenics appear to have more mentally ill fathers than control subjects.

A poor premorbid disposition seems to be related to the development of process (or chronic) schizophrenia. It would seem that such patients embody an increased vulnerability (probably of genetic origin) to environmental stresses. Schizoid personalities are commonly linked with the development of schizophrenia and perhaps even share the same genetic features. Schizoids are oversensitive, rather uncommunicative, rigid, excessive in their intellectualizations and abstractions, and shy and reticent in their contact with others. They appear cold, egocentric, awkward, or exquisite, but always distant and restrained.

PSYCHOPATHOLOGY AND CLINICAL MANIFESTATIONS

The identification of the disease is difficult, particularly in the early states of decompensation. The three most common forms of presentation are an insidious, almost unnoticeable progression lasting several months or years, an acute (less than two months) episode that can be as unexpected and abrupt as dramatic, and an acute decompensation that brings to light previously unnoticed maladjustments.

The patient's entire personality becomes affected by the disease. There seems to exist a pervasive disturbance which variously disorganizes the relationship of the patient with himself, with others, and with the environment. The psychotic disturbance becomes manifest in different forms and with varied intensity. Young persons are more affected by the disease than older persons.

Transformation of the Personality

The initial changes sensed by the patient frequently include feelings of fatigue, depression, and anxiety; unmotivated fears; and a slow reduction of spontaneity, initiative, task concentration, and performance. A vague and ill-defined sense of a basic change in the self brings about uncertainty and confusion about identity. A disturbance of autonomous and synthetic ego functions takes place. An increased, yet unproductive, withdrawal into the self occurs. The self is no longer the source of the patient's autonomous strivings. The patient feels devoid of the familiar, significant connection with himself (depersonalization). Drive and impulses cease to be governed by the patient (disturbances in drive control; "made impulses"). Reality testing becomes disturbed: External events cannot be clearly differentiated from the world of fantasies. The experiences that arise from within are no longer discriminated from those that originate outside of oneself (loss of ego boundaries); the patient may attribute to others his own feelings or thoughts (projection; "made thoughts"), or he may believe that others are experiencing what he is currently feeling (transitivism). The patient frequently feels controlled or possessed, split into two different beings, or as if he has become an entirely different person.

A parallel change in emotions becomes apparent. The affective links with others lose intensity and meaningfulness, and an increasing detachment occurs. The love and concern for others may diminish, disappear, or even be replaced by hatred and hostility. All these changes usually manifest themselves in the form of alterations in functioning in school, at work, and in the area of personal relationships where a retreat from the interpersonal world occurs. Behavior becomes incomprehensible, bizarre. Together with a progressive withdrawal, the patient may neglect his well-being and devote his energies to futile or risky endeavors with an apparent disdain for the consequences.

Symptoms

All of the symptoms present in a schizophrenic patient are interconnected. The clinician needs to identify them without losing the perspective of the experience as a whole. Most symptoms are not constantly present in the patient but change, disappear, and reappear in the clinical picture. Usually, the patient remains lucid and well-oriented in the different spheres and without alterations in memory or intellect.

There is no one specific symptom that can be seen exclusively in schizophrenia. Clinical experience and research, however, have provided useful diagnostic clues. Bleuler [7] made an important contribution by indicating the existence of fundamental symptoms closer to the essence of the disease than the accessory symptoms, which are often encountered in other conditions as well and which are understood as secondary psychological reactions to the experience of the illness (Table 5.1). An especially important aspect is the splitting, or disintegration, of the so-called basic psychological functions: Thought, affect, impulses, and so forth are disassociated from one another and within their own constitutive elements.

Bleuler's [7] fundamental symptoms are autism, ambivalence, associative disturbances, and affective incongruity.

Table 5.1
BLEULER'S CLASSIFICATION OF SYMPTOMS

Fundamental symptoms	*Accessory symptoms*
Autism	Perceptual disorders
Ambivalence	Delusions
Associative disturbances	Behavior disorders (motor, verbal, etc.)
Affective incongruity	Memory disturbances
	Somatic symptoms

Autism means a disjunction between the inner and the outer world, with an experienced predominance of the former. The patient loses contact with reality and removes himself from interpersonal contact, while in his internal life, disconnected from a transactional ratification, he builds up a private world of wishful thinking, dreadful fantasies, or both.

Ambivalence as a symptom means that the patient experiences intense, simultaneous, and opposite wishes, affects, ideas, and volitions, and this may lead to negativism, paralyzing indecisiveness, and other symptoms. For example, pleasant and unpleasant feelings toward the same person can be experienced simultaneously.

In associative disturbances the patient's thinking appears incomprehensible. He is no longer capable of linking his thoughts according to logical relationships, so that thoughts are disconnected or unusually connected and lacking a rational structure.

In affective incongruity the emotional substrate of the conveyed message is inconsistent with the message. The patient may express an emotion which is not relevant to the situation or which expresses inappropriately his affective state. Other times, several different kinds of emotions, even contradictory, may be experienced simultaneously or with unusual intensity. Cosmic feelings may develop. Next to a hypersensitive emotional disposition, a feeling of indifference or an emotional bluntness may coexist.

In addition to the fundamental disorders pointed out by Bleuler, other important symptoms have been recognized, particularly in the areas of thought and affect. Such disorders are significant both in form and content, the latter acquiring particular restorative potential when there is an opportunity to develop a psychotherapeutic relationship with the patient.

Some examples of such thought disorders are overinclusion, alienation of thinking, concretization of thought, magic thinking, blocking, and neologisms. They have their behavioral correlates in the consequent verbal alterations.

Overinclusion means that, in spite of having a normal intelligence, the patient is unable to form clear concepts. He includes in his thinking irrelevant subsidiary ideas which are remote from the main concept and "contaminate" it.

Alienation of thinking may take one of the following forms. In *thought insertion*, the patient claims that thoughts are being put in his mind by somebody or something else. Others may actively "take possession" or "steal" the patient's thoughts in the case of *thought withdrawal*. Or, as in *thought broadcasting*, the patient is convinced that his ideas become known to others, even though he is not communicating them in any way.

Concretization of thought is related to the loss of the patient's ability to think abstractly. It may become manifested by a literal interpretation of proverbs or metaphors. Ideas and symbolic expressions may be reified; that is, understood as possessing a material and concrete quality rather than the representational character that is proper to them.

Magic thinking is archaic, "paleologic" thinking that betrays the patient's immersion in an autistic world. This is manifested, for example, by the conviction that the patient is capable of influencing external events by virtue of his own thinking alone.

Blocking refers to the cessation of the trend of thought for a variable amount of time, after which the patient reiterates fruitlessly the unspoken issue, or he addresses another topic. At times, he feels overwhelmed and becomes silent due to a pressuring flow of thoughts.

The patient may create neologisms; that is, he may condense several ideas or combine normal words in a new word that cryptically represents them, or he may just create an entirely new word on the basis of some idiosyncratic meaning attributed to its components.

In addition to the affective incongruity described by Bleuler as a fundamental feature of schizophrenia, other emotional disorders include: depression, lack of affective contact, apathy, and alienation of feeling.

Depression can be present as a symptom or as a syndrome, and it may mislead the diagnosis. At times flavored with hypochondriacal complaints, depression is seen particularly during the early stages of schizophrenia and in combination with a decline in motivational drives. Also, it tends to occur during the process of recompensation, when the patient gains insight into his clinical situation. Occasionally, depression may develop as a psychological side effect of the neuroleptic medication.

There may be a lack of affective contact, a generalized reduction in the ability to establish empathic rapport with others; a certain shallowness which places the patient at some emotional distance from others. The interviewer's response (praecox feeling) to the failure in engaging emotionally with the patient is said to lead many experienced clinicians to suspect the diagnosis of schizophrenia.

The patient who exhibits apathy remains indifferent even under intense emotional stimulation. Various degress of incapacity to experience sentiments of any kind are usually coupled with a lack of vigor to sustain a decision or even a decision-making effort (apathoabulia).

Alienation of feelings may take one of these forms: insertion of feelings (external agents are imposing an emotion on the patient) or withdrawal of feelings (one's emotional experience is taken away by other).

Bleuler's accessory symptoms [7] include: perceptual disorders, delusions, behavior disorders, memory disturbances (memory gaps, paramnesias), somatic symptoms (e.g., anorexia, bulimia, sleep and sexual disturbances). The first three are described below.

The most common perceptual disorders are hallucinations and illusions. In *hallucinations*, a nonexistent stimulus is perceived as if it were really presented to the patient. In schizophrenia all sensory modalities can be affected, particularly in the acute stages. Hallucinations contribute to the removal of the patient's attention from interpersonal transactions. Usually, several hallucinations are felt concomitantly. Most commonly the auditory field is affected and the voices are heard in a clear state of consciousness. In schizophrenia, as outlined by Schneider, [57] the voices usually talk or argue about the patient in the third person, formulate commands to him, and comment on his actions. In addition, the patient may hear his own thoughts spoken aloud. Visual hallucinations occur less frequently and do not oscillate in time as much as in toxic or organic conditions. Olfactory hallucinations were understood in the past as representing a poor prognosis, but this assertion has not been confirmed. The hallucinated odor is usually an unpleasant one. Tactile hallucinations (i.e., bugs crawling under the skin) can be felt conspicuously with a clear sensorium. Body or somatic hallucinations are usually experienced with severe psychological pain. Strange agents, machines, and others generate torturing sensations. Parts of the body are felt to be mutilated, torn apart, battered, burned, shattered, reflecting the patient's somatic passivity, according to Schneider. [57] *Illusions* differ from hallucinations in that the sensory stimulus exists, yet it is perceived differently, with a different form or with a different meaning.

Delusions represent a basic disturbance in the patient's symbolic activity and are pregnant with significant affective meaning for the patient. They are understood by some as attempts by the patient to solve his emotional problems. The delusional themes vary from patient to patient, but all delusional constructs are false, unshakable ideas or beliefs elaborated by the patient without logical basis and at variance with his cultural and social background. Delusions need not always be well elaborated and can

remain ill defined by the patient, yet they may greatly influence his behavior. The so-called secondary delusions are somewhat understandable
in terms of the primary disturbance affecting the patient (i.e., delusions of
impoverishment in depressed patients who feel everything is coming to
an end). Primary delusions, to the contrary, are completely incomprehensible. Persecutory and grandiose delusions are most common, particularly
among paranoid patients. Characteristically, a schizophrenic patient may
hold the delusion that he is controlled by an external source which renders
him impotent and without autonomy. Usually, schizophrenic delusions
have a bizarre quality.

Behavior disorders, such as motor and action disorders, in the schizophrenic patient include stereotypes, repetitive movements or fixed postures without a useful objective; mannerisms, odd distortions of normal
postures or movement of the face or the body which may correspond to a
delusional experience; echopraxia, replication of another person's action;
verbal disorders, such as speech incoherence, mutism, echolalia (repetition of another person's words); and negativism, active and unfounded
opposition to cooperate that can be manifested by actual lack of cooperation or by behaving opposite to what is expected.

SCHIZOPHRENIC SYNDROMES

There are four classical syndromes: hebephrenia, catatonia, simple, and
paranoid. There is insufficient evidence to sustain sharp distinctions between these types, since features from all four syndromes may appear
simultaneously in one patient and may present themselves in successive
episodes in the same patient. Subsequently, more subtypes and syndromes have been proposed by other authors, both on the basis of prognosis and clinical features (e.g., pseudoneurotic schizophrenia and atypical schizophrenia).

In hebephrenia affect and thought disorders predominate with comparatively scarce participation of motor disturbances and delusional constructs. The patient's behavior and appearance are puerile, eccentric, and
whimsical, and there is marked disorganization of thought and ego synthetic functions. A long-lasting, insidious presentation is usually followed
by a progressive deterioration.

In *catatonia* a disconnection of the normal motor behavior from its
volitional and emotional counterparts is prominent. It usually leads to either excitement or stupor. In the former, the patient, driven by hallucinatory or delusional experiences, may become violently agitated, vociferous,
and destructive to the point of exhaustion. Waxy flexibility, echolalia,
echopraxia, mannerisms, stereotypes, and grimaces are also frequent. The

onset may be acute or subacute, and the course is not as devastating as in hebephrenia. The short-term prognosis is better when organic approaches are applied (i.e., electroconvulsive theraphy (ECT), neuroleptics). It must be remembered that isolated catatonic symptoms may be seen in entities other than schizophrenia.

Secondary symptoms are absent in the *simple* syndrome. The patient's early and progressive apathy and withdrawal often place him in a marginal social role. He lives with blunted affect and impoverished behavior and gradually and quietly progresses to a deterioration. Recent reviews show this syndrome to be less malignant than is widely assumed. This syndrome has been the subject of controversy and is becoming less frequently diagnosed.

The *paranoid* syndrome is marked by a well-systematized disruption of logical thinking and a profound disturbance of relationships with others. Hallucinations and delusions (frequently but not exclusively of a persecutory nature) are prominent, but the patient's personality and intellectual capacity are preserved relatively longer than in the other syndromes. An acute or an insidious onset, beginning at middle age or later, is usually followed by a progressive or intermittent course toward final deterioration, unless treatment intervention mediates.

In addition to the classical types, other syndromes have been proposed including the following: schizoaffective schizophrenia, pseudoneurotic schizophrenia, pseudosociopathic schizophrenia, paraphrenia, late schizophrenia, and atypical schizophrenia.

Next to the typical schizophrenic thought disorders, strong affective components of depression or elation can be identified in *schizoaffective schizophrenia*. A prominent presence of affective elements is said to improve the prognosis (which is not, however, as good as in manic-depressive illness).

In *pseudoneurotic schizophrenia* the experiential changes characteristic of schizophrenia are felt with intense and pervasive, free-floating anxiety. Multiple neurotic symptoms (e.g., obsessions and phobias) resist psychotherapeutic attempts. The course towards a marginal adjustment or permanent psychosis finally betrays the presence of schizophrenia.

In *pseudosociopathic schizophrenia* antisocial behavior is intimately linked with an underlying schizophrenic process that becomes apparent only after careful examination. Many "acting-outers" and alcoholic loners are said to belong to this subtype.

In *paraphrenia* the patient chronically harbors well-systematized hallucinatory and delusional symptoms with few other schizophrenic symptoms and rather firm ego boundaries.

Late schizophrenia is characterized by a typical schizophrenic picture that appears mostly between forty and sixty years of age, but also later. Paranoid syndromes predominate.

In *atypical schizophrenia* schizophrenic symptoms appear with a background of confusional and affective symptoms (clouding of consciousness, disorientation, perplexity, and depression).

Research has evolved new diagnostic concepts for schizophrenia. Data derived from recent research findings tend to support distinctions between acute schizophrenia and chronic, or process, schizophrenia, and between schizophreniform illness and true schizophrenia. Moreover, the concept of schizophrenic spectrum disorder has arisen following research findings in clinical genetics.

Many authors underline the difficulty of establishing a reliable diagnosis of schizophrenia during an acute episode. It is postulated that only a prolonged study of the acutely ill patient can render an accurate diagnosis. Some studies of acute schizophrenic episodes indicate that they constitute a separate group of schizophrenia in terms of their pattern of heritability and good prognosis. On the other hand, it has been contended that the diagnosis of schizophrenia should be reserved for persons with chronic disorganizations. Others believe that there is no disparity between the ultimate course of acute and chronic schizophrenia and that depression and confusion are clearly indicative of pseudoschizophrenia.

According to the view establishing a dichotomy between true schizophrenia and pseudoschizophrenia, "true" schizophrenics have a poor prognosis and pseudoschizophrenics (with symptoms of depression and confusion in relation to a precipitating stress) a good prognosis, even though they might have a recurrent course. The reason for such a good outcome would be that a pseudoschizophrenia (i.e., schizophreniform psychosis, atypical schizophrenia, cycloid psychosis) is possibly a variant of the affective disorders.

The concept of schizophrenia spectrum disorders, arising from adoption studies, attempts to encompass all disorders that show clinical manifestations of chronic schizophrenia. In addition to classic schizophrenia and schizoaffective types, it includes the American Psychiatric Association's acute schizophrenic episode, schizophrenia latent type (or borderline personality), paranoid personality, schizoid personality, and some severe cases of inadequate personality. In one study, the prevalence of spectrum disorders in the biological relatives of schizophrenic patients was about twice as high as in relatives of nonschizophrenic patients. In another project, when both parents suffered from a spectrum disorder, the frequency of spectrum disorders in the offspring was three to five times higher than among the offspring of those couples in which only one parent had a spectrum disorder.

Also, according to Bender [6], schizophrenics, sociopathic, neurotic, and inadequate personalities have been found more among the relatives of schizophrenic children than among those of nonschizophrenic children.

DIAGNOSIS

Most experienced clinicians prefer to formulate the diagnosis of schizophrenia only after a careful evaluation of the patient. This position is
based on the understanding that the profound personality modifications
that take place crystallize only after a progressive process of organization.

The diagnosis is particularly difficult when the symptoms are not
distinctly manifested. This may occur, for example, in *incipient conditions*,
where there is only an ill-defined sense of internal change, perhaps
anguish and a forceful trend toward building imaginary constructs in
order to understand the changing perception of the self and others.

In *acute episodes* where the multiplicity of symptoms and the consequent situational crisis mutually reshape the clinical manifestations, the
diagnosis must be formulated first on a tentative basis, pending more information on the premorbid personality, family background, and subsequent course.

Schneider [57] formulated what he considered to be pathognomonic,
or first-rank, symptoms of schizophrenia:*

1   Audible thoughts (voices speaking one's thoughts aloud)
2   Voices arguing (referring to the patient in the third person)
3   Voices commenting on one's actions
4   Somatic passivity (experiencing externally controlled body
    changes)
5   Thought withdrawal
6   Thought insertion
7   Thought broadcasting
8   "Made" feelings
9   "Made" impulses
10 "Made" volition
11 Delusional perception (a real percept elaborated in a delusional
    way)

Even though not all schizophrenic patients possess these symptoms, they
have been found to be useful to diagnose schizophrenia. However, clinical research has shown that the symptoms postulated by Schneider are not
exclusively present in schizophrenia but are also found in depressed and
neurotic patients and in personality disorder patients.

This and other findings regarding Schneider's symptoms evolved
from the multinational study sponsored by the World Health Organiza-

* From K. Schneider, *Clinical Psychopathology*, Grune and Stratton, 1963. Reprinted by
permission.

tion, the International Pilot Study for Schizophrenia (IPSS) [64]. Departing from this study, a list of twelve differential symptoms have been identified which are believed to be most discriminating and useful in the diagnosis (Table 5.2). It is pointed out that these symptoms describe nine criteria generally indicative of schizophrenia and three indicative of nonschizophrenia." [18] The latter are held to be useful for differential diagnosis.

In the IPSS, it was observed that the identification of certain symptoms increased the probability that the patient would be diagnosed as having schizophrenia. For example, when delusions of control and subjective experience of disordered thought were noted as present, there was a 97 percent chance that the diagnosis would be one of schizophrenic psychoses (Table 5.3). Furthermore, when four of those symptoms (delusions of control, thought alterations, voices about the patient, commentary voices) were put together, they formed a syndrome which gave a 96 percent chance that the patient would receive the diagnosis of schizophrenic psychoses. Patients from different countries who received the diagnosis of schizophrenia and who belonged to clusters selecting patients regardless of clinical assumptions formed a concordant group. The most prominent symptom in this group was lack of insight. The concordant group also had high scores in auditory hallucinations, flatness of affect, experiences (including delusions) of control, and predelusional signs. It seems, therefore, that these schizophrenic symptoms can be identified regardless of cultural influences.

Table 5.2
DISCRIMINATING SYMPTOMS FOR THE DIAGNOSIS OF
SCHIZOPHRENIA (IPSS)

Restricted affect
Poor insight
Thoughts spoken aloud
Poor rapport
Widespread delusions
Incoherent speech
Unreliable information
Bizarre delusions
Nihilistic delusions
Waking early*
Depressed facies*
Elation*

* Symptoms indicative of nonschizophrenia.

Table 5.3

PROBABILITY OF DIAGNOSIS ACCORDING TO THE
PRESENCE OF SYMPTOMS

Symptom	Schizophrenic psychoses	Manic psychoses	Depressive psychoses neuroses, etc.
Voices to the patient	0.91	0.05	0.03
Voices about the patient	0.95	0.03	0.02
Commentary by voices	0.97	0.03	0.01
Thought broadcasting	0.97	0.02	0.01
Delusions of control	0.96	0.02	0.01
Neologisms	0.97	0.04	0.00
Poverty of content of speech	0.95	0.02	0.03

Adapted from W. T. Carpenter, J. S. Strauss, and J. J. Bartko. Flexible system for the diagnosis of schizophrenia: Report from the WHO International Pilot Study of Schizophrenia. *Science* 182:1275–1278, 1973. Copyright 1973 by the American Association for the Advancement of Science.

Once the presence of a psychosis has been established as indicated, for example by the presence of delusions or hallucinations, it is helpful to try to identify Bleuler's fundamental symptoms and Schneider's first-rank symptoms, taking into consideration the recent research findings. However, it must be remembered that they are not specific or present in every schizophrenic condition. Other thought and affective disorders frequently found in schizophrenia contribute to the diagnosis (i.e., overinclusion, blocking, neologisms, apathy, lack of affective contact). An important diagnostic clue is the identification of a deep and progressive personality transformation, a concomitant withdrawal of affective links leading toward the magic world of autism, together with an increasing ego fragmentation. The classic patient shows schizoid traits in the premorbid personality and a family history where relatives have suffered the illness and where communicative disturbances may be discernible. The patient may be reticent, secretive or incoherent, uncooperative or bizarre. His clinical condition is experienced as incomprehensible, the patient is unreachable by the interviewer who finds himself unable to share the meaning of the patient's behavior or to establish a direct emotional link. The reaction of the interviewer to such emotional distance has been frequently held to be a useful diagnostic clue (praecox feeling). Pao [52] maintains that for this reason the diagnosis of schizophrenia should begin with the study of the interviewer's own emotional reactions in the interaction between the patient and himself. However, it is unwise to rely solely on such criteria for

the diagnosis, particularly when the interviewer has not been able to accumulate supervised experience.

The presence of symptoms of organic brain syndrome (i.e., clouding
of consciousness) should exclude the diagnosis of schizophrenia. Alcoholic hallucinosis and amphetamine psychosis can be manifested in a
state of clear consciousness and initially mislead the interviewer because
of their resemblance to schizophrenia. A predominance of visual hallucinations should stimulate the differential exploration of psychotic organic
brain syndrome (i.e., tumors, syphilis, posttraumatic conditions, postpartum psychosis). Visual hallucinations are also frequent in the so-called
hysterical psychosis, where a hysterical personality abruptly reacts with
ego disorganization after a traumatic event. Psychomotor or temporal lobe
epilepsy can also induce a clinical picture resembling schizophrenia.

Marked depressive or manic symptoms are usually suggestive of a
schizophreniform psychosis, but not a schizophrenia. Particularly difficult may be the distinction between schizophrenic excitement and manic
elation and between schizophrenic thought disorders and the associative
disturbances characteristic of mania. The contagious sense of well-being
of the manic, his rapid, however erratic, response to external stimuli can
help to differentiate him from the schizophrenic patient who is responding to internal, idiosyncratic, cryptic motivations. In the manic patient,
flight of ideas is frequently present. In this case, the associative disturbance arises from superficial connections (between the sounds of the
word, for example), a high level of distractability, and accelerated and disorganized sentence production. This associative disorder does not involve
an underlying disruption of logical rules of thinking, which is apparent in
the schizophrenic patient. The latter also presents more cryptic and symbolic activity in thought and speech.

Special caution should be exercised in diagnosing schizophrenia in
the adolescent who is known to respond to very different stresses with
schizophrenialike symptoms, particularly in the experiential, affective,
and motor areas.

Obsessive-compulsive symptoms may precede the onset of schizophrenia or may appear as the patient is consolidating his improvement of
a system of new defenses.

COURSE AND PROGNOSIS

The illness usually follows: (1) an intermittent path with episodic exacerbations, social remissions, and compensations at a lower level of adaptation after each relapse or (2) a progressive and uninterrupted chronic state
with or without schizophrenic defect (a profound personality change with
marked restriction of interests and of the affective life).

Mild chronic courses seem to have increased and severe chronic courses seem to have decreased. At times, a seemingly deteriorated schizophrenic patient can show a clear improvement with modern treatment approaches. In general, however, the total number of patients entering into chronicity (about 25 percent) does not seem to have changed. The severity of the illness or a high intrafamilial incidence appears not to be correlated with dementiation. A course marked by periodic decompensations may have worse prospects in regards to final deterioration than a progressive course or a defective stabilization.

The introduction of neuroleptics has changed the course and prognosis of schizophrenia and, presumably, the clinical manifestations after the first episode. Most likely, neuroleptics help to mask the accessory symptoms without influencing the substantial course of the illness. They help to stabilize the patient, improving markedly the short-term prognosis and, to a lesser degree, the long-term outcome. With drugs, the patients can be maintained in a sort of unstable equilibrium.

Antipsychotic drugs have shortened the length of each hospitalization, but not the total number of admissions, which has actually increased. They also seem to prevent acute exacerbations. The total time span for inpatient and outpatient treatment seems to have remained unchanged.

The young, married, middle- or upper-class patient who develops an acute paranoid or catatonic schizophrenic episode and who has a history of a good premorbid adjustment, particularly in the areas of relatedness and educational and occupational fields, has a better prognosis than the patient who is older, single, separated, or divorced, belongs to a low socioeconomic status, and has a history of poor school and work adjustment and schizoid traits in his premorbid personality.

A more accepting and responsible societal attitude toward the schizophrenic patient has facilitated more rapid treatment interventions with hospitalizations occurring at early stages of the illness. The result is a prevention of grave deteriorations. Rehabilitation programs are also promoting an increased number of social remissions.

Several environmental variables seem to have prognostic value. For example, it has been recognized that when patients are discharged to an unstructured, unsupportive, and negative emotional environment, all treatment results and efforts become undermined and a readmission can be precipitated. It has also been pointed out that "positive" symptoms (i.e., delusions and hallucinations) are of little prognostic value while "negative" symptoms (i.e., blunted affect) are usually indicative of a deleterious course. Disorders of personal relationships may have the most important prognostic implications since they frequently herald an unfavorable recovery from various kinds of symptoms.

The presence of affective elements in the clinical picture usually betters the prospects for outcome. Along these lines, schizoaffective and schizophreniform psychoses have a relatively better prognosis. The traditionally held poor prognosis of olfactory hallucinations does not hold true.

TREATMENT AND MANAGEMENT

The treatment of schizophrenia is a long-term endeavor. The current trend is to offer a diversified, comprehensive approach. The unavoidable psychotherapeutic impact of any treatment modality used must be borne in mind. There are few human conditions as devastating and isolating as schizophrenia. The approach to the patient is restorative and seeks the patient's reengagement in the human group through the exploration and compensation of his developmental lags. Excessive reliance on one treatment modality alone will not do justice to the prevailing notion of the multifactorial origin of this condition and may hinder the patient's opportunities for the resolution of his drama.

Psychotropic drugs, psychotherapy, social therapies (group therapy, milieu therapy), and behavior therapy are examples of modalities at the therapist's disposal. In addition, it has become apparent that there is a need for consistent rehabilitation efforts which seem to depend on the quality of aftercare programs as well as on the nature of the emotional environment surrounding the patient during and after the most critical stages of his illness.

The acute schizophrenic patient (i.e., catatonic excitement) frequently poses an emergency and mobilizes the intervention of various agencies. Treatment usually requires the participation of family and social support, oral or parenteral medication, and brief hospitalization. Medication may not be necessary if support and structure are available and a tactful approach is used. Chronic patients are generally able to avoid exacerbations with indefinite maintenance of medication. The need for medication "holidays" has been emphasized to diminish the incidence of long-term, undesired effects. If outpatient treatment is unsuccessful, hospitalization of schizophrenic patients should be indicated. Hospitalization is also necessary when appropriate social and family supports are not available, when drug treatment needs intensification or reevaluation, and when an adequate resettlement in the community can best be planned from within the hospital (through assessment of the patient and his family's potential and linkage with appropriate aftercare and work programs). The benefits of short-term (three to four week) hospitalization have been highlighted by numerous authors.

Pharmacotherapy

The phenothiazines, the thioxanthenes, and the butyrophenones are the antipsychotics most used in the treatment of schizophrenia. The antipsychotic drugs are not aimed at the treatment of schizophrenia but at some of its symptoms (i.e., agitation and anxiety). The medication ameliorates or masks the productive symptoms allowing for other types of intervention (i.e., psychotherapy, sociotherapy). It has been observed that discontinuation of drug treatment in chronic patients usually results in relapse. There are, however, reports indicating that for certain good prognosis patients chronic drug use may have an adverse effect. Another issue related to the long-term administration of neuroleptics is the increasing number of patients suffering from tardive dyskinesia.

Among recent developments, it is important to note: (1) the utilization of long-acting parenteral preparations and the perspective of long-acting oral compounds for the avoidance of relapse, and (2) the monitoring of plasma levels as guidance for the efficacy of the drugs (different patients may achieve different plasma levels with the same dose).

Other somatic treatments in schizophrenia include megavitamin therapy with large amounts of niacin and nicotinamine, which has produced, at best, controversial results; electroshock which has been shown to be useful particularly in catatonic schizophrenia and in acute schizophrenic episodes; and psychosurgery, very infrequently indicated at present, although some consider it useful for patients who do not benefit from psychotropic drugs and whose symptoms are markedly impairing. Some authors believe that psychosurgery is particularly beneficial for intractable pseudoneurotic schizophrenia.

Psychotherapy

The psychotherapy of schizophrenia, a highly individualized and intuitive process, is based on clinical observations of the psychogenesis of the disease. Such observations have evolved in several theoretical schools. Examples of these schools are the ego defect school, which postulates that a basic organic deficit interferes with appropriate internalization of object representations, which later results in psychosis; and the conflict theory, which postulates that a psychological conflict stemming from early stages of development is responsible for the disease. This theory is related to both the interpersonal approaches and to the object-relation theory position, which suggests a disturbed mother-child relationship as the basis for the schizophrenic development. The technical approaches utilized in psychotherapy with schizophrenics have been influenced by these theories.

For example, the defect theory emphasizes a positive real relationship with the therapist in order to facilitate the process of internalization. Conflict theory proposes techniques much closer to classical psychoanalysis. The interpersonal and object-relationship schools emphasize the need to enhance relatedness in an atmosphere of sensitive acceptance.

Some of the problematic considerations common to all of these schools have been recently summarized by Grotstein [25] such as whether a psychotic patient can formulate free associations, whether the patient is able to understand interpretations in spite of his thought disorder, the impact of interpretations on the weak patient's ego, and the possible restrictive effect of the patient's environment on the individual psychotherapy.

In his review of individual psychotherapy with schizophrenic patients, Brody and Redlich [13] point out that focus should be placed on the particular personality characteristics of the patient (i.e., the patient's oversensitivity). The therapist is confronted with strong emotions arising from the patient and from within himself. Initially, the patient may be in an out-of-contact phase which necessitates skillful and flexible reaching-out techniques. The patient needs support to fortify his ego, and the therapist must search for and find common values with the patient.

A recent survey of experienced psychotherapists indicates five factors considered to hold a good prognostic implication in psychotherapy with schizophrenics: sudden onset, known precipitant, an egodystonic psychosis, pain or depression, and employment or academic success, at some point, outside the nuclear home. Some emphasize duration of psychotherapy as playing a crucial role in the outcome, with a duration of more than four years having a clear positive effect.

Several studies comparing psychotherapy and pharmacotherapy indicate that individual psychotherapy is not essential for the treatment of schizophrenia. However, important methodological weaknesses in such studies have essentially left this question unanswered. A recent report on the psychoanalytic psychotherapy for acute schizophrenic patients stresses the importance of follow-up in order to evaluate long-time results.

Other Treatment Approaches

Family psychotherapy and other sociotherapies as well as behavior therapy have also been utilized in the treatment of the schizophrenic patient.

Family therapy has attempted to apply the general concepts derived from family research. This has been apparent, particularly in the general approach that refuses to deal exclusively with the "identified patient" and sees the family context as a more relevant area of intervention. Family therapists also try to expose and correct transactional disorders and communication disturbances among the family members. Recently, the failure of family therapists to incorporate in their practice more specific hypotheses advanced in research has been discussed. Indications and contraindications for family therapy of schizophrenics have only rarely been established. In the absence of research evidence the opportunity and extent of involvement of different family members is usually determined by the therapist's judgment. Studies of effectiveness are thus far limited and inadequate.

The opportunities for resocialization, support, and correction of reality perceptions are at the basis of the *group therapy* approaches. Against them are the dangers of evoking further withdrawal or intensification of symptoms in the hypersensitive and guarded schizophrenic patient.

The hospital milieu is understood as a collective therapeutic behavior, which may be geared to tactful enhancement of interactions, motivation, and appropriate expression of feelings. The multiple variables involved have prevented an accurate assessment of the effectiveness of *milieu therapy*. One major conclusion of comparison studies suggests that there is a definite interaction between the hospital therapeutic atmosphere and the effectiveness of psychotropic drugs. The prevailing attitudes about the latter may influence the drug therapy outcome.

Occupational therapy must be included in a general treatment plan in order to be beneficial. Very often the occupations engaged in by the patients have not only rehabilitation as an aim but serve as vehicles for less threatening, yet profound interactions.

Behavior therapy has been utilized, particularly in hospital settings. Token economy, a work-payment incentive system, has been the most popular method applied. In selected cases, it appears to have some usefulness in preventing excessive withdrawal and self-neglect. Evaluative studies of long-term efficacy are needed.

HISTORIES

The first case history describes a previously well-adjusted patient with an insidious change of personality — withdrawal, isolation and self-neglect — which finally erupted in an acute psychosis with multiple symptoms (hallucinations, motor disorders, negativism, ambivalence, incomprehensible behavior). Note race, age, and source of referral.

A sixteen-year-old black male patient without previous psychiatric history was brought to the hospital by the police "because he was attempting to divert rush-hour traffic on a busy street." The family reported that he had always been "a good boy" and a good student until about one year prior to admission when they started to notice less dedication to his schoolwork and an increased desire to stay by himself while refusing to communicate with his family. About three months prior to admission, his family related his behavior as becoming "bizarre." The patient began talking to himself, wandering the streets at night, refusing to eat, and hitting his family members. He was picked up once by the police for climbing on a car and standing on it for hours. The second arrest led him to hospitalization. On admission, he was lucid and well oriented in all spheres. He looked restless and kept shifting positions and assuming postures which lasted anywhere from five to ten minutes at a time (i.e., holding his arm behind his neck). Throughout the interview, he was darting glances into the corner of the room, occasionally grabbing at the air and strongly rubbing his arms and thighs. At times, he would smile or laugh for no apparent reason or relation to the conversation. Alternatively, he appeared suspicious, hostile, sad, and frightened. For the most part, he refused to talk and denied knowledge of the recent events related to his hospitalization. He answered most questions with "yes but no" responses and with incomplete, unintelligible sentences. He spoke very softly and avoided eye contact.

After several months of hospitalization, he had to be discharged to a day care center since he was found "unable to function without supervision and structure" at that point.

In the second case history note the early response to a disrupted family environment, maladjustment in school, absence of interpersonal life, and a rigid dedication to music, philosophy, and mathematics. Several acute decompensations were successfully controlled with medication, but the basic disengagement and inability to use his talents constructively continued until he was finally confined to permanent hospitalization.

The patient, a forty-seven-year-old single white male, was an only child. He never met his father. His parents separated before he was born because his father "never worked and liked to stay in the basement all the time." Two weeks before the patient's birth, his maternal grandfather died. The patient was raised by his mother and his maternal grandmother. The latter "ran the house" and was most active in raising the patient "different than" his father. School days were a tormenting experience: his glasses and old-fashioned clothing made him an easy target of scorn and ridicule. He never developed friendships and purposefully failed grades "just to avoid" his cruel peers. In high school, he excelled, however, in mathematics and music. He bought books that taught him how to make violins and spent nine years making one. His workshop was in the basement of his house. In this place, he confined himself practically all day long. He never learned how to play music but became versed in the history of music. Also, he was fascinated by Spinoza and Hitler. Slowly, he developed a complicated "mathematic" theory of the universe. Once in a while he would take a walk around the block but felt observed and criticized by the neighbors and returned quickly to his basement. On five separate occasions, starting at the age of twenty-one, he unexpectedly went on an acute rampage through his house, upsetting the furniture and barricading himself in the basement after throwing furniture out of the windows. He had to be hospitalized and remained under suicide precautions for some time. Voices were ordering him to kill himself as the only way to be free from the machine that was electrocuting, burning, and raping him, causing an agonizing pain. Each hospitalization lasted several months and after the last one, at age forty-three, he could not be discharged because he was considered unable to take care of himself. In the meantime, all of his relatives had died. For some time, he kept his interest in Spinoza and was frequently seen reading the same pages of an old book by him. During most of the recent years, he was just "sitting on the floor and staring at the walls," according to ward reports.

ADDENDUM

The Diagnostic and Statistical Manual of Mental Disorders (DSM-III) [1] draft published in 1977 provides certain operational criteria for the diagnosis of schizophrenic disorders. Such criteria are characteristic delusions, characteristic hallucinations, and formal thought disorder. Schneider's first-rank symptoms [57] have provided the basis for the characteristic delusions and hallucinations. Bleuler's [7] autism and ambivalence are not included. The hallucinatory content must not be clearly related to depression or elation. The thought disorder must be accompanied by "either blunted or inappropriate effect, delusions or hallucinations of any type, or grossly disorganized behavior" [1]. In addition, it is indicated that during the active phase of the illness, several areas of routine daily functioning must be significantly impaired. Chronicity is defined as at least six months of an active phase with characteristic delusions and hallucinations. Also, the following prodromal and residual symptoms are defined: social withdrawal, marked impairment in role functioning, eccentric behavior, impairment in personal hygiene and grooming, blunted or inappropriate affect, mild formal thought disorder, and unusual thoughts or experiences. Patients with full depressive or manic syndromes may not be diagnosed as schizophrenic, and the illness may not be apparently due to any organic mental disorder. The course of the illness is categorized in five types: subchronic (less than two years of continuous signs of active or residual phases), chronic (same as above but longer than two years), subchronic with acute exacerbation, chronic with acute exacerbation, in remission. The following clinical types are listed: disorganized (hebephrenic), catatonic, paranoid, undifferentiated, and residual. The simple type is not included. Pseudoneurotic schizophrenia and paraphrenia are not included.

Schizoaffective disorders are classified separately from schizophrenic disorders. Schizoaffective disorders must meet the criteria for depressive or manic episodes and have at least delusions of control or thought broadcasting, insertion, or withdrawal; characteristic schizophrenic hallucinations, which are detailed in the manual; and formal schizophrenic thought disorder. Typical depressive delusions are permitted. None of the prodromal symptoms of schizophrenia may antedate the depressive or manic syndromes, which overlap temporally to some degree with the schizophrenialike symptoms. The effective syndrome must precede or develop at the same time as the schizophrenialike symptoms. The schizoaffective disorder must not be due to any organic mental disorder or superimposed on schizophrenic disorder, residual type. Finally, schizoaffective disorders can have the following course: single episode, recurrent episode, chronic, in remission.

The paranoid disorders are divided into four groups: paranoia; shared paranoid disorder (folie à deux); paranoid state (when the disorder does not meet the criteria for either paranoia or shared paranoid disorder), and unspecified paranoid disorder. Paranoid psychoses associated with organicity are therefore included in paranoid states. The operational criteria for all paranoid disorders include persistent delusions (persecutory or jealousy); absence of characteristic schizophrenic delusions, hallucinations, or thought disorder; absence of manic or depressive syndromes; absence of organic mental disorder causing the paranoid disorder; and duration of illness of at least two weeks.

REFERENCES

1   American Psychiatric Association. *Diagnostic and statistic manual of mental disorders,* DSM-III Draft. Washington, D.C.: American Psychiatric Association, 1977.
2   Arieti, S. *Interpretation of schizophrenia.* New York: Brunner, 1955.
3   Ban, T. A. "Pharmacotherapy of Schizophrenia." In *Current psychiatric therapies,* vol. 16, ed. J. H. Masserman, pp. 163–175. New York: Grune and Stratton, 1976.
4   Bartko, J. J., Strauss, J. S., and Carpenter, W. T. Expanded perspectives for describing and comparing schizophrenic patients. *Schizophrenia Bull.* 11:50–60, 1974.

5   Bateson, G., Jackson, D. D., Haley, J., and Weakland, J. H. Toward a theory of schizophrenia. *Behav. Sci.* 1:251–264, 1956.

6   Bender, L. "Schizophrenic spectrum disorders in the families of schizophrenic children." In *Genetic research in psychiatry*, R. R. Fieve, D. Rosenthal, and H. Brill, pp. 125–134. Baltimore: Johns Hopkins University Press, 1975.

7   Bleuler, E. *Dementia praecox or the group of schizophrenias.* New York: International Universities Press, 1950.

8   Bleuler, M. The offspring of schizophrenics. *Schizophrenia Bull.* 8:91–107, 1974.

9   Bleuler, M. Conception of schizophrenia within the last fifty years and today. *Int. J. Psychiatry,* 1:501–515, 1965.

10   Boyer, L. B., and Giovacchini, P. L. *Psychoanalytic treatment of schizophrenia and characterological disorders.* New York: Science House, 1967.

11   Bradley, R. J., and Smythies, J. R. "The biochemistry of schizophrenia." In *Biological foundations of psychiatry,* vol. 2, ed. R. G. Grenell and S. Gaby, pp. 653–682. New York: Raven Press, 1976.

12   Brody, E. B. Cultural exclusion, character, and illness. *Am. J. Psychiatry* 122:852–858, 1966.

13   Brody, E. B., and Redlich, F. C. *Psychotherapy with schizophrenics.* New York: International Universities Press, 1964.

14   Cancro, R. *Annual review of the schizophrenic syndrome.* New York: Brunner/Mazel, 4 vols. 1971–1975.

15   Cameron, N. Reasoning, regression, and communications in schizophrenics. *Psychol. Monogr.* 50:1–33, 1938.

16   Carlsson, A. "Pharmacological approach to schizophrenia." In *Schizophrenia: Biological and psychological perspectives,* ed. G. Usdin, pp. 102–124. New York: Brunner/Mazel, 1975.

17   Carpenter, W. T., Strauss, J. S., and Bartko, J. J. Flexible system for the diagnosis of schizophrenia: Report from the WHO International Pilot Study of Schizophrenia, *Science* 182:1275–1278, 1973.

18   Carpenter, W. T., Strauss, J. S., and Muleh, S. Are there pathognomonic symptoms in schizophrenia? *Arch. Gen. Psychiatry,* 28:847–852, 1973.

19   Carpenter, W. T., Strauss, J. S., and Bartko, J. J. Use of signs and symptoms for the identification of schizophrenic patients. *Schizophrenia Bull.* 11:37–49, 1974.

20   Cooper, B., and Morgan, H. G. *Epidemiological psychiatry.* Springfield, Ill.: Thomas, 1973.

21   Fish, F. Leonard's classification of schizophrenia. *J. Ment. Sci.* 104:943–971, 1958.

22   Garmezy, N. Children at risk: The search for antecedents of schizophrenia. I. Conceptual models and research methods. *Schizophrenia Bull.* 8:14–90, 1974.

23   Goldstein, M. J., and Rodnick, E. H. The family's contribution to the etiology of schizophrenia: Current status. *Schizophrenia Bull.* 14:48–63, 1975.

24   Gottesman, I. I., and Shields, J. A critical review of recent adoption, twin, and family studies of schizophrenia: Behavioral genetic perspectives. *Schizophrenia Bull.* 2:360–398, 1976.

25   Grotstein, J. S. "Psychoanalytic therapy of schizophrenics." In *Treatment of schizophrenia*, eds. L. L. West and D. E. Flinn, pp. 115–130. New York: Grune and Stratton, 1976.

26   Group for the Advancement of Psychiatry. *Pharmacotherapy and psychotherapy: Paradoxes, problems, and progress*. New York: Group for the Advancement of Psychiatry, 1975.

27   Gundersen, J. S., and Mosher, L. R., eds. *Psychotherapy of schizophrenia*. New York: Jason Aronson, 1975.

28   Hanson, D. R., Gottesman, I. I., and Heston, L. L. Some possible childhood indicators of adult schizophrenia inferred from children of schizophrenics. *Br. J. Psychiatry* 129:142–154, 1976.

29   Heston, L. L. Psychiatric disorders in foster home reared children of schizophrenic mothers. *Br. J. Psychiatry* 112:819–825, 1966.

30   Hirsch, S. R., and Leff, J. P. *Abnormalities in parents of schizophrenics*. London:Oxford University Press, 1975.

31   Hoch, P. H., and Zubin, J., eds. *Psychopathology of schizophrenia*. New York: Grune and Stratton, 1966.

32   Hollingshead, A. B., and Redlich, F. C. *Social class and mental illness*. New York: Wiley, 1958.

33   Kane, J., Rifkin, A., Quitkin, E., and Klein, D. "Antipsychotic drug blood levels and clinical outcome." In *Progress in psychiatric treatment*, ed. D. Klein and R. Gittelman-Klein, pp. 399–408. New York: Brunner/Mazel, 1976.

34   Kendell, R. G., Cooper, J. G., Gourlay, A. J., Copeland, J. R. M., Sharpe, L., and Gurland, B. J. The diagnostic criteria of American and British psychiatrists. *Arch. Gen. Psychiatry* 25:123–130, 1971.

35   Kennedy, P. F. "The ecology of schizophrenia." In *New perspectives in schizophrenia*, eds. A. Forrest and J. Affleck, pp. 69–79. Edinburgh: Churchill Livingstone, 1975.

36   Kety, S. S., Rosenthal, D., Wender, P. H., Schulsinger, F., and Jacobsen, B. "Mental illness in the biological and adoptive families of adopted individuals who have become schizophrenics: A preliminary report based on psychiatric interviews." In *Genetic research in psychiatry*, eds. R. R. Fieve, D. Rosenthal, and H. Brill, pp. 147–166. Baltimore: Johns Hopkins University Press, 1975.

37   Klawans, H. L., Goetz, C., and Westheimer, R. "The pharmacology of schizophrenia." In *Clinical neuropharmacology*, ed. H. L. Klawans, pp. 1–28. New York: Raven Press, 1976.

38   Kohn, M. L. Social class and schizophrenia: A critical review. *Schizophrenia Bull.* 7:60–79, 1973.

39   Kraepelin, E. *Dementia praecox and paraphrenia*. Edinburgh: Livingstone, 1919.

40   Langfeldt, G. "Schizophrenia: diagnosis and prognosis." In *Schizophrenia: The first ten Dean Award lectures*, ed. S. R. Dean, pp. 207–216. New York: MSS Information Corp., 1973.

41   Lehman, H. E. "The somatic and pharmacologic treatment of schizophrenia." In *Strategic intervention in schizophrenia*, ed. R. Cancro, N. Fox, and L. Shapiro, pp. 153–185. New York: Behavioral Publications, 1974.

42   Lidz, T., Fleck, S., and Cornelison, A. R., eds. *Schizophrenia and the family*. New York: International Universities Press, 1963.

43   McCabe, M. D., Fowler, R. C., Cadoret, R. J., and Winokur, G. Familial differences in schizophrenia with good and poor prognosis. *Psychol. Med.* 1:326–332, 1971.

44   Mednick, S. A., Schulsinger, F., Higgins, J., and Bell, B., eds. *Genetics, environment, and psychopathology*. Amsterdam: North-Holland, 1974.

45   Mellor, C. S. First-rank symptoms of schizophrenia. I. The frequency in schizophrenics on admission to the hospital. II. Differences between individual first-rank symptoms. *Br. J. Psychiatry* 117:15–23, 1970.

46   Meltzer, H. T., and Stahl, S. M. The dopamine hypothesis of schizophrenia: A review. *Schizophrenia Bull.* 2:19–76, 1976.

47   Mendel, W. M.: *Schizophrenia: The experience and its treatment*. San Francisco: Jossey-Bass, 1976.

48   Mitsuda, H. The concept of "atypical psychoses," from the aspect of clinical genetics. Acta Psychiatr. Scand. 41:372–377, 1965.

49   Mitsuda, H., ed. *Clinical genetics in psychiatry*, Tokyo: Igaku-Shoin, 1967.

50   Mosher, L. R., and Gunderson, T. G. Special report on schizophrenia. *Schizophrenia Bull.* 7:10–52, 1973.

51   Odegard, O. Changes in the prognosis of functional psychoses since the days of Kraepelin. *Brit. J. Psychiatry* 113:813–822, 1967.

52   Pao, P. "On the diagnostic term 'schizophrenia.' " In *The annual of psychoanalysis*, ed. Chicago Institute of Psychoanalysis, vol. 3, pp. 221–238. New York: International Universities Press, 1975.

53   Pritchard, M. Prognosis of schizophrenia before and after pharmacotherapy. I. Short-term outcome. II. Three-year follow-up. *Brit. J. Psychiatry* 113:1345–1359, 1967.

54   Romano, J., ed. *The origins of schizophrenia*. Amsterdam: Excerpta Medica, 1967.

55   Rosenthal, D. "The spectrum concept in schizophrenic and manic-depressive disorders." In *Biology of the major psychoses*, ed. D. X. Freedman, pp. 19–25. New York: Raven Press, 1975.

56   Rosenthal, D., and Kety, S. S. *The transmission of schizophrenia*. Oxford: Pergamon Press, 1968.

57   Schneider, K. *Clinical psychopathology*. New York: Grune and Stratton, 1963.

58   Stierlin, H. *Separating parents and adolescents: a perspective on schizophrenia, runaways, and waywardness*. New York: Quadrangle, 1974.

59   Strauss, J. S., Carpenter, W. T., and Bartko, J. J. Speculations on the processes that underlie schizophrenic symptoms and signs. *Schizophrenia Bull.* 11:61–75, 1974.

60   Vaillant, G. E. Prospective prediction of schizophrenic remission. *Arch. Gen. Psychiatry* 11:509–518, 1964.

61   West, L. J., and Flinn, D. E. *Treatment of schizophrenia*. New York: Grune and Stratton, 1976.

62   Will, O. A. "The psychotherapeutic encounter: Relatedness and schizophrenia." In *Interpersonal explorations in psychoanalysis*, ed. E. Witenberg, pp. 235–257. New York: Basic Books, 1973.

63   Wing, J. K. "Epidemiology of schizophrenia." In *Contemporary psychiatry*, ed. T. Silverstone and B. Barraclough, pp. 25–31. British Journal of Psychiatry Special Publication no. 9. Ashford: Headley Brothers, 1975.

64   World Health Organization. *The international pilot study of schizophrenia*, vol. 1. Geneva: World Health Organization, 1973.

65   Wyatt, R. J. Biochemistry and schizophrenia (pt. 4). *Psychopharmacol. Bull.* 12:5–50, 1976.

66   Wynne, L. C., and Singer, M. T. Thought disorder and family relations of schizophrenics. *Arch. Gen. Psychiatry* 9:191–206, 1963.

6

Paranoid Psychoses

José D. Arana, M.D.

The term *paranoia,* traceable to ancient Greek philosophy where it was used to indicate mind beside itself, has undergone many semantic vicissitudes. Vogel and Heinroth in Germany, promoted its modern use in psychiatry and also applied the term as a general word representing mental disturbance or disorganization. Subsequently, other authors narrowed the concept to a meaning much closer to the current popular connotation of persecutory or grandiose delusions. Paranoia was separated from the deteriorating (dementiating) conditions that were later to be known as schizophrenic psychoses. Paranoia was, for Kahlbaum and Kraepelin, a chronic delusional condition that permitted clear and ordered thinking and left the personality intact beginning about middle age (as opposed to paraphrenias which started later). Some authors later elaborated on its psychogenesis and included certain of the most profoundly disorganized paranoid patients among the group of schizophrenias. Kretschmer described the "sensitive self-referential delusions" as constructs psychologically understandable and built on the basis of impressionable and vulnerable personalities undergoing deceiving and frustrating traumatic experiences. He tended to disregard the existence of paranoia as an illness but to understand rather the development of individual "paranoiacs". The notion of paranoia as a psychogenic, reactive process was also endorsed by others who preferred to group paranoia within the schizophrenias.

Others emphasized the development of the paranoid condition as unfolding on the basis of the patient's personality. French authors separated paranoia from schizophrenia, and, in fact, they described instead the chronic hallucinatory states of *délire*. In addition to the disorder of judgment implied by the presence of a delusion, they included all affective and thinking phenomena seen in the paranoid patient. In regard to its etiology, paranoia was first understood as endogenous in nature. Later, paranoia and paranoid syndromes have been mostly recognized as psychologically determined, with the psychoanalytic contributions e.g., making evident many of the underlying unconscious conflicts and dynamics.

Currently, the term paranoia remains loose and vague, mainly because it is indiscriminately applied. No appropriate distinction is usually made of its semantic extent, so that the differential recognition of a symptom, syndrome, or disease becomes blurred. However, most clinicians, it seems, would probably agree on the general characteristics of the paranoid syndromes. The classification of paranoid psychoses and the description of some specific clinical pictures remain controversial.

Paranoid personalities are often difficult to distinguish from certain paranoid psychoses (see chapter 15).

ETIOLOGY

To date, it is not possible to assume either a constitutional liability or a psychological trauma alone as essential for the manifestation of paranoid behavior. Both factors may be necessary, even though the scarcity of genetic studies precludes definitive statements.

Certain personality traits (i.e., hypersensitivity, a tendency to blame others, rigidity, suspiciousness, excessive self-importance) are frequently but not necessarily found in connection with the development of paranoid psychoses. Obsessional and hypochondriacal traits are not unusual. This has led to speculations about the possible nosological relationship between paranoid, obsessive, and hypochondriacal disorders, all of which share a tenacious symptomatology firmly established in a lucid and otherwise well-preserved personality.

Inheritability

At the beginning of the twentieth century, it was emphasized that constitutional, heritable factors were underlying paranoia. This approach is still prevalent in German psychiatry but is not used in France, England, or the United States.

Very few studies have investigated the genetics of paranoid disorders other than schizophrenia. Some have suggested that among relatives of paranoid patients a variety of psychiatric disorders other than paranoia are usually found.

In regard to schizophrenics, several studies have suggested that there are more cases of schizophrenia, undiagnosed psychosis, and paranoid personality in the nonparanoid subjects than in the paranoid ones. Such differences are not always statistically significant. Heritable subtype associations have been suggested. Winokur noted that hebephrenics have been found to have more than three times as many schizophrenic relatives as the paranoids. Children of hebrephrenic patients are more likely to be hebephrenic than paranoid. Children of paranoid schizophrenics, on the other hand, are more likely to be paranoid than hebephrenic. Odegaard also found that the subtype association was strongest for the paranoid form.

The abnormal co-twins of paranoid schizophrenics were found in one study as tending to suffer from depression, suggesting that elements common to the development of schizophrenic and affective disorders can coexist in some paranoid schizophrenics. Within-pair phenotypic similarities have also been found by some investigators. A greater risk of schizophrenia among relatives of paraphrenics than in the general population has been reported.

A high prevalence of schizophrenia among the biological relatives of *induced* psychotics in cases of folie à deux has been reported. This finding would suggest a reassessment of the role played by the induced psychotic in the appearance of this psychosis. Along these lines the jealousy syndrome has frequently been found in conditions that are commonly considered to be constitutionally conditioned.

In summary, there appears to be some degree of heritability for paranoid schizophrenia as a subtype, however, attempts to validate a two-illness concept (nonparanoids versus paranoids) have yielded contradictory results so far. Also, in terms of other paranoid psychoses, no evidence is available regarding their inheritability. Isolated clinical findings involving certain specific paranoid psychoses need replication and more ample study.

Psychodynamic Considerations

The psychodynamic hypotheses of paranoid development are based on subtle and laborious clinical observations. They have enhanced the understanding of the paranoid patient and indicate consequent psychotherapeutic strategies. No one hypothesis has met universal acceptance.

Here, the following postulates will be considered: the role of homo-sexuality, the role of arrested development, the role of aggression, and the role of feelings of inferiority and inadequacy. In addition, psycho-dynamic observations have been made pertaining to the relationship between paranoid symptoms and depression, obsession, hysteria, and hypochondriasis. ·

Freud put forward for the first time the notion that paranoia develops as a result of a conflict over homosexual impulses. As a defense against such repressed homosexual conflicts, projection is utilized. Consequently, a man suffering from persecutory delusions would deny and project his repressed homosexual impulses. He would elaborate the conviction: "I do not love him; he hates and persecutes me" (as opposed to "I love him" — "I do not love him" — "I hate him"). A man suffering from delusions of jealousy would deny and project his homosexual conflicts by constructing the delusion: "She loves him." ("I do not love him", she loves him.") By projecting, the patient preserves an acceptable sense of himself. A number of studies have attempted to evaluate this hypothesis. The objections against it originate in the following observations: Active homosexuality has been found in overt paranoid patients, and indications of homosex-uality are not always recognizable in the paranoid; pseudohomosex-ual conflicts can develop as a consequence of excessive dependence and power needs and the search for their satisfaction through genital activities.

In discussing paranoia in the famous Schreber case, Freud formu-lated several other important contributions; for example, he indicated in discussing projection, the relationship between paranoid and normal pro-cesses of thought. He also pointed out the similarities found in any of the psychoses.

The role of arrested development is related to the sense of worth-lessness that may be fostered by lack of adequate mothering in early phases of development. The consequent narcissistic injuries bring about rage and humiliation that can later be projected onto others. Melanie Klein has described the stages of development dynamically responsible for later elaboration of paranoid and depressive conditions. There is first an early "paranoid position" or stage, where the child can only identify the source of pleasure — or the lack thereof — in an external object, the mother. As a result of faulty mothering at this stage, paranoid patients may remain fixated at this phase. Paranoia had previously been consid-ered a regression to the anal-sadistic phase, a hypothesis related to the aggression compulsions observed in the paranoid patients. More studies are necessary to test the validity of these theories.

The role of aggression — hatred, hostility, and sadomasochistic im-pulses — have been postulated in the development of paranoid condi-tions. Hate may be a defense against libidinal involvement. It has been contended that the fundamental problem in paranoia may really be in the management of hostility. Aggression turned against the self may engender feelings of inferiority and worthlessness. Love may be needed to neutralize intense unconscious hate and the projected love may actually become a means of defending the self against hostility.

Emphasis on an interpersonal approach to the psychiatric phenomena has resulted in focusing on the psychosocial impact of feelings of inferiority and inadequacy. Whatever the source of these feelings, it is contended, they can become unbearable and necessitate either the blaming of others as the source of such limitations or a grandiose elevation of the self as a compensatory device. Either way, the paranoid will meet rejection, which will, in turn, intensify his delusional perception of others.

Some authors believe that the cyclothymic externalizations are qualitatively different from the paranoid projections. Others think that the paranoid projects his feelings of inadequacy and that the depressed person blames himself for them. The feelings of inadequacy are hidden from awareness (denied) in the paranoid patient but usually accepted by the depressive patient. A paranoid elaboration can be seen as a defense against underlying depressive feelings. The deprived child may assume responsibility for his own deprivation or may blame it on others. Manic defenses may be enlisted by paranoid patients to avoid depression. Interestingly, it has been found that many patients diagnosed as paranoid schizophrenics can later be diagnosed as suffering from mania when rigorous diagnostic criteria are applied. Atypical paranoid schizophrenics include strong affective components in the clinical picture. The same is true for a clinical picture called affect-laden paraphrenia. Depressive and paranoid symptoms can coexist in the same clinical condition (e.g., involutional melancholia).

Environmental Factors

A change of values and norms in the immediate environment can result in an unstable relationship with oneself and others. Moreover, the loss of reliable structures and reference groups for the validation of one's psychosocial identity may lead to a faulty evaluation of reality. It has been contended that cultural change, migration, and social isolation (i.e., as determined by deafness, language differences, imprisonment and so forth) can stimulate the development of paranoid psychoses.

Some believe that environmental factors must interact with a vulnerable individual for a paranoid condition to develop. The delusional elaborations are then understood as efforts to build a livable state through the reconstruction of an intolerable situation. In this way, a resolution of the patient's need not to remain isolated is attempted. The existence of paranoid societies or paranoid cultures has been suggested. It must be remembered that environmental factors alone cannot explain the cause of paranoid psychoses.

Organic Factors

Paranoid psychoses frequently develop in connection with organic diseases. A disorganization of one's body image and the perception of the self has been suggested as a common determinant for such development. Addison's disease, Cushing's syndrome, and other endocrine disturbances are examples of conditions that can be associated with paranoid psychoses.

Epidemiology

A satisfactory epidemiological understanding of paranoid conditions has been difficult due to two factors: the patient's reluctance to seek help and the problems defining the patient population under scrutiny. The very mistrust and lack of insight that lie in the case of paranoid syndromes hinders a realistic estimate of their incidence. Moreover, it is often difficult to delineate a distinction between understandable defensive adaptations to life situations and delusional elaborations of the experienced external or internal world.

Paranoid problems come to psychiatric attention usually after the age of thirty and not infrequently during the sixth and seventh decades. It is considered that about 10 percent of all admissions to mental hospitals receive the diagnosis of paranoid psychoses, but this figure is not universally accepted. The total duration of stay in the hospital seems shorter in paranoid than in nonparanoid schizophrenics.

Single, separated, and divorced persons of both sexes seem more susceptible to paranoid syndromes. Unmarried women have the highest incidence rate of paranoid schizophrenia and, perhaps, paranoia. Low socioeconomic status, social isolation, and migration have been found to be factors connected with the development of paranoid syndromes, even though no causal relationships have been determined.

Paranoid symptoms and syndromes can appear in practically every psychiatric entity and in many somatic diseases, e.g., schizophrenia, manic-depressive illness, involutional melancholia, alcoholic psychoses, epilepsy, endocrine disturbances, severe infections, and pernicious anemia.

Chronic paranoid psychoses without other symptoms are rare or rarely reach psychiatric service. The proportion of paranoid patients among chronic schizophrenic populations is smaller than other schizophrenic subtypes.

CLINICAL FEATURES

The general clinical features common to most paranoid conditions will be discussed first. Subsequently, the most common clinical pictures will be reviewed.

Onset

The onset of paranoid conditions can be dramatically acute, acute after an incubation period, and insidious — to the point that an actual distinction between the psychosis and patient's character cannot be made. Thus, in addition to the dramatic "revelations" that suddenly agitate some patients, a slow, quiet, and guarded development of illness can be present.

As a reaction to psychological or physical trauma, or both, the hypersensitive, suspicious, and easily injured patient first denies his vulnerability and hurt. Then, he may increase his isolation before blaming and "counterattacking." He may resort to overcontrol first and then to frenetic defensive action. At the beginning, he may only be certain that "something is going on" that he cannot comprehend. His anxious expectation may revert to focusing on his own inadequacies so that the grounds for insecurity and hypochondriasis become fertilized. Or, he may have always held an obstinate and tenacious mistrust in others. At some point, particularly when threatened by certain situations or events (i.e., that stimulate, isolate, deceive, or humiliate) he may panic and enter into a psychotic turmoil in which he feels utterly helpless, dominated, subdued, controlled by external forces, and at the mercy of them. A "homosexual panic" may develop if an erotic stimulation is registered. Auditory hallucinations may, in certain cases, fustigate and scorn the patient, usually talking *to* him (rather than about him, except in paranoid schizophrenia). It has been postulated that the paranoid patient confronted by ensuing "threats" is driven to form hypotheses to explain the changes that he is perceiving. For example, a "plot" might be "discovered," "coded" signals "deciphered," "hidden" messages "understood" by the patient: Delusions are formed and a new "understanding" of the new surroundings is reached. The delusional system reinterprets the reality to the patient, alleviates his narcissistic hurt, and connects him anew with the world of others. He may then become dangerous if he deems it necessary to "retaliate" in order to preserve himself. Together with the structuring of delusions, the patient transforms the interpersonal environment into a conspiratory machinery which seeks to persecute and annihilate him. Anybody can become a member of this "paranoid pseudo-community." It is basically an imaginary organization but it includes some real persons as well. The therapist is not infrequently included in it.

Thus, when paranoid psychosis develops one may observe an early stage of brooding and mounting suspiciousness, and an increment in the self-referential outlook of the world is observed when a premorbid paranoid personality has preceded the psychosis. Finally, an eruption of a frank psychosis crystallizes, characterized by delusion formation and the organization of a "paranoid pseudo-community.

Predisposition and Vulnerability

There is no consensus regarding either predisposing characterological traits or precipitating events in connection with paranoid psychoses. It appears that a premorbid abnormal personality is not a sine qua non for a paranoid psychosis to develop. Moreover, paranoid psychoses can be understood in many instances as psychotic abnormal developments where an onset cannot be discerned. Not infrequently, it is even difficult to ascertain whether the patient is psychotic or not: In some cases, the symptomatology is most comprehensible; in others, the patient conceals the delusional symptoms; and often, the psychosis is nonpervasive and allows the patient to develop successfully several aspects of his personality (that is, grandiose paranoid persons, when talented, can meticulously "mastermind" important achievements.)

Certain environmental factors (e.g., social isolation, cultural change) seem to stimulate the development of paranoid psychoses. For some patients, a struggle centering on their sexual identity, inadequacy, or aggressive impulses is crucial. For others, early developmental lags lie at the base of their psychoses. Certain situations seem to be frequently involved in the precipitation of paranoid psychoses: stimulation of erotic or hostile impulses, emotional isolation, competitive and rivalry situations, exposure to deceitful interactions, experiences of humiliation and defeat and so forth.

Defense Mechanisms

Very frequently, denial, repression, projection, and rationalization are utilized. Repression loses effectiveness in the psychotic patient, so that unconscious processes invade the conscious life. Denial helps the patient to later project and disclaim his own impulses and take some distance from them. Rationalizations are vastly employed to validate the delusions. Delusion formation seems to protect patients from a more devastating disruption and offers a framework within which the ego is able to retain some degree of organization and coherence.

Essential Features

No consensus regarding the essential clinical features of paranoid conditions has been reached. Cameron postulated that paranoid conditions share three main characteristics: an extreme sensitivity to certain unconscious trends in other people, while they are remarkably insensitive to similar trends in themselves; a notable tendency to self-reference and an inability to correct their false self-reference by empirical, objective reality testing; and severe defects in reciprocal role representation by which normal people may view things from the perspectives of other people. For some authors, paranoid conditions present a certain outlook of life, a certain mode of thinking. Others believe that, essentially, the paranoid patient builds up a certainty that the familiar interpersonal environment and the behavior of others has changed. Schwartz, in turn, contends that the essential constellation consists of underlying feelings of unworthiness and insignificance, the incapacity for self-referral of responsibility, incapacity for ambivalence, and need for recognition. In addition, "the denial of unworth and insignificance takes the form of *centrality:* the assertion of overwhelming and pervasive importance to others." Salzman believes that, essentially, "the paranoid development is characterized by a grandiose development . . . which is an attempt to deal with extreme feelings of worthlessness through a process of denial and reaction formation." As the environment disregards the grandiose claims, the consequent humiliation and rage generates in the patient a feeling of conspiracy, a defensive, projective transfer of the blame.

Swanson and co-workers have described what they consider to be the basic characteristics of the *paranoid mode of thinking*. The features most integrally related to the paranoid approach are as follows: projective thinking, hostility, suspiciousness, centrality, delusions, fear of loss of autonomy, and grandiosity.

Projection is a defense applied by normals and paranoid patients by which one's impulses or feelings are attributed to others. It rests at the core of the distorted connection established by the paranoid with the outside world, a connection which may save him from immersion into autism and gives him the recognition he is lacking, even though it is of negative quality. It might also save the patient from falling into self-deprecation and depression.

Hostility displayed by the paranoid turns against him because it creates adversaries. As the patient's defenses become unstable he increases his explicit aggressiveness and anger. This can also happen as treatment progresses. Hate and aggression may be understood in many patients as a means to retain a distance from the very object that is unconsciously desired. It may also reflect a narcissistic injury inflicted at early developmental stages and which is reactivated in the face of feared and wished objects.

Biased by an acute awareness of his own vulnerability to threat, the paranoid patient increases his vigilance and alertness. Relentlessly and carefully, he searches for hidden, antagonistic, malevolent clues. He has a passion for "truth" and a hate for "hypocrisy."

Suspiciousness goes along with the patient's inability to be trustful, his incapacity to rely on others, his faulty premise that he is constantly under possible attack. It has been contended that the less structured the delusional system, the more guarded and distrustful is the patient.

Ideas of reference are preliminary indications to the patient that he is the center of interest of other people. As the patient becomes more paranoid, his central position in the world continues consolidating itself. Such *centrality*, more explicit in the presumptuous, grandiose paranoid, is nurtured by the real rejection generated by the patient's inflated arrogance or hostility.

Delusions, a feature of paranoid psychoses, are unshakable beliefs elaborated by the patient without logical basis and at variance with the patient's personal and cultural background. They represent a disturbance in the patient's symbolic activity and are pregnant with affective meaning most significant for the individual patient. Often delusional themes challenge credibility. In other instances, they are somewhat understandable in terms of the patient's circumstances. Delusions are held with a high degree of certainty and are kept within a logical structure of varied solidity. Except for the paranoid schizophrenic, delusions are not bizarre and autistic in nature. They usually offer an explanation of the feared reality and alleviate the patient's tense suspiciousness. The elaboration of delusions does not preclude at all the exercise of an impeccable reasoning based on the false delusional premises. It has been recognized that the inability to judge the validity and truth of a delusion is not an impediment to clearly organizing the thought processes. This has been called reasoning madness by some authors.

The paranoid patient fears *loss of autonomy;* loss of control. Frequently paranoid thinking is preoccupied with themes of dominance and submission. He becomes careful, restrained, guarded, and calculating in order to avoid the possibility of others taking advantage of him. There is, therefore, no room for playfulness, humor, or casual interplay, as relaxation can result in total loss of control over what others can do to him and over his own impulses. He comes across as defensively superior, argumentative, and with an air of certainty that seeks to maintain a precarious equilibrium.

The *grandiosity* of the paranoid patient as he elaborates a megalomaniac delusion has an arrogant, presumptuous quality that generates rejection. A mission must be carried out as dictated secretively by certain clues that the patient feels he is given. The patient feels admired, envied, and subsequently persecuted. Almost always paranoid grandiosity follows persecution in the natural course of paranoid illnesses. The reverse is seldom observed. For this reason, some believe that paranoid grandiosity points out to a later stage of dynamic elaboration and, consequently, to more severe pathology than persecutory symptoms.

CLINICAL MANIFESTATIONS

Paranoid psychoses have been classified in many different ways and a semantic confusion prevails in the literature. Here, the clinical manifestations are distinguished as follows:

1   Paranoia
          Involutional paranoia
2   Paranoid schizophrenia
          Paraphrenia
          Late paraphrenia
3   Paranoid states
4   Paranoid psychoses associated with organicity
          With acute OBS
          With chronic OBS
          With somatic illness
5   Other paranoid psychoses
          Delusional jealousy
          Folie à deux
          Erotomania
          Capgras' syndrome
          Unusual and exotic syndromes (Amok, Susto, Whitico, Voodoo death)

Involutional paranoia is mentioned with paranoia and that paraphrenia seems to be better subsumed under schizophrenia.

Most of these clinical forms are usually chronic, with the exception of the paranoid states and those psychoses associated with organic disease. Only paranoid schizophrenia and paraphrenia imply a deficitary evolution. In Scandinavian countries, paranoid states are usually diagnosed as reactive psychoses or psychogenic psychoses. Paranoia, paraphrenia, and paranoid schizophrenia are regarded by many as located in a continuum. Several authors have suggested that hebephrenics have given way to a psychotic disorganization, whereas paranoid patients overreact, organizing their resources to fight disruption.

French psychiatrists differentiate several paranoid psychoses which include: systematized *délires* psychoses, chronic hallucinatory psychoses, and fantastic psychoses, all of which evolve without deterioration. In addition, they consider paranoid schizophrenia as having a deteriorating course. The systematized *délires* include: *délires* — the quarrelsome (délire of honor, property, or rights), the inventor (délire of invention), and the passionate idealist (délire of ideology); passional desires — jealousy (delusional infidelity) and erotomania (the patient believes he is loved by another individual). The chronic hallucinatory psychoses are characterized by the importance and intensity of the hallucinations. In the fantastic *délires* (paraphrenia) a rich production of fictitious constructs predominates over the hallucinations.

Paranoia

A rather rare condition, paranoia is also called true paranoia, paranoia vera, or classic paranoia. Some consider paranoia to be an isolated nosographic entity. It is characterized by chronic highly systematized and inflexible delusions (e.g., persecutory, grandiose) which develop with order, coherence, and clarity, in the absence of hallucinations, and without deterioration of the personality. It has a relatively late age of onset (thirty years old and over). Some authors consider paranoia within the schizophrenic psychoses, yet conspicuous schizophrenic thought disorders are absent. The condition evolves slowly; the patient lacks insight and is frequently bright and displays an elaborated and logical reasoning which departs, however, from false premises. Remarkably, the patient is able to develop his talents, and the rest of his thinking is not affected by the obstinate and unshakable delusional system. This system is well encapsulated or compartmentalized and may be easily overlooked if the sensitive "cords" are not touched by others. Not infrequently, the patient is most persuasive in presenting his delusions in a plausible form. The psychosis is, in a sense, monosymptomatic — delusions only. The nondeteriorating personality shows often psychological rigidity, mistrust, conceitment, and hostility. Along these lines, French clinicians have emphasized that, in paranoia, the delusion plays an active role in the permanent relationship of the person with his world. Paranoia, thus, is the delusional mode of being of an alienated ego. Treatment of the few patients that come to the clinician's attention requires tact, patience, openness, and a clear respect for the distance that the patient seeks to maintain. Very seldom can some alleviation of the paranoid tension be achieved.

Involutional paranoia generally settles in a personality marked by paranoid or schizoid traits. The clinical picture of paranoia appears at the involutional period (between forty-five and fifty years of age approximately). Persecutory themes are common. Hypochondriac symptoms are frequent, which has been related to the dilemmas corresponding to the life period where this condition occurs. The treatment is less challenging than in paranoia vera. Symptoms of organic brain syndrome must not be present for this diagnosis to be considered.

Paranoid Schizophrenia

Next to fundamental or first-rank symptoms of schizophrenia, a well-systematized disruption of logical thinking and a profound disturbance of the relationship with others can be observed in paranoid schizophrenia. Persecutory and grandiose delusions are prominent. Frequently, the auditory hallucinations talk about the patient in the third person. The intellectual capacity and the personality are relatively preserved longer than in other forms of schizophrenia. As opposed to other schizophrenic subtypes, paranoid schizophrenia appears at middle age or later. Some clinical-genetic observations have suggested the possibility of a differentiation of two separate illnesses: paranoid and nonparanoid schizophrenia. Such differentiation may be more evident in chronic cases and when the patients are treated with phenothiazines.

Paraphrenia is a debated term. Involutional paranoia is sometimes called involutional paraphrenia. Originally, it was meant to indicate a condition nosologically intermediate between paranoia and schizophrenia. The delusions are less systematized, more fantastic than in paranoia, and as opposed to paranoia, hallucinations can be present. Many patients later develop schizophrenia. Ego boundaries remain firm.

Late paraphrenia indicates a paranoid state of the elderly (usually fifty-five years of age and over) in which no symptoms of organic brain syndrome or primary affective illness can be identified. Single, socially isolated women with a paranoid or schizoid personality and with severe hearing loss are more vulnerable than other individuals. Delusions and hallucinations are present. A high incidence of late paraphrenia among relatives of paraphrenic patients has been found. In addition, late paraphrenia is generally thought to belong to the group of schizophrenias, given the high incidence of schizophrenia among the relatives of paraphrenics. However, some authors still contend that late paraphrenia may be a distinct clinical entity.

Paranoid States

Paranoid states are frequent paranoid psychoses which do not have an organic basis and cannot be ascribed to either paranoia or paranoid schizophrenia. Less systematized delusions than in paranoia arise as a result of a traumatic precipitating event. Treatment is usually much more successful than in paranoia, and the condition is seldom chronic or deteriorating in regard to personality and intellect. The sensitive, vulnerable individual seems to react to stressful situations with the development of a delusional system. Paranoid states are usually understandable in terms of the dynamic and genetic background of the affected person.

Paranoid Psychoses Associated with Organicity

Paranoid psychoses associated with organicity can be linked with acute or chronic organic brain syndrome (OBS) and somatic illnesses.

Paranoid psychoses associated with acute OBS paranoid syndromes, often with visual hallucinations, evolve with or without cloudiness of consciousness. Some postpartum psychoses and toxic psychoses — following lysergic acid diethylamide (LSD) intake for example — can be accompanied by cloudiness of consciousness. In alcohol hallucinosis, the accusatory or threatening auditory hallucinations are manifested in a state of relatively clear consciousness.

Paranoid psychosis associated with amphetamine consumption presents a clinical picture often indistinguishable from paranoid schizophrenia. The usual signs or symptoms of organic brain syndrome are commonly absent. Amphetamine psychosis is more likely to ensue after long-term consumption of large doses. Often, a heralding symptom is depression. Self-destructive actions and motor agitation, as well as visual hallucinations, when present, differentiate it from schizophrenia. In most cases, the psychosis lasts only about a week after withdrawal but longer lasting conditions have been described. No gradual withdrawal is required, and the drug can be identified with appropriate laboratory tests when suspected. Amphetamine psychosis appears related to a release and excessive activity of dopamine in the brain. Phenothiazines, which block dopamine receptors in the brain, are the treatment of choice. Notably, children treated with amphetamine for minimal brain dysfunction do not develop psychoses.

Marijuana abuse may result in cannabis psychoses. Violence, panic, rapid ideation, and a certain degree of insight are often present.

Paranoid psychoses associated with chronic OBS can be seen in encephalitis, tertiary syphilis, Huntington's chorea, brain tumors, epilepsy, dementias, alcoholic paranoia (which often includes pathological jealousy), and other disorders.

Paranoid psychoses associated with somatic illnesses have been observed in association with pernicious anemia, infections, lead poisoning, endocrine disturbances (i.e., thyrotoxicosis and myxedema, Addison's disease, and other illnesses), and postoperative and postpartum disorders, and so forth. These psychoses may take the form of acute OBS and usually do not last beyond several weeks.

Other Paranoid Psychoses

These are rather rare disorders and include delusional jealousy, folie à deux, erotomania, paranoid grandiosity, Capgras' syndrome, and others, as well as certain unusual and exotic syndromes.

In *delusionsal jealousy* the patient develops delusions of infidelity about his spouse or partner. The tormenting jealousy arises on the basis of long-standing feelings of inadequacy and low self-esteem. The hypervigilant patient becomes hostile and belligerent against the loved and the "rival," and "reparative" measures taken may be dangerous. A misinterpretation of a trivial circumstance or an actual yet magnified event may exist. Pathologic jealousy may occur *as a symptom* of alcoholic hallucinosis, schizophrenia, and so forth.

In *folie à deux* one lucid paranoid patient "induces" the psychosis in a person (for example, spouse, child) closely associated with him so that both share the same delusion. The inductor is usually most persuasive and dominant in the relationship. The induced psychosis rapidly disappears after separation from the inductor. The biological relatives of the induced psychotic appear to include a high prevalence of schizophrenia, a finding that has promoted a reassessment of the role played by each participant. Sharing of the same delusion by more than two persons has been described.

In *erotomania* (Clérambault's syndrome), classically, a female person develops the delusion that a man, usually highly visible, is in love with her. She tries to establish contact with the man, while increasing her expectations and demands for confirmation of such "love."

In *paranoid grandiosity* the patient is convinced that he possesses unusual talents and special (e.g., divine) missions. He believed himself to be the subject of admiration and envy due to his uniqueness. The delusions are very firmly established, and treatment is often unsuccessful. Some patients do accomplish some important realizations, but for the most part they must deal with an increasing rejection and skepticism.

In *Capgras' syndrome*, (the illusion of doubles), the patient is delusionally convinced that a certain person known to the patient is an impostor. He claims that the impostor is skillfully impersonating the real individual. The syndrome may occur in connection with a variety of psychiatric disorders.

Unusual and exotic syndromes are rare. Many of them occur in connection with deeply rooted cultural factors, and some examples are mentioned to illustrate the role played by such factors. *Amok* describes a condition in which the patient suddenly presents a violent, homicidal agitation and begins killing people around him. It is usually seen in patients suffering from some organic disease, particularly an organic brain syndrome. The condition, originally described in Malayan men, is followed by amnesia. In *susto*, depression, weight loss, anxiety, and fright are common. The patient believes that his soul has been captivated by the earth. It occurs frequently in childhood and adolescence and has been described in South America and other continents. In *whitico* the patient believes to have become a Whitico — a legendary cannibal ice monster. It may result in dangerous homicidal actions. It is observed among certain Eskimos. *Voodoo death* is a state of insurmountable fright which leads to prostration and death. It is a situation where death is induced out of panic in the individual who believes himself to be persecuted or the victim of some exorcism.

PROGNOSIS

The very mistrust that lies at the core of paranoid conditions reinforces the patient's isolation, prevents his receiving treatment and perpetuates the symptoms. Generally, acute psychoses last shorter than chronic, insidiously setting psychoses.

Paranoia vera has a poor prognosis. However, at least one series of studies indicates that the course of paranoiac delusions is similar to that of the paranoid delusion of other psychoses.

Paranoid schizophrenics appear to recover more rapidly and completely than nonparanoid schizophrenics. Paranoid schizophrenics are less often found in chronic populations. As the length of illness increases, the proportion of paranoid schizophrenic patients decreases. This differential incidence appears to result, at least partially, from the disappearance of paranoid symptoms with chronicity. The role played by neuroleptic treatment needs to be evaluated. Paranoid symptomatology, as opposed to withdrawal symptoms, seems to change over a long period of time under neuroleptic treatment. Paranoid "reactive" psychoses (Scandinavian nomenclature) have a great tendency to schizophrenic development.

In paranoid psychoses with hypochondriacal delusions, the prognosis usually depends more on the basic type of disease (e.g., schizophrenia, other paranoid conditions) than on the type of the delusions. The personality does not deteriorate, yet the symptoms remain inaccessible to treatment. Senstitive self-reference delusions generally have a good prognosis.

The prognosis of jealousy-paranoid conditions depends on the underlying disease (schizophrenia, alcoholism, for example). It has been contended that the more reactive the delusion, the better the prognosis.

Apparently, acute paranoid syndromes which follow a precipitating event and which include both affective elements and no familial load of similar psychoses have a better prognosis than the syndromes which present different characteristics. A favorable response to psychotropic drugs, solid familial support, and marital status (married) have also been found to imply a good prognosis.

The prognosis of paranoid psychoses is not as good as in affective illnesses. Retterstol found that depressive delusions are more closely related to a favorable clinical course than other types of delusions. He also suggested some unfavorable indicators: hallucinations, ideas of influence, depersonalization, derealization, and psychomotor inhibition. A good emotional control during hospitalization generally indicates a good prognosis.

The schizoid premorbid personality is considered to be an unfavorable factor by many investigators. In general, paranoid psychoses do not lead to a deterioration of the personality, except in certain schizophrenic patients.

TREATMENT AND MANAGEMENT

There is general agreement concerning the therapeutic challenge presented by paranoid patients. Firstly, they seldom feel motivation to enter treatment, least a desire to change their watchful and defensive outlook. Not infrequently, they come to treatment responding to family and societal pressures. Therapeutic efforts have little chance to succeed when the patient has been "tricked" into treatment. Often treatment begins with advice to the anxious relatives who should be encouraged to hold a prudent and frank approach. Dangerous paranoid *actions* must be dealt with firmness, and when necessary, patients must be forced to undergo a psychiatric evaluation. The determination of the patient's dangerousness is particularly difficult in the proper, hyperalert, and well-reasoning patient. Such difficulty may be compounded when the patient's environment has already developed a rejecting attitude towards the patient and when a credible delusional construct appears to be based on real deceitful events. Hospitalization is particularly indicated when the patient is clearly dangerous to himself or others.

The more chronic the condition, the less treatable it is. Cameron has cautioned against unreasonable therapeutic goals and has particularly discouraged the notion of complete recovery as the only acceptable objective of treatment, since social remission remains a desirable goal.

The prevailing practice is to offer an approach where neuroleptic medication is combined with psychotherapy. Treatment of the underlying organic disorder is, of course, necessary when present. This may necessitate the use of psychotropic medication.

Pharmacotherapy

The choice of antipsychotics is based on both the need for sedation and previous favorable response to a neuroleptic. Assessment of the patient's premorbid personality when the patient is schizophrenic has also been suggested.

Sedation is advisable in the agitated, aggressive, panicky paranoid, particularly when the available supportive measures fail to calm the patient. In most instances, however, a nonsedative neuroleptic (i.e., trifluoperazine) is preferred because the patient needs to remain alert and vigilant, if actual intake of the medication is to be secured. A history of disappearance of symptomatology under neuroleptic treatment should encourage the use of it again. Some studies have suggested that in particular the good premorbid paranoid schizophrenic requires medication if improvement is to occur. Seemingly, paranoid symptoms keep responding to neuroleptics for longer periods of time (more than five weeks) than symptoms of withdrawal.

Psychotherapy

Polatin considers that the treatment of the paranoid patient has two aims: the reduction of anxiety and the reestablishment of realistic communication. "One must always remember that it is not the delusion that calls for therapy, but the frightened person" (Cameron). A clear understanding of the therapeutic goals must rule treatment from the beginning.

The therapist's main challenge is to find a way to encourage the development of trust in him. If the therapist succeeds in developing such a relationship, the patient begins abandoning his isolation. A realistic support must be offered at the onset of therapy. Most likely, the patient will reject excessive or premature friendliness or warmth from the therapist. Phoniness and insincerity in the therapist will be rapidly detected by the paranoid patient.

Premature confrontation and interpretation can result in immediate discontinuation of therapy. An examination of the delusional system cannot be started when the patient is acutely ill or has not developed a trusting relationship with the therapist. Firmly objecting to the delusions is as inadvisable as accepting them as if they were real. The therapist must seek to instill doubt and uncertainty in regard to the delusional structure. Alternative explanations for the delusional elaborations should be rationally explored. Interpretations should be infrequent, brief, and concrete. The importance of remembering the protective and adaptational function of delusion formation is often stressed. When delusions begin to lose firmness, the patient may start showing the underlying hostility, depression, and feelings of inadequacy and worthlessness that promoted the formation of the symptoms. Narcissistic wounds and homosexual fantasies may be shared by the patient. At this point, the therapist must exercise particular sensitivity and skills in order to support the patient while examining realistically his essential conflicts.

The therapist's patience, consistency, and openness, sensitively presented to the patient, are major sources of support. The therapist has to avoid becoming defensive, punitive, or rejecting.

Salzman has indicated the need to foster in the patient an experience of satisfaction from real achievements in everyday tasks. He recommends setting realistic goals for the patient in order to enhance his self-reliance and self-esteem.

Other Treatment Approaches

Environmental manipulation (e.g., change of jobs, change in the relatives' response to the symptoms) may be useful in paranoid states. *Milieu therapy* has been found useful in the treatment of paranoid conditions, particularly by a negative reinforcement of the symptoms through the therapeutic atmosphere of the ward. *Group therapy* is controversial. Some therapists prefer to promote a direct confrontation of the patient in a group setting, while others do not due to the risk of increasing the patient's suspiciousness, hostility, or withdrawal. *Electroconvulsive therapy* is, at times, used in acute paranoid-hallucinatory syndromes. The difficult treatment of paranoia has promoted a variety of approaches, ranging from electroshock to lobotomy with varied results. Removal of the precipitating stresses and treatment of the underlying psychiatric or organic condition must be attempted.

RECOMMENDED READINGS

- Cameron, N. The paranoid pseudo-community, *Am. J. Sociol.* 49:32–38, 1943.
- Cameron, N. "Paranoid conditions and paranoia." In *American handbook of psychiatry*, vol. 3, 2nd ed., ed. S. Arieti, pp. 676–693. New York: Basic Books, 1974.
- Carr, A. C. Observations on paranoia and their relationship to the Schreber case. *Int. J. Psychoanal.* 44:195–200, 1963.
- DePue, R. A., and Woodburn, L. Disappearance of paranoid symptoms with chronicity. *J. Abnorm. Psychol.* 84:84–86, 1975.
- Ellinwood, E. H. "Amphetamine model psychoses: The relationship to schizophrenia." In *Biological mechanisms of schizophrenia and schizo-phrenialike psychoses*, eds. H. Mitsuda and T. Fukada, pp. 89–96. Tokyo: Igaku-Shoin, 1974.
- Foulds, G. A., and Owen, A. Are paranoids schizophrenic? *Br. J. Psychiatry* 109:674–679, 1963.
- Fowler, R. C., Tsuang, M. T., Cadoret, R. J., Monnelly, E., and McCabe, M. A clinical and family comparison of paranoid and nonparanoid schizo-phrenics. *Br. J. Psychiatry* 124:346–351, 1974.
- Freud, S. "Psychoanalytic notes upon an autobiographic account of a case of paranoia (dementia paranoides)," 1911. In *Standard edition*, vol. 12, ed. J. Strachey, pp. 1–32. London: Hogarth Press, 1958.
- Freud, S. "Some neurotic mechanisms in jealousy, paranoia, and homosex-uality," 1922. In *Standard edition,*, vol. 18, ed. J. Strachey, pp. 221–232. London: Hogarth Press, 1955.
- Goldberg, S. C., Schooler, N. R., and Mattsson, N. Paranoid and withdrawal symptoms in schizophrenia: Differential symptom reduction over time. *J. Nerv. Ment. Dis.* 145:158–162, 1967.
- Goldstein, M. J. Premorbid adjustment, paranoid status, and patterns of response to phrenothiazines in acute schizophrenia. *Schizophrenia Bull.* 3:24–37, 1970.
- Griffith, J. D., Cavanaugh, J., Held, I., and Oates, J. A. Dextroamphetamine: Evaluation of psychomimetic properties in man. *Arch. Gen. Psychiatry* 26:97–100, 1972.
- Hoaken, P. C. S. Paranoid-depressive relationship. *Can. Psychiatr. Assoc. J.* 18:427–433, 1973.
- Houston, F., and Royse, A. B. Relationship between deafness and psychotic illness. *J. Ment. Sci.* 100:990–993, 1954.

- Judd, L. L., Goldstein, M. J., Rodnick, E. H., and Jackson, N. L. P. Phenothiazine effects in good premorbid schizophrenics divided into paranoid-nonparanoid status. *Arch. Gen. Psychiatry* 29:207–211, 1973.
- Katan, M. A psychoanalytic approach to the diagnosis of paranoia. *Psychoanalytic Study Child* 24:328–357, 1969.
- Kay, D. W. K. and Roth, M. Environmental and hereditary factors in the schizophrenia of old age ("late paraphrenia") and their bearing on the general problems of causation in schizophrenia. *J. Ment. Sci.* 107:649–686, 1961.
- Klein, M. *Contributions to psychoanalysis.* London: Hogarth Press, 1948.
- Kraepelin, E. *Dementia praecox and paraphrenia.* Edinburgh: Livingston, 1919.
- Kretschmer, E. *Der sensitive Beziehungswahn.* Berlin: Springer, 1950.
- Lewis, A. Paranoia and paranoid: A historical perspective. *Psychol. Med.* 1:2–12, 1970.
- Meissner, W. W. Schreber and the paranoid process. In ed. Chicago Institute for Psychoanalysis, pp. 3–40, vol. 4, *The annual of psychoanalysis,* New York: International Universities Press, 1976.
- Ovesey, L. Pseudohomosexuality, the paranoid mechanism, and paranoia. *Psychiatry* 18:163–173, 1955.
- Post, F. *Persistent persecutory states of the elderly.* Oxford: Pergamon Press, 1966.
- Retterstol, N. *Paranoid and paranoiac psychoses.* Springfield, Ill.: Thomas, 1966.
- Retterstol, N. *Prognosis in paranoid psychoses,* Springfield, Ill.: Thomas, 1970.
- Rimon, R., Stenback, A., and Achte, K. On sociopsychiatric study of paranoid psychoses. *Acta Psychiatr. Scand.* 180 (Suppl.): 1965.
- Salzman, L. Paranoid state: Theory and therapy. *Arch Gen. Psychiatry* 2:679–693, 1960.
- Schwartz, D. A. A review of the "paranoid" concept. *Arch. Gen. Psychiatry* 8:349–361, 1963.
- Schneider, K. *Clinical psychopathology.* New York: Harper and Row, 1959.
- Strauss, M. E. Behavioral differences between acute and chronic schizophrenics: Course of psychosis, effects of institutionalization, or sampling bias? *Psychol. Bull.* 79:271–279, 1973.
- Swanson, D., Bohnert, P., and Smith, J. *The paranoid.* Boston: Little, Brown, 1970.
- Tanna, V. L. Paranoid states: A selected review. *Compr. Psychiatry* 15:453–470, 1974.
- Thacore, V. R. Cannabis psychosis and paranoid schizophrenia. *Arch. Gen. Psychiatry* 18:383–386, 1976.
- Tsuang, M. T., Fowler, R. C., Cadoret, R. J., and Monnelly, E. Schizophrenia among first-degree relatives of paranoid and nonparanoid schizophrenics. *Compr. Psychiatry* 15:295–302, 1974.
- Tyhurst, J. S. "Paranoid patterns." In *Explorations in social psychiatry,* eds. A. H. Leighton, J. A. Clausen, and R. N. Wilson, pp. 31–66. New York: Basic Books, 1957.

- Waelder, R. The structure of paranoid ideas: A critical survey of various theories. *Int. J. Psychoanal.* 32:167–177, 1951.
- Weintraub, W. Obsessive-compulsive and paranoid personalities. In *Personality disorders: Diagnosis and management,* ed. J. R. Lion. pp. 85–101. Baltimore: Williams and Wilkins, 1974.
- Winokur, G. Paranoid versus hebephrenic schizophrenia: A clinical and familial (genetic) heterogeneity. *Psychopharmacol. Comm.* 1:567–577, 1975.

7

Affective Psychoses

Gerald L. Brown, M.D., and
William E. Bunney, Jr., M.D.

NOSOLOGY, CLASSIFICATIONS, AND DIAGNOSTIC CONSIDERATIONS

Nosology in psychiatry is largely based on descriptive phenomenology rather than etiological understanding of the disorder. The history of medical nosological classification has generally been from a descriptive to an empirical basis to a more etiological understanding. For example, Parkinson's disease has progressed from the "shaking palsy" [79] to a neuropathological entity with basal ganglia alterations and a clinical response to anticholinergic medication to the specific knowledge of a dopamine deficiency and a hypothesized dopamine-acetylcholine dysbalance. Despite the difficulties of assimilating and integrating the multiple variables in human emotional and behavioral disorder, affective disorders have made some progress on this continuum of understanding.

Affective illness has been defined as an emotional and behavioral clinical entity. Specific pharmacological response to drugs, both those that appear to induce or to treat affective states, are well known. Genetic data

Betty DeBauche, Research Assistant, Biological Psychiatry Branch, National Institute of Mental Health, National Institutes of Health, Bethesda, Maryland, helped in the preparation of this chapter.

indicate a transmittable component of these disorders, and, if so, genetically transmitted abnormalities often involve an alteration in a critical protein.

The incidence of manic-depressive illness is thought to be 3–4/1000; the male-female ratio varies from three-to-two to two-to-one [84]. Kraepelin [62], who in 1896 proposed the name manic-depressive insanity, indicated that 58 percent of first attacks occurred between twenty and thirty-five years of age and 35 percent from age thirty-five to sixty. Later findings [7] show that 88 percent of all cases have an age of onset of less than forty-nine, and the median is thirty-nine. Estimates of morbidity risk percent (MR%) for manic-depressive psychosis in the general population range between an MR% of 0.6 and 2.7 [81].

A number of classification systems and diagnostic categories have been devised for affective illnesses [3]:

1   General concepts
      Primary and secondary
      Endogenous and reactive
      Neurotic and psychotic
      Unipolar and bipolar
2   Diagnostic classifications (DSM-II)
      Manic-depressive (depressed type, circular type, manic type)
      Psychotic depressive reaction
      Involutional melancholia
      Cyclothymic personality
      Depressive neuroses
      Psychosis with childbirth (postpartum psychoses)
3   Other affective states
      Normal depressions
      Grief reactions

A brief description of these groups, their definitions, and their utility are discussed below.

Normal Depression

All depressive episodes need not be considered pathological or maladaptive. For example, Darwin [34] has shown a regular progression of morphological maturation and affective expression utilizing observational data from animals, including primates, primitive peoples, mental patients, infants, and adults. Harlow [48] has discussed adaptive features of

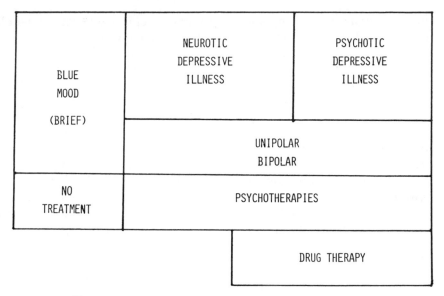

Figure 7.1
Depressive Mood.

depression in infant primates as has Bowlby [16] in infant humans. As Bowlby has discussed the infant's reaction to loss, Mahler [69] has discussed the progression of normal "loss" as the infant individuates himself from his mother. There is a clear difference between depression as a normal, age-appropriate and/or situationally appropriate affect (such as feeling blue or sad) and severe depression as a pathological condition. Figure 7.1 reviews the continuum óf depressive mood which can be experienced. Most of the population experience periods of blue mood. These moods are characterized as being brief, mild, and usually clearly related to a stressful environmental event, i.e., an individual's being turned down for a promotion. These brief periods of feeling blue require no treatment; they often respond to talking with a friend or simply spontaneously remit after a few hours to a couple of days. At the other end of the continuum are severe psychotic depressive illnesses which clearly interfere with functioning; they often require hospitalization and respond to drug or electroconvulsive therapy. There is an intermediate group of depressive illnesses in terms of severity, characterized as neurotic depressions, which are milder and usually do not require hospitalization. Some of these illnesses respond to psychotherapy and do not require drugs, whereas others do. The milder neurotic depressions and the more severe psychotic depression can also be classified as unipolar (patients with a history of depressive episodes only) or bipolar (patients with a history of depressive episodes and manic episodes). Phenomenologically, affective disturbance manifests itself somewhat differently in children than in adults [32].

An example of an ordinarily nonpathological depressive episode which may become of such quality, intensity, or duration as to become pathological is the grief process after a loss, often of a close family member. However, if grief reactions do become intense and extend for six months or longer they may become indistinguishable from clinical depressions. A distinction between nonpathological mourning and pathological melancholia was put forward by Freud [39]. Lindemann [67] later discussed the variations from individual to individual of the grief process and the influence of specific interventions. Parkes [78] studied the clinical picture of 115 bereaved psychiatric patients and classified grief and its variants. Bornstein et al. [15] studied 109 widowers during the year following loss and concluded that grief was a good model for studying depression from a clear-cut loss but was significantly different from clinical affective illness (no cases of fear of losing one's mind, psychomotor retardation, or suicidal attempt).

Unipolar Illness

Among these various classifications for affective disturbance, the unipolar-bipolar distinction appears promising and has come to be used widely in recent years. Leonhard's [65] original use was a distinction between those recurrently depressed patients with and without a previous history of mania. This distinction has perhaps been the most useful in terms of genetic, biochemical, neurophysiological, and neuropsychopharmacological data.

The depressive symptomatology of a unipolar (UP) disturbance, not without considerable variations, consists of the following basic aspects: (1) depressed mood; (2) psychomotor retardation, a general condition consisting of combinations of decreased energy, slowed motor movements, slowed speech, and slowed thought processes; (3) thought processes that may deteriorate to psychotic disturbances in the form of paranoid ideation, accusatory hallucinations, and nihilistic delusions; (4) biological concomitants, i.e., profound sleep disturbances (such as frequent and early morning awakening), marked changes in appetite and weight, decreased sexual and aggressive interest, decreased peristalsis, constipation, other autonomic disturbances, anxiety, and motor agitation; and (5) suicidal wishes, ideation, or, not infrequently, attempts.

Generally unipolar depressions are a diagnosis by exclusion, namely depressive episodes without a history of mania, although this lack of history may be explained often by an insufficient period of observation.

Unipolar depression may be a chronic recurrent disorder with episodes occurring once or twice a year. The unipolar depressions may also be differentiated from the bipolar depressions in that unipolar patients may be agitated; they tend to sleep less, and family studies [6,44] show a lower incidence of affective illness in the relatives. Though the boundaries of unipolar illness are not clinically clear, depressive episodes from the very mild to the quite severe will be briefly discussed below.

Bipolar Illness

The manic phase of a bipolar (BP) disturbance, as is generally true for psychiatric conditions, is not without considerable variation, but the basic aspects are the following: (1) elated, unstable, and fluctuating moods; (2) pressure of speech, with sometimes associated rhyming or punning, clang associating, and circumlocution; (3) flight of ideas as distinguished from the loose associations of the schizophrenic; grandiosity, sometimes elated to increased religiosity; increased distractability and sometimes paranoid thinking; (4) rapid and increased energy and motor activity with minimal periods of relaxation, rest, or sleep; (5) poor judgment, frequently not observable by the patient; and (6) increased aggressive or sexual behaviors, or both.

The depressive phase of a bipolar disturbance is described above. The bipolar depression may be markedly slowed, whereas the unipolar depression may be agitated or retarded. Agitation may actually coexist with psychomotor retardation, giving the patient the appearance of being restless in slow motion. Both bipolar and unipolar illnesses have degrees of disturbance. A hypomanic condition is manifested by buoyant, energetic behavior that may lead to marginal social functioning or, at times, to great bursts of usefully productive activities. The most severe form of mania — referred to as delirious mania — can include hallucinations, delusions, incontinence of urine and feces, exhaustion, and metabolic disturbances of a magnitude that can lead to death without immediate intervention (neuroleptic or electroconvulsive therapy). A depressive disturbance may be manifested by a transient mood disturbance only, or an episode as described above, or by a severe depressive episode during which a patient may refuse to eat or drink, resulting in so profound a metabolic dysequilibrium as to lead to death unless antidepressant or electroconvulsive therapy is initiated. The danger of suicidal ideation being put into action is most likely preceding or during recovery from these most severe disturbances.

Prior to the use of pharmacotherapy or electroconvulsive therapy, the usual manic disturbance would last about 3.5 months and the usual depressive disturbance about 6.5 months [84]. Treated episodes of both unipolar and bipolar illness usually do not last longer than three months,

AGE ----

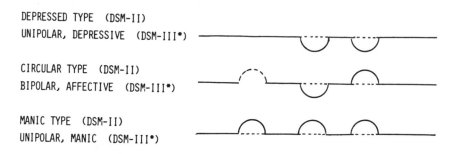

DEPRESSED TYPE (DSM-II)
UNIPOLAR, DEPRESSIVE (DSM-III*)

CIRCULAR TYPE (DSM-II)
BIPOLAR, AFFECTIVE (DSM-III*)

MANIC TYPE (DSM-II)
UNIPOLAR, MANIC (DSM-III*)

*TENTATIVELY PROPOSED

Figure 7.2
Manic-Depressive Illness.

unipolar illness being approximately 20 percent longer. Cycle length, i.e., the time from the beginning of one episode to the beginning of the next, may shorten as the illness progresses. The cycle length in bipolar illness consistently is slightly less than that for unipolar illness when respective episodes are compared. In general, the courses of bipolar illness and unipolar illness show more similarities than differences, namely, both are periodic, the number of episodes appears to be limited in a given patient, the majority of episodes are around three months in length, the episode length for a given patient remains fairly constant throughout his life, and the cycle length becomes progressively shorter in both groups over the course of the illness [7].

According to the diagnostic nosology of the second edition of the American Psychiatric Association's *Diagnostic and Statistical Manual* (DSM-II) [3] manic-depressive illness may be of the depressed type, the circular type, or the manic type. These classifications and their relationship to the proposed DSM-III [4,95] can be visualized in Figure 7.2. One must remember in viewing this schematic diagram that these affective episodes are generally recurrent and vary in severity, duration, and period of remission. These proposals for change appear to be realistic and necessary. When these episodes are mild, but clearly recurrent as a pattern, a diagnosis of cyclothymic personality may be more appropriate than that of a manic-depressive illness ("cyclothymic" means "circular" pattern of mood swings).

Earlier clinical descriptions, nosological systems, and psychodynamic formulations of one phase as a defense against the other all have tended to encourage a mutually exclusive conceptualization of manic-depressive illness and/or the concept that the two conditions are opposite, or at least dichotomous in nature; however, when tridaily behavior and affective ratings of bipolar patients are made in a research setting, depressive ratings may be present at times without manic ratings, but during almost all periods of significant manic ratings, depressive ratings are also significant. More importantly, for both conditions, some of the apparent biological variables and psychopharmacological responses to the same compound (i.e., lithium) vary in the same direction; whereas other responses may vary in the opposite direction. Some genetic studies also hypothesize that unipolar and bipolar illness may be a continuum with an increasing genetic component, despite their being some biological variables that seem specific to one condition or the other. The role of precipitating stresses, both psychological and biological, are discussed below.

Primary and Secondary Affective Disorders

Affective disorders have been distinguished as primary versus secondary by Robins et al. [85]. Essentially, a patient whose affective disturbance is his first, or whose previous psychiatric disturbance has been affective in nature, is considered to have a primary affective disorder. If a previous psychiatric disturbance in a presently affectively disturbed patient has been other than affective, the patient is then considered to have a secondary affective disturbance. According to this model, a secondary affective disturbance is a clinical state, such as congestive heart failure, which may be the final outcome of several conditions; whereas there can be a primary affective disturbance which would warrant investigation as an entity in itself. This classification does not involve the issue of whether an affective disturbance has been precipitated by stressful life events.

Endogenous and Reactive Affective Disorders

Indeed, this distinction of endogenous versus reactive depression is not so much a dichotomy as a supposed predominance of certain findings along a continuum. For example, endogenous depressions have been thought of as those which were unrelated to a stressful event and included biological concomitants, such as disturbances of sleep, appetite, weight, autonomic nervous systems manifestations, and sexual desire. However, reactive depressions (to life stresses) may evince biological symptomatology and most endogenous depressions (with biological concomitants) are preceded by stressful life events [64]. Holmes and Rahe [51] have demonstrated that increased life stresses, such as serious illness, loss of a family member, divorce, or loss of job, occur at greater frequency preceding emotional and medical disturbances. Losses of various types have long been associated with the precipitation of depression, though many — and perhaps most — adults in the general population are able to cope with loss without suffering clinical depression. This classification is still in use in the United States and in Europe; however it seems that no useful and clear distinction can be made from the criteria discussed.

Neurotic and Psychotic Affective Illness

Neurotic versus psychotic depression is a distinction that has been widely used clinically. Generally, *neurosis* has been used to mean either a mild form of functional mental disturbance characterized by symptomatology that does not impair reality testing — i.e., anxiety — or a more specific meaning related to psychodynamic disturbance at an advanced level of psychosexual development and/or internalized, unconscious conflicts. Generally, *psychosis* has been used to mean either a severe functional mental disturbance, which includes symptomatology that impairs reality testing and which may or may not imply psychodynamic disturbance at an early psychosexual level of development and/or externalized primitive psychological processes. The fact that these terms are used in such a varied way relegates the neurotic-psychotic distinction to that of a generality unless the terms are specifically defined by the user. This distinction has given rise to current clinical diagnoses such as depressive neuroses and psychotic reactions.

Depressive episodes that are transient, usually without biological concomitants, and may or may not appear to be precipitated by overt external events may be called *depressive neurosis*. Depressive episodes that reach the severity of those described under bipolar illness may be classified as psychotic depressive reactions, according to DSM-II if there is no history of recurrent depression and if there is a precipitating external stress. Some psychotic depressions — always accompanied by biological concomitants — may or may not be preceded by a clear history of a precipitating event. (External events always appear to have a role, although those events that would not ordinarily be significant to one individual can be quite significant to another.) The classification of psychotic depressive reaction has not been proposed for DSM-III.

Another depressive diagnosis, involutional melancholia, is similar to those described under unipolar illness. This condition was thought to be preceded by an obsessional personality and occur at an involutional period, either biologically, as the menopause (although no clear evidence linking them to hormonal changes is yet at hand), or functionally, as retirement from a job. Frequent somatizations and often a considerable degree of psychotic symptomatology (particularly paranoia) is reported. This disorder was considered as a late onset unipolar depression. Involutional melancholia has not been proposed for DSM-III.

Postpartum Psychoses

Postpartum psychoses may be depressive or schizophrenic in nature. Hallucinations and delusions are not infrequent whether or not the individual manifestations are predominantly those of an affective disorder or those of a thought process disorder. The aspects of the postpartum depression that are different from a usual depressive episode are profound and abrupt endocrine changes and a specific stress, that of becoming a mother with all of the internal psychological and external environmental changes that attend thereto. Although this diagnosis has not been included in DSM-II or the proposed DSM-III as a specific diagnostic subcategory of depression (DSM-II — psychoses associated with organic brain syndrome, other physical conditions, childbirth; DSM-III — not specified) and although its affective aspects are not clearly phenomenologically different from a depressive episode of similar quality, intensity, or duration in a similarly aged nonpostpartum woman, certain clinical and biological observations have raised the possibility of a higher level of nosological specificity than it has been accorded to date.

Some controversy has surrounded an observation by Karnosh and Hope [59] of a three-day latent period postdelivery; but, in any case, such a period would correspond to the full onset of lactation triggered by increased prolactin. Dopamine, a neurotransmitter implicated as being deficient in depression, is thought to be closely related to prolactin inhibiting factor (PIF). No controlled studies have been done relating lactation, its inadequacy, or its iatrogenic prevention to affective disturbance in postpartum women.

Much current work is being focused on the neurotransmitter regulation of hypothalamic hormonal releasing and inhibiting factors, as well as evidence that peripheral changes in hormones can also affect a feedback regulation of neurotransmitters. Also, the same authors [59] have noted as one of their most constant findings a fever ranging from 99° to 102°. Although there can be many causes for a low-grade fever in a postpartum mother, a dysequilibrium of thermoregulation in the hypothalamus can be a determinant. Studies have shown profound decreases in stage-four sleep from early pregnancy to four to six weeks postpartum; these changes are similar to those seen in nonpregnancy-related depression [58].

Two areas of general interest have been the marked increases in corticosteroid and estrogen levels in late pregnancy (and their abrupt decrease postpartum) and the increased protein-bound iodine during pregnancy and its fall during the postpartum period [33]; these changes may be related to the estrogen-induced elevation of the proteins that bind thyroxine and cortisol [35]. In any case, triiodothyronine and desiccated thyroid have been reported to be therapeutically successful in postpartum depression [47]. That steroid and/or estrogen withdrawal can trigger depression may be supported by studies [51] indicating that mild to severe depressive symptoms may accompany withdrawal of oral contraceptive steroids. During the premenstrual period, during which women have undergone a normal relative estrogen withdrawal and concomitant increase in progesterone, there are often transient periods of mild to moderate depression.

PSYCHOLOGICAL ASPECTS OF AFFECTIVE DISTURBANCE

Precipitation of Affective Illness by Life Events

A great deal has been written concerning the relation between stress, separation, loss, and other life events and the various syndromes of depression. Mendelson [75], who reviewed the incidence of early childhood loss of a parent in manic-depressive patients, outlined several conflicting reports. Some studies demonstrated an increased incidence of early childhood loss in manic-depressive patients versus the general population; whereas others could find no significant difference, or that delinquency or shallow interpersonal relationships were the more likely result of such early loss. In his discussion of stress and life events as precipitating factors in depression, Klerman [61] noted that "separation and loss account for only about 25 percent of a large series of depressed patients" and that separation and loss "in themselves . . . cannot account for the total causation (of depression)." He points out that "most persons, when confronted with stress, do cope, and one must look for the factors within the persons that account for those who cope as contrasted with those who develop clinical symptomatic states." Though it may appear that some patients develop an adult depression as a reactivation of childhood experiences, by no means is there a clear relationship that could be generalized to all adult depressions.

Psychodynamics and Affective Illness

Those aspects of depression that might be referred to as psychodynamic have largely come from the field of psychoanalysis or some of its later variants. Abraham [1,2] felt that the initial and primary difficulty lay in a more than usual frustration and lack of gratification from the mothering figure in the first year of life. Freud [39] later discussed the differences between mourning as a nonpathological response to a real loss and clinical melancholia (often precipitated by a real loss). He noted that self-reproach was so great in the depressed patient that often no amount of reassurance or confrontation with the unrealistic aspects of the self-accusations could dissuade the patient from these views of himself. The idea of depression as a defense mechanism has followed from Freud's views of anxiety as a signal to initiate defense mechanisms and the further elaboration of these mechanisms by Anna Freud [38]. Affects have also been described by Sandler and Joffe [91] in a hierarchical fashion with an increasing component from the higher levels of mental functioning (ego) and a corresponding decreasing component from the lower levels of mental functioning (id) — i.e., contempt and disdain as highly evolved and modified affects with complex contributions from the ego and rage as an affect from the id, with little modification from the ego. This hierarchical concept is consistent with Darwin's [34] view of the development of the expression of affect in man and animals. Jacobson [52] has elaborated on the variations that affect and mood have on the concept of one's self and the related vicissitudes of self-esteem. Whether or not aggression is the substrate for clinical depression (as Freud's early hypotheses might indicate), Darwin's studies would indicate that the capacity for aggressive affect precedes the capacity for depressive affect; and Spitz's [94] studies of depression in infants indicated that depressive affects follow the rageful protest at the failure of assertive (aggressive) attempts to attain one's basic needs (an inevitable failure in the situation in which the caretaker is lost). Harlow's [48] primate studies would also indicate that depression follows aggression (despair follows protest); McKinney [71] who studies biochemical correlates of protest and despair in primates has reported that despair does not invariably follow the protest elicited by separation.

The efficacy and limitations of psychoanalysis as a treatment for manic-depressive illness has been most thoroughly documented by Cohen et al. [26].

BIOLOGICAL ASPECTS OF AFFECTIVE DISTURBANCE

Genetic studies have implicated affective illness as a heritable disorder which presumably would express the defect through an altered protein. Drugs can activate either depression or mania. All of the drugs which affect mood and cognition in man have an effect on neurotransmission in the central nervous system. Some of the compounds which function as neurotransmitters, i.e., epinephrine (E), norepinephrine (NE), dopamine

(DA), serotonin (5HT), acetylcholine (ACh), γ-aminobutyric acid (GABA), glutamic acid (GA), and histamine (HA), have been identified and studied in recent years. Much has been learned about their synthesis, storage, release, uptake, and catabolism. The function of these neurotransmitters and their relationship to neuroanatomical structures, neuroendocrinology, neuropharmacology, and electrolytes are important in attempting to clarify the biological contribution to affective disorders.

Genetic Factors

Several lines of evidence have pointed to the possible role of genetic factors in the etiology of affective disorders. Affective disorders can be traced through several generations of the same family. A consistent finding in the studies performed throughout the world has been that the risk of developing a primary affective disorder is about twenty times greater among the first-degree relatives (parents, siblings, and children) of probands (family members who are identified as exhibiting the trait of interest and through whom the families are located) with primary affective disorder than that of the general population [81].

Twin studies have been important in genetic investigations of affective disorders. Monozygotic (MZ) twins have identical genes while dizygotic (DZ) twins, like any other pair of siblings, on the average share half of their genes. Twins of the same age and sex and reared together are considered to provide some control for environmental factors. There are two essential features of the twin study method: (1) to the extent that genetic factors are associated with a trait, the members of MZ pairs will be more alike than DZ pairs, and (2) any differences between the members of MZ pairs will be associated with environment and acquired differences. Studies of MZ and DZ twins have suggested that genetic factors play a significant role in the etiology of affective illness. In a review of six twin studies [41] it was found that the pooled concordance rate (the proportion of pairs in which both members have been found to exhibit the trait in question) for affective illness in MZ twins was 69.2 percent, in comparison to a concordance rate of 13.3 percent for DZ twins. If the assumption that intrapair differences of environment are not essentially distinctive for MZ and DZ twins is tenable, then the significantly higher concordance rate for affective illness in MZ twin pairs indicates a heritable disorder.

Studies of MZ twins are useful in investigating the relative contribution of genetic and environmental factors in the development of affective disorders, but, unfortunately, they cannot be used to elucidate modes of genetic transmission. Family studies may be useful in this regard. Several excellent reviews of family studies of bipolar illness have been written

[13,92,97]. Table 7-1 shows the results of early morbidity studies which were performed to determine the risk of BP illness in the siblings, parents, and children of patients with the disorder. The morbidity risk of developing an affective disorder has been consistently found to be higher among the first-degree relatives of patients with affective disorder than among the general population [86].

Genetic studies have made a contribution to the classification and identification of various subtypes of affective disorders. The BP and (unipolar) UP forms of affective illness have been the subject of genetic investigations. Leonhard [66] hypothesized that these two disorders may be genetically distinct. A clearer distinction between UP and BP affective illness is made when the morbidity risk for the two sexes is compared. The incidence of affective disorders is the same in the male and female relatives with BP illness, but a higher incidence of endogenous depression is observed in the female relatives of UP probands. The overall rate of hospital admissions is higher for females than for males. Evidence favoring X-linkage (a mode of genetic transmission in which a gene of the X-chromosome may be passed from father to daughter or from mother to daughter, but not from father to son) in the subgroup of bipolar illness has been obtained by studies which tested linkage between manic-depressive illness and color blindness [97] and the Xg[a] blood system [98,36]. Perris [80] has shown that a non–X-linked subgroup must also exist because some fathers with BP illness have affected sons. Gershon et al. [45] have argued that it is premature to conclude that BP illness is linked to either color blindness or Xg, or both.

Several psychiatric disorders have been found to be more prevalent in the first-degree relatives of patients with affective illness than in the general population. It may be possible, due to the high heritability of affective disorders, that these other psychiatric disorders are manifestations

Table 7.1

CLASSICAL FAMILY STUDIES OF MANIC-DEPRESSIVE
PSYCHOSIS. MORBID RISK OF DEVELOPING
MANIC-DEPRESSIVE ILLNESS (%)

Investigator	First-degree relatives		
	Siblings	Parents	Children
Slater [93]	—	11.5	22.2
Stenstedt [96]	14.1	7.5	17.1
Kallman [56]	23.0	23.5	—
Cadoret [25]	—	unipolar	30.3
		bipolar	45.5

of the same heritable factors which lead to affective illness [42]. The disorders which have been identified in the first-degree relatives of patients with affective illness include neurotic depressive reaction, involutional melancholia, alcoholism, antisocial personality, and cyclothymic personality.

The specific heritable factors which may predispose an individual to the development of an affective disorder are, as yet, a matter of speculation. The enzymes responsible for the enzymatic inactivation of catecholamines, catechol-O-methyltransferase (COMT) and monoamine oxidase (MAO) are hypothesized to have altered functional activity in the affective disorders. Both platelet MAO [99] and erythrocyte COMT activity [43] have been reported to be heritable; and reduced platelet MAO has been found in both schizophrenia and bipolar illness [77], thus these enzymes are possible candidates for further genetic investigations to determine if the altered enzyme activities are transmitted along with the affective disorder. Other pharmacological, biological, or behavioral studies may yield data that can assist in identifying the *affective genotype*, a specific genetic predisposition to affective illness which might or might not manifest itself as clinical illness

Neurotransmitters in Affective Illness

The catecholamine hypothesis [20,92] has generated much subsequent work in the psychobiological study of depression and mania. In its simplest form it postulates that some depressions are associated with a functional deficit of NE in synaptic clefts in the brain, whereas mania is associated with an excess. This hypothesis is supported by certain pharmacological responses; i.e., reserpine, which depletes central NE, can facilitate depression; amphetamines, which acutely release NE and block its reuptake followed by a depletion, induce an initial stimulation which may be followed by depression when the compound is terminated or if administered chronically; MAO inhibitors which increase functional brain amines, act as antidepressants; tricyclic compounds, i.e., imipramine, which increase synaptic catecholamines by inhibiting their presynaptic reuptake, act as antidepressants; and specific catecholamine synthesis blockers, as α-methyl-p-tyrosine (AMPT), may exacerbate depression or precursors, as L-dopa, may sometimes act as antidepressants. These same compounds, MAO inhibitors, tricyclics, and L-dopa may precipitate mania or hypomania in some patients, particularly those with a history of BP illness. Cerebrospinal fluid (CSF) amine metabolites, which partially reflect cerebral amine metabolism, have been studied in depressives. Two of four studies have shown a decreased 3-methoxy-4-hydroxyphenyl glycol (MHPG), a central amine of NE, but only two of nine studies have shown a decreased homovanillic acid (HVA), a central amine metabolite of DA [82]. A decreased vanillylmandelic acid (VMA), a central amine metabolite of probably both NE and E, has recently been reported [54].

The indoleamine hypothesis states that depression may arise as a result of a decreased brain 5HT [27,63]. Administration of tryptophan, the 5HT precursor, to depressed patients has yielded mixed results, although when combined with an MAO inhibitor, better results are obtained [30,31]. In depression, some CSF amine metabolite studies show a decreased 5-hydroxy-indoleacetic acid (5HIAA), a metabolite of 5HT, while others do not [82]. A bimodal distribution of 5HIAA is compatible with the findings that depressives with a decreased CSF 5HIAA show an antidepressant response to the 5HT precursor, 5HTP, and by a specific response to tricyclics that are more specific for 5HT reuptake blockage [8,83].

The catecholamine and indoleamine hypotheses are not mutually exclusive. Some urinary MHPG studies have indicated that depressed patients with low pretreatment MHPG values respond best to tricyclics whose predominant mode of action is reuptake block of NE; whereas those with higher pretreatment MHPG values respond best to tricyclics whose predominant mode of action is the reuptake block of 5HT — thus two biological and pharmacological subgroups of depression [14,68].

Those hypotheses that indicate an alteration in balance or ratio between neurotransmitters rather than absolute deficits or excesses appear currently to hold promise. A balance system involving NE and 5HT has been proposed [19]. Earlier, for Parkinson's disease, which shares some similar characteristics with depression [17], balance systems between DA and ACh, and 5HT and HA have been proposed [12]. ACh has been implicated as being in excess in depression and in deficit in mania [53]. There are further indications of functional balances between ACh and NE [40] GABA and DA [5] and GA and GABA [76]. There is much yet to be clarified regarding these basic neurochemical systems and their relationships and their possible further relationship to emotions and behavior. An area of related interest is the "switch hypothesis" [21–24]. In brief, the switch into and out of mania has been studied in some detail. Figure 7.3 is a theorized schema to incorporate clinical observations, genetic predisposition, and the various stresses (i.e., environmental or pharmacological) that may be associated with a "switch" [24]. On the day prior to a switch into mania, twenty-four-hour urinary NE was found to increase and remain so during the manic phase. On the day of the switch itself, urinary cyclic-AMP was increased and decreased subsequently. The apparent precipitation of mania by drugs was noted above.

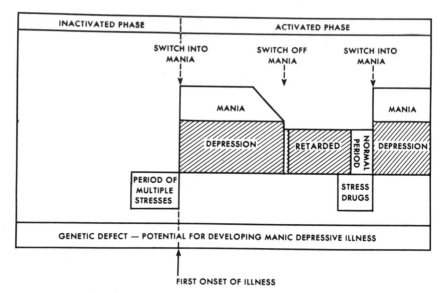

Figure 7.3
Bipolar Manic-Depressive Process (Theorized Schema). From Bunney and Murphy, *Arch. Gen. Psychiatry* 27:312–317. Copyright 1972, American Medical Association.

Several components of manic-depressive illness may best be considered separately in attempting to understand the onset of symptoms: (1) a preexisting defect, possibly of genetic origin, which is necessary for the illness but which is generally insufficient by itself to produce overt symptoms; (2) environmental stresses which contribute to the activation of the illness; such stresses may be exclusively psychological, or, as in the case of psychoactive drugs, may produce psychological changes indirectly via biological changes in the neurochemical mechanisms subserving emotion and psychomotor arousal; in the case of other illness, the environmental stresses may be physical; (3) long-phase rhythms in a biological system pertinent to the illness may be sufficient by themselves to activate the preexisting defect in the uncommon cases of regular periodic illnesses, whereas in irregularly recurrent illnesses they may act in concert with environmental stresses, with overt symptoms only occurring when all three factors are concurrent.

Neuroendocrine Functioning in Affective Illness

Although an attempt to understand the place of the amines in affective illness has largely been based on neuropharmacological techniques and

the analysis of blood, urine, and CSF, another method for viewing hy-
pothalamic-limbic alterations in depression is to study neuroendocrine
changes, as neuroendocrine regulation appears to be related intimately to
the hypothalamic content of amines. Cortisol, growth hormone, and
thyroid hormone have been studied. The cortisol secretory pattern of anx-
ious-depressed patients, who are high cortisol secretors, show several significant variations from normal. Preliminary findings indicate that the
number of secretory episodes is greater; the peaks are higher than normal;
the baseline does not fall to the levels seen in the normal, even in the late
hours of the evening and early hours of sleep; and during this period,
depressed patients may have secretory bursts when normally secretion
ceases [90]. Studies of depressive adults' secretion of growth hormone in
response to insulin-induced hypoglycemia have shown mixed results
[46,88,89]. A possible relative insulin insensitivity in depressed patients
has been shown not to be related to increased cortisol production. The potentiation of imipramine by triiodothyronine in female depressed patients
suggests the possible interaction of thyroid hormone with sex hormones,
altering the cellular receptivity to amines or antidepressants, but there is
no clear picture of the relationship of sex hormones to depression [87].

Electrolyte Factors in Affective Illness

The study of electrolytes in depressed patients dovetails with the interest
in the lithium responsivity of some affective illnesses. Sodium, potassium, calcium, and magnesium have been studied. Coppen and Shaw [28]
have reported an elevated intracellular sodium during depression with a
subsequent decrease on recovery. A problem with this determination is
that it involves the use of multiple isotope dilution techniques to measure
indirectly total body sodium and extracellular fluid volume, from which is
calculated the intracellular sodium. The picture for potassium has varied
from normal to low potassium during depression. Calcium and magnesium studies have yielded no consistent results [9]. Coppen et al. [29]
found that cellular sodium was about twice as high in mania as in depression, but other results [9] did not confirm the finding. One cannot assume
that biological changes in mania and depression will necessarily be opposite to each other. Although the net effect of lithium administration (at
an equivalent dose to that given in manic-depressive patients) in rats is a
reduction in total body sodium and an even greater depletion of brain sodium [11]; how this effect may be related to therapeutic efficacy in man is
unclear. Clinically, a patient on a low-sodium diet will become lithium
toxic on a lesser level of lithium intake, and a patient on a high-sodium
diet will require a higher level of lithium intake to reach a therapeutic

range. Lithium may influence depression by replacing sodium in central nervous system transport systems and it appears not to be so efficiently pumped out of cells as the sodium ion [60,70]; Mendels et al. [74] have shown that lithium affects the sodium pump mechanism in erythrocyte membranes, and they suggest an abnormality in a subgroup of depressed patients in all membrane properties which regulate electrolyte movement. Whether the lithium index (red blood cell/plasma lithium level), as described by Mendels and Frazer [73] will prove to be useful in distinguishing between controls and affectively ill patients, or predicting lithium therapeutic response is still unsettled. The pharmacological mechanisms of lithium are not clearly known nor are its mechanism of action in altering affective disorders.

Neurophysiological Factors in Affective Disorders

Routine studies of electroencephalogram (EEG) patterns have not led to any specific correlations with functional clinical conditions [37]; however, the EEG alterations are associated with modalities used to treat some depressions, such as pharmacotherapy and electroconvulsive therapy. Average evoked responses (AER) have shown augmenting responses in bipolar patients and reducing responses in unipolar patients when both groups are compared to normals [18].

The area in which electroencephalographic study has been used most extensively in affective illness is the study of sleep rhythms. Stage-four sleep has consistently been greatly reduced or absent in studies of depressed patients [49]. Generally rapid-eye-movement (REM) sleep has also been reduced. Tricyclic antidepressant therapy is accompanied by a restoration to a normal sleep pattern which is simultaneously accompanied by an improvement in clinical depression [100]. In depressed patients, when nocturnal patterns of cortisol are correlated with the sleep EEG and the electrooculogram (EOG), the higher than normal peaks of cortisol tend to occur when the patient is awake; and, furthermore, the nocturnal bursts of secretion tend to be associated with periods of awakening [90]. Also, in contrast to normals, a number of depressed patients fail to secrete growth hormone in the early hours of sleep; whether this failure is secondary to the loss of stage three and four sleep or a primary deficit related to depression is unclear [50]. Jouvet [55] has shown considerable evidence that amines, particularly 5HT, play a critical role in sleep mechanisms, although much work remains to be done in understanding the possible interrelationships between sleep, amines, and affective illness.

TREATMENT

Treatment modalities are not the primary concern of this chapter; however, an overall outline of treatment options may be useful in relation to the above discussion. More specific recommendations regarding treatment and management are discussed elsewhere.

The range of treatment for depression, from the "treatment" of talking with a friend to the use of drug or electroconvulsive therapy has been mentioned. Psychotherapy, modified to suit the patient's condition, may also be a useful primary or adjunctive therapy in depressive disorders. A major factor which must be assessed in all depressions is the degree of suicidal risk. If suicide seems to be a risk, the patient should be hospitalized first before necessarily arriving at a specific diagnosis and treatment plan. Since most patients with recurrent depressions or mania have a lifelong vulnerability, following up on these patients on a regular basis — at least every six months throughout life during symptom-free intervals — is appropriate. The critical aspect of regular assessment is most likely to be appreciated by the physician who has treated the patient over a period of time.

CONCLUSION

An attempt has been made in this chapter to give a broad but highly selective review of affective disturbances. No attempt has been made to be exhaustive in terms of particular aspects or perspectives, but an ultimate integrated understanding of affective disturbance in humans must take into account the various aspects that have been discussed. The different classifications of affective disturbance are important as they are an attempt to organize observational data in such a way as to utilize clinical data for a rational diagnostic and treatment approach and to understand the etiological factors in the disorder. In the long run, advances in clinical management are likely to come from an increased basic knowledge of the disorder under consideration.

The psychological aspect of affective disturbance in its broad psychosocial aspects and its internal psychodynamic aspects are crucial for one who is to spend very much time in an intensive way taking treatment responsibility for a patient with an affective disturbance. Acquiring such clinical skills requires a strong interest in patient care.

The genetic, biochemical, and neurophysiological aspects of affective disturbances must be studied in order to gain a grasp of their important role in the understanding and treatment of these disorders. The data described are an indication of the vigorous biological investigation that affective disorders have undergone in recent years. Exciting new understanding of neural transmission and pharmacological specificities are among the areas currently being studied.

REFERENCES

1   Abraham, K. "A short study of the development of the libido, viewed in the light of mental disorders. I. Manic-depressive states and the pregenital levels of the libido." In *Selected papers of Karl Abraham*, ed. E. Jones, pp. 418–433, London: Hogarth Press and Institute of Psychoanalysis, 1948.

2   Abraham, K. "Notes on the psychoanalytical investigation and treatment of manic-depressive insanity and allied conditions." In *Selected papers of Karl Abraham*, ed. E. Jones pp. 137–156, London: Hogarth Press and Institute of Psychoanalysis, 1948.

3   American Psychiatric Association. *Diagnostic and statistical manual of mental disorders*, DSM-II. Washington, D.C.: American Psychiatric Association, 1968.

4   American Psychiatric Association. *Diagnostic and statistical manual of mental disorders*, DSM-III. Draft. Washington, D.C.: American Psychiatric Association, 1977.

5   Anden, N. E. Inhibition of the turnover of the brain dopamine after treatment with the gamma-aminobutyrate 2-oxyglutarate transaminase inhibitor amino-oxyacetic acid (AOAA). *Arch. Psychol.* 283:419–424, 1974.

6   Angst, J. "Zur Atiologie und Nosologie Endogener Depressiver Psychosen." In *Monographien aus dem Gesamtgebiete der Neurologie und Psychiatrie*, no. 112. Berlin: Springer-Verlag, 1966.

7   Angst, J., Basstrup, P., Grof, P., et al. The course of monopolar depression and bipolar psychoses. *Psychiatr. Neurol. Neurochir.* 76:489–500, 1973.

8   Asberg, M., Thoren, P., Traskman, L., Bertilsson, L., and Ringherger, V. Serotonin depression: A biochemical subgroup within the affective disorders? *Science* 191:478–480, 1976.

9   Baer, L. "Electrolyte metabolism in psychiatric disorders." In *Biological psychiatry*, ed. J. Mendels, pp. 199–234, New York: Wiley, 1973.

10   Baer, L., Durell, J., Bunney, W. E., Jr., et al. Sodium balance and distribution in lithium carbonate therapy. *Arch. Gen. Psychiatry* 22:40–44, 1970.

11   Baer, L., Kassir, S., and Fieve, R. R. Lithium-induced changes in electrolyte balance and tissue electrolyte distribution. *Psychopharmacologia* 17:216–224, 1970.

12   Barbeau, A. The pathogenesis of Parkinson's disease: A new hypothesis. *Can. Med. Assoc. J.* 87:802–807, 1962.

13   Beck, A. T. *Depression: clinical, experimental, and theoretical aspects.* New York: Hoeber, 1967.

14   Beckmann, H., and Goodwin, F. K. Antidepressant response to tricyclics

and urinary MHPG in unipolar patients. *Arch. Gen. Psychiatry* 32:17–21, 1975.

15   Bornstein, P. E., Clayton, P. J., et al. The depression of widowhood after thirteen months. *Br. J. Psychiatry* 122:561–566, 1973.

16   Bowlby, J. *Attachment.* New York: Basic Books, 1969.

17   Brown, G. L., Wilson, W. P. and Green, R. L., Jr. "Mental aspects of parkinsonism and their management." In *Parkinson's disease: Rigidity, akinesia, behavior,* vol. 2, ed. J. Siegfried, pp. 265–278. Bern: Huber, 1973.

18   Buchsbaum, M. "Average evoked response: Augmenting reducing in schizophrenia and affective disorders." In *Biology of the major psychoses.* ed. D. X. Freedman, pp. 129–142, New York: Raven Press, 1975.

19   Buena, J. R., and Himwich, H. E. A dualistic approach to some biochemical problems in endogenous depressions. *Psychosomatics* 8:82–94, 1967.

20   Bunney, W. E., Jr., and Davis, J. M. Norepinephrine in depressive reactions: A review. *Arch. Gen. Psychiatry* 13:483–494, 1965.

21   Bunney, W. E., Jr., Goodwin, F. K., and Murphy, D. L. The "switch process" in manic-depressive illness. I. A systematic study of sequential behavioral change. *Arch. Gen. Psychiatry* 27:295–302, 1972.

22   Bunney, W. E., Jr., Goodwin, F. K., and Murphy, D. L. The "switch process" in manic-depressive illness. II. Relationship to catecholamines, REM Sleep, and Drugs. *Arch. Gen. Psychiatry* 27:304–309, 1972.

23   Bunney, W. E., Jr., Goodwin, F. K., and Murphy, D. L. The "switch process" in manic-depressive illness. III. Theoretical implications. *Arch. Gen. Psychiatry* 27:312–317, 1972.

24   Bunney, W. E., Jr., and Murphy, D. L. "The behavioral switch process and psychopathology." In *Biological psychiatry,* ed. J. Mendels, pp. 345–367, New York: Wiley, 1973.

25   Cadoret, R. J. "Genetics of affective disorders." In *Biological foundations of psychiatry,* ed. R. G. Grenell and S. Gabay, pp. 645–652, New York: Raven Press, 1976.

26   Cohen, M. B., Baker, G., Cohen, R. A., et al. An intensive study of twelve cases of manic-depressive psychosis. *Psychiatry* 17:103–138, 1954.

27   Coppen, A. The Biochemistry of affective disorders. *Br. J. Psychiatry* 113:1237–1264, 1967.

28   Coppen, A., and Shaw, D. M. Mineral metabolism in melancholia. *Br. Med. J.* 2:1439–1444, 1963.

29   Coppen, A., Shaw, D. M., and Custain, R. Mineral metabolism in mania. *Br. Med. J.* 1:71–75, 1966.

30   Coppen, A. Shaw, D. M., and Farrell, J. P. Potentiation of the antidepressive affect of a monoamine-oxidase inhibitor by tryptophan. *Lancet* 1:79–81, 1963.

31   Coppen, A., Shaw, D. M., Herzberg, B., and Baggs, R. Trytophan in the treatment of depression. *Lancet* 2:1178–1180, 1967.

32   Cytryn, L., and McKnew, D. H., Jr. Proposed classification of childhood depression. *Am. J. Psychiatry* 129:149–155, 1972.

33   Danowski, T. S., Gow, R. C., Mateer, R. M., et al. Increases in serum thyroxin during uncomplicated pregnancy. *Proc. Soc. Exp. Biol. Med.* 74:323–326, 1950.

34   Darwin, C. *The expression of the emotions in man and animals*. Chicago: University of Chicago Press, 1965.

35   Doe, R. P., and Zinnemann, H. H. The significance of the concentration of the nonprotein bound plasma cortisol concentration in normal subjects, Cushing's syndrome, pregnancy, and during estrogen therapy. Paper delivered at the Forty-second Meeting of the Endocrine Society, 1960.

36   Fieve, R. R., Mendlewicz, J., and Fleiss, J. L. Manic-depressive illness: Linkage with the Xg blood group. *Am. J. Psychiatry* 130:1355–1359, 1973.

37   Fink, M. "The electroencephalogram in clinical psychiatry." In *Biological psychiatry*, ed. J. Mendels, pp. 199–234, New York: Wiley, 1973.

38   Freud, A. *The ego and the mechanisms of defense*. New York: International Universities Press, 1946.

39   Freud, S. "Mourning and melancholia." In *Standard edition of the complete psychological works of Sigmund Freud*, ed. J. Strachey, A. Strachey, and A. Tyson, pp. 237–260. London: Hogarth Press, 1953.

40   Gellhorn, E., and Kiely, W. F. "Autonomic nervous system in psychiatric disorder." In *Biological psychiatry*, ed. J. Mendels, pp. 235–261, New York: Wiley, 1973.

41   Gershon, E. S., Bunney, W. E., Jr., Leckman, J. F., van Eerdemegh, M., and DeBauche, B. The inheritance of affective disorders: A review of data and of hypotheses. *Behav. Genet.* 6:227–261, 1976.

42   Gershon, E. S., Dunner, D. L., and Goodwin, F. K. Toward a biology of affective disorders. *Arch. Gen. Psychiatry* 25:1–15, 1971.

43   Gershon, E. S., and Jonas, W. Z. Erythrocyte-soluble catechol-O-methyl transferase activity in primary affective disorders. *Arch. Gen. Psychiatry* 32:1351–1356, 1975.

44   Gershon, E. S., Mark, A. Cohen, N., Belizon, N., Baron, M., and Knobe, K. E. Transmitted factors in the morbid risk of affective disorders: A controlled study. *J. Psychiatr. Res.* 12:283–299, 1975.

45   Gershon, E. S., Targum, S. D., Kessler, L. R., Mazure, C. M., and Bunney, W. E., Jr. "Genetic studies and biologic strategies in affective disorders." In *Progress in medical genetics*, vol. 2 (new series), pp. 101–164. Philadelphia: Saunders, 1977.

46   Gruen, P. H., Sachar, E. J., Altman, N., et al. Growth hormone response to hypoglycemia in postmenopausal depressed women. *Arch. Gen. Psychiatry* 32:31–33, 1975.

47   Hamilton, J. A. *Postpartum psychiatric problems*. St. Louis: Mosby, 1962.

48   Harlow, H. F. Love in infant monkeys. *Sci. Am.* 200:68–74, 1959.

49   Hawkins, D. R., and Mendels, J. "The psychopathology and psychophysiology of sleep." In *Biological psychiatry*, ed. J. Mendels, pp. 199–234. New York: Wiley, 1973.

50   Hellman, L. Personal communication.

51   Holmes, T. H., and Rahe, R. H. The social readjustment scale. *J. Psychosom. Res.* 11:213–218, 1967.

52   Jacobson, E. *Depression*. New York: International Universities Press, 1971.

53   Janowsky, D. S., Davis, J. M., El-Yousef, M. K., and Sekerke, H. J. A cholinergic-adrenergic hypothesis of mania and depression. *Lancet* 632–635, 1972.

54   Jimerson, D. C., Gordon, E. K., Post, R. M., and Goodwin, F. K. Central

noradrenergic function in man: Vanillylmandelic acid in CSF. *Brain Res.* 99:434– 439, 1975.

55 Jouvet, M. Biogenic amines in states of sleep. *Science* 163:32– 41, 1969.

56 Kallman, F. "Genetic aspects of psychoses." In *Biology of mental health and disease*, Milbank Memorial Fund, pp. 283–302. New York: Hoeber, 1952.

57 Kane, F. J., Jr., Treadway, C. R., and Ewing, J. A. Emotional change associated with oral contraceptives in female psychiatric patients. *Compr. Psychiatry* 10:16–30, 1969.

58 Karacan, I., Williams, R. L., Hursch, C. J., et al. Some implications of the sleep patterns of pregnancy for postpartum emotional disturbances. *Br. J. Psychiatry* 115:929–935, 1969.

59 Karnosh, L., and Hope, J. Puerperal psychoses and their sequelae. *Am. J. Psychiatry* 94:537–550, 1937.

60 Keynes, R. D., and Swan, R. C. The permeability of frog muscle fibres to lithium ions. *J. Physiol.* 147:626– 638, 1959.

61 Klerman, G. L. "Overview of depression." In *Comprehensive textbook of psychiatry*, 2nd Ed., eds. A. M. Freedman, H. I. Kaplan, and B. J. Sadock, pp. 1003–1024. Baltimore: Williams and Wilkins, 1975.

62 Kraepelin, E. *Manic-depressive insanity and paranoia*, ed. G. M. Robertson. Edinburgh: Livingstone, 1921.

63 Lapin, I. P., and Oxenkrug, G. F. Intensification of the central serotonergic processes as a possible determinant of the thymoleptic effect. *Lancet* 1:132–136, 1969.

64 Leff, M. J., Roatch, J. F., and Bunney, W. E., Jr. Environmental factors preceding the onset of severe depressions. *Psychiatry* 33:293–311, 1970.

65 Leonhard, K. *Aufteilung der endogenen Psychosen.* Berlin: Academie-Verlag, 1959.

66 Leonhard, K., Korf, I., and Schulz, H. Die Temperamente in den Familien der Monopolaren und Bipolaren Phasischen Psychosen. *Psychiat. Neurol.* 143:416– 434, 1962.

67 Lindemann, E. Symptomatology and management of acute grief. *Am. J. Psychiatry* 101:141–148, 1944.

68 Maas, J. W. Biogenic amines and depression: Biochemical and pharmacological separation of two types of depression. *Arch. Gen. Psychiatry* 32:1357–1361, 1975.

69 Mahler, M. S. On the first three subphases of the separation-individuation process. *Int. J. Psychoanal.* 53:333–338, 1972.

70 Maizels, M. "Cation transfer in human red cells." In *Membrane transport and metabolism*, ed. A. Kleinzeller and A. Kotyk. London: Academic Press, 1961.

71 McKinney, W. T. *Animal biological/behavioral models relevant to depressive and affecting behavior in humans.* Conference on the Psychological Bases of Early Childhood Depression, National Institutes of Mental Health, Washington, D.C., September, 1975.

72 Mendels, J. *Concepts of depression.* New York: Wiley, 1970.

73 Mendels, J., and Frazer, A. Intracellular lithium concentration and clinical response: Towards a membrane theory of depression. *J. Psychiatr. Res.* 10:9–18, 1973.

74 Mendels, J., and Frazer, A. Alterations in cell membrane activity in depression. *Am. J. Psychiatry* 131:1240–1246, 1974.

75 Mendelson, M. *Psychoanalytic concepts of depression,* 2nd ed. New York: Spectrum, 1974.

76 Menkes, J. H. "Paroxysmal disorders." In *Textbook of child neurology* pp. 420– 462, Philadelphia: Lea and Febiger, 1974.

77 Murphy, D. L., and Weiss, R. Reduced monoamine oxidase activity in blood platelets from bipolar depressed patients. *Am. J. Psychiatry* 128:1351–1357, 1972.

78 Parkes, C. M. Bereavement and mental illness. I A clinical study of grief of bereaved psychiatric patients. II A classification of bereavement reactions. *Br. J. Med. Psychol.* 38:1–26, 1965.

79 Parkinson, J. *An essay on the shaking palsy.* London: Sherwood, Neally, and Jones, 1817.

80 Perris, C. Genetic transmission of depressive psychoses. *Acta Psychiatr. Scand.* 203 (Suppl.):45–52, 1968.

81 Perris, C. "The genetics of affective disorders." In *Biological psychiatry,* ed. J. Mendels, pp. 385– 415, New York: Wiley, 1973.

82 Post, R. M., and Goodwin, F. K. "Approaches to brain amines in psychiatric patients: A revaluation of cerebrospinal fluid studies." In *Handbook of psychopharmacology.* vol. 3, eds. L. L. Iverson, S. D. Iverson, and S. H. Snyder, pp. 147–185. New York: Plenum Press, forthcoming.

83 van Pragg, H., and Korf, J. Endogenous depressions with and without disturbances in the 5-hydroxytryptamine metabolism: A biochemical classification? *Psychopharmacologia* 19:148, 1971.

84 Rennie, T. A. C. Prognosis in manic-depressive insanity. *Am. J. Psychiatry* 98:801– 814, 1942.

85 Robins, E., Munoz, R. A., Martin, S., et al. "Primary and secondary affective disorders." In *Disorders of mood,* ed. J. Zubin and F. A. Freyhan. Proceedings of the American Psychopathological Association, 1970, pp. 33– 45. Baltimore: John Hopkins University Press, 1972.

86 Rosenthal, D. "Genetic studies of manic-depressive psychosis." In *Genetic theory and abnormal behavior,* New York: McGraw-Hill, 1970.

87 Sachar, E. J. "Endocrine factors in psychopathological states." In *Biological psychiatry,* ed. J. Mendels, pp. 175–197, New York: Wiley, 1973.

88 Sachar, E. J., Altman, N., Gruen, P. H., et al. Human growth hormone response to Levodopa: Relation to menopause, depression, and plasma dopa concentration. *Arch. Gen. Psychiatry* 32:502–506, 1975.

89 Sachar, E. J., Finklestein, J., and Hellman, L. Growth hormone response in depressive illness. I. Response to insulin tolerance test. *Arch. Gen. Psychiatry* 25:263–269, 1971.

90 Sachar, E. J., Hellman, L., Roffwarg, H., et al. Disrupted twenty-four-hour patterns of cortisol secretion in depressive illness. *Arch. Gen. Psychiatry* 28:19–24, 1973.

91 Sandler, J., and Joffe, W. G. Towards a basic psychoanalytic model. *Int. J. Psychoanal.* 50:79–90, 1969.

92 Schildkraut, J. J. The catecholamine hypothesis of affective disorders: A review of supporting evidence. *Am. J. Psychiatry* 122:509–522, 1965.

93   Slater, E. Zur Erbpathologie des manisch-depressiven Irreseins: Die Eltern und Kinder von Manisch-Depressiven. *Z. ges. Neurol. Psychiatr.* 163:1–47, 1938.

94   Spitz, R., and Cobliner, W. G. *The first year of life: A psychoanalytic study of normal and deviant development of object relations.* New York: International Universities Press, 1965.

95   Spitzer, R. L., Endicott, J., and Robins, E. Clinical criteria for psychiatric diagnosis. Paper presented at the 128th Annual Meeting of the American Psychiatric Association, 1975.

96   Stenstedt, A. A study in manic-depressive psychosis: Clinical social, and genetic investigations. *Acta Psychiatr. Scand.,* suppl. 79, 1952.

97   Winokur, G., Clayton, P. J., and Reich, T. *Manic-depressive illness.* St. Louis: Mosby, 1969.

98   Winokur, G., and Tanna, V. L. Possible role of X-linked dominant factor in manic-depressive disease. *Dis. Nerv. Syst.* 30:89–94, 1969.

99   Wyatt, R. J., Murphy, D. L., Belmaker, R., et al. Reduced monoamine oxidase in platelets: A possible genetic marker for vulnerability to schizophrenia. *Science* 179:916–918, 1973.

100 Zung, W. W. K. Insomnia and disordered sleep. *Int. Psychiatry Clin.* 7:123–146, 1970.

III
Psychoneurotic Disorders

8

Anxiety Disorders

Ellen McDaniel, M.D.

In the third edition of the *Diagnostic and Statistical Manual of Mental Disorders* (DSM-III) [1], the category anxiety disorders covers the following syndromes: panic disorder, generalized anxiety disorder, phobic disorder, and obsessive-compulsive disorder. The one common element in all of these illnesses is the predominance of the affect of anxiety in the clinical picture. In the obsessive-compulsive disorder, the anxiety is partially controlled by specific compulsive rituals. In phobic disorders, the anxiety is displaced onto particular objects and situations. Anxiety is nonspecific and unfocused in the generalized anxiety disorder, traditionally referred to as anxiety neurosis. Fashion perhaps more than any other consideration has dictated that the phobias and obsessive-compulsive syndromes (to be discussed in separate chapters) are grouped with the free-floating anxiety state under a general category of anxiety disorders. Previously those syndromes were considered separate diagnostic entities.

Theoreticians debate whether fear and anxiety are similar constructs. Usually fear is described as an affective and physiological response to a consciously recognized external source of danger. It is generally short-lived, especially after the danger is removed. Anxiety, in contrast, is an affective and physiological response to a predominantly unconscious internal (intrapsychic) source of danger and is not so easily dispelled [3]. In the panic disorders, the prevalent affect is overwhelming fear, since the danger is typically external and conscious. Fear and anxiety, if viewed as separate constructs, still share many aspects in common, such as the physiological changes and the subjective feeling of danger. Panic disorders probably are more like anxiety states than any other psychopathological syndrome and so are included in this category.

PANIC DISORDER

Definition

The term *panic*, sudden fear without any apparent cause, has derived from the legend of Pan, the Greek god of flocks and shepherds who dwelt in the forests. Half-man and half-animal, with the hair body and lower limbs of a goat, Pan was dreaded by those who had to travel through the forest by night and who superstitiously feared the gloom and loneliness therein [6,12].

Almost everyone has experienced that overwhelming sense of terror in anticipation of an impending personal disaster. This emotional state loosely defines panic. Besides the overall features of anxiety, as described above, there is in addition, as distinguished from generalized anxiety disorder, a specificity of fear and the inability to isolate these fears from the social structure in which it occurs, e.g., fear as a part of an organized or an informal group setting, or fear when in isolation from others.

Etiology

Only in very rare instances, if ever, can panic behavior be attributed to a few factors. There is often a precipitating cause for panic, and that is the immediately perceived danger. This alone, however, cannot explain any individual or group response of panic. Pathogenetic factors are subdivided here into three groups: individual aspects, situational dimensions, and those that apply specifically to organized groups. (McDougall [18] defines an organized group as having the following five characteristics: continuity of existence, awareness of membership, interaction with other organizations, a body of tradition, and differentiation of functions.)

Individual Factors

Critical ability has been described as the "most important single psychological variable related to panic reactions [7]. This ability to evaluate carefully and rationally a situation before jumping to conclusions is related to one's educational level, native intelligence, security and confidence in oneself, absence of superstitious and fatalistic beliefs, and good physical and particularly emotional health. Vulnerability to loss, separation, or annihilation enhance a panic reaction [19]. Developmental problems that render the likelihood of the individual being overwhelmed by narcissistic concerns and sexual (as in homosexual panic) or aggressive impulses heighten the possibility of a chaotic response to stress. Also a previous experience in a crisis may leave a person more likely to interpret a new stimulus as being dangerous [24]. Particularly distressing is the anticipation of suffering or suffocation [31] which, perhaps more than any other physical symptom, conveys the imminency of death [21]. Personality traits as suggestibility, naiveté, and histrionics enhance nonrational behavior.

Situational Factors

A lack of reliable information previous to and concurrently with the occurrence of the perceived threat heightens the possibility of panic. Rumors flourish under those conditions, creating chaos and fear. The perception of a threat for which there has been no previously prepared response adds to the confusion. For example, soldiers under combat sometimes panic when a new weapon is used by the enemy, even though the new weapon may be far less dangerous than the familiar artillery [25]. The cultural existence of a stereotyped situation likely to result in panic contributes to the formation of that type of response [23]. To illustrate, the degree of fear of individuals caught in a movie theater fire may be exaggerated by the cultural notion that people will panic in such a situation. Cues concerning a time allotment before the perceived threat becomes reality and cues concerning the likelihood of escape are further important considerations [10]. A miner trapped underground or a passenger on a plane may not panic because of the keen awareness that flight is not even a possibility. Panic may be delayed or prevented if one believes that there is sufficient time to avoid the disaster. On the other hand, the overly prolonged anticipation of danger is usually more unbearable than the danger itself [19]. A situation where there is the possibility of rapid contagion or mass imitation contributes to the possibility of mass terror [24]. An example of this is a theater audience, which is a physically close but unorganized group. In that setting, one may react with panic to the perception of another's terror without any idea of the source of that individual's fear.

Organized Group Factors

The absence of a leader or the loss of faith in an identified leader renders the individual members of an organized group more susceptible to suggestion, thereby decreasing the members' critical ability [10,24,25]. Organized groups provide for certain physical and psychosocial needs of its members in return for the members' contributions to the groups' goals. Anything which lessens the expectation of support from the group increases the possibility of panic, because there results a deterioration in group cohesiveness and in discipline and a lack of physical or psychological preparation by the group for a crisis. Individual status within a group also affects behavior; the more dominant members of a group are not as impressed by the behavior of less dominant members than is true of the converse situation.

Clinical Description

There are four aspects of the panic reaction: the subjective emotional experience, the cognitive experience, physiological manifestations, and manifest behavior. Emotionally one experiences a sense of a very immediate and direct threat to one's survival, a threat that can usually (but not always) be labeled and localized in space and time. There is an intense fear that something highly valued, as one's physical intactness or psychological stability, is in grave danger. The individual becomes very self-centered, as he begins to lose self-control [23]. Surprise and rage, feelings of powerlessness and helplessness, and an extremely exaggerated sense of vulnerability are typical. Cognitively there is an increased alertness to potential danger. Thinking is nonrational, since alternate courses of action and the consequences of action are not even considered. The collecting and processing of perceptual information fails [5] and a dissociative state may ensue. Physiologically there is increased blood pressure, pupillary dilatation, increased adrenalin output, increased muscle tonus [31], painful vasoconstriction, and increased urinary frequency [23]. Behavior increasingly loses its social dimension. There is a complete breakdown in group cohesion and a lack of any kind of cooperative endeavor [25]. The prominent and usually singular goal is to survive the anticipated danger [30]. This may explain why a devoted mother may abandon her child in a fire. One may witness several different types of behavioral response: sudden immobility or paralysis, passive surrender to fate, sudden death (voodoo death) [20], paradoxical responses as uncontrolled laughter [31] and/or extremely agitated and randomly destructive assaultive behavior [11]. The most typical response is flight towards the direction of perceived safety [2].

Management

Preventive measures can be instituted in many situations where the possibility of panic exists. Once panic has arisen, the presence of empathic, calm, and well-organized leadership becomes essential in management [5,19,20]. Confusion is reduced by the continuing dissemination of information on the local situation, by the squelching of rumors, and the clarification of facts. Anything that enhances a feeling of group cohesiveness assists in decreasing panic, such as activity directed towards assisting one another. Some type of oral gratification (coffee, cigarettes, candy, minor tranquilizers, even aspirin) provides symbolic mothering and heightens the feeling of belonging. Marked physical inactivity can escalate counterproductive fantasy formation. Individuals may need opportunities for immediate ventilation of feeling before being able to calm down. Sedatives can be used but they may have a paradoxical effect and are usually not indicated. Behavior modification (relaxation training, modeling, thought-stopping instructions, and behavior rehearsal) has been successfully tried [26]. The crucial element in management is that reparative measures be instituted as quickly as possible. Prolonged panic may develop into a traumatic neurosis with far-reaching sequelae.

GENERALIZED ANXIETY DISORDER

Definition

The most common definition of a generalized anxiety disorder (anxiety state, anxiety neurosis) recognizes a difference between anxiety and fear. Anxiety in this syndrome is nonspecific, free-floating, and quantitatively beyond the optimal level necessary for adaptive functioning and originates (at least according to prevalent theory) from unconscious conflicts. Anxiety occurs in nearly all psychopathological states, but this affect predominates the symptom picture in the generalized anxiety disorder in the absence of other marked disturbances, such as loss of reality testing, delusions, or specific phobias. The free-floating anxiety is accompanied by physiological symptoms resembling those described for panic disorders.

Epidemiology

Prevalence of generalized anxiety disorders in a normal population varies between 2.0 to 4.7 percent [15]. In a cardiology practice this figure increases to between 10 to 14 percent (a synonym used for anxiety neurosis has been cardiac neurosis). In a study conducted at Maudsley Hospital in London, 8 percent of all outpatients suffered primarily from anxiety states. Females predominate over males in incidence, approximately two to one in a general medical practice. In a psychiatric practice, the sex ratio becomes more equal. The mean age at onset is in the midtwenties although symptoms are often present for about five years before treatment is sought. The age range of patients is from sixteen years to about sixty years; the youngest patients are more likely to be female. Anxiety starting after age forty is much more commonly part of a depressive disorder.

Etiology and Pathogenesis

Since anxiety is actually a theoretical abstraction of a distressing subjective sensation, the etiological factors supposedly producing it are as numerous as are theories on the production of conflict. Fischer [9] describes these different conceptualizations of anxiety. The major viewpoints are summarized here to provide an appreciation of the magnitude of meanings and causes of pathological free-floating anxiety, some of which are contradictory to each other and to the introductory definition of anxiety.

1   *Orthodox Freudian approach.* Neurotic anxiety is derived from childhood conflicts over sexual and aggressive drives. These drives can conflict with the individual's ideal self-image, his prohibitions, and his morals (superego anxiety); they can arouse an anticipation of danger to one's physical or emotional integrity (as in castration anxiety); and/or they can threaten one's attachment to significant others (as in separation anxiety). The anxiety is irrational; the sources are unconscious; and the conflicts are intrapsychic.

2   *Neo-Freudian approach.* The interpersonal conflicts rather than the intrapsychic conflicts are of primary importance here. Anxiety reaches pathological proportions when the expectations of failure in relationships with significant others predominate.

3   *Learning-theory approach.* Learning theorists emphasize the importance of the principle of homeostasis: the tendency of all organisms to maintain a constant and minimal level of excitation. Learning takes place when a drive is reduced as a consequence of some response. Fear and anxiety are considered synonymous (which is not true for the two previous theoretical approaches). Anxiety is an affect which may become attached to previously neutral stimuli; it can motivate or reinforce behavior. Learning theorists postulate that the most common type of neurotic problem is one in which an approach-avoidance type of conflict is present, where the goal has both positive and negative aspects.

4   *Existential approach.* Anxiety is felt to be an inherent part of one's realization of alternatives, of choices in life. An abnor-

mally anxious person is one caught between two mutually exclusive possibilities and is unable to commit himself to choose one.

Regardless of how the production of anxiety is theoretically conceptualized, it is an affect which signals some type of impending inner disaster or loss of self-esteem. It occurs when an individual suffers a breakdown in his defensive and adaptive aspects of his psychological functioning.

Clinical Description

The typical patient suffering a generalized anxiety disorder experiences a very exaggerated sensation of dread, a panicky feeling without any specific external source of stress. Death thoughts are not uncommon [29]. Physiological symptoms, such as increased tone of skeletal muscles, precordial pressure and pain, tachycardia, palpitations, sweating, dizziness, hyperventilation, light-headedness, tremor, nausea, diarrhea, and cramps are typical complaints [3]. There is a general restlessness and irritability, not infrequently accompanied by insomnia and appetite changes. A time perspective to the future has been described [14]; the patient fears that something bad is about to happen rather than a fear that something detrimental has already taken place. The symptoms characteristically occur in identifiable episodes lasting minutes to hours. The patient may feel quite comfortable in between episodes, or he may be chronically anxious with periods of exaggerated terror. The frequency of attacks can vary from one episode every several months to repeated attacks within a day. The intensity of feeling may also vary from mild apprehension to abject terror. The degree of incapacitation can be great, particularly if the individual severely restricts his life in an effort to reduce stress. However with many patients, a casual acquaintance may never notice any disturbance in the patient [17].

Margaret is a nineteen-year-old college sophomore. She is intelligent, attractive, and has always enjoyed a wide circle of friends. One day while walking to class with her boyfriend, she suddenly and without warning developed a sensation of terror. She felt that at any moment something terrible was going to happen to her. Her boyfriend commented on her pallor and confused look, but Margaret denied any difficulty and entered the classroom. Sitting at her desk was barely tolerable. She felt that at any moment she was going to scream or run aimlessly from the room. Chest pains and gastrointestinal distress accompanied the feelings. Within ten minutes the anxiety subsided. Margaret could not identify any cause for the panic feeling, but when the attack occurred a week later in her apartment and shortly after that in the middle of the night, she went to the emergency room of a community hospital. Medical history, physical examination, and an electrocardiogram (EEG) gave no evidence of an organic cause. She was referred to a psychiatrist for insight-oriented psychotherapy.

Differential Diagnosis

The first differential diagnosis that must be made is from organic illness. Anxiety attacks can be a typical symptom in alcohol or drug intoxication or withdrawal. For example, patients on amphetaminelike anorectic drugs can have symptoms of anxiety and agitation. Withdrawal from minor tranquilizers, narcotics, and barbiturates can produce symptoms similar to anxiety states, and so may even excessive caffeine intake [4].

An allergic response can cause psychological manifestations. Allergic etiology should be considered if the symptoms clear with steroid treatment, if bowel symptoms predominate the clinical picture, or if there are concomitant nasal symptoms, hives, vertigo (not light-headedness), or seizures [13]. Paroxysmal tachycardia is another differential to be made. Usually in anxiety states the heart rate is less than 140 beats per minute, whereas in paroxysmal tachycardia, the heart rate is usually between 140 to 220 beats per minute. In the history, sometimes one hears an association of these attacks with postural changes. An ECG is diagnostic. Thyrotoxicosis can resemble anxiety attacks with the following differences: In thyrotoxicosis the tremor is fine (it is coarse in anxiety), the palms are warm and pink (versus cold and clammy in anxiety), and the tachycardia does not slow to normal during sleep. Diagnosis is made by laboratory tests, e.g., increased protein-bound iodine, increased uptake of radioiodine, and raised levels of serum triiodothyronine. Pheochromocytoma, a very rare disease, may likewise appear like an anxiety state, but one also sees other signs of illness, such as very high blood pressure. Large amounts of catecholamines and vanillylmandelic acid are found in the urine [15]. Hyperinsulinism and hypoglycemia are two further considerations.

Another type of differential to be made is from the depressive reactions. Neurotic depressions often manifest symptoms of insomnia, agitation, a sensation of impending doom, and appetite disturbances. Some clinicians feel that all of the nonpsychotic affective disorders are in fact one continum rather than separate disease entities. In some recent studies [8,22] results indicate that a separation of patients into different diagnostic groups (depressed and anxious) is warranted.

Prognosis

Positive prognostic signs include the use of defense mechanisms which do not lead to a serious loss of reality testing, whether the anxiety is determined more by current environmental circumstances than by long-standing personal conflicts, and the awareness by the patient of external and internal cues to the production of anxiety. Unfavorable prognostic signs include the use of projection, a paranoid sensitivity in interpersonal relationships, and the prominent use of a primitive defensive structure [28].

Generally speaking, the greater the degree of the presenting anxiety, the more effective any given therapy is [18]. This disorder is not considered to be commonly debilitating or one of the more serious psychiatric illnesses. However, some patients who suffer from anxiety attacks may be unable to function in any productive or meaningful way.

Management

Most commonly patients with a generalized anxiety disorder are treated as outpatients. Three major therapeutic approaches are used by different clinicians — supportive psychotherapy, insight-oriented psychotherapy, and behavior therapy. The particular choice of therapy depends on the patient's desires, the therapist's orientation, and practical issues, such as availability of time and of trained personnel. Some of the behavior modification techniques used include assertive training, role playing, and teaching relaxation [15]. Behavior therapy and insight-oriented psychotherapy were rated as essentially equal in benefiting work and social adjustment in one study conducted on outpatients [27]. Insight therapy (psychoanalysis or psychoanalytic psychotherapy), however, is the only treatment approach that offers the hope of resolving intrapsychic conflicts in such a way as to permit the individual more long-term flexibility and relief from symptoms. Supportive therapy involves the positive effects of the relationship with a nonjudgmental, interested, and tactful therapist [16]. This type of treatment also can include environmental manipulation to reduce stress. Minor tranquilizers may be used but their application is very debatable because of the addictive potential of these drugs.

REFERENCES

1   American Psychiatric Association. *Diagnostic and statistical manual of mental disorders,* DSM-III. Draft. Washington, D.C.: American Psychiatric Association, 1977.

2   Arana, I. "Prognostication of psychiatric disorders." In *Psychiatric foundations of medicine,* vol. 5, eds. G. U. Balis, L. Wurmser, E. McDaniel, and R. G. Grenell. Boston: Butterworths, 1978.

3   Branch, C. H. H. Preface of *Aspects of anxiety.* Philadelphia: Lippincott, 1968.

4   British Medical Journal. Editorial: Anxiety symptoms and coffee drinking. *Br. Med. J.* 1:296–297, 1975.

5   Brosin, H. W. "Panic States and Their Treatment." *Am. J. Psychiatry* 100:54–61, 1943.

6   Bulfinch, T. *The Age of Fable.* New York: Heritage Press, 1942.

7   Cantril, H. *The invasion from mars.* Princeton, N.J.: Princeton University Press, 1952.

8   Downing, R. W., and Rickels K. Mixed anxiety-depression: Fact or myth? *Arch. Gen. Psychiatry* 30:312–317, 1974.

9   Fischer, W. F. *Theories of anxiety.* New York: Harper and Row, 1970.

10   Gaten, S., and Allen, V. L. Likelihood of escape, likelihood of danger, and panic behavior. *J. Soc. Psychol.* 87:29–36, 1972.

11   Goldston, J., ed. *Panic and morale.* New York: International Universities Press, 1958.

12   Grimal, P., ed. *Larousse world mythology.* New York: Hamlyn, 1973.

13   Hubbard, R. C. Acute anxiety reactions secondary to food allergy. *Conn. Med.* 40:188–189, 1976.

14   Krauss, H. H. Anxiety: The dread of a future event. *J. Individ. Psychol.* 23:88–93, 1967.

15   Lader, I., and Marks, J. *Clinical anxiety.* New York: Grune and Stratton, 1972.

16   Manekshr, S., and Harry T. Anxiety neurosis in general practice. *Br. J. Clin. Pract.* 28:65–66, 1974.

17   Marks, I., and Lader, M. Anxiety states (anxiety neurosis): A review. *J. Nerv. Ment. Dis.* 156:3–18, 1973.

18   McDougall, W. *The group mind.* Cambridge: Cambridge University Press, 1920.

19   Meerloo, J. A. M. *Patterns of panic.* New York: International Universities Press, 1950.

20   Meerloo, J. A. M. First-aid in acute panic states. *Am. J. Psychother.* 5:367–371, 1951.

21   Nayyar, R. A night of panic in the high Sierras. *Am. J. Nurs.* 73:1218–2119, 1973.

22   Prusoff B., and Klerman, G. L. Differentiations depressed from anxious neurotic outpatients. *Arch. Gen. Psychiatry* 30:302–309, 1974.

23   Quarantelli, E. L. Abstract of "A Study of Panic: Its nature, types, and conditions." Master's thesis, Chicago: University of Chicago, 1953.

24 Sargent, S. S., and Williamson, R. C. *Social psychology.* New York: Roland Press, 1958.

25 Schultz, D. P. Panic in organized collectivities. *J. Soc. Psychol.* 63:353–359, 1964.

26 Shelton, J. L. Murder strikes and panic follows: Can behavior modification help?" *Behav. Ther.* 4:706–708, 1973.

27 Sloane, R. B., Staples, F. R., Cristol, A. H., Yorkston, A., and Whipple, K. Short-term analytically oriented psychotherapy versus behavior therapy. *Am. J. Psychiatry* 132:373–377, 1975.

28 Smith, G. J. W., Sjoholm, L., and Nielzen, S. Individual factors affecting the improvement of anxiety during a therapeutic period of 1.5–2 Years. *Acta Psychiatr. Scand.* 52:7–22, 1975.

29 Spalt, L. Death thoughts in hysteria, antisocial personality, and anxiety neurosis. *Psychiatr. Q.* 48:441–444, 1974.

30 Titchener, J. L., and Kapp, F. T. Family and character change at Buffalo Creek. *Am. J. Psychiatry* 133:295–299, 1976.

31 Trautman, E. C. Fear and panic in Nazi concentration camps: A biosocial evaluation of the chronic anxiety syndrome. *Int. J. Soc. Psychiatry* 10:134–141, 1964.

9

Hysterical Neurosis

Ellen McDaniel, M.D.

Hysteria is a term used to describe a wide variety of behaviors which have been grouped together by perhaps no more than a shared historical background. For the reader to appreciate fully how all of these diverse and sometimes unrelated manifestations of mental life can be grouped under the umbrella of hysteria, a comprehensive study of the history of this "disease" would be necessary.

Common definitions of hysteria include (1) a relatively unchanging pattern of behavior called a character type (the hysterical or histrionic personality disorder), (2) a psychological conflict which is expressed somatically (conversion reaction), and (3) an altered state of consciousness or identity (amnesia, depersonalization, fugue, and multiple personality, collectively called dissociative reactions). Three less common but not unfamiliar uses of the designation hysteria include (4) a transient psychotic reaction precipitated by an environmental stress (hysterical or factitious psychosis), (5) an old term once used to refer to phobias (anxiety hysteria), and (6) a syndrome describing patients with multiple physical complaints, frequent hospitalizations, and polysurgery (Briquet's disorder).

Slater [61], whose position is considered extreme, questioned whether anything could be found that was particular to the diagnosis of hysteria. He investigated hereditary factors, family history, early developmental experiences, physical aspects, psychodynamic aspects, symptomatology, and concurrent but different psychiatric diagnosis. He concluded that nothing seemed specific to being labeled hysteric except that most of the patients so labeled were clinically difficult patients. Slater commented that if the diagnosis was obscure or if treatment was unsuccessful, the doctor might be more prone to label the patient as an hysteric, adding that hysteria, of all diagnoses, is least apt to be made in a spirit of detachment.

Other writers have addressed themselves to particular subgroups of hysteria. Chodoff [14] was one of the earlier skeptics who questioned the validity of including conversion disorders under the hysteria label. He observed that conversion phenomena are seen in many and diverse personality structures. In a later paper he and Lyons [16] recommended that conversion hysteria be relabeled conversion reaction and that a conversion disorder need not be a primary diagnosis but can be regarded as a symptom in other illnesses. It is interesting however, that in the *Diagnostic and Statistical Manual of Mental Disorders-II* (DSM-II) [3] published in 1968, and in the proposed DSM-III [4], drafted in 1977, conversion disorder is still placed under the heading of hysterical neurosis or hysterical disorders.

The confusion continues when the dissociative disorders are examined. As far back as 1943, Stengel [64] commented that one would not be correct to call a fugue state an hysterical symptom, as fugues are seen in a variety of psychiatric disorders. Kirshner [42] concluded from his studies that, like conversion reactions, dissociative reactions are more a symptom than a specific diagnostic category, in that people with this diagnosis "do not share any important characteristics apart from being psychiatric patients."

If one were to examine the other definitions of hysteria, the controversy does not cease. Perhaps the most that can be said about all six "scientific" meanings of hysteria is that they share no common etiology, pathogenesis, epidemiology, clinical picture, or prognosis; thus, they cannot be rigidly defined as a group. The singular element tying all of these phenomena together is their history. In my opinion, to group these symptoms (or syndromes) under the heading of hysterical disorders perpetuates the historical accident; and yet the state of knowledge and tradition in psychiatry is such that it still seems to be the most acceptable grouping for conveying information. As Lewis [46] stated in his discussion of the confusion over the term, "despite great controversy and little data to validate the use of the term, hysteria as a word seems solidly entrenched."

HISTORY

The history of psychiatry is in large part an elaboration of the history of hysteria. Hysteria was first associated with sexual problems as far back as

1900 B.C. In ancient Egyptian medicine conversion symptoms were etiologically attributed to the migration of the uterus to the affected body parts. This began a 4000-year-old association of hysteria with the female sex. In Hippocratic writings about 400 B.C. the word hysteria was coined. It derives from the Greek word *hystera* which means uterus. Aretaeus of Cappadocia around A.D. 100 observed that conversion symptoms also occurred in men, but his work on this aspect was completely ignored. Galen (A.D. 129–199) postulated retention of uterine secretions due to sexual abstinence as the cause of hysteria and also recognized a similar syndrome in males. What is interesting and puzzling about that era of hysteria is that, although hysteria is and was then attributed at least in part to sexual problems, the sexual drive was considered a very natural and open issue in ancient Egypt and Greece.

From the time of Augustine in the fourth century until the Renaissance of the fourteenth and fifteenth centuries, hysteria changed from being considered an illness, which was the business of physicians, to being a state of bewitchment and possession by devils, thus making hysteria a religious matter. Symptoms remained unchanged and consisted primarily of loss of diverse functions and convulsions, but now sex became a highly conflictual matter. Sexual delusions started to appear in the clinical picture.

As the Dark Ages passed hysteria once again became a medical matter. Paracelsus (1493–1541) rejected supernatural explanations for the disease but returned nonproductively to the ancient uterine theories. He did stress the importance of the unconscious, but this idea was ignored until Freud's investigations over four centuries later. Edward Jorden (1578–1632) was one of the first physicians to place the hysteric's difficulties in the brain rather than in the uterus. However, like others of his time (Charles Lepois, William Harvey, and Thomas Willis), he combined uterine and cerebral theories when formulating treatment plans. An understanding of the emotional difficulties in hysterical patients thus remained very limited by this essentially anatomical and neurological approach.

The picture began to change when Franz Anton Mesmer (1734–1815) introduced hypnosis in the treatment of hysteria. Jean-Martin Charcot (1825–1892) used hypnosis to reproduce hysterical symptoms in his patients and soon recognized the importance of suggestibility and psychological stress in producing the clinical manifestations. Sigmund Freud's analytic investigations into the psyche of hysterical patients revolutionized psychiatry. Freud's earliest patients had classical loss-of-function symptoms but also manifested considerable ego pathology. He labeled these patients as hysterics, although clinically they resembled more closely the hysterical (factitious) psychotics of today. Freud originally gave some credence to Breuer's theory, that these patients had had some early psychologically traumatic sexual experience which had occurred while the patient was in a hypnoid state, i.e., an altered state of consciousness, although he stressed the role of conflict already in his first publications about this topic. This experience remained unconscious and exerted a detrimental effect on the individual. One can see at this point the connection of dissociative reactions (i.e., those characterized by an altered state of consciousness) and of psychotic illnesses with conversion disorders. At any rate, Freud revised his psychodynamic theory as he began to appreciate the importance of fantasy and childhood sexuality. Briquet's syndrome is the most recent addition to the disorders grouped under hysteria. In my opinion the focus on physical symptoms may be the thin string which ties the syndrome to conversion disorders, the oldest definition of hysteria.

COMMON MANIFESTATIONS

Five common definitions of hysteria are examined: hysterical personality disorder, hysterical (factitious) psychosis, dissociative disorders, conversion disorders, and Briquet's disorder. The first two share some pathogenetic and descriptive features: conflict over sexuality, varying degrees of oral developmental difficulties, and a dramatic and provocative social presentation. The last two disorders involve somatic expressions of psychological problems. The appropriateness of classifying all of these disorders in one group has been questioned by many writers, but tradition has kept them nosologically linked.

Hysterical Personality

DEFINITION AND CLASSIFICATION
The hysterical or histrionic personality refers to a constellation of behavior traits that are relatively characteristic and habitual for an individual, regardless of the quality of the external reality. Most commonly these traits include [16] egocentricity, exhibitionistic behavior, a dramatic and exaggerated form of communication, frequent and unpredictable mood swings accompanied by emotional outbursts, low frustration tolerance, emotional shallowness in relationships, sexualization of nonsexual matters and relationships, and a dependent and demanding quality in the latter. Other traits [21] include an active and direct engagement with humans, increased suggestibility, and a dislike or avoidance of the exact and mundane.

This disorder actually is included in chapter 15; however, because I believe that the hysterical (histrionic) character type may be the most appropriate clinical entity to warrant the diagnosis of hysteria, it is included here for further emphasis and exploration. The hysterical personality, unlike conversion disorders, dissociative reactions, or Briquet's disorder, has been intensively investigated for etiological factors, pathogenetic mechanisms, quality of object relationships, and prognosis. It can be more rigorously defined and thus may facilitate the understanding of a more cohesive group of individuals than the other subgroups of hysterical disorders seem to be.

EPIDEMIOLOGY

Hysterical personality disorders are found in all adult age groups. Women are much more frequently diagnosed with this disorder than men. Sociocultural class in Western civilization does not seem to be significantly correlated.

ETIOLOGY AND PATHOGENESIS

Character disorders can be conceptualized as behavioral defenses against dysphoria that originates from unresolved intrapsychic conflict and furthermore reflect a partial failure of ego development in the various stages of psychosexual growth. Finally, the behavior can be seen as a type of adaptation to the demands of the outer world and the individual's psychic environment. Based on these concepts, one widely held dynamic explanation of the hysterical personality states that the patient has unresolved conflicts from the oedipal period of development. Unconscious incestuous fantasies interfere with current object relationships. Anxiety results over sexual issues in heterosexual relationships. Repression and regression become the predominant defenses used. Behavior caricatures the oedipal age child, i.e., Daddy's little girl or Mommy's strong boy. People are not appreciated as separate others but instead are seen more as transference figures with whom the childhood conflicts can be reenacted.

Preoedipal determinants have also been emphasized and sometimes are even considered of greater importance in the development of the hysterical personality. Among the preoedipal elements stressed are the insufficient development of anxiety tolerance, impaired reality testing, and defective organizing function of the ego [44]. One writer [49] spoke of the presence of excessive gratification of oral-receptive needs in family histories, whereas another writer [34] described significant maternal deprivation in the oral stage which encourages the female child to turn to the father for both maternal needs and sexual needs.

Sociocultural factors in the development and diagnosis of hysteria include greater cultural acceptance and, more importantly, encouragement of dependency, helplessness, and moodiness in females.

Mrs. P, a forty-two-year-old housewife sought psychiatric help after her oldest son was picked up for illicit drug use. She appeared for the interview dressed in a fashion popular with the teenagers. She wore a lot of makeup and took considerable interest in her physical appearance. Although socially poised, engaging, and quite intelligent, she portrayed herself as helpless and confused when confronted with the demands of handling an adolescent child. Mrs. P spoke in a dramatic manner, constantly building up to an emotional climax in her story but never quite reaching the conclusion because of her distractions with unnecessary details and subplots. She seemed genuinely concerned about her child but never remained at the same emotional plane for long in the interview. Anger, humor, sadness, and apathy were easily communicated. Mrs. P. would occasionally ask the interviewer personal questions about himself which were unrelated to the presenting problem. She seemed very concerned about the impression that she was making. Thought associations were coherent and logical, and there was no evidence of delusions or hallucinations.

DIFFERENTIAL DIAGNOSIS

Hysterical personality disorders have been subdivided by the severity of the pathology. Easser and Lesser [21], differentiated a group of individuals who employ hysterical mechanisms and behave as an exaggerated example of the hysteric but who differ in several important aspects. These patients, referred to as hysteroids, have more erratic and less successful adaptational functioning in work and other critical areas of living. The quality of their object relationships reflects very infantile needs; the patients often are loners and vacillate in their few ongoing relationships from extreme idealization to unrelenting depreciation of the persons involved. Family life is much more disturbed and chaotic for the hysteroid, particularly in the preoedipal stages of development. Oral problems predominate. Fantasies are a major source of gratification and reflect, in addition to the other factors mentioned, less development and integration of ego functions. Zetzel [70] divided hysterics into four clinical groups, the latter two groups resembling the hysteroid and the other two including quite engaging and successful individuals. In regard to the fairly recent surge of literature on narcissistic and borderline personality disturbances, many of those previously classified as sick hysterics or hysteroids could be reclassified into these newer diagnostic categories.

PROGNOSIS AND MANAGEMENT

Prognosis is favorable for the healthier hysterics. Social success and ability to cope with reality may remain, even if the patient receives minimal treatment. However, internal distress may significantly interfere with the person's capacity to experience much of life in a positive way, and then long-term insight-oriented therapy is recommended. Therapy should be directed at clarifying the defensive meanings of the behavior patterns and at connecting affects with events. As the character defenses are worked through, the underlying conflicts could be examined and resolved. For the hysteric not motivated for long-term treatment or for an individual too psychologically vulnerable to tolerate an uncovering approach, supportive therapy would be in order. This includes encouragement of adaptive behavior, empathic nonjudgmental reflections of understanding, advice, provision of reality testing, and an opportunity to ventilate feelings and attitudes.

One needs to be alert to severe underlying ego pathology in an hysteric who does not appear psychotic but is rapidly escalating in the portrayal of confusion, self-destructive exhibitionistic behavior, and manipulativeness. The escalation may signal the breakdown of the hysterical defenses in a fragmenting ego structure. Countertransference reactions require careful monitoring. The clinician is sometimes tempted to respond in a parental, seductive, or rejecting manner to the provocative communications of the hysteric.

Hysterical (Factitious) Psychosis

DEFINITION AND CLASSIFICATION

Hysterical (factitious) psychosis is a functional psychosis with an acute onset precipitated by environmental stress. The clinical picture is dramatic and includes bizarre behavior and thought content. Recovery is usually rapid and recurrence is unusual.

In the final form of the DSM-III, to be published in 1979, factitious psychosis will be given official recognition for the first time. This disorder is considered a psychosis because the patient experiences ego fragmentation with loss of reality testing. If the association of this disorder with hysterical character formation is emphasized, it correctly belongs under hysterical disorders. If one emphasizes the precipitating agent (the acute environmental stress), then this disorder is classified under stress-related disturbances (i.e., a brief situational psychosis). If the cultural influence on the type of symptoms manifested is stressed, the disorder might be considered a culturally determined psychosis. The nosological differences reflect the divergent ways of conceptualizing mental illness.

EPIDEMIOLOGY

Statistics are very difficult to obtain for this disorder because of the lack of official recognition. In the cases in the literature, hysterical psychosis occurs in both men and women although females predominate; it is more likely to occur in the young adult years and is slightly more common in the lower socioeconomic groups.

ETIOLOGY AND PATHOGENESIS

The individual who develops an hysterical psychosis is most commonly described as an hysterical character type. The psychosis results from the collapse of this adaptation [37]. Several authors emphasize the importance of oral developmental problems in the etiology of this illness but add that the orality is better integrated than in schizophrenia. Noble [52] described these patients' mothers as being superficially efficient but inwardly rejecting and dependent. The fathers are commonly inadequate and depreciated family members. Noble hypothesized that the hysterical defenses (repression and regression) are utilized in defending against intense oral anxieties. He felt that these patients do not develop schizophrenia because they had a significant loving relationship somewhere in their childhood, as with a household employee or a relative, and that the maternal relationships had positive as well as destructive qualities. Richman and White [59] placed a central role on the family dynamics and viewed the psychosis as an acting-out of a shared fantasy, with the psychotic symptoms covertly if not overtly sanctioned by the family. Pankow [55] emphasized the importance of the body image and felt that the psychosis is connected with difficulties in self-identity.

Most authors agree on the importance of current environmental stress as a precipitating factor. Bower [8], describing the dynamics of this condition, wrote that there is an incomplete and temporary withdrawal as an adaptive maneuver when confronted with an overwhelming environmental stress. The patient becomes symptomatic because the usual environmental escape routes are barred and the patient cannot change the stressful situation. If, however, the stress is removed, a high rate of recovery without recurrence is typical. Precipitating environmental stresses vary. Actual or anticipated object loss is a common one. Greenberg [27] reported a case of a patient who had an acute psychotic episode immediately after watching a suggestive television program. Interpersonal difficulties with significant others, such as a spouse, are cited by others [50,63].

CLINICAL DESCRIPTION

Hollender and Hirsch [39], writing a representative description of the hysterical psychosis, concluded that the illness begins suddenly and dramatically, usually as a reaction to a traumatic event. Symptoms may include hallucinations, delusions, feelings of depersonalization, and other grossly unusual behavior. Affect may be quite appropriate. If it is disturbed, it is usually in the direction of volatility rather than depression or flatness. If a thought disorder is present, it is circumscribed, transient, and frequently occurs during an emotional outburst. The thought disorder is more reality connected, with more wish-fulfilling qualities, than one sees in schizophrenic patients. However, its very presence indicates ego disruption. The acute episode rarely lasts longer than three weeks and may recede suddenly. No residue remains, and the chances are very great that there will be no recurrence.

Ann is a twenty-six-year-old housewife. She was raised by relatives after the age of six years because her mother was institutionalized following a psychotic breakdown. Ann's marriage was stormy, and she became involved in an affair. On the day of her breakdown, Ann's affair was discovered by her husband, who threatened to leave. Ann became very agitated and anxious. She felt that people were poisoning her food, that her deceased father was calling her name, and that her blood was turning into ice. She complained of feeling like she was watching herself act, as though she was standing at a distance from her body. She was hospitalized. Family members expressed their concern, and her husband decided to work at improving their marital relationship. The patient was ready for discharge at the end of two weeks.

DIFFERENTIAL DIAGNOSIS

Two main differentials may be made — from culturally determined psychotic episodes and from schizophrenia. Various authors debate whether a culturally induced psychosis might in fact be the same phenomenon as an hysterical psychosis. Langness [43] is one of many who describe a form of behavior which appears bizarre to an outsider of a particular culture and is referred to as a culturally determined psychosis but has also been referred to as an hysterical psychosis. Hirsch and Hollander [37] in a second paper on this subject stated that the cultural psychosis is a different entity than the true hysterical psychosis. They wrote that the culturally sanctioned dramatic behavior communicates a difficulty in coping with environmental stresses because of individual psychopathology but that the communication of this distress appears psychotic only to the outsider. Within the cultural setting, the behavior represents good reality testing in a particular sociocultural context. The true hysterical psychosis, in contrast, is a disruption and breakdown of ego boundaries.

Bower [8] gave some criteria differentiating hysterical psychosis from schizophrenia. He states that (1) regression never proceeds to a deep level; (2) deterioration is conspicuously absent; (3) recovery with or without treatment is the rule, with the return of the personality to its premorbid level; (4) recurrence is unusual; there is not a cyclical pattern, as in the

manic-depressive psychosis, or the common pattern of remissions and exacerbations, as in chronic schizophrenia; (5) onset is usually preceded by
an obvious traumatic environmental event; and (6) the disorder often
presents as a paranoid state, a pseudoschizophrenic reaction, or a confusional state resembling that which accompanies organic disease.

PROGNOSIS AND MANAGEMENT

If the environmental stress is removed or if assistance is given to the patient in coping with the acute situation, the psychosis should recede from
within hours to approximately three weeks. The underlying characterological difficulties of course remain. No residue from the psychosis
should be anticipated.

The immediate stress has to be clarified and dealt with, either by environmental manipulation or by a directive kind of counseling. Medication with a minor or major tranquilizer to reduce anxiety may be tried.
Brief hospitalization is indicated if suicide is a serious threat or if the patient cannot function in the outside community. Depending on the assessment of the family situation, family therapy may be indicated. If the underlying characterological difficulties are to be resolved, long-term
treatment must be instituted. One may decide, however, to limit the therapy goals to management of the acute crises.

Conversion Disorders

DEFINITION

In 1950 Franz Alexander [2] divided psychosomatic illnesses into three
categories: conversion hysteria, vegetative neurosis, and psychogenic
organ disturbances. Conversion hysteria, which was clearly differentiated
from the other two, was considered to be a symbolically meaningful attempt to resolve unconscious psychological conflict. The illness involved
either those body parts under voluntary nervous system control or those
parts concerned with sensory perception. Typical symptoms included
blindness, muteness, numbness and paralysis, i.e., the classical loss-of-
function symptoms. Alexander's other two categories of psychosomatic
diseases, vegetative neurosis and psychogenic organ disturbance, reflected
chronic emotional stress, had no specific symbolic meaning, and involved
structures under involuntary innervation. Rangell [58] was one of the first
writers to question this definition of conversion, as did Alexander himself
in his later works. Rangell proposed separating the conversion process
from the concept of hysteria. Although he felt that the somatic changes
symbolically represented unconscious conflict, he recognized that this
could occur in any psychopathological condition. Rangell conceptualized

conversions as a regressive movement which reflected many different psychological problems and not as a specific syndrome. He stated that these conversion processes involved both the autonomic and voluntary nervous system but excluded somatic-to-psychic phenomena. George Engel [12, 23] broadened the concept of what was by then called conversion reaction. He wrote that any body part capable of achieving mental representation could be involved in a conversion process; in fact, the conversion process is but one component in the development of many diseases which heretofore have been considered as exclusively organic, e.g., infections and neoplasms. The ultimate organic pathology manifests the effects of a combination of psychological factors, predisposing biological factors, nervous system feedback mechanisms, the environmental situation, and a plethora of other events. Loss-of-function symptoms would thus be a very restricted example of conversion disorders.

CLASSIFICATION

Traditionally conversion reactions are classified as a neurotic illness, symbolically representing intrapsychic conflict in a person with good reality testing. However, since the 1950s numerous studies have supported the proposition that conversion reactions occur in every conceivable psychiatric illness as well as accompany other stressful situations. Two questions can be raised: How should conversion disorders be defined? Should they be conceptualized as a particular psychological process which *may* manifest itself in symptom formation, or should this phenomenon be given a diagnostic rank of its own?

EPIDEMIOLOGY

Statistics vary according to how conversion disorders are defined. The mean age of patients given that label is close to 40 years old [71,47,51]. The age range reported, excluding pediatrics, is from 14 to 80. Female patients are recorded three to four times more frequently than male patients. Intelligence scores follow a normal distribution curve. Classical loss-of-function symptoms are found more in patients from comparatively backward rural areas, whereas more expert simulation of some complicated diseases are seen in patients from medically sophisticated subcultures. One study [45] found educational level and somatization of emotional problems inversely proportional. Ziegler [71] found patients with conversion reactions not infrequently occupying a special role position in their families, for example, the youngest child or the only daughter.

ETIOLOGY AND PATHOGENESIS

Pathogenetic factors can be divided into five groups: sociocultural, intrapsychic, iatrogenic, secondary gain, and situational. Conversion symptoms, perhaps more than any other hysterical disorder, reflect the cultural surroundings. Certain sick roles are socially sanctioned or tolerated [38], and during different historical periods specific impulses and attitudes may be variously forbidden or encouraged. For example, during the Victorian Era of repressed sexuality, orgasmic convulsions were common and tolerated. Today this symptom is discouraged and uncommon. Exposure to specific disease entities influence the patient's choice of symptoms. If a culture's understanding of a disease is so widespread that the individual patient would find it nearly impossible to deny consciously the psychological origins of his conversion illness, that disease is not likely to be commonly mimicked. This in large part accounts for the progressive disappearance of the classical loss-of-function symptoms. However, some exotic diseases are expertly imitated by medically sophisticated patients.

> Mr. W was hospitalized for food-poisoning while on vacation. Because of a bed shortage, he was placed on a ward where a prominent neurologist had a group of research patients with myasthenia gravis. The following year Mr W was in and out of the intensive care unit of his small community hospital with a diagnosis of myasthenia gravis. A critical reevaluation of his case was made when he failed to respond in a typical fashion to medication. The psychological etiology was then discovered.

Intrapsychic conflict has long been considered a cause of conversion disorders. The conversion symptom may symbolically represent both the conflictual wishes and the defenses used for protection.

> Mrs. B presented with a two-week history of aphonia. She was supposed to present her version of the problems created by her chronically intoxicated and physically abusive husband to a judge who was considering permanent institutionalization for him. At her moment in court Mrs. B became extremely anxious. She felt overcome by her intense rage, her prohibition against expressing anger, her sense of duty, and her vacillating self-esteem. She opened her mouth to talk and found that she could only whisper. Her rage came out "softly," and her sickness made it impossible for her to continue working to support herself and her husband. Her self-image remained that of a quiet and concerned wife.

Frank [26] emphasized the communicative aspect of a conversion symptom. He viewed it as a revival of a past psychological trauma that is expressed in a nonverbal form. He stressed the importance of the unconscious fantasy of the extreme dangerousness of one's impulses and the physical symptom as a defense against its expression. Sperling [62] described a special form of symbiotic relationships in patients wherein their mothers encourage the sick role to minimize their children's autonomy and aggressiveness. Many other dynamic interpretations have been made which will not be elaborated upon, but one can glimpse the richness of possible dynamic meanings of conversion symptoms.

Iatrogenic factors [71] and secondary gain may encourage symptomatology. If the physician displays a special interest in a patient's physical symptoms, he may inadvertently communicate approval and information for the elaboration of the simulated illness. He in effect teaches the patient how to play better a certain sick role. Secondary gain is never a cause for a conversion disorder but can certainly influence the recovery time. If a patient receives monetary compensation or is able to escape an undesired responsibility because of the illness, the investment to maintain the symptoms is enhanced.

Situational determinants have recently gained more attention. Engel and Schmale [23] wrote of the affects of hopelessness and helplessness (the "giving-up–given up" complex) which often precede the onset of a broad group of physically ill patients. There is no direct causal relationship, since the complex is not always followed by a somatic disorder. In fact, almost any environmental stress can rekindle unresolved intrapsychic or interpersonal conflicts which may then result in a conversion disorder.

CLINICAL DESCRIPTION

There are four common types of clinical presentation [71]: (1) the nineteenth-century type of symptom, whereby a patient experiences either a loss of voluntary motor function or sensory modality or has a grand pseudoseizure; (2) simulation of known organic diseases with varying degrees of naiveté or sophistication; (3) pain; and (4) illnesses in which conversion processes are a component together with organic and/or physiological disturbances. Guze, Woodruff, and Clayton [32] listed anesthesia, aphonia, and ataxia as occurring most frequently in their clinical studies. Ziegler, Imboden, and Meyer [71] cited pain as a common presenting complaint. Lewis and Berman [47] found that the stereotyped *belle indifférence* was uncommon in their conversion patients, as was a predominance of any particular character types. Physicians, however, are more likely to call an unexplained physical symptom in a patient with histrionic characteristics a conversion disorder, responding more to the character style than to the symptom.

PROGNOSIS AND MANAGEMENT

A widely accepted axiom is that patients with conversion reactions respond very poorly to psychiatric intervention. These patients often fail to follow through on recommendations for psychotherapy [8,71]. They view themselves as physically ill, and the few who do agree to see a psychiatrist not infrequently assume a passive and essentially nonproductive role in treatment. Despite this pessimistic picture, most clinicians can readily recall patients with conversion symptoms who benefited considerably from psychiatric intervention. Because of the occurrence of conversion processes in a variety of psychiatric illnesses (including depression, addictions, anxiety disorders, and schizophrenia), valid generalizations about prognosis cannot be made, except to say that the greater the investment in being physically ill, the worse the prognosis. Therapeutic approaches used are varied and include environmental manipulation [35], operant conditioning techniques [6,9,28], and every form of the talking psychotherapies (brief therapy, analysis, family counseling, and so on). Medication is indicated if depression is pronounced or if the conversion is considered a defense against psychotic disintegration.

DIFFERENTIAL DIAGNOSIS

Conversion reactions first and foremost need to be clearly differentiated from any suspected organic or physiological disease. Of course, both can be concurrently present. Malingering is very hard to differentiate from a conversion reaction. One needs to be aware that the conversion symptoms may mask significant depression, anxiety, and/or an impending psychosis.

Dissociative Disorders

DEFINITION

Dissociative disorders are grouped together by one shared clinical feature: the presence of an altered state of consciousness or identity. The four most well-known dissociative disorders are fugue states, amnesia, depersonalization episodes, and multiple personalities. There is very little in the current literature on the first three as specific clinical syndromes. Paradoxically articles on multiple personalities, the least common entity, are numerous. In part this reflects the fact that many workers conceptualize episodes of amnesia, depersonalization, and fugues as symptoms found in a wide range of psychopathological conditions and not as separate syndromes. The popular press has also directed attention to multiple personalities from classics, such as Robert Louis Stevenson's *The Strange Case of Dr. Jekyll and Mr. Hyde* [65] to the more current bestsellers, *Three Faces of Eve* [66] and *Sybil* [60].

   Fugue states are brief periods of wandering for which the patient appears to be conscious but has no recall on recovery. *Amnesia* describes a circumscribed period of time that has been lost to memory. *Depersonalization episodes* are altered states of consciousness during which the person is aware of where he is and what he is doing but experiences the situation as though someone else was involved rather than himself. *Multiple personality* [16] is the presence in the same person of one or more auxiliary personalities which are substantially different from the usual personality yet capable of intermittently replacing it to the extent of carrying out daily activities for extended periods of time. Aside from the curiosity aroused by the multiple personality disorder, it phenomenologically also includes fugue states, amnesic episodes, and periods of depersonalization. It is important to realize, however, that the converse is not true. The presence of any one of these conditions does not warrant a diagnosis of multiple personality.

CLASSIFICATION

Typically, these disorders are classified as neurotic problems. As with conversion reactions, this classification is debatable. Kirshner [42] and others [1,25] regard dissociative phenomena more as a transitional social role that is culturally determined and protectively utilized to cope with environmental stress. Jaffe [41], in a study of former concentration camp inmates, felt that dissociative states in these survivors were residues of traumatic events which were experienced in abnormal states of consciousness during the imprisonment, such as being in a semistuporous condition due to starvation. The events experienced were never fully integrated by the ego. Jaffe did not consider this condition as a traumatic neurosis or as hysterical psychosis but seemed instead to be reviving the concept of the hypnoid state.

The classification of multiple personality remains confusing. It has been considered a rare form of a fugue state [20], a neurological problem [19,40], an iatrogenic phenomenon [36], a prepsychotic character disorder [29,24], and as representing a wide range of aberrant behavior (including unequivocal psychotic behavior) which does not fit any current conceptual scheme [10].

EPIDEMIOLOGY

Most of the cases of multiple personality reported in the literature were described around the turn of the century; the first case was described in 1816. Since the 1940s no more than a dozen cases have been reported. The other dissociative disorders occur infrequently. Kirshner reported 1.3 percent of patients diagnosed as having a dissociative disorder in 1795 psychiatric admissions. The age range varies widely, the young adult being the most common age group. Females predominate in reported cases, although males are certainly well represented.

ETIOLOGY AND PATHOGENESIS

A variety of etiological factors have been cited: organic, developmental, situational, and iatrogenic. Organic and iatrogenic causes are mentioned only for multiple personality. The most commonly accepted explanation for dissociative states is summarized by Bychowski [12], who wrote that fugue states (although also true for the other conditions) reflect an impairment in the organizing and integrating functions of the ego, whereby antiethical strivings are acted out with various degrees of conscious awareness.

Organic factors are considered as related to multiple personality. If one examines some cases in the literature [18,20,40,48], one not uncommonly finds listed among the clinical symptoms such problems as headaches, visual disturbances, seizure disorders, and electroencephalogram (EEG) abnormalities. One can raise the question whether at least some of these patients have a type of seizure disorder which appears phenomonologically as a separate identity. Iatrogenic influences pose additional questions. Harriman [36], in his noteworthy paper, described the experimental induction of almost all of the manifestations of multiple personality by hypnotic procedures or through ordinary suggestibility. Carrying this idea further, one notes that many (but not all) cases of multiple personality in the literature were only discovered while the person was in a hypnotic trance. Orne [53] contemplated whether a patient either in a trance (or even in an ordinary interview) may preconsciously perceive the demand characteristics of the interview situation and whether the so-called multiple personalities emerge from the dissociation of ego parts in response to the interviewer and to the procedure of hypnosis itself. For example, in questioning the diagnosis of Sybil in the book *Sybil,* could the therapist be labeling different personality characteristics of the patient as though each characteristic represented a distinct personality? The patient would then respond to the suggestions and interest of the therapist by elaborating on each characteristic and eventually develop a "person" for each personality trait.

A number of developmental and dynamic formulations have been offered for multiple personality, which can apply for the other dissociative disorders. The effect of mood states has been cited [33]. Ludwig and associates [54] theorized that one's mood affects one's perception of the self and others. An individual with alternate personalities has experienced altered states of consciousness because different mood states have accumulated different histories and experiences. These authors conclude that "all individuals, no matter how well adjusted, have at least a touch of multiple personality within them" [54] Congdon et al. [19] discussed the importance that role playing or an imaginary playmate might have as a precursor to the development of an alternate personality. These authors observed that everyone fantasizes having another identity and that under appropriate conditions, for example, hypnosis, these fantasies may appear as a separate personality. It is important to stress though that amnesia for the auxiliary personalities may be the distinguishing feature of the multiple personality. Horton and Miller [40] discussed family dynamics, emphasizing the absence of a satisfactory same sex model for identification, a finding in many sorts of psychopathology. Almost all authors mention that the alternate personality is a way for an individual with poor ego integration to express otherwise unacceptable feelings and behavior in an environment which does not permit the conflict to remain repressed.

CLINICAL DESCRIPTION

Dissociative reactions have been described as lasting from seconds to months or even years. The individual may appear briefly as if he were engrossed in a daydream at one extreme or to the other extreme of being psychotic with delusions and hallucinations. The only common descriptive element in these patients is the presence of an altered state of consciousness.

Three criteria have been used for suspecting a multiple personality [10]: (1) time distortions are present which are reported as time lapses, blackouts, or spells; (2) the patient has been told by others of behavior that the patient does not remember; and (3) notable changes in behavior patterns are observed by others, during which time the patient may label himself with different names or speak of himself in the third person. Different types of amnesia are reported. One personality may be aware of the other (usually the secondary aware of the primary) but not the reverse; the alternate personalities may be unaware of one another; or least common, the personalities are acquainted with one another.

MANAGEMENT

Almost uniformly, investigators agree that therapy has to be directed toward the merger of the personalities, which in essence means that intrapsychic conflict has to be resolved. The major disagreement about treatment is on the use of hypnosis. Should hypnosis be used to "bring forth" the alternate states, or should hypnosis be definitely avoided because of the problems with this technique previously mentioned?

PROGNOSIS

Many authors, describe a successful course of short-term therapy for patients with multiple personalities. There has been only one case of a long-term follow-up reported [20], and so one questions whether these successful cures were more descriptions of temporary symptomatic relief, i.e., transference cures, and whether in fact the diagnosis was accurate.

Briquet's Disorder

DEFINITION AND HISTORY

This syndrome describes a group of patients, primarily women, who have recurrent symptomatic distress in many different organ systems, are hospitalized repeatedly, and undergo a high number of surgical procedures.

In 1859 Briquet [11] described this syndrome which was reintroduced in the literature by Savill in 1909, and by Purtell [57]. Researchers from the Washington University School of Medicine began studying this syndrome in 1962 [56]. The St. Louis group, as these researchers are called, has been writing the majority of publications on Briquet's disorder ever since. This syndrome will be officially recognized in the final form of the DSM-III.

CLASSIFICATION

Clarification of different approaches used to classify psychiatric illnesses is in order here. Guze and Perley [30] stated that, ideally, a diagnosis should predict etiology, pathogenesis, prognosis, and family disorders. They felt that etiology and pathogenesis are never clear in psychiatry and so rested the validity of a diagnostic category on prognosis and family disorders. Woodruff, Clayton, and Guze [69] set up very specific criteria for inclusion and exclusion in the diagnostic category of Briquet's disorder. The research centered primarily on investigating prognosis and family disorders for this homogeneous group in terms of clinical symptoms.

An analyst, when making diagnostic categories, would use different criteria. Aufreiter [5] succinctly described this in his discussion of the controversy over hysteria and nosology. He illustrated three additional criteria used for classifying psychiatric illnesses: psychosexual development and libidinal fixation points, ego defenses and ego development, and object relations development. These criteria are not considered in the St. Louis group's definition for Briquet's disorder. Chodoff [15] questioned whether this group is really a separate group of patients or rather part of a larger category of emotionally unstable patients of many diagnostic types who have physical complaints.

Returning to the original question of how to classify Briquet's disorder, one is faced with a dilemma. It is difficult to describe a neurotic illness without some regard to intrapsychic conflict or to refer to character disorders and psychosis without addressing oneself to ego development and object relationships. In my opinion the classification of Briquet's disorder remains an open question.

EPIDEMIOLOGY

The St. Louis group regards this disorder as a syndrome occurring almost exclusively in females [33], although this criterion will be modified so as to eliminate any bias towards making this diagnosis only in women. Various studies [7] agree that the syndrome usually begins before age twenty and almost always before thirty.

Family studies [31] of patients with Briquet's disorder show a significant incidence of this disorder in female relatives and sociopathy in male relatives. There is also a higher incidence of Briquet's disorder in convicted women felons than in the general population [17]. One study stated that 10 percent of all women psychiatric inpatients appear with Briquet's disorder [7]. Prevalence rates for the general population run around 2 percent of all females and seem independent of socioeconomic status.

CLINICAL DESCRIPTION

This syndrome is characterized by recurrent symptoms [30] in many different organ systems. These patients often present their vague and multiple somatic complaints in a colorful and dramatic way. History reveals menstrual and sexual difficulties, excessive hospitalizations, excessive operations, frequent conversion reactions, overuse of medication, and signs of anxiety. Specific diagnostic criteris [69] include: (1) a complicated and dramatic medical history with onset prior to age 35, (2) a minimum of 25 symptoms in at least 9 of 10 symptom groups, and (3) a minimum of 25 symptoms in a minimum of 9 groups without somatic medical explanation. (Sample groups would be group one: headaches, sickly most of life; group seven: a list of menstrual problems, and so forth.) Many patients have accompanying symptoms of depression [61].

DIFFERENTIAL DIAGNOSIS

The criteria for inclusion are so specific that a differential is not a problem. Cassidy and associates [13] described similar polysymptomatic, medical presenting complaints in manic-depressive patients, but the St. Louis group felt that this differential can be made by considering age at onset, sexual distribution, presence or absence of episodes of illness with complete remission, and differences in the mental status exam [56]. Patients with Briquet's disorder may have conversion symptoms, but this is not a requirement for inclusion.

PROGNOSIS AND MANAGEMENT

This illness has a chronic course of many years without remission. Most patients reject a psychiatric approach to their illness.

This is another aspect of the syndrome not dealt with to any degree in studies to date. Clarification of the environmental stresses and developmental difficulties seem important in formulating any treatment plan. Also important is the avoidance of encouraging illness by cooperating with the patient's desires for hospitalization and surgery. The patient needs a "united medical front," which means open communication and cooperation among all the personnel involved in the patient's management. Finally, the depreciation of these patients (i.e., "She's a crock") has to be eliminated and the patient approached as any other distressed and depressed individual.

REFERENCES

1   Abeles, M., and Schilder, P. Psychogenic loss of personal identity. *Arch. Neurol. Psychiatry* 34:587–604, 1935.
2   Alexander, F. *Psycosomatic medicine.* New York: Norton, 1950.
3   American Psychiatric Association. *Diagnostic and statistical manual of mental disorders,* DSM-II. Washington, D.C.: American Psychiatric Association, 1968.
4   American Psychiatric Association. *Diagnostic and statistical manual of mental disorders,* DSM-III. Draft. Washington, D.C.: American Psychiatric Association, 1977.
5   Aufreiter, J. Psychoanalytic nosology and hysteria. *Can. Psychiatr. Assoc. J.* 14:569–571, 1969.
6   Bhattacharya, D. D., and Singh, R. Behavior therapy of hysterical fits. *Am. J. Psychiatry* 128:602–606, 1971.
7   Bibb, R. C., and Guze, S. B. Hysteria (Briquet's syndrome) in a psychiatric hospital: The significance of secondary depression. *Am. J. Psychiatry* 129:224–228, 1972.
8   Bower, H. M. Transient Psychosis. *Third World Cong. Psychiatry Proc.* 2:842–845, 1961.
9   Brady, J. P., and Lind, D. L. Experimental analysis of hysterical blindness. *Arch. Gen. Psychiatry* 4:331–339, 1961.
10 Brandsma, J. M., and Ludwig, A. M. A case of multiple personality: Diagnosis and therapy. *Int. J. Clin. Exp. Hypn.* 22:216–233, 1974.
11 Briquet, P. *Traite clinique et therapeutique de l'hystérie* Paris: Balliere, 1859.
12 Bychowski, G. Escapades: A form of dissociation. *Psychoanal. Q.* 31:155–173, 1962.
13 Cassidy, W. L., Flanagan, N. B., Spellman, M., and Cohen, M. E. Clinical observation in manic-depressive disease. *J.A.M.A.* 164:1525–1546, 1957.
14 Chodoff, P. A reexamination of some aspects of conversion hysteria. *Psychiatry* 17:75–81, 1954.
15 Chodoff, P. The diagnosis of hysteria: An overview. *Am. J. Psychiatry* 131:1073–1078, 1974.
16 Chodoff, P., and Lyons, H. Hysteria, the hysterical personality, and hysterical conversion. *Am. J. Psychiatry* 114:734–740, 1958.
17 Cloninger, C. R., and Guze, C. B. Psychiatric illness and female criminality: The role of sociopathy and hysteria in the antisocial woman. *Am. J. Psychiatry,* 127:303–311, 1970.
18 Condon, W. S., Ogston, W. D., and Pacoe, L. V. Three faces of Eve revisited: A study of transient microstrabismus. *J. Abnorm. Psychol.* 74:618–620, 1969.

19   Congdon, M. H., Hain, J., and Stevenson, I. A case of multiple personality illustrating the transition from role playing. *J. Nerv. Ment. Dis.* 132:497–504, 1961.

20   Cutler, B., and Reed, J. Multiple personality: A single case study with a fifteen-year follow-up. *Psychol. Med.* 5:18–26, 1975.

21   Easser, B. R., and Lesser, S. R. Hysterical personality: A reevaluation. *Psychoanal. Q.* 34:390–405, 1965.

22   Engel, G. L. A reconsideration of the role of conversion in somatic disease. *Compr. Psychiatry* 9:316–326, 1968.

23   Engel, G. L., and Schmale, A. M. Psychoanalytic theory of somatic disorder: Conversion, specificity, and the disease onset situation. *J. Am. Psychoanal. Assoc.*, 15:344–365, 1967.

24   Fast, I. Multiple identities in borderline personality organization. *Br. J. Med. Psychol.* 47:291–300, 1974.

25   Fisher, C. Amnesic states in war neurosis. *Psychoanal. Q.* 14:437–458, 1945.

26   Frank, R. L. Conversion and dissociation. *N.Y. State J. Med.* 69:1872–1877, 1969.

27   Greenberg, H. R. Television-induced "psychosis." *N.Y. State J. Med.* 67:1188, 1967.

28   Grosz, H. J., and Zimmerman, J. Experimental analysis of hysterical blindness. *Arch. Gen. Psychiatry* 13:255–260, 1965.

29   Gruenwald, P. Hypnotic techniques without hypnosis in the treatment of dual personality. *J. Nerv. Ment. Dis.* 153:41–46, 1971.

30   Guze, S. B., and Perley, M. J. Observations on the natural history of hysteria. *Am. J. Psychiatry* 119:960–965, 1963.

31   Guze, S. B., Woodruff, R. A., Jr., and Clayton, P. J. Hysteria and antisocial behavior: Further evidence of an association. *Am. J. Psychiatry* 127:957–960, 1971.

32   Guze, S. B., Woodruff, R. A., Jr., and Clayton, P. J. A study of conversion symptoms in psychiatric outpatients. *Am. J. Psychiatry* 128:643–646, 1971.

33   Guze, S. B., Woodruff, R. A., Jr., and Clayton, P. J. Sex, age, and the diagnosis of hysteria (Briquet's syndrome). *Am. J. Psychiatry* 129:745–748, 1972.

34   Halleck, S. Hysterical personality traits. *Arch. Gen. Psychiatry* 16:750–757, 1967.

35   Hammer, H. M. Astasia-Abasia: A report of two cases at Nest Point. *Am. J. Psychiatry* 124:671–674, 1967.

36   Harriman, P. L. A new approach to multiple personalities. *Am. J. Orthopsychiatry* 13:638–643, 1943.

37   Hirsch, S. J., and Hollender, M. H. Hysterical psychosis: Clarification of the concept *Am. J. Psychiatry* 125:909–915, 1969.

38   Hollender, M. H. Conversion Hysteria *Arch. Gen. Psychiatry*, 26:311–314, 1972.

39   Hollender, M. H., and Hirsch, S. J. Hysterical psychosis. *Am J. Psychiatry* 120:1066–1074, 1964.

40   Horton, P., and Miller, D. The etiology of multiple personality. *Compr. Psychiatry* 13:151–159, 1972.

41   Jaffe, R. Dissociative phenomena in former concentration camp inmates. *Int. J. Psychoanal.* 49:310–312, 1968.

42　Kirshner, L. A. Dissociative reactions: An historical review and clinical study. *Acta Psychiatr. Scand.* 49:698–711, 1973.

43　Langness, L. L. Hysterical psychosis in the New Guinea highlands: A Bena Bena example. *Psychiatry* 28:258–277, 1965.

44　Laplanche, J. Panel on "Hysteria Today." *Int. J. Psychoanal.* 55:459–469, 1974.

45　Lerner, J., and Noy, P. Somatic complaints in psychiatric disorders: Social and cultural factors. *Int. J. Soc. Psychiatry* 14:145–150, 1967.

46　Lewis, A. The survival of hysteria. *Psychol. Med.* 5:9–12, 1975.

47　Lewis, W. C., and Berman, M. Studies of conversion hysteria. *Arch. Gen. Psychiatry,* 13:275–282, 1965.

48　Ludwig, A. M., Brandsma, J. M., Wilbur, C. B., Bendfeldt, F., and Jameson, D. H. The objective study of a multiple personality: Or, are four heads better than one? *Arch. Gen. Psychiatry* 26:298–310, 1972.

49　Marmor, J. Orality in the hysterical personality. *J. Am. Psychoanal. Assoc.* 1:656–671, 1953.

50　Martin, P. A. Dynamic considerations of the hysterical psychosis. *Am. J. Psychiatry* 128:745–748, 1971.

51　McKegney, F. B. The incidence and characteristics of patients with conversion reactions. *Am. J. Psychiatry* 124:542–545, 1967.

52　Noble, D. Hysterical manifestation in schizophrenic illness. *Psychiatry* 14:153–160, 1951.

53　Orne, M. T. The nature of hypnosis: Artifact and essence. *J. Abnorm. Soc. Psychol.* 58:277–299, 1959.

54　Orzeck, A. Z., McGuire, C., and Longenecker, E. D. Multiple self-concepts as effected by mood states. *Am. J. Psychiatry* 115:349–353, 1958.

55　Pankow, G. W. The body image in hysterical psychosis. *Int. J. Psychoanal.* 55:407–414, 1974.

56　Perley, M. J., and Guze, S. B. Hysteria: The stability and usefulness of clinical criteria. *N. Engl. J. Med.* 266:421–426, 1962.

57　Purtell, J. J., Robins, E., and Cohen, M. E. Observations on clinical aspects of hysteria. *J.A.M.A.* 146:902–909, 1951.

58　Rangell, L. The nature of conversion. *J. Am. Psychoanal. Assoc.* 7:632–662, 1959.

59　Richman, J., and White, H. A family view of hysterical psychosis. *Am. J. Psychiatry* 127:280–285, 1970.

60　Schreiber, F. R. *Sybil.* Chicago: Henry Begnery, 1973.

61　Slater, E. The Thirty-Fifth Maudsley Lecture: "Hysteria 311." *J. Ment. Sci.* 107:359–371, 1961.

62　Sperling, M. Conversion hysteria and conversion symptoms: A revision of classification and concepts. *J. Am. Psychoanal. Assoc.* 21:745–771, 1973.

63　Spoerl, O. An unusual monosyptomatic psychosis featuring feelings of coldness. *Am. J. Psychiatry* 124:551–554, 1967.

64　Stengel, E. Further studies on pathological wandering (fugues with the impulse to wander). *J. Ment. Sci.* 89:224–241, 1943.

65　Stevenson, R. L. *The strange case of Dr. Jekyll and Mr. Hyde.* New York: Putnam, 1961.

66 Thigpea C., and Cleckly, H. *Three faces of Eve.* McGraw-Hill, 1957.

67 Veith, I. *Hysteria: the history of a disease.* Chicago: University of Chicago Press, 1970.

68 Victor, G. Letter: Sybil: Grande hystérie or folie à deux? *Am. J. Psychiatry* 132:202, 1975.

69 Woodruff, R. A., Jr., Clayton, P. J., and Guze, S. B. Hysteria: Studies of diagnosis, outcome, and prevalence. *J.A.M.A.* 215:425–428, 1971.

70 Zetzel, E. R. The so-called good hysteric. *Int. J. Psychoanal.* 49:256–260, 1968.

71 Ziegler, F. J., Imboden, J. B., and Meyer, E. Contemporary conversion reactions: A clinical study. *Am. J. Psychiatry* 116:901–909, 1960.

10

Phobic Neurosis

Leon Wurmser, M.D., and
Ellen McDaniel, M.D.

Terminologically phobia, phobic neurosis, and phobic character traits must be distinguished. Phobia is a term derived from the Greek word *phobos* which, interestingly enough, means originally flight, only secondarily fright as well as real threat. In psychiatric terminology *phobia* denotes a fear, usually recognized as irrational, of an *object* or group of objects (e.g., snakes or dogs, thunderstorms), of a type of *situation* (e.g., enclosed space or free open space), or of certain functions, movements, or aspects of the *body* (blushing, eating, bathing, traveling, supposed ugliness). Although one specific phobia may be leading in the symptomatology, it is far more typical (perhaps regularly so) that one deals with an entire phobic syndrome, the phobic neurosis. It consists of a primary complex of overt and covert phobias, and the secondary adaptive and defensive layers of general attitudes, character deformations and cover-up symptoms. This concept of the phobic neurosis is thus far more complex than commonly described [34]. The character traits derived from largely hidden unconscious phobias form an enduring pattern, e.g., that of the claustrophobic character [4].

HISTORY

In the Old Babylonian incantation "Shurpu," probably from the second millennium B.C., the priest tried to exorcize various phobias: "Be the (mystery?) resolved in that he does not know why . . . he has a phobia of meeting an accursed person or of an accursed person meeting him, or of sleeping in the bed, sitting in the chair, eating at the table, or drinking from the cup of an accursed person . . . of leaving or entering (such and such) city, city gate, or house, or of (such and such) a street, temple or road" [43:294]. Though mentioned in medical writings through the ages, scientific interest focused on phobic states only in the late nineteenth century. A whole slew of terms was coined to categorize the many types, terms which now appear far less relevant than the overall state and the specific dynamics of phobic neurosis. The latter were studied and pathogenetically elucidated by Freud in a number of papers now basic for all of psychoanalysis, e.g., "Obsessions and Phobias" [18], "Little Hans" [19], "Repression" [20], "Lines of Advance in Psychoanalytic Therapy" [21], and "Inhibitions, Symptoms, and Anxiety" [22]. Freud first separated the phobic neurosis from conversion hysteria, then from obsessive-compulsive neurosis, and named the syndrome anxiety hysteria. He also distinguished it from anxiety neurosis in that in the latter anxiety was free floating and all pervasive, while in phobic neurosis ("anxiety hysteria") anxiety was attached and restricted to certain situations and objects [34]. In recent decades learning theory and behavior therapy have devoted particular attention to experimental creation and therapeutic elimination of circumscript phobic symptoms [31].

EPIDEMIOLOGY

Accurate information about the incidence, distribution, and natural history of the phobic neurosis does not exist. Estimates are that these patients form less than 5 percent of all neurotic disorders in adults [34]. If one considers its complexity, however, it is likely that the incidence of this syndrome may be much higher since it tends to be masked by secondary layers of symptom formation and character disorders. Transient isolated phobias are not only very frequently (and normally) seen in children between three and five years but may occasionally occur in otherwise quite healthy adults after particularly frightening experiences (e.g., a very dangerous airplane ride or a life-threatening attack, such as a rape or an acute physical catastrophe) [28].

Agoraphobia is probably the most prominent form of phobias, not because it is particularly frequent, but because it is one of the most crippling and conspicuous neurotic illnesses.

ETIOLOGY

Psychodynamic and family dynamic considerations emphasize the role of early childhood conflicts in the genesis of phobic neurosis. These conflicts were for a long time seen as typically centered around the love-hate relationships with the closest relatives during the oedipal period and as resulting in particularly severe castration anxiety. Since the 1940s, however, interest has more and more shifted to earlier (preoedipal) levels of conflict and anxiety and to overall family dynamics [11,12,41].

In contrast, behavior therapists see in phobias learned responses due to exposure to a single intensely painful or frightening situation or, more probably, to repeated exposures to subtraumatic situations [28].

PATHOGENESIS

This discussion of the pathogenesis (psychodynamics) of phobic neurosis in general is elucidated from the psychoanalytic point of view as it emerges in intensive psychotherapy or in psychoanalysis.

The basic dynamic principle of phobic neurosis consists in replacing a vague undefined inner anxiety, originating in unconscious conflicts that appear unavoidable, by the fear of a localized or concrete outer object, action, or situation which then can be *avoided*. One can flee from an outer threat but not from an inner danger [22]. The feared object or event may be connected by many experiences and symbolic resemblances or by sheer contiguity in time with the original conflict-related object. The process of this substitution is quite complicated and needs a more detailed presentation.

Dynamically the starting point is either an intense but unacceptable wish and intolerable excitement or the frustration of and punishment for this wish. The wish may be of a sexual or an aggressive nature, stemming from childhood. Unless originating in severe trauma later, phobic neuroses in adults usually have their direct forerunners in infantile neuroses. The most primitive (infantile) type of phobia consists in just this: "In a situation which unconsciously represents an instinctual temptation, anxiety is felt instead of excitement, and subsequently the situation (and therewith the anxiety) is avoided" [11:278]. This requires a process of *projection*, for example: "The dangerous (sexual) excitement or the threatening competitive even murderous feelings which I cannot tolerate really do not belong to me, but to the outside world which evokes them." To illustrate, rhythmical noises and movements (dripping of water, a clock, the railroad) may thus directly represent the rhythmic sensation of sexual excitement, while thunderstorms, darkness, animals, and so forth, may come to stand for aggressive wishes (among others).

A second step in most, though not all, phobias is *displacement*, ensuing after projection. Sexual excitement in children is often induced by sensations of a changing equilibrium, especially by sudden falling, lifting, or rotation (as occurs in much playing and entertainment) [11]. Thus the eroticism of falling can substitute for directly sexual (phallic) excitement. The excitement is thus displaced from the body sensation onto situations of floating in space, falling, rotation, flying — or falling asleep. Subsequently the pleasure in these sensations and fantasies is turned into its opposite: unpleasure, specifically anxiety, even terror.

Why this occurs requires a third defense: *repression* of pleasure. First of all, the excitement may, by its sheer force, be unbearable for the little child. "I cannot stand it anymore; I'm going to burst," one patient cried whenever she felt intense pleasure: joy, satisfaction, tickling (see chapter 12). Or since the desire is unfulfillable and its goal unreachable, the wish has to be pushed out of consciousness. Finally, the threat of punishment (real or fantasied) may make the fulfillment of the wish inadvisable. In all these instances when repression occurs, the pleasure felt or anticipated turns into anxiety or its three major derivatives: guilt, shame, and disgust. Since the threat of punishment is the most likely motive to initiate and maintain repression, the phobic situation most frequently "combines an unconscious temptation with an anticipation of punishment" [11:278].

This last notion, the anticipation of punishment, however, really entails yet a fourth defense, a *reversal* in the direction of the wish: "Instead of me wanting to remove father, he is going to destroy (or mutilate) me." Aggression (of many forms) switches its target: from the object to the subject. Furthermore, the form of the wish also may be altered with the help of a fifth form of defense, *regression*. For example, in this statement: "Instead of my wanting to sleep with mother and to penetrate her with my penis I would like to bite her," the regression is from a phallic to an oral wish. "No, it is not I who wishes to bite her, it is she who wants to devour me" represents the use of reversal. "No, it is not my mother either; how could I think that! But it is a monster, an ugly witch, a robber — or Death who is coming to get and devour me"; this is an example of displacement. A similar, more frequent transition would occur (in the male child) with aggression: "Instead of my wanting to remove father, I'd like to bite him and to swallow him up. No, he does it to me. No, it is a horse (or a dog, or a snake) which is going to bite, castrate (or otherwise mutilate), blind, or devour me" [19].

Moreover, this regression is expressed in that "all phobic patients behave like children whose anxieties are allayed by a comforting mother whose presence dispels fear" [11:279]. This wish fulfillment is secondary to the original conflict, a helplessness experienced as loneliness and lack of human contact, i.e., the absence of the protection against the frightful wishes and punishments [11:279].

In 1977 Anna Freud added yet another defense as obligatory for the symptom formation: *condensation* preceding projection. "This means that fears and anxieties do not remain diffuse but are compressed by the child into one encompassing symbol" [17:87]. Without condensation one would encounter diffuse anxiety, as in anxiety neurosis.

All or most of these defense mechanisms (condensation, projection, displacement, repression, reversal, and regression) can eventually be found in the full constitution of a phobic symptom.

A word more about displacements: They occur according to the rules of the primary process (mythical thinking, as described in volume 1, chapter 2 [44]); e.g., similarity in even one trait makes for identity; contiguity in time makes for causal relation; natural occurrences are seen as expressing supernatural will; thought, fear, and wish are equated with concrete outward action, evoking retaliatory counteraction.

In a second stage, during the actual development of the phobic neurosis, the phobias themselves may largely disappear and remain just as minor vestiges under the shell of several layers of additional defenses. With the help of enduring character traits, e.g., attitudes or activities, the patient protects himself against the underlying fears. One possibility is a spreading, that is, where a concrete, limited fear becomes a more and more generalized timorousness: Everywhere dangers are seen lurking. Another possibility is a kind of identification with the aggressor [16], in this case with the frightening, already phobically viewed object, for example: "Instead of my being afraid of the monster (or the dead relative), I play the monster (or the dead) and, in fantasy, I really am it!" This may be done in compulsively playing games of frightening other people, in a basic generalized aggressiveness, defiance, stubbornness, and even in criminal violence (going from sparring to assault if a face-saving device cannot be found — an attack out of phobic fear). A most fascinating sequel of this coping with a very general phobia, that of death, is the universal custom of mask wearing.

Yet another most important secondary layer of defense against a phobia is the overcompensation against fear, more exactly what Fenichel called the counterphobic attitude, "a never-ending attempt at the belated conquest of an unmastered infantile anxiety" [12:167]. Instead of fleeing the source of anxiety it is sought out again and again. Somebody who is phobically afraid of falling takes to flying and skydiving; one who is afraid to be attacked turns into a war hero. The aim: "The experience that imaginary ideas connected with a certain situation actually do not prove true, is precisely the basis of most counter-phobic attitudes" [12:171].

Many other forms of such secondary coverups against partly hidden phobias may be found in apparently independent problems: homosexuality, drug or alcohol abuse, or a general fear of human closeness and intimacy or of distance (character defenses against claustrophobia and agoraphobia respectively).

It often takes very long work in psychoanalysis or psychotherapy to unravel the complex structure of such a phobic neurosis with its defensive overlays that deceive patient and physician alike.

Finally, it should be noted that not only are several forms of closely related phobias often combined (e.g., vis-à-vis several animals) but also quite different types very often coexist: In one patient, phobias of dogs, flying, situations of social exposure, and blood and meat emerged during various periods of his life, mostly traceable to helpless exposure to overwhelming rage of an oral (cannibalistic) nature, experienced throughout early and later childhood as sequels of traumatic abandonments and typically triggered later on by separation, rejection, and humiliation. In a second patient a phobia of being discovered as ugly (which in reality she was not; this is called dysmorphophobia) [3] coexisted with both a quite related fear of being stared at (and also a less clearly connected one of being caught while spying) and one of blushing (erythrophobia). In the case to be presented shortly fears of snakes, of sexual involvement with women, and of closed and crowded buildings, as well as of any intimate friendships were all present (mostly variations on the theme of claustrophobia).

Not too rarely fear and wish are intermingled, e.g., the claustrophobic may also be claustrophilic in some more secret areas; the one afraid of the dead and ghosts is fascinated by tales about them. Fascination and thrill are often just anxiety turned around; they are the return of the repressed.

Due to the multiformity of underlying, largely covert phobias, it is not possible to describe a generally valid *phobic character*, except in a circular and overly general way, as one whose major character traits are determined by hidden phobias of whatever nature. Certainly anxiety and fears play a very prominent part in the makeup of the phobic character, but this is not specific enough. Study of the literature indicates that this problem needs to be explored in systematic psychoanalytic research; it has hardly been touched as yet [4,13]. Possibly the centrality of the defense mechanism of displacement could be one of the distinguishing marks of this character. Most crucially it is marked by compulsive avoidance as a widespread behavior pattern. Continually small or large areas of life have to be shunned in order for the person not to be uncomfortable, ill at ease, or, lastly, frightened. In certain areas the avoidance is replaced by an equally compulsive search for what is at bottom dreaded (the counterphobic character trait). The necessary avoidance leads perforce to the often noticeable massive restriction of ego activities in these patients: Despite high intelligence and emotional sensitivity they are blocked, for example, in their ability to read or to enjoy the arts, literature, or music, creating thus an almost bizarre discrepancy within their character between extraordinary keenness and playing the dunce, the empty headed dimwit. Yet another aspect of the phobic character (and of great social relevance) may be in some the inclination to ethnic and racial prejudice where all of the defense-mechanisms described above are clearly involved. Of course, in regard to all these character derivatives of phobias, rationalizations abound and at times make it rather difficult to distinguish the phobic from the obsessive-compulsive character.

MAJOR SUBTYPES

The special categories, marked by one or the other major phobia, are striking in their cultural equivalents, bespeaking the generality of the problems that find most marked expression in this disease. The discussion takes the psychoanalytic mode of explanation.

Claustrophobia

One of the few large types of phobias in need of separate study is the fear of an enclosed space (claustrum). Since it is particularly often well shielded by character traits it is often misdiagnosed. Therefore no reliable data as to incidence, etiology, and other factors are known to exist. This is due to the fact that claustrophobia usually is displaced further to metaphorical enclosures: Many feel stifled, smothered, uncomfortably hemmed in by human warmth, by physical or emotional closeness, and have to beat a frightened or angry retreat as soon as somebody gets too close (the word close is Latin *clausus*, which means closed in, from the same stem as claustrum); any gesture of such closeness is experienced as a suddenly concrete threat of being engulfed and swallowed up by the other (often seen also in schizoid and schizophrenic patients; this was specifically the case with Andreas, described in chapter 18). Another symbolic variant [23,24] is manifested by procrastination and indecision: Every deadline, every chore or task becomes a confining limit, and thus represents a claustrum, evoking both fear and anger; "a definite decision excludes the possibility of escape" [11:283].

It also may eventuate in the fear of death (to be buried alive, to be enclosed in the tomb, to be devoured by the earth) or of being helplessly closed in within vehicles (cars, trains, especially airplanes).

Yet another character variation can often be traced back to a hidden claustrophobia: These patients have to escape any commitment (e.g., marriage), show insufficient perseverance in tasks, and are perpetually peregrinating (compulsive travelers). Such severe forms of claustrophobic characters have been particularly noted in children of psychotic or absent mothers. Only during deeper exploration (specifically psychoanalysis) is the phobic core unveiled.

According to Lewin [25,26], this phobia's content is derived from childhood fantasies about the prenatal state. The enclosure stands for the mother's body, the intruding object for the father's penis. "The idea of being within the closed space is not an anxiety fantasy, but one of safety, of being in hiding. The anxiety arises from the threat of interruption" [26:108]. It is by no means certain that this interpretation is valid for all cases. In our experience Fenichel's explanation seems more applicable: "any state of anxiety is physiologically accompanied by feelings of being closed in; and thus reversely, an external closeness (or the idea of it) facilitates the mobilization of the entire anxiety syndrome" [11:283]. This leads back to the state of inner tension (excitement, rage, and so on) with which the discussion of the psychodynamics was opened — a tension over which all control has been lost, as, for example, "represented by a moving vehicle uninfluenced by the wish of the passenger, by a room which cannot be left at will, and also by the mounting sexual excitement approaching orgasm." [11:284]. We may add passively suffered death, in contrast to suicide.

> Mr. A, a successful architect in his early thirties, entered psychoanalysis because he felt bothered by his compulsive drivenness, overactivity, frenzy, and the subsequent chaotic way of life and lack of privacy, although he also hated to be hemmed in by structure, order, and organization. His countless relationships with others were superficial, unauthentic; he was a compulsive rescuer and confidant but felt very lonely. Sexually he did not know where he stood: When he had been involved with a girl, he felt he had to perform in bed and to commit himself to something deep; so he had shunned heterosexual ties for several years and turned instead to transient passive-homosexual relationships. A few anxiety attacks occurred

while in a crowded shop; a snake phobia was remembered from childhood and resurfaced in a few dreams.

He was the younger of two sons. The crucial event of his childhood was that his father had to undergo surgery for a brain tumor twice, when the patient was three and eight years old. The father came out a sullen, bitter, irascible man whose wrath the patient often tried to appease (a fantasy important in his homosexual encounters, in which he tried to "please" a "surly" man). From the long-time analysis only a brief vignette germane to the topic should be presented.

The last remainder of a broad neurosis, resistant for a long time to analytic elucidation, was his fear of women, more specifically his fear of being committed to a woman. He felt it to be like "gooey" molasses by which he would be engulfed, stuck, swallowed up, or overcome by his own "greediness" and selfishness. The vagina was like a velvety cloak opening into an abyss into which his penis would disappear. (Thus, for example, during intercourse his penis was depersonalized, felt to be detached from himself, like a separate person.) Quite late in his analysis the crucial connections emerged. In the context of a funeral he felt: "All the older men in my family died off, my father disappeared and returned mutilated while all the women survived." The hidden feeling: Women are dangerous, because they are invulnerable, immortal, and lastly in control. Men are always threatened by mutilation, castration, disintegration, and death. One sequel: "This is perhaps the fear of being engulfed and devoured by the vagina: The man can be consumed, he would disappear." He felt envy and anger at the (fantasied) power of women. He fought it off by avoiding physical contact with them (the hallmark of the phobic character being avoidance), by being angry at them (reasserting power), and as a general trait — his frantic overactivity. The latter proved that he was not threatened by the ultimate passivity — in sexuality as well as in death. His housebuilding proved to be counterphobic. He mastered his fear of the "devouring inside space" by building houses and especially by redesigning the interior of houses and cities, a constant obsessive preoccupation since early childhood: "I always redesign the interior to make it controlled by me what always had been controlled by mother." The crucial fear was that of his own consuming murderous rage, originally at his irritable, disappointing father, then displaced onto mother ("I am furious at her") and reversed in direction ("She is devouring"): "She is the treacherous Jezebel. How can I feel lust for a woman when I am afraid to be swallowed up?"

That the anxiety is not banned by the counterphobic frenzy was shown by a feeling of disintegration. "Either I feel smothered by that velvety 'security-claustrophobic cloak', or I feel superfragmented in a whirlwind of activities." He was also almost always late to the analytic hour. "Fifty minutes in here are too oppressive" (another derivative of his claustrophobia).

In short: His own rage and oral (devouring) wishes were projected onto mother, with the reversal described before, then displaced onto the vagina of and emotional relation with all women. Secondarily he hides this phobia with a pseudohomosexuality and, counterphobically, with a frenetic overactivity involving houses and entire cities. Etiologically the mutilation (castration) of his father in the middle of the oedipal period was probably truly traumatic (disintegrating).

Agoraphobia

This particular subgroup of phobias recently has received considerable attention. One speculation about this rise of public concern involves the changing cultural roles of women. Females (who make up the majority of agoraphobics) are being confronted with more external pressures to explore the world beyond the home, and these cultural changes, in turn, help create different internalized expectations (and conflicts) as well as weaken cultural acceptable defensive behavior.

HISTORY AND DEFINITION

The term *agoraphobia* derives from the Greek root *agora*, which means an assembly, the place of assembly, and marketplace. It was first used by Westphal [42] to describe the "impossibility of walking through certain streets or squares or the possibility of so doing only with resultant dread of anxiety."

A frequent misusage of the word agoraphobia interprets it as being a fear of open spaces. Westphal [42] actually picked the term to illustrate its more specific meaning; it is not so much a fear of open spaces as it is a fear of public places of assembly.

Generally speaking, the term can include all those fears that relate to distance and space. Patients suffering from these space phobias experience a panicky feeling when they leave a safe space or enter into a forbidden one. The territory defined by the phobia can be global (e.g., any place away from home), discrete (e.g., cars, buses), expansive (e.g., downtown) or confining (elevators) [14]. Other authors define the term in a more restricted way. If another specific fear is the cause of being home-bound (e.g., fear of trains or fear of meeting a dog), then this is not agoraphobia [7].

Commonly agoraphobia can be defined as a fear of leaving home. Patients most frequently report that their subjective fears are of becoming physically ill, of causing a public disturbance, of being stared at, and of losing control, screaming, or going mad [15].

EPIDEMIOLOGY

Prevalence rate is estimated to be 6.3 per 1000 in the general population. Agoraphobia is the most common subgroup of phobias comprising 50 percent of psychiatric patients diagnosed as having a phobic neurosis. From 70 percent [2] to 95 percent [32] of these patients are women. Age of onset is between 18 to 35 years [30]. Family histories reveal a high incidence of emotional disorders (especially amongst the siblings) [8]; most striking is the significant reporting of school phobias in the childhood of the adult agoraphobics, as well as a significant occurrence of school phobias among the patients' children [5].

ETIOLOGY AND PATHOGENESIS

Earliest formulations explained the fear of leaving home as a symptomatic expression of unconscious conflicts over sexual fantasies. Women with this problem were said not uncommonly to have a wish to engage in prostitution, men in homosexuality [9]. The agoraphobia was the symptomatic resolution of both the wish to engage in such sexual endeavors and the defense against it.

As ego psychology developed, the defensive aspect of the symptom received increased attention. Furthermore, pregenital components were emphasized as pathogenetic factors, particularly those maturational processes most closely associated with the separation-individuation phase of development [29]. The child of one to three years of age uses locomotion as a means of separating physically from mother and returning to her when the anxiety becomes too great. If the mother is tolerant of the child's explorations out into the world, the child develops an increasing ability to master his anxiety about separation and gains autonomy and individuation. If the mother is negligent in protecting the child from real dangers or is overprotective, the child fails to master his anxiety upon separating and needs mother's presence to ensure his feeling of safety.

Adult patients with agoraphobia often are symbiotically tied to another person. This companion is used by the patient to reenact the earlier incompleted phase of development of leaving and returning to mother and to safety [14]. The symptom ("I cannot leave the house unless you go with me") ensures the patient his dependency source (his mother surrogate). Rather than the satisfaction of the dependency need being the secondary gain of the illness, it can be viewed as the primary gain: The conflict is over attachment, dependency versus autonomy, individuation [36].

The dependency conflict and the phobic companion can be explained further. Just as the toddler experiences rage, frustration, and an insufficient development of self-esteem in his clinging dependency on a restrictive mother, so are the adult agoraphobic's important relationships colored by significant amounts of hostility, demandingness, fearfulness, and dependency [35]. Whereas with claustrophobia, there is a flight from destructive attachment, in agoraphobia there is flight from an equally devastating separation.

One issue not infrequently debated is the importance of a precipitating factor in the onset of the symptom. Studies give an incidence of from 10 percent to 83 percent [37]. Although learning theory has stressed the role of accidental conditioning in causing agoraphobia and of a similar stimulus reactivating the symptoms, in experimental tests and clinical cases this hypothesis does not seem to hold true.

Families of these patients are described as unusually stable, close-knit [37] and overprotective [40]. A common (but not consistent) background history includes childhood enuresis, night terrors, and shy, dependent personalities [30].

The effect of agoraphobia on present family life also has been investigated. Some studies report that the illness may not produce any striking impact on the patient's family, that the performance of the children and husband at school, work, and in social situations is the same as in the general population [3]. Predictably, however, such factors as occupation, financial resources, social class, greatly influence the effect of the illness. One sometimes sees families wherein much of the activity is focused around one member's agoraphobia.

CLINICAL DESCRIPTION

The onset of agoraphobia can be sudden (developing over a period of hours) or gradual (over weeks, months, or years). There is a prodromal stage of vague intermittent anxiety. Remissions and relapses are variable; e.g., a patient can be completely house-bound for one month and be able to move about freely the next, or the fear may persist for years with only partial remissions. Most commonly the patient finds it easier to travel in the presence of a close person or an animal or by any variety of security maneuvers [30] (e.g., a bus that stops by a friend's house is safe to use but other buses are not; the carrying of an umbrella or a particular coat eases the fear). Anxiety and depression are very common associated symptoms.

The following examples demonstrate the variations seen in clinical pictures as well as some clues to pathogenesis.

Ms. B is a twenty-six-year-old secretary who first came for psychiatric help after a panic attack. She reported a history of depression and free-floating anxiety throughout her teens and early twenties. However, she dated, worked regularly, and experienced no awareness of any specific fears until one week before her consultation. On that day, she had gone swimming with two girlfriends. While undressing in the locker room, she suddenly became overwhelmed by a fear of vomiting and embarrassing herself. She got back into her street clothes, called her parents to bring her home, and had not been able to leave her house for the next seven days.

Mrs. C is a forty-five-year-old housewife who sought psychiatric help for an increasing sense of depression. She complained of feeling bored with her domestic routines and yet not interested in pursuing a career in law — something that she was professionally trained to do. Her description of her activities sounded quite ordinary, i.e., nothing that would point to phobic difficulties, and she had no history of previous emotional illness.

Over the course of the next year, the patient was seen for weekly visits. What emerged was not a picture of a "bored housewife" but rather that of a very frightened woman who had so disguised her phobia of leaving home that even she was unaware of it. She had "safe territories" well defined, and these were sufficient to cover what later appeared as extensive fears. For example, the little neighborhood grocery store down the block was safe to go to, but none other. Her ten-year-old car was likewise safe, but when her car was in the garage being fixed, she stayed home. Traveling with one of her children or accompanied by her dog was possible; otherwise she invited others to her house (and so appeared quite outgoing and relaxed). Her husband frequently was away on business and appreciated his wife's lack of demands.

Her family of origin was described as "very close; we always were together." Mother told the patient how to dress, what and how much to eat, whom to date, what to read, and so forth. Father treated her like a "little china doll." Anger was forbidden in the home. Both parents insisted on cheerfulness, optimism, and obedience from their offspring.

As Mrs. C reached adulthood, she became terrified of her murderous impulses towards her parents for "suffocating me, treating me like an imbecile, using me for their own needs." As the agoraphobia (in all of its ramifications) was uncovered during the course of therapy its defensive protection against both intense separation anxiety and hostility became clearer. The patient's safe places had transitional object qualities to them — her car was old, worn, familiar, and comforting; the little grocery store was an extension of her kitchen and likewise small, familiar, and comforting. Other cars were weapons of aggression; the big bustling supermarket was like a battlefield.

During therapy, much time was spent discussing her anger, which came out in the transference as well as in her family relationships. As she explored her own feelings more and became more emotionally individuated, her agoraphobia lessened.

Phobic Fear of the Dead and Ghosts

This is a fear barely brought up in the psychiatric literature and yet is quite frequent in children, less so in adults. Everything pertaining to death is for these people unusually frightening. Cemeteries and belongings of deceased are avoided or approached only with a quiet fear. In corners, under the bed, in the attic, and in forests ghosts are feared to hide, or there roam the vengeful spirits of the dead, against which security is sought in the company of the living. This is an exaggerated form of what we all dread. As Plato said in the Phaedo: "There is a child within us who is frightened (*phobeitai*) of such things (like death); him too I try to persuade not to be afraid of death, like of ghosts."

This widespread phobia, rooted obviously in the frightening wishes to see someone else die and the subsequent guilt and dread of vindictive punishment (again projection, reversal, and displacement), is more important for its sociocultural than its clinical relevance. As Meuli [33] has shown, "the main mass of primitive *masks* represent spirits, and the main mass of these spirits are those of the dead" [33:71]. "They are malevolent, vengeful, obscene; they kill, beat and demand, but they also protect the existing order with the help of punishment and scolding . . . It is a ceremony of atonement deeply satisfying both for player and onlooker, an expiation vis-à-vis the dead. It brings fertility and blessing to all areas of life and presents, often symbolically, gifts, in return for receiving reverence and sacrifices from the public" [33:77–78, our translation].

Eventually these horrifying masks turn from the deadly serious and potentially murderous into comical derivatives where the fright is partly overcome. Still they appear in times when the dead are expected to return and to demand symbolic sacrifice under threat of reprisal: Halloween (that is, the evening before All Hallows' Day), around the winter solstice and New Year's Day, and during carnival. Many of the words used still show the macabre origin: The word mask itself is Old German and related to the word mesh (enmeshed) — the net in which the corpse is shrouded, according to ancient tradition, so that the dead person is prevented from returning. Harlequin derives from Harilo-King, the leader (king) of the Wild Host, the army of the dead riding through the stormy night and killing or maiming who stands in their way [33:226].

Spider and Bug Phobia

This is a very frequent, often very well hidden symptom of phobic neurosis. Many patients (see chapters 12 and 18) are inordinately frightened of crawling cockroaches or of spiders touching them or falling into their mouths during sleep. When they encounter such an insect, they may immediately trample it to death with a vengeance. Andreas (see chapter 18) felt even the thought of a cockroach more horrifying than his homicide or severe depression. The insect, with its long moving legs, was a disturbing reminder of, among other things, the frequently watched intercourse of his parents, an event which was profoundly traumatic for him, evoking rage, hatred, disgust, helplessness, but also excitement. It brought out, moreover, memories of an anal nature about his father's dirty body habits.

In a thorough study of spider phobia in eight analytic cases (children as well as adults) Sperling [39] described rather uniform features and pathogenesis of this symptom: strong anal fixations, often of a psychotic nature; sadomasochistic relationships with rejecting mothers (inability to separate from them, intense wishes to kill them, strong feelings of breast and penis envy); traumatization in the second year of life, leading to severe sleep disturbances and very early to this phobia. The spider is chosen because of its (anal) repulsiveness; its murderous, devouring image; its similarity with the pubic hair surrounding the female genital. The many legs and threads with their smothering strangling quality symbolize very poignantly the actual character of the mother (overprotective, while hostile and rejecting). Moreover its image serves well that of the parents in intercourse (a violent act, many legs) [27].

It is interesting to note that in folklore, like in the symbolization of the core problem in these patients, the spider is often connected with craziness, the very central and justified dread in these patients. In Switzerland, for example, the main expression for craziness is *Spinnen*, i.e., to spin (a web or for the rocker). "To be off the rocker" uses at least a related metaphor.

School Phobias

Many forms of school phobias are not real phobias. In a recent study [41] four often overlapping types are distinguished. In type one, the problem is the fear of separation from the mother, not a school phobia proper. Only type two is a classical phobia with projection and displacement. In type three, it is fear of what would happen to the parent while the child is away, and in type four, the fear concerns real situations in school that threaten the child with failure, loss of self-esteem, or bodily harm. The findings from family studies reveal "fairly close links among a mutually hostile-dependent relationship between mother and child, excessive importance of the child to the mother, marked separation anxiety in the child, and faulty development of autonomy and self esteem leading to the child's having an impaired capacity for autonomous functioning" [41:807]. Thus school phobias actually appear to be, in appearance as well as dynamically, precursors to agoraphobias.

Other Phobias

Many other important forms of phobias include the phobia of heights and flying (related to erotic feelings connected with equilibrium and contributing to this symptom). In stage fright and erythrophobia (fear of blushing) the problem of wanting to be seen and the profound shame attached to it are central. In phobias of eating, e.g., anorexia nervosa and avoidance of meat, oral sadistic wishes are warded off. Phobias about contamination, dust, bacteria, and venereal disease (VD) are rather part of the obsessive-compulsive neurosis or even precursors of a schizophrenic psychosis. Snake phobia is connected with oral sadistic (devouring, strangling) and phallic wishes but much is still unclear about it.

Sleep phobia is often overlooked as a cause for insomnia. The patient is afraid to lose control over his thoughts and feelings, because he fears he might go crazy or die if he relaxed his vigilance.

DIFFERENTIAL DIAGNOSIS

The borders to all other forms of neurosis are not sharply delimited. The connections to conversion hysteria and to obsessive-compulsive neurosis especially have been stressed [34]. In severe cases of multiple phobias one has to consider differentially the possibility of a schizophrenic psychosis, especially of the paranoid type, since the mechanism of projection is central to both states. The prevalence of little-disguised aggression over fear, however, distinguishes the paranoid from the phobic state.

To be more specific, there are numerous transitions of phobias mainly to the obsessive-compulsive syndrome. Often the two merge and cannot be clearly distinguished. Many taboos in the latter can also be viewed as phobias. In turn, phobic avoidances may become rigidly supported by compulsive rituals. The differentiation from anxiety neurosis and hysteria is usually easily established by the prevalence of phobias as against all-pervasive, "unattached" anxiety in the former and conversion symptoms in the latter.

Diagnostic difficulties arise, however, if symptoms of all three other neurotic categories are also present. Some may diagnose, therefore, pseudoneurotic schizophrenia; others may use the nowadays fashionable label of a borderline condition. It may be more appropriate to see in such a mixture the polysymptomatic decompensation of a severely disturbed (but not psychotic) narcissistic character disorder, one which also is not likely to develop an overt psychosis.

The most difficult differentiation is that from depressive neurosis and other superimposed, secondary illnesses, such as drug abuse or alcoholism. Only careful analytic exploration can elucidate this; but the major practical consequence of such a distinction relates only to questions of thoroughness, of being correct in interpretations, and of timing of termination of psychoanalytic treatment, not to questions of other types of management. If the phobic state expands more and more and if anxiety increasingly changes to enmity, hostility, and rage, the differential diagnosis vis-à-vis paranoid schizophrenia may become difficult. Phobias may actually be precursors of this condition.

Of course, phobias are not limited to phobic neuroses but may occur in many other forms of neurotic and in psychotic disorders. To call a disease a phobic neurosis, phobias must be particularly prevalent and the defense mechanisms specified above especially characteristic for this patient.

PROGNOSIS AND MANAGEMENT

As was true in regard to epidemiology, the findings about the natural history of this syndrome are unreliable, sparse, and contradictory. Most patients apparently remain unchanged [10:1]. With stress on the role of behavior therapy in management, there are several major courses of action open: insight-oriented psychotherapy (specifically psychoanalysis), supportive therapy (including hypnosis), and behavioral psychotherapy.

As to the success rate of analytic therapy in these patients no data are available. But studies, as those of Sperling [39], show that even in very severely ill patients (including psychotics) astonishing successes are possible, given early beginning of treatment and perseverance. On the other hand, Freud noticed that the analyst had to take a stand that was more active than usual in psychoanalysis: "One can hardly master a phobia if one waits until the patient lets the analysis influence him to give it up"

[21:165]. With agoraphobic patients who have ceased to go out "one succeeds only when one can induce them by the influence of the analysis . . .
to go into the street and to struggle with their anxiety while they make the
attempt. One starts, therefore, by moderating the phobia so far; and it is
only when that has been achieved at the physician's demand that the associations and memories come into the patient's mind which enable the
phobia to be resolved" [21:166]. This is actually a method that is central
also to behavior therapy. Today Freud's recommendation is, in the opinion of many, to be discarded if one wants to give psychoanalysis the
chance to resolve the basic conflicts of this syndrome (not just to wipe out
the phobias themselves); in the interim great strides have been made in
defense analysis which may indeed obviate such an active intervention [6].

Supportive therapies (exhortation, encouragement, and so forth); relaxation techniques, including antidepressant and anxiolytic agents like
diazepam (Valium) and chlordiazepoxide (Librium); and autogenic training have been used with moderate success. Several authors reported effective use of hypnosis in the treatment of phobias; moreover, the very good
hypnotizability of these patients was emphasized. Therefore, Frankel and
Orne have suggested "that the capacity for spontaneous trance-like occurrences is related to the origin of phobic symptoms" [15:1260]; they recommend use of hypnosis "to facilitate the patient's understanding of a special mode of mental functioning" [15:1261], one that represents an asset as
well as a liability (the latter is the risk of leading to rapid induction of
phobic symptoms, the former an ability to increase inner mastery) [15].

Finally the various methods of behavioral therapy seem to have an
encouragingly high rate of success with phobias. Marks [31] has described
the various methods employed (in a case of acrophobia, fear of heights):
"We can ask him to close his eyes, relax, and imagine himself slowly putting his foot on the first rung of the ladder and then relaxing again, and to
imagine this several times until that inspires no anxiety, after which he
can imagine himself on the second rung of the ladder, etc. That is *desensitization in fantasy*. If we asked the patient to carry out the same maneuvers
in real life rather than in fantasy, that would be *desensitization in vivo*"
[31:258].

Marks himself, however, apparently prefers the first two among the
following methods: "An alternative strategy would be to ask the patient to
close his eyes and imagine himself standing right at the top of the ladder
looking down, swaying, and feeling dizzy and scared at the same time,
and to continue to imagine this until he feels better. This is *implosion* or
flooding in fantasy. The *real-life flooding* variant would be (with his permission) to grab him by the scruff of his neck and thrust him to the top of the
ladder and keep him there, sweating out his fear, until he becomes used to
the situation" [31:258]. This he refers to as *exposure in vivo*. "If for any of

these procedures we first demonstrate to the patient what to do, e.g. if we precede him up the ladder, we would call this *modeling*. If we praise the patient each time he takes a step up the ladder this is *operant conditioning* or *shaping*. If we ask the patient to close his eyes and imagine himself persuading another patient with a height phobia that it is good for him to go up the ladder, this would be *cognitive rehearsal*. If the patient is asked to say to himself: 'This is not so bad, I can really tolerate this fear' — that is *self-regulation*." [31:258]. He considers behavioral psychotherapy the approach of choice in phobic disorders but emphasizes the importance of first clearly delineating the treatment goals and thus of singling out the target problems. "Several targets are commonly needed for each patient." The in vivo exposure should each time be carried out for several hours. Relaxation techniques are, in his opinion, superfluous.

In our opinion, the choice of therapy comes down to the question of which goal one sets for it: If the clinician wishes the relatively rapid removal of often debilitating or constricting single, precisely defined phobias, behavioral therapy is the method of choice, although symptom removal may be followed by other neurotic compromise formations. If he wants, however, to resolve the phobic syndrome in its entire complexity and many-layeredness, psychoanalysis is preferable, although it too has shown failures. Clearly the two methods do not present a choice between right or wrong but are mutually complementary and compatible, although certainly not so, if carried out by the same therapist with the same patient.

REFERENCES

1   Agras, W., Chapin, H., and Oliveau, D. The natural history of phobia. *Arch. Gen. Psychiatry* 26:315–317, 1972.
2   Agras, W., Sylvester, D., and Oliveau, D. The epidemiology of common fears and phobias. *Compr. Psychiatry* 10:151–156, 1969.
3   Andreasen, N. C., and Bardach, J. Dysmorphophobia: symptom or disease. *Amer. J. Psych.* 134:673–675, 1977.
4   Arlow, J. A. "Character traits and perversion." Unpublished paper.
5   Berg, I. School phobia in the children of agoraphobic women. *Br. J. Psychiatry,* 128:86–89, 1976.
6   Brenner, C. Some comments on technical precepts in psychoanalysis. *J. Am. Psychoanal. Assoc.* 17:333–352, 1969.
7   Buglass, D., Clarke, J., Henderson, A. S., Kreitman, W., and Presley, A. S. A study of agoraphobic housewives. *Psychol. Med.* 7:73–86, 1977.
8   Burns, L. E., and Thorpe, G. L. Fears and clinical phobias: Epidemiological aspects and the national survey of agoraphobics. *J. Int. Med. Res.* Suppl. 1, 5:132–139, 1977.
9   Chesser, E. Behavior therapy: Recent trends and current practice. *Br. J. Psychiatry* 129:289–307, 1976.

10 Errera, P., and Coleman, J. A long-term follow-up study of neurotic phobic patients in a psychiatric clinic. *J. Nerv. Ment. Dis.* 136:267–271, 1963.

11 Fenichel, O. "Remarks on the common phobias," 1944. In *The collected papers*, pp. 278–287. New York: Norton, 1954.

12 Fenichel, O. "The counterphobic attitude," 1939. In *The collected papers*, second series, pp. 163–173. New York: Norton, 1954.

13 Ferber, L. Panel report: Phobias and their vicissitudes. *J. Am. Psychoanal. Assoc.* 7:182–192, 1959.

14 Frances, A., and Dunn, P. The attachment-autonomy conflict in agoraphobia. *Int. J. Psychoanal.* 56:435–439, 1975.

15 Frankel, F. H., and Orne, M. T. Hypnotizability and phobic behavior. *Arch. Gen. Psychiatry* 33:1259–1261, 1976.

16 Freud, A. *The ego and the mechanisms of defense. The writings of Anna Freud*, vol. 2. New York: International Universities Press, 1936.

17 Freud, A. Fears, anxieties, and phobic phenomena. *Psychoanal. Study Child* 32:85–90, 1977.

18 Freud, S. "Obsessions and phobias," 1895. In *Standard edition*, vol. 3, ed. J. Strachey, pp. 71–84. London: Hogarth Press, 1962.

19 Freud, S. "Analysis of a phobia in a five-year-old boy," 1909. In *Standard edition*, vol. 10, ed. J. Strachey, pp. 3–149. London: Hogarth Press, 1955.

20 Freud, S. "Repression," 1915. In *Standard edition*, vol. 14, ed. J. Strachey, pp. 143–158. London: Hogarth Press, 1957.

21 Freud, S. (1919) "Lines of advance in psychoanalytic therapy," 1919. In *Standard edition*, vol. 17, ed. J. Strachey, pp. 147–168. London: Hogarth Press, 1955.

22 Freud, S. "Inhibitions, symptoms, and anxiety," 1926. In *Standard edition*, vol. 20, ed. J. Strachey, pp. 77–175. London: Hogarth Press, 1959.

23 Gehl, R. H. (1964) Depression and claustrophobia. *Int. J. Psychoanal.* 45:312–323, 1964.

24 Gehl, R. H. (1973) Indecision and claustrophobia. *Int. J. Psychoanal.* 54:47–59, 1973.

25 Lewin, B. D. Claustrophobia. *Psychoanal. Q.*, 4:227–233, 1935.

26 Lewin, B. D. *The psychoanalysis of elation*, 1950. New York: The Psychoanalytic Quarterly, 1961.

27 Little, R. Spider phobias. *Psychoanal. Q.* 36:51–60, 1967.

28 MacKenzie, K. R. The eclectic approach to the treatment of phobias. *Am. J. Psychiatry*, 130:1103–1106, 1973.

29 Mahler, M. *On human symbiosis and the vicissitudes of individuation*. New York: International Universities Press, 1968.

30 Marks, I. M. Agoraphobic syndrome (phobic anxiety state). *Arch. Gen. Psychiatry* 23:538–553, 1970.

31 Marks, I. M. The current status of behavioral psychotherapy: Theory and practice. *Am. J. Psychiatry* 133:253–261, 1976.

32 Marks, I. M., and Herst, E. R. A survey of 1200 agoraphobics in Britain. *Soc. Psychiatry* 5:16–24, 1970.

33 Meuli, K. *Gesammelte Schriften*, vol. 1. Basel: Schwabe, 1975.

34 Nemiah, J. C. "Phobic neurosis." In *Comprehensive textbook of psychiatry*,

2nd ed., ed. A. M. Freedman, H. I. Kaplan, and B. J. Sadock. Baltimore: Williams and Wilkins, 1975.

35   Reutsch, H. The genesis of agoraphobia. *Int. J. Psychoanal.* 10:51–69, 1929.

36   Rhead, C. The role of pregenital fixations in agoraphobia. *J. Am. Psychoanal. Assoc.* 17:848–861, 1969.

37   Roth, M. The phobic-anxiety-depersonalization syndrome. *Proc. R. Soc. Med.* 52:8, 587, 1959.

38   Sim, M., and Houghton, H. Phobic anxiety and its treatment. *J. Nerv. Ment. Dis.* 143:484–491, 1966.

39   Sperling, M. Spider phobias and spider fantasies. *J. Am. Psychoanal. Assoc.* 19:472–498, 1971.

40   Terhune, W. The phobic syndrome: Its nature and treatment. *J. Ark. Med. Soc.,* 58:230–236, 1961.

41   Waldron, S., Shrier, D. K., Stone, B., and Tobin, F. School phobia and other childhood neuroses: A systematic study of the children and their families. *Am. J. Psychiatry* 132:802–808, 1975.

42   Westphal, C. Die Agoraphobie: Eine neuropathische Erscheinung. *Arch. Psychiatr. Nervenkr.* 3:138–161, 1871; 3:219–221, 1872.

43   Wilson, J. V. Kinnier *An introduction to Babylonian psychiatry.* Assyriolian, Studies, no. 16, Oriental Institute. Chicago: University of Chicago Press, 1965.

44   Wurmser, L. "Historical development of psychological thinking in medicine." In *Psychiatric foundations of medicine,* vol. 1, eds. G. U. Balis, L. Wurmser, E. McDaniel, and R. G. Grenell. Boston: Butterworths, 1978.

11

Obsessive-Compulsive Neurosis

Anne C. Redmond, M.D.

Man has been trying to control his future throughout history. Central to all religious beliefs is the acquisition of a better future through adherence to rules and ritual in a difficult present. Obeying the rules is man's attempt to influence a power (deity, saint, force, cosmic consciousness) which has the ability to improve the next moment (day, year, lifetime, life after death).

Not only is this theme in religion, but it also pervades all of culture. Shakespeare's sonnets, published in 1609, illustrate this struggle. Time and aging are major themes in 48 of the 154 sonnets. In sonnet 19 [24:1752] the first five lines portray time as "devouring" and cruel. Life is in a constant state of decay. Then time is acknowledged as being omnipotent: "And do what e'er thou wilt, swift footed Time,/To the wide world and all her fading sweets," however, the author makes himself more omnipotent: "But I forbid thee one most heinous crime," which is reinforced by a ritualized address:

> O, carve not with thy hours my love's fair brow,
> Nor draw no lines there with thine antique pen;
> Him in thy course untainted do allow,
> For beauty's pattern to succeeding men.

This is followed by a line which again acknowledges time's omnipotence (undoing man's) but immediately reestablishes man's superiority by the command for time to progress: "Yet do thy worst, old Time." Finally the author magically withdraws his lover from time's effects, "despite thy wrong,/My love shall in my verse ever live young."

This poem beautifully illustrates obsessive-compulsive thinking and feeling. Individuals with an obsessive personality style are chiefly concerned with the issue of control — the most obvious and relentless struggle being with time. Since all living things are prisoners of the life cycle, man is constantly aging. For the obsessive personality this process of change is particularly abhorrent; therefore, he strives to create a static world — perfect without change [28].

CLINICAL DESCRIPTION

A personality style represents an individual's characteristic ways of (1) receiving information from both his internal and external environment, (2) processing this information, and (3) transmitting new information to the self and others. This information may be perceptions, affects, cognitions, or motor actions. Most of the time people are unaware of their personality patterns in daily living [25]. A functional personality style allows the individual to obtain attention, affection, and achievement. Expressing this in the psychoanalytic framework, a healthy person is able to work and to love [10].

In order to function comfortably, one must be able to adapt to the changes which occur with time, especially the transition from childhood to adulthood. The way small children process the world is entirely different than the way of the functional adult. A child must gradually separate himself from the external world. The initial assumption is that his thoughts cause external events, since there is no boundary between self and other. This magical thinking is accompanied by strong fluctuating feelings, ranging from euphoria to extreme dysphoria, and by a very short attention span for any thought or activity. Moreover, the child is realistically dependent upon adults who are bigger, stronger, more capable, and more successful for his life support, e.g., food, clothes, shelter, education, and love. As the normal child matures he gradually recognizes that he is separate from others, one among many, and gaining in size, education, and an ability for self-care. The magical thinking is largely abandoned, being encapsulated in permissible adult activities such as religion, astrology, gambling, and superstition. The desperate life sustaining need for other people (his parents) also recedes in favor of autonomy. The vicissitudes of daily living, especially those adverse events which none of us can completely prevent (a broken toilet, a car which will not start, the onset of illness, another world crisis, death of a relative), require coping flexibility within the personality structure. This coping flexibility is learned during childhood if parents are flexible and protective of their children [23].

If a child is overwhelmed by external events such as dysfunctional parents or early death, there is regression to magical thinking and other early ways of processing information. One group of characteristic ways of coping with internal and external demands, called *ego defenses* in psychoanalytic theory, are learned in early childhood. These are usually modified with age and experience. The overwhelmed child desperately holds on to early defenses even as he matures. Hence an adult emerges with exaggerated, rigid characterological defenses which do not allow for the effective attainment of attention, affection, and achievement [7,23]. This adult may be diagnosed at sometime as having a personality disorder. He himself may not be uncomfortable with his style; however, he may not be able to work and may be creating considerable discomfort in other people or the society, i.e., breaking laws. He may have no personal relationships. If this same person experiences dysphoria then he is symptomatic. Anxiety is usually the first symptom. Other symptoms are an attempt to cope with this anxiety when the usual defenses in the personality style no longer can contain it [14]. Neurotic symptoms, such as depression, obsessive-compulsive rituals, phobias, are alien and may be debilitating to the patient. These are generally the presenting symptoms of a patient voluntarily seeking psychiatric help.

An important point not to be overlooked is that in any one person's life time he may have intermittent symptoms interspersed between relatively symptom-free functioning. Other people have a marginally functional existence with fluctuations; still others are chronically severely impaired.

Obsessive Personality Disorder

It is not known if there is an infantile temperament which predisposes to an obsessive personality style in later life, although these people possess character traits which may be traced back to infancy. Cognition is sharply focused on a very narrow spectrum; minute details are carefully examined, whereas major trends are not perceived. Rigid rules are created for perceptions, thoughts, feelings, and actions. Experiences not conforming to those rules are handled by the ego defense system using reaction formation, isolation, undoing, displacement, intellectualization, rationalization, and/or denial. These defenses permit the individual to have little conscious awareness or concern about material which contradicts the obsessive's belief system, hence the missing of the essentials [4]. The obsessive has very ritualistic ways of thinking, feeling, and acting, which are attempts to conform to rules. Although the belief system becomes a part of the obsessive, in his thinking the rules are "out there somewhere." His herculean task is to discover and adhere to these rules. If he can accomplish this, he will have security in the future and be in control — the ultimate goal. He is compelled to strive for perfection, that is, the state of no change. Since a state of no change is unrealistic there are lapses in his logic; for example, he may ponder for months about a decision, painstakingly balancing all the factors, then impulsively make the choice based on a factor not at all related to his well being; e.g., a man spent eight months reading literature on new cars, then suddenly bought a used truck for which he had no need because it had a new engine installed. Since making decisions implies change as well as an increase in the degree of freedom of the individual, obsessives frequently have trouble choosing between alternatives [21].

Feelings seem overwhelming. The predominant feelings states are anger, fear, shame, guilt, and disgust [15,26]. In the nonsymptomatic obsessive these feelings, although present, are syntonic. There seems to be a deficit of happiness, joy, and love, and spontaneity is frightening. Feelings may oscillate in a fashion similar to thoughts and actions. The effort to control all experience generally brings about an exaggerated pendulum effect [13]. For example, the obsessive who will not permit himself to get angry and then may finally have a temper tantrum over a minor event. This loss of control makes him feel fear and shame, which leads to more anger. This affect explosion is similar to the decision-making process, where tremendous time and thought have been spent weighing the alternatives, but the actual decision is made on irrelevant impulse. Instead of remaining fixed in the neutral zone, the obsessive experiences wide oscillations and thus tries harder to remain static in the middle [21].

Actions are also carefully regulated. Much attention is given to eating, bowel, dressing, and cleanliness routines. Daily activity may be highly ritualized. Paradoxically there may be orderliness and messiness relating to the same or similar functions. A patient may have a clean desk surface and chaotic drawers or may consistently always be one-half hour late. A student may begin the semester taking twenty credits (a very heavy load) and drop twelve after three weeks, leaving an insufficient load of eight [26].

Interpersonal relationships present difficulty for the obsessive [4,21]. First and foremost he has trouble controlling his spouse. Power struggles are common. Second, intimacy requires a decision to be committed. Since decision making is so hard the obsessive "straddles the fence," leaving his partner insecure and angry. Because the spouse can never achieve perfection (his internal concept), he is constantly angry, critical, and demanding that the spouse try harder. His partner is not recognized as a person who has needs, hopes, and a different set of values [3].

Obsessive women frequently are anorgasmic because they cannot give up monitering the sexual act. Obsessive men tend to be goal oriented, striving for climax without awareness of their partner's needs [12]. Tenderness is not a comfortable emotion; therefore, courtship, sexuality, and marriage assume the aura of a business arrangement. Child rearing may also be awkward. As children's spontaneity can be threatening to the obsessive's need to control, child rearing is approached with rules allowing for little deviation: The children are expected to conform to the parent's expectations from earliest infancy. Achievement in school usually is demanded. Since the negative feelings — anger, fear, shame, disgust — are not admitted to by the obsessive parent, the children are raised with the cognitive message being different from the affective message. The obsessive father may delegate all parental responsibility to his wife: "That's her job, mine is to earn money." This also protects him from personal decision making [2,3].

The obsessive functions more comfortably in society than in his personal life. He is a diligent worker, being meticulous, thorough, and organized. He follows rules easily, has impeccable integrity, is cautious and thrifty. He is usually formal in his interpersonal relations at work. He is able to make decisions and has definite opinions which in some way reflect the code of the work. With friends he is stilted, spends much time discussing work or politics, and does not relax. He may have his entire social life regimented, e.g., bridge on Friday, shopping on Saturday. He pays his bills, follows the law, and keeps the house relatively neat. Time and money are major preoccupations. Again there may be pockets of disorder in his social functioning — e.g., a report not finished which was due a month ago [16].

The preceding character traits will be more exaggerated and rigid as the severity of the obsessive personality disorder increases. It is not unusual for a patient with an obsessive personality disorder to present with depression, anxiety, or phobias as the chief complaint. He is unaware of how his personality style has contributed to his problems [20,21].

Obsessive-Compulsive Neurosis

The compulsive neurotic experiences an inability to prevent himself from thinking, feeling, or acting in certain repetitive, nonsensical ritualistic forms. Accompanying these is usually a belief that these thoughts and actions can influence the future in a magical way. Brooding doubt is intermingled with an anxiety-laden search for certainty. Finally, there is usually a conscious preoccupation with unacceptable aggressive impulses, such as fear of killing someone or of being killed. All of this is accompanied by anxiety, anger, fear, shame, guilt, and disgust, causing much discomfort to the patient [15,21,28] and may be so severe as to disrupt his work and interpersonal relationships. Phobias are frequent additional symptoms and are a sign that the obsessional mechanism is not working to bind the anxiety from the intrapsychic conflict. The phobias may relate directly to the obsessive fantasy, i.e., a man who had an obsession about strangling his wife with a rope was terrified when he saw ropes. It is another attempt by the ego to gain control of the hostile impulses. The effects of these phobias may range from very mild to very severe [20] (see chapter 10).

The following case illustrates a compulsive neurosis in an individual with an obsessive personality style.

A twenty-three-year-old white single woman, Ms. K, first sought psychiatric help two months after her mother had ordered her to move out of the family home because of her depression and obsessive thoughts about killing her twenty-six-year-old brother who continued to live at home. "I think about poisoning my brother over and over." She also had a compulsion to count all of the oncoming cars in the center lane when she was driving. This was done to prevent her brother from having an auto accident. She had been left by a boyfriend, with whom she had lived, one month before returning home. She had not worked since age twenty-one, when she had become anxious teaching first grade. "I kept thinking about smashing the children's heads together." She had many daily routines — bathing, dressing, and bathroom habits were ritualized. She was almost always ten minutes late. She wanted to paint but was overwhelmed with what subjects and colors to use. She lived alone in a room from which she wanted to move but had been unable to decide upon a new living arrangement. She experienced extreme anxiety when she tried to look at "for rent" or "roommate" ads. She was very self-critical: "I should be working"; "I hate myself"; "I'm so lazy." She had unpacked seven out of ten boxes with the contents neatly arranged three days after she moved. The other three boxes had been sitting near the middle of the rooms since that time. She had been furious with her previous boyfriend for not taking care of her: "He should have worked so I could stay home and do housework." "I should have been able to figure out the right way to get him to marry me." Her intrapsychic life was highly organized. She had a fantasy of the "perfect" mother, father, daughter, and son which she tenaciously guarded. "I was the perfect child — my mother did not take care of me right." She was acutely ashamed as she discussed these totally foreign murderous thoughts. During the first visit, she was meticulously groomed, wearing clean elaborately embroidered jeans and an indian blouse. Her affect was highly controlled as was her speech style. She was courteous. There was no evidence of delusions or hallucinations. She had a fear of flying.

EPIDEMIOLOGY

Studies by Rudin (1953) and Woodruff and Pitts (1964) estimate a 0.05 percent incidence of obsessive-compulsive disorders in Western culture. China has the same incidence. It is rarely found in underdeveloped countries [5].

There are three reliable published accounts of four sets of identical twins with obsessive-compulsive neurosis. This is greater than the law of probability; however, the numbers are so small that no conclusion can be reached about a genetic predisposition for this illness. Between 5 and 10 percent of parents and 2 and 14 percent of siblings of obsessional neurotics have pronounced obsessional traits. Seven studies provide evidence of obsessive-compulsive traits occurring in 64 to 83 percent of the patients prior to the onset of the full-blown obsessive compulsive neurosis [5]. Ingram's [11] study of 89 inpatients demonstrated substantial obsessional symptoms during childhood in 25 percent of his obsessive-compulsive neurotics.

Obvious precipitating factors are present in over half of these cases. An analysis of eight studies indicated that the first symptom occurs prior to age 15 in 30.5 percent of 667 cases; 41.9 percent have their first symptom before age 20; 55.3 percent before 25; 73.6 percent before 30; 84.1 percent before 35; 91.3 percent before 40; 95.3 percent before 45; and 96.3 percent before 50 [5]. Clearly this is an illness which begins early. There is no male-female or social-class skewing. There seems to be a higher intelligence level among obsessives when compared to other neurotics. The course of the illness is variable. The literature is scant and has not correlated outcome to initial severity of illness or treatment modality. The types of courses noted are improving, remaining the same for years and then improving, fluctuating with or without periods of complete remission, and becoming worse [5,11]. Research is minimal on how treatment affects outcome; however, clinicians and patients both note improvement from treatment [5].

ETIOLOGY AND PATHOGENESIS

For purposes of learning fundamentals, the obsessive spectrum will be examined using psychoanalytic, interpersonal, and behavior theories. In
psychoanalytic theory a personality disorder develops as the ego tries to
contain the anxiety produced by unresolved psychic conflicts. Neurotic
symptoms develop when the ego's characteristic set of defenses are not
binding the anxiety. New defenses may suddenly be mobilized, the results of which are experienced as ego-alien and/or dysphoric [7,10]. The
major conflicts for obsessives first occur in infancy during the anal stage
which coincides with toilet training [1:370]. Erikson [6] called this the
stage of autonomy versus shame. According to Kestenberg [13], the infant
from six months on has been playing cyclic holding and releasing games,
i.e., holding and releasing the sphincter during diapering, peek-a-boo,
holding and dropping toys. As the infant grows the mother increasingly
frustrates these games so that the infant learns to prolong holding. This
coincides with an increasing physiological ability for bowel and bladder
control as well as an increasing separation of self from other. The child at
two is alternately approaching the mother lovingly (relaxed) or hostilely
(tense), which is another example of holding and releasing. At this time
mother (father) begins to demand control over holding and releasing of
bowel movements. The child, however, still experiences his feces and
urine as a part of himself and so is reluctant to cooperate. Mother (father)
and child are now in a power struggle over control of bowels, one which
fluctuates in a rhythmical fashion over time as bowel and bladder fill and
are released. The child must give up pleasant, warm feces, whereas before
he was giving up a cold, soggy diaper. As the child explores his boundaries, he is not only in a power struggle about toilet training but also in
other areas of life, e.g., what to eat, when to sleep. Magical thinking and
fantasy predominate his thoughts. He feels omnipotent. If mother is so
rigid in her demands that it exceeds the infant's capacity or if she is overly
angry and punitive with the child, the child's rage is increased along with
his sadistic impulses. The infant with a punitive mother will toilet train
out of fear, rather than becoming clean for the sake of mother. This always
occurs if these demands are made before the infant has a capacity to do
things for another person [1:370,19]. The mother's rigidity, anger, and
punishment are incorporated within the infant and become the rudiments
of a very sadistic superego. The child not only fears the parent but fears
himself. This is the origin of the preoccupation with issues of control,
time, rules, ritual, feelings of omnipotence, sadistic fantasy, and bowel
functions always seen in the obsessive [9,18:196]. The lack of fusion of
aggression and sexual energy, characteristic of a two-year-old child, remains present in the adult obsessive [9]. The obsessive is constantly trying

to cope with the affects of rage, fear, shame, guilt, and anxiety. The raging punitive superego creates the shame, fear, and guilt. The anxiety is a symptom of the marked intrapsychic conflict, as the superego forbids gratification of id instincts, even those made acceptable to the ego [7,14]. The magical belief in omnipotence makes the internal rage seem especially dangerous to the external world. All subsequent developmental stages are distorted by these dynamics. At some point in time a combination of external events and internal responses lead to symptom formation.

The major ego defense mechanisms which are developed to handle this conflict in the obsessive-compulsive are regression, reaction formation, isolation, undoing, and displacement [8]. When an individual is stressed at any age by intrapsychic and external events, *regression* to an earlier mode of functioning occurs. In the obsessive, regression proceeds to the anal stage. *Reaction formation* is the ego's attempt to contain rage. The rage is *repressed* (placed into the unconscious) and the opposite attitude substituted. Hence, obsessive individuals are usually gentle, nonviolent people, and the preoccupation with cleanliness hides a wish to play in feces and dirt. *Isolation* is employed: The cognitive content of an experience is remembered, but the accompanying affect has been dissociated from that memory. An obsessive will talk with a calm affect about being beaten severely at age seven by his father. Later he may be overwhelmed with rage but not know the content. The obsessive thought of murdering someone is experienced as foreign and guilt-producing by the patient but is not accompanied by anger. *Undoing* is another defense, which is related to magic and expiation. Something is performed or thought which is the opposite of what preceded it. Either or both may be thoughts or actions. The opposite action or thought magically changes the first. The hand-washing ritual made famous by Lady Macbeth is an example of a compulsion to undo the murderous wish. Obsessive thoughts and compulsions stem from this mechanism. *Displacement* is another defense found in compulsions and phobias. The affect is moved from one thought to another. Strong dysphoria may be associated with an innocuous compulsion, such as a ritual for putting on shoes. A woman may experience terrible fear if she encounters a cockroach (cockroach phobia). In both cases the feeling is not related to the event [7].

Barnett [2–4] emphasizes the interpersonal genesis of the compulsive syndromes. He believes that the central dynamic is the need to maintain innocence about oneself and one's relationships. He states that one or both parents are hostile and engaged in severe power struggles with the child, who must not only conform to parental demands for performance but also must acknowledge neither his own nor his parent's hostility. The cognitive pattern of making things static prevents the processing of information about ongoing interpersonal relationships, thus the family dynamics can be camouflaged in a facade of love and concern. The emphasis for life achievement is placed on school and work performance, not on interpersonal relationships.

Obsessive-compulsive behavior can also be explained by learning theory. Avoidance learning is a procedure in which a noxious stimulus is avoided by the learned behavior. The greater the noxious stimulus, the more the behavior is resistant to extinction. Administration of other stresses during the learning process increases the resistance to extinction. In the extinction phase, the noxious stimulus is removed. Obsessive rituals are considered to be avoidance responses in the acquisition or maintenance phase if severe emotional dysphoria occurs when the behavior is resisted. The obsessive is unable to discriminate when the behavior is appropriate, which is when he will receive a noxious stimulus for not performing the behavior (thought). Also, any noxious stimulus — even one completely unrelated to the avoidance ritual — will increase the frequency of the ritual. When both the ritual and the consequences of not performing it are dysphoric it is called an avoidance-avoidance conflict [29:197,30].

Phobias are classically conditioned anxiety responses. A neutral stimulus, i.e., bug, is paired in time with fearful events, i.e., horror movie, which elicits strong fear responses. In the future the bug alone elicits the fear. This is not extinguished because the patient avoids the bug. Why some people develop these obsessive symptoms and others do not is being studied. It is hypothesized that some individuals are in a state of hyperarousal by temperament and are more prone to the acquisition of these learned behaviors [29:197,30].

DIFFERENTIAL DIAGNOSIS

If depression is the presenting complaint, the clinician must differentiate between depressive illness in an individual with a functioning obsessive style and depression as the dysphoric symptom of an obsessive personality disorder. Usually depression, although currently increased in the latter, is of a chronic, long-standing nature, accompanied by interpersonal and social disruptions. Patients with involutional melancholia or a discrete episode of psychotic depression frequently have an obsessive style but have experienced little conscious dysphoria or inability to work in the past [21].

Phobias may be present in obsessive conditions or may be the predominant symptom. In the phobic neurosis the patient fears that he is in danger from the phobic object or situation. The obsessive on the other hand, fears that he will harm others and the phobia is another attempt to control this harmful impulse [20].

Some patients with obsessive personalities and/or symptoms have schizophrenia. This genetic illness probably affects the development of the child from conception. Obsessive mechanisms are employed to try to control the distorted thinking process. Usually these mechanisms are more fragile and primitive in the patient with schizophrenia than in the non-schizophrenic obsessive. As the acute psychosis emerges, obsessions may pass into delusions and superego rules may become hallucinations telling the patient what to do. Schizophrenia is not the underlying process of obsessive-compulsive neurosis. These are two distinct entities even though the schizophrenic may have rituals and destructive fantasies. The obsessive may have a fear of "going crazy," but for him this means a loss of control of emotions or actions, not psychosis. Schizophrenia is diagnosed by mental status and history. Delusions, especially of mind control, thought broadcast, and thought insertion, in addition to hallucinations, loosening of associations, and agitation characterize the acute psychosis [21].

TREATMENT

Psychotherapy with the obsessional initially must be aimed at the distortions in the cognitive sphere. These patients confuse every issue with much intellectualization, reaction formation, and doing and undoing. As the crux of the matter is being approached, the patient will become even more elusive, especially if a decision is evolving, since this increases anxiety. The therapist must avoid getting into a power struggle with the patient, who will unconsciously always be in one with the therapist. Although committed to keeping the surface rules of time and payment, the patient will distort the boundaries, such as being chronically late. In essence, all of the obsessional traits will be used in the relationship with the therapist [17]. The therapist's job is to help the patient observe his traits and explore his life both past and present. He also must monitor his work and countertransference. The symptoms which brought the patient into therapy provide motivation for the initial commitment. It is only after the patient begins to resolve his cognitive distortions, including his attempts to fix everything in a static position, can he meaningfully examine his interpersonal relationships. Also, underneath the defenses is a vulnerable person who is being consumed by rage, fear, shame, and guilt from his sadistic superego and id impulses. Exploring this and working through the distortions more thoroughly is usually the middle-stage work in therapy. A person who is resolving his conflicts experiences change in his actions and interpersonal relationships as well as in his cognition. Symptoms such as rituals diminish, self-esteem rises, and the individual is less dysphoric. The patient gives up much of his striving for perfection. The end stage of therapy is the termination process where separation anxiety is worked through [2,4,21,22]. The therapist's explanation of the dynamics will vary according to the model used to describe the origins of obsessive behavior. The techniques used will also vary somewhat. Group psychotherapy has been effectively used to treat obsessives [22].

With respect to *behavioral therapy*, two behavioral strategies have been used to treat obsessions. The first involves anxiety reduction and counter conditioning. The patient is taught deep relaxation, then introduced to a systematic desensitization format. Relaxation is paired with thinking about the obsessions and/or phobias, hence the anxiety, shame, and guilt are extinguished. The second group of techniques involves extinguishing the obsessive thought or behavior. One technique involves the signaling to the therapist when a thought is occurring, and the therapist then claps his hands loudly or yells "stop." Repetition of this inhibits the disturbed thoughts [29:197,30].

Among the *physical treatments*, no medication seems to be especially effective in treating obsessional states. However, severe depression and anxiety should be treated with appropriate medication. In some instances the obsessional symptoms clear as the affect in disturbances are treated. The results from leukotomies performed in Europe in the 1940s and 1950s are ambiguous. This treatment is now almost never used [27].

REFERENCES

1   Abraham, K. "Contributions to the theory of the anal character." In *Selected papers on psychoanalysis*. New York: Basic Books, 1953.
2   Barnett, J. On cognitive disorders in the obsessional. *Contemp. Psychoanal.* 2:122, 1965.
3   Barnett, J. On aggression in the obsessional neurosis. *Contemp. Psychoanal.* 6:48, 1970.
4   Barnett, J. Therapeutic intervention in the dysfunctional thought processes of the obsessional. *Am. J. Psychother.* 26:338, 1972.
5   Black, A. "The natural history of obsessional neurosis." In *Obsessional states*, ed. H. Beech. London: Methuen, 1974.
6   Erikson, E. *Childhood and society*. New York: Norton, 1963.
7   Fenichel, O. *The psychoanalytic theory of neurosis*. New York: Norton, 1945.
8   Freud, A. *The ego and mechanisms of defense*, rev. ed. New York: International Universities Press, 1966.
9   Freud, A. Obsessional neurosis: A summary of psychoanalytic views as presented at the congress. *Int. J. Psychoanal.* 47:116, 1966.
10   Freud, S. *A general introduction to psychoanalysis*. London: Liveright, 1935.
11   Ingram, I. M. Obsessional illness in mental hospital patients. *J. Ment. Sci.* 107:382, 1961.
12   Kaplan, H. *The new sex therapy*. New York: Brunner/Mazel, 1974.

13   Kestenberg, J. Rhythm and organization in obsessive-compulsive develop-
      ment. *Int. J. Psychoanal.* 47:151, 1966.
14   Lesse, S. Anxiety: Its relationship to the development and amelioration of
      obsessive-compulsive disorders. *Am. J. Psychother.* 26:330, 1972.
15   Monroe, R. *The compulsive phenomenology of will and action*, ed. E. Straus and
      R. Griffith. Duquesne University Press, 1967.
16   Monroe, R. "Obsessive behavior: Integration of psychoanalytic and other
      approaches." In *American handbook of psychiatry*, eds. S. Arieti and E. Brody.
      New York: Basic Books, 1974.
17   Morgenthaler, F. Psychodynamic aspects of defense with comments on tech-
      nique in the treatment of obsessional neurosis. *Int. J. Psychoanal.* 47:203,
      1966.
18   Rado, S. "Obsessive behavior: So-called obsessive-compulsive neurosis." In
      American handbook of psychiatry, eds. S. Arieti and E. Brody. New York: Basic
      Books, 1974.
19   Ramzy, I. Factors and features of early compulsive formation. *Int. J. Psycho-
      anal.* 47:169, 1966.
20   Salzman, L. Obsessions and phobias. *Contemp. Psychoanal.* 2:1, 1965.
21   Salzman, L. *The obsessive personality.* New York: Jason Aronson, 1973.
22   Schwartz, E. The treatment of the obsessive patient in the group therapy set-
      ting. *Am. J. Psychother.* 26:352, 1972.
23   Serban, G. The process of neurotic thinking. *Am. J. Psychother.* 18:418, 1974.
24   Shakespeare, W. *The riverside Shakespeare.* Boston: Houghton Mifflin, 1974.
25   Shapiro, D. *Neurotic styles.* New York: Basic Books, 1965.
26   Stekel, W. *Compulsion and doubt*, vols. 1 and 2. New York: Liveright, 1949.
27   Sternberg, M. "Physical treatments in obsessional disorders." In *Obsessional
      states*, ed. H. Beech. London: Methuen, 1974.
28   Straus, E. *On obsession.* Nervous and Mental Disease Monograph, no. 73,
      1948. New York.
29   Teasdale, J. "Learning models of obsessional-compulsive disorder." In *Ob-
      sessional states*, ed. H. Beech. London: Methuen, 1974.
30   Wolpe, J. L. *Behavior therapy and techniques.* New York: Pergamon Press,
      1966.

12

Depressive Neurosis

Leon Wurmser, M.D.

As so often in psychopathology, we clinicians must confront a paradox: On the one hand we undoubtedly encounter very frequently and clearly severe and clinically interfering forms of depression, both in private life and in medical and psychiatric practice. On the other side, boundaries, subgroups, and even the usefulness of the distinction of both neurotic depressions and depression as a diagnostic category in general are unclear and controversial. One must ask what are the obligatory criteria for depression.

The criteria I have chosen — and on which this chapter is based — to explain depression and its ramifications are very briefly that

1   There are normal, not neurotic (or psychotic) forms of depression.

2   Neurotic depression is not a homogeneous illness but a fairly well ordered group of forms which have a leading symptom group in common. However, for practical and theoretical reasons, depression can be differentiated into a number of psychodynamically quite varied forms.

3   The transition to affective psychoses (called melancholia in earlier terminology) may be very unclear. Considerable somatic

symptoms (e.g., insomnia, eating disturbances, and rhythmicity, like greater severity in the morning and partial withdrawal from social functioning) are often used as criteria for the psychotic forms but may still be part of neurotic depression. Only if intensive enough, they verge into an indubitably psychotic state. Still this differential diagnosis may in concrete cases remain in doubt, even in psychoanalysis, for a very long time and for very experienced observers [28]. In contrast the differential diagnosis between neurotic and schizophrenic depression is far easier.

4   As in nearly all emotional disturbances, the concept of the complementary series and the continuous spectrum [35] proves to be of particular value. It was proposed by Freud in [17] but circumscribed already much earlier, e.g., in the famous "Three Essays on Sexuality" [13]: "Neurosis will always produce its greatest effect when constitution and experience work together in the same direction" [13:170]. He defined it in 1920 as a spectrum in "which the diminishing intensity of one factor [constitution] is balanced by the increasing intensity of the other [experience]" [13:240], without denying the existence of extreme cases at the two ends of the series. Thus the possible finding of biological predisposing factors, even in neurotic depression, would not invalidate psychodynamic scrutiny nor psychotherapy but might broaden the access to and deepen a comprehensive understanding of depressive disorders.

Although Brenner [9,10] has questioned the usefulness of the entire diagnostic category of depression (normal, neurotic, psychotic), his summarizing definition is very helpful:

"Depression" as a diagnostic entity is characterized by an alteration of affect. It is, indeed, often referred to as an affective disorder. The most common and most obvious symptoms of depression, the symptoms which have given it its name, are what are commonly called depressive affects: grief, despair and guilt, in varying degrees and combinations. Not only are these affects painful in themselves, they are also often associated with an inability to function normally and with self-injurious or even with self-destructive tendencies. It is doubtless this fact — that the emotions of depression are both painful and associated with serious behavioral abnormalities — that has resulted in their being used as a basis for diagnostic classification [9:25].

Thus it is important to distinguish between depression as affect and depression as syndrome. Depression as affect is in itself probably a compound emotion, not a simple and basic ego state, as Bibring [7] postulated. Brenner [9] stated that depression has a complex structure, of composite and manifold ideational content. The common denominator is the response to what is experienced as disaster that has occurred (while anxiety refers to an impending calamity).

More specifically, depression belongs to that type of affects which are called moods; these are generalized and enduring affects, defined by Jacobson as "ego states characterized by generalized discharge modifications which temporarily influence the qualities of all feelings, thoughts, and actions" [28:80].

In order to define the mood of depression three cardinal and specific features (according to most, though not all theoreticians), which follow each other in a temporal and psychodynamic sequence, are required: (1) a sense of unacceptable loss and change [25,38], (2) a severe drop of self-esteem [7,28], and (3) strong, but conflicted wishes for aggression which are dealt with by the well-known defense of turning against the self [18,28]. Wherever this compound mood of depression is the major symptom, the emotional state as a whole is called a depressive state, e.g., a depressive neurosis. If depressive states are examined more carefully, a large number of components and derivatives can be distinguished. Some of the leading feelings and behavior traits which mark the depressive mood or originate from it are derived from the first feature, the sense of loss: sadness, a painful feeling of being deprived of an integral part of one's life. A second group is related to the drop of self-esteem — feelings like despair, helplessness, loneliness, emptiness, and boredom. Still others reflect the third part, the self-attack: guilt, shame, irritability, and provocativeness. The prominent coloring by some of these derivative affects may be of assistance in subdividing the large group of nonpsychotic depressions.

HISTORICAL EXAMPLES

Depressive moods of all types (healthy, neurotic, and psychotic) are encountered throughout the literature of mankind and probably exist in all cultures.

Among the most ancient examples is a famous, impressive though not unambiguous papyrus from Egypt 2200 B.C., which presents the inner dialogue of a desperate man, desiring suicide, with his *Ba*, a concrete representative of his own soul. This inner dialogue represents an inner conflict and split between the wish to give in to the "fire of despair" and opposition to this suicidal yearning, expressed by "the voice of personal, individual truth" and ascribed to the Ba. The fragment ends with a reconciliation of these two inner voices in a new inner unity, leaving the decision (suicide or continued endurance) open. The detailed description of the depression often sounds modern, e.g.: "Death stands today before my eyes as if it were recovery for a sick man, freedom for one afflicted." He suffers under limitless loneliness, is desperate about the collapse of justice, tradition, wisdom, and friendship and about trustlessness and anarchy. His own name (his essence) has the foul smell of corpses or excrements, he feels "dumb unto despair," and he pleads with his Ba to relieve him of his anxiety about the sin of suicide [27]. Another source showing clear evidence for the universality of the depressive syndrome is the Biblical book of Job, itself probably reaching back to far older Egyptian and Babylonian sources; even the name Job is Egyptian.

A more modern document, more explicit and therefore far easier to compare with many of today's patients, is Goethe's *The Suffering of Young Werther* [21], the love of a young poet for a woman already promised to another man, a woman both encouraging and rejecting this love. Hundreds of quotes can be adduced which are similar to statements made by depressed patients. Even before Werther meets the girl he complains about his abrupt changes from "sweet melancholy to pernicious passion, from grief to debauchery," his feelings of depersonalization ("life of man is but a dream . . . merely the painting of colorful shapes and views on walls which imprison him"), later the narcissistic flavor of his love ("how I adore myself since she loves me"). Passion, suffering, pain beyond endurable limit is an illness to death, (a concept put in the center of philosophical experience by Kierkegaard [24]), no less a sickness than a malignant fever. Werther compares despair with an abyss: "All is darkness, no hope, no consolation, no comprehension." To be left without the loved one deprives him of worth and of the very sense of existence: "alone, abandoned by everyone, blind, pushed into a corner by the horrible distress of the heart — into the embracing death." Without his love he feels like a ghost returning to a burned out castle; life is empty and estranged, "the flowers of life are only appearances . . . I am played with like a puppet and touch the other's wooden hand." Murderous fury against his rival, but mostly against himself is overflooding like a dammed up river (Goethe's symbol, one taken up and elaborated later on by Freud) and cast into innumerable metaphors and fantasies, ending eventually in suicide. "One of the three of us has to leave, and that must be I. Oh my dearest! In this torn heart it has angrily been creeping around, often — to kill your husband —you! — me! — So be it!" He accuses himself of his sin of wanting and trying to take her from her husband, the punishment for it, and the hope of eventual reunion in eternal embrace with her in death.

Another, also well-known version of the same problem can be traced through Hesse's *Steppenwolf* [26]: "days of headache, days of the dying of the soul, those evil days of inner emptiness and despair . . . where the world of man and culture . . . grins at us like a nauseant." He is desperate with loneliness, meaninglessness, disgust, hatred — and, still, terrified of suicide. "New suffering and new guilt were towering up. Every time, the tearing off of a mask, the collapse of an ideal had been preceded by this ghastly emptiness and silence, this mortal constriction, loneliness and lack of relatedness, this void, a devastated hell of lovelessness and despair . . . a burning, endless suffering . . . a lowness and worthlessness of one's own self, but also this horrible anxiety about succumbing, all this fear of death" He uses alcohol, opium, and cocaine to escape for a few hours from the conflict between despair and anxiety, between the wish to die and the fear of death.

NORMAL AND NEUROTIC DEPRESSION

If one turns from literature to clinical practice, it is apparent that the vast majority of outpatients seen today by psychiatrists prominently complain about depression; in particular, many, perhaps most patients seen in intensive or in supportive psychotherapy or in psychoanalysis can fairly be subsumed under this symptomatically described group.

To distinguish between healthy forms of depression, and neurotic and psychotic forms the excellent book by Jacobson [28] is useful.

For example, if a close friend or relative leaves or dies, a person may feel a deep sense of loss, grief, and sadness. The world for a while may appear empty, triste; its worth, its color, its meaning seem to have faded, and with that those of the self. One may weep, seek out the same enjoyments shared with the departed, and try to rebuild life, often integrating into it particular interests and skills of the lost person [28:96,243]. This is best called *a reaction of grief, of mourning, of sadness.* Despite the sense of helplessness and hopelessness and the decrease of well-being, self-esteem, and esteem for the surroundings, it is not yet a depressive reaction.

But even if the condition proceeds to a clear form of depression, the person has not yet crossed over into neurotic territory: "We easily lose sight of the fact that both depressed and elated states may well develop within the range of normal mood conditions" [28:92]. If one assumes that the lost person, e.g., one's parent or spouse, has not only been loved but that a considerable dose of hostility is also present in one's mind, this anger and disappointment and the ensuing sense of guilt and regret about the other's passing are predominantly conscious. Thus there results a combination of feelings: on the one hand, a deep sorrow, sadness, and a sense of loss, gloom, focused helplessness and hopelessness, and loneliness (the grief reaction); on the other hand, anger, guilt, and memories of murderous thoughts, and withal a bad conscience, self-accusations, and self-deprecation. Anger and guilt usually refer less to the other's death or leaving and more to a personal failure for not having shown the departed enough love during his lifetime or presence. They eventually lead to an attempt to alter the self to make up for these past failings. This prevalently conscious, normal form of depression gradually loses its intensity and is overcome by the usual "work of mourning" and the ensuing inner change, often by some symbolic forms of reparation and restitution (e.g., by an upsurge of creativity) [18:244–245, 25:93–101]. In this form of depression a low level of compulsiveness, drivenness, of irresistible, fixed, stereotyped processes are typical. Conscious effort or external change relatively easily breaks through the pall of gloom.

Another instance for such a normal depression can be experienced if a person does a bad job, knows it, feels not up to the task, and is angry at himself for not having "shaped up" or for having placed himself into a position which he was unable to perform well. Of course, many neurotic processes may be operating too, e.g., the need to overreach one's abilities, the insistence to do the impossible, while raging at oneself for continued inability. On the other hand, a person may either find ways to grow into the task or to leave the overtaxing job. In this case the depression has been resolved by a rational action.

A third example is of particular importance for the physician: the depression induced by severe, especially terminal, illness or other situations of hopelessness (e.g., facing inevitable extermination during political persecution). In such cases even suicide may not automatically be a sign of pathology but a rationally reached decision.

Such forms of normal depression have been called by many (especially in Europe) a *reactive depression*. (On the other hand, Jacobson has a very different meaning of this term: "the kind of psychotic depression which, in contrast to endogenous depression, clearly develops in 'reaction' to a precipitating event" [28:168].

However, these same processes, as witnessed in the normal depression, may also largely go on unconsciously and be connected with deeply repressed conflicts: conflicts about wishes for symbolic union and fears of living a separate, detached, unfulfilled life; conflicts about yearning for something one cannot have (masculinity or femininity, penis or breasts, father or mother, beauty, power, or glorious intelligence) and ensuing envy and jealousy; conflicts about wanting to use, depend upon, and exploit others, while also trying to attain autarchic independence. All these unfulfillable demands and irreconcilable conflicts may lead to a largely unconsciously motivated depression: no hope, a helplessness about ever attaining the forbidden or unreachable, a deep need and want, a lowered self-esteem, and the much bruited-about feeling of inferiority (used by A. Adler as cornerstone of his theory). The angry, greedy, grabbing demands to correct the wrong are also largely unconscious as to their correct meaning and original target. Instead they are displaced (e.g., on to social success and money) and turned against the self (the insistent demands imposed on oneself and the ensuing fury that one never can live up to these goals): The depressive self-reproaches, self-condemnations, and self-destructive actions. As it befits the largely unconscious nature of this syndrome, no outer success and gratification can fill the inner void, the gap, in any lasting way. No sexual gratification, no joy about one's children, no attainment even of the highest professional rewards or awards, lifts the neurotic-depressive misery permanently. On the contrary, as Freud [16] demonstrated with the help of Shakespeare's *Macbeth* and Ibsen's *Rosmersholm*, there are many persons who, out of unconscious, overwhelming guilt, destroy themselves precisely at the moment when they have reached the very pinnacle of what they had worked for all their lives (including, e.g., Nixon and the presidency!). Freud called them "those wrecked by success" [16]. Thus quite a few patients decompensate into a severe depression, not when they are disappointed and deprived in outer reality but when they meet apparent fulfillment and satisfaction. As Freud stated: the frustration is not on the outside but remains internal and unconscious. A very similar process is encountered in psychotherapy or psychoanalysis: every new insight, every step out of the pit of neurotic misery is followed by a crushing sense of defeat and aggravation of symptoms, the so-called negative therapeutic reaction, a feeling that "I do not deserve to feel better and to succeed in therapy and life."

LEADING AFFECTS

By examining the major components of the syndrome of neurotic depression, some clusters of affects present in more or less intense form in most patients can be discerned. Dependent on the prevalence of one or the other cluster, patients, most of whom have always considered themselves ill, may be subdivided into groups. It must be clearly understood that all the feelings to be described may be encountered in varied intensity and combination in all neurotic depressions. Despite this overlap, however, it makes sense to use the most prominent clusters of feelings for a phenomenological (descriptive) differentiation which also might indicate the major defenses used. Moreover, how far a cluster reflects a deeper, perhaps etiological distinctiveness (e.g., level of causative conflict) still largely remains to be explored, but it makes sense to assume a link of leading core conflicts → leading group of defenses → most prominent symptomatic cluster of affects.

    1. In the *lonely depression*, the clinician may be struck by the intensity of feelings of abandonment, lovelessness, solitude and loneliness, isolation, unrelatedness, and the deep sense of helplessness about change

and loss. Hence, wishes for clinging symbiotic dependency, a restless search for an all-fulfilling partner, and an ideal of total fairness and acceptance mark the life of such a patient. Since a "perfect" partner either cannot be found or, if apparently encountered, inevitably disappoints or rejects the patient, life moves between brief states of apparent fulfillment of his fantasy and, with that, boundless bliss and elation, and long periods of profound, often suicidal depression.

In a lonely depression these feelings are prevalent in a conscious form. It may be surmised that conflicts about separation (especially separation traumata in the first few years of life with strong oral fixation) would represent the core of this form of depression. The major defenses are idealization (an absolutely good object), turning passive into active ("It is better for me actively to provoke rejection than to suffer it passively."), and turning rage against the self ("I am to blame, I do not want to kill the other who has forsaken me; I kill myself."). This latter defense is based on the defense by introjection: "Not the other (e.g., mother) is the bad, cruel, selfish, callous, worthless, weak one, but I am the one who has all those odious traits."

2. In the *empty depression*, feelings of emptiness, impoverishment, and neediness, and with that an attitude of demandingness and entitlement, greedy claiming, desperate surrender, and apathy prevail. If these feelings are very intense, disappointment and abandonment were particularly deep, massive and early, affecting the very core of one's self-feeling and self-esteem.

3. In the *angry depression* (Asch [4] "depression with rage") feelings of rage, envy, jealousy, demands for all-or-nothing often reflect as well as defend against a depressive core of helpless despair and the feeling that one has been angrily rejected. There are indeed many depressives whose depression is most noted by a nagging quarrelsomeness and complaining, or by violent and explosive outbursts of fury or lastly self-defeating rage precisely against those whom they are closest to (children, spouses, parents). Many an angry "explosive psychopath" has taken on such a chronically distempered attitude and mood as a defense against despair. (Obviously the clinician has to be careful not to declare every angry neurotic a depressive). The conflicts may lie on very early or much later levels. The leading defenses are turning passive into active (and with that "identification with the aggressor" [12], and projection ("I do not want to remain the bad and evil one, I want the other to be the source of my misery").

4. In *bored, apathetic depression* the feelings of boredom and, if more intense, hopelessness, form the leading complaint: "I have no meaning, no goal, no value, no hope in my life; I might just as well die." Often this state is expressed also by fatigue, ennui, a sense of weakness, a constant complaint: "I am harassed, chronically tired, uninterested." The patients

in this group seek excitement, change, distraction; sometimes they throw themselves into a frenzy of activity and obligations, of running after a cause or drugs, or even committing crimes or at least social transgressions as a counter-depressive defense. Most authors see the core conflict in this group on an oedipal level that might be stated: "I never can have the incestuous fulfillment I crave for, but life without it is not worth living." Still one might wonder whether even these oedipal conflicts reflect not also much deeper (oral) problems. The major defenses probably are repression and denial, perhaps often isolation and other obsessive-compulsive defenses.

5. Very closely related to the bored apathetic depression category is the group in which a ceaseless sense of tiredness, exhaustion, weakness, usually somatically experienced, prevails. This depression was known in earlier times as *neurasthenia*, and Freud noted the close relationship between chronic sexual dissatisfaction, unfulfillment, and this illness. The clinician might wonder whether these patients do not really suffer from a form of neurotic depression, i.e., a *neurasthenic depression*, in which both drop of self-esteem and aggressive conflicts are precipitated by sexual frustration and hence lived out on the level of the so-called body ego: "I am impotent, my entire body is impotent, that is, without power and without energy."

6. In *hypochondriacal depression* feelings are far more focused than in other depressions and indeed approach paranoid proportions. The patient feels that something is wrong with a part of his body, usually a particularly important organ or group of organs. (heart, gastrointestinal tract, liver). Both great danger and particular importance and specialness are attributed to this frightening, bad, dangerous part, which nevertheless also demands all the loving and tender attention and care so well described by Molière in *Le malade imaginaire*. Hypochondriasis is a type of depression very close to and often leading into a schizophrenic psychosis, but it also forms a typical part of the depressive (melancholic) psychosis. It is far less characteristic of but by no means absent from neurotic depressions. Still, the clinician who encounters a depressive neurotic with a predominance of hypochondriasis must be very suspicious of an incipient psychosis. Throughout the literature, from Freud [14] to Kohut [30], this symptom has been explained, with the help of the energy metaphor (the economic model of psychoanalysis), as withdrawal of emotional investment (cathexis) from the outside world unto the self, as a change of object libido and object-directed aggression into narcissistic libido and self-directed aggression. In this theory the major defense would be regression (Nemiah [33], referring to Schilder, 1930). Indeed, far too little is known about the psychodynamics of hypochondriasis.

7. In *sin-fraught depression* the feelings of a vague but all-pervasive

guilt, of sinfulness, unworth, and evilness nearly take over; self-condemnation and self-reproaches for all kinds of evil thoughts and deeds abound (Blatt's [8] "introjective depression"). This prevalence of consciously experienced (albeit not consciously understood) guilt leads to nearly continuous fantasies of self-destruction and suicide and to milder acts of self-sabotage and complaining ("Woe is me! I am so bad and worthless! Everyone treats me horribly because I am so unlovable."). Sin-fraught depression, rather than the term guilt-ridden depression, avoids any possible misunderstanding that unconscious guilt is not also very important for many (though not all) other depressives. This prevalence of feelings of guilt and sinfulness may be particularly encountered in patients with an obsessive-compulsive personality. Some symbolic actions and attitudes of expiation and atonement (e.g., the vegetarian who would have liked so much to kill and eat his rival brother "because he took away mother's breast and ate it" but who now does not dare to eat any meat and is scared of all blood) are currently being sought. The leading conflicts may be of anal or oedipal origin. Leading defenses are repression of incestuous and aggressive conflicts, introjection ("It is I who is bad and deserves punishment."), turning against the self, and reaction formation ("No, I am not murderous, on the contrary, I am particularly considerate, conscientious, thoughtful, and sensitive to the suffering of others; I even bend over backwards and become a rescuer and healer.").

This guilt-dominated depression has been the most described and studied form and, because of the particularly important role of guilt in depression in general, may indeed be the central, most typical and frequent neurotic depression. Some authors, e.g., Beres [6], go so far as to call only those states depressions in which a sense of guilt is an essential determinant: "I would maintain that without the sense of guilt and the structured superego we do not have what I would consider to be true depression" [6:484]. Jacobson [28] objects that in most manic-depressive patients the guilt problem was not even the predominant clinical feature [28:172]. Be that as it may; at least in many, particularly neurotic depressives, unconscious guilt plays a crucial role; but beyond this, in a good number conscious guilt and related feelings (of course, still veiling their real origins) prevail. These would be counted under this seventh group.

8. In *shame-oriented depression* shame, embarrassment, self-consciousness, and fear of humiliation and of being exposed as weak, a failure, defective, ugly, worthless, inferior, dominate the inner scene. In many depressives (and not even necessarily more massively dysfunctional or regressed ones) shame, even in its unconscious versions, may be far more important than guilt. It lends always a paranoid tinge to the clinical picture; thus, one has to be very careful not to mistake such a strongly

shame-oriented depression for a beginning paranoid psychosis; yet the reverse also holds true: The clinician should take heed not to overlook a possibly brewing paranoid psychosis. The leading defenses are the same as in sin-fraught depression but with the addition of projection.

9. Very close, though probably not identical to the particularly shame-oriented depression is the *depression with severe depersonalization* (the sense of strangeness, detachment, unreality of the self) *and derealization* (the same, but regarding the outside world). Often there is a kind of inner split into an observing, neutral part versus all the rest, especially feelings and body, which is repudiated as unreal, unworthy of existence, and doomed to invisibility. In turn, the estrangement of the outside world indicates a repudiation not only of the sexually seductive or aggressively luring or threatening world but also of seeing and hearing in general. Thus it appears likely that one of the important meanings in this form of depression lies in most intense unconscious shame: "I do not want to see (or feel or hear) nor to be seen." To perceive and to be perceived is equated with intensely frightening exposure, in its most regressive forms an exposure which petrifies (turns into stone, inanimate matter) or annihilates; in less intense forms the patients often use the multidetermined image of being separated (and protected) by a glass wall, a fine veil or curtain, or cotton or wool from shameful, disappointing reality. The major defenses are denial and repression. It is likely that all neurotic states of depersonalization (see chapter 13) belong into the large group of depressive neuroses, just like the two other forms often treated separately but integrated in this chapter — hypochondriasis and neurasthenia.

10. In the *psychosomatic form of neurotic depression* patients have clearly psychosomatic symptoms (e.g., constipation, chronic back pain, asthma, hypertension, peptic ulcers, cardiac problems, autoimmune diseases, recurrent colds). In some, such a psychosomatic problem may indeed be the only or main manifest symptom of an underlying depression. Although not all psychosomatic illnesses are a symptom of depression, it appears justified to single out a psychosomatic form of neurotic depression, where these physiological abnormalities represent a true equivalent of depression. Internists especially are familiar with this connection: A majority of all cases seen in outpatient medical practice are said to suffer basically from emotional disturbances, mostly depression (with or without anxiety states).

11. A separate group is that of *hysterical depressions*. Usually the two syndromes, depression and hysteria, can be distinguished quite clearly, but certainly there are also depressions in a hysterical character — depressions with a particular demonstrativeness (e.g., profuse crying, weeping, and pleading or dramatic suicidal gestures which nonetheless have to be

taken very seriously) or with outright conversion symptoms. Such hysterical depressions are a transition group to hysterical neurosis (as hypochondriasis and shame-oriented depression are to paranoid forms of pathology, the bored and sin-fraught types to obsessive-compulsive neurosis, or the following group to anxiety neurosis).

12. The twelfth subform may be called *anxious depression*. Although anxiety is an affect different from depression ("something bad is going to happen" versus "something bad has already happened"), it is nevertheless often (by no means always) part of the depressive states, including neurotic depressions. For example, Brenner [9] states: "Depressive affects and anxiety are also often present in the same patient, as witness the diagnostic category of agitated, i.e., anxious depression" [9:25].

13. A sense of mild to *paralyzing inhibition*, a feeling of being blocked, held back as if moving through molasses, being slowed down in thinking is common to all depressions, to some extent even in normal depressions where it usually can be overcome by a conscious effort, to a considerable degree in most neurotic depressions, to a massive degree in psychotic depressions. The inability to concentrate is part of this inhibition. It is well possible, as Jacobson [28] writes, that at least the severer feelings of inhibition are of a somatic origin. She quotes a particularly good example for this depressive retardation, which indeed is felt like a somatic illness: "You know, this is a real 'illness.' One morning I wake up and have no appetite. I cannot think, I cannot move, but I can control it enough to be able to work. And then, one day I wake up, and I know it is over" [28:173–174]. These features of severe psychomotor retardation that color the quality, not the content, of the depression are seen by Jacobson as signs of a psychotic depression, not of a neurotic form ("simple depression" without delusional ideas, without manic swings, but still part of the cyclothymic psychosis).

14. The more in-depth work is being done with compulsive drug users, the more apparent the importance becomes both of the depressive affect and of the whole depressive syndrome as part of the underlying pathology. *Depression underlying drug abuse* holds particularly true for abusers of stimulants (e.g., amphetamines), but an overwhelming depressive mood can also be discerned in many as one of the primary affects leading to drug use and reemerging with virulent force after withdrawal. This depression underlying drug abuse is often combined with other severe psychopathology (severe anxiety states, near psychotic states of confusion and various forms of "splits," instability of mood, violent rages, and often states of hypomanic elation).

15. *Fate neurosis*, described by Deutsch [11], pertains more to a consistent set of actions dictated, at least in many instances, by a depressive character structure and is more a feature of several of the aforementioned

groups than forming a distinctive group in its own right. At least some cases of depression fall under this category, although Deutsch subsumed it under hysteria because of its mainly oedipal origin: "The fate neurosis is a form of suffering imposed on the ego apparently by the outer world with a recurrent regularity. The real motive of this fate lies . . . in a constant, insoluble, inner conflict" [11:27] which leads to a repeated disastrous choice of partners or life situations (patterned after early childhood prototypes) and accompanied by guilt. "This guilt forced the patient [described by Deutsch] to continual renunciations, penance reactions, and ultimately to attempt suicide" [11:27].

A much more archaic, more clearly depressed and masochistic constellation has been noticed rather in literary criticism and philosophy than in psychiatry or psychoanalysis: the so-called *tragic character*, a suffering to the core, continually replicated in a tragic fate full of rejection, defeat, and hurt; a constant search for a high value which keeps being thwarted; an exaggerated, at times heroic, but self-defeating pride [39].

NEUROTIC, BORDERLINE, AND PSYCHOTIC DEPRESSIONS

All fifteen groups of affects found in neurotic depressions and used in this chapter, in addition, to differentiate subgroups, can be mild to very severe. In the instance of very deep depression, it is often nearly impossible to draw the line towards a psychotic form, mainly of the cyclothymic depression. Expression of this uncertainty and doubt is the diagnosis of a *borderline depression*. It has to be clearly understood that this condition does not deal with the "border" towards schizophrenia but towards depressive psychosis (or melancholia), i.e., that the criterion is that of an extensive affective withdrawal from outside reality (as opposed to a cognitive-perceptual one in schizophrenia). In a depressive psychosis this affective withdrawal is, usually only temporarily, nearly total.

The diagnosis of borderline depressions is really a diagnosis out of embarrassment: It is known that the depressive state is more severe, more interfering with functioning than is usually found in depressive neuroses and yet it is not clear how much investment in external reality has been retained. The manifest behavior of total withdrawal does by no means have to reflect an equally profound emotional withdrawal which alone signifies a psychotic detachment. It is precisely such a discrepancy between behavioral and emotional withdrawal which keeps observer and therapist puzzled and leads to the compromise solution of the borderline depression.

Jacobson [28] goes much further: Wherever "the typical triad of symptoms — periods of depressed mood, of inhibition of thinking, and of psychomotor retardation, or the opposite" [28:173] is encountered, she found it useful to emphasize the psychotic nature of pathology. In my opinion this seems too broad a definition. Mild forms of this triad, especially of a transitory nature, are nearly ubiquitous so that these criteria may have to be somewhat modified, e.g., by stating their intensity, pervasiveness, paralyzing nature, their long duration, and their general massive impact on functioning. Such specification may indeed have been provided by Jacobson [28] when she wrote that we do not always have sufficient criteria to distinguish at first sight between neurotic and psychotic mood conditions. Only if observed over a prolonged period and studied psychodynamically, the distinction between neurotic and psychotic may become clear in her view psychotic disorders are characterized by severely regressive processes involving all systems, particularly leading to a tremendous surplus of "deneutralized" (unmitigated, unsublimated) aggression which may invade all systems. "Eradicating the superego functions, these aggressive forces may flood the ego and provoke it to destructive actions; or they may accumulate in the superego, thus smothering all ego functions, and possibly lead to self-destruction . . . The crucial distinction is that the experiences of disillusionment and abandonment occur in borderline and psychotic depressions at an early time when the boundaries between object and self-images are not yet firmly established [28:225–226]. There is overexpectation with regard to the love objects as well as the self; they are overvalued, idealized; any new disappointment leads to a radical denigration of the object and hence of the self as well [28:226]. Jacobson considers the superego pathology in depressives as a form of restitution by a double introjection: the image of the disappointing, deflated, bad, worthless parents becomes equated with that of the self, whereas the image of the glorified, omnipotent, inflated, punishing parents is equated with that of the superego. "This restitutive attempt must fail, however, and the boundless hostility turned to the self may lead to self-destruction" [28:226]. However, in milder form a similar process occurs in all neurotic depressions. The difference is that, according to Freud [18:251,19:51–59] and Jacobson [28], "what guarantees the safety of the ego is the fact that the object has been retained" [19:53]. To put it in simpler terms: the emotional investment still remains partially attached to some parts of the outer world or memories of them, and is not all withdrawn unto the self and archaic fantasy figures. But even this formulation shows how extremely difficult it is to distinguish between such partial and full emotional withdrawal, and hence between severely neurotic and psychotic forms of depression.

Finally in regard to schizophrenic depressions Jacobson [28] notes "the enormous cathectic fluidity . . . and their inability to tolerate ambivalence . . . schizophrenics tend to discharge their instinctual drive impulses, and especially their destructive ones simultaneously or in rapid alteration on external objects and on the self" . . . Thus schizophrenics, unless they are in a paralyzing depression, "may easily alternate between suicidal and homicidal impulses and actions" [28:258,281]. In simpler terms: love and hatred in most primitive forms rapidly shift in schizophrenic depressions from one person to the other or to the self. "Love," or what appears as love, is all-engulfing and yet is suddenly replaced by equally consuming rage and murderousness.

Thus it appears that the cardinal difference between depressive neuroses and both types of psychotic depression lies in the partial and limited versus total emotional withdrawal from the outer world. The difference between schizophrenic and melancholic depression can mainly be found in the rigidity of the equation self = total badness and worthlessness in the latter, whereas the former shows sudden switches from self = abysmally bad to self = grandiose, entitled to everything and omnipotent (and obverse switches in the object-images).

Beyond what has already been described one has to agree with Jacobson: "With regard to psychotic depressions, I have conjectured that their very special qualities may be determined by the underlying neurophysiological pathology." . . . [28:183] She emphasizes especially the psychosomatic features in the depressive retardation which color the quality — not the content — of the depression. . . . Cyclothymics seem to be aware that there is a somatic quality to this phenomenon. They commonly feel that the retardation, as well as the keyed-up state, befalls them like a physical illness" [28:183,173].

It has become painfully evident that the problem of differential diagnosis still harbors many unsolved questions that pervade the entire field of depressions.

It should be added here that for the physicians working outside of psychiatry it is particularly important also to consider organic causes in the differential diagnosis of depressions. With that, I do not mean the earlier mentioned reasons: the hopelessness and helplessness vis-à-vis suffering and dying and the ensuing psychogenetically motivated depression, but depression directly caused by somatic processes [37].

These somatic processes include a great many endocrine disorders (e.g., hypothyroidism, corticosteroid imbalance, including treatment with these so important drugs), tumors of the pancreas and brain, and other illnesses of the central nervous system (CNS). Therefore, a thorough physical workup in chronic depressions is always indicated.

It should also be added that many infectious illnesses (especially flu in the narrow medical sense) lead to a lingering depressive state, usually of the neurasthenic type, often for a number of weeks.

PSYCHODYNAMICS

Although the above considerations of this chapter have gone deeply into psychodynamic deliberations, some of the essentials can be recapped: "Most analysts are in general agreement with Fenichel's (1945) summary of the psychological factors which he considered to be of major importance in the pyschopathology and pathogenesis of depression. He included orality, object loss, self directed aggression, identification with an ambivalently loved object, guilt and preoedipal fixation or regression, or both" [9:25].

Jacobson [28] has described a basic conflict underlying all depressed states: "Frustration arouses rage and leads to hostile attempts to gain the desirable gratification. When the ego is unable (for external or internal reasons) to achieve this goal, aggression is turned to the self image. The ensuing loss of self-esteem is expressive of the narcissistic conflict, i.e. a conflict between the wishful self image and the image of the deflated, failing self. The nature of the mood condition that then develops depends on the intensity of the hostility and the severity and duration of frustration and disappointment" [28:183].

This is the common denominator for all depressions, specifically also for the fifteen clinical pictures previously described. Instead of going any deeper into theoretical discussions, the elucidation of the processes with the help of one case, described in great detail, may be more helpful.

The patient, Irene, suffered from a severe chronic depression with particularly "tragic" features (a tragic character [39]). She was seen for seven years (1100 hours) in psychoanalysis and eventually, after numerous setbacks, successfully terminated treatment. For a period of several years she was unable to work and lived on small amounts given by various social agencies. She might be considered a "borderline" patient, showing nearly the entire spectrum of pathology of depressive neurosis, however without convincing evidence for a psychotic depression. She may be best seen as a particularly severe form of the first type, the lonely depression.

She was a white, thirty-year-old (at inception of therapy), unmarried, Catholic woman of Mediterranean extraction, who was short and rather slim, with long, falling reddish hair, blue eyes, and pale complexion.

The immediate reason for referral to a woman colleague was that she had consulted a local female gynecologist with the request for a prescription for contraceptives as medication against acne. When the physician refused to do this without an internal examination, the patient requested general anesthesia. The gynecologist refused and started talking with her instead. The patient indicated that she had a deadly fear of an internal examination for reasons not entirely clear to her but partly due to the humiliation. It also became evident that she never had had intercourse and had led a rather solitary, fantasy devoted life. The gynecologist, psychologically a very perceptive and sensitive woman, sent her to Dr. P. During the five months of psychotherapy with her, it emerged that the patient had had an almost exclusively fantasy based relationship of seven years duration with a navy officer. She had seen him altogether about half-a-dozen times but was, all the time, deeply preoccupied by marriage plans and pursuing him with gifts, letters, phone calls, and quasi-unintentional encounters. According to her description, he left her dangling in the air, never giving her an outright "no" but offering her just enough nice words which she could take as signs of encouragement and hope. In the few encounters there was some petting but nothing more. While she was in psychotherapy with Dr. P and at her therapist's prodding, she followed up a long series of letters to her "boyfriend" by a phone call, only to find out that her fantasy husband was about to marry another girl. She was completely crushed by the collapse of her fantasy, around which she had arranged her entire life, including her move to the city where she lived. At the same time, she also started questioning the nature of her unrealistic attachment.

In the initial interview with the analyst, she expressed her intense feelings of inferiority, ugliness, and worthlessness, and her inability to establish meaningful relationships, especially with men. She had never had any heterosexual contact beyond petting, neither with the officer nor with boys and other men she dated.

It may be added that in one of the first analytic sessions, she suddenly indicated that she believed she might have a tumor in her abdomen. To quote her: "When I went to see the gynecologist, I was convinced I had a cancer inside which was growing and filling up the inside and that therefore I didn't have my menstruation. I am still sure I have a growth inside, for years already. Intellectually, I am not always certain but emotionally I am convinced." This sounded awfully suspect for a hypochondriacal delusion, but why this could not be confirmed will be seen.

Irene is the youngest of three children. The other two are brothers with age intervals of two years. Her real father was allegedly a compulsive gambler, an alcoholic, and a sailor in the navy. He left her mother while she was pregnant with Irene. Several years later the mother married another man in the navy who served on the same ship as the real father and had the same family name. Irene's stepfather left the navy when she was about four and worked as a crafts-man since. His actual return to the family occurred probably at that time, although there is much evidence that he came on frequent weekend furloughs long before, while the family trekked from port to port where he was stationed (perhaps already in the first or second year of our patient's life) — reconstructed experiences which will prove to be of high significance. He allegedly was unable to have any children of his own. He was always experienced as her own father. She found out between six and ten ears of age that he was not her real father, allegedly during a severe altercation between mother and stepfather when the latter accused mother of unfaithfulness and the mother, shouting that he was anyway not even their real father, went with a butcher knife at him, while the children tried to keep them apart.

The mother, described as an aggressive, domineering woman, was the driving force behind the college education which all three children received. Whenever she is together with our patient, they quickly get into fights. The saying in the family goes that the two can never be together without arguing, and her mother at times tells her, "It's about time you come home because we have not had a good fight in a long time."

It should be added that the stepfather was not successful in his work, and when the patient was about nineteen, he lost all his sav-ings in a deal where dishonesty on his part may have forced the fam-ily to flee from their village. Because of this, there was subsequently a good deal of moving to all parts of the United States until they settled down again in the East, where the father built a house for himself, his wife, and his daughter, (our patient) and where "a stu-dio is just waiting for me." He seemed to be very authoritarian, not tolerating the children talking at the table and punishing the boys violently with his fists. At first, she spoke about him rather with fondness and described how much he always treated her as his dar-ling whom he could not deny anything. Later in the analysis, how-ever, she talked with swelling bitterness about how he never listened to her, always told her to "shut up your sassy mouth," how he derided her as a "French whore" when she used makeup, how she never counted for anything at home, how she still is called and treated by both parents as a "baby," or called by her father "stink-weed" or "stinky," in a mixture of tenderness and devaluation.

The oldest brother, John, is a very successful businessman. He had relatively little contact with the family, including the patient, until his marriage collapsed. He was always a very hard-driving, successful person, even in childhood. He is said to have been a hero as a spy in the armed services. The second brother, Tony, called a "slob," is an alcoholic, and is in intermittent psychiatric treatment, which he fails to pay. He is debt-ridden, unsuccessful, and still asking for support from his quite impoverished parents. He is married to a wife who severely abuses their children and keeps the house like a pigsty.

Early memories include one very vivid recollection when she was about five: Her parents had gone to the neighboring house where the grandparents lived. She woke up; it was pitch-dark. Irene started to call for the parents. Nobody came and she began screaming for help. She still remembers herself standing in the crib, crying hysterically.

Two other memories are of an anal nature and from two-and-a-half years of age. She remembers sitting under the kitchen table eating her own feces. Another memory involved her riding her sled down the slope behind her house. In the middle of the road, there was the pail from their outhouse, which she plowed into. It was filled with excrements, which plastered over her face and filled her mouth. Her mother's reaction allegedly was wild laughing.

When four or five she underwent two eye operations for strabismus on both eyes. Both were unsuccessful. A reoperation at age twenty-five did not fare any better. Equally at age four she underwent a tonsillectomy, probably simultaneously with the first eye operation.

The patient occasionally referred to the fact that she had heard her parents having intercourse when she was a little child and that she spoke with her brother Tony about it. She particularly vividly remembered that the mother kept telling the stepfather in the adjacent room, "That's all you men want." There are screen memories of having walked in on them at eight and of having heard heavy breathing earlier. A derivative memory: When she was ten or twelve, she saw two dogs (the female belonged to the patient) having intercourse on the driveway of their house. She screamed at them at first, then started spanking the male cur, and finally grabbed and pulled on his penis, to free the female dog — in vain. She felt particularly ashamed that "it" happened on their lot.

In regard to her professional background, she went to college at great sacrifice. It took her about eight years to finish because she had to alternate one semester studying with one working as a waitress. Again contributing to her rage, bitterness, and envy, she had to send most of her money to her next older brother, Tony, who thus was put through university, although he kept flunking his courses and blowing his money on drinking parties. Still her parents insisted that "his education" had to take priority over hers, even after a severe car wreck in which he was severely injured and his closest friend killed. It was likely that Tony was the driver and certain that both were drunk.

Right from its inception, the analysis mired down into a complex web of acting-out on the patient's side. It was clear that a massive, widespread transference neurosis with many facets was being built up very rapidly.

From the first hours it was very difficult to maintain an analytic stance since she kept asking questions, wishing usually to get assurances, guidance, decisions, and further clarifications and angrily insisting and badgering the analyst to answer her. He tried to cope with it in many ways: with direct interpretations, with silence, with returning the question — to no avail. Long periods were mired in angry, deprecating attacks, which then usually turned into a morass of self-condemnation or depressive attacks upon herself, that over the first three years of analysis assumed more and more a suicidal taint. The analyst's failure to answer her directly was a confirmation of her feeling "used" and rejected: "I cannot stand the big silence in analysis; I just do not want to be nothing and meaningless to anybody."

Eventually it emerged that the transference aspect relevant to this form of intra-analytic acting-out was: "You are not listening, you are shutting me out, you are paying no attention to me, you are not caring about what I have to say."

Behind this there was the probability of a well-founded conviction that her family never paid much attention to her when she had something to say. Her opinion did not count. To disagree always meant: "You just want to fight. You always want to argue." Women in general, her mother, and she in particular were "stupidos" in her father's eyes. Already as a child she had often tried to gain a hearing by such insistent asking.

Yet there were deeper levels to this combination of insistent angry curiosity and the persistent demand to be listened to: her sense of being left out from primal scene experiences (watching parental intercourse) of massive early dimensions and later stimulated by the sexual explorations with brother Tony and the neighbor's boy.

There is so much information to tie in with this deep layer of the affect storm surrounding very early primal scenes, which must have occurred repeatedly between age two and five, that some of the evidence needs to be given here [23,24]. A series of suggestive screen memories (well remembered rather banal events which are a coverup for very painful or frightening memories that are repressed) were already mentioned: the scene with the butcher knife, standing in the crib (at two and five), not being heard, and screaming hysterically for her parents, the scurrilous scene about the copulating dogs which she could not separate. When she witnessed a mock rape on a stage play, about four years into the analysis, she was so overwhelmed with rage, terror, and confusion that she wanted to intercede, and talking later that evening to her (platonic) boyfriend, she "lied" to him that she had undergone something like that herself. Both phases (stage scene and later talking with her boyfriend) were accompanied by intense crying and trembling. There were a number of highly exciting dreams with heavy breathing in her right ear. The hearing of sexual intimacies by her roommates in college filled her with most intense rage and an excited watchfulness so that she could not sleep at all. ("I was furious, I wanted to go in and say: If you want to screw, go some place else.")

Akin to this was the general oversensitivity to noise which made it necessary for her to hide in a tunnel to prepare for college examinations. And even more, there was a curious propensity for compulsive lying. Very often its content was that some terrible accident and injury had happened to her, a nonexistent sister, or a girlfriend (clearly substitutes for her). Any pleasure and excitement was accompanied with a sense of bursting: "I cannot stand it anymore" — as a child and now.

And may then not her eye operations at age four have also been experienced as a mutilating punishment for her horrified, yet fascinated watching of the primal scene? When she sees the analyst from afar she has to hide: Her intense curiosity to see, to find out, to listen, is covered by the sense of shame, "as if I had been caught in something forbidden, in staring at something that I should not have seen."

And then there is the strongest screen memory of all which seems like a masochistic negative of the primal scene, including a kind of negative acoustic "halo" [22] — in the form of a strange quiet. This memory emerged during the crisis of the transference neurosis (session 529) and had a peculiarly delusional quality — an "event" from age five or six. One evening she saw her parents whispering together. Irene "knew" that they were going to murder her. "I was not afraid. They were looking at me. I just knew they wanted to get rid of me, but I was not afraid. Only: Tonight is the night. Just as I feel now that I am a bother to everybody; I feel that, I know I am." How she thought she might be killed, she does not know, although she had dreams pointing in this direction.

The analysis of her primal scene memories and fantasies led to a complete disappearance of this and many closely related feelings and symptoms (e.g., her noise sensitivity, the rage about phone calls during the therapy hour, or a delay by the analyst of a few minutes).

Closely related to this first piece of transference neurosis and acting-out is a very pervasive symptom which has not merely served as a most powerful expression of resistance but also as a tool of self-wrecking throughout her life: her *pseudostupidity*, a symptom of fluctuating severity. Yet, it made it nearly impossible for her to get the necessary reading done in school; it blocked most of her professional aspirations. In detail it consisted of an "inability" to read — more exactly, a compulsive rereading of each sentence or word, because she might have missed something. As soon as she had a page or a chapter finished, she felt she had completely forgotten it. The same often held true in lectures. And it worked at its most efficient best in wrecking the analyst's interventions. There were literally weeks and months where none but the most simple comment was intelligible to her. She described as getting all "hung up" on the first word or part of a sentence and missing the rest. In turn, even if the analyst tried to keep his comments as terse, simple, and straightly tied to what she had said, she did not understand what he referred to, how he came to such a conclusion — even when it may have been a literal repetition of an earlier comment of hers. Not a coy not-understanding, it was filled with a perplexed sense of foundering and confusion and with massive anger at herself and the therapist.

Occasionally the therapist pointed to the aggressive aim, the wish to defeat him, to make him helpless, impotent, castrated — the chewing up and making into hash what was communicated to her, but these interpretations did not seem to hit the core of the symptom.

Again the solution arrived on several levels. Directly in the transference it was that she felt attacked, nagged, condemned by the therapist. It was he, not she, who was quibbling, viewing her as worthless. It led back in stages over the many traumatic events of aggressions in her family, to early and incomprehensible over-stimulation, to bloody violent castration and mutilation memories (penis and eyes) in her preoccupation with the idea that "something is missing." The major meanings seem to be these: Every comment is a penetration and with that an aggressive and sexual act upon her which she has to fight off. In a dream she saw the therapist intruding in her eye with a lighted ophthalmoscope looking like a penis: "Insight" has to be warded off like the awe-inspiring frightening, cruel, and envied penis (and the instruments of operation). In addition one may note again the halo effect described by Greenacre [22], which occurred in a few other dreams too.

The not understanding and subsequent quibbling is a direct castrating attack against the analyst, against everyone in authority (not just men), and lastly against the three men in her family. It is a vengeful rebuff which made analysis almost impossible. The therapist felt quite keenly that she was "breaking" his analytic instrument.

Yet a particular form of the not-understanding finally opened up the crucial level. Many comments and experiences within and without the analysis evoked a sense of "tilt", that "my computer goes bananas," "the intake is shut off," "there is too much input." Dreams often ended in a similar state equated by the patient with this "tilt," "a sense of fainting," a "numbness coming down my forehead like molasses," a "blackout from which I always wake up and feel my heart racing." Is this blackout (coinciding in area with that of nearly daily headaches [22]) not a form of a dream within a dream? And is with that the numbing, blinding confusion not an actual historical memory?

The expression of "tilt" for confusion and perplexity, probably a form of partial depersonalization and derealization, is in itself an interesting metaphor: It is a signal on a pinball machine when the "system is overcharged" or the "ball goes in the wrong hole."

Thus, not to hear, read, or understand expresses not only her fear of succumbing passively to intrusion, of passive surrender and merger, but above all to be passively overwhelmed by the storms of primal scene and the other traumata. "I want to see and hear and understand it, and I cannot and do not want to grasp it. It is too painful. I do not see what I see, I do not hear what I hear." Just like mother's denial: "you could not have seen what you have seen" ([2:40–41]). The result: perplexity, confusion. The same feelings in an association with the eye operations: the terror of the closing in of the ether mask, her attempt to tear it off — the fainting, the "molasses," the numbness in dream after dream. "I could almost cry now, I feel like a frightened little child."

The following is a discussion of the central, depressive part of the transference neurosis: the frenzy of self-condemnation, accusation, and regression. This triple feature of the transference neurosis was indeed its center and the greatest menace to treatment. With a crescendo from month to month, she read into nearly every event outside the analysis and into most comments within the analysis a condemnation, ridicule, put-down, and humiliation — yet further proof that she was worthless, ugly, bad, incurable, a freak, a loser, dead inside, defeated, stupid, boring, unlovable, a slob. In its extreme form she felt dead, totally isolated, practically without feeling, only wishing never to have been born and to die as soon as possible. It is fair to presume that here once again the severe depression was also marked by deep depersonalization.

For the analyst to ask and to question her was in itself an attack on her narcissistic position and a global condemnation. To be questioned meant to be torn apart, to be ridiculed, and condemned. Her reaction was rage: She questioned his right to question her. In a "holier than thou" huffiness, she told him "there is nothing to look into, I am right"; then the generalization: "Who in the hell are you to question me? You just dump on me, you make fun of me and put me down. You have not listened to me and have not understood ever anything I said. Now I turn the tables: You are no good; analysis is a ridiculed profession. I do not believe you a word, I never could trust you. No one can be trusted." And it ended: "You will kick me out of the analysis."

This was made explicit at the peak of the negative transference, at the end of the third year [in session 530], but it accompanied in somewhat less harsh forms dozens and dozens of sessions throughout the analysis. There was much evidence for the disappointment behind this violent storm of rage about him and herself: "when I find out things about myself, I hate myself even more. I do not do anything right." This ascribing of her own vicious self-deprecation to the therapist and then continually trying to provoke him into an angry rejection and putting down of her (typical for depressed patients) became very massive after she dropped her job (at the end of her second year in analysis) because she could not take it when she felt humiliated by repeated transfers and unable to handle the violence at work. She gloried in the defiant feeling that she had made the right decision by stopping work, spurned any consideration of alternate jobs, refused haughtily even to consider that her complete financial dependency on family and agencies (and her very low fee arrangement in analysis), her intensity of rage and indignation about the work situation, and her staying in bed until the afternoon could be more than a perfectly acceptable natural reaction to insufferable insults inflicted upon her. Her sinking into deeper regression was also noticeable in her living-out of oral and anal wishes (e.g., her eating gallons of ice cream in bouts, her reveling in scatological language and vilifications — much like her parents).

This led finally up to a period of about five-months duration when she repeatedly contemplated suicide and emphatically stated that analysis had not only not helped her but harmed her, that she could count the hours on the fingers of one hand when she had felt helped. During this severe crisis culminating at the end of the third year of analysis (sessions 528–540), the therapist raised the possibility of a change from analysis to psychotherapy and that she was "very successful" indeed in destroying what he could do for her in analysis. This (and especially his emphatic and probably sharply sounding "and you are very successful at it!") brought a most dramatic change. She told herself: "You are trying to get kicked out of the analysis. You are awful and difficult to deal with. He is going to take just so much to carry on for just so long. If someone has been put down from childhood, he then behaves so to bring it about." And she added (to him): "I beat you to the punch: that I reject you or provoke you to reject me before you do it on your own." She turned passively suffered rejection into active rebuff and actively provoked rejection. Thus the not-hearing and not-understanding also assumed a disguised aspect of turning passive into active rejection. And: "The nicer someone is, the more vulnerable and dependent I'd feel, and thus the higher the fear of rejection, and the more need to provoke it actively, and the more terrified of trusting anyone." Her complete social isolation subsequent to the inception of analysis and still deepened after her retreat from work appeared in a new light (instead of being just explainable as part of her narcissistic orientation): It was her rejecting the world first. After the crisis, there were a few months of excellent work and very little acting-out. She ventured out of her bunker of solitary living, started with deep interest some new studies, and began dating.

One might wonder, however, what ever happened to the "delusional" idea of having cancer. About four months after the crucial crisis and lysis she finally dared to make an appointment with the original gynecologist. The finding was a shock: She indeed had a large tumor in her lower abdomen which required immediate surgery.

Anxiety before and resentment after the operation, resentment about being a woman and being now mutilated too, probably infertile as well, led to a new period of intense emotional storming within the hour, much acting-out, little working through. Much of her rage and envy remained focused on the analyst. "It is always the woman who has to suffer — and you men have only the pleasures." Her envy at him, at men in general, which had been an undercurrent noticeable all along, became a devouring furor. Certainly envy about not being a boy, of not being able to urinate far ("I wish I had 'one'."), rage about the obvious preferential treatment of her two brothers, humiliation about her and mother feeling "just used" by men, a sense of envious bitterness and resentment toward all men, dim and potentially frightful memories about abdominal operations of her mother during childhood, and the pale memories about her own operations — all these elements emerged clearly.

Equally important was the immediate employment of the actual mechanism of how she reacts to the not-hearing and the perplexity — namely, her usual counterattack of disjunctive and dismembering isolation and her turning passive into active by provocation when finally faced, in a comprehensive reconstructive interpretation, with the vast array of the evidence for her profound penis envy. The quibbling was recognized by her as part of the very problem she was working on. She disconnected, tore to pieces the interpretation, as she had felt mutilated herself. Thus it opened up a new avenue to elucidate her pseudostupidity — connections she was able to recognize mostly on her own.

And yet it is clear that her castration shame and penis envy must have been so traumatic for the deeper, earlier (pregenital) reasons, — mainly the primal scenes, the operations, the severe aggressions at home, and the betrayal by mother in the symbiotic fusion. Again the transference neurosis proved to be the lens in which archaic fusion fantasies were collected and brought to focus.

Much of her anger at the analyst and her compulsive asking and quibbling with him ("Do you hear, do you understand?") was really a protest: "When I know it, you have to know it." She saw him as a mindreader who would have to know everything from minute hints. "And I get very angry if you do not understand me, or if I think you do not understand me." She needed constant confirmation that he indeed was with her, part of her, approving and accepting her, a counterbalance against the crushing weight of her constantly condemning superego.

It appeared that the whole traumatic sequence of primal scenes, operations, and castration equivalents had yet a prehistory which represented the deepest layer of her feeling shut out and shut off and which had given the later events such a particularly intense and tragic pathogenetic vehemence: the still earlier lived-out symbiotic fusion with mother prior to her stepfather's definitive return. Not only was Irene the baby sleeping in mother's bed until her stepfather returned (at age four) from the navy, but she remembered that during his later long absences she often slept snuggled up against mother's body with mother's hand resting in the girl's crotch. Even up to recently when mother came to visit (with or without father), mother and daughter slept in the same bed together. Only as an adult did she succeed in fighting off her mother's insistent demand.

It is likely that she originally was overstimulated and seduced by the lonely, depressed mother, that she then felt betrayed by her, hated her intruding father (and all men), and identified with the bitter, haughty, pseudostupid, pseudohumble, but really resentment-laden and indeed deeply depressed mother. This would entail that the basic narcissistic injury was not that of castration but to have been rejected by mother in favor of father and the identification with the sadistically tormented mother. After her mother's betrayal, no one could ever be trusted again or expected to be faithful, except for herself (her perseverance in the fantasy love!). Nothing and no one could be good enough after the grievously wrecked union with her mother. In this aspect, her sailor boyfriend (the fantasy lover) and a later repetition of the same during analysis are thus on the one hand her mother representatives. On the other hand, they took on also the father's image. The early, seductive attentive stepfather turned out to be, upon his return, an extremely brutal, rejecting, vicious man whom she loathed and hated. Besides that she developed the fantasy of an extremely idealized fantasy father who would totally accept her and with whom she could merge, who was all-giving, all-powerful, and omniscient. Him she would only love, in a clinging, sticky form of dependency, bare of any conscious aggression. It was only about 950 hours into the analysis that she could clearly recognize and reexperience this nearly complete split into the monstrous and the godlike father. At first this latter image was displaced onto the unknown "real father" who became in her fantasy a loving superman and hero. When he really showed up (around age fourteen) he was a total disappointment, but then this image became attached to a very select sequence of men, attachments which usually lasted each about seven years (including eventually the duration of the analysis). Both extremes were reexperienced with the analyst: He was godlike, a rescuer and protector, omniscient; he was a sadist, condemning her to death and whom she would like to kill; a greedy, despicable, dirty Jew, a vile man out to humiliate and to degrade women, absolutely insensitive. But he also was, at least, for most of the time, something in between: neither God nor the Devil, but a man with his limitations, helping, neither extolling nor destroying her, neither merged with her nor totally aloof and isolated from her.

She learned to tolerate more and more this profound ambivalence, thus narrowing the split, worked through much of her profound masochism (particularly vis-à-vis her superego), and successfully entered a heterosexual relationship.

TREATMENT

The treatment of depressive neuroses may span virtually the whole spectrum of psychiatric treatment (except for electroconvulsive therapy and similar gross physical interventions).

The method of choice is psychotherapy, if possible psychoanalysis or psychoanalytically oriented psychotherapy. In quite a few cases, short-term, focal, insight-oriented psychotherapy with the use of psychoanalytic knowledge [20] can be surprisingly helpful.

Supportive psychotherapy combined with antidepressant or antianxiety agents and regular discussions of life's problems with the family physician or a social worker can bring significant relief, although the underlying illness is not causally removed.

Since depression of any kind has, like most other psychopathological problems, a peculiar self-confirming quality, the nature of a vicious circle, of "a feeding on itself," the breaking of such a circle can in itself be of great help. For example, the more depressed a patient, the more disturbed in his sleep and the less efficient at work, the more depressed about realistic shortcomings he becomes. To step in at any of these points breaks the chain which pulls the patient down.

REFERENCES

1　Anthony, E. J. Two contrasting types of adolescent depression and their treatment. *J. Am. Psychoanal. Assoc.* 18:841–859, 1970.

2　Arlow, J. A. Fantasy, memory, and reality testing. *Psychoanal. Q.* 38:28–51, 1969.

3　Arlow, J. A. Unconscious fantasy and disturbances of conscious experience. *Psychoanal. Q.* 38:1–27, 1969.

4　Asch, S. S. Depression: Three clinical variations. *Psychoanal. Study Child* 21:150–171, 1966.

5　Asch, S. S. Wrist scratching as a symptom of anhedonia: A predepressive state. *Psychoanal. Q.* 40:603–617, 1971.

6　Beres, D. "Superego and depression." In *Psychoanalysis: A general psychology*, eds. R. M. Loewenstein, L. M. Newman, M. Schur, A. J. Solnit, pp. 479–498. New York: International Universities Press, 1966.

7　Bibring, E. "The mechanism of depression." In *Affective disorders*, ed. P. Greenacre, pp.13–48. New York: International Universities Press, 1953.

8　Blatt, S. J. Levels of object representation in anaclitic and introjective depression. *Psychoanal. Study Child* 29:107–157, 1974.

9　Brenner, C. Depression, anxiety, and affect Theory. *Int. J. Psychoanal.* 55:25–32, 1974.

10　Brenner, C. Depression, anxiety, and affect theory: A reply to the discussion by Paula Heimann. *Int. J. Psychoanal.* 56:229, 1975.

11   Deutsch, H. "Hysterical fate neurosis." In *Neuroses and character types*, pp. 14–28. New York: International Universities Press, 1965.

12   Freud, A. "The ego and the mechanisms of defense," 1936. In *Collected writings*, vol. 2. New York: International Universities Press, 1971.

13   Freud, S. "Three essays on sexuality," 1905. In *Standard edition*, vol. 7, ed. J. Strachey. London: Hogarth Press, 1968.

14   Freud, S. "Psychoanalytic notes on an autobiographical account of a case of paranoia," 1911. In *Standard edition*, vol. 12, ed. J. Strachey. London: Hogarth Press, 1958.

15   Freud, S. "On narcissism: An introduction," 1914. In *Standard edition*, vol. 14, ed. J. Strachey. London: Hogarth Press, 1957.

16   Freud, S. "Some character types met with in psychoanalytic work," 1916. In *Standard edition*, vol. 14, ed. J. Strachey. London: Hogarth Press, 1957.

17   Freud, S. "Introductory lectures on psychoanalysis," 1916–1917. In *Standard edition*, vols. 15–16, ed. J. Strachey. London: Hogarth Press, 1963.

18   Freud, S. "Mourning and melancholia," 1917. In *Standard edition*, vol. 14, ed. J. Strachey. London: Hogarth Press, 1957.

19   Freud, D. "The ego and the id," 1923. In *Standard edition*, vol. 19, ed. J. Strachey. London: Hogarth Press, 1961.

20   Gillman, R. Brief psychotherapy: A psychoanalytic view. *Am. J. Psychiatry* 122:601–611, 1965.

21   Goethe, J. W. v. *Die Leiden des jungen Werthers*, vol. 13. 1774. Reprint. Munich: Dtv. Gesamtausgabe, 1970.

22   Greenacre, P. "Vision, headache, and the halo," 1947. In *Trauma, growth, and personality*, pp. 132–148. New York: International Universities Press, 1970.

23   Greenacre, P. "The influence of infantile trauma on genetic patterns," 1967. In *Emotional growth*, vol. 1, pp. 260–299. New York: International Universities Press, 1971.

24   Greenacre, P. The primal scene and the sence of reality. *Psychoanal. Q.* 43:10–41, 1973.

25   Haynal, A. Le sens du désespoir: La problématique de la dépression dans la théorie psychanalytique. Paris: Presses Universitaires France, 1976.

26   Hesse, H. *Der Steppenwolf*. Berlin: Suhrkamp-Verlag, 1927.

27   Jacobsohn, H. "Das Gespräch eines Lebensmüden mit seinem Ba." In *Zeitlose Dokumente der Seele*. Studien aus dem C. G. Jung Institut Zürich. Zürich: Rascher Verlag, 1952.

28   Jacobson, E. Depression: Comparative studies of normal, neurotic, and psychotic conditions. New York: International Universities Press, 1971.

29   Kierkegaard, S. *Krankheit zum Tode*. 1849. Reprint. Düsseldorf: Diederichs Verlag, 1954.

30   Kohut, H. *The analysis of the self*. New York: International Universities Press, 1971.

31   Mahler, M. S. Notes on the development of basic moods: The depressive affect. In *Psychoanalysis: A general psychology*, pp. 152–168. New York: International Universities Press, 1966.

32   Miller, F., and Bashkin, E. A. Depersonalization and self-mutilation. *Psychoanal. Q.* 43:638–649, 1974.

33   Nemiah, J. C. "Depressive neurosis." In *Comprehensive textbook of psychiatry*, 2nd ed., eds. A. M. Freedman, H. I. Kaplan, and B. J. Sadock, pp. 1255–1264. Baltimore: Williams and Wilkins, 1975.

34   Peto, A. Body image and depression. *Int. J. Psychoanal.* 53:259–263, 1972.

35   Rangell, L. Aggression, oedipus, and historical perspective *Int. J. Psychoanal.* 53:3–12, 1972.

36   Schmale, A. H. "Depression as affect, character style, and symptom formation." In *Psychoanalysis and contemporary science* vol. 1, eds. R. R. Holt and E. Peterfreund, pp. 327–351. New York: Macmillan, 1972.

37   Shochet, B. "Laboratory diagnostic procedures." In *Psychiatric foundations of medicine*, vol. 5, eds. G. U. Balis, L. Wurmser, E. McDaniel, and R. G. Grenell. Boston: Butterworths, 1978.

38   Smith, J. H. Identificatory styles in depression and grief. *Int. J. Psychoanal.* 52:259–266, 1971.

39   Wurmser, L. A Clinical study about the tragic character. Presented to Baltimore — District of Columbia Society for Psychoanalysis, 1975.

40   Wurmser, L. "The range of behavior: Concepts of normality and pathology." In *Psychiatric foundations of medicine*, vol. 3 eds. G. U. Balis, L. Wurmser, E. McDaniel, and R. G. Grenell. Boston: Butterworths, 1978.

13

Neurotic Depersonalization

Leon Wurmser, M.D.

INTRODUCTION

The experience of depersonalization must be distinguished from the syndrome or state of depersonalization, in which the former is merely the leading symptom. And, like depression, depersonalization goes far beyond neuroses. Jacobson [14:141–148], in a most impressive study, has described severe experiences of this kind in normal people who, suddenly placed in a Nazi prison, were exposed to massive external and internal pressures and experienced an abrupt split in their identity. Fever, epilepsy, fatigue, and intoxications, as well as acute and chronic psychoses of all types may be accompanied by this symptom. Schilder is quoted as stating that in every depression there is depersonalization [24]. As a matter of fact it was called one of the most frequent psychiatric symptoms, ranging third in frequency, after anxiety and depression [34]. Moreover, the opinion has been expressed that depersonalization as a process may actually accompany each dream and precede every neurotic symptom [18,19], a precursor both of "dreamwork" and repression.

It is preferable to use estrangement as a superordinate term for depersonalization and derealization, designating an experience as being changed, as lacking its familiar reality-feeling, and, perhaps most typically, as having a characteristic "as-if" quality. In depersonalization this feeling of strangeness affects oneself, in derealization the experience of strangeness is of the outer world. As to depersonalization, the more prominent affect: Janet [15] defined it "as the negative feeling of not being one, of not being sufficiently alive, not real enough" [15:326].

Jacobson [14] described *depersonalization* particularly aptly: In the case of depersonalization of the physical self

> the person will complain that his body, or rather certain parts of the body, do not feel like his own, as belonging to him. He may describe them as being estranged from himself or as being dead. This experience may go along with subjective sensations of numbness and changes in size and volume of the estranged body parts. The person may try to touch and feel them in order to convince himself that they are really his. There are states of depersonalization pertaining to the genitals and to the sexual act, which at first sight may impress us as cases of impotence or frigidity. When carefully questioned, such patients will report that they experience their genitals as dead, as estranged, as not being their own . . . Whenever the depersonalization extends to the mental self, there is a feeling of unreality of the self and of being "outside of the self." The depersonalized patient will think, react, act; but his experience is that of a detached spectator who is observing another person's performance. Not only his actions but his own thought processes appear to him unfamiliar and strange" [14:137–138].

Thus, it is characteristic that one feels split into two parts. "He feels as if he were two selves at the same time. One self appears to be standing off at a distance in a detached and relatively objective manner observing another representation of the self in action. To the observing self the latter appears separate and estranged" [3:456–457].

In *derealization* the outer world seems not quite real. Sounds are perceived as if they came from far away; what is seen looks blurred, distorted, removed. Many describe "feelings of being surrounded or enveloped by transparent substances that create a sense of being separated from the world" [33:844] — dreamlike, as if hidden by a glass wall, cotton, or a veil. "Depersonalization and derealization are usually found together, although one or the other may be more prominent" [3:460]; it is possible that derealization generally precedes depersonalization [18:101].

Finally, three modes can be differentiated: In the *first modus* the experienced thing (or part of self) may be as if not existing, as if strange, remote, dead; in the *second modus* it may be as if blurred, fused, and indefinite, as if not separated; or in the *third modus* it may be like scattered, chaotic, as if not connected. A differentiation can be made in regard to intensity and duration; there is a wide range of experiences of estrangement — from the mild fleeting feelings over severe and prolonged nondelusional forms to delusional extremes. Furthermore, estrangement may affect different areas: external perceptions (derealization) as contrasted with perceptions of one's body, thoughts, feelings, or one's own identity (depersonalization); derealization is the estrangement of the object-representations; depersonalization is the estrangement of the self-representations [14,31]. This chapter is restricted to the chronic, severe, yet nondelusional, i.e., neurotic, forms of depersonalization and derealization.

In order to get a feeling for this state as well as for its underlying meaning a case is presented in considerable detail.

The patient is a woman in her late thirties, an artist, who had been hospitalized for eighteen months before the beginning of psychotherapy. Treatment consisted of intensive psychoanalytically oriented psychotherapy and lasted a little more than one year (four to six hours a week); half of this time, the patient was still hospitalized. She seems now symptomatically recovered. She suffered from marked depression, severe anxiety attacks, and feelings of estrangement: of feelings of numbness all over her body or of weightlessness, of feelings that everything around her and within her was empty, not quite real and hazy. Her self seemed unreal: "What am I? Am I? Where am I?" Often — in the characteristic split of the depersonalized patient — she looked at herself with the eye of an inner observer, spying at herself like a stranger incessantly despising and scorning her that she was without core, empty, only facade and shell.

This state of depersonalization gave way when anxiety and depression became overwhelming. In such panic attacks she was afraid she would kill herself by jumping out of a skyscraper window ("floating" out) or throwing herself under a train; or she was frightened she would kill her boy with a knife, or, in turn, would be dismembered by an intruding man at night. More frequently, the anxiety attack consisted of the fear of losing her mind. These anxiety attacks often occurred when she was among other people: on the street, in the bus, in her office. She felt everyone looked at her as at a fake, a phony, and a failure.

Some information about the background of this woman: She was unusually beautiful, almost always very neatly dressed and groomed. She was divorced and had a child five years old; her husband had left her during the pregnancy and returned only for a brief period at the time of childbirth. She was the older of two children; apparently, her unplanned conception had necessitated her parents' marriage. Her father was a designer, but he had wanted to be a painter all his life and was very bitter about not being able to follow an artistic career. He accused in a covert way his wife and his two children for having spoiled his life plan. He left his wife before the patient's birth but returned shortly afterwards. He died when the girl was eleven years old. She described him as a very angry person. "The memories I have of him are of rages and temper tantrums at myself, my brother or at my mother. Besides these outbursts, there seemed to be controlled anger — much teasing, some of which hurt me more than the actual rages. My brother and I used to rush to meet him when he came home from work, but he would cross to the other side of the street and pay no notice to us. Although I knew it was a joke, it hurt."

Her mother is described as a deteriorated, neglected alcoholic. "She seems even more hazy in my memory. She stands out as being overly protective of our very lives. Yet, she had little interest in us as persons. We were not permitted to go to and from school alone, like our friends. Physical dangers seemed to lurk everywhere. She put bars up at our windows after the Lindbergh kidnapping. I only remember her being attentive when I was ill. The only punishment was for being 'impudent,' for talking back. To speak up was to be rude."

Her brother, two years her junior, is, like father, a disappointed artist, angry and bitter that he had to give up his artistic career in order to sustain a family.

The patient had been highly successful in her profession, although always feeling she was an impostor and one day would be unmasked. She had many changing relationships; usually she went with two men at the same time, one whom she despised and who accompanied her to parties and the second whom she conquered during the party and started a relationship with. Soon she began despising him too, and then she turned to a new friend.

Her husband whom she met when she was around thirty was again a frustrated artist, angry at society and resentful of its conventions.

After the separation from him she led a professionally, socially, and sexually hectic, self-forgetting life. Her son had severe fits of screaming, kicking and destroying and thus contributed his share to the whirlwind of her life.

Her disease erupted suddenly when she thought she finally had taken care of her main problems (in the job and with her child). She was to have a date the evening of that day with an attractive man with whom she had performed fellatio on the previous date. At noon, she went to a restaurant and ordered milk and tuna fish for a small lunch. At once, while sitting at the counter and waiting for the food, she got an overwhelming anxiety attack — the first in her life. This anxiety attack consisted of the fear of losing her mind. She saw it in the form of an inner image: Her mind was like a thread, and this thread would be cut; and she would fall into infinity, into empty space. She became extremely panicky, paid without eating her meal, ran out, went to a friend, then to a doctor, felt the almost irresistible impulse to jump out of the window of the skyscraper. Since then she was hospitalized in different institutions, suffering from frequent attacks of panic, despair, and suicidal impulses and from the almost constant feeling of emptiness and unreality.

During the course of therapy one of the first themes covered was the conflict between frightful separation and the hope to overcome this abandonment and loneliness by personifying an ideal. Her recollections of childhood events — how her father prepared to leave the family after an argument with her mother and how the little girl screamed and implored him to stay; how the father ridiculed her mother by strewing pepper on her palm when she stretched out her hand for reconciliation — cannot be examined deeply.

A first breakthrough in the therapy was when she reported with very intense emotion a particular incident: She was about seven years old and was doing her homework. Her father was helping her. Her brother angered her with some prank and she threw father's silver pencil at him. Father reacted with immediate rage to her outburst and shouted: "You can never have this (silver pencil) again — never, never." She pleaded: "In six months — in one year?" He remained firm: "Never!" The next morning, the father, without having talked to her anymore, left with the brother and went to the shore; she had to stay at home with her mother. This "never-never," the feeling of "lost forever," continued resounding through her life and seemed revived in the feeling of infinity and emptiness of the anxiety attack. For hours she cried in the therapy over the loss of the silver pencil which had come to symbolize for her the love and recognition of father, her brother's penis, and all the possible love and acceptance. In turn, being accepted the way she really was meant for her the degradation of the lover: "To love me — that means that he is no longer a man. If it is so easy to get their affection for me, it points up how miserably I failed to get Daddy's affection." Thus, by despising the men, as soon as they started to love her, she was justifying her father and his rejection of her.

Her father's death finalized the conflict: "The day he went to the hospital I was unaware that he was really so ill. I was very casual when he left. I did not even kiss him good-bye. His last words were, 'Be a good girl.' " This (preconscious) conflict was between the need to live up to an ideal, to the expectations of her parents, to be very neat and clean, submissive and mild—and the vague awareness of what is really going on "behind the wall of silence," the wall of denial, hiding, and forgetting.

The ideal she had for herself and for others was almost godlike: to be complete, perfect, and in total control. She was thrown into a rage of disappointment if she or the others did not live up to these expectations. In her depressive periods she turned this anger and contempt against herself and hammered at herself with self-reproaches: "You are worthless, decaying, weak." The function of this ideal was, of course, to be so perfect and good and free of anger in order to be finally acceptable to her father. Only when she despised herself as she really was, his rejection appeared justified and could be overcome. She had not given up the hope of gaining his love, although he had been dead for so many years: Her hope was that he would return and accept her, if only she were a good girl.

Sharply conflicting with this largely unconscious ideal was all that went on "behind the wall," not only within herself but also in the family: She recalled a scene where she had walked into the parents' bedroom, surprising them in a scene of fellatio. Then there was a blackout in her memory, a feeling of dizziness, of extreme shame, embarrassment, and frozen rage. She was shoved out of the room, while she tried to save the situation by claiming that she also had a milky secretion, namely from her breast. This was one of the first instances in therapy where the looking appeared as an activity, in which desires and pleasure, shame and grief, jealousy and guilt, converged; an activity also, which could lead to sudden identification in a traumatic situation — as evident from the false memory of her own milk secretion [8:I-389]. In particular, it was a crystallization point for all her feelings of shame for her parents, with whom she was deeply identified, and the subsequent shame for herself.

This, by the way, also elucidated her sudden anxiety after she had ordered milk and fish (with their symbolic value!) and prior to another anticipated scene of fellatio: It was above all the frightening realization of her being just as despicable (shameful) and dirty as mother (the *devalued identification*). And then it was the impending emergence of her overwhelming sexual desires, breaking through the "wall of silence": her genital and oral sadistic wishes, her pleasures in showing her naked body and in looking at father's nakedness. And finally, seen from this primal-scene experience, her anxiety attack covered an angry protest: "If I can not have what I want, I throw away what I have. It is only a poor substitute for what I long to possess and what was denied to me: penis and milk, love and recognition." So, even now at work, when she e.g. did not find the eraser or the pencil on their place she became furious and at the same time panicky — and she wanted to throw herself out of the building. Yet, since anger would lead to complete rejection and abandonment, she had to "forget about it." Thus, her anxiety attack used to decrease markedly when she realized that she was angry and at whom she was angry.

Returning to the first point — the fight against being similar to her mother — one sees that her ideal was a counteridentification: not to be dirty like her mother, not to be exposed like her, not to bite off the penis. It may be presumed that her mother represented her *antiideal* (the negative ideal) [16], devouring, slobby, rejected. It was a shame to be her daughter. Basically, her loyalty belonged not so much to the real figures of her parents but rather to their expectations. When she could not live up to their highest standards — to be a little princess, an aristocrat — then she was all bad, dirty like mother. Yet in turn, when she could not be like mother and thus possess father, envy and jealousy were gnawing at her, emptiness and hopelessness were overwhelming.

Although depression, anxiety, and hidden rage had decreased significantly, her vague feelings of worthlessness and estrangement continued more or less unchanged.

It was only about one year after beginning therapy that she, quite suddenly, remembered three interrelated groups of incidents which seemed to offer the key to the basic conflicts. The first memory was: When she was about four, she was moved out of her room which was larger — to make place for her brother. She felt very hurt and humiliated to have now two darker and smaller rooms for the one big room. She also had to give away her toy box to the younger rival, as she was not supposed to play with it anymore. But, at times, she could return to the old room. On occasion, at twilight, she was sitting with her brother by the window, and there was truce after the incessant fighting during the day — it was "peace" (just as her anxiety frequently quieted down in the early evening). Sometimes, she was even allowed to sleep in the brother's room; and it was then, as she remembers now, that she wet her bed. She suddenly recalled what a release it was in the dream, the flowing of the urine, and reexperienced the free harmonious feeling of flowing and floating. But soon after the awakening came the shame and exposure — not only about having wet the bed, about having been a baby again, but also to discover that she was not complete again, as she had felt in the dream where she was squirting: The shameful realization that, after all, she was still without a penis — the experience of what may be called *castration shame*. With this memory, not only did the primal scene described before receive its traumatic background, but it was better understood how shame and embarrassment became connected with all looking, exposing, and showing. Another consequence for her life was the equation of orgasm with infinity and emptiness, and here the bridge was the "free floating" of the urine in the dream — translated into the floating out into the infinite space (falling through space) — a release, a self-loss, a giving in, but accompanied by exhibition, shame, and degradation, and prevented from happening in the orgasm by her frigidity [8:I–264].

This led to the second aspect of her shame experiences: This second memory concerned seeing her brother's penis. Mother told her not to touch or hurt it, because "there is so much feeling there." She had been conscious intellectually of her envy and sullen anger, derived from her assumption that her brother was more liked and higher valued because of his penis; but it was only after recalling the shame-experience that she became aware of her impulses to cut it off. She remembered how she used to be in the bathtub together with him: "He has a penis, I have not. Why do not I have one? It was cut off from me. I want to cut off his penis." And then the retaliation: "I would be cut to shreds myself." (Or in a modification: "I want to bite off his penis" — and the fear to be devoured by the sarcastic looks of others.) This cutting returned in the impulses to kill her little son, in the retaliatory fears of being lacerated by a man, and in the murderousness of self-exposure in jumping from a skyscraper. On the basis of the body-phallus-equation [8:II–3–18,20] she had to exhibit and to destroy her body. Thus, castration shame, penis envy, angry attack, and guilt formed a chain of emotions repeated over and over again.

A third related memory was the observation of her infant brother at the breast. It meant to her something like: "Mother and brother are a unity: I am left out." She was cut off from this oneness. He had the milk — and she was eaten by jealousy (as indeed her anxiety often was triggered by eating). Separation and exclusion ran like a thread through her life — and shame became the color of this thread. Not only was she excluded and therefore worthless and rejected, but this memory of union was a symbol for the lost ideal: The ideal of herself and her mother represented something like a background to her deep disillusionment about the castrated, weak, dirty mother, her shame for a mother whose offspring she was, her shame for herself. This shame again covered other affects, mainly rage about her exclusion and disappointment, and guilt for her jealousy.

These experiences of shame were like concrete and specific crystallization points and served as rationalizations for the vague ambiguities and humiliations suffered mainly from her father.

It was also evident how shame led to rage, and rage in turn evoked not only guilt but also heightened feelings of shame. Thus, shame and anger can be mutually potentiating emotions, bound together in a kind of "reverberating circuit."

Here one could object: All this may explain her anxiety, her frozen anger, her depression; but what about estrangement? It became evident, after clarification of these core elements, that shame and exposure, looking and being looked at, were of central importance in her feelings of estrangement: instead of shame, she felt strange, unreal, not fully existing, numb. Therefore, the observation which needs more clarity was that the feeling of shame seemed to be the key unlocking the phenomenon of estrangement. How can this be understood in motivational terms?

In the depersonalization, she saw herself from the outside. "It is like a puppet, at strings — I can not make me to be myself — as I want to be. I go around with a frozen face. I am not really anxious, but like trapped into observing myself. It is like mother telling her child, 'Say something. Do not say the wrong thing.' It is my trademark: 'They are going to discover —.' I suddenly wonder — very far back — that they discover I am a girl. Or that I act like Mother. Suddenly now, I see my contour at the wall — it is Mother's. I shudder. She always looks frightened and scared to death." She despised herself like she detested mother. This confirms E. Jacobson's remark in a personal communication that some patients with depersonalization show the "wish to *disidentify*, i.e., to counteract an undesirable identification. I believe this plays quite a role in the patient who suddenly saw the mother performing fellatio on the father." This wish to deny or undo her identification was actually expressed by our patient: "I do not want to be like my mother — and, still, I come from these rotten roots." Thus, she expressed in the symptom of estrangement: I am not like mother, and yet I am not myself. When she is *aware* of her shame (her identification with the devalued mother), she feels satisfied: "I know who I am, I can wallow in shame." Then she is not depersonalized, but depressed. And, in turn, when she feels elated, close to her ideal, free of her identification with the mother she feels the compulsion to eat, "to weight me down." "In all happiness, one thing was disturbing: Why was I so alone? I felt like betraying my mother." Either she is independent, elated, but alone — or she is close to mother, but dirty and full of shame.

However, it was not only the identification with her mother which made her ashamed and thus, if denied or repressed, depersonalized. All her wishes from "behind the wall" — all the aspects of her self which did not fit her ideal — evoked shame, and with that estrangement. It was shame of her being "castrated" [9] — and, regressively, of her being dirty [17] and dependent [12]; it was shame of her desires — particularly to let her urine flow in a warm, pleasant, orgastic relaxation and liberation — and, again regressively, of her wishes to attack her brother and take his penis and her desires to be one with an idealized mother-figure.

In short, in these periods of depersonalization she fought against awareness of the basic discrepancy within herself: the discrepancy between the image she had of herself as a clean, neat, and self-controlled person and a contrasting image which threatened to be exposed: that of a dirty, weak, demanding, or a murderously jealous, cutting child. *This discrepancy between ideal self and real self* [14], between rigorous observer-me and contemptible-me, was felt as shame and self-contempt, as frightening inferiority and worthlessness and was covered by the feeling of unreality.

In summary, in the psychoanalytically oriented therapy of a hospitalized patient with a severe neurotic depersonalization and anxiety neurosis was found, besides the dominant elements in her conscious life-history of separation, loss, and worthlessness, largely unconscious underlying conflicts which best can be described as shame conflicts. Three forms of anxiety determined character and symptoms: the fear of being like mother; the fear of being rejected because of exposure of her dirtiness, especially the bedwetting; and the basic fear of being excluded and left alone. All three of these fears converged in the feeling of shame, although only the second one is the experience of shame or shame anxiety par définition.

Thus, underlying the estrangement was a denial of the all-pervasive disappointment and shame feelings, whereby neither the "bad" nor the "good" poles were conscious. This denial could be put in words like: "I am not really this dirty girl in a shameful environment, but I want to be and can be something else and somewhere else, I don't know what and where." Or more specifically: "I am not dirty like Mother" (denial of the devalued identification) and yet, "I am not the ideal I want to be; I cannot see the ideal and do not want to be seen by my conscience" (denial of the counteridentification); so: "I have to hide and be no one."

When denial and repression could not be maintained, the previously denied bad, devalued side appeared exposed and conscious:

In the predominantly apathetic form of depression the general feeling of shame and worthlessness (but not so much of guilt) were not denied anymore and became conscious: "I am all bad, rotten and decaying. My life is aimless and hopeless."

In the episodes of elation, the same denial of the experience of disappointment and rejection, of deprecation and shame (as in the depersonalization) took place (and with that indeed a feeling of estrangement, of weightlessness, of floating appeared); the "bad," shameful side itself was also denied, while the previously preconscious, denied parts of the "good" (ideal) side were now consciously experienced and identified with.

After many of these connections were worked out and in one of the last sessions, she reported an incident never mentioned before, which seemed to be a confirmation of some of the correlations just described: When she reentered her school, right after the death of her father, she was consciously deeply ashamed for having her leader badge rusty ("that was my image") and also for being accompanied by her mother. "It was the same fear of discovery, of losing my position as a leader." And there, she suddenly went "blind": The vision was reduced to a pinpoint and blurred. In the recess, she fell — due to this hysterical "blindness" — and hurt herself. It was the same lightness and blankness, the feeling of emptiness and of falling through space, as in the earlier primal scene and in the later states of depersonalization and anxiety, namely, to disappear out of shame.

DYNAMICS OF DEPERSONALIZATION

Depersonalization, as such, is — like depression — a relatively nonspecific affective state, encountered wherever there is the feared or actual experience of loss. The loss may consist in the loss of an object (by separation, abandonment, death) or of a part of the self (degradation of the self esteem, castration), and in particular the loss of control over the inner or outer reality. In this broad form, estrangement as denial of loss expresses: "The present is not real — I want to return to the past."

As example for the *loss of an object*, seen in the patient, was her father's death, constituting the preconscious foil to the state of estrangement; but, as recognized in the course of treatment, this was only a segment of the decisive, essentially unconscious conflict.

Quite frequently it is the *loss of a part of the self*, which is defended against by depersonalization — whether it concerns the sudden devaluation and invalidation of a part of the conscience and of the wishful self-image or the realization of the incompleteness (castration) and the sub-sequent deprecation of the real self.

And finally, every dreaded or actual experience of an overwhelming trauma [7] can lead to the feeling of *loss of control* and, with that, to an at-tempt to deny the emotional impact, with the help of estrangement, and thus to regain control.

Three Layers of Conflict

1. *Identification and depersonalization.* Jacobson [14] concludes that the sub-stratum of estrangement lies in "a narcissistic conflict caused by discrep-ancies between opposing identifications" [14:161] and narrows this dis-crepancy further: "the deflated, castrated ego part becomes estranged, dead, because it is identified with devalued, castrated object images" [14:163]. She specifies: "In both depression and depersonalization, iden-tification processes bring about an inner schism. In depression, however, the schism develops between the punitive sadistic superego and the ego or the self-image. In depersonalization the superego need not even take part in the conflict . . . Instead of a punishing superego accusing the worthless self, we find in depersonalization a detached, intact part of the ego observing the other — emotionally or physically dead — unaccept-able part" [14:163]. In a personal communication she added: "Regarding the question of identification in depersonalization, I meant that these pa-tients got depersonalized when they tried to *undo* an unacceptable regres-sive type of identification."

To put in other words: "I am not really as worthless (dirty, castrated, weak, and so on) as father or mother was (or is)." Or: "I am not feminine, like mother is." The patient chooses an ethereal ideal identity instead, denying everything that is identical with the parents [3].

2. *Shame conflict.* It appears likely that in most cases the repudiation and disowning of a part of the self is dictated by a specific kind of inner condemnation, i.e., that initiated by shame. There may be a similar corre-lation between depersonalization and unconscious feelings of shame as there is between depression and unconscious guilt feelings, both in re-gard to the broad, unspecific nature of the symptom itself and the partic-ular type of conflict underlying the severe chronic states.

The wish (the goal) inherent in the feeling of shame is: "I want to disappear as such a person, as I have shown myself to be." Or, simpler, but less precise: "I want to be (seen) different than I am." Corre-spondingly, in depersonalization the patient indicates: "I am not this, this is someone else, not I" [11:37]. This "being different" or "being looked at as a different person" is a direct fulfillment of the demands of the superego, inherent in shame. But at the same time, part of the warded-off wish forces its way through: the "being seen," the exposure — namely, in the form of the "self-observation-compulsion," one of the cardinal symptoms of typical states of depersonalization [2,14].

The *split* in the experience (*die Widersprochenheit im Erleben*, Hartmann, [13] especially the split of the self-experience (*le sentiment du dédoublement*) [15:319] was encountered in the case history as a characteristic of the state of depersonalization. Patients have not only lost their self [15:318] but also watch themselves: "My true personality cries at the side of myself" and "I am like two persons, I give myself as a spectacle to myself" [15:320]. In other words, the part of the self for which the patient is most ashamed, appears as most estranged, as not real, as lost, whereas the "eye" of the (otherwise hidden) conscience can remain open and unrelentingly staring.

Similarly, it would often not be specific enough to translate the experience of derealization into words like: "The world is not so disillusioning and frustrating as I see or hear or sense it. It cannot be true—it is really better." Although this interpretation of the denial of disappointment may be often correct, generally it is too broad and vague. In the case of severe, chronic estrangement the more specific and therefore more accurate explanation is: "The world, in front of which I stand exposed (with my body, my voice), does not really look at me or listen to me." In that form it would be the denial of the shame anxiety directed against exhibitionistic wishes. As another patient with a severe psychotic break in her history put it: "People don't look real to me; they look as if they did not have eyes. If they were real, they would hurt me by humiliating me." And correspondindingly: "My looking or hearing or touching cannot be done by myself; I would feel ashamed for it." Here, the perceptual processes are covered by shame anxiety. Still another type of interpretation is: "I would feel ashamed if this were true what I see or hear." To quote Arlow: "What is happening has nothing to do with me. I am only an observer" [2:20]. In these last two instances it is not specified further what the shame is directed against: whether against perceptual or exhibitionistic wishes which are experienced as danger.

More generally "the perceptions of the external world are taken as representatives of the internal danger and, accordingly, are repudiated" [3:471]. A third patient described the double experience of depersonalization and derealization, the veiling of perception and self-exposure, translucently: "I felt I was completely disappearing, and my awareness of everything was disappearing."

So, the symptom of estrangement fulfills the wish for both the magic hood and the magic looks — not to be seen and to make unreal, invisible;

but it also reflects the fear of both — to turn into lifeless stone [8,I-373-397] or into another nonhuman being [32,6] and the fear of becoming blind. The wishes warded off by shame and experienced as frightening are: 'I want to see, know, hear" (curiosity) and "I want to be seen, heard, known" (exhibition). In borderline or psychotic patients this conflict assumes a peculiarly devouring, total quality. This brings the discussion to a brief consideration of the deepest layer, seen rather in prepsychotic or psychotic patients than in neurotics (although it may occur in them too).

3. *Depersonalization as denial of totality.* As just alluded to shame may take on quite global features: The impulses which have to be warded off are wishes to devour by looking and to petrify by fascinating self-exposure. Accordingly, the rejection feared in shame can be that of total isolation and annihilation. Thus, the shame problem merges with the more general conflict of devouring to union and self-protective isolation. In severely regressed patients this becomes the basic conflict; the other two layers of conflict are mere differentiations out of this broad and encompassing configuration.

In this most archaic layer, depersonalization is the denial of everything which is not absolute. Everything that is not total union and merger — or its opposite, total isolation and destruction — is denied, is unreal. Only the absolute gratification or the absolute Nothingness and Emptiness would be real.

The sequence (as, for example, indicated in the examples given by Arlow [1], Mahler [22], Mahler and La Perriere [27], Rubinfine [30], and Rochlin [29]) would be: a wish for total union → the premature and threatening separateness (standing also for other types of frustration) → the reaction by total aggression and destruction → estrangement as protection against this flooding with the all-pervasive, fragmenting rage. The denial inherent in this type of estrangement could be put into words: "The object has not hurt (left or overwhelmed) me, I do not need to destroy it. It is inanimate, a thing which I can control" (derealization). And, similarly, the own feelings (of anguish and anger) are muted by the robotlike emptiness: "I do not want total satisfaction, I am not hurt, I do not want total isolation and annihilation. If I am a machine, nothing can happen to me" (depersonalization). In this connection, the *denial of separation* seems to be of particular practical importance: "If I am already detached, no separation can hurt me anymore." As if to say: "I have cut the ties myself, I am abandoned and strange, I am already dead and in the Nothingness — no abandonment can destroy me anymore." Denial of separation is in this case a kind of defense against a symbiotic bond and prevents the dread of (passive) abandonment. At the same time it is not only active separation and negation but also has a positive aim: "If I am away from reality, I am close to the object with whom I want a symbiotic unity. If I destroy the world, I am alone with mother." This double aspect of depersonalization: expressing both the wish and the anxiety, is, as already seen, quite typical.

TREATMENT AND PROGNOSIS

In most instances of neurotic and chronic (or repeated, acute) depersonalization and derealization intensive psychotherapy or psychoanalysis leads to relatively quick symptomatic recovery (several months), although the underlying pathogenic conflicts may need far longer treatment. If depersonalization is indeed the lead symptom of neurotic nature and treated in psychotherapy, the prognosis is favorable. If, however, it is accompanied by a severe depression or underlying hidden psychotic conflicts, or if intensive psychotherapy is not available, this state tends to deteriorate and become more and more dangerous.

Still there are many untreated, chronically depersonalized patients who go through life without feelings, neither joy nor grief, for example: "His main complaint was that his emotional life was so dull and subdued . . . His craving for any kind of emotional experience, even though it might be profoundly upsetting, proved to be a longing for a 'frank' conflict between violent emotional and instinctual strivings on the one hand, and an audible, strong, convincing inner voice of conscience on the other" [14:110,114]. Some of these may injure or even mutilate themselves, just in order to feel [21,4,25]; or they provoke angry fights for this purpose: to break out of this dullness and bored, empty, feelingless state. Still others resort to drugs: to feel, to be one again [35]. In most of these the true syndrome is not recognized and hence not treated with the specific knowledge required to bring about a resolution of the pathogenetic conflicts.

Psychotropic medication (antidepressants, antipsychotic drugs, even minor tranquilizers) often increases the experience of estrangement. In contrast depressant drugs (alcohol, narcotics, especially barbiturates) as well as their opposites, stimulants (especially amphetamines), often tend to reduce the painfulness of depersonalization, both apparently by reducing the gap between wishful and realistic self-image and by magically wiping out shame and isolation.

In all these instances efficacious treatment and, with that, improved prognosis hinge on the proper recognition of the underlying syndrome and the focusing on its components, whereas treatment with most psychopharmacological drugs may be contraindicated, and the view that drug abuse is the crucial problem in such cases is inadequate.

Organic causes (e.g., intoxication, endocrine disturbances, temporal lobe epilepsy) always have to be excluded.

REFERENCES

1   Arlow, J. A. "Discussion of Dr. Fromm-Reichmann's paper." In *Psychotherapy with schizophrenics,* eds. E. B. Brody and F. C. Redlich, pp. 112–120. New York: International Universities Press, 1952.

2   Arlow J. A. Conflict, regression, and symptom formation. *Int. J. Psychoanal.* 44:12–22, 1963.

3   Arlow J. A. "Depersonalization and derealization." In *Psychoanalysis: A general psychology,* ed. R. M. Loewenstein, et al., pp. 456–478. New York: International Universities Press, 1966.

4   Asch, S. S. Wrist scratching as a symptom of anhedonia: A predepressive state. *Psychoanal. Q.* 40:603–617, 1971.

5   Bergler, E., and Eidelberg, L. Der Mechanismus der Depersonalization. *Z. Psychoanal.* 21:258, 1935.

6   Bradlow, P. A. Depersonalization, ego-splitting, nonhuman fantasy, and shame. *Int. J. Psychoanal.* 54:487–492, 1973.

7   Federn, P. *Ego psychology and the psychoses.* Basic Books, New York: 1952.

8   Fenichel, O. *The collected papers,* 2 vols. New York: Norton, 1954.

9   Freud, S. Lecture thirty-three, 1932. "New Introductory lectures on psychoanalysis," vol. 22. London: Hogarth Press, 1968.

10   Freud S. "Splitting of the ego in the defensive process," 1938. In *Standard edition of the complete psychological works of Sigmund Freud.* Standard edition, vol. 23. London: Hogarth Press, 1968.

11   v. Gebsattel, V. E. *Prolegomena einer medizinischen Anthropologie.* Berlin: Springer Verlag, 1954.

12   Grinker, R. Growth, inertia, and shame. *Int. J. Psychoanal.* 36:242–253, 1955.

13   Hartmann, H. Ein Fall von Depersonalization. *Z. ges. Neurol. Psychiatr.* 74:593–601, 1922.

14   Jacobson, E. *Depression.* International Universities Press: New York, 1971.

15   Janet, P. *Les obsessions et la psychasthénie,* 2nd ed. Paris: Alcan, 1911.

16   Kaplan, S. M., and Whitman, R. M. The negative ego-ideal. *Int. J. Psychoanal.* 46:183–187, 1965.

17   Kubie, L. S. The fantasy of dirt. *Psychoanal. Q.* 6:388–425, 1937.

18   Levitan, H. L. The depersonalizing process. *Psychoanal. Q.* 38:97–109, 1969.

19   Levitan, H. L. The depersonalizing process: The sense of reality and of unreality. *Psychoanal. Q.* 39:449–470, 1970.

20   Lewin, B. D. The body as phallus. *Psychoanal. Q.* 2:24–47, 1932.

21   Lower, R. B. Depersonalization and the masochistic wish. *Psychoanal. Q.* 40:584–602, 1971.

22   Mahler, M. S. Thoughts about development and individuation. *Psychoanal. Study Child* 18:307–324, 1963.

23   Mahler, M. S., and La Perriere, K. Mother-child interaction during separation-individuation. *Psychoanal. Q.* 34:482–498.

24   Meyer, J. E. *Die Entfremdungserlebnisse.* Stuttgart: Thieme Verlag, 1959.

25   Miller, F., and Bashkin, E. A. Depersonalization and self-mutilation. *Psychoanal. Q.* 43:638–649, 1974.

26   Modell, A. R. On having the right to a life: An aspect of the superego's development. *Int. J. Psychoanal.* 46:323–331, 1965.

27   Oberndorf, C. P. The role of anxiety in depersonalization. *Int. J. Psychoanal.* 31:1–5, 1950.

28   Piers, G., and Singer, M. *Shame and guilt.* Springfield, Ill.: Thomas, 1953.

29   Rochlin, G. The dread of abandonment. *Psychoanal. Study Child* 16:451–470, 1961.

30   Rubinfine, D. L. Maternal stimulation, psychic structure, and early object relations. *Psychoanal. Study Child* 17:265–282, 1962.

31   Sarlin, C. N. Depersonalization and derealization. *J. Am. Psychoanal. Assoc.* 10:784–804, 1962.

32   Searles, H. F. *The nonhuman environment.* New York: International Universities Press, 1960.

33   Slap, J. W. On waking screens. *J. Am. Psychoanal. Assoc.* 22:844–853, 1974.

34.   Stewart, W. A. Depersonalization (panel report). *J. Am. Psychoanal. Assoc.* 12:171–186, 1964.

35   Wurmser, L. Drug abuse: The hidden dimension. New York: Jason Aronson, 1978.

14

Hypochondriasis: A Symptom Complex

Bernard Shochet, M.D.

Concern about health and preoccupation with bodily symptoms has been an undeniably human characteritic for thousands of years. However, the first recorded perception of these human concerns date at least to 350 B.C. In the seventh century A.D. these concerns were first related to melancholy [4]. Bright's treatise on melancholy in 1586 specifically mentioned hypochondriasis as a marked preoccupation with physical health, and by 1733 hypochondriasis had become so fashionable in England that it was being called the "English malady." Griesinger in 1861 pointed out again the close relationship between hypochondriasis and depression. Freud considered this problem in 1895 and concluded that hypochondriasis lay somewhere between the psychoneuroses and the psychoses; and he labeled it an *actual neurosis* [7].

Numerous investigators since Freud have disagreed as to the nature of this ailment, with opinions ranging from Kraepelin's view (1919) that hypochondriasis is part of a psychotic syndrome; Fenichel (1945) that it is a transitional state between reactions of a hysterical character and those of a delusional and clearly psychotic one; Kenyon [7] in 1966 and Mayou [9] in 1976, who called hypochondriasis an arbitrary syndrome, a reaction of wide ranging significance [3].

For a definition, then, hypochondriasis can be considered a persistent preoccupation with symptoms of physical or mental discomfort, without apparent foundation, or excessive disproportionate preoccupation with existing disorders. It may be acute or chronic, alone or in association with other illness. It may occur in neurotic illness or psychotic illness or with paranoia. On the other hand, excessive preoccupation with bodily symptoms may also develop as neurotic reaction to stress in an otherwise normal person, representing somaticized psychic distress and is the commonest malady the primary physician is called upon to treat [6].

When someone is having difficulty maintaining the homeostatic balance in their life, they may decompensate with an illness — physiological, psychological, or both. Stress produces different reactions in different people depending on the individual's specific past and present life history and vulnerabilities, both inherited and learned, and the symbolic meaning of the current stressful situation to the individual. That person then consults a physician and becomes a patient. The way in which the patient offers the initial complaint to the physician is a function of social learning and is offered with the vocabulary available to that person and in the terms consistent with his world view. Conversely, the physician interprets the symptoms offered in terms of his own life experience, concepts of illness, and world view.

The patient in psychological distress but lacking a psychological vocabulary may present his anxiety in terms of diffuse physical symptoms [10]. This may become a repeated pattern of behavior and so evolve into a chronic and fixed behavior pattern in which physical symptoms are substituted for anxiety with elimination of the affect [11]. This is more likely to occur in those patients with poor self-esteem and guilt who have a great need to be cared for and who exhibit underlying depression. The patient then tends to cling to his symptoms, which become defensive in nature. The patient's goal becomes that of maintaining the relationship with the doctor. He neither expects nor desires relief of symptoms [2]. This can be a preventable or reversible syndrome but often becomes chronic. Precipitating factors frequently are in the sphere of personal, social, or economic stress.

Thus, hypochondriasis is a symptom complex which may be acute or chronic, may vary in severity, and may appear as a reaction to stress in relatively normal people [3]. Or it may be a symptom heralding a severe psychotic illness, a depressive or a paranoid state. It is thus an unconscious process used in an attempt to solve conflicts, helping the patient deal with anxiety and guilt and with a great potential for secondary gain. Indeed it may become a way of life.

Treatment of the patient who presents this chronic symptom complex may be extremely difficult and frustrating for the practitioner, especially if the goal is to cure the patient.

The treatment program should be an active one designed to be supportive. The physician acts as a benevolent authority figure, who is warm, sympathetic, and listens attentively. The symptoms are not challenged, diagnostic studies are limited, and the patient is protected against surgical intervention. Credible instructions offered in a sympathetic and supportive way and that avoid new reasons for anxiety are more helpful than blanket reassurances. It is helpful to arrange specific subsequent visits, with the goal being to help the patient maintain as much normal function as possible, even though the patient may not and usually does not give up the physical symptoms. Usually referral to a psychiatrist is seen by the patient as rejection by the doctor and is refused and resented.

On the other hand, should a patient develop the symptoms of hypochondriasis acutely in an acute stress situation, treatment should be active and aggressive psychotherapy, and pharmacotherapy is indicated to prevent the development of a chronic state. If the symptoms develop acutely and herald a decompensating psychotic, depressive, or paranoid state, then the treatment should be actively directed at the major underlying illness. Bebbington [1] has described two cases of monosymptomatic hypochondriasis of a delusionary nature which terminated in suicide, despite multiple efforts at intensive treatment. Serious suicide potential is frequently associated with psychotic depressions presenting with hypochondriasis.

The use of psychopharmacological agents can be very helpful as adjunctive therapy in hypochondriacal syndromes. An underlying specific illness will call for a specific neuroleptic agent, such as a tricyclic compound in depression and a phenothiazine in a schizophrenic paranoid psychosis. For the chronically hypochondriacal patient who is not manifesting a specific underlying illness the major treatment is sympathetic support on the part of the physician. However, frequently, small doses of amitriptyline, 50–75 mg per day, will be quite helpful in reducing anxiety and consequently reducing the intensity of the physical symptomatology.

REFERENCES

1   Bebbington, P. E. Monosymptomatic hypochondriasis, abnormal illness behavior, and suicide. *Br. J. Psychiatry* 128:475– 478, 1976.
2   Brown, F. The bodily complaint: A study of hypochondriasis. *J. Ment. Sci.* 82:295–359, 1936.
3   Busse, E. W. Hypochondriasis in the elderly: A reaction to social stress. *J. Am. Geriatr. Soc.* 24:145–149 1976.
4   Dorfman, W. Hypochondriasis revisited: A dilemma and challenge to medicine and psychiatry. *Psychosomatics* 15–16:14–16, 1974–1975.
5   Gillespie, R. D. Hypochondria: Its definition, nosology, and psychopathology. *Guys Hosp. Rep.* 8:408– 460, Oct. 1928.

6   Idzorek, S. A functional classification of hypochondriasis with specific rec-
     ommendations for treatment. *South. Med. J.* 68:1326–1332, 1975.
7   Kenyon, F. E. Hypochondriasis: A survey of some historical, clinical, and
     social aspects. *Int. J. Psychiatry* 2:308–326, 1966.
8   Kenyon, F. E. Hypochondriacal states. *Br. J. Psychiatry* 129:1–14, 1976.
9   Mayou, R. The nature of bodily symptoms. *Br. J. Psychiatry* 129:55–60, 1976.
10   Mechanic, D. Social psychologic factors affecting the presentation of bodily
     complaints. *N. Engl. J. Med.* 286:1133–1139, 1972.
11   Rittlemayer, R. F. Caring for the hypochondriac. *Am. Fam. Physician*
     14:98–101, 1976.

IV
Personality Disorders

15

Personality Disorders

John R. Lion, M.D.

The student of psychiatry may well wonder whether personality disorders exist at all or whether all human beings have some degree of a personality disorder. Indeed, the average person probably has some elements of an obsessive-compulsive personality; that is, he or she is probably concerned with orderliness and conformity, is somewhat inhibited, and puts a premium on logic, punctuality, and thoroughness. These are traits which serve a person well in life; many successful people are obsessive in nature and have distinct compulsive traits. Is a person so described an obsessive-compulsive personality, particularly if one considers that an obsessive-compulsive personality is listed in the American Psychiatric Association's (APA) *Diagnostic and Statistical Manual of Mental Disorders (DSM-II)* [2] as a mental disorder?

Consider the Hysterical personality. The characteristics of this personality are excitability, emotional instability, overreactiveness, attention seeking, and dependency. These are traits we have seen in many patients and probably in our friends and relatives. Do they constitute a mental disorder? The same question, of course, can be applied to the term cyclothymic personality, an individual described as showing mood swings

Portions of this chapter are reprinted from John R. Lion, ed., *Personality Disorders: Diagnosis and Management.* Copyright 1974 by The Williams and Wilkins Co. Reproduced by permission.

Table 15.1

V. PERSONALITY DISORDERS AND CERTAIN OTHER NONPSYCHOTIC
MENTAL DISORDERS (301–304)

301 *Personality disorders*
This group of disorders is characterized by deeply ingrained maladaptive patterns of behavior that are perceptibly different in quality from psychotic and neurotic symptoms. Generally, these are life-long patterns, often recognizable by the time of adolescence or earlier. Sometimes the pattern is determined primarily by malfunctioning of the brain, but such cases should be classified under one of the non-psychotic organic brain syndromes rather than here. (In DSM-I "Personality Disorders" also included disorders now classified under *Sexual deviation, Alcoholism,* and *Drug dependence.*)

301.0 *Paranoid personality*
This behavioral pattern is characterized by hypersensitivity, rigidity, unwarranted suspicion, jealousy, envy, excessive self-importance, and a tendency to blame others and ascribe evil motives to them. These characteristics often interfere with the patient's ability to maintain satisfactory interpersonal relations. Of course, the presence of suspicion of itself does not justify this diagnosis, since the suspicion may be warranted in some instances.

301.1 *Cyclothymic personality* ((*Affective personality*))
This behavior pattern is manifested by recurring and alternating periods of depression and elation. Periods of elation may be marked by ambition, warmth, enthusiasm, optimism, and high energy. Periods of depression may be marked by worry, pessimism, low energy, and a sense of futility. These mood variations are not readily attributable to external circumstances. If possible, the diagnosis should specify whether the mood is characteristically depressed, hypomanic, or alternating.

301.2 *Schizoid personality*
This behavior pattern manifests shyness, over-sensitivity, seclusiveness, avoidance of close or competitive relationships, and often eccentricity. Autistic thinking without loss of capacity to recognize reality is common, as is daydreaming and the inability to express hostility and ordinary aggressive feelings. These patients react to disturbing experiences and conflicts with apparent detachment.

301.3 *Explosive personality* (*Epileptoid personality disorder*)
This behavior pattern is characterized by gross outbursts of rage or of verbal or physical aggressiveness. These outbursts are strikingly different from the patient's usual behavior, and he may be regretful and repentant for them. These patients are generally considered excitable, aggressive and over-responsive to environmental pressures. It is the intensity of the outbursts and the individual's inability to control them which distinguishes this group.

Cases diagnosed as "aggressive personality" are classified here. If the patient is amnesic for the outbursts, the diagnosis of *Hysterical neurosis, Non-psychotic OBS with epilepsy* or *Psychosis with epilepsy* should be considered.

301.4 *Obsessive compulsive personality ((Anankastic personality))*
This behavior pattern is characterized by excessive concern with conformity and adherence to standards of conscience. Consequently, individuals in this group may be rigid, over-inhibited, over-conscientious, over-dutiful, and unable to relax easily. This disorder may lead to an *Obsessive compulsive neurosis* (q.v.), from which it must be distinguished.

301.5 *Hysterical personality (Histrionic personality disorder)*
These behavior patterns are characterized by excitability, emotional instability, over-reactivity, and self-dramatization. This self-dramatization is always attention-seeking and often seductive, whether or not the patient is aware of its purpose. These personalities are also immature, self-centered, often vain, and usually dependent on others. This disorder must be differentiated from *Hysterical neurosis* (q.v.).

301.6 *Asthenic personality*
This behavior pattern is characterized by easy fatigability, low energy level, lack of enthusiasm, marked incapacity for enjoyment, and oversensitivity to physical and emotional stress. This disorder must be differentiated from *Neurasthenic neurosis* (q.v.).

301.7 *Antisocial personality*
This term is reserved for individuals who are basically unsocialized and whose behavior pattern brings them repeatedly into conflict with society. They are incapable of significant loyalty to individuals, groups, or social values. They are grossly selfish, callous, irresponsible, impulsive, and unable to feel guilt or to learn from experience and punishment. Frustration tolerance is low. They tend to blame others or offer plausible rationalizations for their behavior. A mere history of repeated legal or social offenses is not sufficient to justify this diagnosis. *Group delinquent reaction of childhood (or adolescence)* (q.v.), and *Social maladjustment without manifest psychiatric disorder* (q.v.) should be ruled out before making this diagnosis.

301.81* *Passive-aggressive personality*
This behavior pattern is characterized by both passivity and aggressiveness. The aggressiveness may be expressed passively, for example by obstructionism, pouting, procrastination, intentional inefficiency, or stubborness. This behavior commonly reflects

Table 15.1 (Continued)

hostility which the individual feels he dare not express openly. Often the behavior is one expression of the patient's resentment at failing to find gratification in a relationship with an individual or institution upon which he is over-dependent.

301.82* Inadequate personality*

This behavior pattern is characterized by ineffectual responses to emotional, social, intellectual and physical demands. While the patient seems neither physically nor mentally deficient, he does manifest inadaptability, ineptness, poor judgment, social instability, and lack of physical and emotional stamina.

301.89* Other personality disorders of specified types (Immature personality)*

301.9 [Unspecified personality disorder]

Current personality disorders reproduced from the Diagnostic and Statistical Manual of Mental Disorders-II. American Psychiatric Association, Washington, D.C., 1968.

that are high and low and alternate between sadness and elation. But do not all of us have mood swings? Are not most creative people cyclothymic?

These questions strike at the heart of the problem of making diagnoses of personality disorders, a problem which has plagued psychiatry for many years and dates back to the earliest stages in medicine, when Hippocrates defined the sanguine, melancholic, phlegmatic, and choleric temperaments. European psychiatry in particular regarded various personalities and characterized them in a variety of ways. For example, one early European clinician described no less than ten kinds of psychopaths, such as the hyperthymic psychopath, the depressive psychopath, the insecure psycopath, the fanatic psychopath and the explosive psychopath [30]. Another clinician discussed ectomorphic, endomorphic, and mesomorphic personality [31], while yet another labeled personalities according to traits, such as alaxia, which refers to a trusting individual who is free from jealousy; praxernia, which refers to a careful and conventional personality; and a low ergic personality, which refers to a relaxed and tranquil and unfrustrated personality [11].

It is quite obvious from the above that a variety of classification systems have been used to study people. Realizing that the classification of personality traits is highly subjective, it is not difficult to appreciate that a classification of personality disorders is also quite subjective. Of all the syndromes in psychiatry, personality disorders generally have the least data base to support their existence.

The concept of premorbid state has been used to formulate the various diagnostic entities for the personality disorders. Thus, the schizoid personality is seen as a potential precursor of schizophrenia, whereas the obsessive-compulsive personality is seen as one prone to develop an obsessive-compulsive neurosis. This rule is not invariable, however, and certain personality disorders do not progress to other kinds of psychiatric illness or, more precisely, cannot be conceived as being part of a continuum. Thus the explosive personality is an entity unto its own.

Current psychiatric nomenclature lists several personality disorders, which are described in Table 15.1. These disorders have been revised over the years and are presently undergoing revision by the APA's Task Force on Nomenclature, which is considering a tentative list of personality disorder classifications as follows:

Avoidant personality	Dependent personality
Asocial personality	Paranoid personality
Histrionic personality	Labile personality
Compulsive personality	Cyclothymic personality
Antisocial personality	Depressive personality
Narcissistic personality	

There are several factors which the student should keep in mind when studying personality disorders. First, although it is implicit in the definition that personality disorders are "characterized by deeply ingrained maladaptive patterns of behavior . . . and are lifelong patterns" [2:41], it must be remembered that these disorders are not immune from other forms of psychopathology. That is, a person with a personality disorder can become depressed or even psychotic, and other coexisting pathology may exist.

Second, it is very usual for the clinician to see admixtures of personality disorders rather than pure types. For example, explosive personalities are often paranoid and show passive-aggressive mannerisms in addition to paroxysmal outbursts of rage. Similarly, certain schizoid individuals also show asthenic and paranoid traits, and so on. Therefore, it is often difficult to make a single primary diagnosis.

Third, the clinician should be aware of the fact that personality traits are generally exaggerated by certain organic and psychopathological processes. For example, people tend to become less flexible as they get older, and if one were at all somewhat suspicious in younger years, one is apt to become more suspicious, not less, as one grows older. Therefore, in senility there is an exaggeration in certain instances of what might be termed premorbid personality traits. Chronic organic brain syndromes of aging bring out these traits, and it is often noted that a quarrelsome person becomes more quarrelsome and irritable as he gets older. Organic brain syndromes in general and toxic conditions resulting from impaired circulation or the use of drugs may bring out underlying psychopathology. A person who has shown certain schizoid traits may, under the influence of certain drugs such as the amphetamines or hallucinogens, become grossly autistic and paranoid and show distinct features of a schizoid or paranoid personality or may even later show psychotic manifestations. Alcohol often precipitates the explosive rages in an explosive personality. Generally, if a patient's personality changes or becomes worse — that is, his mannerisms become exaggerated or caricatured — the clinician should consider an underlying organic process, such as the above-mentioned organic brain syndromes, toxic states, or other central nervous system pathology, as a brain neoplasm.

Fourth, the clinician should remember that the environment also conditions the way a patient behaves. Indeed, in some instances it is difficult to make a diagnosis if one takes a person living in a particular community out of his social or cultural contacts. Such a person might appear very passive and schizoid (or the opposite), when in reality he is conforming to his community's social and cultural expectations [1]. By the same token, certain personality disorders decompensate when subjected to social situations such as confined military settings or prisons, which are characterized by sensory deprivation and which do not allow free behavioral outlets. The personality disorder generally reacts to this stress by some kind of regressed behavior, such as temper or social withdrawal. When such behavior cannot be physically or verbally expressed, depression or anxiety may set in. Clinicians tend to label given personality disorders in a way which connotes an immutability to any kind of psychopathological change. When seen in emergency rooms or outpatient clinic settings, the patient is given a once-and-for-all diagnosis of, for example, a schizoid personality, and those who see him later in time are apt to overlook the fact that a variety of changes in intrapsychic or external life may produce a depression or a psychotic decompensation [25].

Many of the personality disorders are extremely manipulative. They utilize certain personality traits and social skills in obtaining their ends. The antisocial personality (previously called psychopath) is often very charming and facile in his handling of interpersonal relationships. He may be a confidence man and try to persuade his clinical examiners to give him medication or write letters to the court excusing his behavior. It is partly these manipulative skills that lead personality disorder labels to be used in a distainful manner. Such a pejorative perception of certain personality disorders obscures good clinical judgment and may lead the observer to be insensitive to shifts in mood, affect, or thought process changes.

Personality disorders are not diagnosed very frequently. Roughly, they comprise about 10 percent of diagnoses made in state mental hospi-tals [23]. A primary diagnosis of neurosis may be more often given to middle-class patients. A patient in a lower socioeconomic group with the same psychopathology would be called a personality disorder. In this regard, antisocial personality is a diagnosis frequently made in prisons, whereas depressive reaction is a diagnosis frequently made in the thera-pist's office. The latter middle-class group of patients happen to be those who make their way into long-term therapy, whereas the former lower-class patients make their way into incarcerated settings. Again, the milieu shapes the diagnosis [13].

Throughout this chapter, the term personality is used, rather than character. The latter was the word first used by early workers in the field of psychoanalysis, whereas the word personality is the formal term used in current nomenclature. For clarity of presentation the various personality disorders, described in more detail, are grouped together.

EXPLOSIVE, ANTISOCIAL, AND PASSIVE-AGGRESSIVE PERSONALITIES

The *explosive personality* is an individual who demonstrates gross out-bursts of rage. The rage may be verbal or physical, generally paroxysmal in nature, and is very sudden or impulsive in quality. In contrast to the rage outbursts, the patient may be generally quite passive, compliant, or docile, and these rage outbursts are superimposed upon a baseline quies-cent state. Yet, patients with explosive personalities are generally over-responsive to environmental pressures and become easily excitable. Com-monly they react with hostility whenever something goes wrong.

Typically, explosive personalities face frequent problems with the law because of their volatile tempers; they are apt to talk quite freely about their temper tantrums. Quite typically, people with explosive personal-ities are dependent and require a good deal of nurturance because of early childhood deprivations. When their spouses withhold love and affection or, in bad marriages, threaten to leave them, these patients react by an all-or-none rage outburst in which they lose control of their ability to monitor their aggression, destroying furniture, striking out impulsively at any-thing in their way, or physically attacking their spouses or other family members. This diffusion of ego boundaries is a manifestation of an almost transient psychotic state which accompanies the rage outburst. In addi-tion, patients with explosive personalities may, during the uncontrolled rage outbursts, make suicidal gestures [8], for example, overdosing on pills. This overdose may represent an attempt to quench a painful affective rage state rather than a desire to kill oneself. Patients with rage outbursts are at risk around weapons and also tend to misuse the automobile by driving at high speeds when angry. Their histories reveal temper tantrums which date back into childhood and reflect themselves in poor adjustment to school, jobs, the military, or their work. These patients cannot stand criticism of any kind and react with rage toward employers. Their unstable job histories coupled with their tendency towards assaultiveness make them prone to multiple legal actions. A history of incarcerations is quite often obtained.

Because the paroxysmal and impulsive nature of their rage outbursts is reminiscent of an epileptic disturbance, consideration of underlying brain dysfunction, such as psychomotor epilepsy, should be considered, and sleep electroencephalograms (EEGs) are utilized in these patients [27]. Diagnostically, a careful history, with emphasis upon possible central nervous system injury, must be taken (similar to the type of history one takes from a mentally retarded patient in whom one wants to establish the etiology of brain damage). Patients with explosive personalities often have sustained head injury due to their involvement in physical abuse, and multiple head trauma with episodes of unconsciousness may lay the groundwork for temporal lobe dysfunction, which gives rise to psychomotor seizures [4].

A certain type of explosive personality uses alcohol in such a way as to exacerbate his violent propensities. Alcohol, in fact, is a commonly used agent which has toxic properties for this group of patients. Whether the alcohol has some pharmacological activating properties or simply increases vulnerability to psychological stress is unsettled by observers, who have described the phenomenon as "pathological intoxication" [5].

An organic etiology does not rule out a psychodynamic etiology. Many patients with explosive personalities become explosive under easily defined and repetitive psychological stresses. Maternal deprivation often leads to a high sensitization to any kind of rejection by the spouse and a preoccupation with fidelity. When, in such patients, the spouse "neglects" the patient, rage can ensue. Thus careful probing into the precipitants of the explosive outbursts is mandatory.

The *antisocial personality* is a term reserved for individuals who are unsocialized and in conflict with society. These patients are incapable of loyalty to individuals and groups, and are selfish, irresponsible, and unable to feel guilt or benefit from punishment. The term antisocial personality is the more recent term for what was once called a psychopath. Early English law was devoted to the concept of moral insanity, denoting a form of illness in which a person was not psychotic but suffered from an inability to know right from wrong [14]. Thus early in psychiatry the psychopath was conceptualized as someone who had a psychiatric illness, though the term remains elusive. Generally, psychopaths have been viewed as confidence men, people who can trick others into believing what psychopaths want them to believe, and it is probably true that many hoaxes and swindles in modern and older society have been performed by psychopaths. On the other hand, the charming aspect of the psychopath and his extremely adroit ability to mobilize people and manipulate them to his own ends is a trait which is not unuseful in certain occupations. It is not difficult to understand how persons in various professions may use these same skills within the framework of the law and the sanctions of society to achieve high standards and success. Therefore, the question arises as to when an individual is really sick. A cynical answer may be that a psychopath is mentally ill when he gets caught. The student of personality disorders will see that it is very difficult to make the diagnosis of psychopathy and indeed, certain moral and social judgments are involved.

The term antisocial personality should not be used just because a person is in jail, not all criminals are antisocial personalities. As an extension of the term psychopath, the diagnosis of antisocial personality is reserved for the particular individual who cannot profit from punishment and who shows peculiarly and specific guiltless patterns to his behavior. Many criminals are repentant for their acts and, although they may deny guilt on a superficial examination, do show remorse on some level of thinking. A typical antisocial personality does not show genuine remorse, and, in fact, tends to be recidivistic with regard to commission of antisocial acts.

A good deal of research by sociologists, psychologists, and criminologists has been carried out on antisocial personalities because these personalities come into so much contact with authorities and agencies and hence the literature is quite extensive [28]. Studies of this disorder have revealed a family history of emotional deprivation, early onset detectable at puberty with multiple involvements in juvenile delinquency, school truancy, and poor work performance. Antisocial individuals may be quite intelligent and creative. The peculiar deficit in their ability to respond to the same guilt that stops others from committing criminal acts is noteworthy, and a study of such failure of guilt mechanisms has been undertaken in some early classic work by Cleckley [12], who approached the problem by conceptualizing a lack of guilt as analogous to an aphasic process in neurology, whereby an individual simply could not think of the right word. Cleckley therefore postulated that there was a central nervous system deficit in antisocial personalities which explained their typical and strange inability to experience guilt. A sociological view of the same phenomenon has been given by workers who have put forth the theory of *superego lacunae*, which states that families tend to act out their own pathology in very covert ways by inciting various potential antisocial personalities to criminal acts. Such covert provocation comes about through tacit admiration of criminals, through subtle suggestions regarding thievery, or through simple modeling of parental behavior. Electroencephalographic studies of antisocial personalities have also been carried out in an attempt to find an organic reason why these patients lack guilt. Such studies [32], have never shed light on the problem, and the basic process of the psychopathological development of the antisocial personality remains a matter of speculation.

Many of these patients give reasons for their behavior, which on first inspection sounds quite legitimate and plausible. The patient's appearance may be so good that the clinician must obtain background information from other sources, including a report from the Federal Bureau of Investigation (FBI), before he comes to the conclusion that the patient has psychopathology. It is surprising how often a clinician is fooled by a well-dressed articulate individual who was sent for evaluation and who relates in a guiltless manner that he is quite innocent of any wrongdoing, only to discover later from a subsequent FBI report that the patient has been involved in a variety of highly violent criminal activities. Corroborative evidence is always necessary in interviews with a spouse or a probation officer, as these patients obviously use a good deal of denial in discussing their past.

The *passive-aggressive personality*, commonly seen in bureaucratic settings, very effectively uses the obstructionistic traits of pouting, stubbornness, and ignorance as ways of dealing with his unwillingness to perform a certain act. Patients who are passive-aggressive handle aggressive traits in a passive way. They retreat into negativism and a refusal to do work. In the older literature, a variant of this disorder was labeled passive-dependent, which generally referred to an individual who could not deal with his aggressive drives but instead retreated into passivity, which led to clinging helplessness and reliance upon other people. This term has now been deleted, and the passive-aggressive personality disorder remains.

Passive-aggressive behavior often can be extremely effective. Many of the changes in civil rights have come about through organized passive-aggressive movements on behalf of certain racial groups. The purposeful inefficiency and procrastination that one sees in the passive-aggressive personality is a forceful method of expressing rebelliousness and defiance. The same kinds of traits often are seen in certain adolescent patients, who demonstrate stubbornness and obstructionism as a part of a general adolescent adjustment reaction. The diagnosis of passive-aggressive personality can be difficult to make. The clinician is more apt to find passive-aggressive traits among an admixture of explosive, antisocial, and passive-aggressive mannerisms.

The treatment of patients with explosive, antisocial, and passive-aggressive personalities is aimed at reducing hostility and aggressiveness which are globally present as traits among all three character disorders [22]. Treatment of the explosive personality is basically aimed at teaching the patient to deal with aggression through verbal means rather than physical outbursts of rage. To this extent, pharmacological and psychotherapeutic measures are indicated. Pharmacological agents [24] such as anticonvulsants are indicated and are useful when there is an epileptoid basis for the disorder. The clinician will have to decide whether or not he requires electroencephalographic confirmation of such a disorder or whether he will accept a possible epileptoid diagnosis on purely clinical grounds. The subject of whether or not violence can ever be an epileptic phenomenon remains controversial in the scientific literature and has been reviewed in recent publications [19]. The point here is that for clinical purposes, medications which reduce impulsivity in patients bothered by such a trait are useful. Other medications, such as the benzodiazepines (including diazepam, oxazepam, or chlordiazepoxide), may be useful in reducing the anxiety which leads to aggressiveness, and because of their anticonvulsant properties. The psychotherapeutic treatment of the explosive personality involves making the patient aware of premonitary signs and symptoms which cause him to erupt. Patients who respond in all or-none fashion to certain stimuli need to be made aware of means by which they can verbalize their anger in order to avoid physically destructive outbursts of rage. Educating the spouse or other family members as to when the patient is going to explode makes intervention possible.

The treatment of antisocial personalities has been one of the most problematic in psychiatry. Because of the chronic lack of guilt in this type of patient, milieu confinement has traditionally been seen as the only way in which a patient can learn right from wrong. It takes a great deal of time to acquire a sense of guilt — something which most people learn from childhood. Coercive treatment regimens have traditionally been advocated for these personality disorders, but the value of coercion appears to lie not in any psychodynamic enlightenment which comes from treatment but rather in the close follow-up and watchfulness that become part of the therapy. Coercive treatment is always difficult due to split allegiances; the clinician who undertakes to help such a patient must be aware of the fact that the patient always sees him as an agent of the law, a fact which impairs trust and must be dealt with. Milieu indeterminate-sentence treatment for certain antisocial individuals has been attempted in both the United States and abroad with certain success [21]. The premise of such treatment is that the antisocial personality cannot con those who treat him but must earn his way out of incarceration through meaningful change. Indeterminate sentence facilities make release contingent upon dynamic change and marked personality improvement and probably offer the best hope for reform in this regard.

The passive-aggressive personality is often quite unaware of the tactics he uses in dealing with others and a group therapy approach may be useful by virtue of its strongly confronting nature. Videotape confrontation may also be useful, but these patients are rather refractory to change, since they possess such powerful means of dealing with people.

HYSTERICAL AND CYCLOTHYMIC PERSONALITIES

These disorders are grouped together because both show emotional instability, lability of mood and affect, and a tendency toward mood swings and shifts in levels of feeling.

The *hysterical personality* is characterized by emotional overreactiveness, dramatization, and attention-seeking behavior. This disorder is probably overdiagnosed, particularly in seductive females who are falsely perceived by clinicians as being "hysterical," although it *is* a disorder more prevalent in females than males. However, not every attention-seeking, flamboyant, and sexually seductive individual is a hysterical personality, and there are very marked cultural and subcultural differences in this regard.

What helps the clinician in making this diagnosis? Basically, in addition to the traits outlined above, there are certain psychodynamic features which are important for the establishment of this diagnosis. The hysterical personality was one of the first personality disorders described by early psychoanalytic workers, including Freud [17], who felt that the basis for the disorder lay in an unresolved oedipal situation. For example, unable to deal with incestuous wishes for her father, the daughter relinquishes true sexuality and flirts and plays with men, rather than obtain true sexual gratification from them. Many hysterical personalities are sexually frigid, and the women act in a childlike and coy manner which bespeaks their infantile orientation toward sexuality. In addition to the above dynamic, hysterical personalities may put a premium on personal sexual attractiveness as a way of reassuring themselves, through the admiration of others, that they are desirable and feminine. This trait also springs from an inner uncertainty about sexual identity, derived from the same unresolved and forbidden oedipal incestuous wishes. In effect, the patient in part supresses her femininity in deeper fantasy, then takes pains to reaffirm it in daily life.

These psychodynamic explanations are somewhat a luxury for the clinician who must make the diagnosis of hysterical personality in a female, for they are rarely obtainable unless the patient enters into an extensive and intensive psychotherapeutic experience where such unconscious data can be gathered. Instead, the clinician should gather some information about the patient's relationship with her mother, father, and other men and make a prudent assessment of her various traits. In addition to the traits already mentioned, hysterical personalities may somatize and exaggerate their pain and suffering as a way of getting attention. It is not infrequent to find such patients have undergone needless surgery and make repeated visits to doctors with real or imagined complaints of an exaggerated nature [33]. The clinician must realize that it is attention that the patient wants and make an appropriate referral in cases where demands are excessive and somatic illness is absent. Somatic illness, of course, always needs to be ruled out in these patients and is often made difficult by the fact that they "cry wolf" so often.

Because these patients crave attention so badly and because female patients are preoccupied with their identity as females and with their attractiveness, they are quite prone to depression during bodily changes in menopause or subsequent to any medical or surgical procedures. Under the same circumstances depression also occurs in male patients. The incidence of this disorder is much higher in women than men, and this is believed to be attributable to the psychodynamics outlined above. Hysterical personalities among males do exist and tend to have a homosexual basis.

There is a condition among the hysterical personality disorders often referred to as a *borderline hysteric*. This refers to a personality disorder which is sicker than the ordinary hysterical personality. The borderline hysteric has had deficits in early object relations and is not merely fixated at the genital stage but has suffered deprivations at the oral stage. These patients are quite empty and lonely and tend to translate their emptiness and loneliness into a craving for insatiable attention. It is often very difficult to clinically differentiate a borderline hysteric from an ordinary hysterical personality [18]. Briefly, the desperate and urgent need for attention and approval and the exaggerated level of despair and emptiness within the patient should alert the clinician to the fact that the patient has more severe psychopathology than in the hysterical personality.

Clinicians are apt to find that these patients are quite troublesome to treatment. Attending physicians or surgeons may complain that these patients ask repeatedly for pain medication and that they are never content with any kind of help received in the hospital. The clinician must be aware of the fact that the hysterical personality is highly invested in her or his body and does require a good deal of supportive intervention in this regard. Verbal reassurance rather than antidepressants is the answer for intervention. The female hysterical personality, because of her appearance and seductiveness, may pose countertransference problems for the male clinician who may find himself attracted to a particular patient who flatters him and makes frequent office visits. In such cases, dilution of the intensity of the relationship by the intervention of a colleague or nursing personnel, or appropriate discussion with or referral to a colleague is in order.

The *cyclothymic personality* is defined as one who shows recurring and alternating periods of depression and elation. The elation may be characterized by a good deal of enthusiasm and optimism, together with a very high energy level and productivity, whereas the periods of depression are characterized by ruminations, sadness, passivity, and worry. The mood variations do not relate to environmental circumstances but occur endogenously and for no apparent reason [33].

Many highly productive people are cyclothymic and it is within the nature of mankind to show some alterations in mood. It should also be noted that some individuals are consistently hypomanic and able to enthusiastically engage in a variety of activities with high levels of energy, whereas other individuals are more chronically depressed and anhedonic. It remains a question in psychiatry whether the cyclothymic individual really does exist or is a simple variant of true manic-depressive illness, which is an affective disorder characterized by severe or recurrent mood swings. It seems likely that the latter is the case and that a cyclothymic personality, if one defines it as a person who shows periodically alternating mood swings, is a milder form of a manic-depressive illness and should be diagnostically considered and therapeutically treated as such. It is relatively rare to see a cyclothymic personality in clinical practice, and those who are seen are generally diagnosed as having a manic-depressive illness.

In order to make the diagnosis, if it can be made, the clinician should be aware of the fact that these mood swings occur for no apparent reason and are relatively self-limited. It is not necessarily axiomatic that a patient must swing from high to low, but he may also show simple swings to high from a baseline state or swings to depression from a baseline state. That is, he may show hypomanic mood swings or depressive mood swings. During the high phase, the patient shows enthusiasm, an ebullient mood, a high activation level, little need for sleep, and a tendency to work very hard. When the work becomes driven and unproductive and when the patient begins to spend too much money, makes poor business decisions, or gets himself in debt or otherwise engages in destructive activity with impaired judgment, a more malignant process such as a manic-depressive psychosis should be considered. Likewise, when the low is characterized by suicidal thoughts and a depression of immobilizing quality, the diagnosis of manic-depressive psychosis should also be considered.

The treatment of hysterical and cyclothymic personalities is quite divergent. Traditionally, the hysterical personality has been considered an excellent candidate for long-term intensive psychotherapy. There is a discrete psychodynamic basis for the disorder and a developmental arrest phase which can be corrected through intensive therapy by review of conscious and unconscious material. Group therapy is often used in confronting these patients with their behavior and its consequences. Patients who are diagnosed as borderline hysterics are to be considered as closer to psychosis and may be treated along more supportive psychotherapeutic lines with medication. Attention should be paid to the patient's need for excess medication or surgery and proper intervention to prevent needless "treatment" is necessary.

The cyclothymic personality may be treated with lithium carbonate, with the rationale that the personality disorder is a manifestation of a manic-depressive affective illness. Lithium carbonate is the drug of choice for manic-depressive psychosis and is also useful in the prophylaxis of mood swings. The clinician should realize that the patients often enjoy being high and will resist treatment. If for some reason lithium cannot be used, antidepressants may be required to deal with the lows and minor or major tranquilizers may be necessary to deal with the highs (see chapter 7).

OBSESSIVE-COMPULSIVE PERSONALITY AND PARANOID PERSONALITY

These disorders are grouped together because both of these personalities use isolation as a way of dealing with their anxieties about the world [34]. The obsessive-compulsive personality relies only upon himself and not upon others. The paranoid personality mistrusts everyone around him and also relies only upon himself. Both personalities are generally patients with a good degree of intelligence and are potentially capable, by virtue of their self-reliance and achievement, of a good deal of industry. Both personalities use denial and rationalization; thus, they deal with inner loneliness and depression by working hard and valuing logic and order. The paranoid personality also uses the defenses of projection, seeking the blame for his troubles in the outside world.

The *obsessive-compulsive personality* shows excessive concern with conformity and adherence to standards of conscience. The patients in this group are characterized as being overinhibited, with a severe conscience, and driven to work compulsively and unable to relax. This personality disorder is relatively easy to diagnose. The obsessive-compulsive personality is concerned with logic, punctuality, orderliness, and the rational approach to the world. He is less concerned with spontaneity and dislikes the murky world of emotions, which he cannot organize into some systematic theory of logic. Obsessive-compulsive personalities are often people who accomplish a great deal, and their general intellectual level enables them to achieve high professional status.

Early psychoanalytic workers postulated that patients with this disorder had difficulties at the anal psychosexual stage of development. They tend to be obstinate, retentive, and frugal and are obsessed with orderliness and adherence to time schedules. The obsessive-compulsive personality may find himself working harder and harder on a certain problem, for these patients perceive that the answer to the world's problems lies in hard work. They cannot effectively deal with loss, death, problems in marriage, child rearing, or other emotional issues, and they divest themselves of the difficulties by staying at the office longer, working harder and harder, and displacing their anxiety onto something else in an attempt to cope with that which they cannot handle. It is at this point that they often voluntarily come in for treatment. Obsessive-compulsive personalities like hysterical personalities, are prone to depression — and are also prone to paranoid decompensation. The obsessive-compulsive personalities value their own integrity and ability to get things done and do not easily trust others. Thus, when their work and own efforts fail them, they become suspicious of those around them and may develop the feeling that the world is against them. This feeling may subsequently attain exaggerated proportions concomitant with a paranoid psychotic decompensation. The obsessive-compulsive personality craves work, industry, and achievement. His esteem rests upon his accomplishments at the expense of inner satisfaction. He is preoccupied with ambition, control, and other external manifestations of his achievements. Although his traits keep him in good stead and functioning well, they also pose a certain vulnerability to loneliness, isolation, and as previously mentioned, depression and paranoia.

The *paranoid personality* is an individual who shows jealousy, envy, a certain self-importance, a tendency to blame other individuals, and a need to always be on guard. Paranoid personalities can be loud or quiet. In many instances it requires several interviews with a patient to ascertain how suspicious he is about the world, for he will not admit his suspicions to anyone as a matter of his own paranoia. Other paranoid individuals are quite openly suspicious about the world, and the clinician should have no difficulty in making this diagnosis. There is a relatively thin line between a paranoid personality and a paranoid psychosis. Many paranoid personalities may become psychotic transiently without the examiner being aware of it, and delusions of persecution or actual hallucinatory episodes may occur which invalidate the diagnosis of a simple personality disorder. The differential diagnosis between paranoid personality and paranoia and the various paranoid states is made on the basis of delusions, and it often requires a good deal of intimate knowledge to determine whether or not an apparent paranoid personality has delusions or not (see chapter 6).

Paranoid personalities may have social relationships which are satisfactory but limited to a small nucleus of friends, while they distrust the rest of the world. Alternately, they may be loners who shun the environment and never achieve close intimacy. Paranoid personalities tend, if they are married, to be very jealous and possessive of their spouses and often harbor continuous suspicions of infidelity. Male patients are particularly sensitive to any slurs about their masculinity and self-esteem, and this may in part reflect the psychodynamic formulation that homosexuality is the basis for paranoia as initially formulated by Freud [9]. Again, this dynamic may not be accessible to the clinician, who needs only to be aware of the fact that paranoid personalities have difficulty tolerating close intimacy with people (particularly of the same sex) and need to maintain a defensive posture to protect themselves from the anxiety which such intimacy breeds. Paranoid personalities can be quite intelligent and hypervigilant. By virtue of the fact that they notice small details in their environment, they become astute observers of people and events and can occasionally put such knowledge to productive use. The hypervigilance which accompanies paranoia is something that everyone experiences at times; for example, when a person travels to a foreign country whose language he does not speak, he finds himself constantly on guard for people who may take his money or otherwise exploit him. The paranoid personality operates in everyday life like that. He rarely rests and must maintain a constant alertness as to what occurs in the environment.

The use of alcohol may either reduce the paranoid personality's anxieties or increase his suspiciousness. The results of alcohol are relatively idiosyncratic but should be monitored by clinicians who are interested in working with these groups of patients. In addition, illicit use of central nervous system stimulants such as methylphenidate or amphetamines may exacerbate the symptoms and produce a paranoid psychotic condition; thus these drugs must be avoided by the paranoid personality.

Paranoid personalities have a great deal of trouble in maintaining stable relationships with people at work or with their families. Their constant need to defend themselves and their constant mistrust tend to alienate them from others. Thus, a simple remark by an employer may be misinterpreted to the extent that an argument ensues, leading to the patient's quitting his job. Marital arguments may be the rule rather than the exception. The patient's entire functioning in society can revolve around his need to prove others wrong and to ensure that he is not taken advantage of. There is a mildly grandiose flavor to this type of orientation, which, of course, becomes more pronounced in actual psychotic decompensation. When paranoid patients become sicker (and such decompensation often is quite insidious and difficult to detect), the delusional and self-centered thinking becomes evident to the observer.

The treatment of obsessive-compulsive and paranoid personalities is psychotherapeutic, though secondary symptoms may be treated with medication. The obsessive-compulsive personality becomes a hard-working patient in the therapeutic situation because of his desire to master therapy the same way he desires to master any other job. This in itself produces problems with control and passivity within the treatment setting. In addition, the obsessive-compulsive personality has trouble dealing with emotions in a spontaneous and forthright fashion. Indeed, the thrust of psychotherapy is to enable him to deal with his emotions at the expense of logic [29]. Such psychotherapy is a long-term venture. In those instances where anxiety and/or depression are prominent features, appropriate medications may be considered. Psychotherapeutic treatment for the paranoid personality is theoretically desirable but practically rare, due to the fact that these patients will not come to therapy spontaneously because of their mistrust and the syntonic nature of their symptoms. Should they enter into the treatment process, therapy is made difficult by this mistrust, and a working alliance requires time to be established. Eventually, the paranoid personality must learn to put some reliance upon the therapist and to put himself in a somewhat dependent position within treatment. In cases where suspiciousness and hypervigilance are extreme, medication of the antianxiety type may be indicated. Drugs of the benzodiazepide class, such as oxazepam, diazepam, or chlordiazepoxide, are useful adjuncts in treatment and do not produce too many side effects that would cause the paranoid personality to discontinue medication. On the other hand, severe suspiciousness approaching psychotic proportions may be benefited by the administration of small amounts of major tranquilizers with antipsychotic properties, such as trifluoroperazine. Both the paranoid and the obsessive-compulsive personalities do not like medication. The paranoid does not like medication because it may render him weak and helpless, and the obsessive-compulsive may not like medication because he values his own integrity and his own ability to master problems. Therefore, the clinician has difficulties administering drugs unless symptoms of anxiety are severe enough to produce a desire for relief within the patient. With the paranoid personality, administration of drugs must be given in a scrupulously honest manner, and one should be very clear in explaining to such patients what the administration of medication entails. One should err on the conservative side and give a small amount which will cause minimal side effects.

Ruminations are common features of both the obsessive-compulsive personality and the paranoid personality. Ruminations are thoughts of a repetitive nature which plague these patients in a "tape recorder" style. Thus both of these patients stay awake at night, mentally reviewing over and over again a particular event, the significance of that event, and the possible injustice done them by that event. This type of rumination can be affectively painful and can benefit from the administration of an antianxiety agent or, if severe, an antipsychotic agent. Excessive ruminations may signal decompensation and may represent defenses which usually protect the patient from helplessness and passivity, but which are now failing.

Paranoid personalities may feel extremely uneasy when suffering from medical illness. In such instances, the clinician must explain procedures in great detail to them and be aware of their litigious qualities and appropriately address the underlying anxieties of such patients. On rare occasions, paranoid patients may request elective surgery for certain deformities such as a deformed nose or varicocele. In such instances, the clinician should realize that the patient has a more basic inner difficulty with self-esteem which he translates into an external deformity. The clinician should further realize that correction of the nose or the varicocele will not be accepted gratefully and is apt to lead to enhanced disappointment rather than relief, since the patient can no longer blame his problems on his deformity. Consequently, he is apt to become more paranoid. Clinicians should refer such patients for psychiatric consultation.

SCHIZOID, AESTHENIC, AND INADEQUATE PERSONALITIES

These patients show similarities with regard to their difficulties in adjusting to society and their social withdrawal, isolationism, seclusiveness, and general passive responses to environmental demands. Two of these disorders, the schizoid personality and the inadequate personality are, in fact, on the continuum of the schizophrenic disorders, and in the diagnostic typologies in certain countries, such as those of Scandinavia, they are listed as forms of schizophrenia [3]. It is relatively easy to understand why, since a severely schizoid person who demonstrates autistic withdrawal and seclusiveness may very much resemble a schizophrenic person. Likewise, the inadequate personality who simply cannot function in society but requires constant support and nurturance also appears to be very similar to a psychotic person who requires a sheltered environment.

Like the hysterical personality, there are strong cultural and subcultural influences which lead to the making of this diagnosis. People such as "hippies" or "religious freaks" may demonstrate schizoid features because of their social isolationism, passivity, and emotional withdrawal. Such asocial traits need to be considered when making the diagnosis. It is very likely that all three terms may be deleted in the forthcoming revision of the APA psychiatric nomenclature glossary, since they are all so similar and quite ambiguous in nature. In fact, the differential diagnosis of the three conditions is exceedingly difficult, and the diagnoses of the inadequate personality and asthenic personality are very rarely made.

The *schizoid personality* is characterized by an individual who shows shyness, seclusiveness, and the avoidance of intimacy. While the schizoid personality may daydream, show an impoverished ability to deal with emotions, and respond to environmental events by coldness and aloofness, he does not retract to the degree seen in a schizophrenic who hallucinates or dissolves himself in his own delusional thinking. Schizoid personalities may be quite productive, and their aloofness and detachment from emotions leads them to perform well in isolated settings, such as outposts in the military, scientific or geological explorations in isolated areas, or other environmental situations where there is little companionship. Indeed, such individuals thrive on loneliness and often have an inner resourcefulness which, when coupled with obsessive-compulsive traits, makes them highly desirable people for certain professional work. However, the schizoid individual is the only one of this group who shows a potential for professional achievement in contrast to the asthenic and inadequate personalities who share the common denominator of not being able to function in society. Yet most schizoid personalities do show some difficulties in coping with environmental stresses. The schizoid personality is typically a walking "robot" or a cold and indifferent individual who shows a remarkable nonchalance to highly charged emotional situations. His inability to respond to stress in this manner, although occasionally being an asset, is more often a liability in that he fares poorly in interpersonal relationship [15]. Since most of us deal with people by responding to their comments and emotions, it can be seen that an individual who operates as a machine has few friends and does poorly when called upon to perform in the emotional sphere of the world. Schizoid individuals often have trouble handling aggression and may respond to hostilities in a manner reminiscent of that seen in explosive personalities; i.e., they remain ostensibly indifferent until a certain threshold is reached, at which point they respond in an all-or-none fashion. Schizoid personalities are often bizarre and can show ritualistic types of behavior, such as laughing or talking to themselves, behaviors which are not psychotic but very close to it and which are reflective of internalized thought processes. Schizoid personalities are bland, speak in monotones, and tend to intellectualize their problems similar to the intellectualization seen in the obsessive-compulsive personality. This common defense of intellectualization bespeaks a vulnerability when confronted with intimacy from which he cannot escape, such as a military barracks. Unable to fathom the emotions in which they are immersed and unable to run from such close intimacy by using the various defenses of social withdrawal and autism, they may become psychotic or depressed. The schizoid personality is typically a loner who has few friends or cares to socialize. He may show eccentric mannerisms but is generally capable of sustaining himself within a certain context, provided that he can make "a nest" for himself in an environment such as a school or college. In work situations, he may function well in a laboratory or in a professional situation conducive to isolation and privacy.

Somewhat in contrast to the schizoid personality, the *asthenic personality* is characterized by a person having an extremely low level of energy. Asthenic personalities are always tired, complain of being fatigued, and cannot enjoy the events of the world around them [16]. A weakness of libido and difficulties in interpersonal relationships and occupations are paramount, and this type of personality disorder may be seen in clinic settings, complaining of somatic concerns which are found to have no organic basis. These patients are basically individuals who show a chronic low energy level and function on a rather marginal level in life. The formal diagnosis of an asthenic personality is rarely made, although the trait is occasionally seen in certain personalities and the differential diagnoses of depression and physiological illness are necessary.

The *inadequate personality* shows a behavior pattern characterized by ineffectual responses to emotional, social, intellectual, and physical demands. The patient is not mentally deficient or physically diseased but does show an ineptness and poor judgment, together with a lack of physical and emotional stamina. This diagnosis, like that of the asthenic personality, is rarely made. Most inadequate personalities are probably akin to schizophrenia of the simple type and are so hampered in their functioning in society as to be functionally psychotic [26], yet without evidence of a thought disorder. The term passive-dependent personality, although no longer a formal diagnosis as it once was in earlier psychiatric typologies, may be applicable to describe some inadequate personalities, since this type of patient typically responds in a clinging and helpless fashion to the world around him. In military settings, for example, the inadequate personality may show a total inability to adjust to training, barracks life, or any facet of his environment. Patients with inadequate personalities do poorly in school, camps, or any kind of setting that requires stress and often lead seclusive and sheltered lives within the context of their home, never wandering far from it. Somatic preoccupations may be present, and again this disorder requires differentiation from depression and from somatic illness.

The treatment for the above three conditions is basically similar and requires a resocializing experience. These patients must be taught over time to interact with people and deal with the anxieties which accompany such interaction. Group therapy or therapy within a milieu setting or hospital must of necessity be long-term and is the requisite form of treatment. These patients evoke a good deal of distaste in those who view their maddening helplessness with disdain, and treatment is problematic in this regard. The anxiety which accompanies social interaction or the depression which accompanies the frustrations of the social experiences may be treatable with certain medications, but the fact remains that these patients must be educated to respond and adapt to society and its demands. In the case of the schizoid personality, antipsychotic medication may occasionally be indicated if withdrawal becomes too extreme and signals psychotic decompensation.

GENERAL CONSIDERATIONS

The personality disorders must always be differentiated from their neurotic counterparts. This is particularly true of the obsessive-compulsive personality who may develop an obsessive-compulsive neurosis. The obsessive-compulsive neurosis is characterized by distinct ruminations and ritualistic behavior such as hand washing, pacing, and other signs indicative of a neurotic process (see chapter 11). Likewise, the hysterical personality may develop a hysterical neurosis characterized by dramatic exaggerations in body dysfunction, including paralysis, blindness, deafness, and other conversion symptoms. The asthenic personality may develop a neurasthenic neurosis which is characterized by chronic weakness and fatigability with exhaustion, but in this instance the course is transient and not chronic as seen in the personality disorder. A hypochondriacal neurosis may develop in certain hysterical or asthenic or inadequate personalities, and such a neurosis is characterized by a preoccupation with a body disease or dysfunction of an organ.

Depression and anxiety are not infrequently seen in personality disorders subjected to external stresses, as previously mentioned. In addition, psychotic decompensation is always a potential development in personality disorders subjected to stress. In all of the personality disorders, organicity and underlying somatic disease should be carefully considered by the observer.

The basic premise of therapy for a personality disorder lies in intrapsychic change and the modification of the traits of the individual concerned. There are occasions, however, where personality defenses need to be upheld and strengthened, rather than changed. In acute crisis situations, such as on a medical ward, the clinician is apt to see anxiety in an obsessive-compulsive personality who has undergone a surgical operation and cannot deal with the helplessness concomitant with the recovery period. There are so many unknowns that this patient, who values mastery of his environment, becomes anxious when he cannot deal with all of them. The treatment in this case is to give the patient an active participation in his medical management. Thus, one tells the obsessive-compulsive to approach the nursing station at a specific hour and take the medication at a specific time, in addition to engaging in a specific routine set of exercises. Such obsessive-compulsive directions enhance his defense structure and help him overcome the anxiety resulting from passivity and helplessness. The hysterical personality often complains loudly of discomfort and the clinician must be aware of the fact that the pains such a patient experiences are more easily alleviated by discussion than by analgesics. Often, such patients tend to discourage staff and nurses from spending time with them as a result of their frequent requests and demands, and simple reassurance as well as acknowledgement of the patient's complaints do more to calm the patient and uplift his mood than does antidepressant medication. The tactics of dealing with these patients in medical settings has been reviewed elsewhere. [20].

Psychological testing of personality disorders is often very helpful in distinguishing these diagnoses from psychotic counterparts [10].

Finally, students of personality disorders should be aware of the fact that certain organic lesions are accompanied by specific personality traits. The frontal lobe personality can show apathy and indifference accompanied by a tendency toward infantilism and euphoria. Such changes may indicate an underlying cortical lesion [7]. An epileptoid personality has been described as showing a deepening of emotional responses with episodic discharges of rage and anger and an increased obsessiveness; these traits may bespeak underlying temporal lobe disease [6].

REFERENCES

1   Albert, J. S. "Sociocultural determinants of personality pathology." In *Personality disorders*, ed. J. R. Lion. Baltimore: Williams and Wilkins, 1974.

2   American Psychiatric Association. *Diagnostic and statistical manual of mental disorders*, DSM-II. Washington, D.C.: American Psychiatric Association, 1968.

3   Azcarate, C. "*Schizoid, asthenic, and inadequate personalities.*" In *Personality disorders*, ed. J. R. Lion. Baltimore: Williams and Wilkins, 1974.

4   Bach-y-Rita, G., Lion, J. R., Climent, C. E., and Ervin, F. R. Episodic dyscontrol: A study of 130 violent patients. *Am. J. Psychiatry*, 127:11, 1971.

5   Bach-y-Rita, G., Lion, J. R., and Ervin, F. R. Pathological intoxication: Clinical and electroencephalographic studies. *Am. J. Psychiatry* 127:698, 1970.

6   Blumer, D. "Organic personality disorders." in *Personality disorders*, ed. J. R. Lion. Baltimore: Williams and Wilkins, 1974.

7   Brickner, R. M. *The intellectual functions of the frontal lobes.* New York: Macmillan, 1936.

8   Cain, A. C. The presuperego "turning inward" of aggression. *Psychoanal. Q.* 30:171–243, 1961.

9   Cameron, N. *Personality development and psychopathology: A dynamic approach.* Boston: Houghton Mifflin, 1963.

10   Carney, F. L. "Psychological testing of the personality disorders." In *Personality disorders,* ed. J. R. Lion. Baltimore: Williams and Wilkins, 1974.

11   Cattell, R. B. "Personality theory derived from quantitative experiment." In *Comprehensive textbook of psychiatry,* eds. A. M. Freedman and H. I. Kaplan. Baltimore: Williams and Wilkins, 1967.

12   Cleckley, H. *The mask of sanity.* St. Louis: Mosby, 1950.

13   Craft, M. J. "The moral responsibility for Welsh psychopaths." In *The mentally abnormal offender,* ed. A. V. S. De Reuck and R. Porter. *Int. Psychiatry Clin.* 5:91, 1967.

14   Craft, M. J. *Ten studies in psychopathy.* Bristol: Wright, 1965.

15   Deutsch, H. Some forms of emotional disturbance and their relationship to schizophrenia. *Psychoanal. Q.* 11:301–321, 1942.

16   Freedman, A. M., Kaplan, H. I., and Sadock, B. J., ed *Modern synopsis of comprehensive textbook of psychiatry.* Baltimore: Williams and Wilkins, 1972.

17   Freud, S. "Hysteria." In *Collected papers,* vol. 1. London: Hogarth Press, 1955.

18   Gallahorn, G. E. "The borderline personality." In *Personality disorders,* ed. J. R. Lion. Baltimore: Williams and Wilkins, 1974.

19   Goldstein, M. Brain research and violent behavior. *Arch. Neurol.* 30:1–35, 1974.

20   Kahana, R. J., and Bibring, G. L. "Personality types on medical management." In *Psychiatry and medical practice in a general hospital,* ed. N. E. Zinberg. New York: International Universities Press, 1964.

21   Liebman, M. C., and Hedlund, D. A. "Therapeutic community milieu therapy of personality disorders." In *Personality disorders,* ed. J. R. Lion. Baltimore: Williams and Wilkins, 1974.

22   Lion, J. R. *Evaluation and management of the violent patient.* Springfield, Ill.: Thomas, 1972.

23   Lion, J. R. "Diagnosis and treatment of personality disorders. In *Personality disorders,* ed. J. R. Lion. Baltimore: Williams and Wilkins, 1974.

24   Lion, J. R. Conceptual issues in the use of drugs for the treatment of aggression in man. *J. Nerv. Ment. Dis.* 160:76–82, 1975.

25   Lion, J. R., and Leaff, L. A. On the hazards of assessing character pathology in an outpatient setting. *Psychiatr. Q.* 47:104, 1973.

26   Monro, A. B. The inadequate personality in psychiatric practice. *J. Mental Sci.* 105:44–50, 1959.

27   Monroe, R. R., *Episodic behavioral disorders.* Cambridge: Harvard University Press, 1970.

28   Pasternack, S. A. "The explosive antisocial, and passive-aggressive personalities." In *Personality disorders,* ed. J. R. Lion. Baltimore: Williams and Wilkins, 1974.

29   Saltzman, L. *The obsessive personality*. New York: Science House, 1958.

30   Schneider, K. *Psychopathic personalities*. Springfield, Ill.: Thomas, 1958.

31   Sheldon, W. H., and Stevens, S. S. *The varieties of temperament*. New York: Harper, 1942.

32   Stafford-Clarke, D., and Taylor, F. H. Clinical and EEG studies of prisoners charged with murder. *J. Neurol. Neurosurg. Psychiatry* 12:325, 1949.

33   Tupin, J. P. "Hysterical and cyclothymic personalities." In *Personality disorders*, ed. J. R. Lion. Baltimore: Williams and Wilkins, 1974.

34   Weintraub, W. "Obsessive-compulsive and paranoid personalities." In *Personality disorders*, ed. J. R. Lion. Baltimore: Williams and Wilkins, 1974.

16

Borderline Personality Disorder

George E. Gallahorn, M.D.

Borderline personality disorder is a diagnosis that has been used only since the 1940s, and considerable confusion remains regarding the criteria for diagnosis. All authors agree that the patient occupies a position between neurosis and psychosis. The patient makes use of multiple neurotic defenses (such as phobias, compulsions, and dissociative episodes) to sustain a fragile ego, but also there are transient episodes of regression and impaired reality testing. These episodes are precipitated by stressful situations, alcohol, and drugs, or at times by intensive psychotherapy (transference psychosis).

HISTORY

The first author to use the term borderline was Stern [17], although such patients had been described for many years prior to this and were first diagnosed by Bleuler [3] as latent schizophrenia. The diagnosis became more common following a paper by Hoch and Polatin [9] on pseudoneurotic schizophrenia in 1949 and two papers by Knight [11,12] in 1953.

Since then there has been a plethora of articles on borderline state, borderline character, borderline personality organization, and borderline schizophrenia. The label borderline also was dropped at times in favor of psychotic character [6], "as if" personality [4], ambulatory schizophrenia [19], latent schizophrenia, and many others. The American Psychiatric Association included the diagnosis of latent schizophrenia in its diagnostic manual for the first time in 1968 [1].

EPIDEMIOLOGY

There are no good epidemiological studies of borderline personality disorders. Most of the patients described in the literature appear to be in the middle or upper classes. One reason for this may be a tendency on the part of diagnosing physicians to see lower-class patients as having acting-out character disorders. If criteria for diagnosis could be agreed upon and established, it should be possible to obtain epidemiological data.

ETIOLOGY AND PATHOGENESIS

The theories of etiology are based partly on the patient's history and partly on current difficulties in object relations. The latter are manifested by the patient having mental representations of himself and significant others as "all good" or "all bad." The patient is unable to synthesize these contradictory images of himself and others. In addition to these images there are the affects associated with the image. The all-good self or other is loved, and the all-bad self or other is hated.

Under normal circumstances the synthesis of good and bad images takes place during the first thirty-six months of life. The infant originally perceives self or others as the borderline patient does. Eventually, the normal infant is able to have contradictory images (good and bad) and experiences contradictory affects (love and hate) with regard to himself and others. The borderline patient does not achieve this synthesis either in infancy or later life.

Kernberg [10] has stated that there are two major factors that lead to the lack of synthesis of contradictory images and affects. He feels that some borderline patients have a constitutional (inborn) excess of aggression. Because this drive is so intense, the infant fears that its rage and hate toward the "bad" mother will overwhelm its love for the "good" mother, and the mother will be destroyed. Thus, in order to preserve the good mother, two separate mental images of the mother are maintained — all-good and all-bad. A similar process occurs in relation to the image of the self resulting in an all-good and all-bad image.

In addition to his concept of a constitutional defect, Kernberg [10] states that some patients are subjected to extreme frustrations in the first year of life by their mother and develop an excess of oral aggression toward the frustrating mother. Again, to preserve the image of the good mother, the image of the bad frustrating mother is kept separate.

Masterson [16] and Mahler [13] have theorized that the borderline patient encounters difficulty during the rapprochement subphase of separation-individuation (eighteen to thirty-six months). The child is traumatized at this time by a mother who is often borderline herself. She cannot tolerate the child's separating and growing, and as the child attempts to grow she withdraws her love. The child experiences a feeling of abandonment, accompanied by depression, rage, guilt, fear, passivity, helplessness, emptiness, and void [15]; in later life the borderline patient becomes symptomatic when faced with separation.

Although Kernberg [10] and Masterson [16] disagreed on the etiology, they both agreed that the borderline patient in later life continues to use the same primitive defenses that were available to him as an infant and indicate that the borderline patient is more likely to use these defenses when aggressive feelings are intensified. This frequently occurs when the patient is under stress or under the regressive influence of drugs, alcohol, or a transference psychosis.

CLINICAL DESCRIPTION

These patients present such diffuse pictures clinically that often a number of interviews are necessary before the diagnosis is established. One way of assessing the patients involves looking at their interpersonal transactions, symptom clusters, and ego defects and defenses.

Grinker [7] studied borderline patients and found there were four subgroups based on their interpersonal relations. Group one: Patients undertake attempts at relationships but at the same time overtly, in behavior and affect, react negatively and angrily toward other people and their environment. Group two: Patients inconsistently move toward others for relations; this is followed by acted-out repulsion and moving away into isolation where they are lonely and depressed. Group three: Patients seem to have given up their search for identity and defend against their reactions to an empty world; instead they passively await cues from others and behave in complementarity — "as if." Group four: Patients search for a lost symbiotic relation with a mother figure which they do not achieve and reveal what may be called an anaclitic depression (anaclitic-dependent for survival). One may elicit historical data to place the patient in one of these groups, or the transference may manifest itself in a manner similar to one of the groups.

Multiple neurotic symptoms are one of the original hallmarks of the borderline patient. Chronic diffuse free-floating anxiety is frequently encountered. Kernberg [10] has listed a number of polysymptomatic neuroses. He feels the presence of two or more of these particular neurotic symptoms is strong evidence of a borderline personality. They include: (1) multiple phobias which inhibit the patient's life in all aspects — especially social (fear of crowds, fear of open spaces); (2) obsessive-compulsive symptoms which are ego-syntonic and are rationalized by the patient; (3) chronic, multiple, and bizarre conversion symptoms that may resemble bodily hallucinations (e.g., painful-pleasurable sensation a patient developed in her vagina when her only son left home); (4) dissociative reactions, including hysterical twilight states and fugues; and (5) hypochondriasis, with giving up of social contacts because of symptoms. At times in dissociative reactions the patient responds to intense feelings of unreality by self-destructive activities — especially wrist cutting. A patient frequently will explain the wrist cutting as an attempt to make himself feel real. Although this may be so, the therapist should not take this explanation at face value; the conflict leading to feelings of unreality must be understood [2] as well as the patient's need to discharge aggressive impulses toward himself by wrist cutting.

Pansexuality or the presence of polymorphous perverse sexual trends is found in borderline patients. There often are several perversions, such as masochism and transvestism, although in patients with impoverished object relations the perversions exist in fantasy only. These patients also may have bizarre perversions involving extreme aggression or eliminatory functions. This latter group of perversions is consistent with the patient's difficulties with aggression.

The borderline patient often manifests nonspecific ego weakness [10]. This weakness is demonstrated by: (1) lack of anxiety tolerance — the patient responds to any increase in anxiety by an increase in neurotic symptoms, inappropriate behavior, or ego regression; (2) persistently weak impulse control with the activity being ego-syntonic (The patient engages in impulsive and destructive acts, during which he does not experience guilt but may feel guilty later. In contrast, an impulse-ridden personality such as the antisocial personality experiences no guilt during or after the act. The borderline patient also impulsively may use alcohol or drugs); and (3) lack of developed sublimatory channels so that the patient is unable to engage in and enjoy creative activity.

There are five major primitive defenses used by the borderline patient: splitting, primitive idealization, projective identification, denial,

Review new
cards
_____

Shim Wolman

_____

Review
old cards
Look over notes (old)

~~Neurosis~~

~~Delinquent~~

Develop.

Epilogue ± / card nots off notes.

book notes taken

~~Speech~~ ~~finish.~~ stuttering

& behav. prob in Sch.

card.

Rd. for notes

Skim Last chapt

re Sc. ~~course~~ in

Wolman

omnipotence, and devaluation [10]. *Splitting* is the primary defense, with the others used to support this defense. Splitting, as defined by Kernberg [10], refers to keeping separate all-good and all-bad mental images both of oneself and others. For example, at any particular time the patient may be aware of an all-good mental image of himself and his therapist. Others may be seen as all-bad. This situation may be reversed at another time, and the patient and therapist are all-bad while others are all-good.

Primitive idealization is utilized by the patient to prevent significant others from being seen as all-bad or contaminated by all-bad objects in the environment.

Projective identification is a defense for handling unacceptable aggressive impulses. The patient projects all-bad aggressive feelings onto a significant other. This other is then seen as all-bad with intense aggressive feelings toward the patient. In order to protect himself against the perceived threat from this all-bad aggressive object, the patient identifies with the object and thus sees himself as such, as bad and aggressive as the object. Thus, there is a complete circle of aggression which begins in the patient, is projected onto an outside object, and is taken back into the patient by identification. This process is accompanied by a confusion of the boundaries between self and object with the same aggression being present in both.

Denial is used to ignore the emotional meaning of a previous mental image of an all-good or all-bad self or object. For example, the patient may see the therapist as all-good, and although he can recall an image from before of the therapist as all-bad, it has no meaning or relevance for him.

Patients make use of *omnipotence* and *devaluation* in order to maintain an all-good and powerful image of self and an all-bad devalued image of another.

At times the borderline patient fears feelings of fusion between himself and a significant other. Some authors feel that if fusion is actually experienced, the patient is schizophrenic and not borderline. Kernberg [10] has stated that borderline patients are fearful of fusing with another and that the feelings of fusion are related to loss of a sense of self. This loss often is precipitated by projective identification in which a significant other and the patient are both perceived as all-bad; it is unclear to the patient what is inside himself and what is outside himself.

Finally the borderline patient may show evidence of primary process thinking, i.e., psychoticlike thinking, which is irrational and makes use of primitive symbolism, condensation, and displacement. This thinking is most obvious on projective tests such as the Rorschach.

Amy was a nineteen-year-old single caucasian female who had been ill since the age of thirteen. At that time, following her menarche, she developed a number of symptoms, including free-floating anxiety, compulsive rituals at bedtime, which involved arranging her sheets and bed clothes a certain way, and repeated handwashing. These rituals often would last two hours a night. The patient developed an intense fear of cockroaches and would rationalize that she engaged in the bedclothes rituals to be certain that no roaches were in the bed. She also developed a fear of vomiting, would take a variety of medications, and go to bed whenever her stomach felt queasy. The patient began to experience dissociative episodes during which she felt as though she and her surroundings were unreal.

She lost interest in her studies and had difficulty concentrating. She began to have intense rage reactions toward her parents. She would have episodes of feeling empty and separated from the world. Often during these episodes she would cut herself with a razor blade or stick pins in herself. Amy had several close friends whom she idealized and whom she felt could do no wrong. It was because of the urging of these friends that she sought psychiatric help.

After evaluation the patient was hospitalized for several months and treated with phenothiazines and psychotherapy with some improvement in her anxiety. She was discharged from the hospital and began individual psychotherapy. During the next two years she was hospitalized on three occasions because of increased anxiety and self-destructive behavior. Finally, long-term hospitalization with intensive psychotherapy was arranged. The patient remained in the hospital for three years.

During her long hospitalization many of the patient's conflicts became clearer and were worked through in therapy. Amy was an only child whose mother was extremely ambivalent about any movement toward separation the patient would make. Most of the time Amy was openly hostile toward her parents but occasionally would be clinging and dependent. She had a few intense relationships in the hospital. They also were characterized by marked swings in feelings toward the individuals, and at times she loved them and at times she hated them. Her attitude toward her therapist was similar — either hostility or extreme idealization. When the patient was hostile, she felt that the therapist was feeling angry and hostile toward her. It was at these times that she feared fusion with the therapist.

This case illustrates many of the aspects of the borderline patient. The patient's family history was consistent with the typical family dynamics of these individuals. Her object relations were poor and she would fit into group two of Grinker's [7] patients. She had multiple neurotic symptoms, including free-floating anxiety, compulsions, phobias, dissociative reactions, and hypochondriacal concerns. The patient used the typical defenses associated with the borderline patient. Splitting was a prominent feature of all interpersonal relations and was especially evident in the relationship with the therapist. In addition the therapist was idealized at times and devalued at other times by the patient. When confronted with her alternating views and feelings toward the therapist, the patient would deny the significance of any past feelings and insist that the current one was the only valid one. Projective identification was evident in her hostility toward the therapist and perception of him as a threatening hostile figure at the same time.

DIFFERENTIAL DIAGNOSIS

The diagnostic entity most often confused with borderline patients is schizophrenia. If the patient has defects in reality testing, i.e., hallucinations or persistent delusions, most authors would agree that the patient is schizophrenic and not borderline. The borderline patient may have transient hallucinations or delusions, but they are limited primarily to the therapy hours. If there is a formal thought disorder (loose associations), the patient is not borderline. Finally, Kernberg [10] and others believe that the borderline patient develops a different type of transference psychosis from the schizophrenic patient. The borderline patient experiences a loss of identity between himself and the therapist, but there is no sense of complete fusion with the therapist. The schizophrenic patient, on the other hand, experiences himself and the therapist as fused — with a total loss of identity and sense of self. Other authors, however, feel that this latter distinction is not correct and that both categories of patients have fusion experiences.

Narcissistic personality disorders may be confused with borderline patients because similar defense mechanisms are present. However the narcissistic personality's ego is more intact, and therefore the symptoms are less severe. Because of the more intact ego, these individuals function fairly well socially, have better impulse control, and have some areas of achievement in their lives [10].

Adolescents who are experiencing severe problems with identity diffusion [5] may appear similar to borderline patients. If the patient's problems persist over a significant period of time, the diagnosis of borderline should be considered.

Personality disorders where acting-out is prominent, such as in the explosive personality or the passive aggressive personality, may be confused with the borderline patient. Acting-out engaged in by these patients is more ego-syntonic than the acting out of a borderline patient, who is more likely to see his acting-out problems as his, rather than feeling that he is blameless and accusing the external world.

Minimal brain dysfunction at times may present a clinical picture similar to the borderline patient. These patients can be differentiated by soft neurological signs and evidence of brain dysfunction on psychological testing.

PROGNOSIS AND MANAGEMENT

The prognosis is fair to good, depending on a number of factors, such as the patient's capacity to make use of psychotherapy [10]. A five-year follow-up study of Grinker's [7] original patient sample was done. Even with a minimum of psychiatric contact, none of the patients showed deterioration to schizophrenia, but many had socially (with regard to friends and recreation) impoverished existences [7].

Long-term psychotherapy is the primary treatment modality. For those patients who are in an acutely disorganized state with a high potential for acting-out, hospitalization is recommended. The hospitalization should either be very short and crisis oriented or long-term (a minimum of nine to twelve months). Any hospitalization induces regression, and when borderline patients are in the hospital for more than just a few days, it is difficult for them to shift rapidly out of this regressed state. Because of the patient's use of splitting, problems may develop in which staff are identified as all-good or all-bad (Main's syndrome) [2].

In the psychotherapeutic situation the therapist faces the difficult task of allowing the patient autonomy and at the same time must set limits on dangerous acting-out in which the patient may engage [10,12].

Phenothiazines are sometimes helpful in low doses — especially for patients with difficulties in thinking and concentrating. However for patients who are experiencing dissociative symptoms, the phenothiazines may aggravate the symptoms and make the patient feel out of contact [5].

No other medication has been effective in treating borderline patients. These patients often complain of depression, but it is the type of depression that rarely responds to tricyclic antidepressants. Minor tranquilizers should not be prescribed because of these patients' potential for addiction. Tolerance to the antianxiety effect of the minor tranquilizers develops rapidly, and the dose must be increased. This may continue until the patient is physiologically addicted.

REFERENCES

1   American Psychiatric Association. *Diagnostic and statistical manual of mental disorders*, DSM-II. Washington, D.C.: American Psychiatric Association, 1968.

2   Arlow, J. Conflict, regression, and symptom formation. *Int. J. Psychoanal.* 44:12–22, 1963.

3   Bleuler, E. *Dementia praecox, or the group of schizophrenias*, trans. J. Zinkin. 1911. Reprint. New York: International Universities Press, 1950.

4   Deutsch, H. Some forms of emotional disturbance and their relationship to schizophrenia. *Psychoanal. Q.* 11:301–321, 1942.

5   Erikson, E. The problem of ego identity. *J. Am. Psychoanal. Assoc.* 4:56–121, 1956.

6   Frosch, J. The psychotic character: Clinical psychiatric considerations. *Psychiatr. Q.* 38:81–96, 1964.

7   Grinker, R., Werble, B., and Dryder, R. *The borderline syndrome: A behavioral study of ego functions*. New York: Basic Books, 1968.

8   Havens, L. Some difficulties in giving schizophrenic and borderline patients medication. *Psychiatry* 31:44–50, 1968.

9   Hoch, P., and Polatin, P. Pseudoneurotic forms of schizophrenia. *Psychiatr. Q.* 23:248–276, 1949.

10 Kernberg, O. *Borderline conditions and pathological narcissism*. New York: Jason Aronson, 1975.

11 Knight, R. Borderline states. *Bull. Menninger Clin.* 17:1–12, 1953.

12 Knight, R. Management and psychotherapy of the borderline patient. *Bull. Menninger Clin.* 17:139–150, 1953.

13 Mahler, M. A study of the separation-individuation process and its possible application to borderline phenomena in the psychoanalytic situation. *Psychoanal. Study Child* 26:403–424, 1971.

14 Main, T. The ailment. *Br. J. Med. Psychol.* 33:39–31, 1960.

15 Masterson, J. *Psychotherapy of the borderline adult*. New York: Brunner/Mazel, 1976.

16 Masterson, J., and Rinsley, D. The borderline syndrome: The role of the mother in the genesis and psychic structure of the borderline personality. *Int. J. Psychoanal.* 56:163–178, 1975.

17 Stern, A. psychoanalytic investigation of and therapy in the borderline group of neuroses. *Psychoanal. Q.* 7:467–489, 1938.

18 Werble, B. Second follow-up study of borderline patients. *Arch. Gen. Psychiatry* 23:3–7, 1970.

19 Zilboorg, G. Ambulatory schizophrenia. *Psychiatry* 4:149–155, 1941.

17

Addictive Disorders: Alcoholism

Willem G. A. Bosma, M.D.

Alcoholism is the most frequently encountered medical problem in the United States today. About 9 million of the estimated 95 million drinkers in the United States are considered to be alcohol abusers, which means that 9 percent of the adult population manifests the behavior of alcohol abuse and alcoholism [27].

Since Prohibition alcohol has established itself as the most abused drug in the United States. Many specialists maintain that alcoholism is a more significant problem than all other forms of drug abuse combined [15:294]. Until recently the medical profession has paid little attention to the problem of alcoholism, but this attitude is fortunately changing.

The realization that alcoholism is a disease has not had long acceptance. For centuries alcoholism was considered to be a moral weakness and the alcoholic a moral degenerate. Especially among the lower classes drunkenness was considered a vice and the topic of many a sermon. Gradually it began to be understood that there was more involved in alcoholism than merely the consumption of alcohol, and in 1956 the American Medical Association took the progressive step of officially recognizing alcoholism as a disease.

Alcoholism is a complex disease involving physical and psychosocial elements. In both areas the physician has an extensive role to play. Since alcoholism has become demystified for members of the medical profession, the danger is that it will be considered the exclusive domain of psychiatry, whereas the basic orientation to a health problem of this magnitude should involve the whole medical profession rather than a particular specialty.

DEFINITION

In the official classification of psychiatric disorders, alcoholism is placed under personality disorders with the subheadings episodic excessive drinking, habitual excessive drinking, alcohol addiction, and other alcoholism [17]. Alcoholism does not allow easy definition or classification. Medical definitions, ever striving to be scientifically precise, concentrate on the physical aspects of the disease — on the tolerance and withdrawal syndrome, mainly because these can be observed and to a certain extent measured.

Still the psychological dependence is far more important, especially in regard to the onset and the development of the disease and the difficulties in abstaining from alcohol and maintaining sobriety.

Basic to the understanding of the psychological aspects of alcoholism are the following definitions:

1   *Addiction* is a behavior pattern of compulsive use characterized by tolerance, physical and psychological dependence, overwhelming involvement with securing the drug, and a great tendency to relapse after withdrawal.
2   *Tolerance* is acquired resistance to addictive substances that occurs by increasing dose so that sudden withdrawal of drugs or the administration of a specific antagonist results in a predictable sequence of withdrawal signs.
3   *Psychological dependence* is an irresistible urge to seek the effects of the drug regardless of the consequence.

The above definitions are rather complicated and confusing. Each specialist seems to have his or her own definition, depending on his or her orientation. A random perusal of some works on alcoholism produced thirty-eight definitions, each with its own merits. The easiest to remember and in general the most comprehensive is the definition used by Alcoholics Anonymous (AA). An *alcoholic* is a person whose life has become unmanageable because of the use of alcohol, or similarly, any use of alcohol that interferes with the physical, psychological, or social functioning of an individual. The American Psychiatric Association (APA) has a similar definition: Alcoholism is the diagnosis "for patients whose alcohol intake is great enough to damage their physical health, or their personal or social functioning or when it has become a pre-requisite to normal functioning" [2:45].

The APA further lists the following patterns of drinking alcoholically: (1) *episodic excessive drinking,* when an individual becomes intoxicated as frequently as four times a year with impaired coordination or altered behavior; (2) *habitual excessive drinking,* when an individual becomes intoxicated more than twelve times a year or is recognizably under the influence of alcohol more than a week at a time, and (3) *alcoholic addiction,* when there is direct or strong presumptive evidence that the individual is dependent on alcohol through withdrawal symptoms, inability of the patient to go one day without drinking, or heavy drinking that continues for three months or more.

DRINKING TRENDS

Wine and beer have been used since prehistoric times. Originally these spirits were prized not only for their euphoria-producing qualities but also for their nutritional values — which was preserved in early preparations. Nowadays, these vitamins and minerals are distilled out, but alcohol continues to be valued at an infinite number of social and solemn occasions for its relaxing and euphoric effects.

Most people have drunk alcohol at one time or another, and drinking is an acceptable pastime in most circles. Three studies conducted in 1964–1965, 1967, and 1969 by a social research group of the George Washington University of 4105 persons over age twenty-one [5–7] and a 1971 Harris survey for the National Institute of Alcoholism and Alcohol Abuse [13] arrived at the following information about alcohol and drinking in the United States.

Sixty-eight percent of the adult population drinks at least once a year, 77 percent of men and 60 percent of women. Not all these people are regular drinkers. When the infrequent drinkers and abstainers are added together the adult population is rather evenly divided between 45 percent who drink less than once a month and 53 percent who drink once a month and more. Of the 32 percent abstainers, one-third drank at one time but stopped, and two-thirds never had tasted any alcoholic beverages at all. The Harris survey showed much the same figures. Both studies found that not only is drinking increasing, particularly among young women, but also that heavy drinking is increasing. The studies further reported the following:

1   Drinking patterns seem to be dependent on sociocultural variables, such as sex, social status, religion, degree of urbanization, and region. Thus, an upper-class Jewish male's attitude towards drinking is different from a farmer's wife from Kansas who attends the Baptist church.

2   The factors which determine who will become an alcohol abuser are probably established early in life.

3   The single greatest determining factor of future alcoholism is parental alcoholism.

Teenage drinking in the United States also is increasing [4]. This increase is attributed mainly to the ever larger numbers of female adolescents who drink. It also seems that since the early sixties drug abuse has shifted from the use of soft drugs and hallucinogens to alcohol abuse among the young.

The research group of the George Washington University also compiled a profile analysis of different types of drinkers [5–7]. Abstainers from alcohol are most likely to be older people who are lower than average on the socioeconomic scale. Relatively more abstainers or teetotalers live in the South and in rural areas, have native-born parents, belong to conservative or fundamentalist Protestant churches, and take part in religious activities frequently.

Compared with other groups, heavy drinkers report more drinking by parents and friends. Heavy drinkers are apt to drink because it helps relieve their anxiety and depression. Compared to moderate drinkers, both abstainers and heavy drinkers tend to feel alienated from society and unhappy with their lot in life.

THEORIES OF ALCOHOLISM

The causes of alcoholism are unknown, but many theories have been formulated, usually based on the background and clinical experiences of the developer of the theory. Needless to say, these are often biased and limited.

Psychoanalytic Viewpoint

Freud [11] and his contemporaries tried to develop a dynamic formulation. Freud spoke of strong oral childhood influences and considered the change of mood which alcohol causes in an individual as the main reason for the excessive drinking. He [11] mentioned the reactivation of repressed homosexual traits as the basic conflicts causing the extensive use of alcohol.

More recently, Knight [21] emphasized early childhood development as leading to alcoholism:

> These childhood experiences have given him a personality characterized by excessive demands for indulgence. These demands are doomed to frustration in the world of adults. He reacts to the frustration with intolerable disappointment and rage. This reaction impels him to hostile acts and wishes against the thwarting individuals for which he feels guilty and punishes himself masochistically. As reassurance against guilt feelings and fears of dangerously destructive masochism and reality consequences of his behavior, he feels excessive need for affection and indulgence as proof of affection. Again, the excessive claims, doomed to frustration, arise and the circle is complete" [30:546].

He sees the alcohol as alleviating disappointment and rage. It is used as a means to carry out repressed impulses in order to secure masochistic debasement and as a symbolic gratification of the need for affection.

Menninger [24] emphasized the self-destructive drives of the alcoholic and terms alcoholism chronic suicide. This is supported by the notion that in untreated alcoholics the life span is shortened by twelve years. Kendell and Stanton [16] found that the suicide rate among alcoholics is fifty-eight times that of the normal population.

Tiebout [31], in his studies, believes that the alcoholic has an unconscious wish to dominate his environment. He feels that a pervasive feeling of loneliness and isolation is one of the main characteristics of the alcoholic.

Fenichel [10] maintains that alcoholics are passive-dependent and have a predominantly oral-narcissistic orientation.

Learning (Reinforcement) Theory

This theory basically postulates that if an action leads in a relatively short time to a desired effect, the individual is induced to repeat the action to get the same or an even more desirable effect. Therapy based on learning theory sometimes uses negative stimuli to unlearn undesirable behavior, since people tend to be attracted to pleasant situations and repelled by unpleasant or tension producing ones. In this view, alcohol is the ideal reinforcer of drinking behavior. Alcohol reduces fear and anxiety in an individual, due to its tranquilizing effect. The individual tranquilized by alcohol is regarded by society as convivial and manly. In other words, alcoholic consumption reduces an individual's feelings of tension and unpleasantness and replaces these feelings with ones of well-being and euphoria, which can be observed in people after one or two drinks.

The difficulties experienced by most alcoholics — such as family discord, ill health, loss of employment — would appear to contradict the learning theory. However, the pain and discomfort of the alcoholic are easily overcome by more alcohol. Alcohol has the immediate effect of reducing tension, while the unpleasant consequences of continued drunken behavior do not come until later. In addition, conditions or events occurring at the time of reinforcement tend to acquire the characteristic of conditioning stimuli. Alcohol is consumed because of a state of anxiety. The emotional state itself takes on the properties of a stimulus, thus triggering another drinking bout.

Frequently the negative stimuli of the withdrawal syndrome — severe anxiety, panic, physical and emotional discomfort — keep many alcoholics from attempting to abstain from alcohol. Alcohol-induced discomfort is not considered as great as the unknown discomfort of the abstinence from alcohol.

Learning theory can shed some light on the dynamics of alcoholism. The application of learning theory in treatment has been discussed by Kepner and others [1,17,19].

Personality Trait Theory

Many have attempted to define the causes of alcoholism in terms of an "alcoholic personality." Although it is felt that all alcoholics do not have the same personality structure, it is postulated that in the prealcoholic stage a personality pattern could be recognized as a predisposition toward alcoholism. Unfortunately, the studies performed in this area are usually done with people that already have gone through the throes of alcoholism, and it is not easy to determine whether these characteristics are prealcoholic or are the consequence of alcoholism.

Blane [3] has presented some of the personality characteristics commonly seen in alcoholics. They include low frustration tolerance and sociability and feelings of inferiority combined with attitudes of superiority, fearfulness, and dependency.

Lisansky [20] suggested that the alcoholic personality has (1) an intensely strong need for dependency; (2) a weak and inadequate defense against this excessive need, leading to intense dependence-independence conflicts; (3) a low degree of tolerance for frustration or tension; and (4) unresolved love-hate ambivalences.

Cultural Theory

In the Western world, where the various cultures are much the same, drinking behavior varies considerably. In the adjoining countries of France and Italy the per capita consumption of alcoholic beverages is nearly similar, but the rate of alcoholism is quite different. France has the highest rate of alcoholism in the world (which is the reason so many liver diseases have French names), whereas in Italy the rate of alcoholism is quite low. In Italy alcoholic beverages are integrated into daily life. Children start drinking early in life, alcohol is mainly consumed at mealtime, and, above all, drunken behavior is scorned. On the other hand, in France, drunken behavior is not only accepted but, one can even say, encouraged. Wine is consumed like water by people of all ages, but there are no societal or familial guidelines, as in Italy, for the enjoyment of reasonable quantities of alcohol.

In the United States the various subcultures tolerate different drinking habits, which usually correlate with those of their native country of origin. In one group of problem drinkers analyzed in New York City, where the total population roughly consists of 10 percent Irish, 15 percent Italian, and 23 percent Jewish, 40 percent of the alcoholics were Irish, 1 percent Italian, and 0 percent Jewish [30].

Genetics do not explain these differences in the rate of alcoholism, since an increase in alcoholic drinking has been noted among Jews, especially as they tend to change from Orthodox to Reformed attitudes [29]. The Irish in Ireland do not have many alcoholism problems, while the immigrated Irish in the United States are known for their high rate of alcoholism.

The rate of alcoholism is low in those groups in which drinking customs and sanctions are well established, known and agreed upon by all, and consistent with the rest of the culture. By contrast, those groups, such as the Anglo-Saxon Protestant group in the United States, with a marked ambivalence toward alcohol and with no well-established ground rules for the consumption of alcohol, tend to have a high rate of alcoholism. The conflict, to drink or not to drink and under what circumstances, with its pressures, guilt feelings, and uncertainties, produces the ideal climate for alcoholism to flourish [32].

Physiological Factors

A great deal of research has concerned itself with trying to find a physiological basis for a person's abuse of alcohol, in the expectation of finding a nutritional, metabolic, or allergic defect. None of this research seems to have produced substantial indication of any such factors. There is, however, one area that has been given particular attention lately, which may prove to produce some worthwhile findings — that of parental alcoholism as an indicator of future alcoholism.

It has been known for decades that the incidence of alcoholism is higher among children of alcoholics. For some researchers this suggests the possibility of a genetic factor [25]. A recent famous study of twins in Denmark [12] seems to indicate that there is an inherent disposition toward alcoholism. Twins raised apart from their natural alcoholic fathers showed a greater rate of alcoholism than adopted twins with nonalcoholic natural fathers. However, another study indicates that the children of alcoholics are no more prone to alcoholism than the average child if they are raised away from their parents [26].

The argument between those favoring environmental influences over genetic influences, and vice versa, as dominant in alcoholism will undoubtedly continue. The fact remains that the children of alcoholics are more vulnerable to future alcoholism, but the reasons for this are unclear at best.

The miseries and grief the alcoholic brings upon himself by his continued drinking is difficult for the moderate drinker to understand. The miseries of the drinking process in themselves, the constant hangovers, blackouts, and so forth, make it incomprehensible for the moderate drinker, who derives pleasure from his drinking, to understand why the alcoholic would continue drinking. It may be that indeed the alcoholic has a special response to alcohol that the normal drinker does not have, a special response, furthermore, that destines the alcoholic to drink abusively [12]. Many more studies are needed before this can be determined conclusively.

Alcoholism may well be caused by the environment of the child. As the above mentioned studies indicate, however, a combination of genetic predisposition and conducive environment most probably leads to this enormously complicated problem.

Final Common Pathway Theory

Any of the countless theories on the nature and cause of alcoholism only gives an incomplete picture of this pervasive disease. It is possible to say there are as many types of alcoholism as there are alcoholics. Therefore, many alcoholists have come to embrace the holistic view of the causes of alcoholism.

This view takes into account all of the above theories and integrates them into one view, which could be called the final common pathway of

the different characteristics and systems that have come together to produce the addictive drinker. All aspects of an individual's life play a part
here: his childhood traumas, familial structure, peer group, and social
group. Stated reversely, absence of these factors will probably prevent an
individual from abusing alcohol.

This theory is a result of recent data which support the view that
there is indeed a so-called addictive personality, that there are personality
correlates common to addictive persons. The inability to delineate and,
therefore, identify the prealcoholic personality has limited prevention and
treatment programs in this area up until now [23].

PREALCOHOLIC PERSONALITY
A severe conflict in the early oral stage of the child is undoubtedly a factor
leading to later addiction. Chafetz writes:

> In our patients the fixation at this early level of emotional development
> seems to be the result of deprivation in a significant emotional relationship
> during the early period of development. Many of the addicted alcoholics
> were abandoned, illegitimate children. Others were children of psychotic
> mothers. Still others had a parent die shortly before or after their own birth
> while some were the progeny of parents who were severely alcoholic during
> the patient's early years. A few addicted alcoholics were children of exces-
> sively indulgent or overly protective mothers, with underlying disguised
> hostility existing in both cases [8:9].

The deprivation of a significant relationship in early childhood is
due frequently to a drinking parent. If it is the mother, clearly she cannot
relate in a warm, motherly fashion. If the father is the alcoholic, the
mother is not very effective either, since she must cope with the pressing
problem of an alcoholic husband and her ability to function as a mother
decreases proportionately. Children of an alcoholic parent are deprived
of a loving, warm, and safe relationship with a mother figure in early
childhood.

This lack or loss of a meaningful relationship obviously has a great
influence on the later development of the child, especially as the alcoholic
parents provide only an unrewarding, inconsistent, and distant relationship to the child. It might be said that in becoming an alcoholic later in
life, the child exchanges one bottle for the other — milk for alcohol — to
relieve the feeling of emptiness and the lack of safety and seeks peaceful
oblivion in alcohol, which reminds him of the only time he was satisfied
as a child. He satisfies two oral needs at the same time, one relief from the
tensions of the world and the other a unique fusion with it, in which he is
the central and dominating figure. This theme, oral narcissism, is extremely important in understanding the alcoholic.

This does not explain why alcoholics prefer alcohol, schizophrenics choose their symptomatology, others choose to overindulge in food, or still others, heroin, while some people talk incessantly or become great orators. All of these people show a strong orality and experienced an evident trauma during the oral period. The ways in which people significant to the individual's development dealt with frustrations would probably lead that individual to express or relieve his tensions or escape from frustrating reality in similar ways. In the case of alcoholism, up to 58 percent of investigated alcoholics revealed a significant family figure who was dependent on alcohol in an unhealthy way [30].

McClelland and associates [22] have presented a wealth of empirical data indicating that "power needs" are important motivational factors in male drinking. Women, however, were found to react differently. Drinking enhanced their feelings of warmth, loveliness, consideration, affection, and sexiness — in short, their womanly feelings [9].

Prior to entering school, the prealcoholic child does not seem to cause a problem to the parents. He is frequently described as having been easy to handle. Separation from family upon going to school caused more stress for this child, however, than for the average child. The results were usually recurrence of bed-wetting, anxiety, hyperactivity, or withdrawal, accompanied by indifference or aggression toward peer groups and, above all, poor scholastic performance.

After the first year of school, the child adjusts adequately, and the latency period passes uneventfully. The problems arise in early adolescence. The child feels very insecure and is unusually preoccupied with his appearance and self-image. His accumulated anger at his parents is frequently acted-out in school. The roots of the problem seem to be his complete lack of self-worth and sexual identity caused by earlier and ongoing lack of parental love and approval.

In late adolescence, a superficial change comes about. The boys seem self-confident and boisterous: Often they project themselves as leaders. They are more rebellious than their peers, more disapproving of their parents, and unrestrained in their aggression. The girls are passive, even shy, and either sexually promiscuous or sexually withdrawn.

Both boys and girls may overcompensate for identity problems and inferiority feelings by projecting the image of a super male or female.

At this point, the prealcoholic finds that alcohol seems to solve many of his problems and relieve much of his anxiety and depression and from then on comes to rely more and more on this magic substance.

DEVELOPMENT OF ALCOHOLISM

It usually takes the alcoholic between five and fifteen years to develop what is called chronic alcoholism. During this time, alcohol is used more frequently to relieve anxiety and tensions in order to cope with the world. As one alcoholic said, "When I am frustrated, I drink. Then I get more frustrated, so I drink more."

As the individual begins to rely increasingly on alcohol most of the "coping mechanisms" fall into disuse. It is as if he is stripped of most of his defense mechanisms. As a result, the most diverse pathology becomes evident in the alcoholic. As a result, many psychiatrists approach the alcoholic with the full array of diagnoses. One man was diagnosed as follows: schizophrenic reaction paranoid type, passive-aggressive personality, grand mal epilepsy. The diagnosis of alcoholism was completely overlooked. After two years of sobriety, minimal counseling, and attendance at AA meetings, this man showed only a passive-dependent personality and some identity problems. The grand mal seizures were associated with withdrawal. As happens all too frequently, the diagnosis of alcoholism is not made, leading to a host of complications for both the patient and the doctor.

ALCOHOLIC PERSONALITIES

For practical reasons, it is possible to divide the chronic drinker into three categories: the reactive or neurotic drinker, the psychotic drinker, and the addictive drinker. In addition there is another type of chronic drinker who usually does not come to the attention of the physician — the "normal" alcoholic.

Neurotic Drinker

The reactive or neurotic drinker has a rather normal ego structure; social investigation and evaluation show normal development, school achievement, marital adjustment, and so on. He seems to turn to alcohol, however, whenever outside stresses become too severe for him. This drinking episode runs a predictable course and stops by itself, whether through pressures from the environment or through inner strengths. This does not mean that this type of alcoholic does not need attention. The dependency on alcohol tends to increase over the years, and finally it is difficult to determine whether this person is a reactive or an addictive drinker. These people, however, react very well to treatment as given to anybody with a neurotic disorder.

> A quite hysterical woman started drinking in early adolescence; her drinking was strongly reinforced by the family's approval of her antics when she became high at parties. This led to heavy drinking at

parties in later life, which, except for occasional unpleasant incidents, did not lead to trouble. However, after her first child was
born, she drank heavily for several months, even frequenting bars.
She became promiscuous. This drinking bout ended by itself, and
the patient adjusted to routine again. A similar bout occurred after
the family moved because of her husband's promotion. When she
was threatened with a divorce, she abused alcohol over such an extensive period that she finally was taken to a doctor who referred her
to a psychiatrist. She had three years of intensive psychotherapy,
and although on two occasions she went through another short
drinking bout, she has been sober for five years and is well adjusted,
though still quite hysterical. She is convinced she is an alcoholic and
will not drink at all, although she probably could drink socially.

Psychotic Drinker

The psychotic alcoholic uses alcohol either as a tranquilizer or to get relief
from inner pressures or acute panic situations.

As with the chronic alcoholic, mental and social functioning deteriorate through the long-term abuse of alcohol. It is sometimes difficult to determine whether, in fact, there is an underlying psychosis which he attempts to control with alcohol or whether mental deterioration caused by
long-term chronic alcoholism is itself the cause of the psychosis. Usually a
good social history will clarify this, especially if it is found that sometime
in the past there is evidence of adequate psychological and social adjustment. The psychotic alcoholic, who is quite rare, responds well to psychotropic drugs and therapy. If he stays in treatment, his drinking can be
curbed quite easily. Cases of pathological intoxication fall under psychotic
alcoholics. These are patients who, when they drink alcohol (sometimes
the amount of alcohol is minimal), behave extremely inappropriately, either in an aggressive way, attacking people or destroying property, or
becoming sexually abusive. In most cases, they have retrograde amnesia
for the episode. In some of these cases, a relationship with temporal lobe
epilepsy is to be suspected and needs further investigation.

A clear case of pathological intoxication was a man who, after drinking one can of beer, would terrorize his family and the neighborhood
by destroying property and chasing people with any weapon available. Aside from these episodes, which brought him to jail regularly,
he was a good provider, a good husband and father, and well liked
by his neighbors. It seemed that nothing could stop his taking his occasional can of beer, until he was given small doses of a phenothiazine, which, together with group treatment for alcoholics, has prevented this behavior for over seven years.

Addictive Drinker

The addictive drinker constitutes by far the largest group of people with drinking problems that come to the attention of the physician and psychiatrist. No specific personality disorder can be described, although most patients do have many traits in common. Feelings of inferiority combined with attitudes of superiority are a very common phenomenon. There is nothing as disturbing to the doctor, for example, as the patient who knows it all, wonders aloud whether the therapist knows what he is doing, whether a nonalcoholic can ever understand alcoholism. If the physician is aware, however, that the basis for this type of attitude is the patient's feeling of inferiority and severe insecurity, mixed with some very strong narcissistic tendencies, it becomes possible to overcome the original feelings of antipathy toward the patient.

> The patient, a forty-nine-year-old, very successful business executive, came for treatment after much cajoling by his wife and threats from his company. In the first session, he expressed his doubts about psychiatry, denied having any real problems, and blamed his visit on the sickness of his wife and his company, which had been doing quite badly lately and for which the president was trying to find a scapegoat, namely him. It took months of psychotherapeutic sessions and a few bouts of uncontrolled drinking before he suddenly changed his attitude and transferred the megalomania to the therapist. This transference progressed to the point that he tried to force the therapist to make business decisions for him. This was accompanied by expressions of intense feelings of inferiority and an inability to handle any stress or make decisions, which seemed to date back to adolescence. This was also the time that the patient accepted attendance of group treatment for alcoholics and joined AA. A year of therapy was necessary for the patient to overcome at least partially his low self-esteem and resulting dependence on the therapist.

Other disturbing traits of the alcoholic include the deadly combination of a low frustration tolerance and poor impulse control.

> The patient explained his slip from sobriety this way: "The bus was ten minutes late, so I stepped in a bar and was drunk for two weeks as a result."

The alcoholic tends to interpret ordinary frustrations as personal rejection. If the therapist has to cancel an appointment, it takes many sessions to overcome his feeling of rejection, anger, and hostility. The alcoholic is a great storyteller. He is convivial and charming and talks about his interesting life experiences and gives long explanations about his failures, which never seem to have much to do with his lack of abilities or insight. If one spends much time with him, one will be impressed, however, by his lack of depth. It is very difficult for him to have a close relationship. This hampers personal therapy and undoubtedly is the reason group therapy seems much more to his liking and is often more effective.

In all the literature about alcoholism, dependency needs of the alcoholic are always mentioned and stressed. Indeed, dependency is a central issue in the personality makeup of the alcoholic. Many alcoholics will use their environment to fulfill their needs, marry strong and independent persons who will take care of them, and depend heavily on the therapist or the group. Many of them have a strong fear of dependence, and many men will go to great lengths to ensure and express their independence, to assert their "manliness." This is clearly a reaction formation. For the therapist, this can be very disturbing, as the alcoholic often uses hostility as a means to fight his dependence on his environment. Inappropriate telephone calls which express dependency and anger, demands that cannot be met, and impulsive breaking of appointments with too short or no notice are common in the treatment of alcoholics.

Of course, between the two extremes of being openly dependent and the inability to accept dependency needs lies a vast array of combinations. Obviously, the more extreme the situation, the more difficult the treatment.

Associated with his superiority-inferiority complex is the tendency for the alcoholic to set extremely high goals for himself. In other words, the ego ideal is very unrealistic.

> A professor in one of the best-known schools and a well-known specialist in his field was horrified at having to admit to alcoholism. Aside from many other problems, the patient set unbelievable goals for himself. Although he obviously had been very successful, his expectations could never be met, which resulted in depression and very heavy drinking. A great deal of therapy time was spent assessing the unrealistic nature of his goals and his need to prove to himself that he could not live up to them.

"Normal" Alcoholic

The three categories of chronic drinkers, which speak to the underlying psychological disorders, omit what might be called the normal alcoholic, if this were not such a contradiction of terms. This is the alcoholic who usually does not come to the attention of the physician because he stops drinking by himself or with minimal support, usually from AA or an empathetic friend, wife, or minister. Alcoholics try to stop drinking when the effects of their drinking become more painful than the relief the drinking offers. These are people who have no severe underlying pathology and have enough ego strength to realize their growing dependence on alcohol and do something about it. They are called "high bottom" alcoholics in AA circles, as opposed to those who really have to hit a low bottom before they realize the necessity of giving up alcohol.

CONCLUSION

Unfortunately, it is not only the alcoholic that suffers from his disease. Most specialists see alcoholism as a family disease. Obviously the wife or husband of an alcoholic is usually not only unable to cope with the alcoholic spouse, but also has his or her own pathology. Women with alcoholic fathers frequently marry men who become alcoholics and, although not drinking, do not escape alcoholism. The children are the really defenseless victims. Not only is their chance of becoming alcoholic markedly increased, but they also have more behavioral problems during their formative years. Children of alcoholics comprise more than 50 percent of the following problems: school adjustment problems, truancy, drug abuse, juvenile delinquency, adolescent suicide, premature marriage.

The disease of alcoholism has a far-reaching effect on all our lives. The immediate and the extended family are involved; numerous man hours of work are lost due to alcoholic workers; the majority of fatal automobile accidents are caused by drunken drivers. Furthermore, it has now become obvious that alcoholism is treatable and is, in fact, the chronic disease that has the best results in treatment.

REFERENCES

1   Abrams, S. An evaluation of hypnosis in the treatment of alcoholics. *Am. J. Psychiatry* 120:1160–1165, 1964.

2   American Psychiatric Association. *Diagnostic and statistical manual of mental disorders,* DSM-II. Washington, D.C.: American Psychiatric Association, 1968.

3   Blane, H. T. "The personality of the alcoholic" in *Frontiers of alcoholism,* eds., M. E. Chafetz, H. T. Blane, and M. J. Hill, pp. 115–138. New York: Science House.

4   Bosma, W. G. A. "Adolescence and alcohol " in *Medical care of the adolescent,* 3rd ed., eds. J. R. Gallagher, F. P. Heald, and D. C. Garell, pp. 701–708. New York: Appleton-Century-Crofts, 1976.

5   Calahan, D., *Problem drinkers*. San Francisco: Jossey and Bass, 1970.

6   Calahan, D., Cisin, I. H., and Crossley, H. M. *American drinking practices: A national survey of drinking behavior and attitudes.* New Brunswick, N.J.: Rutger's Center of Alcohol Studies, 1969.

7   Calahan, D., and Room, R. *Problem drinking among american men* Monograph no. 7. New Brunswick, N.J.: Rutger's Center of Alcohol Studies, 1972.

8   Chafetz, M. E., Blane, H. T., and Hill, M. J. *Frontiers of alcoholism.* New York: Science House, 1970.

9   Dexter, M. Toward the new chastity. *Reflections* 8:2, 1973.

10   Fenichel, O. *The psychoanalytic theory of neurosis.* New York: Norton, 1945.

11   Freud, S. "Mourning and melancholia," 1917. In *Collected papers*, vol. 4, pp. 152–170. London: Hogarth Press, 1925.

12   Goodwin, D. *Is alcoholism hereditary?* New York: Oxford University Press, 1976.

13   Harris, L., and Associates, Inc. American attitudes toward alcohol and alcoholics. Report prepared for the National Institute on Alcohol Abuse and Alcoholism, study no. 2138. Washington, D.C.: Government Printing Office, 1971.

14   Jaffe, J. H. "Drug addiction and drug abuse." In *Pharmacological basis of therapeutics*, eds. L. S. Goodman and A. Gilman, chap. 16. New York: Macmillan, 1965.

15   Jones, M. C. (1967): Personality antecedents of drinking patterns in adult males. *J. Consult. Psychol.* 32:2–18, 1968.

16   Kendell, R. E., and Stanton, M. C. The fate of untreated alcoholics. *Q. J. Stud. Alcohol* 27:30–41, 1966.

17   Kener, E. Application of learning theory to the etiology and treatment of alcoholism. *Q. J. Stud. Alcohol* 25:279–291. (1964)

18   Knight, R. P. The psychodynamics of chronic alcoholism. *J. Nerv. Ment. Dis.* 86:538, 548, 1937.

19   Lemeze, F., and Voegtlein, W. L. "An evaluation of aversion treatment of alcoholism." In *Management of addictions*, ed. E. Podalski, pp. 238–243. New York: New York Philosophical Library, 1955.

20   Lisansky, E. S. The etiology of alcoholism: The role of the psychological predisposition. *Q. J. Stud. Alcohol* 21:314–343, 1960.

21   Lolli, G. Schesler, E., and Golder, G. M. Choice of alcoholic beverage among 105 alcoholics in New York. *Q. J. Stud. Alcohol* 21:475, 482, 1960.

22   McClelland, D. C. et al. *The drinking man.* 1972. Collier-Macmillan. New York.

23   McCord, W., and McCord, J. "A longitudinal study of the personality of alcoholics." In *Society, culture and drinking patterns*, eds. D. J. Pittman and C. R. Synder. New York: Wiley, 1962.

24   Menninger, C. A. *Man against himself.* New York: Harcourt-Brace, 1938.

25   Partane, J. Bruun, K. and Markkanen, T. *Inheritance of drinking behavior.* Helsinki: Finnish Foundation for Alcohol Studies, 1966.

26   Roe, A. "Children of alcoholics raised in foster homes." In *Alcohol, science, and society.* New Haven, Conn.: Quarterly Journal of Studies on Alcohol, 1945.

27   Secretary of DHEW. First special report to the United States Congress on alcohol and health, Washington, D.C.: U.S. Department of Health, Education and Welfare, 1971.

28   Sherfey, M. J. "Psychotherapy and character structure in chronic alcoholism." In *Etiology of chronic alcoholism*, ed. O. Diethelm, pp. 16–42. Springfield, Ill.: Thomas, 1955.

29   Snyder, C. R. *Alcohol and the Jews*. New Brunswick, N.J.: Rutger's Center of Alcohol Studies, 1958.

30   Terry, J., Lolli, G. and Golder, G. M. Choice of alcoholic beverage among 531 alcoholics in California. *Q. J. Stud. Alcohol* 18:417–428, 1957.

31   Tiebout, H. M. The role of psychiatry in the field of alcoholism, with comment on the concept of alcoholism as a symptom and as a disease. *Q. J. Stud. Alcohol* 12:52–57, 1951.

32   Ulman, A. D. "Attitudes and drinking customs." In *Mental health aspects of alcohol education*. Washington, D.C.: U.S. Public Health Service, 1958.

18

Addictive Disorders: Drug Dependence

Leon Wurmser, M.D.

This area of disturbances stands out both by its particular complexity, involving in every case compound biological, intricate psychological, and obvious social, cultural, and legal factors (in origin as well as consequence) and by the ensuing difficulties of treatment.

DEFINITIONS

For purposes of this chapter the definitions given by the World Health Organization (WHO) [18:14–16] are most useful and entail the broadest (though not the deepest) understanding.

Drug: "any substance that, when taken into the living organism, may modify one or more of its functions"

Drug dependence: "a state, psychic and sometimes also physical, resulting from the interaction between a living organism and a drug, characterized by behavioural and other responses that always include a compulsion to take the drug on a continuous or periodic basis in order to experience its psychic effects, and sometimes to avoid the discomfort of its absence. Tolerance may or may not be present. A person may be dependent on more than one drug"

Psychic dependence: a condition in which a drug produces "a feeling of satisfaction and a psychic drive that require periodic or continuous administration of the drug to produce pleasure or to avoid discomfort"
Physical dependence: "an adaptive state that manifests itself by intense physical disturbances when the administration of the drug is suspended . . .
These disturbances, i.e., the withdrawal or abstinence syndromes, are
made up of specific arrays of symptoms and signs of psychic and physical nature that are characteristic for each drug type"
Dependence-producing drug: "a drug having the capacity to interact with a living organism to produce a state of psychic or physical dependence or
both. Such a drug may be used medically or nonmedically without
necessarily producing such a state. The characteristics of a state of drug
dependence, once developed, will vary with the type of drug involved.
Some types of drugs, including those present in tea and coffee, are
capable of producing drug dependence in a very broad sense. The existence of such a state is not necessarily harmful in itself. There are, however, several types of drugs that, because they can produce *substantial
central nervous stimulation or depression or disturbances in perception,
mood, thinking, behaviour, or motor function,* are generally recognized as
having the capacity, under certain circumstances of use, to produce individual and public health and social problems. Drugs of the types
listed below can produce substantial effects and problems of the kinds
mentioned above. As used in this report, the term 'dependence-
producing drug(s)' means one or more drugs of the following types:

1   Alcohol-barbiturate type — e.g., ethanol, barbiturates, and certain other drugs with sedative effects, such as chloral hydrate,
chlordiazepoxide, diazepam, meprobamate, and methaqualone.
2   Amphetamine type — e.g., amphetamine, dexamphetamine,
methamphetamine, methylphenidate, and phenmetrazine.
3   Cannabis type — preparations of *Cannabis sativa* I., such as
marihuana (bhang, dagga, kif, maconha), ganja, and hashish
(charas);
4   Cocaine type — cocaine and coca leaves.
5   Hallucinogen type — e.g., lysergide (LSD), mescaline, and
psilocybin.
6   Khat type — preparations of *Catha edulis Forssk.*
7   Opiate (morphine) type — e.g., opiates such as morphine,
heroin, and codeine, and synthetics with morphine-like effects,
such as methadone and pethidine.
8   Volatile solvent (inhalant) type — e.g., toluene, acetone, and
carbon tetrachloride"

Tobacco. "Though not listed above, it clearly is a dependence-producing
substance with a capacity to cause physical harm to the user, and its
use is so widespread as to constitute a public health problem. However, unlike the types of dependence-producing drugs just noted, it

produces relatively little stimulation or depression of the central nervous system or disturbances in perception, mood, thinking, behaviour, or motor function. Any such psychotoxic effects produced by
tobacco, even when it is used in large amounts, are slight compared
with those of the types of dependence-producing drugs listed above. It
is for this reason that dependence on tobacco — perhaps the most
widespread form of drug dependence — is not given specific attention
in this report. Attention has been restricted to the use of dependence-
producing drugs capable of exerting major psychotoxic effects"

As we go to a more detailed study, several other issues have to be
clarified.

Drug abuse, a very widely employed term, is not contained in the
above definition. Because of its heavy sociolegal implications, many (perhaps most) experts opt for its abolition. Others, myself included, find
some usefulness for the term. Jaffe [9], for example, defines as drug abuse,
any use of a drug for reasons which are medically not accepted and are
against the prevailing social and legal standards. However, from a psychiatric point of view, it is probably more consistent with medical tradition,
to define as *drug abuse* proper the use of any mind-altering drug for the
purpose of inner change if it leads to any transient or long range interference with social, cognitive, or motor functioning or with physical health,
regardless of the legal standing of the drug.

This definition puts the focus on the person instead of arbitrary societal standards. Why should for example, the drunkenness of a physician
at a party or driving under the influence of alcohol not be drug abuse,
whereas the often ineffective smoking of one marijuana cigarette should
be? Or why should compulsive smoking be any less a form of drug abuse
than heroin addiction? There are some alternate, less burdened words. A
term which lacks all sociolegal connotations, typically used in Europe, is
Toxicomania (the craving for toxic substances). A third term, even less
devaluing in meaning, is Pharmacothymia. Rado [14] used this in a narrow sense to denote a mood disorder akin to manic-depressive illness but
marked by the use of drugs. In a broader sense this term can mean the use
of drugs for emotional reasons, without any relationship to cyclothymic
illness. In this sense the concept is eminently useful and rich in meaning.

So far several criteria used to describe drug dependence have been
distinguished: psychological dependence or compulsiveness, the development of tolerance (the need to take increasingly higher dosages in order
to attain the same result), withdrawal symptoms (suffering if the dosage is
reduced), sociolegal repudiation (a particularly unsatisfactory criterion),
and interference with functioning (a useful dynamic concept). These give
the term drug abuse more sensible meanings but leave out an important

area of drug dependence: the often medically induced dependency which enhances, not decreases, overall functioning.

PSYCHOLOGICAL DEPENDENCY

In the sweeping sociolegal considerations and the political pronouncements (as well as in the fears of parents and physicians) one crucial fact is often obliterated: the clear and quite radical distinction between experimental and occasional users on the one side and intensive and compulsive users on the other side. The first group rarely presents problems (with the exception, for example, of "bad trips" or accidental overdose), but they represent the vast majority of the so-called drug problem. All of the medical, social, and legal concentration devoted to the casual user is drawn away from the real problem that needs infinitely more attention: the compulsive drug user. In him the use of drugs is the tip of the iceberg, the indicator of all the deeper troubles that beset him. Only a relatively few casual or experimental users proceed to predominantly compulsive use, and these individuals carry a set of rather specific predispositions. That latter much smaller category must be detected and treated early.

A derivative myth is the frequently heard belief that "once heroin, always heroin," that to take it once or a few times "hooks" the person. In reality there are very many heroin users who, for years, take it irregularly, occasionally, (the so-called chippers), or in binges. Furthermore, all these thoughts can be applied without alteration to alcohol consumption.

A far more sophisticated classification of drug dependency is defined in the Second Report of the National Commission on Marijuana and Drug Abuse [16:95–97]:

1   *Experimental use* is . . . the short-term non-patterned trial of one or more drugs . . . with a . . . maximum frequency of ten times per drug, used either singly or in combination.

2   *Social or recreational use,* like experimental drug use, occurs in social settings among friends or acquaintances who desire to share an experience perceived by them as both acceptable and pleasurable.

3   *Circumstantial-situational use* is generally task-specific, self-limited use which may be variably patterned, differing in frequency, intensity and duration. The distinguishing feature of this pattern is that use is motivated by the perceived need or desire to achieve a known and anticipated effect deemed desirable to cope with a specific, sometimes recurrent, situation or condition of a personal or vocational nature. Such users include students whose drug use is attendant to examination preparation, long distance truckers who rely on drugs to provide extended endurance and alertness, military personnel using drugs in stress and combat situations, athletes who use drugs to improve their performance or to extend their endurance, and most forms of self-medication in response to a particular task or situation.

4   *Intensified use* is generally a long-term, patterned use of drugs at a minimum level of at least once daily and is motivated by an individual's perceived need to achieve relief from a persistent problem or stressful situation or his desire to maintain a certain self-prescribed level of performance.

5   *Compulsive use* is patterned at both high frequency and high intensity levels of relatively long duration, producing physiological or psychological dependence such that the individual cannot at will discontinue such use without experiencing physiological discomfort or psychological disruption. It is characterized primarily by significantly reduced individual and social functioning.

For practical purposes those in the first two groups, experimental and social users, appear not to be particularly associated with serious preexisting psychopathology, whereas those in the latter two most definitely are, and very many in the circumstantial-situational use category as well. Obviously, drug use should be understood as a continuum.

However, since this division is based on external behavior one is led into a semantic quandary because compulsiveness in a subjective and psychoanalytically relevant sense is present wherever significant psychopathology is found. Therefore, the nomenclature needs to be changed. The fifth group should rather be called psychologically or physically addicted (*addictus* in Latin originally meaning sentenced to servitude because of indebtedness), thus symbolizing rather aptly an extreme form of compulsive behavior: the "enslavement" to the external master, the drug.

After this revision the continuum can be put into the following graph:

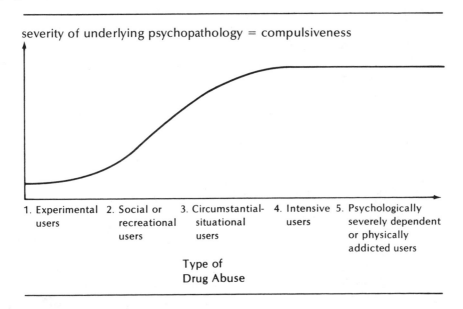

severity of underlying psychopathology = compulsiveness

1. Experimental   2. Social or   3. Circumstantial-   4. Intensive   5. Psychologically
   users   recreational   situational   users   severely dependent
                     users   users   or physically
                                                                            addicted users

Type of
Drug Abuse

This simple curve has to be modified: accessibility, legality, and acceptability by the immediate surroundings tend to *flatten* the curve. Good examples are the use of nicotine and alcohol throughout society, the use of cannabis amongst graduates from the youth culture, and heroin amongst the youngsters in some particularly degraded areas of the ghetto. The extent of the flattening of the curve is not known.

Of course the reverse is equally true: The more inaccessible a drug is and the more laden with social and legal opprobrium, the more severe is the psychopathology of the user. In other words, a compulsive alcohol or nicotine abuser usually shows far less preexisting psychopathology than a compulsive (or even casual) user of heroin, lysergic acid diethylamide (LSD), or cocaine. It might be suspected that the reason lies in the inner resistance against jumping over the hurdles of illegality and massive social disapproval. The more severe the inner pressure for relief and the extent of pathology is, the lower this hurdle appears.

A striking example for the often veiled nature of compulsive drug use, which was at first puzzling, surfaced when the just-described framework was presented to a group of second-year medical students. Heinrich, a twenty-three-year-old white man protested that he had used marijuana and hashish two to four times a day during college, studied with amphetamines for the exams, taken occasionally all the other major drugs short of heroin, and still quite commonly used cannabis as a relaxant at bedtime or on weekends. He felt driving a car, playing his guitar, and tasting food were enhanced by the use of marijuana. He denied ever having had perceptual distortions with it but allowed for a quite severe interference with his short-term memory and attention and ascribed it to the extensive cannabis use. Therefore, he had reduced his drug use to such an extent that he took the drug only when he did not have to learn and sometimes before finals went without it altogether. He stated his whole dorm engaged in similar drug use and felt that he was "using, not abusing" the drug, that it was partly recreational (a social leisure activity), partly situational, but certainly he had no psychological "compulsion" to use it. He believed that it was completely under his control to leave it or take it according to his rational judgement. This case appeared both typical (in phenomenology) and yet bewildering (as to claimed and overt absence of psychopathology). In a tête-à-tête with the teacher Heinrich denied all psychopathology: He had a happy family life and no social problems — only a very irascible younger sister, "a typical problem child." The first conclusion was that statistical and general findings do not have to encompass the individual case. However, it developed that he had a constant need, not just for various stimuli, but to try fate, to gamble with mind and life (e.g., by skydiving). These activities contained considerable compulsive elements. All his extracurricular activity had the aim: "Either I gain control against all odds over what I experience, or I avoid it altogether." His reckless curiosity and drivenness to discover "new experiences" seemed to be part of this *counterphobic activity*, the frantic efforts to prove he was in control. Characteristically when challenged in outside reality to prove those controls, as in the case of exams, he reduced his counterphobic activities very much. Why should he need them? After all, the exam was, like skydiving and getting "high," a test of proving to himself that *he* was indeed in control of fate and of his life against all thrilling dangers. This general counterphobic theme is a reckless, audacious stand against death, insanity, against losing ultimate control. Each challenge becomes an ultimate proof.

As a counter example, a typical case of a severely compulsive drug user, "Black Rose," is presented. She was a twenty-one-year-old woman, unskilled but rather intelligent, not unattractive, who came for temporary methadone maintenance and detoxification from heroin (diacetylmorphine) and Dilaudid (hydromorphone). The therapist saw her intermittently in psychotherapy for about half a year — intermittently because, as soon as she was withdrawn from methadone, she dropped out of treatment, came back, stayed perhaps two to three months and left again.

Here is a synopsis of what Black Rose said: "When I was sixteen, I started off with LSD, then smoked grass or hash, then took amphetamines and barbiturates. About four years ago I started taking heroin on weekends, out of curiosity, I guess. I was raped about the same time, when drunk with a boy, and got pregnant but got an abortion. I really have no sexual desires. My mother hates sex, sees it as a bad thing. She did not want me to be born (patient is second of three girls). She tried to kill herself when she was pregnant with me. She is overprotective; she loves me too much. She threatened to beat me up if I had sex with a boy — even today. She said if I did not shape up — with sex or drugs — she would shoot mé and herself. She slit up my clothes so that I cannot leave the house. She is afraid of losing me. I would like to have a baby (she thought she was pregnant again), even if it is only to spite my mother. I never fought her. I tried to kill myself before with barbiturates, after fights with my mother about going out. If you had to live with her you would also try to kill yourself to get away from her."

After an interruption in treatment and, after an additional suicidal attempt with Tuinal (secobarbital and amobarbital), she mentioned that she was back on Dilaudid. "When I got off methadone, I felt sick. Father went and bought me dope, I hate him: he tried to molest me, his own daughter, when he bought me the dope. He tried it once before, after the abortion. I hit him and was screaming and crying. My mother threatened to kill him. Then I forgave him. Mother and father always yelled at each other. He used to whip us with a belt. If he tried again to sleep with me I'd kill him with a butcher knife; I have it ready. I do not go near him, do not talk to him . . . Mother threatened again to shoot me if I took drugs again. If I'd die she would bury me the same day. She has already bought three burial plots, one for herself, one for father, one for me." All those ghastly stories (which were confirmed by her mother) were told with a flatness — not a schizophrenic flatness, but a depressed, sad, apathetic one.

She tried unsuccessfully to find a job and live with an aunt but was not accepted because of her drug history. In order to get away from the stifling presence of her mother, she wanted to get off methadone and go far away. Her request for withdrawal could not be refused. Two weeks later she was brought back by her mother who protested to the therapist: "*You* told her to move out. She was not yet ready. She kept taking sleeping pills, fell and busted her head open. I would rather see her institutionalized than dead. My love is all for her."

The patient was hospitalized but continued the psychotherapy with a very perceptive, warm female medical student who had sat in during some of the previous therapy sessions. Half a year later, on a leave of absence from the state hospital, she killed herself with an overdose of barbiturates. Real threats of incest and murder formed the foil to compulsive drug use and eventual suicide.

EFFECTS OF DRUG ABUSE

Two large groups of dependency-creating drugs (and hence classes of drug-dependent persons) can be distinguished: those which clearly are physically addicting and those which solely or mainly bring about psychological dependency. To the first large grouping belong (1) narcotics (the opiates and the synthetic narcotics); (2) alcohol; (3) barbiturates, other sedatives (e.g., chloral hydrate, paraldehyde), and the so-called minor tranquilizers; (4) phenacetin (in analgesics); and (5) nicotine. In all these one finds the hallmarks of tolerance and withdrawal (besides a psychological overlay and dependency), hallmarks which are strictly of a physiological nature. Even isolated cell cultures can show these two signs.

Parenthetically it should also be mentioned that tolerance, withdrawal, and, even to some extent, psychological dependency can be created artificially in animals as well as in patients who are (for good medical reasons) put on addicting medication. However, it has to be stressed that in this latter instance the iatrogenic drug dependence is commonly a self-limited state if the specific psychopathology needed for compulsive drug use is not present. Gradual withdrawal from the addicted state proceeds without difficulties.

Another corollary of the tolerance phenomena is *cross-tolerance;* that is, certain drugs can freely substitute for each other without any marked difference in effect; e.g., when a patient is addicted, heroin can be substituted at once and without problems with morphine, methadone, or Demerol, provided a pharmacologically similar dosage is given. The only differences lie in length of duration, slowness of withdrawal, side effects, and intensity of euphoria.

A similar grouping according to cross-tolerance exists for alcohol, all hypnotics, and minor tranquilizers. Thus, theoretically and often practically, one can withdraw an alcohol addict with high doses of diazepam (Valium) or chlordiazepoxide (Librium), or an ethchlorvynol (Placidyl) or glutethimide (Doriden) addict with the help of barbiturates. In contrast, stimulants and psychedelics belong to the second grouping, entailing only, or mainly, psychological dependence.

Narcotics

It is an error to assume that addiction to narcotics causes, by itself, physical damage. It does not. This does not imply that there may be no long-lasting or enduring physiological changes. Rather, there are indications that following a state of addiction and withdrawal proper, some physiological functions remain changed at least for a number of months, although this does not mean there is any physical disease. For several months increased blood pressure, hyperthermia, mydriasis, and increased respiratory rate can be found; still later, and again for a number of months, one observes decreased blood pressure, hypothermia, bradycardia, miosis, and increased sensitivity of the respiratory center to carbon dioxide (CO_2). It is more and more dubious that the continued craving has any relation to these minute physiological alterations.

However, much more important are the indirect consequences, many due to the illegal status of narcotics use. This type of addiction is usually not compatible with full social functioning. After one shot, the patient may start to "nod" or to retreat into his pleasant dreams. If he is at the wheel of a car, this dreaminess conflicts with traffic safety. In his job he may neglect his duties to some degree. Yet even this is true only to a limited degree, i.e., as long as the dose is not stabilized. "The fact that many successful persons have been chronic addicts and were able to lead worthwhile, constructive lives is often forgotten in discussions of the addict's ability to work," writes Kolb [10:10]. "Prior to the enactment of the Harrison Narcotic Law in 1914, there was no feeling among the general public that opiate addiction had appreciable adverse effects on work habits. At that time, addicts worked as regularly and as efficiently as any other group of people. The need for regulatory laws arose from the enslaving, difficult to cure physical dependence and not from addiction's economic meaning" [10:10]. Still the crucial variable is dosage stabilization. Once a level of tolerance is attained the addict's functioning may not only be normalized but may actually improve because of factors to be described.

Another consequence is self-neglect. The addict, especially if not on a stable dose, may not care as much about his physical needs — such as eating, cleanliness, and dental care. Again the reason may rather lie in the incessant "hustling" than in the drug's effect. A third and most dangerous group of consequences is directly due to the illegality of drug use. The addict can acquire drugs only at very high costs. The chasing after drugs in itself is a full-time profession and precludes most steady work. Other aspects (criminality, prostitution) dictated by the illegal status are obvious. It is a misapprehension that drug addicts, because of their drugs, favor violence and sexual crimes. Actually the opposite is true. The addicted person is too happy and mildly tranquilized; the person during the withdrawal state is too miserable. Norman Kerr wrote in the last century: "Opium soothes, alcohol maddens. Those intoxicated by opium are serene, sedate, and lethargic" [10:17]. Again Kolb [10] states that "it is conceivable that the number of violent crimes could be drastically reduced if all habitual criminals were addicts and would obtain sufficient morphine or heroin to keep sedated at all times. The effect of addiction on the behaviour of the mentally abnormal criminal is to *inhibit* his impulse to crime" [10:17]. This was confirmed by observations on patients on compulsory abstinence which will be described later on.

What are the health hazards induced by the illegal status of opiate use? The main risks are overdose, contamination, and infection. The dose, of course, is not known, nor can the addict himself accurately estimate his own tolerance. This is due in part to the various strengths of the "bags" he has had. Deaths from overdose are quite frequent (between 1000 and 1500 annually in New York City alone). Overdose leads to respiratory arrest. The ensuing hypoxia causes softening and cystic defects of the globus pallidus and rapid death or, if checked, may result in lasting brain damage. Since no one checks the content of the bags, the opiates may intentionally be adulterated with strychnine, digitalis, and other substances. It is commonly observed that patients who had been informers have been finished off simply with an unusually and unexpectedly potent dosage. Infections such as hepatitis, subacute bacterial endocarditis (which has an especially high mortality, since it is often caused by staphylococci), and phlebitis are common.

Withdrawal from opiates "cold turkey" (without substitution by methadone), is quite unpleasant, like a strong flu, but usually not life threatening, except in cases of congestive heart failure or other serious disease (including a severe depression or schizophrenia).

Sedatives and Alcohol

Again sedatives and alcohol are as truly addictive as narcotics proper. Intoxication with them leads, as with most of the other depressant substances, to sleepiness and impaired functioning. Speech is slurred and the gait atactic. Driving a car is very hazardous. It is most important to know, however, that withdrawal (in contrast to that from narcotics) is highly dangerous. If any of these drugs are withdrawn too rapidly, first tremulousness, then epileptic seizures, and eventually delirium ensue. These withdrawal symptoms frequently lead to death unless treated properly. What has been said about the barbiturates is valid also for meprobamate and other minor tranquilizers (diazepam, chlordiazepoxide). There is psychological as well as physical dependence, with epileptic seizures as withdrawal symptoms and, in higher doses, severe interference with psychomotor functioning. Daily intake of 100 mg of Valium leads after a few weeks to physical dependence (compare: 400 mg of pentobarbital (Nembutal) or secobarbital (Seconal).

> Several years ago the author was consulted by a professional for severe anxiety attacks and depression. The patient mentioned in passing that he suffered from severe insomnia, and despite moderate use of ethchlorvynol (Placidyl), he had an almost total day-night reversal. He asked for psychotherapy and withdrawal from the drug. Overconfidence on the physician's part let him assume only a mild and relatively harmless form of drug dependency. He slowly reduced the dosage from two to one capsule and then stopped. After total withdrawal, the patient felt fine for about three days. He then began to hear music in the air conditioner and car and suffered from increasingly severe anxiety attacks. In the light of the rest of his psychopathology these symptoms were explained (wrongly!) as the overreaction of an extremely anxious man who was terrified about the loss of his artificial prop. Twenty-four hours later he had two epileptic seizures (one in the bath tub), was injured, became unconscious, and then developed in the hospital a most severe psychotic episode of a clearly exogenous type (withdrawal delirium) which lasted about three days.

Few words need to be added in regard to alcohol. As Lemere [13] stated "alcohol outranks all other dangerous drugs by a wide margin in its total damaging effect on millions of people and society in general. After all, alcoholism is our fourth largest public health problem" [13:11].

The following groups evoke only psychological, not physiological dependency:

Stimulants

Besides the desired effects (antidepressant, especially massive boost of self-esteem and activity) there is a dangerous potential with all these stimulants (e.g., amphetamines, cocaine): acute episodes of violence, delusional misperception, and a paranoid state accompanied by auditory hallucinations. It should also be mentioned that physical side effects have been reported: Cocaine sniffers show perforated nasal septa, methamphetamine injectors develop a form of periarteritis nodosa and fatal cerebral vascular accidents. Overdose of cocaine may lead to sudden cardiac arrest due to ventricular fibrillation.

To examine the psychopathology with intensive prolonged use of these drugs it is useful to quote from E. H. Ellinwood [5], who examined amphetamine users that had been involved in homicide:

> The phase of chronic abuse often sets the stage: it includes changes in the individual's frame of mind involving suspiciousness, paranoid thinking, and fearful regard of his environment. It is during this period that he obtains and begins to carry a concealed weapon . . .
>
> The second phase, involving a sudden change in emotional arousal and/or a loss of intellectual control, is often secondary to a variety of factors, including a sudden increase in the dosage level (or acute use in a person with low tolerance), chronic loss of sleep, and the use of other drugs, especially sedatives and alcohol. In this emotional and cognitive framework, the person often misinterprets his environment and becomes increasingly fearful . . .
>
> Within this framework, a minor singular incident can trigger the violent act. Often the threatening incident is half real and half misinterpreted. Thus, although chronic amphetamine abuse may set the stage for violence, it is the phase of acute change in sensibilities that is actually associated with misinterpretation and the violent act [5:1174–75].

Such correlations between use of stimulants (cocaine, amphetamines, phenmetrazine) with paranoid symptoms and violence have been known for many years. Very often it is difficult later on to distinguish the original amphetamine psychosis from the continued schizophrenic psychosis and to determine whether there was any causal relationship between drug use and later chronic paranoid symptomatology.

From the past it is also reported that severe abuse of cocaine has these effects. The notion of the "dope fiend," which is commonly used to describe narcotic addicts, is said to originate with the observation that severe cocaine abuse can lead to such "crazed," "fiendish" behavior. In contrast, however, I have personally known many narcotics addicts who also used cocaine. In no case could I convincingly witness what the literature reported. And then there are many illustrious cocaine users such as Halstead, Conan Doyle, Stevenson, and Freud who have not been known for violence or persecutory delusions during the periods of their taking cocaine.

Psychedelic Drugs

A very large number of drugs has to be counted here, all of which may cause vivid hallucinations, dreamlike states, and a subjective sense of consciousness expansion, with greater appreciation for art and nature and (similar to the trema state in schizophrenia) a sense of cosmic meaningfulness.

The best known are LSD, peyote (mescaline), morning glory seed, psilocybin, di-methyl-tryptamine (D.M.T.), dimethoxy-methyl-amphetamine (STP), phencyclidine (PCP, "animal tranquilizer," angel dust, Sernylan), anticholinergics (atropine, scopolamine, muscarine), and solvents of plastic cements ("glue sniffing, the ten-cent hallucinogen") — and high doses of cannabis.

Acute intoxication with any of these may lead to bad trips from a few hours up to ten days' duration. The occurrence of such an acute, panicky state of severe confusion and breakdown of all perceptual, cognitive, and emotional structures depends on the dosage of the drug, the preexisting personality (set), and the immediate surrounding (setting). It has been claimed that if the latter is supportive enough, no bad trips occur.

As to chronic use of psychedelics it was observed [17] in standardized techniques of Rorschach evaluations that there existed "a clear tendency for drug users regardless of diagnosis to have more signs of increased intrusion of primitive-drive material, higher penetration scores, and higher responsivity.

"There were indications of conceptual boundary disturbance in the drug users although their scores on this variable were influenced by their increased responsivity. These select features of thinking and responsivity marked the drug users as different than other patients . . . The length of drug use over time was more strongly related to these thinking disturbances than variety or amount of drug use" [17:443].

Cannabis

Marijuana and hashish in higher dosages belong to the psychedelics, in very weak dosages perhaps simply to the mild relaxants and euphoriants. They should be treated separately, however, because of the enormous spread (30 million Americans have at least tried it), the many unsolved scientific problems, and the particular controversies the marijuana question raises legally, socially, politically, in medical training, philosophically, and in psychotherapy and psychoanalysis.

In the last fifteen years a large number of clinical, epidemiological, and laboratory studies have appeared which focus mainly on the possible consequences of long-term use of marijuana. The claimed consequences may be described in five categories. (1) affect disturbances, particularly panic reactions which reach sometimes psychotic proportions; (2) perceptual and sensory distortions and hallucinations affecting world and body image, sometimes recurring after prolonged abstinence; (3) cognitive and attentional disturbances with fragmentation of thinking, inability to attain the goal of a single thought process and a flight of thoughts and ideas; (4) disturbance of the sense of reality, like depersonalization (estrangement of the outer world and a split of the self); (5) changes in the psychomotor sphere and, with that, in the outward appearance of the personality, mainly in the form of apathy and neglect, loss of effectiveness, and a diminished capacity to carry out long-term plans and to endure frustration, the so-called amotivational syndrome.

In most studies the role of the underlying personality is emphasized. Despite this, however, many studies about drug effects are presented with the implicit and apparently very scientific premise that there exists a clear cause and effect relationship between drug intake and symptom. I am reminded of Freud's criticism of "the restricted nature of what men look for in the field of causation: in contrast to what ordinarily holds good in the real world, people prefer to be satisfied with a single causative factor" [6:99].

As is usual in psychology one is dealing with a complex hierarchy of causes and motivations. If the jumble of findings relevant for the theme at hand is sorted out (leaving out rightly contested claims as effects on testosterone level and sexual performance, possibility of reduction of immunity, genetic damage and teratogenicity, visible brain damage, carcinogenic as well as anticancer potential), the current knowledge can be summarized in the following points:

1. *The amotivational syndrome.* Diminished drives, lessened ambition, decreased motivation, apathy, shortened attention span, and fragmentation in thought and speech — the amotivational syndrome — has been described by many researchers [4], doubted by the Shafer Commission [16], and possibly refuted [15].

2. *Short-term effects on cognition, perception, and memory.* The excellent report by Hollister [8] summarized: "Sleepiness was constantly observed . . . *Time sense* was altered, hearing was less discriminant, vision was apparently sharper with many visual distortions. Depersonalization, difficulty in concentrating and thinking, and dream-like states were prominent . . . The drawing test . . . showed *reduced accuracy* . . . probably indicating some loss of finer judgment" [8:23; italics added]. Also: "whereas long-term memory . . . was maintained, *short-term memory . . . was impaired*" [8:23; italics added]. *"Temporal disintegration"* has been described both by Hollister [8] and by Casswell and Marks [2]; the latter two authors have stated. "Temporal disintegration, that is, the inability to keep track of goal-relevant information over time, as measured by the GDSA (Goal Directed Serial Alternation) has been demonstrated in this study to be a consequence of cannabis intoxication within the range expected to occur following social use of the drug" [2:805]. Hollister [8] has described other test impairments as explainable "by *loss of selective attention*, immediate recall, and systematic thinking" [8:24].

In contrast to short-term memory loss, recent memory and long-term memory appear not significantly affected, but one may wonder whether not all organic noxae of this nature bring along, if severe and repeated enough, a mild organic, amnestic syndrome. Chronic severe cannabis users have complained about some such memory loss, just like those with equivalent alcohol abuse (which usually remains within socially acceptable bounds). This double question as to *lasting* long-term memory deficiency in the wake of both frequent marijuana and equally frequent alcohol use urgently needs longitudinal careful research.

3. *Psychomotor abilities.* As psychomotor abilities affect driving, NORML, the protagonist group for decriminalization of marijuana, stated unequivocally on March 26, 1975: "As the tests have become more sophisticated in this area, it has become more and more obvious that it is not safe to smoke marijuana and drive a car. Though clearly not as debilitating as alcohol, nonetheless, the marijuana smoker makes more errors on driving tests than the non-smoker."

4. *"Marijuana Psychosis."* Cohen [4] has stated: "The literature on chronic marihuana use leading to psychosis is completely confusing. While it can be said with assurance that a few people, usually neophytes, who smoke potent materials can have an acute psychosis, the incidence and nature of long lasting psychotic reactions is strongly disputed" [4].

PSYCHODYNAMICS

The crucially important psychological aspects [19,20] of compulsive drug use are vastly neglected. Social and biological theories and explorations preempt the field.

The central place the concept of psychological dependence, i.e., of compulsion, assumes has been noted. If one carefully studies, on the one hand, history and treatment experience and, on the other hand, the interesting observations in medically and psychiatrically induced addictions (e.g., when opiates were used to treat melancholics), one is forced to assign very little valence in the long-range to the factor of physical dependence. The crux is that "the readiness is all."

Everyone who works closely and personally with a compulsive drug user has had the experience that if his drug of predilection is taken away the user desperately tries to substitute another symptom. A kind of natural experiment occurred during the dock strike in 1971 which lasted fifty-nine days and led to a shutdown of imports, including opiates. Although the underworld had apparently enough stockpiles, these were held back in order to drive up the price. The result was a severe shortage of narcotics. Those addicts who could not get methadone from unscrupulous physicians or from programs or illegally turned mainly to barbiturates and related sedatives (e.g., Quaalude [methaqualone]). The same phenomenon of drug, or symptom, substitution precedes and accompanies compulsive drug use. Most frequently, other symptoms have a similar compulsive quality: use of alcohol and hypnotics, stealing and running away, occasionally violence or suicidal depression. A similar and very valuable set of observations is gained in programs of compulsory abstinence.

What then is the meaning of this compulsive need to take drugs — either a specific type of drugs or promiscuously? Above all, one notices fluctuations. Under any psychological or physiological stress the compulsion to take drugs (or to show other forms of symptoms) increases. In turn, it can be observed that the emotional dependency on the drug is overcome if the psychological dependency and commitment is displaced to other objects, e.g., to a concrete community (as Synanon), to a cause (Black Muslims), or to a therapist (positive transference). In other words, potent meaning-giving factors can replace, in highly motivated individuals, the compelling role the drug exerts.

This implies a most important fact: that there is a continuum of compulsiveness — ranging from zero to total. Compulsiveness is a relative, not an absolute concept. Most importantly, when one speaks about compulsive drug users no clearly defined group comes to mind but simply one where the extent of compulsion most of the time is very prominent.

The drugs are used as a form of self-treatment and most specifically as a way to cope with *overwhelming affects*. Although many other determinants enter, this function of drug use as an *affect defense* may be the most prominent.

This phenomenon which is shared by all toxicomanics and by many other borderline patients as well can variously also be described as generalization, radicalization, and totalization of affects. The feelings become suddenly and irresistibly overwhelming, fearfully out of control. Words cannot do them justice, nor can they be clearly differentiated from each other. Anxiety, anger, despair, pain, all flow into each other [11,12].

All compulsive drug users have the following affects in common, which must be warded off by all means (not only by drugs). All these feelings are the direct outcome of narcissistic frustration. Some of them are more prevalent in one type of drug use, but basically all these affects are present. These basic moods and affects are: disappointment, disillusionment, rage, shame, loneliness, and a panicky mixture of terror and despair. Depression (comprising a number of these affects) and depersonalization as feeling states and of near psychotic proportions are particularly frequent underlying affective disorders.

In a short review the correlation of specific affects denied, the nature of the narcissistic wish-fulfillment attained, and the preference for certain types of drugs can be surveyed.

1. The narcotics user has to cope with the emotional pain and anxiety flowing from the entire array of affects mentioned above. Among them rage, shame, and loneliness seem particularly prominent. What he attains on the side of wish-fulfillment is a sense of *protection, warmth, and union,* of heightened self-esteem and self-control.

2   The user of barbiturates and other sedatives has to deal with nearly the same task. Perhaps the feelings of humiliation, shame, and rage are particularly prominent and need the most powerful form of denial, that contained in estrangement (partial or total depersonalization and derealization). A study of the barbiturate addict will have to pay particular attention to that peculiar form of compromise formation; depersonalization is not simply a defense. The particular wish-fulfillments are those contained in this symptom. (However, this does not mean that hints of this very important symptom are not present in most other toxicomanics also. It is most prominent in the use of hypnotics.)

3   In psychedelic users the major affects denied are boredom, emptiness, and lack of meaning; disillusionment and loneliness are also "walled off" with the drug's help. What is attained as gratification is a sense of meaning, value, and admiration and a state of *passive merger* — concerning the self as well as ideals.

4   The users of stimulants fight against a particularly intense form of depression, despair, sadness, and loss. Shame about weakness and vulnerability, boredom and emptiness, are quite prominent. The narcissistic gain lies in the feelings of strength,

victory, triumph, invincibility, and invulnerability, in some (but by far not all) nearly a manic state. The importance of magical control, so ubiquitous in all categories, is particularly eminent and obtrusive in this group.

5   Alcoholics are less subject to the primary feelings listed above; the main feelings denied appear to be guilt and loneliness, also shyness, shame, and social isolation. The narcissistic gratification lies in the expression, not in the denial, of anger which had been so long suppressed or repressed. In many there is also the feeling of company and togetherness, of *shared regression* and acceptance in a childlike status, and the overcoming of being an outcast, when alcoholized.

These manifold negative affects break through with unrestrained force when archaic narcissistic demands are thwarted. Many of them are already expression of aggression, the twin of narcissism.

There are also important differences in regard to the lead defenses and the underlying conflicts between various forms of compulsive drug use, but these are omitted here.

With regard to the family constellation, clinically one cannot fail to notice that there is hardly any compulsive drug user who does not hail from a family with massive problems. Not only are broken families common, but this fact in and by itself is less of a problem than the overall family atmosphere, the life-style in which the child grew up. The various family constellations are described as follows:

1   The most constant family features are the absence of consistency in setting, enforcing, and sticking to limits and the undermining, undercutting power struggle between the parents. In other words, it is the lack of structure and the amount of overt or covert aggression which is striking in these families.

2   One very frequent constellation (and a special variant of the inconsistency), is the vacillation between seduction and vindictiveness. On the one side, there are virtually no limits to living out material gratifications, in the forms of eating, drinking, and sex and in providing money, cars, and luxury. Even in many slum families this type of spoiling, a permissive granting of wishes and lack of discipline can be seen. On the other side, the parents engage in wild temper tantrums (including physical violence) to enforce a particular limit. They like to justify their outbursts or rage as "discipline," but clearly they are the opposite.

3   In the same or other families, the conflict is between an intrusive form of pseudolove and overprotective "care" and a complete disregard for the individuality of the child and his real emotional needs.

4   Particularly in upper middle-class families, the self-centered preoccupation with success and prestige on the parent's part is matched by the self-centered retreat into a drug-induced dream world by the child and supported by the parent's guilt-ridden giving-in to all demands of the child.

5   Very often the parents themselves are deeply involved in using prescribed or not prescribed drugs and alcohol to sustain their own versions of what Ibsen called the "lifelie" and other attempts to cover over or to deny the tragic dimensions of their own entanglements, their sense of being lost. Often one senses, as if shrouded in a mist, profound family secrets, forms of family shame and family guilt, of rifts and broken loyalties, putting an almost unbearable burden on the parents, on the children, and on the family as a unit.

6   Occasionally it was noted in the literature [3] how severely neglected and deprived many drug users were. Going over the cases in our own methadone program it is striking how many patients were illegitimate, bastards, and/or scapegoats; always outcasts, degraded in their own immediate surrounding which hardly can be called "family" anymore (so much of a parody it is). The sheer amount of criminality, mayhem and murder, alcoholism and drug use, and just all-pervasive neglect is staggering. The result for the child is horrifying and disastrous.

     Perhaps one might come closest to the clinical truth by saying that the symptom of drug taking by the child is a derivative of the whole family's attitude of inconsistency, self-centeredness, and, most importantly, of inner and outer dishonesty. The deceptiveness and wiliness of many drug abusers is a reflection of their parents' denial or deviousness and power-hungry manipulations, or it is a frantic escape from disillusionment and anger about the unavailability of their parents as persons during the crises of growing up.

Thus one sees in the families the crucial features of the major problems of these patients preformed: narcissism, denial and splitting, externalization, and superego split. This allows the pretense of maintaining magical powers, omnipotence, and self glorification (supreme narcissistic gratifications) to stand. The vicious circle is closed in them, as in their offspring.

The following case history provided by Dr. Gerson in New York and treated there in the sixties is particularly instructive because it shows all the complex factors in combination.

Andreas, a man in his early thirties married, with two chidren, was seen for four years in psychotherapy; at the beginning attendance was very sporadic, only after one and one half years psychotherapy gained momentum and intensity.

He entered the methadone program when his doctor, who for a few years had prescribed 100–200 mg methadone daily to him, was forbidden to practice by the authorities. He wanted to see the psychiatrist because he was suffering from severe anxiety attacks and insomnia when starting on the program: "I am afraid of dying. These feelings of near-insanity and panic come over me several times a day and particularly at night. Some time ago, I tried to be withdrawn from methadone in a mental hospital, but they put me on Thorazine (chlorpromazine). I started hallucinating, was overwhelmed with fear, and had convulsions. Yet the more frightened I became, the more Thorazine they gave me, once 400 mg for the night alone! I was never as close to killing myself as then. That was far worse than any withdrawal; so I signed myself out." As to his immediate history: "I have never stolen. Either I got my drugs from a physician or I worked in construction or in the shipyard. Before that I was in college but broke it off, worked a while as a computer programmer. I have to tell you something which still haunts me, and my life has never been right since — nor really before. When I was nineteen, I killed a man." Then in bits and pieces he told me his life history over the weeks and months. "I am the younger of two; my sister is ten years older than I am. My father was unhappy and chronically ill. However, a nagging wife and a job he completely loathed kept him from dwelling on his other misfortunes. Although my parents never physically hit each other, they either argued violently, or they sulked in silence. The fights were always for silly or no reasons.

"When I was four or five my next-house neighbor and playmate was killed before my eyes as a truck ran over him while we were playing in front of my house. I had no real conception of death; I ran down the street thrilled that something important and exciting had happened. While playing with toy soldiers I would fantasize that I had been captured by the enemies and was tortured until I would give up the secrets. The fantasizing pleasure was from two sources: the physical pain itself and the concept of bravery resulting from withstanding the pain in a manly fashion.

"At a preschool age I had several sexual experiences with two girls about my age. Among other things we acted out sexual intercourse. We knew, I suppose instinctively, that what 'I had' should go into what 'she had.' Of course I didn't have an erection; actual intercourse was not taking place. I had no shame or guilt feelings; it seemed like a natural thing to do. We were finally discovered and made to feel what we had been doing was very wrong.

"In the first or second grade, I became aware of the word claustrophobia, or, if not the word itself, the concept. I would panic if I were closed in a small space and was uanble to get out, or if I were held and unable to break the hold in a wrestling match. I experience life only in tragic situations — as if I created a novel. I do not know how many young children feel that. But already by eight or ten when I was walking all by myself on a Saturday or Sunday morning, I had that lonely, haunting feeling. And that it was appealing to me was crucial — otherwise I would have avoided it. It is a perverse fascination: to walk through the ghetto, seeing people drunk, whiskey bottles in alleys, hearing 'the Blues'. It sounds sentimental, but there was a heartache, something odd, haunting, a pain and sadness that permeated the air. It attracted me — it sounds like a novel — it drew me to alcohol and drugs. That was definitely one of the reasons why I eventually became an addict. If anyone tells you there is *one* reason why somebody takes drugs, he is stupid. I have found perhaps eight or more, and each was part of it and true."

Around that same time of age fifteen he was part of a roaming gang of rather wild "friends." When they were attacked with snowballs, one of them (the Whelp) stabbed two of the "attackers" to death. Andreas was not with them but came upon the scene shortly thereafter. The Whelp was sent to jail for four years. A little later, Andreas had improved very much in school — emulating the first consciously remembered ideal he had — his sister's husband, a scientist. Tragically, however, shortly thereafter this young man died of a malignancy, and Andreas, who was now in college, good, but not outstanding, lost all interest in studying.

Already by age sixteen and seventeen, he had earned some money by serving as a homosexual "hitchhiker," being "sucked" by men of respectable standing. "It screwed me up a lot with adult males, not having much respect for my father to begin with." He suddenly dropped out of college, "because I was not the best anymore," engaged in several homosexual adventures, and got in with the same group of friends, including eventually again the Whelp. By now the patient was nineteen.

One evening three of them had group sex with a girl in a club room. She taunted them that one of them had not been a "good lover." The Whelp felt ridiculed and tried to pick a fight with the patient and finally spat in his face because Andreas would not give him a ride home. "I did not fight back because I felt stunned by shame, paralyzed." About a week later when they ran into each other again, the Whelp told Andreas: "You are okay, I am sorry." Strangely enough this semiapology was the crisis point which led up to the conviction in Andreas: "Now he has shown himself to me to be weak — now you can get back at him!" Repulsion and scorn were added to the long accumulated shame and rage in Andreas. One week later the Whelp challenged Andreas again, taunting him as a coward. The patient went home and got a gun and eight bullets. He drove around throughout the night, afraid of coming upon his enemy and scared of his own anger, even consciously avoiding places where he might run into the Whelp. Finally, in early dawn, he came upon his antagonist when the latter, after yet another brawl, tumbled out from a barroom. "I was not upset, not trembling; I had convinced myself that I was as insane as I could be. I shot him twice through the chest. It was like a slow motion movie, frame after frame, strobe-like. Ten seconds appeared like a lifetime. My first feeling was humor, surprise; it sounds terrible. I thought he was just play acting. He began to stagger and appeared overly dramatic. Then he was falling toward me. I had the fear that he was falling on me. I wanted to fight him off and tried to shoot again, but I did not have any more bullets. I was puzzled. I went to the car looking for the additional six bullets but could not find them. Then I went straight home for more bullets. I did not assume at all that he was dead. It was a complete feeling of unreality when I was driving home — no sorrow, not one emotion, nothing. I was definitely going now for all out war — that 'it' was about to happen, not that 'it' had already happened. The thing that changed it completely and got me suddenly stuck in the tracks was that my mother had left food out for me with a note. It made me sick! I suddenly realized 'Someone loves me, shows me human kindness! What have I done! 'I went back with the car and looked at what had happened. There was a lot of police there. I rode by. Then I told myself: 'You have not done anything wrong — but something justifiable.' But then I recalled my old claustrophobia. That kept me running. Then I said: 'What the hell, I can handle it. Or I always can kill myself when it becomes too bad.' I felt completely fearless. Dying had absolutely no meaning. I went to the police station after driving around all night and told them I had shot that guy. At first they did not want to believe me. They had already arrested the guy with whom the Whelp had been fighting. When I came in that room where that guy was sitting — I never saw anybody so relieved. Why did I kill the Whelp? I was afraid of him, and I did not want him to know it. And he wanted to see himself as this underworld hitman and be respected as a killer. I felt the streets were unsafe with him walking on them; he was a looming presence, a menace."

Acquitted because of temporary insanity a year later, while adjudged sane in the institution for the criminally insane, Andreas was set free after one year in jail and went back to college. But soon his moods of emptiness, boredom, dullness, loneliness, and sadness took over again. He also felt very much an outsider, out of place, ill at ease with the "normal" students. During that dark period he married his present wife.

Yet at that point there were two exciting things which made life worthwhile again: a homosexual liaison and narcotics. These two, by their very "wrongness," broke through the empty, sad mood. He dropped out of college.

To be a drug user at first was a triumph: to break society's laws. "Heroin was the cement of a secret group of people, like a conspiracy. I was not alone. I suddenly felt very special and in control." But this triumph soon turned into a humiliating dependency.

Similarly, when he started succeeding in life, he felt a sense of triumph and recklessness and yet a deep compulsion to wreck what he built up (family and professional achievement). The narcotics had many functions, besides the vague breaking of society's laws in spiteful challenge. They muted the shame about his homosexual propensities, his social defeat, and his passive-dependent drifting. They soothed his despair, loneliness, and his guilt. But most of all they calmed the attacks of terror and anxiety inherent in the unsolvable tragic conflicts haunting his life and forestalled the welling up of murderous rage and guilt-fed self-wrecking, all of which appeared puzzling and out of control. Whenever he withdrew from narcotics, anxiety and violent anger became unmanageable.

Henceforth, for about eight years, he was on illegal heroin and Dilaudid, then methadone, working only irregularly as an unskilled laborer. About half a year after entering methadone maintenance he withdrew himself from methadone, went to Lexington, could not stand the regimentation and structure there, hurried back, and wanted to be readmitted to the program. He was told to return the next day. He felt he could not wait, broke into a drug store in a most inept and self-sabotaging way, and was arrested. For the following fifteen months he lived under the thundercloud of the trial, worked a little, but mostly sat passively around. He came to see the therapist but all was fear, despair, and passivity. He was unable to start anything as long as he was waiting for the trial. He drank and ruminated about his self-destructiveness and being closed in. It was embarrassing to him to speak about his problem. "I am good at being a failure. I can't be an average person. I can't deserve to have a good time." Then, about four months after resumption of therapy and a brief period of work in the dry docks, his murderous and tragic fate nearly repeated itself a second time. During a period of unemployment he gave a coworker of his, Sleezy, and some others a ride home from a tavern late one night. The other reviled an old homosexual friend of his. The patient burst out in verbal anger and was in turn slapped in the face by Sleezy. The jump from humiliation to blind rage was instantaneous. He got out of the car, knocked his foe unconscious, and broke his own hand. A warrant was issued for Andreas' arrest. Sleezy did not appear before the magistrate to press charges against Andreas, who thus went free once more. Brooding idleness, gambling, and betting filled the following year till his trial for his drug store break-in. Still he recognized the pervasiveness of shame in his life — especially about his homosexual impulses. "I picture myself as masculine, and at the same time I have these homosexual feelings. Before the homicide and drug use, I had an episode of homosexuality. And with Sleezy again it was about homosexuality; he touched on my most sensitive spot; in all these situations my rage becomes uncontrollable. I am ashamed of these still present wishes and acts (fellatio on boys about eighteen); I cannot reconcile them with my self-image as a man. The boys are like me when I was that age; *it's like a split in me — a big brother and another kid which is in trouble.*" He compared himself to his father who also had been passive, inactive, and had given up on life, defeated and humiliated.

The homosexual escapades were exciting, forbidden, very shame-ridden and led to severe anxiety attacks and a lot of guilt; and so did his childlike dependency and passivity towards his wife, his wish to be treated as special, as he was with mother.

Then the trial came. The therapist testified for him and suggested to the judge continuation of psychotherapy and methadone maintenance as the only hope for this man; a long jail sentence would probably finish off most chances for rehabilitation. It was only then, a little more than two years after inception of treatment, that psychotherapy started in earnest. The therapist gave him a near-ultimatum: that he would resume his studies, thus making use of his very high intelligence and adding skills to gifts in a field where he would really find inner satisfaction. With a stipend from a state's agency he resumed his studies in a scientific field and became within a few months an honor student, enthusiastic about his new life, "happier than ever in my life," but also fearing that "what is so good cannot last, something might happen — a disaster, a catastrophe. . . . It reminds me of dreams from childhood where I was drowning. This unknown force in me which always destroys what I built up entered time and again: When I started college it was such a happy point in my life — but I felt it had to change. And all collapsed. And when I left jail it was the same: I was back in college and married — and both times there was this combination of homosexuality and self-destruction. Precisely because it was wrong, it was sexually exciting. When I was about to kill the Whelp, I was so disgusted by myself that I wanted to commit suicide. *It was almost an accident that I killed him, not me.* I remember since I was four or five I have thought of suicide."

These remarks touch on the unknown "inner demon" who always wrecks life. "I remember the terror and the feeling of death. The first time that I was in contact with death was when the neighbor next door who had been very fond of me and treated me like a son, and whom I liked very much, was very sick in the hospital. He jumped out of the window and killed himself. All that was when I was less than six." Here the therapist reminded him of the child who was crushed to death. He immediately responded: "But there was nothing emotional, I was too young to understand it. I was not upset, only excited." The therapist asked him directly whether he might not have repressed the intense anxiety and ensuing rage which later emerged in the claustrophobia (being pinned to the ground like the child whose importance he kept emphasizing). "That's a very good point. I hate feeling crushed, especially in sports. But I was a tremendous football player, because I could run over people; it was relief for my aggression." Therapist: "You did to others what the truck did to the little boy." He came in very depressed the next hour, in a mood of loneliness, irritation, and emptiness, "as if I was avoiding something. It was precisely this mood which preceded my starting with drugs and with my homosexual liaison. They made life again exciting and worthwhile. There is definitely something masochistic: the enjoyment precisely because it was wrong." In the following sessions he talked more about this demonic force in him which kept condemning and sabotaging him but as soon as he felt insulted would break out in murderous rage.

After his first startling successes at his resumed studies and following an interruption in psychotherapy, he said: "Every week I feel I am growing, I am becoming something, but the problem is still the underlying anxiety that I will ruin things, that there is something about me that is uncontrollable. Just under the surface the animal is working, under a thin veneer of civility, the part which shot the Whelp. The worst now is that I have that feeling precisely with those people I am closest to and I care for most, my family, some friends, you: to strike out where there is no justification, to hit, to kill, for no reason at all. This is the most horrible thing for a person to have. It feels good to be physically injured (he was just then!) and weakened — so I don't feel as dangerous." He talked about his narcissistic rage in the present as well as in his childhood — how he "got away with murder" with his very inconsistent, spoiling, extremely materially indulgent parents, which only increased his deep sense of guilt.

Then he brought up that until age eight he slept in his parents' bedroom and vaguely remembered having witnessed their intercourse: "I thought that mother was crushed by father. There was never any privacy. This sounds crazy, as a child I felt as if there were hidden microphones or concealed cameras so that the parents always knew what I did. It was my fantasy that the parents had only the best in mind for me and never would harm me." (Thus he dealt with frightening looking, exhibition and attacking by reversals.)

The following hour he returned to the "crushed boy": "I spoke the other day with my mother about that memory. She told me that I was so upset at the time when I came home that I was unable to talk. It is odd how differently I remembered it. I remember the boy who died was a very good kid. We played a lot together. He shared his toys, but I did not want to share my things with him. I have never thought about that before, but he was my best friend and best enemy; I competed so much with him and was jealous. I wonder whether I felt responsible for his death? We were not allowed to go on the street, but I went with him anyway. I turned around and saw the truck behind me. If I could have given him a warning? I wonder what really happened. I have felt guilty, especially because I had felt aggressive towards him anyway."

He tied this guilt up with his lifelong need to repeat both aggression and self-punishment; he never got the punishment he expected for the boy's death, for his stealing, for his outbursts with his parents, or for his murder, and he was still haunted by the fear that the monster was catching up with him. "After the homicide I wanted jail and expected seven to ten years and did not get it. Instead the following ten years were as if I had been in jail, wasted, on drugs." He questioned his sanity and self-control and felt a close connection between homosexual and murderous impulses. The tie-in was "masochism": "In the homosexual act I only play-act, as if I were controlled and exploited. If I really lost control, it would turn into something unpleasant. *I want to be masochistic, but I want to dominate the situation.* If I lost control, if a girl or man really takes the whip out, I get furious. It is paradoxical. I enjoy a homosexual act where I pretend that the person has me under control and forces me to fellatio, that I am subjugated by someone stronger than me, but as soon as they really believe it, it turns my mood off." It is indeed a very precarious balance between two nearly equally strong parts, which are not really conflicted with each other but coexist in a curious split with most abrupt flip-flops: the illusion of total power and the illusion of masochistic subjugation.

Thus, scenes of parental intercourse and fights, of the crushed boy, and of forced fellatio, are turned from situations of extreme passivity, helplessness, and powerlessness into a situation of merely played subjugation but real, complete control and power. It combines sexual excitement and fascination with a curiously split experience of brute force and violence, masochistically replayed and reenacted, but secretly controlled and mastered by him, followed by a sense of guilt, repentance and shame, while feeling relaxed and freed of his boisterous anger and combativeness, and able to work! The shame part is the reaction to the replay of the early scene in its masochistic version (identification with the mastered and castrated mother); guilt, relaxation, and freedom of anger are the response to his own sense of force and power (the identification with the controlling, castrating father). So the later split reflects the double identification with both the sadistic father and the masochistic mother in the primal scene. His lifelong, most destructive sense of self-punishment in the many forms of humiliation and self-murderousness repeats the original traumata in split, double form. And so does his drug addiction. It gives him a sense of power and specialness, accompanied by guilt, and a sense of dependency, weakness, enslavement, filling him with shame. Thus his life is like a constant dangerous journey between the Scylla of shameful defeat and humiliation, leading to blind rage and murder, and the Charybdis of guiltful success, triumph, and self-sabotage.

He remembered how the very negligence and unconcern of father in several episodes had a murderous quality (e.g., risking Andreas' drowning). This aspect had not occurred to Andreas before but was both surprising and convincing, and he himself connected the mutual murderousness between his father and him with that between the Whelp and him. He then remembered how his father used to reproach him for every minor infraction, like coming home fifteen minutes late: Andreas was "killing" him. Later he added that if Andreas took drugs this would be the worst thing he could do and would kill him. It was indeed only about one year before his father's death that Andreas started taking narcotics — evidently unconsciously a magical means to finish once and for all his father's blackmail in form of these death threats.

"Often everything is such a tragedy for me, so dark and gloomy despite all the insight. Then I feel I am living a tragedy and that people are aware of it; then I use homosexuality, violence, or drugs to boost my self-esteem and remove the pain. I am leading a double life — tragedy and success."

More than four years after the beginning of psychotherapy and one and a half years into his most successful professional studies, he felt ready to be detoxified (withdrawn) — very slowly, with an increase in psychotherapy (from two up to four to five hours a week). Despite greatest care he felt worse and worse: very depressed, unable to do anything, empty, lonely, a vague nervousness, uneasiness, apprehension, a "general sense of nothingness." From this deepening depression with clear anhedonia, depersonalization, and all the physical signs of a somatically felt depression he went (when the medication was down to 10 mg methadone) into violent despair. He threatened to kill his wife, himself, and his therapist and to rob a bank (just to break out of the depression). Valium and Librium did not help. He used all kinds of illegal drugs (heroin, methadone, methamphetamine). Only the latter seemed to help for a few hours. He got drunk every afternoon but to no avail. Eventually his methadone dosage was increased, back in steps to 40 mg. The severe depression continued. Thereupon it was decided to put him on a tricyclic antidepressant. Ten days went by without change and then almost overnight, the depression went, to his complete surprise. He suddenly broke off psychotherapy, eventually finished his studies and worked at last report successfully as a professional for the city government in a large mid-western city.

The underlying psychopathology in this case was a possibly biologically founded depression (a psychotic depression?) which had haunted him through life. The psychodynamically accessible and yet not fully resolvable conflicts which were presented only in brief excerpts were offshoots of this depressive core problem. Nonetheless it may be helpful to select his two interrelated main problems as they can be understood psychologically.

First of all, the use of narcotics (including the yearning for it) was above all a regressive gratification in the form of a directly observable increase in self-esteem. Before his daily methadone dose, he felt low, as if depleted of self-worth and interest in the world; afterwards, he showed a stable, healthier level of self-regard, a more realistic outlook on the future, an ability to put past and present more in perspective. This effect was vastly enhanced by the antidepressant. It was not an elation or an unrealistic overoptimism. The narcotic clearly had to function as a regulator of self-esteem. Of course, the sadomasochistic gratifications were another very important determinant. The drugs (as objects and symbols) were a compromise formation: They were the badge of glory of a select, esoteric, feared in-group and conspiracy, a playing with fire (the excitement cited before), a revenge on the norms of society (externalizing by transgression) and on the family (especially father), plus a stigma of his shame, dependency, being an outcast. The drugs (in regard to their pharmacological effect) represented a compromise formation too: boosting of self-esteem, denial of the archaic affects mentioned (especially massive depression, shame, and rage), a sense of power via action and magical substances (the particular mode of externalization); a masturbation substitute and protection against shame-laden sexual impotence, and a feeling of being freed up, "unfrozen" in his object relations. Finally, the drug use was a form of symbolic jail sentence and expiation for the murder.

His acts of violence — which, significantly enough, preceded the taking of drugs (except for considerable drinking and marijuana) — especially the murder, were above all a vindication of his masculinity, a protest against the shame of being not quite a man. The murder was also a concrete crime as an instrument to bring about real expiation in jail for his most massive and still-enduring unconscious guilt, which in turn stemmed from the murderous events around father, mother, and crushed boy. Third, it was a suicide, an aggression turned back again from the self; as he felt, he could just as well have killed himself. Fourth, it was a sadistic counterattack and murder against the humiliating father in a condign substitute figure. And thus fifth, it was a direct defense against unconscious homosexual feelings within the oedipal triangle against these two "disgusting" figures (after all he had had group sex, together with his victim to be). And finally, since the murdered had been a murderer himself, one might wonder whether this was not itself a triumph: to kill the killer, to exact vengeance, revenge supposedly in behalf of society but really in behalf of all the crushed victims on the crushing assassins: the truck driver, father.

This is (except perhaps for his intelligence and articulateness) a typical case history of a patient with the lead symptom of drug dependence. The latter indeed is merely the tip of the iceberg of a most complex, intricate psychopathology, which in turn is intertwined with massive family and social as well as neurophysiological problems. It is obvious that only an equally complex, combined approach can dare to resolve some of this severe pathology.

If anyone doubts that the clinical picture is that dark, it should be added that 90 percent of the patients on a methadone maintenance program show clinical depression and 50 percent abuse alcohol or diazepam while on methadone. Case histories of similar complexity, severity, and tragic depths could have been adduced from all types of compulsive drug use (barbiturates, amphetamines, LSD) — and with no selection. These are very sick patients, most typically combining characteristic features of (near-) psychotic depression, depersonalization, and sociopathy and often of explosive personality disorder. Dynamically narcissism and masochism are most prominent. The whole gamut of defenses are employed, but denial, splitting, and externalization are most marked.

TREATMENT OF DRUG DEPENDENCE

This is in itself a large and important topic and, if treated thoroughly, would encompass a good part of psychiatric therapies. It may be best to subdivide treatment according to the drugs preferentially abused — narcotics, sedatives, stimulants, and psychedelic drugs — acute versus long-term treatment, and treatment of the underlying problems common to all these patients.

Abuse of Narcotics

SHORT-TERM TREATMENT

A number of measures are legally required if one wants to provide a patient with narcotics for conditions not related to severe physical pain. Although the attitude towards these patients has changed from a strictly punitive to a more sympathetic and medically oriented approach, it is still largely encumbered with legal threats, often barely known to the physician. The shadow of official opprobrium still either induces physicians not to treat these people at all or to commit errors which tarnish their reputation, if not their ability to practice.

To verify narcotics addiction one has to note (in writing) "tracks" (discolored scars along the veins) and fresh needle marks, acute withdrawal symptoms (gooseflesh, muscle spasms and twitching, retching, nausea, vomiting, diarrhea, profuse sweating, yawning, running nose and frequent sneezing, insomnia — although all these can occasionally be faked), the results of a urine specimen (24–48 hours after last intake; it may however become negative, which does not preclude addiction), and confirmation from other sources (other agencies, institutions, jail, even friends and relatives). Not all of these may be found, but several of them are necessary to justify appropriate treatment.

Once addiction is ascertained, one may either decide on withdrawal or narcotics maintenance (legally maintained narcotics addiction). Withdrawal is legally restricted to 21 days and often can be completed, without undue hardships, within 7–14 days. Regardless of dosage claimed it is absolutely mandatory not to give a potentially lethal dosage.

A patient who comes for withdrawal or maintenance is never given more than 30 mg methadone (usually 20 mg); in the former instance this dosage is gradually reduced by 5 mg (e.g., every 2–3 days), in the latter the dosage is increased by 10 mg every 3 days until the maintenance dosage is reached (usually 50–80 mg). With narcotics the great danger is overdose, with barbiturates underdosing. Although there is no cross-tolerance, some of the withdrawal symptoms can be alleviated (but not fully removed) with unspecific medication: Valium and Librium, antiemetica (e.g., Compazine) [prochlorperazine] and general sedatives.

The question is often asked what is roughly the equivalence between various narcotics. 10 mg of morphine correspond to 7.5 to 10 mg of methadone, 1.5 mg of Dilaudid, 80 to 100 mg of Demerol (meperidine) and 3 mg of heroin. The content of a "bag" of heroin varies enormously but has been put at 1 to 3 mg (average).

The prognosis of withdrawal treatment, even if combined with intensive rehabilitative efforts, is very poor. Most patients drop out even before completion; nearly all the rest return to drugs shortly thereafter. The success rate is at best a few percent.

The results may, however, be considerably better if such withdrawal is carried out on an inpatient basis, and the patient remains for several months hospitalized, undergoes intensive, combined psychotherapy (individual, group, family Alcoholics Anonymous (AA) and is after discharge followed under strict supervision and therapy. In such instances success rates of 30 to 50 percent have been reported.

Incidentally, withdrawl with the help of methadone is chosen over that with heroin or morphine, due to indications that withdrawal symptoms with the former, though more protracted, are far milder. (This is contested by some patients however.)

LONG-TERM TREATMENT

As just noted, physiological-medical withdrawal treatment in and by itself is hardly successful in the long run and at best merely a first step. Even if a patient can be treated on abstinence, in almost all cases far more treatment is needed, preferably once more a whole array of modalities. Therapeutic communities (e.g., Synanon, Daytop, and many variants), narcotics antagonists (Nalline [nalorphine], cyclazocine, naloxone, naltrexone), behavior modification and threats of punishment, various types of psychotherapy, vocational counseling or rehabilitation, legal and family counseling — all these may become necessary props to prevent a patient from relapsing into street use, criminality, or other severe forms of decompensation (suicide, homicide). Even with these "life-support systems" only a minority of patients are successful; no reliable data are extant to give more than estimates: With therapeutic communities and antagonists the success rate is said to be about 5 percent, if these methods are used alone; in compulsory abstinence, a form of punishment-reward systems, about 25 percent.

The rationale for methadone maintenance simply lies in the factor of cross-tolerance. Once a patient is stabilized on a relatively high narcotics dosage he is tolerant, quasi-immune, to any other high, even lethal dosage of a narcotic. Thus patients on 80 mg of methadone may take as much as 500 mg of additional methadone without killing themselves (ordinarily 50 mg is the lethal dosage) and perhaps 100–200 mg without getting markedly "high." Once stabilized, patients usually do not nod (dream off in an intoxicated sleepy state). It takes 2–4 weeks until stabilization is reached. It is self evident that methadone tolerance is ineffective vis-à-vis drugs of other groups, e.g., Valium, barbiturates, alcohol. Methadone is preferred over other narcotics only because it is effective for 24–36 hours (heroin, 4–8; morphine, 6–12) and can be taken by mouth (it is not rendered ineffective in the liver).

For the nonspecialist it is only important to know that this treatment modality is ruled by very stringent regulations which are simultaneously enforced by an entire group of agencies: the Food and Drug Administration, the Drug Enforcement Agency, and the various states' funding and regulatory agencies. Often these supervisory interventions are ill-coordinated, even haphazard, and occasionally in contradiction to standards of medical ethics. Some of the most important rules are at least two years of addiction, written verification (as spelled out above), minimum age of eighteen, at least one prior attempt at detoxification (verified), and no take-home medication for at least three months on the program. Further requirements are annual physical examinations and a reevaluation after two years by the physician, documenting why the patient should *not* be withdrawn. No private physician can start a program on his own but must have a special license to run such a program on the specific location. Some of the many preconditions are guarantees for minimum coverage by physicians on the premises of the program in directly patient-related (i.e., nonadministrative) activities (currently 24 hours a week for 200 patients), regularly controlled security measures (safes, alarms), and a minimum supportive staff. There are frequent inspections by the state and federal agencies to scrutinize the compliance in all regards (most painstakingly in regard to the charts). It is wise for anyone involved in such a program regularly to check whether the regulations have been altered and also whether very many apparently day-to-day decisions of an emergency nature (change in dosage, take-home schedules, staffing) abide by the official, at the moment valid laws. It is no exaggeration to state that the "sponsor" (the legally responsible physician) walks continually on the edge of illegality and of forfeiting his license.

He also should be aware that the lures of corruption and abuse of power in such a program are so great that many of the less well paid employees (nurses and counselors), and even some prominent people involved succumb to the temptation but that misdeeds are most difficult to prove and eliminate because of the often prevailing conspiracy of silence between patients and staff. It takes often years (if that!) to document malfeasance which had been suspected all along and to take remedial action.

Finally, it also has to be reemphasized that in methadone maintenance only an individually adjusted combination of treatments will be successful, as far as full social rehabilitation is concerned. Dependent on initial selection of patients, stability of structure, and combination with the above mentioned, misleadingly dubbed "ancillary" services (psychotherapy, counseling, other psychotropic drugs), the success rate varies between 50 percent and 90 percent.

Addiction to Sedatives

Since all of these drugs (barbiturates, other sleeping medication, minor tranquilizers) are highly addictive (with Nembutal and Seconal 400 mg/day, with Valium 100 mg/day, with meprobamate about 1600 mg/day) careful attention to physical dependence and very cautious treatment are mandatory.

The American Medical Association's (AMA) Committee on Alcoholism and Addiction and Council on Mental Health [1] (*JAMA* 193:673–677, 1965; copyright 1965, American Medical Association) describes the withdrawal syndrome as follows:

> Sudden and abrupt withdrawal of barbiturates from a person who is physically dependent results in definite abstinence signs and symptoms. Their intensity varies according to the dose taken, the length of time the patient has been physically dependent, the degree of intoxication produced by doses consumed, and individual factors which remain incompletely understood. During the first eight hours after abrupt withdrawal, signs and symptoms of intoxication decline and the patient appears to improve. As these signs and symptoms recede, increasing anxiety, headache, twitching of various muscle

groups, nervousness, tremor, weakness, impaired cardiovascular responses when standing, and vomiting become evident. They become fairly intensive after 16 hours of abstinence and are rather severe after 24 hours. Between the 30th and 48th hours of withdrawal, convulsions of grand mal type are very likely to occur. Occasionally, convulsive seizures are observed as early as the 16th hour and as late as the eighth day. Frequently, there is a period of post-convulsive confusion lasting for one or two hours. At times, there will be increasing insomnia culminating in a state of delirium, closely resembling delirium tremens and characterized by confusion, marked tremors, disorientation, hallucinations, and delusions. Ordinarily the delirium lasts less than five days and ends with a prolonged period of sleep.

Even though no treatment is given, the entire withdrawal syndrome is usually a self-limited condition. Clinical recovery appears to be complete and no organic sequelae are known to occur. However, patients have died during uncontrolled, untreated barbiturate-withdrawal syndromes [1:676].

On treatment of the withdrawal syndrome the AMA committees made the following statement:

Since significant abstinence symptoms and signs do not occur even after long-term ingestion of comparatively small doses (less than five therapeutic doses in 24 hours), it is *theoretically* possible to withdraw patients on a small-dosage regimen on an ambulatory basis. However, this is rarely successful, as it requires the complete cooperation of a person who probably has a strong psychological dependence on the drug.

Withdrawal of persons with strong physical dependence may be life-threatening and can only be accomplished satisfactorily, and with reasonable safety, in a drug-free environment where hospital and nursing facilities are available.

When barbiturates are the addicting drug, withdrawal must be accomplished very slowly and carefully. Manifestations of mild barbiturate abstinence, such as anxiety, weakness, nausea, and tremor, signal the danger of impending convulsions and/or psychosis. Patients in this condition should be given a short-acting barbiturate at once. Experience has demonstrated that sodium pentobarbital, 200–400 mg (3–6 grains) orally or parenterally, is extremely effective. If the syndrome is not relieved within one hour, the dose should be repeated. Subsequent withdrawal consists of a graduated, four-times-daily administration of barbiturates, at the dose level which just maintains a mild degree of intoxication. Usually 200–300 mg (3–4 grains) of sodium pentobarbital, four times a day, will suffice. Clinical evidence of sedation is essential. Further reduction can begin after one or two days of observation, but the dosage should not be reduced more than 100 mg (1½ grains) daily. If abstinence signs or symptoms recur, the dosage should be temporarily increased. Close observation is required because of concomitant mental confusion, lethargy, muscular incompetence, apprehension, and possible convulsions. Supportive measures such as restoration of electrolyte balance, proper hydration with I.V. fluids, and vitamins are also in order.

The usual nursing care and ward routine applicable to patients with convulsive disorders, confusion, or delirium states should be maintained [1:677]. Recently the use of the longer acting phenobarbital has been recommended.

On Definitive treatment and aftercare the AMA committees advised:

The role of the physician does not terminate when withdrawal of the drug from the patient has been completed. This is actually the real starting point for meeting the problem of any patient's drug dependence. Continuing contact and help are essential and must be maintained over a long period. If such help is not forthcoming, relapse to the use of drugs is almost inevitable. Each drug-dependent person must be treated as an individual and should have a complete medical, psychological, and sociological assessment. He should receive the best available treatment in terms of his own particular psychological, physical, and sociological needs.

Psychiatric referral, as indicated and feasible, should be made on either a public or private basis. The general practitioner can also administer such forms of psychotherapy as he is qualified to carry out. Even in cases where specific psychotherapy is not feasible, the physician can function effectively in a supportive and rehabilitative role, helping the drug dependent patient to develop ways of handling tensions and anxieties without resorting to drugs.

Physicians should play an important role in the mobilization of social resources for aftercare and in providing supervision and follow-up treatment. The use of community resources, such as voluntary and governmental social agencies, can be of great value to the physician in his treatment of the drug-dependent person. Any effort that may contribute toward better adjustment in social, cultural, economic, and industrial spheres is specifically indicated in the rehabilitation of the patient.

State civil statutes providing for compulsory in and out-patient treatment, rehabilitation, and follow-up of persons suffering from dependence on sedative drugs have been very helpful. Unfortunately, few states have such laws. In general, such statutes should be comparable to the modern and enlightened statutes for the commitment of mentally ill persons [1:677].

Psychological Dependence on Stimulants

Often very high doses of stimulants — amphetamines, Ritalin (methylphenidate), and cocaine — are taken (e.g., 100–200 mg of amphetamines) which may lead to the earlier described states of severe psychopathology. Since there is no physiological dependence, withdrawal can be carried through at once. The paranoid symptoms are signs of the overdose, not of withdrawal; hence no substitution with stimulants is needed; but, if severe enough, phenothiazines (as with an ordinary schizophrenic psychosis) are indicated. The usual severe fatigue and depression following withdrawal may necessitate antidepressant therapy if massive enough.

Indeed, patients may become suicidal because of the underlying depression which prompted the compulsive use of stimulants in the first place.

Psychological Dependence on Psychedelic Drugs

Acute states of hallucinosis and delusions (bad trips) need mostly supportive psychotherapy (talking down) in a quiet, calm environment (e.g., not in the emergency room). Usually it is not necessary to give phenothiazines either in acute or chronic states, but they are recommended in serious states. In PCP intoxication, however, they are contraindicated. Instead, diazepam, 10 mg im repeatedly is useful.

Treatment Common to All Types of Compulsive Drug Users

One thing is clear above all: the clinician cannot do "business as usual" with compulsive drug users. They resemble in many regards psychotic patients. Despite the usually dismal prognosis it is important to state that I have seen a number of very severe chronic drug abusers successfully in long-term therapy. For example, there were several patients who had been dependent for ten to twenty years on very high doses of amphetamines (100 mg and more) or similar stimulants or of narcotics (with dosages of 100–800 mg of methadone daily) who were seen for one or several years. Reviewing these I can recall one precondition of treatment that has facilitated successful treatment in several instances: the readiness on both sides for intensive, analytically oriented work and to stick it out no matter what. Intensive means, often, in times of crises, three to seven sessions a week, and sometimes much longer than one hour, in addition to telephone availability in times of lesser urgency. Some cases decompensate repeatedly and necessitate brief hospitalizations (e.g., for suicidality in the case of amphetamine abstinence — often many months after withdrawal) but are able to work out their problems sufficiently in such very intensive psychotherapy so that they are not only capable of assuming highly responsible positions but eventually also to enter psychoanalysis proper. Given the severely regressive nature of the entire personality organization, it becomes clear that the treatment situation has to encompass the following built-in transference elements:

1. It has to have strongly nurturing, supportive elements without, however, feeding into the often overwhelming fears in the toxicomanic patient of engulfment. The therapist has to be far more active, warm, interested, personally involved (yet again without becoming intrusive, as very often the mother was).

2. Also in all instances the exact counterpart has to be observed as well: to maintain distance, to be very patient, not pressuring, almost detached (without, however, supporting the profound sense of abandonment and despair so deep in these patients). One has to create a clear boundary of separateness, an atmosphere of nonsymbiosis and respect for individuality, while still allowing symbiotic conflicts to be expressed, to become interpretable, and not have the patient feel exploited and treated as a nonhuman object, no matter how much he tries to do that himself unto the therapist.

3. Limit setting, external structure, is absolutely crucial. Time and again the patient needs to be faced with the alternative of curtailing some particularly noxious form of acting-out or of forfeiting any true benefit from therapy and even the gains already attained. Each intervention is a crisis for the therapy. The patient may concur and work on the intense anger this limitsetting evokes, with additional gain in self-control and, with that, in the ability to observe himself and in the working alliance. Or he may revolt and vanish, seeing the guardianship of the therapist over boundaries and limits yet as a new form of entrapment. Therefore such interventions have to be used sparingly and without any moralistic implications: transgression of ethical or of any other boundaries has to be treated strictly as a symptom with severe self-destructive potential, the compulsiveness of which is the sole concern, not its antisocial (or socially positive) valence.

4. This leads to problems of countertransference. Outrageous disregard of limits is often enacted precisely to provoke rage, punishment and scorn from the therapist and thus to reconfirm the masochistic triumph: "No one can ever be trusted. I am suffering again betrayal and degradation, and thus I prove the basic unworth of human relationships; I can rely only on my actions and on nonhuman substances."

Or, in turn, the therapist becomes a masochistic partner, forced by the ostentatious suffering of the patient into endless giving and giving-in, or into going along with and thus once again indulging the severest, most pernicious regressions.

Again the therapist has to find a golden means: to set actively limits, but without anger, sadism, shaming, and vindictiveness, and yet to be very flexible, patient, always oriented not towards ethical values in a narrow sense but towards the central psychoanalytic value outlined elsewhere [20].

5. This *demand for giving* and indulgence may in some cases be overwhelming, especially in massively spoiled or severely neglected patients. The transference-countertransference bind may turn into a sadomasochistic nightmare, a severe negative therapeutic reaction and hence into defeat: Rage, pain, hopelessness alternate with insatiable demands. Here

the dilution of the dyadic therapy relationship may save both treatment and life. In a number of cases the splitting up of the therapeutic approaches, e.g., into a combination of individual, family, and group therapy, carried out by different therapists, proved far superior to individual psychotherapy alone.

6. Whereas the just-mentioned type of transference-countertransference constellation is a kind of perversion of intimacy, the next is a type of distancing which can reach extreme proportions. In many patients it may take a real therapeutic moratorium of months (even years) of passive drifting, boredom, interrupted treatment, apparent endless stagnation, a deep gloom, despair, and hopelessness (and at times effectively transmitted to the therapist) until a solid basis of trust has grown to start therapy in earnest.

This moratorium of passivity might be necessary not just because of the deep fear of intimacy, of the claustrum, and thus of the devouring, englutting mother but also (and connected with it) of the dread of the murderous aggression unleashed in the submission to the power of the stronger "other."

In order to tolerate such a lengthy moratorium the therapist has not only to be patient and rather at peace with his own narcissistic needs, but it is likely that he needs two additional traits: First, he has to see in the patient strongly redeeming features, e.g., in the case of Andreas there was an intense feeling in the therapist through the years of despair: "What a waste of a capable, likeable, highly gifted, basically honest person!" In this feeling of respect and esteem for him, there was of course a lot of hope, which kept outweighing nearly always the massive despair. Secondly, the therapist has, as Freud stressed, to subordinate his therapeutic zeal to the scientific curiosity: to understand, to help, to understand must take precedence over the wish to heal, to mold according to one's own value priorities. To wait may mean to build up trust and to show caring; but then to step in and to set the right limits at the right moment may be critically important.

7. The working alliance was defined by R. Greenson as "the relatively nonneurotic, rational rapport which the patient has with his analyst" [7:46]. I believe this concept to be equally applicable to the analytically oriented psychotherapy chosen with these patients. In most instances these patients are too sick, too self-destructive, too demanding, to leave much room for such rational cooperation. At first it merely consists of a gut reaction: "I have suffered enough; I want to start anew. The price I paid in the past I am not willing to pay in the future." Thus it is not so much the value of rationality which attracts them but the fear of further pain and suffering which pushes them from behind. But as the time

passes (again often years) an identification with the value of inner free-dom, of self-mastery, of noncondemning exploration and knowledge, as represented by the therapist, may replace the more archaic ego ideals, and gradually lend more and more force to rationality and thus to the work-ing alliance. Hence, shame and guilt may become associated with such a standard of reason instead of the grandiose self-image which had ruled supreme.

Large-scale Treatment Policy

Heavy (compulsive) drug use is coexistensive with moderate to severe psychopathology underlying the drug use, not caused by it. The crisis in the treatment of these patients who are either rejected or inadequately treated by the currently existing programs is also coextensive with the crisis in the treatment of emotionally disturbed or outright mentally ill pa-tients in general. Innovative facilities should be created, employing the gamut of already known psychiatric techniques to this class of patients; it appears imperative to develop and implement innovative psycho-therapeutic techniques specifically for this type of pathology — combin-ing in-depth dynamic (psychoanalytic) understanding and leadership, structure building and limit setting, family treatment, vocational retrain-ing (or new training), opening up of creative or recreational avenues of gratification, and the flexible use of psychopharmacological agents. In other words: Instead of one track modalities, combinations of four to seven methods for each individual patient in a methodical specific way is needed.

Such a plan calls for the avoidance of many of the current faddish short-cuts and fashionable new simplistic techniques because of their de-structive potential with these severely ill patients. It requires a deeper in-volvement, in the positions of leadership, by psychiatrists and psychoan-alysts in dealing with the majority of the problems of compulsive drug use. The current debunking of a thorough training in psychiatry — and especially in intensive individual psychotherapy — and, with that, the nearly total lack of understanding for the psychodynamics of these pa-tients and their families has been devastating for psychiatry in general; but it has left the field of treatment of these patients almost entirely to paraprofessionals and to specialists from other fields who are naive about the gravity and nature of the psychopathology in the majority of these cases as well as the measures on devising rational treatment strategies for each individual case.

DIFFERENTIAL DIAGNOSIS

To pose the diagnosis of acute drug influence is not too difficult: Incoherence, slowness in talking, slurred speech, and atactic gait are indicative for intoxication with any depressant drug: sleeping medication of any kind, moderate to high doses of tranquilizers, alcohol, narcotics. Pinpoint pupils are characteristic for any narcotic (opiate and opioid), bloodshot sclerae for alcohol. Lower dosages can, however, be easily dissembled, and all too frequently the physician does not think of this possibility and overlooks a dangerous state. The differential diagnosis reaches to nearly all organic types of intoxication and brain dysfunction — from inhalation of noxious gases over endocrine disorders to brain tumors and strokes.

Chronic use of these depressant drugs is often unsuspected because the established tolerance gives a picture of emotional stability. All signs of acute intoxication may be absent, except, for example, for the pinpoint pupil in narcotic addicts, dilated capillaries in alcohol addicts, and some slurring of speech in barbiturate addicts. Here the clinician has to resort to indirect signs which we shall come back to shortly.

The pressure of speech, paranoid ideation, incoherence evoked by stimulants (cocaine, amphetamines) may mimic manic or paranoid states, hyperthyroidosis and a few other organic illnesses. But amazingly often intensive use can go undetected even by a seasoned observer.

Mild to severe use of psychedelics (including cannabis) may be marked by slight to moderate disjointedness of talking, a slight disintegration and incoherence, and a rambling quality of talking, of missing the point, and not getting to the point. Some are "spaced out," silent for brief or longer periods. In such severer states the picture may resemble those of milder thought disorders in schizophrenics. But once again, even severe users may lack all of these signs.

The best way to obtain a clear diagnosis is a thorough physical examination. It is obvious that most patients who inject drugs (narcotics, stimulants) show severe track marks all over their body, mostly in the cubital fossae, the forearms, and the dorsal side of hands and feet. Often signs of old and new abscesses, lymphedema, and elephantiasis are unmistakable.

In all cases of possible drug involvement a urine test should be done. It requires specialized methods (mostly thin layer and gas chromatography, enzyme tests); every local drug abuse program can advise the physician on where to send the urine. The costs are very modest.

The urine should be taken under supervision. Not only may they give the urine of someone else, but they may prick their finger while urinating to feign kidney stones. It may be advisable to have such a urine drugscreen in all patients who request strong pain medication because the ruses to lure physicians into prescribing narcotics or other strong analgesics are innumerable. Some patients are extremely knowledgeable: feigning convincingly serious, very painful illnesses (trigeminus-neuralgia, nephrolithiasis, angina pectoris, Crohn's disease) and skillfully mispronouncing "helpful drugs" which had alleviated their suffering in the past.

PROGNOSIS

All types of compulsive drug users (except where the drug dependency was induced during a severe physical illness and in the absence of the specific psychiatric predisposition) are a priori severely disturbed patients, as the case examples showed. Therefore both the lead symptom of drug dependence as well as the underlying serious psychopathology has often as dismal a prognosis as a chronic or recurrent psychosis. And still it is striking that, given the patience and skill and the afore described combination of treatment methods, a good many severely ill patients can be rehabilitated. However, just like with most other psychiatric or somatic illnesses, the best that may be hoped for is not a total cure but social rehabilitation and emotional recompensation which may collapse again from time to time. Expectations must be modest and cannot demand of these severely disturbed people to jump over their often very dark shadows.

This particular illness has been given large space because more and more forms of psychopathology are complicated, coped with, hidden, with the help of drug dependency, due to the near universal accessibility and availability of psychotropic, habituating substances, legal or illegal. Moreover, many cultural and social factors support the resorting to this magical means for dealing with otherwise intractable inner problems. Thus drug abuse in general, and drug dependence in particular have become as widespread and obtrusive a problem for physicians as hysterical, psychosomatic, and depressive disorders in the past. As a matter of fact, these latter forms may nowadays be masked by the drugs at discussion.

There is no question that the many faces of drug dependence will form an ever expanding part of psychiatric and medical practice — though unduly neglected still by current training of future physicians.

REFERENCES

1   American Medical Association Committee on Alcoholism and Addiction and Council on Mental Health. Dependence on barbiturates and other sedative drugs. *JAMA.* 193:673–677, 1965.

2   Casswell, S., and Marks, D. F. Cannabis and temporal disintegration in experienced and naive subjects. *Science* 179:803–805, 1972.

3   Chein, I., Gerard, D. L., Lee, R. S., and Rosenfeld, E. *The road to H.* New York: Basic Books, 1964.

4   Cohen, S. Marijuana today. *Drug Abuse Alcohol. Newsl.* 4:1, 1975.

5   Ellinwood, E. H. Assault and homicide associated with amphetamine abuse. *Am. J. Psychiatry* 127:1170–1175, 1971.

6   Freud, S. "The Dynamics of Transference," 1912. In *Standard edition,* vol. 12, ed. J. Strachey, p. 99. London: Hogarth Press, 1958.

7   Greenson, R. R. *The technique and practice of psychoanalysis.* New York: International Universities Press, 1967.

8   Hollister, L. *Marijuana in man: Three years later. Science* 172:21–29, 1971.

9   Jaffe, J. H. "Narcotic analgesics" In *The pharmacological basis of therapeutics,* 3rd ed., eds. L. S. Goodman and A. Gilman, pp. 247–311. New York: Macmillan, 1965.

10 Kolb, L. *Drug addiction: A medical problem.* Springfield, Ill.: Thomas, 1962.

11 Krystal, H. "The genetic development of affects and affect regression." *The annual of psychoanalysis,* vol. 2, pp. 93–126. New York: International Universities Press, 1974.

12 Krystal, H., and Raskin, H. A. *Drug dependence. Aspects of ego functions.* Detroit: Wayne State University Press, 1970.

13 Lemere, F. Communication in *Hospital Tribune,* Dangers of Alcohol. 29 January 1968.

14 Rado, S. The psychoanalysis of pharmacothymia (drug addiction). *Psychoanal. Q.* 2:1–23, 1933.

15 Sassenrath, E. N. Test monkeys display marijuana syndrome. *J.A.M.A.* 233:1251–1255, 1975.

16. Shafer, R. P. Second report of National Commission on Marijuana and Drug Abuse. Washington, D.C.: Government Printing Office, 1973.

17 Tucker, G. J., Quinlan, D., and Harrow, M. Chronic hallucinogenic use and thought disturbance. *Arch. Gen. Psychiatry* 27:443–447, 1972.

18 World Health Organization. Twentieth report of the Expert Committee on Drug Dependence. Geneva: World Health Organization, 1974.

19 Wurmser, L. Psychoanalytic considerations of the etiology of compulsive drug use. *J. Am. Psychoanal. Assn.* 32:820–843, 1974.

20 Wurmser, L. *Drug abuse: The hidden dimension.* New York: Jason Aronson, in press.

V
Psychophysiological and Other Psychiatric Disorders

19

Psychophysiological Disorders

Eleanore M. Jantz, Ph.D.,
Virginia Huffer, M.D., and
Daniel J. Freedenburg III, M.D.

The designation *psychophysiological disorder* attempting, as it were, to combine psychological and physiological phenomena, refers to a distinct class of disorders of vast complexity requiring a multidisciplinary approach for their study. A comprehensive review of what is an enormous body of literature will not be presented here; rather, an attempt will be made to present the basic theoretical issues from an historical perspective and to mention studies of special significance in the area of psychiatry. Readers interested in a general view of the field are referred to Lipowski [14], Reiser [18], and Freedman and colleagues [8].

It is only relatively recently — since the 1930s — that there appeared the first systematic theory of what were then called psychosomatic disorders but which are today more commonly termed psychophysiological disorders. Currently a distinction is often made in the usage of these terms, and it is useful to clarify this distinction in order to avoid confusion. The original designation psychosomatic is synonymous with the present psychophysiological as used in this chapter, whereas today the concept of psychosomatic represents the broad view in medicine that psyche and soma are indivisible, so that, regardless of etiology, every illness has a psychological component which may be either antecedent or secondary to the illness and which is viewed as a complicating factor to be included in the treatment. The term psychophysiological, on the other hand, is restricted to certain physical disorders of presumed psychogenic origin, involving organ systems that are under the innervation of the autonomic and neuroendocrine systems [3].

The assumption underlying the contemporary concept of these disorders is that the direction at the onset of illness is from a dysphoric emotion (for example, anxiety or hostility) to a physical symptom as an outcome. As if to underscore this assumption, the *Diagnostic and Statistical Manual of Mental Disorders* (DSM-II) defines psychophysiological disorders as "characterized by physical symptoms that are caused by emotional factors" [3:46–47]. It is important to recognize this assumption for what it is and to realize that all the data so far gathered are strictly correlative and, in fact, tell nothing about causes. Indeed, the evidence to date suggests that the phenomenon is so complex and multifactored that we may not be able to unravel the mechanisms subserving the process.

In psychiatry the theoretical concepts have been addressed to the psychological determinants of why and under what circumstances these correlations occur. This is the main focus of the present chapter. The question of how and by what mechanisms psychophysiological disorders occur seems more in the province of physiology and neurobiology.

As an illustration of the problems and questions that arise in treating a psychophysiological disorder, consider the following actual clinical history of a patient with ulcerative colitis.

> Mary was a twenty-year-old student in her third year at a small liberal arts college for women. She was seen in psychiatric consultation about a week after being admitted to a general hospital for treatment of a massive rectal hemorrhage, diagnosed as acute, fulminating ulcerative colitis. In addition to the involvement of the colon there was painful arthritic-type swelling of some of her joints.
>
> The precipitating events were immediate: Midyear examinations were to be given several days hence. The students, already tense, were further disturbed by new conditions for passing that had just been laid down by the dean. They decided to protest; five were nominated as a group to represent the student body with their complaints to the dean. When they entered the dean's office, Mary was pushed ahead to become the speaker. She had barely stated their complaints when she was interrupted by a vituperative tirade from the dean that Mary perceived as directed toward her alone. "How dare she question the dean's wisdom and be so impertinent as to

complain, etc., etc." The five students quickly backed out of the office; within three or four hours Mary developed massive rectal bleeding.

Of the five students, why was Mary the only one to show such intense reaction? Why did she not perceive the dean as unreasonable, even tyrannical, and judge the rebuke as a manifestation of the woman's personality? Indeed, she might have reacted in any number of different ways. For example, she might have responded with anger or hostility; she might have become anxious or depressed with transient insomnia and loss of appetite; she might have manifested phobic fear if required to leave the security of her room. Instead, she developed a classical psychophysiological illness. One must ask why Mary developed a physical illness rather than a neurosis? And finally one must ask why did she develop this particular illness rather than some other, such as migraine or asthma, for example. Thus there are three major questions: Why this student? Why a physical rather than an emotional symptom? And why this particular organ system?

The background information gathered over a period of about a year in psychotherapy sheds some light on why Mary alone had such a profound psychophysiological reaction. Some of the antecedent circumstances that made her psychologically vulnerable in this instance are described here.

Mary was the only child of a middle-class family, born and raised in a small town about fifty miles from the college. She described her mother in terms that suggested a suspicious, somewhat paranoid personality, while the father was described as a quiet, emotionally distant person. Since childhood, Mary had been aware that she wished her parents had been different, more warm and giving of affection. However, she found these qualities in neighboring families whom she unconsciously perceived as surrogate parents. In growing up she was liked by her neighbors, peers, and school teachers, and as far as could be determined, she had progressed through her developing years to young womanhood with no evidence of personality problems. In retrospect it can be understood that she had certain emotional and dependency needs that were only partially fulfilled and that she was still trying to satisfy in an immature manner.

After high school Mary had first studied at a large university where she had met a young man, Paul, to whom she became informally engaged. She frequently visited Paul's parents, whom she liked tremendously: She felt that she had found her ideal family. After two years at the university, Paul transferred to a distant school where he could pursue a course of study not offered by the university, and Mary transferred to the women's college. Ostensibly she transferred because she considered the Romance language department to be superior to that of the university; actually, and probably not coincidentally, the college was closer to where Paul's parents lived. She continued to visit them frequently in Paul's absence.

In November of that year Mary visited Paul at his new school for the weekend of an important dance. When she returned, she sensed a distance and coldness on the part of Paul's parents because they disapproved of her having spent the weekend without a chaperone. This tension continued even during Paul's return during the Christmas recess, so that she felt unwelcome to visit them after he left in early January.

Then, too, the dean had acquired a personal significance for Mary. Dean Smith had been born in the same small town as Mary. For that reason, the dean had paid special attention to her and had even hinted that she felt that Mary was like a daughter to her. Mary obviously had responded with delight to this implied parent-child relationship and had suppressed any recognition of the authoritarian and autocratic characteristics of this woman. It was in the context of Mary's dependence on surrogate parents for emotional support and the seeming rejection by Paul's parents that the verbal denunciation and rejection by the dean was experienced as an overwhelming threat, with more emotional meaning for Mary than for the other students.

Few would doubt the temporal relation between the psychic stress brought on by the threat of loss of support and the onset of physical illness in Mary's case. But why ulcerative colitis? As far as Mary could remember she had never had any prior bowel difficulties to suggest a predisposition; nor could she recall any childhood problems related to bowel training to suggest that colitis was a symbolic expression of her hostility toward the frustrating parent figures. One might speculate that Mary's available ego defense mechanisms of identification and substitution were inadequate to cope with rejection from those upon whom she depended for approval. However, why a psychophysiological rather than a more restricted psychological reaction, and why colitis rather than some other disorder are questions still to be answered by investigators in the field.

HISTORICAL PERSPECTIVE

The association of physical changes and states of emotionality has been recognized since ancient times. However, even today the precise nature of this relationship is only just beginning to be clarified. It is accepted subjectively that psychological events (emotions) are normally expressed physiologically, so that one speaks of weeping in sorrow, blushing with embarrassment, paling with fear, or of experiencing a flutter of the heart in excitement. Beyond these normal and temporary physiological changes, however, in some individuals pathological and often irreversible changes in organ tissue functions resulting in illness can occur in relation to stressful conditions of extreme intensity and/or duration.

In the early twentieth century Cannon [4] demonstrated that physiological changes occurred in association with emotional responses to various conditions. His observations led him to postulate that the bodily changes seen in emotional states such as rage and fear constituted an "emergency reaction" that activated an organism for "fight or flight." His hypothesis that the autonomic nervous system acted as an emergency response system may be said to have ushered in the era of psychosomatic medicine.

Franz Alexander [2], using Cannon's activation physiology as a base, developed the specificity hypothesis which stated that intrapsychic conflicts blocked an effective release of tension and that specific conflicts gave rise to disorders of specific organ systems. Alexander and his colleagues identified seven diseases which they considered to be typical psychophysiological reactions: essential hypertension, hyperthyroidism, neurodermatitis, peptic ulcer, rheumatoid arthritis, ulcerative colitis, and bronchial asthma. There are, to be sure, many other disorders in which emotional factors may play an exacerbating role in their overt onset. These include migraine, tension headaches, paroxysmal tachycardia, irritable bowel syndrome, and anorexia nervosa, to name only a few. By means of the other unique aspect of this theory, the introduction of organ specificity, Alexander hoped to demonstrate that a specific psychodynamic constellation subtended a specific disease. Moreover, the dynamics of one disease should not be seen in any other disorder. It should be noted that the theory attempts to explain only the etiology of the various disorders, not their pathogenesis.

An important distinction was made early by Alexander in the separation of psychophysiological reactions (PPR) from hysterical conversion reactions by the following criteria [1]:

PPR	*Conversion reactions*
1. Organs and viscera innervated by the autonomic nervous system affected.	1. Organs of special sense and body parts under control of voluntary nervous system.
2. Symptoms fail to relieve anxiety.	2. Symptoms bind anxiety.
3. Symptoms have no symbolic meaning.	3. Symptoms are symbolic of the underlying conflict.

<table>
<tr><td>4. Structural change that may be life threatening frequently produced.</td><td>4. No structural change produced, unless secondary to atrophy of disuse.</td></tr>
</table>

Alexander postulated three essential elements for the development of a psychosomatic (psychophysiological) symptom [1,2]:

1   A specific psychodynamic constellation, i.e., a particular personality configuration with a certain defense structure, and the existence of an unconscious psychic conflict. The conflicts central to the psychodynamic formulation are the wish to incorporate, receive, or take in; the wish to eliminate, soil, or attack; and the wish to retain or accumulate. Simply stated, the unconscious conflict is dependency versus aggression.

2   A specific onset situation, i.e., a situation that exacerbates the psychic conflict for a given individual.

3   An X factor or a constitutional factor, i.e., the contribution of genetic, constitutional, and developmental predisposing conditions.

Alexander claimed that no single element was sufficient; all three had to be present for a symptom to occur. Stemming from a psychoanalytic tradition, Alexander concentrated on the psychodynamic element and paid little attention to the other two. To the present day the three elements postulated by Alexander are generally accepted as necessary for the development of a psychophysiological disorder. Other investigators have chosen to follow one or another of these lines of approach to an understanding of how these disorders are caused, and they shall be grouped according to which avenue they have followed.

FURTHER PSYCHODYNAMIC FORMULATIONS

Like Alexander, the early investigators of psychophysiological disorders sought for specific cause-and-effect relations, and many present-day investigators continue in this tradition even though they may focus on elements that were given scant attention by Alexander and his immediate followers.

Flanders Dunbar [6] attempted to show that certain personality constellations were associated with specific psychophysiological disorders. As an example of continuity, many years later, Friedman and Rosenman [9] proposed two personality types. Type A personalities manifest an intense, sustained drive for achievement and are continually involved in competition and deadlines, both at work and in their avocations. They are much more likely to suffer cardiac disorder than Type B personalities, who show a pattern characterized by relative absence of drive, ambition, sense of urgency, and desire for competition.

Other investigators, such as Grinker [10], Deutsch [5], and Schur [20], differed from Alexander in that they emphasized not so much the presence of conflict but the breakdown of ego defenses in the presence of threat. Although Grinker and, later, Engel were concentrating on psychological defense mechanisms, the concept of a breakdown in the defense structure is somewhat analogous to Hans Selye's [21,22] theory of a physiological breakdown of the body's normal adaptive mechanisms during prolonged stress.

Engel and Schmale [7,19] proposed that psychophysiological disorders developed from the individual's state of hopelessness and helplessness in a situation in which loss is experienced. It was felt that helplessness represented a feeling of deprivation of gratification as a result of a change in the relationship with another individual in which nothing could be done to correct the situation. Hopelessness became a feeling of frustration, despair, and futility resulting from a loss of satisfaction that had been provided by another object (source). As a result, the individual feels that he is unable to cope or find a solution. They concluded that disease was a breakdown of the positive adaptive mechanisms of the organism when homeostasis could no longer be maintained or restored. Psychologically, it represented an attitude of giving up all resistance to threat. Engel postulated that the physiological responses associated with psychological "giving up" may be a fundamental biological danger response state, *conservation withdrawal,* teleologically to conserve energy. He considered that such physiological responses would act in a nonspecific fashion by making the organism less resistant to many kinds of pathogenic factors. Furthermore, the giving-up process could become generalized to include all types of disease.

Psychogenetically, Engel and Schmale [7] hypothesized the subjective state of helplessness relates to the infant's early awareness of dependence on others for his source of gratification (nine to sixteen months); whereas the child aged three to six years experiences hopelessness when he perceives he cannot be in the preferred love relationship with the mother or father. By substituting other objects for these early sources of satisfaction, the individual may thwart the feelings of hopelessness and helplessness after a loss. The Engel-Schmale theory is very neat and attractive, since it attempts to correlate psychic mechanisms with clinical presentation and seems to form a concise explanation. The main objection to this theory is the absence of any control study of individuals who experience the same affects without developing disease.

CONSTITUTIONAL FORMULATIONS

Just as Cannon [4] is the originator of the concept of homeostasis, Selye [21] is the acknowledged father of the concept of stress.

Since the introduction of this term, stress has been used to signify many things. To some it has meant a noxious stimulus or external threat to which the organism could be expected to react with pain and anxiety or other dysphoric emotion. Much confusion resulted from psychological experiments in which individual subjects failed to respond uniformly in expected ways to such externally controlled "stress." A careful distinction must be made between the stimulus as a stressor and the response of the organism as a state of stress. In reading the literature in this area, it is helpful to bear in mind from what point of view the author defines stress.

In Selye's [21] theory, stress is defined not as a stimulus condition but as a general adaptive response of the organism to a variety of stimuli which may be psychological or physical. It is thus not a theory of specificity. In this view, stress is defined as the response of the body marked by adaptive changes in the homeostatic balance such as occur in strong emotional states and disease. These changes involve the autonomic and neuroendocrine systems, principally the pituitary-adrenal cortical system, in what Selye termed the *general adaptation syndrome* (GAS). Rejecting the notion of specificity, he carried Cannon's concept of the emergency reaction one step further by postulating that the GAS was activated in all arousal conditions, whether they be physiological, psychological, or environmental; pleasant or unpleasant.

It is interesting that in his most recent formulation, Seyle [22] views the higher cortical functions (cognitions) as having a role in the inhibition or modification of the stress reaction. In this view, psychological as well as genetic and constitutional factors come to play a key role in determining how the organism may respond to a stimulus that is potentially a stressor; and in this way Selye accounts for individual differences in responding to specific situations. Psychological attitudes are perceived by Selye to be potentially capable of minimizing the stress reaction and of enhancing resistance. The reverse is also possible; negative attitudes can enhance stress. This is because psychophysiological stress is determined by one's perception or interpretation of an event or situation.

Attacking the problem of individual differences from another approach, Lacey and Lacey [12] investigated the hypothesis of individual autonomic response-stereotypy, according to which individuals could be characterized by the consistency of their idiosyncratic response patterns to a wide range of stimuli. Using such physiological measures as blood pressure, skin resistance, and heart rate, among others, they found that some subjects responded with increased skin resistance, others with increased heart rate, and so forth, whatever the stressor. From this they speculated that symptom specificity in psychophysiological disorders is the end result of an exaggerated and rigidly stereotyped response which may be evident long before frank psychophysiological disorders occur. Thus, individuals could be identified as "muscle reactors" or "cardiovascular reactors," and so forth.

The experimental work of the Laceys appears to support the concept of organ vulnerability as a predisposing X-factor in Alexander's three essential elements. According to this concept, the specific organ affected in a psychophysiological disorder may be likened to a weak link in a chain. Whatever the cause, it is vulnerable to strain and thus more likely to dysfunction when the body is subjected to a stressor. For example, the allergic factors in bronchial asthma and in neurodermatitis are necessary, if not sufficient, conditions for the onset of these illnesses.

Increasingly, the results of research have led away from theories in which a single or specific factor was thought to induce a specific disorder to theories in which it is recognized that in man there are multiple levels of interaction contributing to his being a functional or dysfunctional organism at any given moment. Mason [15] has been perhaps the most articulate proponent of this point of view. In discussing psychological aspects of psychosomatic disorders, he has pointed out that psychological studies have focused on too narrow a line of inquiry; i.e., no single or isolated psychological parameter is alone relevant. He has suggested that five categories of observations should be considered concurrently in any psychological study: the previous developmental history of the individual; the emotional or affective state of the subject; the organization of the psychological defenses; the actual, overt behavior of the individual in everyday life, particularly in light of psychoanalytic formulations; and the social and physical environment for its relevant idiosyncratic factors.

The physiological aspects of psychophysiological disorders are at least as complex as the psychological factors delineated by Mason [15]. Mirsky's [16] formulation of the psychosociophysiological interaction in the development of peptic ulcer represents an attempt to account for and integrate these divergent elements. Mirsky, investigating the constitutional or X factors in psychophysiological illness, found high levels of pepsinogen in the blood plasma to be correlated with, and even predictive of, the development of duodenal ulcers. Mirsky has developed the most comprehensive hypothesis concerning this psychophysiological disorder. He viewed patients who develop duodenal ulcer as having primary physiological factors; i.e., the capacity for excessive (elevated) hydrochloric acid and of blood pepsinogen. These constitutional factors may determine the end-organ of disease and, under certain circumstances, may contribute to the evolution of distinctive psychological characteristics in the ulcer-prone patient.

Using Alexander's psychodynamic formulation for ulcer patients, Mirsky stated the following theory: Children differ genetically in their plasma pepsinogen levels; the assumption is made that those with higher pepsinogen levels will have greater oral needs leading to a greater amount and intensity in the pattern of their oral drive (sucking). If the mother cannot satisfy these intense oral needs, not only will the infant experience repeated frustration, he will also learn to anticipate frustration of his oral dependency needs. As a result, his personality structure will develop in such a way that in adulthood he may either continue to seek gratification or may develop a reaction-formation against these dependent needs and thus appear to be excessively independent.

ONSET SITUATION

A broader and somewhat less direct approach to the genesis of psychophysiological reactions has been taken by Holmes and Rahe [17]. Developing their theory out of the work of Engel and Schmale [7] these men did not claim a direct causal effect but rather hoped to demonstrate that there is a general emotional climate or series of environmental changes which affect the individual prior to the onset of his disorder. The concept of disorder in this theory has expanded to include psychophysiological reactions, physiological and emotional disturbances. It should be noted that Holmes and Rahe concerned themselves only with psychological parameters and did not take into account physiological ones.

Rahe [17] reported the results of several studies dealing with recent life changes and their associated illnesses; these studies were both retrospective and prospective in design. Using a questionnaire containing forty-two categories of events that commonly occur in an individual's life and that may have a psychological effect upon the person, the researchers demonstrated a statistically significant correlation between important life changes and the onset of illness. The validity of these observations has been supported by studies in such divergent cultures as those of Japan and Sweden. Rightfully, the authors have pointed out that the questionnaire does not measure long-term life difficulties, nor can it be used to predict future life change. Their work measured only one aspect of the etiological factors in the determination of near-onset illness.

An area of investigation not even contemplated by Alexander and his followers, but perhaps loosely related to onset situation, is the demographic aspect of disease which has been considered by Lipowski [14] and Hinkle [11]. Social turmoil becomes intrusive on the homeostatic mechanisms of the individual and affects him in the following manner: (1) increased sources of stimuli and arousal; (2) increased emphasis on goal-directed competitive behavior; (3) overwhelming stimulation of somatic and psychic perceptions; and (4) alteration in the factors which govern the adaptive mechanisms of the individual. Needless to say, contemporary society is bombarded by a never-ending series of insults from the physical and psychic spheres which promotes the pathogenesis of disease. Unfortunately, this does not explain the existence of these same disorders in previous ages; the increased incidence of these disorders may reflect a better system of measuring the incidence of these diseases.

CONCLUSION

Having reviewed the psychodynamic, psychosocial, specific versus nonspecific theories it must be borne in mind that contemporaneous with these theories was the continuing work in the neurobiological and psychoendocrine mechanisms. The influence of this work on the more psychodynamic theories becomes ever increasing and has caused considerable alterations in previous conceptualizations of disease process. Stated succinctly, there is no coherent nor satisfactory theory to explain the etiology, pathogenesis, and pathological mechanisms of psychophysiological disorders. Although many unanswered questions and considerations remain, the few general conclusions which research has produced are perhaps easier to list:

1   The psyche and the soma are descriptive aspects of the unitary organism: A dysfunction in one area has a potential for a dysfunction in the other.
2   Preconditions of psychophysiological disorders are varied but can generally be classified into one of three categories: constitutional, environmental, and intrapsychic.
3   No one category has provided a sufficient explanation for the etiology and pathogenesis of any disease process.
4   Most psychosomatic disorders appear to result from an alteration in all three categories.
    These generalized and somewhat vague conclusions reflect the state of the science and art of psychosomatic medicine.

In the investigation of anything as complex as human behavior there is a tendency for a great many seemingly unrelated facts to accumulate. This is essentially the stage in which the area of psychophysiological disorders rests at present. Current knowledge is fragmentary and incomplete, perhaps even erroneous in part. But it is the nature of mankind to need to gather the bits and pieces of information into some logical order around a unifying or integrating concept. Nowhere is this need more evident than in the controversy around the concept of specificity of cause and effect in psychosomatic disease. This issue has split the field into opposing camps, supporting either specificity or nonspecificity. However, as is usually the case, it has not been possible to solve this problem in an either-or manner. It is highly probable that there are both specific and nonspecific effects, depending on the phase of the disorder. This unifying approach has been suggested in different ways by Selye, Reiser, and Mason. Striking parallels of thought and analogies occur between, for example, Selye's stages of resistance and exhaustion on the one hand, and Engel's phase of giving up or Grinker's concept of the ego defense systems and their breakdown. What this portends is that ultimately the theoretical gap between mind and matter will be bridged in such a way that psychological and physiological events can be related in a systematic approach that will permit their being treated as a single phenomenon.

REFERENCES

1   Alexander, F. Fundamental concepts of psychosomatic research: Psychogenesis, conversion, Specificity. *Psychosom. Med.* 5:205–210, 1943.
2   Alexander, F. *Psychosomatic medicine: Its principles and applications.* New York: Norton, 1950.
3   American Psychiatric Association. *Diagnostic and statistical manual of mental disorders,* DSM-II American Psychiatric Association, 1968.
4   Cannon, W. B. *Bodily changes in pain, hunger, fear, and rage.* New York: Appleton, 1929.
5   Deutsch, F. *The psychosomatic concept in psychoanalysis.* New York: International Universities Press, 1953.
6   Dunbar, H. F. *Psychosomatic diagnosis.* New York: Hoeber, Harper and Row, 1943.
7   Engel, G. L., and Schmale, A. H. "Conservation withdrawal: A primary regulatory process for organismic homeostasis." In *Physiology, emotion, and psychosomatic illness,* pp. 57–85. CIBA Foundation Symposium no. 8. Amsterdam: Scientific, 1972.
8   Freedman, A. M., Kaplan, H. I., and Sadock, B. J., eds. *Comprehensive textbook of psychiatry,* 2nd ed. Baltimore: Williams and Wilkins, 1975.
9   Friedman, M., and Rosenman, R. H. Association of specific overt behavior patterns with blood and cardiovascular findings. *J.A.M.A.* 169:1286, 1959.
10   Grinker, R. R. *Psychosomatic research.* New York: Norton, 1953.

11   Hinkle, L. E. Ecological observations of the relation of physical illness, men-
      tal illness, and the social environment. *Psychosom. Med.* 23:289, 1961.
12   Lacey, J. I., and Lacey, B. C. Verification and extension of the principle of au-
      tonomic response specificity. *Am. J. Psychol.* 71:50–73, 1958.
13   Lipowski, Z. J. Psychosomatic medicine in a changing society: Some current
      trends in theory and research. *Compr. Psychiatry* 14:203–215, 1973.
14   Lipowski, Z. J., ed. Current trends in psychosomatic medicine. Special
      issue. *Int. J. Psychiatry Med.* 5(4), 1974.
15   Mason, J. W. "Some general implications of peptic ulcer research for psycho-
      somatic medicine: Discussion." In *Advances in psychosomatic medicine: Duo-
      denal ulcer*, vol. 6, ed. H. Weiner. Basel: Karger, 1971.
16   Mirsky, A. Physiological, psychological, and social determinants in the eti-
      ology of duodenal ulcers. *Am. J. Dig. Dis.* 3:285–314, 1958.
17   Rahe, R. H. "Subjects' recent life changes and near-future illness suscepti-
      bility." In *Advances in psychosomatic medicine*, vol. 8, Basel: Karger, 1972.
18   Reiser, M. F. "Changing Theoretical Concepts in psychosomatic medicine."
      In *American handbook of psychiatry*, vol. 4, 2nd ed., ed. S. Arieti, pp. 477–500.
      New York: Basic Books, 1975.
19   Schmale, A. H. Giving up as a final common pathway to changes in health.
      Psychoanal. Study Child 10:20–40, 1955.
20   Schur, M. Comments on the metapsychology of somatization. *Psychoanal.
      Study Child*, 10:119–164, 1955.
21   Selye, H. *The story of the adaptation syndrome*. Montreal: Acta, 1952.
22   Selye, H. *Stress without distress*. Philadelphia: Lippincott, 1974.

20

Common Sexual Dysfunctions

Anne C. Redmond, M.D.

The common sexual dysfunctions may be categorized as disorders of performance and disorders of satisfaction. *Disorders of performance* prevent or significantly alter functioning during the sexual cycle. *Disorders of satisfaction* decrease enjoyment during the sexual cycle.

Successful performance for males is defined by the ability to obtain an erection sufficient for penetration followed by ejaculation in the vaginal vault. Successful performance for females is defined by the ability to be penetrated and to accept male thrusting to ejaculation without intolerable pain. Because successful performance is more physiologically complex for men than for women, men have more disorders of performance than women [10,11]. Satisfactory performance may occur with or without a feeling of pleasure. The loss of pleasure is the common denominator of the disorders of satisfaction. More women than men experience disorders of satisfaction because of the longstanding sociocultural mores proscribing sexual pleasure for women, especially prior to marriage [3].

There is some disagreement among researchers and clinicians concerning the definition of specific sexual dysfunctions. This disagreement is partly due to the fact that serious research in the field has taken place only in the past thirty years [4]. The definitions presented in this chapter are consistent with those used by most sex therapists [3,9,10,12].

DISORDERS OF PERFORMANCE

In men disorders of performance include impotence and premature, retarded, and retrograde ejaculation.

Impotence is the inability to achieve or maintain an erection sufficient for penetration and ejaculation. This definition includes loss of erection during coitus, but prior to ejaculation.

Premature ejaculation is either ejaculation during a process of foreplay understood by both partners to be leading toward intercourse or ejaculation just before, during, or immediately after the act of penetration.

Retarded ejaculation is the delayed or virtual inability to ejaculate. This condition is usually limited to an essential inability to ejaculate intravaginally.

Retrograde ejaculation means that orgasm occurs without ejaculation being externally expelled. The ejaculate flows into the bladder through the internal vesical sphincter.

In women disorders of performance include *dyspareunia* — vaginal or pelvic pain associated with penetration and coitus, very often leading to termination of the sexual encounter; and *vaginismus*, which is a spasm of the perivaginal musculature rendering penetration difficult or virtually impossible.

DISORDERS OF SATISFACTION

Disorders of satisfaction may lead to a withdrawal from sexual activity — decrease in sexual frequency by either or both partners which may eventuate in no sexual contact.

In men these disorders include *split orgasm*, in which the emission phase of orgasm occurs, but the ejaculatory phase, which includes .8 sec contractions of the perineal muscles and the subjective pleasurable sensation of orgasm, is blocked, and the semen leaks from the urethra; and *orgasm without pleasure*, in which both phases of orgasm occur but without concomitant pleasure. This is usually caused by intrapsychic difficulties.

In women these disorders include *general sexual dysfunction*, inhibition of the sexual cycle with neither psychological erotic feeling nor genital vasocongestive response [2]; *sexual anesthesia*, a conversion reaction in which a woman "feels nothing" on sexual stimulation but lubricates, which is not the case in general sexual dysfunction; and *anorgasmia*, the inability to reach orgasm although sexual arousal is present.

DIAGNOSIS AND ETIOLOGY

A comprehensive diagnosis includes sexual diagnosis, psychiatric diagnosis, and medical diagnosis; any differential diagnostic problem must be clearly outlined.

Sexual dysfunctions are either primary or secondary. *Primary* is used to describe a dysfunction which has always been present; *secondary* indicates that the disturbed function was once intact.

A secondary dysfunction may be constant or specific to a particular situation. For example, it is not uncommon for women to have orgasms through masturbation but be anorgasmic with a partner. A man may be impotent with his wife but not with his lover.

Accurate diagnosis and the determination of appropriate treatment depends upon the gathering of a detailed and comprehensive sexual and interpersonal history. Of particular importance are details of the last satisfactory sexual encounter, life events which coincided with the onset of the dysfunction, the course of the dysfunction, whether anything improves the difficulty or makes it worse, and the outcome the patient desires from treatment.

It is not uncommon for a patient to consult a physician for vague symptoms, such as backache or headache, and when questioned about his or her sexual life, reveals a sexual problem which has been a major source of concern for some time. Those patients who develop symptoms after a period of what is for them normal sexual functioning usually contact their family physician or gynecologist believing that the trouble is caused by organic illness. Physicians must be familiar with the common sexual disorders and provide an atmosphere which permits him or her to elicit specific details about sexual functioning.

The common sexual dysfunctions are syndromes having one or more etiologies—biological, intrapsychic, interpersonal, and sociocultural.

Biological

Impotence and dyspareunia frequently have an organic basis, whereas premature ejaculation and anorgasmia rarely are caused by physical problems. A dysfunction which is experienced with all partners and has a steady downhill course is usually organic. An organic etiology for impotence is indicated when rapid eye movement (REM) sleep and morning full-bladder erections are absent or of poor quality. Dyspareunia which occurs in all coital contacts and with manual manipulation during physical examination is usually organically based. Burning pain during intercourse often accompanies vaginal infections. Women who do not enter the excitement phase of the sexual cycle prior to intromission will experience pain due to the lack of lubrication [9,10].

Retrograde ejaculation can be caused by medication—thioridazine is the most common offender — or transurethral prostate resection. Retarded ejaculation in a young man in whom masturbation achieves rapid ejaculation is almost never organic; however, men over forty do experience a lengthening of the time required to reach ejaculation.

An existing illness may lead to sexual dysfunction even though it does not biologically impair sexual functioning. For example, an amputation or colostomy may be repulsive to one or both partners. Chemotherapy for cancer may produce nausea incompatible with sexual functioning. It is especially important to discuss explicitly sexual functioning with cardiac patients because many fear dying during coitus. Intercourse with a familiar partner and climbing one flight of stairs place equal demand on the cardiovascular system [15].

A careful physical examination of the sexual organs must be performed as part of the workup for a sexual dysfunction to rule out organic pathology. A neurological examination is also essential [7].

Finally, age is a very important biological factor in sexual functioning. Although men's sexual desire peaks in late adolescence to early twenties and women's peak in late thirties to early forties, sexual functioning changes with aging in both sexes. Biology merges with intrapsychic, interpersonal, and social issues related to stages in the life cycle [16].

Intrapsychic

Freud's psychoanalytic observations about infantile psychosexual development are fundamental to modern theories of behavior. According to this theory, adults must have successfully worked through the oral, anal, and oedipal periods of infantile sexuality before being able to enjoy normal, conflict free, mature sexuality. Sexual dysfunction will occur in those individuals who regress in intimate relationships, treating and reacting to their partner as if she or he were the parent. Anxiety from incest taboos, fear of castration, or anger about mistreatment from one or both parents are other examples of intrapsychic issues which impair sexual functioning. Sexual anesthesia, anorgasmia, and impotence are common sexual symptoms with intrapsychic etiologies [12].

Sexual dysfunctions may be secondary to other psychiatric illness in one or both partners. In manic-depressive illness, sexual promiscuity is a frequent symptom of mania, whereas in the depressed phase sexual desire is lost. One common symptom of severe depression of any type is loss of libido. Delusions and hallucinations may alter the sexual functioning of psychotics. Also, anxiety or anger aroused by the psychotic symptoms may impair the partner's sexuality.

Interpersonal

The common sexual dysfunctions occur within the context of an interpersonal relationship; therefore, both partners must be interviewed together and separately in order to assess the interaction between their sexual experience and other interpersonal behaviors.

Frequently both partners have a sexual dysfunction. A man with premature ejaculation often has a partner who is anorgasmic. A woman with vaginismus may have a spouse who is impotent.

The emotions anxiety, fear, anger, and sadness are usually incompatible with sexual performance and enjoyment. The emotions experienced may be secondary as a result of a sexual problem, or the sexual dysfunction may be secondary to these emotions, which arise from conflicts in the relationship.

As a rule, partners in a relationship marked by interpersonal problems feel misunderstood, fear retaliation, lack trust, and communicate in indirect ways. Affect and verbalization are frequently incongruent. What is communicated privately to the physician may be substantially different from what is communicated together. In these relationships sexuality fares no better than other major issues [1].

Some common interpersonal problems which generate dysphoric feelings and interfere with sexual functioning are as follows:

1 *Ambivalent commitment to relationship.* In many relationships when one partner is trying to increase intimacy, the other pulls away and vice versa; therefore, no trust can be developed. If one or both partners are ambivalent about the degree of commitment to their relationship either or both may experience dysphoria sufficient to cause common sexual dysfunctions. Ambivalence is often caused by fantasy-reality incongruency or competition.

2 *Fantasy-reality incongruency.* Each person has fantasies about what he or she wants and needs from a mate. These fantasies are about protection and care-taking. For example, if a woman believes that getting married means being financially secure, she may be resentful if she has to work to help pay the bills.

3   *Competition.* Severe competition between mates may produce marital discord. A couple may not be aware of their competitiveness, but it will be evident in their communications. Problem solving may be very difficult for the couple. Issues such as what type of new car should be purchased, who should climax first, or where the children should be sent to school becomes battles which last for months, sometimes years [3,13].

Sociocultural

Sexual expression is strictly controlled by religious and secular laws in most societies. Universally, there are taboos against incest and laws about premarital, marital, and extramarital intercourse. Women's sexuality is almost always restricted more than men's. This may be a result of the interest in protecting property, inheritance, and kinship ties [4].

Effective birth control, which has been available only in the twentieth century and widely used only since the advent of the "pill" in 1960, has markedly affected female sexuality. These changes have occurred despite the fact that prohibitions against sex were part of the childhood experience of most adult women. The Kinsey study of human sexuality disclosed that of women born before 1900 only 14 percent had premarital intercourse. This figure is only about one-quarter of that for women born after 1900. In the same study most men in both birth cohorts had premarital intercourse [5,6]. Moreover, Hunt's [2] study published in several 1973 and 1974 issues of *Playboy* stated that 95 percent of married men and 81 percent of married women under twenty-five participated in premarital sex. Today many people feel increasing pressure to satisfy sexually their partners. This pressure often generates performance anxiety or the closely related phenomenon of "spectatoring" and may lead to sexual dysfunction.

Common misperceptions about sexual anatomy described in chapter 21 are often the basis for performance anxiety. For example, a man may be anxious about the size of his penis, obtaining an erection, ejaculating too soon, or satisfying his partner. A woman may worry about the choice to have premarital or extramarital sex, the possibility of pain during intercourse, the size of her breasts, whether her partner will be able to perform, or her ability to have orgasm. This anxiety interferes with the sexual cycle, since the accompanying sympathetic arousal prevents parasympathetic discharge necessary for an erection in men and sexual arousal in women [15,3,9].

Spectatoring is a term coined by Masters and Johnson [9] to describe the dissociation between the thought and action which takes place when a person is "watching" what happens during a sexual encounter. This interferes with the feeling of sexual excitement and concomitant physiological response. This is different from the use of a fantasy of watching the sexual act in order to enhance one's pleasure. The pleasurable fantasy does not remove the person from the action, as the spectatoring does.

TREATMENT

The treatment which is most likely to repair the sexual dysfunction depends upon the sexual, psychiatric, and medical diagnoses and their major etiological factors. Usually several etiological factors are important; however, commonly one area (biological, intrapsychic, interpersonal, sociocultural) is most pronounced. The treatment method selected is the one which is most effective in correcting the factors which are causing the problem.

Any biological etiological factors require medical treatment. Residual or chronic medical problems must be explained to the couple with a discussion of how they can enjoy sex within the limits the illness imposes. For example, retrograde ejaculation secondary to prostatectomies performed for cancer causes sterility, since the semen is ejaculated into the bladder. Both partners should be informed about the infertility but should also be encouraged to have normal sexual relations.

If the main cause of the sexual dysfunction is intrapsychic, the goal of such treatment is the working through of the conflict so that the sexual symptom diminishes. Appropriate individual psychotherapy is the treatment of choice. Psychotropic medication should be used if indicated to alleviate depression, mania, and psychosis, keeping in mind that these medications may have side effects such as impotence, retarded ejaculation, or decreased sexual desire [3,9,10,12].

For sexual dysfunction which is secondary to marital maladjustment, couples therapy is the treatment of choice. The therapist explores with the couple the issues which are causing the marital unhappiness [13].

Sexual dysfunction which occurs without substantial biological, intrapsychic, or interpersonal basis usually results from sociocultural factors. Residual dysfunction after treatment for biological, intrapsychic, and interpersonal problems responds well to the treatment formats pioneered by Masters and Johnson [8,9], which have since been modified by other sex researchers [3,10,12]. The treatment is a short-term couple therapy format which relies heavily on behavior modification. The therapists are psychiatrists, psychologists, psychiatric social workers, psychiatric nurses, or gynecologists. Treatment may be provided by a male and female team or one person of either sex knowledgeable about the technique. Advocates of an approach utilizing a male and female therapist believe that it is advantageous for each partner to have a member of his or her own sex in the therapy session. Advocates of a single therapist cite monetary savings and more effective manpower utilization as outweighing the advantage of a dual team. No definitive data exist proving one approach superior to the other; therefore, this should be individualized according to the couple's needs and the therapists' experience.

Treatment consists of twelve to twenty daily or weekly sessions. During the first two sessions, a complete sexual history is gathered including exploring any sensations or fantasy material which is pleasurable or erotic for each person. If physical examinations including genital exam have not already been performed, this is provided. Frequently both spouses are present so that any misconceptions about sexual anatomy may be corrected. In the third session the therapist(s) explain to the couple what factors seem to be the main ones causing their particular difficulty. A contract is negotiated defining price/session, time of sessions, number of sessions, and adherence to the instructions. Assurance is given that sexual activity will only occur between the couple in their private surroundings. Then, sexual anatomy and physiology is taught using pictures. Myths and sexual mores are discussed. At the end of this session, intercourse and genital touching is forbidden, and special instructions are given called "sensate focus" exercises. The couple is instructed to take turns pleasuring each other. The one being pleasured must teach the other verbally and with manual guidance what feels sensual to him or her. When he or she feels dislike of being touched, he or she must immediately tell the other to stop. Then roles are reversed. When sessions are held weekly, the couple is generally instructed to do the exercises three times each week.

In the fourth session, the therapists and couple examine in detail what happened during the exercises. Some typical questions follow: How did the partners decide when and where to do the exercises? What were the physical surroundings? How free from interruption were they? What clothes, lotions, pictures, books, etc., did they use to enhance sensuality? How did they decide who would be pleasured first? Was each partner able to instruct the other? If so, how? What felt sensual? What was each thinking when they signaled the other to stop? How did they feel at that time? How were things for them outside the bedroom? Other aspects of their individual lives or marriage will be explored as they impact on the exercises. Depending on the result of this discussion, the exercise may be assigned again or a new instruction may be added to the first one, i.e.: "You must pleasure each other as before but may include genital touching. You may not have intercourse."

The therapists are using the behavioral techniques of desensitization and reciprocal inhibition. In each session the therapists are trying to extinguish performance anxiety and decrease spectatoring. The exercises progress thorough penile containment with no movement to penile containment with one or both partners moving and then to intercourse in different positions. These are individualized according to the sexual dysfunction presented [3,9,10,12].

Prognosis for the common sexual dysfunctions treated with this format are good. Masters and Johnson's [9] data, presented in table 20.1, are consistent with data from other sex research centers.

Success rates for all disorders are impressive, and some failures may be due to lack of sufficient screening of candidates for this therapy, e.g., using the format with a couple whose primary problem is marital dysfunction.

As a rule, sexual dysfunctions do not improve when there is no stable sexual partner. However, some individuals without partners respond favorably to treatment. Anorgasmic women can be taught to masturbate to orgasm with and without a vibrator. Furthermore, group therapy has been used successfully with anorgasmic women. Men with high anxiety levels can sometimes be desensitized. Also, intensive individual psychotherapy reduces sexual dysfunction in certain cases [10].

Three case examples will help clarify how treatment modes are selected and used.

A twenty-five year-old man consulted his internist about asthmatic episodes which occur when he tries to have intercourse with his twenty-three year-old wife of two years. A careful history re-

Table 20.1
PROGNOSIS FOR COMMON SEXUAL DYSFUNCTIONS

Disorder	Success rate after five years (%)	Number
Impotence — primary	59.4	32
Impotence — secondary	69.1	213
Premature ejaculation	97.3	186
Retarded ejaculation	82.4	17
Vaginismus	100	29*
Anorgasmia — primary	82.4	193
— secondary	75.2	149
Totals — male and female	80.0	790

From W. H. Masters and V. E. Johnson, *Human Sexual Inadequacy*. Little, Brown, 1970.
*These individuals are also included in the group of anorgasmic women.

vealed that he gains a partial erection with foreplay but becomes impotent when he attempts entry. His wheezing begins one to two minutes prior to coitus and becomes worse when he loses his erection. He has full erections upon wakening in the morning as well as full erections with masturbation. His wife lubricates and occasionally has an orgasm with foreplay. Both are unhappy about the impotence. However, they interact comfortably with each other in a supportive manner. They have few marital difficulties and no significant psychiatric signs or symptoms. This has been an intermittent problem for him since his first sexual contact but has increased in the last six months after he received a promotion to foreman at a General Motors assembly plant. He notes increasing wheezing at work.

Sexual diagnosis: Secondary impotence
Psychiatric diagnosis: None
Medical diagnosis: Asthma
Treatment: The internist must regulate the patient's medication to treat the exacerbation of his asthma. Furthermore, he may recommend the prn use of bronchodilator medications just prior to sexual activity to prevent wheezing with exertion. Finally, it is important for the physician to educate both husband and wife about the sexual response cycle and how anxiety produces impotence as well as asthmatic attacks. If this does not alleviate the problem, this couple should be referred to competent therapist(s) for short term sexual format therapy. The prognosis is good [8,11,14].

A moderately plump forty-four-year-old woman complained to her gynecologist that her forty-eight-year-old husband has stopped all sexual contact with her. Sexual activity slowly diminished from two times a week five years ago to the last intercourse four months ago. She burst into tears during the interview. She complained of her husband's twelve-hour work days. She is physically normal, and she has been intermittently orgasmic until the past year.

The gynecologist arranged to interview both husband and wife. The husband accuses his wife of becoming "fat like a hog, for the last eight years"; furthermore, she has never liked any of his hobbies such as football. She yells that he "neglects her and their two children. You're a sham as a father." The gynecologist has difficulty interrupting their tirades. The husband states "she doesn't turn me on — she doesn't like oral sex." The wife counters, "Why don't you leave?" It is difficult to elicit specific details, but both agree that he had difficulty ejaculating intravaginally in their last two sexual encounters. He is healthy, has no difficulty obtaining firm erections, or ejaculating with masturbation. Mental status reveals no significant psychiatric illness.

Sexual diagnosis: Nonspecific sexual withdrawal
Psychiatric diagnosis: Marital maladjustment
Physical diagnosis: None
Treatment: The treatment of choice for this couple is marital couple therapy. The sexual problem is secondary to the severe interpersonal difficulties that have been present for some time. However, some change has occurred to bring them to medical attention. The therapist must be aware of the life-cycle stresses on each partner [16]. Sexual format therapy will fail with this much hostility between partners. If couple therapy allows them to improve the quality of their interpersonal relationship but some aspect of the sexual problem remains, sexual format therapy might then be indicated [1,12,3].

A thirty-seven-year-old white Catholic male, Mr. X, consulted his internist for medicine to "make me last longer." He had been married ten years to his thirty-four-year-old wife. They have two children. His physical examination was normal. The internist told him that no medication could delay ejaculation; however, he referred the couple to a university-based sexual behaviors clinic for further evaluation.

History revealed that Mr. X had not been able to thrust more than ten times after intromission before climaxing. This began during his first attempt to have intercourse. He and his cousin convinced a girlfriend to "go all the way" during a family reunion. They were in the basement. Since their parents were on the first floor, all three were very anxious. He climaxed just prior to intromission. His wife was orgasmic with foreplay but had never climaxed during intercourse. In the year prior to their evaluation she returned to college. This substantially increased her work load, but she had not been willing to share child and housekeeping responsibilities with her husband. She felt overburdened. She had a brief affair in which she was multiorgasmic with a man who was able to thrust for twenty minutes before climaxing. This experience increased her anger toward her husband. She talked with him about her wish to date other men. This raised his anxiety; he experienced several episodes of impotence during the week before the sexual consultation. Neither he nor his wife demonstrated any major intrapsychic pathology.

MR. X
Sexual diagnosis: Premature ejaculation
Psychiatric diagnosis: None
Medical diagnosis: None

MRS. X
Sexual diagnosis: Secondary anorgasmia (during intercourse)
Psychiatric diagnosis: Adult adjustment reaction
Medical diagnosis: None

The evaluator had a conference with this couple. She explained that Mr. X's premature ejaculation was largely caused by his first sexual encounter, which was bound to fail because of the fear of being caught by the parents upstairs. This failure caused him to be anxious in his next sexual encounter, and so again he ejaculated prematurely. A pattern was established. His recent impotence was a response to his wife's increasing demands. Mrs. X's return to school had caused her to become more aware of having an unsatisfactory sexual relation. She was also working hard to pass her courses but was refusing to change her role in the marriage by sharing housekeeping and child care functions with her husband. This increased her anxiety and anger, as she became overburdened. Sexual format therapy was recommended. This therapy concentrated on understanding and altering the stress-inducing factors. Three sets of sensate focus exercises were assigned each week in a graduated fashion. These deemphasized performance. Intercourse was prohibited in the first eight weeks. In the early weeks Mrs. X was able to give her husband major household responsibilities, which he happily accepted. Both felt more comfortable with their relation. Nongenital sensate focus exercises were satisfactorily accomplished during the third and fourth week. In the fifth and sixth week he learned to masturbate focusing on his genital sensations so he could stop penile stimulation just prior to ejaculatory inevitability. He was instructed to allow his desire to subside, then masturbate to this point again prior to stopping. He was given permission to ejaculate following three such arousals. His wife obtained orgasm with manual and oral stimulation during these weeks when she was being pleasured. In the seventh week his wife masturbated him in this fashion and in the eighth week she added lotion. In the ninth week they had female superior intercourse using this method of arousal-stop-start for twenty minutes prior to ejaculation. By the twelfth and last session they were having successful intercourse for as long as one-half hour in any position, during which she was multiorgasmic. She felt less pressured by school, and both were delighted with their success and the renewal of their relationship. Sixth month follow-up demonstrated sustained results.

REFERENCES

1   Green, B. *A clinical approach to marital problems.* Springfield, Ill.: Thomas, 1970.
2   Hunt, M. *Sexual behavior in the 1970s. Playboy* 20, 21 (October–February) 1973, 1974.
3   Kaplan, H. *The new sex therapy.* New York: Brunner/Mazel, 1974.
4   Katchadourian, H., and Lunde, D. *Fundamentals of human sexuality.* New York: Holt, Rinehart, and Winston, 1975.
5   Kinsey, A. C., Pomeroy, W., and Martin, C. *Sexual behavior in the human male.* Philadelphia: Saunders, 1948.
6   Kinsey, A. C., Pomeroy, W., Martin C., and Gebhart, P. *Sexual behavior in the human female.* Philadelphia: Saunders, 1953.
7   Lundberg, P. Neurological examination of patients with sexual dysfunction. *Med. Aspects Hum. Sex.* 11(5), p. 59–60 1977.
8   Masters, W., and Johnson, V. *Human sexual response.* Boston: Little, Brown, 1966.
9   Masters, W., and Johnson, V. *Human sexual inadequacy.* Boston: Little, Brown, 1970.
10   Meyer, J. ed. *Clinical management of sexual disorders.* Baltimore: Williams and Wilkins, 1976.
11   Meyer, J. *The treatment of sexual disorders.* Symposium on Psychiatry in Internal Medicine, Medical Clinics of North America, vol. 61, no. 4, 1977.
12   Sadock, B., Kaplan, H., and Freeman, A. *The sexual experience.* Baltimore: Williams and Wilkins, 1976.
13   Sager, C., and Kaplan, H. *Progress in group and family therapy.* New York: Brunner/Mazel, 1972.
14   Straus, S., and Dudley, D. Sexual activity for asthmatics. *Med. Aspects Hum. Sex.* 10 (11), 1976.
15   Wagner, N *"Sexual activity and the cardiac patient,"* In *Human sexuality: A health practitioner's text,* ed. R. Green. Baltimore: Williams and Wilkins, 1973.
16   Wise, T. N. Sexuality throughout the life cycle. *Psychosomatics,* in press.

21

Sexual Disorders

Anne C. Redmond, M.D.

Western culture covertly or overtly emphasizes sexuality in almost every aspect of living. Advertisements link consumer products with sexual seductiveness; spas, beauty salons, and health clubs capitalize on our wish to remain young, beautiful, and sexy. Explicit sexual material is becoming more prominent in popular literature, theater, film, and television. Effective birth control, which has been developed only recently, allows both men and women to engage in nonprocreative sex. The Gay Liberation movement is openly placing pressure on physicians and legislators to end medical, social, and legal discrimination against homosexuals.

Since many common beliefs about sexuality have been proven wrong, it behooves the physician to obtain a full understanding of sexuality and to develop a nonjudgmental attitude about patients' sexual practices. Kinsey and co-workers [12,13] published data on sexual practices from 1938 to 1952; this initiated sexuality as a respectable area for research. William Masters and Virginia Johnson [18,19] pioneered the method of direct observation in order to study the physiological and psychological aspects of sexuality. Following the publication of their landmark book, *Human Sexual Response,* in 1966, this area of research and education grew rapidly. Now there are a multitude of professional books, articles, and teaching films available not only for professional groups but also for the lay public. Sexuality has been taught in the majority of medical schools only since the early 1970s; therefore, many practitioners have not had current, accurate information about sexuality; however, in the last five years continuing education courses in addition to the publication of journals whose content exclusively pertains to sexual issues — *Archives of Sexual Behaviors* and *Medical Aspects of Human Sexuality* — have helped to teach those physicians.

NORMAL SEXUALITY

Before the clinical syndromes related to sexual dysfunction can be understood, it is necessary to have an understanding of normal biological sex, gender identity and sexuality in the context of the life cycle.

Biological Sex

The normal developing fetus has either XX or XY chromosomes. Without androgen all fetuses develop into anatomic females. The XY configuration of the primordial germ cells stimulates the development of the testes whose cells of Leydig produce testosterone. The presence of testosterone stimulates the Wolffian duct to develop into the ductus deferens, seminal vesicles, and epididymis. The XX configuration permits the sex gland to differentiate into the ovaries while the Müllerian duct develops into the oviducts, uterus, and inner third of the vagina [26].

In the eighth week the primordial external sexual structures begin to differentiate. Without androgen the genital tubercle becomes the clitoris; urethra folds become the labia minora; the labioscrotal swellings become the labia majora and the urogenital sinus becomes the lower two-thirds of the vagina, Bartholin's glands, and Skene's glands. With androgen the genital tubercle develops into the penis and the urethral folds into the corpus spongiosum and penile urethra. The labioscrotal swellings become the scrotum, and the urogenital sinus turns into the prostatic utricle and bulbourethral glands [26].

Gender Identity and Life Stages

At birth the child begins its gender indoctrination. Gender identity is the individual's sense of being a male or female person. The family members, especially the parents, have been preparing themselves for the birth. An important part of this preparation concerns the sex of the infant. Parents convey attitudes and expectations concerning gender from the time of birth when the obstetrician or midwife announces "It's a girl" or "It's a boy." It is unclear what percentage of observable sex-determined differences in infancy is caused by biological parameters and what percentage is caused by differential treatment of boys and girls by their parents [36,6].

According to psychoanalytic theory, in the first 1.5 years of life both sexes experience the oral stage, during which the child focuses most attention on the feelings of the mouth. With the advent of toilet training the child shifts attention to the perineum which includes bowel, bladder, and genitalia. Usually gender identity is firmly established by the end of the anal phase, approximately 2.5 to 3 years [36] although new research shows that about the middle of the second year very strong gender consciousness and awareness of genital sensation arise.

During the oedipal stage (3–5 years) the external genitals receive much attention from children. Also, the child wants to possess the parent of the opposite sex; however, he or she is afraid of retaliation from the same sex parent. For boys this means castration anxiety followed by identification with the perceived aggressor, father. This demands a shift from the feminine introjected mother to identification with the masculine father. For girls this means giving up a wish for a penis and substituting a wish for a baby from father, followed by more intense identification with the primary object, mother [35,32].

Because male children have to switch from introjection of the mother to identification with the father, the gender identity and sexual preference is more frequently disturbed in males than in females. Castration anxiety is fundamental to these disturbances [36].

Sex play among boys and girls starts around age 4, usually under the disguise of playing "doctor" or "show me." Parental attitudes about these normal games as well as about genital touching greatly influence children's attitudes towards their bodies and sexuality. During the latency period (5–11 years) children are forming same-sex friendships in order to further solidify their gender identity while exploring intimacy. Television, movies, radio, and billboards expose the child to the fantasy world of adult sexuality. Recently, sex education has become part of the normal elementary school curriculum [25].

Puberty occurs any time between 11 to 18 for boys and 9 to 16 for girls. In males the sequence is beginning growth of the testes and penis, appearance of straight pigmented pubic hair, early voice changes, first ejaculation, kinky pubic hair, period of maximum growth, axillary hair, marked voice changes, and development of the beard [11,31]. In females the sequence is breast development, growth of external genitals, emergence of pubic and axillary hair, and the beginning of menstruation [11,29]. Pressure to become sexually active early is placed upon those who develop secondary sexual characteristics early. Those who develop late feel abnormal. Both of these phenomena are reinforced by the intense peer pressure during adolescence. The sexual drive of adolescent males is very strong, peaking at 18 to 20. Almost all adolescents experiment with sexuality or intimacy, or both. "Scoring" becomes an important symbol of manhood. The fear of being caught is strong when foreplay or coitus or both occur in the parent's home or car in a "parking area." This guilty initiation into sex frequently influences the performance and satisfaction of coitus between consenting adults [10].

Young adults according to Erikson [3] are dealing with the issues of intimacy versus isolation. Commitment in relationships is sought after, and marriages or long-term liaisons are formed. Couples focus on the quality of their relationships with each other, especially in the sexual area. The dyad becomes a triad with the birth of the first child. In the late twenties and thirties men decrease sexual overtures to their wives, in part due to the normal decrease in the male libido, as well as the loss of sexual excitement with a familiar wife, who is a mother, and increased career striving. Women may begin to assert their needs beyond being a wife and mother by going to school or getting a job. This may threaten the male's self-esteem, causing difficulties in sexual performance. Extramarital relationships may be established by one or both partners [38].

Divorce may occur anytime in the twenties through fifty age range. Not infrequently one or both members is unprepared for being single, especially for the lack of a sexual partner. Many divorced women and men feel guilty about their sexual needs.

During the forties and early fifties most men will be in the highest career position which they can obtain, which may cause low self-esteem. Since our culture values power, youth, and beauty, men commonly seek out much younger women to enhance failing self-esteem. Women in their forties and fifties are experiencing menopause, which causes irregular menstrual periods and physical and emotional changes with hot flashes, due to the changing hormone levels. These factors may lead to a decrease in sexual relations between marital partners or may even precipitate separation [31].

Men and women can continue to enjoy sexual relations throughout old age, although American society discourages sexuality among the aging. For example, little privacy is available in nursing homes for coitus. Older women may need oral estrogen replacement or an estrogen vaginal cream to prevent dysparunia secondary to thin, friable vaginal mucosa [10].

Sexual Anatomy and Physiology

SEXUAL MYTHOLOGY

Sexual mythology about human anatomy and physiology is rampant in Western culture; therefore, it is necessary for the clinician to know the myths (listed below) as well as the facts [7].

1   Women "ejaculate" during orgasm. *False:* A transsudate from vascular engorgement in the vagina occurs during excitation through orgasm [18].

2   A vagina may be too small to accommodate a large penis. *False:* The vagina lengthens and distends, with the cervix and uterus pulled up during excitement phase, accommodating any size penis. Rarely, a woman with an unusually small vagina will need to be in plateau phase before intromission is comfortable [18].

3   A vagina may be too large to adequately stimulate or be stimulated by a penis. *False:* This occurs only if there has been damage to the vagina while the woman was giving birth. This can be corrected with perineal exercises or, if severe, with surgery [19].

4   A big penis is more satisfying to a woman during intercourse. *False:* The vagina accommodates to the size of the erect penis. Penis lengths when flaccid range from 8.5–10.5 cm in length and 2.5–3.5 cm in diameter. When erect the penis is 15.0 ± 2.5 cm in length and 3.0–3.5 cm in diameter [18].

5   Size of the flaccid penis directly correlates with the size of the erect penis. *False:* There is an insignificant difference in erectile penile size between large and small flaccid penises [18].

6   The penis can be trapped inside the vagina. *False:* This is anatomically impossible [18].

7   Penis size is dependent on masculinity or body build or race. *False:* There is no relationship between virility, race, and body size or build and penile size [18].

8   Uncircumcised males can control ejaculation more easily than circumcised males. *False:* During coitus the foreskin generally retracts exposing the glans. Also, there is no difference between circumcised and uncircumcised males in glans sensation or incidence of premature ejaculation [18].

9   The penis and clitoris enlarge with frequent masturbation or sexual experience. *False:* There is no increase in the size of either [18].

10   One can assess virginity by examining the hymen. *False:* The hymen can range from minimal tags to imperforate prior to intercourse [11].

11   Simultaneous orgasms are the goal for intercourse. *False:* Simultaneous orgasms occur infrequently due to the individuality of each person's sexual cycle [19].

12   There are some effective aphrodisiacs. *False:* People keep looking for these substances, but without notable success [23].

13   Sexual desire is lost following hysterectomy and oophorectomy. *False:* There is no physical correlation; however, the loss of estrogen may cause the vaginal mucosa to become painful with intercourse. This can be controlled with replacement estrogens [31].

14   A woman with inverted nipples will not be able to breast-feed. *False:* As the nipples are suckled they become erect, as they do in the excitement phase of the female sexual cycle [18].

15   Urine is "dirty" or is "full of germs." *False:* Urine is sterile unless a urinary tract infection exists [29].

FEMALE ANATOMY

A woman's mons pubis is a hair-covered, soft fatty tissue which rests on the symphysis. The labia majora are folds of skin containing subcutaneous tissue which extend from the mons to the anus. The median edges nearly cover the genitalia when a female is not sexually excited. The labia minora form a single fold of skin lying over the clitoris called the prepuce, then divide meeting again below the vagina. Bartholin's glands, contained in the labia minora, contribute little to vaginal lubrication but are prone to infection. The clitoris consists of two corpora cavernosa which are attached to the pubic bone. The tip, which is called the glans, is generally very sensitive and is exposed, whereas the main body of the clitoris is covered by the labia minora. The clitoris contains many nerve endings with Paccinian corpuscles. Clitoral engorgement during the sexual cycle occurs but is frequently so small as not to be noticed [18].

The urinary meatus lies between the clitoris and vaginal opening. Its function is to transport urine. It is not connected in any way with the vagina. "Honeymoon cystitis" may occur with intercourse in women who are not in excitement phase prior to penetration, because the urethra is traumatized, allowing bacteria to reach the bladder [18].

The introitus is the visible opening of the vagina. It is partially covered by a pinkish membrane called the hymen. Historically, the hymen has been important in many cultures because its intact presence was equated with virginity. Medically, it is now observed that prior to intercourse the intactness of the hymen ranges from minimal tags to a firm membrane covering the entire introitus. The hymen has no known physiological function [11].

The resting vagina is a potential space with a mucosal lining like that inside the mouth. The middle muscular layer consists of predominantly longitudinal muscles. Few nerves are present except in the outer one-third of the vagina which is surrounded by erectile tissue and bulbo cavernous muscles. The uterus is generally tilted forward. It is suspended by ligaments which allow movement for uterine expansion in pregnancy. The cervix is in contact with the posterior vaginal wall when a woman is not sexually excited. The ovaries produce both ovum and female sex hormones (estrogen and progesterone). The Fallopian tubes transport ova to the uterus. Since fertilization generally occurs in the infundibular area, the tubes also protect the developing zygote during transport [18].

Sterilization by tubal ligation, oophorectomy and/or properly performed hysterectomy does not physiologically decrease libido or prevent satisfactory intercourse. However, the psychological impact of sterilization may severely affect desire and performance [31].

MALE ANATOMY

A man's external genitalia consists of the penis, scrotum, testicles, epididymis, and some of the vas deferens. The parts of the penis are the glans, shaft, and root. Two corpora cavernosa lie above the corpus spongiosum which contains the urethra. The corpus spongiosum extends from the root where it is called the bulb to the tip where it becomes the glans which covers the cavernosa bodies. These cylinders contain many irregular venous spaces, which fill with blood during sexual arousal. The glans, however, remains soft during complete arousal, thereby insuring no physical damage during intercourse [18].

The scrotum contains the testes and epididymis, with the left testis usually hanging lower than the right. The dartos muscles in the scrotum, together with contraction of the spermatic cord, raise the testicles closer to the body during cold temperature, stimulation of the inner thigh (cremasteric reflex), and sexual arousal. The testicles produce the male hormone testosterone and spermatozoa, which are transported to the epididymis. This continues into the vas deferens which enters the abdomen through the inguinal canal. The seminal vesicle joins with the vas to form the ejaculatory duct, a tube less than one inch in length surrounded by the prostate. This is joined by the urethra to form one tube with two purposes — transporting urine and transporting ejaculate. The seminal vesicles add fluid to the sperm, as does the prostate. Two bulbourethral glands at the base of the penis are responsible for the clear sticky fluid which emerges in drops at the tip of the penis during sexual plateau [18]

Sexual Response

Any stimulus may cause sexual arousal, depending on the life experiences of the individual; however, for most people touch, sight, and fantasy predominate. Societal and individual factors influence what a person finds sexually stimulating. [4] Each culture, society, and ethnic group defines differently what is sexually stimulating. Robert Stoller [37] observes that fantasies which are erotic to an individual are based upon traumatic childhood events which are reworked to allow for a happy ending — orgasm.

Certain body areas are called *erogenous zones* because touching them most readily stimulates the sexual response. Since the type of touching which is most pleasurable as well as the location of erogenous zones vary among individuals, it is important to share personal preferences with one's sexual partner. Common erotic zones for men are the glans and corona of the penis and the scrotum. Common erogenous zones for women include the clitoris and labia minora. Both men and women are sexually responsive to stimulation of the perineum, inner thigh, nipples, anus, mouth, and ears [9]. A man achieves orgasm by manipulation by hand or movement of the shaft within the vagina, mouth, or rectum of his sexual partner. For women, clitoral stimulation by hand, mouth, vibrator, and vaginal thrusting provide the main sensory stimulus leading to orgasm. There is no difference between clitoral or vaginal orgasm. The clitoris is the sensory organ, whereas the perineal muscles and uterus contract due to sympathetic and motor stimulation [18]

Masters and Johnson's [18,19] research demonstrated four stages of sexual arousal in both sexes. These are excitement, plateau, orgasm, and resolution [18].

EXCITEMENT
Both sexes experience the onset of erotic feelings; increased pulse, respiration, and blood pressure; the beginning of myotonia, nipple erection; and skin "sex flush" [18].

In women early vascular engorgement of the sex organs cause the following:

1   Venous expansion of the breast
2   Expansion of the labia, which causes them to open exposing the vagina
3   Slight thickening of the clitoris
4   Lubrication, lengthening, and distension of the vagina
5   Elevation of the cervix caused by enlargement and rising of the uterus into the false pelvis

Men experience vascular engorgement also, which causes the following:

1   Penile erection
2   Thickening of the scrotum, which binds the movement of the testes
3   Partial elevation and rotation of the testes

Erection is analogous to lubrication in a woman. Erection depends on an intact parasympathetic reflex from S2–S4 in response to penile and scrotal touching as well as an intact vascular system. There is a central nervous system (CNS) mechanism in the limbic system and midbrain which can cause erections from psychic stimulation via a reflex higher in the cord. Anxiety, anger, stress, and pain will impair the ability to obtain an erection, since these emotions inhibit the parasympathetic reflexes [10].

PLATEAU

In both sexes pulse, respiration, blood pressure, sex flush, and vasocongestion continue to increase [18]. The entire clitoris turns upward and is retracted to a flat position beneath the labial hood against the anterior border of the symphysis. This explains why the clitoris seems to "disappear" in foreplay manipulation. The vagina continues to engorge, becoming red, and the orgasmic platform develops in the outer third. There is only a slight increase of lubrication and vaginal expansion.

The penis reaches maximal erection and firmness during the plateau stage. The testicles become 50 percent larger than their normal size and are tightly held against the perineum. Cowper's gland fluid appears.

ORGASM

In both sexes pulses range from 110 to 180 beats per minute, respirations reach approximately 40 per minute and blood pressure is increased systolically above resting blood pressure by 30 to 80 mm/hg (women) and 40–100 mm/hg (men) and increased diastolically above resting blood pressure 20 to 40 mm/hg (women) and 20–50 mm/hg (men). Intense pleasure is experienced during rhythmic contractions of the pelvic musculature of 0.8 sec duration. Striated muscular spasm may occur, especially carpopedal spasm. Females experience 4–8 contractions in the uterine, vaginal platform, and other perineal musculation. There is no refractory period for women; thus it is possible to have many climaxes varying between plateau and orgasm until orgasm is no longer desired. Usually the second orgasm is more pleasurable than the first. Males experience two phases in orgasm. The first is a lumbar sympathetic reflex which causes contractions of the internal sexual organs responsible for adding seminal fluid to the spermatozoa. This is called the sensation of ejaculatory inevitability. The second phase is the rhythmic 0.8 sec contractions of the periurethral, ischiocavernosus, bulbospongiosus, and anal musculature controlled by nerves of the voluntary motor system. This is accompanied by an intense feeling of pleasure while the ejaculate is being expelled. Masters and Johnson noted that orgasms were perceived as more pleasurable when the volume of ejaculate was larger. The volume is directly related to the time between ejaculations; therefore, the first climax is more pleasurable than the second one, after the obligate refractory period. In males under thirty years old the ejaculate may be expelled 25–50 cm. This distance declines with age. Also, age related is the male refractory period between orgasms. This is very short in a young man; however, it may be several days before a man over 55 can reach orgasm again.

RESOLUTION

During the resolution phase [18] pulse, respiration, blood pressure, and vasocongestion return to normal. The clitoris returns to its normal position immediately, but the vagina may take 20–30 minutes to return to its resting state, during which the cervical os is opened slightly. The penis gradually returns to its flaccid state in two states, losing 50 percent of its erection immediately, then taking approximately 30 minutes to detumesce completely. Certain physiological changes during the sexual cycle enhance the chance of insemination. Female lubrication in the excitement phase buffers the acid in the vagina from pH3.5–4.0 to 4.25–4.5. Moreover during the male orgasm, spermatozoa are expelled in an alkaline solution which further neutralizes the acid vagina for 6–7 hours, allowing for maximum spermatozoic mobility. Also, if penile withdrawal occurs quickly after ejaculation, the cervix drops into the seminal pool. It should be noted that supine intercourse is reproductively most effective in women with normally positioned uteri. For a retroverted uterus the knee-chest position allows the cervix to come in contact with the seminal pool on the anterior wall.

DIAGNOSTIC ASSESSMENT

Before one can diagnose the sexual problem, one must be able to gather the pertinent information. It is common for a patient to present an entirely different chief complaint, such as depression, diabetes, alcoholism, or backaches, rather than the sexual problem which may be bothering him or her. Patients require a matter of fact, nonjudgmental attitude from the physician before they are able to discuss sexual difficulties. Usually the physician initiates the discussion of sexuality while taking a comprehensive history; however, if the patient perceives discomfort in the physician's voice or manner he or she will be reluctant to pursue the topic [15].

It is very important to ask questions which will *elicit specific details*. For example: "What were you thinking at the time you lost your erection?" or "What fantasies do you think about when you masturbate?" or "Do you need anything present in order to become aroused?" It is also useful to phrase a question in a manner that assumes it is a normal occurrence as in the following: "What is your wife's response when you ask her for oral sex?" This question brings up another important point about sexual history taking, namely, one should use words that the patient will understand. Few people know what fellatio means — many understand the term oral sex.

Finally, it is very important to *interview the sexual partner*. Frequently the person who initiates discussion of a sexual problem is the more functional partner. If not included, the other partner may subvert any treatment. Also, since sexuality is one expression of interpersonal relating, it is useful to observe the dynamics between the partners as one gathers information [7].

A guideline for taking a sexual history, detailing specific areas of concern, is as follows:

Present problem: sex and gender
1 Onset and course of problem
2 Results desired
3 Sexual experiences and preferences — fantasies, required objects
4 Recreation and/or procreation issues
5 Last sexual encounter — usual partner/different partner
6 Last autoerotic experience — fantasies, required objects
7 Gender identity
Concurrent events
1 Life stage issues
2 Intimate relationships
3 Family of origin
4 Children
5 Friends
6 Career
7 Finances
8 National concerns
Medical history
1 Diseases
2 Surgery
3 Hospitalizations

4   Medications; alcohol and drug abuse
5   Physical symptoms — genital/nongenital
6   Worries concerning health
7   Psychiatric problems

Past history gender and sexual growth — attitudes

1   Sense of gender
2   Early sexual experiences with adult reaction
3   Sexual information — specifics and sources
4   Latency experiences
5   Puberty
6   Adolescent experiences prior to intercourse
7   First intercourse
8   Family of origin relationships
9   Intimate relationships
10   Courtship and marriage
11   Pregnancy
12   Affairs

CLINICAL SYNDROMES

The above review of normal sexuality provides a foundation for discussing the following clinical syndromes: disorders of performance, disorders of satisfaction, paraphilias, homosexual syndrome, gender dysphoria syndrome, physical developmental disorders, disease-related disorders, iatrogenic disorders, and traumatic disorders [21,34]. For a discussion of disorders of performance and satisfaction — the common sexual disorders — see chapter 20.

Paraphilias

Paraphilias are sexual disorders which are found almost exclusively in men. The deviant behavior provides sexual gratification which substitutes for normal intercourse. Psychoanalytic theory states that the deviation is a fixation at or regression to an infantile level of development. The behavior is viewed as a repetitive attempt to deal with castration anxiety arising from difficulty in switching from an introjection of the mother to identification with the father. Paraphilias may be classified in three groups: (1) exhibitionism, voyeurism, obsene phone callers, and obscene letter writers, who have no physical contact with the victim but who attain sexual gratification with the act or with masturbation shortly thereafter; (2)

fetishism and bestiality, which involves sexual gratification with nonliving objects, body parts, or animals; (3) frottage, pedophilia, incest, sadomasochism, lust murders, necrophilia and rape, which are deviations involving a human victim. Sexual gratification occurs within the context of the specific situation [5].

Exhibitionists, voyeurs, and obscene phone callers and letter writers are generally public nuisances. Sexual gratification is obtained by masturbation or the act itself. The victim is not approached for intercourse. The offender does not commit more serious sexual offenses, although he may be repeatedly apprehended for his compulsive sexual behavior. His victims almost always are female adult strangers [31].

Some exhibitionists will simply reveal a flaccid penis. Others will expose themselves while masturbating an erect penis. In general, exhibiting begins in midpuberty or early twenties. When older men begin exhibiting it is usually a symptom of other problems, such as alcoholism, pedophilia, or organic brain syndrome. Most exhibitionists are socially isolated and have difficulty maintaining intimate relationships. Legally, exhibitionism is considered a minor offense though it represents approximately one-third of all sexual offenses. Reported recidivism ranges between 17 and 22 percent and increases with the number of previous convictions [24].

Voyeurs are also usually young men who are socially isolated. Although they are very careful about not being seen by the victim, they may be reported by neighbors for prowling [31].

Fetishists require the presence of a specific object — usually an article of female clothing — in order to obtain sexual gratification. Masturbation with the object present is most common; however, this may be incorporated into heterosexual or homosexual sexuality. Furthermore, body parts such as feet, even amputation stumps, may be given fetishistic significance. The object is symbolic protection against castration anxiety. Achieving sexual gratification by intercourse or masturbation with animals is called bestiality (zoophilia). This is most common among rural male adolescents with farm animals. It also occurs with house pets [33].

Frottage is sexual gratification through touching the breasts or buttocks of anonymous women in crowded public areas.

Men who engage in exhibitionism, voyeurism, fetishism, and frottage almost never commit serious sexual crimes. In other deviations people are more seriously victimized, such as in *pedophilia*. The pedophile may be heterosexual or homosexual. The heterosexual male chooses girls who are known to him, such as stepchildren or neighbors. The sexual act performed represents the fixation point of the offender's sexual development and is generally age appropriate for the child. These are often acts the child is engaged in with his peers; therefore, unless some violence is associated with the act, it is often the reaction of parents and adults to the act and not the experience itself which has the most detrimental consequences for the child. Children who are willing participants commonly have strong needs for affection and attention. The victims of pedophilia are usually from 6 to 11 years old, and most are between 8 and 10. Looking at and fondling each other's genitals is the most common practice. Pedophilic intercourse is rare. Homosexual pedophiles tend to choose victims between 12 and 15. Masturbation, fellatio to orgasm, and anal intercourse are the most common sexual acts. Again, these are practices common among children of this age. By age, pedophiles tend to cluster into three groups, with peaks at puberty, mid-to-late thirties, and early sixties [24].

   Sadists and masochists frequently find each other. Many prostitutes are willing to inflict pain with whips, spiked heels, and other devices. Fewer are willing to have pain inflicted. Bondage is the practice of being tied in ropes and chains, sometimes with a noose around the neck, during the sexual cycle. Some men find perverse pleasure in choking themselves almost to unconsciousness prior to orgasm. Occasionally accidental death occurs. Many people with normal sexuality have sadomasochistic fantasies. *Lust murders* fortunately are infrequent but receive much publicity. *Necrophilia,* or intercourse with a dead body, occurs most commonly following murder or in mortuaries [33].

   Rape is a violent, often life-threatening assault in which a man uses his penis or other objects to penetrate, without consent, the orifices of another person, usually a woman. The rapist's purpose may be to inflict pain, obtain sexual gratification, or a combination of the two. The aggressive intent seems to be most prominent [1,8].

   Besides whatever physical damage may be inflicted, the victim is often severely traumatized psychologically. The trauma can be as severe as that experienced secondary to natural disasters, severe accidents, diagnosis of a fatal illness, and the unexpected death of relatives or friends [1,28].

THE "RAPE TRAUMA SYNDROME"

Burgess and Holmstrom [1] who have studied the "rape trauma syndrome," describe a two-phase reaction. The acute phase, which they call disorganization, is characterized either by initial denial of the severity of the trauma — the victim gives a calm, composed account of the crime — or by an initial expression of anger, fear, and tearfulness. Initial physical reactions are general body soreness with pain specific to traumatized areas, sleep disturbance, decrease in appetite, and nausea. Initial emotional reactions consist of pronounced fear of physical injury, mutilation, or death; humiliation; guilt; shame; embarrassment; anger; revenge; and self-blame. Frequent nightmares about the rape interrupt sleep, and the victim of a rape often ruminates uncontrollably about her experience, trying to think of a way that it could have been avoided. Interpersonal relationships, especially with men, are anxiety laden. Because of the regression which occurs after this trauma, responsibilities which are normally easy for the rape victim to perform, such as child care or work, become overwhelming. These acute symptoms last from a few days to five to six weeks and overlap the onset of the second phase.

The second phase of the rape trauma syndrome is a long-term process which consists of reorganizing one's life and thoughts to accommodate the traumatic event. Many victims continue to have difficulty functioning in their usual routine because of anxiety and fear which generalizes to all aspects of living. Courses may be dropped at school or a job may be lost. Changing one's telephone number and moving are common. Victims frequently visit relatives. Women fear sex with their husbands or boyfriends and may experience severe sexual dysfunction. Phobias specific to the rape situation are pronounced. Nightmares continue which rework the traumatic material. Depression is common.

The resolution of the syndrome depends substantially upon the individual's personality before the rape. For those individuals predisposed to psychiatric illness, such as psychotics, the rape may precipitate or exacerbate the illness. Even the most well-adjusted person will carry residual effects of fear and anxiety.

TREATMENT OF RAPE VICTIMS

Since the mid-1960s concerned women developed rape crisis centers in many metropolitan and suburban areas. When a rape is reported to the police or hospital, a female rape-crisis counselor is summoned to be with the victim during the police interrogation and medical examination. All victims should be seen by a member of a mental health team if no rape counselor is available. Some police departments have female officers who are responsible for gathering details of the rape. The attending physician is responsible for documenting the victim's general appearance and state of clothing, as well as the character and position of marks of violence on the body and the condition of the affected parts (genitals, mouth, rectum, breasts). The physician must also collect pubic hair and secretions for microscopic examination and culture, medically treat injuries, prescribe for venereal disease, and give an antipregnancy medication if necessary. The physician or his records may be subpoenaed for court proceedings; therefore, the records must be legible and complete. The rape crisis counselor in most programs also accompanies the victim to court. Since long-term psychological effects may be significant, a six-month and year follow-up by the mental health team is advisable [1,19,28].

Homosexual Syndrome

Those persons who feel most sexually stimulated by members of their own sex may accordingly choose their partner of their own sex. Their sense of gender matches their biology. All cultures seem to have some members who are homosexuals. Historically in the United States homosexuals have been very negatively stereotyped. The recent emphasis on minority group rights have permitted the growth of "gay rights," social places to meet partners, and more public acceptability. However in 1977, a fundamentalist antihomosexual group in Florida completed a successful campaign to repeal an equal rights bill for homosexuals.

Approximately 4–5 percent of American males and 2–2.5 percent of American females are exclusively homosexual. Many more people are actively bisexual. Some individuals, especially women, with a predominant heterosexual desire choose homosexual partners in order to find understanding, warmth, and intimacy that they were unable to find with the opposite sex. Many homosexuals establish lasting intimate relationships; however, negative social pressure which instills fear and disapproval prevents others from forming stable relationships. Therefore, multiple brief relations are common. Homosexual women tend to have more stable relationships than homosexual men [16,17].

Homosexuality by itself is not an illness, a fact publicly acknowledged in 1974 by the American Psychiatric Association. It is a minority orientation having the same assets and problems as other minority traits. Homosexuals have the same job histories, psychological problems, illnesses, and religious beliefs as heterosexuals. Some homosexuals seek treatment because they are unhappy about their sexual orientation; most, however, seek treatment not for sexual preference change but for help in forming intimate relationships and adjusting to the societal discrimination. The etiology of homosexuality — the role of biological, intrapsychic, and familial factors — is not known at this time [16,17].

The stereotype of the totally active or totally passive homosexual is no more meaningful than these labels applied to a heterosexual relationship. Sexual practices among homosexuals include kissing, tongue play, nipple caressing, mutual masturbation, oral sex, and, among men, anal intercourse [17].

It is important for the physician to ask questions concerning sexual preference and practices in a nonjudgmental manner. Rectal symptoms may be secondary to anal intercourse. Also, contrary to popular belief, it is very difficult to guess sexual preference from appearance and mannerisms.

Gender Dysphoria Syndrome

An increasing number of people are approaching physicians for a sex-change operation. They initially present a history similar to the highly publicized stereotype of the transsexual. However, very few of these people have a gender disturbance which would be cured by surgery. Most have major intrapsychic disturbances. In the Sexual Behavior Consultation Unit at the Johns Hopkins Medical Institution, Jon Meyer and his co-workers [21,22] have identified eight different syndromes in people who request a sex change. These are stigmatized homosexuals, young transvestites, aging transvestites, sadomasochists, polymorphous perversity, persons with schizoid personality disorders, psychotics, and eonists. The eonists, or true transsexuals, are rare but present themselves as stable people who from their earliest memories felt that they were trapped in a body of the opposite sex. They have usually independently taken steps to live and work full-time successfully as a member of the opposite sex. Their ambivalence while doing this is low; moreover, their family of origin is supportive of the change, having desired a child of the opposite sex [6]. These individuals are most likely to meet the rigorous requirements of the Gender Identity Clinic at the Johns Hopkins Medical Institutions for sex-change surgery. These requirements are (1) to live, dress, and work as the opposite sex for two years; (2) to have financial autonomy and the ability to pay for the surgery; and (3) to take hormones of the opposite sex.

Eonists are most likely to have a good postsurgical prognosis. Individuals of the other seven categories have a much more ambivalent gender and sexual orientation. Transvestites have a core gender identity and biological sex that is male. Historically they have cross-dressed with parental approval or as a punishment in childhood. The young transvestite obtains sexual gratification while cross-dressed either through masturbation or with a homosexual or heterosexual partner. The clothes are fetishistic. The aging transvestite generally seeks sex change surgery at a time of crisis — after his wife who approved of or accepted his cross-dressing, has deserted or died, or he is in a middle-age life crisis. Sexual preference is heterosexual. Stigmatized homosexuals have a gender identity consistent with their biological sex and a sexual preference for members of their own sex. However, they experience so much guilt about homosexuality that they request surgery. They do not cross-dress except for external clothing. Stigmatized female homosexuals usually wear women's underwear and do not bind their breasts. No dildos (artificial penis) are used in sexual relationships, nor socks in pants for penile bulge as is common among female eonists [20].

Sadomasochistic males with same-sex gender identity sometimes request sex-change surgery when masochism is a prominent feature. The same is true for the polymorphous perverse male whose diverse erotic activities are based on what is available, i.e., homosexuality, sadomasochism, pedophilia. Sociopathic elements usually predominate in this syndrome, with a history of many short jobs, many different living arrangements, and multiple relationships [20].

The schizoid applicant for sex-change surgery has an impoverished relationship history with sexuality confined to fantasy. The fantasy is that if he or she could be of the opposite sex, he or she would receive much care from others. There is much gender confusion, but the stronger element is the gender consistent with biologic sex [20].

The reasons psychotic applicants offer for seeking surgery depend upon their delusions. Depressed and schizophrenic psychotic individuals of both sexes may seek surgery, although more commonly psychotic applicants are men [20].

As mentioned earlier, the most important point about the gender dysphoria syndrome is that very few people suffering from the syndrome are true eonists. A conservative approach is needed in determining who is appropriate for surgery [20].

The term transsexual is appropriately applied only to individuals who have undergone surgery, although it is not always used in this manner.

Physical Developmental Disorders

There are abnormalities in all phases of prenatal sexual development. John Money and his co-workers [25,26] have done extensive research in this area. Abnormalities include sexual genotype disorders, sexual phenotype disorders, disorders of maternal endocrine influence on the developing fetus, and endocrine disorders in the fetus.

Turner's and Klinefelter's syndromes are the most common sexual genotype disorders. The sexual karyotype in Turner's syndrome is XO. These children do not develop functioning ovaries or testes. They appear female at birth, since the female phenotype is fundamental. At the age of puberty they remain sexually immature, except for developing some pubic or axillary hair. Rudiments of the internal sexual organs are found with surgery. Because people with Turner's syndrome are raised as females from birth, their gender identity is female [25,26]. Klinefelter's syndrome is defined by a karyotype XXY. Since these children appear to be male at birth they are raised as males. At puberty the clinical features are manifested. There is testicular atrophy, androgen deficiency, and gynecomastia. However, gender identity is clearly male.

Genetically male (XY), children born with Testicular Feminizing Syndrome appear to be normal females at birth because there is an end-organ cellular insensitivity to androgen. These children are raised as girls and have normal female gender identities. The syndrome is usually discovered at puberty when menstruation does not occur and there is no uterus [26].

Female fetuses exposed to various progestational substances which are similar to testosterone and fetuses with adrenogenital syndrome may have external genitalia that are partially or fully masculined. These children are generally raised as girls unless a full penis with urethra exists; then they can be successfully raised as boys who at puberty can be given testosterone, have their ovaries removed and testicular protheses implanted. Gender confusion exists only if the parents were confused or ambivalent about the chosen sex [26].

The most important point is that intersexed children with genitals resembling female should always be assigned female because there is no surgical way to construct a penis, but there are successful techniques for constructing a vagina. John Money recommends surgical removal of the penile-appearing organ in the neonatal period in order to prevent sexual ambiguity for the parents and the child, if the child is to be raised as a girl.

Disease-related Disorders

Sexuality may be disrupted by primary symptoms of a disease of the sexual organs or by the secondary impact of a nonsexually related illness.

Primary dysfunctions impair the neurological pathways, vascular supply, musculature, and tissues of the internal and external sexual organs [2]. A physical examination of the sexual organs, testing sensation, and reflexes is required to evaluate thoroughly any sexual complaint [15]. The common sexual disorders which frequently have an organic basis are impotence in males and dyspareunia in both sexes. Historically the organically impotent man and his partner will both agree that there is no erection or only partial erection (1) upon awakening with a full bladder, (2) during REM sleep, (3) during masturbation to climax, and consistently during attempts at intercourse with any partner. Finally there is generally a prolonged downhill course from partial to no erection even though desire is unimpaired. In contrast, men whose impotence is psychogenic in origin commonly experience erections under these circumstances.

Organic causes of impotence, divided into endocrine, neurological, vascular, local genital, and systemic diseases, are as follows:

Endocrine
Diabetes mellitus
Myxedema
Thyrotoxicosis
Pituitary disease
Addison's disease
Cushing's disease
Feminizing tumors
Klinefelter's (XXY) syndrome

Neurological
Temporal and frontal lobe illness
Vitamin deficiencies
Tabes dorsalis
Amyotrophic lateral sclerosis
Syringomyelia
Multiple sclerosis
Spina bifida
Surgery or trauma to lumbosacral area

Vascular
Leriche Syndrome
Thrombosis of veins or
    arteries of penis
Leukemia
Sickle cell disease
Trauma

Local genital
Priapism
Chordee
Peyronie's disease
Balanitis
Phimosis

Systemic
Decreased libido with impaired erections in
    acute or chronic severe illness

Diabetes mellitus is a major cause of organic impotence.

Treatment for organically based impotence may involve surgical implantation of a silastic rod in the penis, providing a constant semierection, or counseling designed to encourage alternate forms of sexuality, namely, oral sex, dildos, vibrators, and so forth [23].

Priapism, a painful, sustained, involuntary nonsexual erection, is a surgical emergency. The venous stasis must be removed before arterioles are also occluded with subsequent gangrene and fibrous adhesions [23].

Dyspareunia in females may have a physical cause. The symptoms are persistent during each attempt at coitus, with all partners. The woman consistently experiences (1) pain with penile insertion, (2) burning in the vagina and/or aching in the pelvis during and after intercourse, and (3) severe pain upon deep insertion with contraction of the abdomen. This may have started following childbirth. Causes of dyspareunia in women, listed by site of problem, are as follows:

1 *Vaginal outlet*
    Scars
    Bartholin cysts
2 *Clitoris*
    Smegma
    Adhesions
3 *Vagina*
    Infection
    Inadequate lubrication
    Postmenopausal sensitivity reactions
4 *Pelvic structures*
    Traumatic laceration of broad ligament
    Infections
    Endometriosis
    Tumors

Occasionally dyspareunia is secondary to broad ligament laceration from obstetrical procedures, illegal abortions, or traumatic rape. Dyspareunia may follow a hysterectomy where the vaginal cuff is not maintained in its superior position. Postmenopausal women may experience dyspareunia secondary to senile atrophic vaginitis. A persistent coliform vaginal infection may be caused by rectal, then vaginal penetration occurring without washing. A rectal examination may help with the diagnosis since the rectal sphincters will reflexively tighten around the inserted finger when there has been no rectal intercourse. These muscles relax in those who are regular participants [19].

Male dyspareunia, though not common, does occur due to the following causes:

Smegma, infection under foreskin
Phimosis (foreskin cannot be retracted)
Peyronie's disease

Chordee
Testicular pain
Chemical irritation

Peyronie's disease, asenile vasculitis, accompanied by pain and curvature upon erection, is one example. Trauma also may produce a similar response [19].

The secondary impact of disease on sexuality is frequently traumatic to the sick individual and his or her partner. All major illnesses tend to cause a decrease in libido because the person is physically debilitated. Furthermore, many illnesses are disfiguring or cause pain with movement. The partner may feel repulsed by the appearance of his or her mate, viz., severe weight loss secondary to carcinoma, colostomy, amputations, scars, or foul-smelling infections. The act of intercourse may inadvertently cause pain, raising anxiety in one or both partners, and causing loss of sexual excitement. Both partners may fear that sex will make the illness worse or may even cause death. This is common in people with cardiac conditions, especially those whose physicians make comments such as "Don't strain your heart." Physicians very seldom sit down with patients and his or her sexual partner to discuss sexuality in the context of whatever illness is present, although this may be critical to the well-being of the couple [31].

Persons with physical symptoms that interfere with their sexuality should understand that there are many ways to enjoy their sexuality and to be intimate. They particularly need concrete suggestions about how to do this and a person with whom they can ventilate their fears. Masturbation, fellatio, cunnilingus, vibrators, penile protheses, and other substitutes for intercourse need to be given medical sanction. Some paraplegics have active sexual lives as do many people with amputations. There is a developing body of literature and films concerning the sexual aspects of rehabilitation [29].

Iatrogenic Disorders

Many medications affect sexual performance. Retrograde ejaculation, where the ejaculate enters the bladder rather than being pumped out by the urethra, can be a side effect of thioridazine (Mellaril).

Drug-induced impotence may be caused by phenothiazines, monoamine oxidase inhibitors, tricyclic antidepressants, and anticholinergic drugs, i.e., banthine and atropine. Antiadrenergic drugs, for example, guanethidine, reserpine, and aldomet, may prevent ejaculation or impair erection. Alcohol, narcotics, and sedatives frequently depress desire as well as erection. Antiandrogens, e.g., estrogens and steroids, decrease desire; amphetamines initially increase libido but with chronic use diminish sexual functioning [10,23].

Traumatic Disorders

Included in this category are accidents and disfiguring operative procedures.

Occasionally during circumcision a baby's penis is amputated. It is critical that this child be raised as a female, since female genitalia can be surgically constructed and the individual can have orgasms. There is no satisfactory operation to construct a penis. The parents require much support in accepting and adapting to the need to raise the child as a female. Parental attitudes will determine the child's sense of gender—not the XY chromosomes. Castration that occurs after puberty will not physically affect sexual functioning. The adrenals supply sufficient androgen to maintain libido. Psychologically, however, the sexual relationship may be affected, especially since castration is performed for malignancies which are androgen sensitive, which means they must assimilate the impact of the cancer as well as the castration. Carcinoma of the penis which necessitates penectomy is particularly traumatic, as are accidental or war-related penile amputations. Autocastration occurs in some psychotic males. Vasectomy has no physical effect on sexual function but may trigger a psychologically induced disorder [31].

Women and their partners may experience changes in their sexual performance and attitudes after hysterectomy. Physiologically, the hysterectomized and oophorectomized women should experience no change in libido or ability to experience orgasm. But . . . psychologically this may have significant impact.

Traumatic lesions of the vagina during childbirth may cause cystocele, rectocele, or uterine prolapse. The repair of these should be directed toward returning the structures to a condition where intercourse can be enjoyed [31].

It is hoped that the following concepts have become elucidated:

1   Gender identity is one's basic sense of being male or female. This seems to be determined by postnatal experience, not genotype, phenotype, or prenatal hormonal influence.
2   A person's sexual preference is the person or thing he needs in order to achieve sexual gratification. This is also probably learned behavior.
3   Exhibitionists, voyeurs, obscene phone callers, and letter writers practically never escalate to more serious sex crimes.
4   Homosexuality is not an illness per se.
5   Illness has a profound effect on people's sexuality, both for the patient and his or her partner.
6   It is important that the physician have a nonjudgmental atti-

tude, asks factual questions about sexuality and takes the time to discuss sexuality with his patients.

7   Finally, if the physician wonders how important sex is to the patient, he has to consider how important it is to himself. It is probably of even more concern to the patient, since that person is seeking the services of a physician for a problem and at that moment the latter is not.

REFERENCES

1   Burgess, A., and Holmstrom, L. *Rape: Victims of crisis.* Bowie, Md.: Brody, 1974.

2   Cooper, A. J. Factors in male sexual inadequacy: A review. *J. Nerv. Ment. Dis.* 149:337–357, 1969.

3   Erikson, E. *Childhood and society.* New York: Norton, 1963.

4   Friday, N. *My secret garden.* New York: Trident, 1973.

5   Gebhard, P., Gagnon, J., Pomeroy, W., and Christenson, C. *Sex offenders.* New York: Harper and Row, 1965.

6   Green, R. *Sexual identity conflict in children and adults.* New York: Basic Books, 1974.

7   Green, R. *Human sexuality: A health practitioner's text.* Baltimore: Williams and Wilkins, 1975.

8   Hilberman, E. *The rape victim.* New York: Basic Books, 1976.

9   Hite, S. *The Hite report.* New York: Macmillan, 1976.

10   Kaplan, H. *The new sex therapy.* New York: Brunner/Mazel, 1974.

11   Katchadourian, H., and Lunde, D. *Fundamentals of human sexuality.* New York: Holt, Rinehart, and Winston, 1972.

12   Kinsey, A. C., Pomeroy, W., and Martin, C. *Sexual behavior in the human male.* Philadelphia: Saunders, 1948.

13   Kinsey, A. C., Pomeroy, W., Martin, C., and Gebhart, P. *Sexual behavior in the human female.* Philadelphia: Saunders, 1953.

14   Lief, H. "Obstacles to the ideal and complete sex education of the medical student and physician." In *Contemporary sexual behavior: Critical issues in the 1970s,* eds. J. Zubin and J. Money. Baltimore: Johns Hopkins University Press, 1973.

15   Lundberg, P. Neurological examination of patients with sexual dysfunction. *Med. Aspects Hum. Sex.* 11:59–60, 1977.

16   Marmor, J., ed. *Sexual inversion: The multiple roots of homosexuality.* New York: Basic Books, 1968.

17   Marmor, J., and Green, R. "Homosexual behavior." In *Handbook of sexology,* ed. J. Money. North-Holland: Elsevier/Biomedical Press, 1977.

18   Masters, W., and Johnson, V. *Human sexual response.* Boston: Little, Brown, 1966.

19   Masters, W., and Johnson, V. *Human sexual inadequacy.* Boston: Little, Brown, 1970.

20   Meyer, J. K. Clinical variants among applicants for sex reassignment. *Arch. Sex. Behav.* 3:527–558, 1974.

21   Meyer, J. K. Training and accreditation for the treatment of sexual disorders. *Am. J. Psychiatry* 133:389–394, 1976.

22   Meyer, J. K., ed. Sex Assignment and reassignment: Intersex and gender identity disorders. Special issue. *Clin. Plast. Surg.* 1(2), 1974.

23   Meyer, J. K., ed. *Clinical management of sexual disorders.* Baltimore: Williams and Wilkins, 1976.

24   Mohr, J., Turner, R., and Jerry, M. *Pedophilia* and *exhibitionism.* Toronto: University of Toronto, 1964.

25   Money, J. *Sex errors of the body.* Baltimore: Johns Hopkins University Press, 1968.

26   Money, J., and Ehrhardt, A. *Man and woman, boy and girl: The differentiation and the dysmorphism of gender identity from conception to maturity.* Baltimore: Johns Hopkins University Press, 1972.

27   Money, J., and Tucker, P. *Sexual signatures on being a man or a woman.* Boston: Little, Brown, 1975.

28   Nadelson, C., and Notman, M. Emotional repercussions of rape. *Med. Aspects Hum. Sex.* 11(3), 1977.

29   Nelson, W., ed. *Textbook of pediatrics.* Philadelphia: Saunders, 1966.

30   Pinderhughes, C. A., Grace, E. B., Reynad, Anderson, R. Interrelationships between sexual functioning and medical conditions. *Med. Aspects Hum. Sex.* 6:52–76, October 1972.

31   Sadock, B., Kaplan, H., and Freedman, A., eds. *The sexual experience.* Baltimore: Williams and Wilkins, 1976.

32   Salzman, L. "Sexuality in psychoanalytic theory." In *Modern psychoanalysis,* ed. J. Marmor. New York: Basic Books, 1968.

33   Schmidt, C. W., Jr., Meyer, J. K., and Lucas, M. J. "Sexual deviations and personality disorders." In *Personality disorders,* ed. J. Lion, pp. 154–177. Baltimore: Williams and Wilkins, 1974.

34   Sharpe, L., Kuriansky, J. B., and O'Connor, J. F. A preliminary classification of human functional sexual disorders. *J. Sex Marital Ther.* 2:106–114, 1976.

35   Sherfey, M. The evaluation and nature of female sexuality in relation to psychoanalytic theory. *J. Am. Psychoanal. Assoc.* 14:28–128, 1966.

36   Stoller, R. *Sex and gender,* 2nd ed. New York: Jason Aronson, 1974.

37   Stoller, R. Sexual excitement. *Arch. Gen. Psychiatry* 33:899–909, Aug. 1976.

38   Wise, T. N. Sexuality throughout the life cycle. *Psychosomatics,* in press.

22

Stress-Related Disturbances

Ellen McDaniel, M.D.

Stress is an ambiguous concept. It implies an event or predicament which causes increased tension in a person, e.g., the stress of unemployment. It also refers to the physiological and subjective experience produced by such an event, e.g., "I feel stressed, tense, pressured." Such definitions usually have a negative connotation attached to them. The devaluation speaks to the universal fantasy of man to be able to avoid experiencing anything unpleasant; thus, anybody or anything which produces dysphoria is called stressful. However, another implication of stress is the accentuation of something important. In this sense, stress can be viewed as a positive, stimulating, exciting situation. For example, the anticipated birth of one's first grandchild can be a stressful period and still a very joyful one.

A discussion of conflict and crisis enters into a discourse on stress. Rapoport [19] speaks of a crisis as an upset in the usual homeostatic balance; i.e., in the usual adaptive, defensive, pleasure-seeking, and problem-solving mechanisms an individual maintains. When a situation (a stress) changes the balance, the person strives to find an equilibrium again, first trying his usual coping methods. If these do not work, the person creates new adaptive and problem-solving measures or regresses to the employment of older and previously discarded ones. One often experiences conflict between the desire to master the stress and the desire to regress in the face of the tension.

Research into the field of stress has been growing fairly steadily since World War II. The range of emphasis has been enormous, from physiological responses to the understanding of very specific environmental stress-producing situations to developmental concerns. Stress is a field investigated by people in all of the behavioral sciences: psychiatrists, physiologists, anthropologists, sociologists, educators, and others. As a result, the phenomenon of stress can be examined from many perspectives.

The emphasis in this chapter is on the clinical situation. In 1968 the Committee on Nomenclature and Statistics of the American Psychiatric Association (APA) used a diagnostic category called transient situational disturbances [1]. The definition stated that the symptoms may be of any severity, from mild anxiety or depression to a full-blown psychotic picture. The crucial aspect was that the symptoms represented an acute reaction to an overwhelming environmental stress and that the symptoms should recede as the stress diminished. The category was divided into developmental stages, i.e., adjustment reactions of infancy, childhood, adolescence, adult life, and late life. This shows consideration for two important facts. First, one's reactions to upheavals is very dependent upon the psychological resources potentially available to that person at a moment of stress. For example, during the bombing of London, young children did not seem as traumatized by the physical danger and chaos as they did by separation from their parents, which was made so their children could be "secure" in the countryside. Second, each stage of life has its own predictable as well as unique set of stresses. Many people do not seek psychiatric help when confronted with these stresses but enough do to warrant an additional discussion.

There is one major problem in discussing stress-related disturbances. Since one's reaction to stress (particularly developmental stresses, as parenthood and retirement) depends so much on one's psychological equipment, it sometimes becomes difficult to differentiate a response within the range of fairly healthy behavior and that which indicates more deep-seated problems. There seems to be greater uniformity of response in people involved in a life-threatening external danger, as a tornado, perhaps because attention is focused on survival or withdrawal, with little opportunity for symbolic elaboration. However, in the more prolonged responses to stresses, symbolic elaboration occurs, and the influence of previous characterological and neurotic difficulties becomes a consideration. In the third edition of the *Diagnostic and Statistical Manual of Mental Disorders (DSM-III)* a separation of developmental and external stress-related disturbances is made for children [3]. For adults, there remains no adequate way yet for describing the variety of responses to developmental stresses or challenges if these responses are not so structured as to be considered characterological, neurotic, or psychotic disturbances. Perhaps this reflects psychiatry's neglect of adult developmental issues.

There is another kind of stress-related disturbance which mirrors in part the culture of the individual. These are a group of syndromes, found in very specific subcultures, which partially reflect the folklore, adversities, and guidelines for behavior in the culture. In part, these syndromes describe behavior considered extreme and pathological even within the culture, which means that they also have an origin in intrapsychic problems. These disorders (amok, koro, and others) are grouped under stress-related disturbances because of their relationship to stresses in the external environment. Many of these disorders are of more historical than current clinical interest, and the present classification scheme does not readily include them.

For this particular chapter, stress-related disturbances are classified under three major headings: developmental stresses, situational stresses, and cultural stresses. The emphasis is on adults, as childhood disturbances are treated elsewhere.

DEVELOPMENTAL STRESS-RELATED DISTURBANCES

Definition

These are the variable reactions to the expectable passing of life's milestones (emancipation from home, marriage, moving, parenthood, loss of family and friends, career decisions, aging, retirement, widowhood, dying). These reactions convey the upset of the homeostatic balance of the individual as he is faced with a new set of challenges appropriate for his physical and psychological development. The symptomatic behavior usually recedes with time as the individual integrates and adapts to the permanent change in his life-space. The symptoms may, however, be the initial sign of more significant regression and more internalized and structuralized difficulties. In such a case, another diagnosis is indicated. The reactions considered here, however, are within the range of normal behavior and are not necessarily evidence of a psychiatric illness. Therefore, strictly speaking, this discussion does not belong under the section on psychiatric disorders. It is included here, however, to give a dynamic perspective to the spectrum of stress-related disturbances.

History and Classification

In twentieth century Western civilization one would not be too far astray in saying that the average individual must confront over a lifetime a variety of complicated intrapsychic, interpersonal, bureaucratic, and technological situations. This actually understates the complexity of our times. Although each person's particular experiences in growing up are similar to those of a great many others, each person nevertheless has the individual stamp of the unique set of influences (genetic, constitutional, familial, and sociocultural) which make him different from anyone else and different in his capacity to master the various challenges over his lifetime. In Western civilization, the majority of people pass some, if not most, of the previously mentioned milestones as adults. Each of these milestones has inherent in it all of the ingredients to provoke conflict, regression, and growth. The treatment of the variation of responses to these normative crises were not within the province of the practicing psychiatrist until recently. People turned instead to family members, friends, religious leaders, and family doctors for support and guidance during whatever upheaval these crises provoked in the homeostatic balance. Psychiatrists also did not see these responses as part of their work. In the late nineteenth and early twentieth centuries, psychiatry concerned itself primarily with the severely ill and institutionalized patients. As Freudian theory became increasingly accepted and after two world wars demanded focus on less severe psychological disturbances, psychiatry turned its attention more also to neurotic and characterological problems. In recent years several other developments have occurred. Cultural patterns have changed so that along with increased mobility, decreased extended family commitments, declining church involvement, and increased focus on attaining self-fulfillment, people have turned more to "outsiders" for help. Psychiatry, meanwhile, became more involved in learning about normal development (particularly ego development), extended itself to prophylactic work with people not considered to be patients, and essentially opened the limits of its interests. This expansion of the field has resulted in a necessity on the physician's part to appreciate once again the variability of normal behavior and to be able to respond in a clinically appropriate manner to healthy individuals. In thus describing these developmental variations, a diagnostic category is being artificially constructed.

Epidemiology

There are statistical reports on isolated phenomena, but one can safely say that it is a rare individual indeed who goes through any of the developmental milestones mentioned without a fair share of ambivalence and strain. Those who seek psychiatric assistance are either individually or socially oriented towards using a mental health professional in such a manner. Another group of people who seek psychiatric help at a time of developmental stress consists of those either referred by others or those who have long-standing difficulties that begin to surface under the stress of a particular developmental situation.

Clinical Description

The following selected developmental stresses are briefly described here, the purpose being more to illustrate the variation of conflicts and responses common to each than to investigate comprehensively the challenges of adulthood.

MARRIAGE

The wedding ceremony signifies both legally and socially the changing commitments from parents to spouse. The months and years to follow demand from the two partners a modus operandi within which each can establish a mutually acceptable and adaptive psychological equilibrium. Each is required to learn to respect their differences and to handle disagreement in as constructive a manner as possible. The fantasies of the courtship period at some point will need to be faced and brought into a more realistic perspective. An illustration may help to clarify some of these commonplace issues.

> Mrs. J, an intelligent and extroverted woman, grew up in a wealthy old Californian family. She materially had most anything that she wanted and she lived a very self-centered existence, oriented to a socially acceptable pursuit of pleasure. Mr. J's parents were poor and hard-working people. Mr. J described himself as similar in personality to his parents: compulsive, aggressive, and overly conscientious. The two young people saw in each other the fulfillment of qualities that each sensed personally lacking. Mrs. J saw in her husband someone who would provide her with control, stability, and a family life which she felt missing. Mr. J believed that his bride would give him social acceptance and greater opportunities for a carefree life-style.
>
> What happened over the next few years was not atypical. The preconscious reasons why each married the other became irritating after a while. Each felt considerable disruption in the continuity of their lives after marriage relative to their lives before marriage. Mrs. J resented the financial and household restrictions placed upon her, and Mr. J resented his wife's lack of appreciation for his career advancements. She felt that her husband was too conservative and controlling, whereas Mr. J felt that his wife was frivolous. Each tried to get the other to change. Mr. J began having temper tantrums and Mrs. J became depressed. At this point, psychiatric intervention was

considered. Before committing themselves to asking for professional help, the couple tried to resolve their own difficulties. Mrs. J became involved through a friend in a difficult and competitive sport which gave her a sense of personal satisfaction and a structure to her life. Mr. J, meanwhile, became increasingly accomplished in his profession and received considerable recognition from his colleagues. Each became less demanding of the other. Also, both were committed to making the marriage work and talked out their disappointments and anger with each other as they reestablished a new equilibrium in their relationship.

PARENTHOOD

Perhaps an even greater strain on an individual is the developmental stage of parenthood. The demand to be even less self-oriented makes adjustment difficult. Gone is a considerable degree of privacy and spontaneity in life-style. The dependency needs of the children claim priority. Dependency is used here in its broadest sense. It means the need for parental involvement in the children's physical and psychological well-being, including issues such as the provision of affection, consistency, autonomous activity, discipline, recreational, and educational opportunities. As the children go through their "growing pains," parents experience parallel "pains." The issues significant for each developmental phase of childhood have their dynamic meanings for each parent. Some parents are more comfortable with infants, others with adolescents. A mother may feel useless and rejected when her youngest goes off to school; another may feel guilty because she seemingly can not wait for that to happen. Each parent once again has to come to terms with his own experiences in being parented as he responds to his offspring's needs. Each has to make peace with his image of the ideal parent and his own capabilities and limitations in this role. Not insignificant either is the effect of parenthood on other roles, as the marital one.

RETIREMENT

Part of one's adult self-concept relates to the work he or she does (e.g., one may identify himself as a husband, father, golfer, and engineer). After spending sometimes as much as three-fourths of one's life working, retirement can be experienced as a personal and cultural shock. Life loses its previous structure, relationships with work-related friends are altered, difficulties with one's spouse may increase because of the changed life-style; one's sense of being productive is threatened and a whole variety of other factors accumulate to make this a troublesome stage. After the initial excitement of a long vacation trip or finishing some long-neglected projects is over, a period of depression is not uncommon. There is a mourning

for the past as it was and the future that never will be. With time, many re-
tirees adjust and develop a new structure to their lives. Others remain de-
spondent and lonely, and more active measures of help are needed for
these people.

The three examples picked are only a few of the adult developmental
challenges which are handled with varying degrees of distress and comfort. These challenges are rarely, if ever, faced without some amount of
conflict. What becomes important is not the presence or absence of
distress but rather whether the individual can again attain a satisfactory
equilibrium without experiencing too heavy a psychological burden or
without seriously jeopardizing others involved.

Differential Diagnosis

The most important differential is between that which is a normal variation of response to a developmental stress and behavior which indicates
more internalized, longer-standing disturbances that have become reactivated by the developmental stress. A psychotic reaction is severe and in-
capacitating and would not be considered a normal variation of response.
Neurotic illness is accompanied by considerable anxiety, guilt, or depression that persist despite a rational understanding of the situation or feelings. The prolonged affect disturbances indicate inner structuralized conflicts. People will handle new challenges within their characterological
framework for adapting and coping. If the responses to a new developmental challenge are rigid and inappropriate for the situation, one is dealing then with a characterological problem.

Prognosis and Management

Most of those going through adult "growing pains" do not seek psychiatric assistance. Their distress is seen mostly by family members, friend,
and working associates, but the symptoms are usually not seriously
disruptive and they wane as the conflicts are resolved. Support, clarification of issues, and an opportunity for ventilation are the most effective
means of handling such patients.

SITUATIONAL STRESS-RELATED DISTURBANCES

The disturbances of affect and behavior described in this section are precipitated by environmental stresses. The symptoms vary in severity from

mild agitation or depression to a full-blown psychotic state with hallucinations and delusions. When the particular stress ceases, the symptoms
should recede as the individual reestablishes his psychological equilibrium. If the individual has had previous and persisting psychological difficulties or if treatment has been mismanaged, a prolonged reaction to the
stress may be observed. This often reflects the resurgence of the underlying emotional disorder, and another diagnosis would be indicated. Two
case histories may clarify the distinction between situational disturbances
and other functional disorders.

Mrs. W came to the emergency room stating that she was going to
commit suicide. She had most of the classical symptoms of a neurotic
depression: agitation, anorexia, insomnia, and tension. Two days
previously, she had been fired from her job which was her only
means of support. She had applied for social-service assistance but
because of bureaucratic difficulties, she could not obtain financial aid
for another month. With one dollar left, she faced eviction from her
apartment the next morning. Her youngest child, a five-year-old
daughter whom she had kept with her, was ill. A psychosocial history unfolded many years of maladaptive behavior. This woman had
dropped out of high school and moved aimlessly around the country
"when things started to close in." She could not keep a job, had
abandoned four of her five children, and was involved in minor legal
difficulties.

The social worker who interviewed the patient was able to obtain emergency funds from the Social Service Department. She also
convinced the landlady to let the patient remain in her apartment,
and she referred the daughter to a pediatric clinic. A followup visit
two weeks later portrayed a woman who was mildly belligerent and
evasive but who gave no evidence of depression. In this case the
symptomatic depression was an affective response to an environmental crisis, and the symptoms abated when the stress was relieved. There were no signs of guilt, remorse, loss of self-esteem, irrational anxiety, or other manifestation of an intrapsychic structural
conflict. The patient certainly had characterological problems but the
acute illness was a situational disturbance.

Mr. A presented with aphonia to his family doctor. A thorough
workup excluded all conceivable organic etiologies. A history of the
present illness connected the onset of symptoms with a disagreement
with his mother. There was a moment in the argument when the patient wanted to yell obscenities at her and suddenly found himself

unable to talk. Superficially, this episode might appear as a temporary situational disturbance, the result of a disagreement. However,
discussions with the patient brought forth many other examples in
which this man since childhood felt his anger as an uncontrollable
rage. He experienced tremendous guilt and loss of self-esteem at any
recognition of his angry feelings. He used a repertoire of rigid and
ultimately self-destructive defenses to keep his feelings under control and his self-esteem at a tolerable level. The aphonia was not a
situational disturbance, although the symptom became evident after
an external stress. In this patient the aphonia represented a long-
standing neurotic problem.

In addition to gross stress reaction and traumatic (war) neurosis, also
included under situational stress-related disturbances are two quite rare
but historically well-known syndromes, folie à deux and Ganser's syndrome. The pathology of the patients in these two disturbances extends
beyond a situational reaction, but the syndromes are included here because each requires a unique set of circumstances to unfold.

Gross Stress Reaction

DEFINITION AND HISTORY
A severe disruption in the homeostatic equilibrium of an individual by an
event which is perceived by the person to be a major threat to his well-being. The event, often enough, is a momentous one, like a flood or fire or
the loss of a home or country.

Gross stress reaction describes mankind's most elementary and automatic response to a major psychological disruption. It thus has a history
dating back to the beginning of the time when man began to be affectively
tied to his past and his future.

CLASSIFICATION
Until recently, this stress reaction was widely accepted clinically but not
officially. With the proposed DSM revision [2] a category called stress
disorders will include this extreme situational illness (i.e., acute and
chronic catastrophic stress disorders). Traumatic neurosis (war neurosis)
is sometimes considered a synonym for gross stress reaction. Although
it is very similar, in this chapter stress reactions secondary to war are considered separately because of the unique culture of the military. Gross
stress reactions can be short-lived or much more chronic. If a reaction
becomes prolonged, older psychological difficulties will come to play an

increasingly important role. Gross stress reaction has no descriptive boundaries for the severity of symptoms.

ETIOLOGY AND PATHOGENESIS

What exactly happens when confronting a catastrophic experience? There is usually an abrupt and unexpected alteration in the world that one has known and expected. A feeling of vulnerability is greatly accentuated by the assault of events sometimes beyond the scope of one's imagination and certainly beyond one's control. There is a sudden tearing off from old ties, with the realization that life may be permanently altered by the occurrence of the catastrophe, yet at the same time one has a heightened need to be taken care of and directed. The most elementary concern is for physical survival and the survival of those people most significant to one. All of these factors create a marked disturbance in the homeostatic balance. An event has occurred for which there may have been little anticipatory work; the usual coping mechanisms are not equipped to deal with the magnitude of stress; dependency and security needs may be minimally satisfied if at all; and the whole physical, emotional, and social future of the person and his loved ones is jeopardized.

CLINICAL DESCRIPTION

Different authors emphasize different aspects of a gross stress reaction. For example, Bowlby [4] wrote about the reaction to separation in youngsters, Lindemann [16] described an acute grief reaction, Parkes [18] emphasized the change in one's assumptive world, and Tyhurst [21] discussed a crisis from the perspective of time. Tyhurst gave a very broad overview of an individual's reaction to severe stress and his outline is used here.

Tyhurst divides the syndrome into three phases. The first is named the *impact phase.* It begins with the onslaught of the stress and ends when that stress no longer exerts a direct effect. The impact phase may last from seconds to hours or even days. The individual is oriented entirely to the present. Behavior becomes almost automatic in response to the current reality demands. Tyhurst estimated that between 12 percent to 25 percent of all the people facing a civilian disaster will be able to assess the situation and carry through an appropriate plan of action. Another 10 percent to 25 percent of the people involved will react with extreme and maladaptive behavior, manifesting panic, immobility, and uncontrollable affective expressions. The rest of the population will be stunned and bewildered, with a narrowed field of attention, unawareness of any subjective feelings, and automatic behavior responses.

The second phase, the *period of recoil,* begins with the removal of the impact stress and lasts approximately until the point when life takes up its routine existence again. The time duration of this is variable also, lasting from days to weeks. The individual then begins to experience fully and subjectively what he has just been through. He begins to think of his immediate future and takes steps to find shelter, contact relatives, and get emotional support. Victims in this phase have a significant need to "abreact" the experience and to be taken care of by others. Dependency needs are greatly accentuated and the survivor, in his search to have his own needs met, has difficulty giving support to others.

The third phase, the *posttraumatic period,* is ushered in by the return of stability and routine to each day. It is in this phase that the full impact of the disaster is most keenly felt, particularly those changes that are permanent. It is at this point that the mourning of lost family and home begins. The survivor appreciates now the irreversible alteration in his life. The person thinks in all of the time perspectives: past, present, and future. He may have periodic episodes of depression or insomnia, but generally he returns to the day-to-day business. For those unable to make the transition, the term traumatic neurosis is sometimes used. This neurosis reflects a combination of responses from the impact and recoil phase plus premorbid personality traits and problems.

DIFFERENTIAL DIAGNOSIS
As is true for many of the stress-related disturbances, the most important differential is from other more internalized psychological difficulties. However, a longer-standing emotional difficulty does not preclude another more situationally related disturbance and, in terms of immediate management, may even be irrelevant.

PROGNOSIS AND MANAGEMENT
The period of recoil is the best time for intervention. Survivors have withstood the immediate physical danger to their well-being and during the recoil, they are in need of and receptive to direction and empathy. They want a listener and a parental figure to help them reintegrate their lives. As in the war neurosis, it is inadvisable to isolate an individual from the stresses that he must confront, unless he truly cannot handle them. But one can be of enormous psychological assistance by being available to listen and to guide a survivor through the stresses.

Factors which enhance a favorable prognosis are an anticipatory period, available help during the period of recoil, a relatively adaptive personality structure, and the minimization of secondary gain. If one has time to prepare for a major stress, some of the psychological work can be done before the crisis. For example, when a war causes a large migration from one culture to another, those who have been able to begin the grief work beforehand and make preparations for their new futures, such as learning the new language, will probably weather the shock better than those who experience the forced migration unexpectedly. The factor of secondary gain is elaborated upon in more detail elsewhere.

Traumatic (War) Neurosis

DEFINITION

There are three general categories of meaning for the term *traumatic neurosis*. One group of definitions refers to those psychological problems encountered in a military and, more specifically, in a combat environment. This group of problems is the focus here. Traumatic neurosis has also been used to describe an emotional upheaval secondary to experiencing a single, time-limited, overwhelming situation — a gross stress reaction. The third category of traumatic neurosis covers that individual who has experienced an accident with personal injury (real or imagined) and has a prolonged recovery which may be complicated by the possibility of financial compensation.

The war neuroses have been referred to by a variety of other terms, such as battle fatigue, shell-shock, and operational fatigue. Authors disagree on whether the acute symptoms of distress or only the chronic problems should be considered a traumatic neurosis. Whatever position one takes, most writers agree that the term refers to a noticeable psychological upheaval in response to the particular environmental stress of war, and the upheaval interferes with the soldier's ability to function in that setting. The acute symptoms usually relate to the fear of the real possibility of being killed or mutilated. The chronic symptoms are those which persist despite the removal of the environmental threat of injury.

HISTORY

The history of the traumatic neurosis repeats much of the history of hysteria (see chapter 9). It also has a background which reflects military history and sociology, since the psychological expression of stress under combat cannot be isolated from the sociocultural milieu of the combat area. One can probably appreciate that a war fought in one's own country will be viewed with a different attitude than one in a country never previously heard of; or a soldier fighting during the Victorian Age will probably bring to the military setting a different way of expressing difficulties than a soldier of the 1960s.

During the Civil War and in the beginning of World War I, psychological problems were not recognized and the symptoms were attributed to microscopic lesions of the central nervous system. The oft-used term battle fatigue is reminiscent of the term brain weariness used to describe war neurosis in the Civil War. By the end of World War I, at which time Freudian theory was just beginning to be recognized, and certainly by World War II, a psychodynamic understanding of men's reactions to combat began developing. During the successive wars interest and research into this area have developed considerably, and the knowledge gained has had significant applicability to the understanding of stress in civilian populations.

CLASSIFICATION

Two areas need discussion at this point; one is the differentiation of the acute and chronic phases; the other is the differentiation of the traumatic neurosis from any other nosological entity. Most writers agree that there are two phases to the traumatic neurosis. The acute phase is sometimes referred to by another designation, as a traumatic syndrome or battle fatigue. The chronic phase is the more definitive and structuralized establishment of a neurotic illness. However, the term traumatic neurosis sometimes refers specifically to either the acute or the chronic phase, and sometimes is used to include both aspects.

How does the traumatic neurosis differ from any other neurotic or characterological illness? Kardiner [13] feels that the traumatic neuroses are different from psychoneuroses in that there is usually a small number of symptoms in the former and that these symptoms are very similar for all individuals. He wrote that there is very little symbolic elaboration in the traumatic neurosis, unlike the psychoneurosis. Kardiner has stated that a traumatic event can provoke an old psychoneurotic conflict with symbolic extension expressed through displacement and condensation. He does not consider this a traumatic neurosis but acknowledges that both aspects can be present. Grinker [12], another well-known authority on the war neurosis, has stated that the neurosis of war is psychoneurosis, with some quantitative differences. He has implied that if one is referring to the chronic phase of the traumatic neurosis, the illness will show the same characteristics as any other neurosis. He does feel that the war neuroses are different from other types of traumatic neurosis because in the latter the trauma is usually single and short-lived and the psychological response is significantly complicated by considerable secondary gain and minimal superego conflict.

A final comment warrants attention when trying to classify this disorder. The word neurosis is a misnomer unless it is used loosely to refer to any psychological disturbance. In World War I, psychological distress was commonly expressed somatically and was diagnosed as a problem of internal medicine, although one would categorize many of the symptoms as psychosomatic or psychophysiological. In the Viet Nam conflict, the majority of psychiatric referrals were characterological problems. Thus, war neurosis includes not only neurotic problems but any other form of functional mental illness attributed to combat.

EPIDEMIOLOGY, ETIOLOGY, AND PATHOGENESIS
The development of a war neurosis can be examined from the three time perspectives: past, present, and future. The most important past contributing factor is the precombat character structure. Although the literature gives widely differing opinions on the significance of this factor, the general trend favors the position that the greater the difficulty in adapting to life as a civilian, the greater the likelihood of problems while in the military. Theoretically at least, this makes the most sense.

The present factor, the particular stress of the military community and of combat, is the one emphasized here for the purpose of clarification. The soldier in a combat situation has to cope with the constant possibility of being mutilated or destroyed. He lives in fear that the next mission or the next explosion will bring about his premature demise. In the environment of combat, fear has a utilitarian function. It alerts the individual to danger, heightens his state of vigilance, increases his sensory receptiveness to trouble, and provides a motivating force for mastery of the situation. However, one basic feature of the military culture is that no one individual can master a battle entirely by himself. The individual soldier depends on the very large military institution, including even policy-forming and law-making branches of his government, for his lone survival. In a much more real sense, he depends on his own relatively small combat group. In exchange for his commitment to the group, he expects them to support him. Grinker [12] discussed this aspect of military life very poignantly in his book. If there is a lack of group cohesiveness or poor leadership, there is an awareness of decreased support which increases the individual's anxiety. If the group is a cohesive one, the individual soldier may experience conflict between his ego-ideal of being a good group member (by accepting the military situation) and his wish to run away from the task confronting him. Even if problems with his military unit are minimal, a very important consideration, perhaps the most important, is the degree of stress one has to endure, the exposure to combat being the most severe. The longer the time spent in combat, the greater the likelihood for a psychological catastrophe. Also related to being increasingly psychologically vulnerable are the emotionally depleting effects of physical illness and discomfort, fatigue, and isolation from others. The quality of combat plays an additional role. Statistics [3] reveal that in the World Wars, psychiatric casualties were at least five times higher in combat units than in noncombat units. This was not true for the Viet Nam conflict wherein psychiatric casualties were the same in the support units and in the combat units. When the combat situation is such that the individual soldier feels some action is taking place that will end the stress, the incidence of psychiatric attrition decreases. For example, soldiers fare better psychologically when they can see the enemy and when the troops are moving, even if it is in retreat [5]. Should prevailing circumstances be such that the duration and intensity of the stress are beyond the individual's ability to integrate and his support system falters, he begins to withdraw and regress, becoming more oriented towards self-preservation than towards any other commitments. If the problem goes beyond the acute stage, old characterological and neurotic problems come increasingly to the fore and become interwoven with the present difficulties.

The future factor at this point becomes significant. Treatment has to keep one part focused on the present, i.e., the dilemma of satisfying both the military's needs and the individual's needs and one part focused on the future. The greater the secondary gain and the more overt and covert permission to regress, the stronger the possibility for an acute reaction to become chronic. Although the most expedient immediate solution to a soldier's symptomatic behavior may be to remove him from battle, one may be encouraging a dragging out of recovery by this decision.

Once the soldier returns home, he is confronted with a wholly new set of problems. Old psychological difficulties exert their effect particularly at this time, but there are other unique difficulties, such as a "return cultural shock," survivors' guilt, problems in adapting to changed family members, and so forth.

CLINICAL DESCRIPTION

During the acute stage, Kardiner [13] described a rather universal and characteristic reaction to overwhelming stress: irritability, anorexia, insomnia, carelessness, short attention span, and a predominant feeling of fear. As the fear increases the soldier becomes disorganized and hypersensitive to noise. Sleep continues to be disturbed and is frequently interrupted by recurring dreams of combat. The chronic phase begins when the external stress is no longer present and the influence of previous methods of handling anxiety is more obvious. These methods are invariably regressive since more mature methods have been tried and have not succeeded. Examples of regressive methods include phobic avoidance, compulsive rituals, and withdrawal into fantasy. Dreams become more elaborate as older conflicts are symbolically expressed. Characterological defenses are accentuated, such as escalation of one's stubbornness or passivity. Secondary gain increases since the illness often results in the removal from the military and may even mean financial compensation.

The clinical manifestations may vary enormously, particularly in the chronic phase. One sees all of the richness of the individual personality in the expression of symptoms, plus a sociocultural dimension which helps explain the group differences from one war to another.

DIFFERENTIAL DIAGNOSIS

As is true for other stress-related disturbances, it is valid to ask what symptoms reflect primarily a temporary response to the situation and what indicate more structuralized difficulties. Malingering should also be considered. A clue to this latter possibility is a significant difference in behavior with peers and with authority figures, or more appropriate behavior when no one seems to be watching.

PROGNOSIS AND MANAGEMENT

Since etiological factors include physical deprivation, prolonged combat, and fatigue, treatment in the acute stage involves removal from extreme stress, rest, and improvement otherwise in physical conditions. However, during World War II, the crucial importance of treating patients on or very close to the combat scene was realized by the poor results of those removed. By sending soldiers away for treatment, the secondary gain was accentuated, group loyalty was lessened, and the symptoms became more organized. During the Viet Nam conflict, Bourne [5] stated that officers tried to treat psychiatric casualties on the spot by lessening the extreme environmental stress, allowing for ventilation, and supporting appropriate dependency needs. Every soldier was entitled to one week of "R and R" (rest and recreation). To minimize the stress of prolonged combat and to decrease secondary gain, a tour of duty lasted only twelve or thirteen months. A soldier then knew that sickness or death was not the only way to get back home. However, because of the short tour of duty, there was much less group cohesiveness than was true for previous wars and hence much less support for sustaining stress.

Prognosis is excellent for those soldiers in the acute stage, prognosis here meaning ability to function in the military. Factors which worsen the prognosis are increased secondary gain, previous history of civilian maladaptiveness, prolonged stress of combat, and lack of a military support system.

Folie à Deux

DEFINITION AND HISTORY

Folie à deux describes a shared delusional system between two or more persons living in intimate association with one another. One of the partners is domineering over the other and is considered the more ill member. He is the one who is initially delusional and imposes his beliefs on the passive person involved.

With respect to the history [8] of this illness, Baillarger wrote in 1860, about a family in which two members were hospitalized at the same time, each beset by the same delusional beliefs as the other. He called their malady *folie communiquée*. Seventeen years later, Lasègue and Fabret [15] in their classic paper, used the term folie à deux. Between 1877 and 1885 four subcategories of folie à deux were described. Lasègue and Fabret coined the first one "folie imposée," which described the imposing of the delusions of a psychotic person onto a mentally healthy individual. If the two are separated, the delusions of the recipient will diminish or disappear. In 1880, Régis described *folie simultanée* as a paranoid psychosis which appeared simultaneously in two predisposed persons who, like in all the other subcategories, lived in intimate association with each other. In 1881, the term *folie communiquée* was resurrected by Marandon de Montyel who differentiated the subcategory *folie imposée* by adding that the recipient, once delusional, maintained his system of beliefs even after being separated from the originally psychotic person. Finally, in 1885, Lehmann separated out *folie induite* as an illness wherein new delusions are acquired by one psychotic person under the influence of the other.

CLASSIFICATION

Usually folie à deux is classified as a particular form of paranoid psychosis. It is placed under stress-related disturbances here because of its occurrence only under the particular situational arrangement described under etiology.

EPIDEMIOLOGY

The literature does not contain a great number of these cases. In an average psychiatrist's practice, one may see only one such occurrence during his or her professional career. Dewhurst and Todd [8] described the highest incidence in sister-sister combinations, whereas Lasègue and Fabret [15] felt that a child-parent combination was most likely.

ETIOLOGY AND PATHOGENESIS

Several conditions seem necessary for this illness to occur. Dewhurst [8] described this as a situation wherein an active, more intelligent, and truly delusional individual lives in very intimate association with a passive, often borderline intelligent person, and the two people are relatively isolated from outside influences. The active member imposes his frankly delusional system on the receptive member. This latter person discards the more bizarre aspects of the system, eventually supports the more plausible ones, and fills in the gaps with coherent links. The final delusional system may not initially appear too fantastic and both members end up sharing very similar delusions which are usually persecutory, although they may be more religious or grandiose in content. Deutsch [7] postulated three psychodynamic explanations of this phenomenon: (1) the members are struggling with latent homosexual problems, (2) the receptive individual has not psychologically separated from the active person but rather overidentifies with him, and (3) the delusions of the active one are very similar to the fantasies of the receptive person.

A mother and her twenty-year-old mildly retarded son were brought to the evaluation clinic by a social worker who was concerned about the frequent absences of the son from a sheltered workshop. Mother and son were interviewed separately. Mother was frankly paranoid. She was intensely involved in a delusional system in which the neighbors, the police, and her son's teachers were accusing her of sexual crimes. The son spoke somewhat more coherently. He commented that he had to stay home in order to protect his mother from "spies" who lived in the neighborhood. He explained their social isolation as necessitated by the difficulty in knowing whom to trust. He was concerned that the police and the neighbors could be "criminals or informers pretending to be someone else." Mother was institutionalized in a state hospital. The son went to live in a foster-care home. He became more outgoing and less suspicious of others.

DIFFERENTIAL DIAGNOSIS
Dewhurst and Todd [8] questioned both the clinical usefulness as well as the theoretical validity of the subcategories of this illness. It is important to recognize the situational contribution to the psychosis of the receptive members. Otherwise the delusional system may be misinterpreted as indicating paranoid schizophrenia or some other paranoid psychosis.

PROGNOSIS AND MANAGEMENT
The longer the recipient person has been delusional and has remained in contact with the active member, the poorer the prognosis. A poor prognosis is also anticipated if the delusions are felt to be of some value to the recipient.

The first step in treatment is to separate the individuals involved. Treatment then is similar to that for schizophrenic psychosis; i.e., hospitalization, drug therapy, and supportive psychotherapy.

Ganser's Syndrome

DEFINITION
This syndrome describes the reactions of a patient who is under significant external and internal stress. He answers simple questions with incorrect responses. His answers convey his understanding of the meaning of

the questions, which are within his ability to solve. This syndrome is associated with prisoners awaiting sentencing.

HISTORY

In 1898 Ganser [10] described four patients, three of whom were prisoners awaiting trial, who answered simple questions with a related but inappropriate answer. The central symptom which is often written *vorbeireden* was called *vorbeigehen* [11]. It means "to pass by"; referring to the passing by the correct answer, which the patient most probably knows, to an answer close to the right one but nevertheless incorrect. Ganser did not feel that the responses were consciously prepared. Other symptoms mentioned in the initial paper were auditory and visual hallucinations, spatial and temporal disorientation, amnesia for the period of the inappropriate response, hysterical motor and sensory problems, and a lack of insight. Ganser wrote a second paper in 1904. He had collected twenty cases by then and discussed the association of psychotic symptomatology in addition to the hysterical one.

CLASSIFICATION

The biggest problem in classifying this disorder is whether to consider the main symptom by itself or as part of a more comprehensive syndrome. In the literature the illness has been classified under many different categories, including psychosis, neurosis, affective disorders, and organic problems. Generally, the illness, with emphasis on the symptom, can be considered in a position intermediate between malingering and hysteria [23].

EPIDEMIOLOGY

Ganser's syndrome is extremely rare and is usually superimposed on a psychotic disorder. Although this illness is commonly thought to be associated with a prison population, studies do not bear this out. Estes and New [9] found less than 1 percent incidence among 8000 army prisoners and there has been a significant number of reported cases that occurred in a noncriminal population. The patient involved is usually of borderline intelligence.

ETIOLOGY AND PATHOGENESIS

The main symptom and the altered state of consciousness have been explained dynamically by Weiner [23] as an unconscious attempt by the patient to hide his intellectual and personal identity in a situation of severe emotional stress in which the patient feels completely helpless. The care that enters into making an inappropriate but approximate answer is explained as an attempt on the patient's part to show the effort that he is exerting to answer the question. Basically, the symptoms are thought to be hysterical in nature although with more conscious conflict involved than in a true conversion reaction. Most often a situation in which the patient would derive benefit from appearing unintelligent or crazy (as an impending trial) is the precipitating factor.

CLINICAL DESCRIPTION

Goldin [11] included the following list of symptoms in the Ganser syndrome. The main symptom is answering a simple question by an incorrect response, which nevertheless conveys that the meaning of the question has been understood and that the correct answer was or still is in the patient's fund of knowledge. For example, to the question, how much is three plus four, the patient will answer ten; or to the question, what are you wearing on your feet, the patient replies, a hat. Other minor symptoms include auditory and visual hallucinations, amnesia for the time of the inappropriate answers, hysterical analgesia or hyperaesthesia, spatial and temporal disorientation, depression, anxiety, and excitement. The Ganser syndrome lasts roughly between one and ten days.

DIFFERENTIAL DIAGNOSIS

Three illnesses may mimic the Ganser syndrome. A malingerer may act more appropriately when he feels that he is not being watched. A schizophrenic patient will not give a regularly coherent and evasive answer to questions, and his negativism will persist throughout the interview and not just to the questions. An organically ill patient would have to be so intellectually handicapped not to know the answer to such simple questions that his organic illness would be very obvious before any questioning.

PROGNOSIS AND MANAGEMENT

The Ganser syndrome is an acute disorder. When the situational stress is removed, the syndrome disappears. Any underlying or accompanying disorder, like a psychosis, would be treated in the usual manner. The Ganser state can recur but it never lasts longer than several days.

CULTURE-BOUND DISTURBANCES

The disorders included in this section are extremely rare, some currently found only in the records of history. They are grouped together here because these diverse syndromes share one feature in common; they all are heavily influenced by the culture of the people in whom they occur. Most are acute reactions which partially reflect the individual's psychodynamics and partially portray the stresses and mores of a well-defined sociocultural group. These syndromes are of interest from historical and cultural perspectives. The symptoms manifest universal conflicts (castration anxiety, difficulty with aggression, cannibalism), but the expression of these conflicts are much more obvious than one usually sees in patients today.

Piblokto

DEFINITION AND HISTORY
Piblokto [6] is an acute attack of increased psychomotor activity and an altered state of consciousness in Eskimo women. The first written description of this disorder was made in the book, *The North Pole*, published in 1910, which detailed Admiral Peary's [6] expedition of 1908–1909.

CLASSIFICATION
This disorder is considered to be a form of hysteria, resembling a dissociative reaction with an alteration in the patient's state of consciousness and in her personal identity.

EPIDEMIOLOGY, ETIOLOGY, AND PATHOGENESIS
Piblokto occurs almost exclusively in adult women Eskimos and is very rare today, in fact probably nonexistent. No satisfactory explanation has been made to explain this illness.

CLINICAL DESCRIPTION
The woman begins the attack by screaming and tearing off her clothing. Although the weather may be subzero, she seems unaffected by the cold and becomes increasingly agitated, often running naked for a few minutes to an hour or so. The screaming continues and often resembles a cry of a familiar animal or bird. Each woman lends her own individual expression to the form of the verbal and motor behavior. After the screaming, the patient may have a period of singing to herself. The attack ends in about 1 to 1.5 hours by sobbing or sleep. The woman awakes from the sleep in her usual normal state.

PROGNOSIS AND MANAGEMENT
The attack is short-lived and return to a normal state is predictable. The Eskimos believed the disease was connected to the influence of an evil spirit and were thus reluctant to touch the patient during an attack.

Koro

DEFINITION AND HISTORY
Koro [26] is a state of acute anxiety, occurring in certain Southeast Asian subcultures, wherein the male patient becomes convinced that his penis will shrink and he will subsequently die.

In 1897, this syndrome was first described in patients in South Celebes by Van Brero. Van Wulften Palthe, in 1934, mentioned it again, later including cases of women patients who complained of their labia and breasts shrinking. Koblen in 1948, described one case in South China. Three authors (Kraepelin, 1921; Schilder, 1950; and Byshouski, 1952) have described similar cases among Westerners.

The background of this illness is interesting, as it reflects from an historical perspective the common concern of genital injury and many of its psychodynamic meanings. Koro means the head of a turtle or tortoise in Malay. There is the obvious similarity between the head of a turtle and the glans of the penis. Also, the turtle was a literary symbol for longevity and vital forces in Chinese art until the Ming dynasty. There was an old Chinese belief that during normal coitus a healthy exchange of vital male and female humors took place. During masturbation and nocturnal emission, there occurred an unbalanced loss of the male humors which would result in koro. Another belief was that a corpse did not have a penis and so penile shrinkage would be a sign of impending death. Later in a Ming treatise, a tortoise's head was used as a simile to encourage coitus reservatus (i.e., without ejaculation) which was believed to increase one's life span.

CLASSIFICATION AND EPIDEMIOLOGY

This disorder has been variously classified as an unusual form of anxiety neurosis, obsessive-compulsive illness, hysteria, and a schizoid phenomenon.

Koro has been described in Chinese subjects living in South China, in the lower Yang-tse valley, and in Southeast Asia, especially Malaysia, Indonesia, and West Borneo. Scattered reports elsewhere probably reflect migration patterns. Yap [26], in a study of 19 cases in Hong Kong, described the age range from sixteen to forty-five years, with a mean of thirty-two years. Also, 18 out of his 19 cases were working-class people, 16 of whom had no more than a primary school education.

ETIOLOGY AND PATHOGENESIS

A typical patient with Koro has been described as a shy, timid, self-effacing, dependent, and anxious individual who is of average or below-average intelligence. He lacks confidence in his sexual capacity and worries about being sexually excessive. Koro reflects what analytically is called castration anxiety.

CLINICAL DESCRIPTION

The attacks are episodic, each lasting several hours and most attacks occurring at night. Usually a precipitating circumstance can be found, most often this being a sexual activity, as coitus or masturbation. The patient appears in a state of panic about the shrinkage of his penis and its withdrawal into his abdomen. Patients are observed checking out the size and presence of their penis by frantically touching and visually inspecting it. If the relatives share the belief in Koro, they may support the patient's fears and hold onto his penis or tie it to a special contrivance so as to prevent its withdrawal.

PROGNOSIS AND MANAGEMENT
The acute episode subsides within hours. Treatment may be supportive for the immediate episode (tranquilizers, hospitalization). Long-term treatment would deal with the underlying difficulties.

Whitigo

DEFINITION AND HISTORY
Whitigo [20] is a psychosis involving cannibalism in certain old Canadian Indian tribes. Whitigo has two meanings. In mythology, whitigo refers to a cannibalistic monster who lives as an ice skeleton in winter and dies each spring, reviving with the return of cold weather. This monster eats humans and symbolically represents the dread of the cold season during which many people starve and cannibalism becomes tempting. The second meaning of whitigo is a human being who has cannibalistic desires and becomes a man-eater.

EPIDEMIOLOGY
The syndrome has been described in specific Canadian Indian tribes, as the Chippewa and the Cree tribes. It no longer is present.

ETIOLOGY, PATHOGENESIS, AND CLINICAL DESCRIPTION
The individual is faced with the reality of starvation and the taboo of cannibalism. He alternates between a severe retarded depression and an aggressive angry state. During nonpsychotic moments, he is aware of his desire to devour family members and may ask them to kill him in order to limit the acting-out of his wish. When the depression lifts and the patient becomes aggressive, he may devour his own family and seek other human prey.

PROGNOSIS AND MANAGEMENT
A shaman's cure required that the patient had to vomit his "heart of ice." Usually the patient is killed by his fellow men, who burn the corpse in order to melt the ice skeleton or ice heart, which corresponds to the mythological cannibalistic monster.

Latah

DEFINITION AND HISTORY
Latah [24,25] is an illness in which after a sudden fright a patient exhibits automatic obedience, echolalia, and echopraxia. The disorder was first described among the Malay races where *latah* means ticklish. It is not confined to this culture and has been referred to by a variety of names such as myriachit or Arctic hysteria in Siberia, mali-mali in the Philippines, and imu in northern Japan. In the past it has been linked with Gilles de la Tourette's disorder, to which it is not related. It is very similar to the behavior of the Jumpers of Maine, more commonly known as the Shakers or the Holy Rollers.

CLASSIFICATION
In Malay, Latah had been considered more as eccentric behavior than as a mental disorder. Most commonly it is considered related to hysteria, although the cultural influence and the factor of the specific fear-producing stimulus make this not a typical hysterical disorder.

EPIDEMIOLOGY
Latah has been described in many cultures and climates, from the Arctic areas of Siberia to the temperate zone of North America to the tropical environment of Africa. Most commonly it is seen in Southeast Asia. Patients are most often female, usually of middle age or elderly, and typically are uneducated and living in a rural community.

ETIOLOGY AND PATHOGENESIS
The personality structure of a typical patient is that of a naive, self-effacing, shy, and passive individual. After being frightened this person does not reorganize to a normal state of purposeful activity and coherent thinking but instead remains disoriented and helpless, with an obliteration of ego boundaries. Latah can be seen in children, and one sometimes can obtain in older patients a history of a progressive increase in the severity of the disorder. Factors as repetition and habituation as well as secondary gain are felt to be important in those patients.

CLINICAL DESCRIPTION
The patient is unexpectedly frightened by what may be a trivial stimulus like a bell ringing and falls into a state of cloudy consciousness and exhibits, in order of preponderance, symptoms of echolalia, coprolalia, echopraxia, automatic obedience, and echomimia. The frightening stimulus may be partially culturally determined. The patient is completely at the mercy of those around her. In severe cases of latah, the patient will try to hide from others so as to protect herself. In younger women, echolalia and

echopraxia may be manifested after being tickled, but the patient seems to be more pleased than distressed in those cases.

PROGNOSIS
Some individuals are subject to repeated attacks. At times, if there is a group of women who are prone to latah attacks and one in the group does have an attack, the rest will follow suit. The severity of the illness increases with age, although not all cases are progressive. A minority of patients will show a gradual deterioration until they are chronically under the influence of others. As urbanization, educational opportunities, and other cultural changes influence the communities of these patients, the incidence progressively drops.

Amok

DEFINITION AND HISTORY
Amok [22,20] is an acute outburst of rage during which the patient runs about wildly and kills anyone in his path. The disorder most commonly was found in the Malay culture although occasionally it was described as occurring in other tropical climates. In the decade before World War II it virtually disappeared. This has been attributed to the progressive civilization of the regions involved with the concomitant cultural changes, and specifically to the change in handling amok cases, from killing the patient to capturing him alive. Such management prevented the use of amok for committing suicide after free expression was given to aggressive impulses.

CLASSIFICATION
Amok used to be considered either a socially accepted way to express anger or a sign of witchcraft. During the years when the attacks became infrequent, it was more often associated with an organic or functional psychosis, the particular behavioral expression being culturally influenced. Some authors consider amok a form of hysteria.

ETIOLOGY, CLINICAL DESCRIPTION, AND PROGNOSIS
After a prodromal period of depression, the patient, who is almost always male, will suddenly run about wildly. He is usually armed and kills anyone in his path indiscriminately. After the attack, he is exhausted and has amnesia for the event. The attack seems unprovoked and can be considered an unrestrained expression of unconscious aggression and a particular form of suicide. The latter was especially true when the only management approach was to overpower and kill the patient during his rampage. "Running amok" has virtually disappeared.

REFERENCES

1   American Psychiatric Association. *Diagnostic and statistical manual of mental disorders*, DSM-II. Washington, D.C.: American Psychiatric Association, 1968.

2   American Psychiatric Association. *Diagnostic and statistical manual of mental disorders*, DSM-III. Draft. Washington, D.C.: American Psychiatric Association, 1977.

3   Appel, J. W. "Preventive Psychiatry." In *Neuropsychiatry in World War I*, vol. 1, eds. A. J. Anderson and R. J. Bernucci. Washington, D.C.: Office of the Surgeon General, 1966.

4   Bowlby, J. Separation anxiety. *Int. J. Psychoanal.* 41:89–113, 1960.

5   Bourne, P. G. Military psychiatry and the Viet Nam experience. *Am. J. Psychiatry* 127:481–488, 1970.

6   Brill, A. A. Piblokto or hysteria among Peary's eskimos. *J. Nerv. Ment. Dis.* 40:514–520, 1913.

7   Deutsch, H. Folie à deux. *Psychoanal. Q.* 7:307–318, 1938.

8   Dewhurst, K., and Todd, J. The psychosis of association: folie à deux. *J. Nerv. Ment. Dis.* 124:451–459, 1956.

9   Estes, M. M., and New, J. S. Some observations on prison psychoses. *J. Med. Assoc. Ga.* 37:2–5, 1948.

10   Ganser, S. Ueber einen eigenartigen hysterischen Dämmerzustand. *Arch. Psychiatrie* 30:633, 1898.

11   Goldin, S., and MacDonald, J. E. The Ganser state. *J. Ment. Sci.* 101:267–280, 1955.

12   Grinker, R., and Spiegel, J. *Men under stress*. Philadelphia: Blakiston, 1945.

13   Kardiner, A. *War stress and neurotic illness*. New York: Hoeber, 1947.

14   Krystal, H. "Severe psychic trauma and psychogenic death." In *Psychiatric foundations of medicine*, vol. 6, eds. G. U. Balis, L. Wurmser, E. McDaniel and R. G. Grenell. Boston: Butterworths, 1978.

15   Lasègue, C., and Fabret, J. La folie à deux ou folie communiquée, 1877, trans. R. Michand. *Am. J. Psychiatry* 121 (Suppl.):1–23, 1964.

16   Lindemann, E. Symptomatology and management of acute grief. *Am. J. Psychiatry* 101:141–148, 1944.

17   Linton, R. *Culture and mental disorders*. Springfield, Ill.: Thomas, 1956.

18   Parkes, C. M. Psychosocial transitions: A field for study, *Soc. Sci. Med.* 5:101–115, 1971.

19   Rapoport, L. The state of crisis: Some theoretical consideration. *Soc. Serv. Rev.* 36:211–217, 1962.

20   Stitt, E. R., and Strong, R. *Diagnosis, prevention, and treatment of tropical diseases*. New York: Blakiston, 1945.

21   Tyhurst, J. S. "The role of transition states — including disasters — in mental illness." In *Proceeding of symposium on preventive and social psychiatry*. Washington, D.C.: Government Printing Office, 1958.

22   Van Wilfften, P. P. "Psychiatry and neurology in the tropics." In *A clinical textbook of tropical medicine*, ed. A. Liechtenstein. Batavia: DeLangen, 1936.

23 Weiner, H., and Braiman, A. The Ganser syndrome: A review and addition of some unusual cases. *Am. J. Psychiatry* 111:767–773, 1955.

24 Yap, P. M. Mental diseases peculiar to certain cultures. *J. Ment. Sci.* 97:313–327, 1951.

25 Yap, P. M. Latah reaction: Its pathodynamics and nosological position. *J. Ment. Sci.* 98:515–564, 1952.

26 Yap, P. M. Koro. *Bri. J. Psychiatry* 111:43–50, 1965.

VI
Psychiatric Disorders of Childhood and Adolescence

23

Developmental Deviations of Childhood

Mary Joan Albright, Ph.D.

The classification proposed by the Group for the Advancement of Psychiatry [4] divides developmental deviations into two categories: broad deviations or lags in a child's maturational patterns and deviations in specific aspects of development. Only the second category is described in this chapter. Specific deviations in development include deviations in motor development, sensory development, speech development, cognitive functions, social development, psychosexual development, affective development, and integrative development. Since these areas of development are interrelated, there may be some overlap in the discussion of the various categories.

MOTOR DEVELOPMENT

Deviations in motor development include long-standing disturbances in psychomotor functions, activity levels, coordination, and handedness which are not due to brain damage. Some hyperkinetic children would be included here [14].

Some infants exhibit deviant drive endowment from the beginning. There are children who exhibit a very low activity level. As infants, they are apathetic, cry little, and fail to signal their needs. They sleep too much, are lazy to grasp, and may spend hours taking a bottle. Such hypoactive babies may be found in the same position in which they were left. They usually are content to stay in bed or in a playpen for longer durations and up to older ages than most children.

In contrast, other infants are hyperactive and may engage in excessive crying despite good caretaking. They may sleep little and be highly restless. Some infants exhibit extremes of autoerotic or autoaggressive behaviors, e.g., sucking, rolling, rubbing, head banging. Later, they may show extremes of hyperactivity and aggressivity.

Thomas and Chess [14] have described how environment and temperament interact to exacerbate or ameliorate deviations in motor activity. There was a high incidence of hyperactivity in Puerto Rican, working-class children compared to middle-class children. The authors attributed some if not all of this excess motor activity in the Puerto Rican children to the fact that the families lived in small apartments and did not allow the children to play outside because of a reality-based fear of accidents. Being cooped up in this way was stressful for children with a temperamental disposition to high activity. Middle-class children having the same temperament usually lived in large apartments close to nice playgrounds or in large suburban homes with yards which provided an outlet for their energies.

In general, children who had a high activity level tended to react to pressure by increasing nonproductive motor activity. This finding suggests that if a child is exhibiting such activity, one should try to identify the pressure and reduce it. What constitutes pressure for one child may not be pressure to another.

Children having the temperamental trait of low activity level were easy to care for and usually adapted well at home and with peer groups during the preschool years. However, as they got older, their motor slowness could elicit impatient responses and criticism when the child's slowness in dressing, eating, or getting ready for school, church, or a family outing held up everyone else. During the school years, such slowness might invite the teacher's displeasure and the ridicule of peers.

SENSORY DEVELOPMENT

Deviations in sensory development consist of problems in stimulus management in screening and monitoring stimuli of a visual, auditory, perceptual, tactile, or social nature. Such children may overreact, underreact, or give uneven responses to ordinary sensory input, consequently they have difficulty in maintaining equilibrium [4].

If a child has unusually sensitive skin, he may react negatively to being held. If he is unusually sensitive to sounds, bright lights, or temperature, he may react with distress to many common situations. This makes the child less of a joy to parents or other caretakers and may provoke negative reactions in them.

Thomas [13] has described the child who has irregularity in biological functions, gives predominantly intense reactions to things, gives uneven responses to ordinary sensory input, responds negatively (i.e., by rejection or withdrawal) to new stimuli, and takes a long time to adjust to new routines as "the difficult child." Since it is difficult for the adult caretaker to meet the needs of such a child, the child may experience difficulty in establishing a sense of basic trust and hence may have problems in interpersonal relationships.

Escalona [2] has pointed out that a very low-keyed approach is sufficient to stimulate inactive babies if they are highly sensitive. In contrast, very vigorous stimulation may cause such children to become disorganized. In self-defense, the children may tend to withdraw. The child who underreacts, has a low activity level, withdraws from new stimuli, and takes a long time to adapt, only becoming interested and involved gradually over a long period of time, is described as the "slow-to-warm-up" child [13]. Such children may have difficulty in getting adequate or appropriate stimulation. Adults may assume the child is dull or may become annoyed with the child's slowness or seeming lack of responsivity. They may assume the child is not interested and hence may give up too quickly.

SPEECH DEVELOPMENT

Children who exhibit delayed speech development that is not due to deafness, oppositional behavior, elective mutism, brain damage, or early childhood psychosis fit into the category, deviations in speech development. The most severe deviation is developmental aphasia. Children who are precocious in their speech development, who have persistently infantile speech, or who exhibit difficulties with articulation, phonation, rhythm, or speech comprehension belong in this category as well. Disorders in *articulation* include distortion of sounds — lisping or gammacism (difficulty with gutterals); elision of sounds; infantile speech; insertion of sounds; omission of sounds; substitution, e.g., lalling (*l* to *r* difficulties) and burring (difficulty with *r*'s). Disorders in *phonation* include changes in voice, monotonic speech, nasal speech, whining speech, high-pitched speech, dysarthria, and anarthria (the inability to express words or symbols properly). Disorders in *rhythm* include cluttered speech, hesitant speech, rapid speech, repetition of words, slurring, and stuttering [4].

Healthy young preschoolers often repeat words as a part of normal development. This is not a deviation. When stuttering is a conversion symptom, it does not fall into this category either.

As pointed out by de Hirsch [5], the more complex a function, the more vulnerable it is. Language is a highly differentiated function having many aspects in which deficits or disturbances can occur. From the earliest age, linguistic difficulties interfere with the development of ego functions that are crucial for the child's learning and for adapting to the world. The emergence of the ego as a psychic structure and the beginnings of verbalization occur at approximately the same time, fifteen to thirty-six months, during the last two phases of what Mahler [8] calls the separation-individuation process. Individuation seems to be a prerequisite for the development of language. If the child does not have a fairly well-developed sense of self as a separate person, dialogue cannot take place. On the other hand, development of the ability to use words as symbols is one of the most important steps in individuation. It seems that individuation and linguistic development are reciprocal processes, with disturbance in one being reflected in disturbance in the other [5].

DISORDERS RELATED TO CNS IMPAIRMENT

Developmental Aphasia

Developmental aphasia is the most severe language disability. It consists of extreme difficulties in processing and generating language in children who have no gross deficits in auditory acuity, no primary psychopathology, no significant mental retardation, and no history of cerebral insult or positive signs on the classical neurological examination. Their early history may be unclear and they may show soft neurological signs and evidence of central nervous system irregularity. It seems these children were affected during crucial developmental processes, resulting in interference with integration and maturation, both physiologically and psychologically. Aphasoid children exhibit maturational imbalances and their organizational schemata tend to be primitive and unstable [6].

Some writers [6] believe that the aphasoid child's primary difficulty is with the processing of auditory input. They cite problems such as trouble with auding (the integration and management of acoustic information by the brain), difficulties in handling complex feedback mechanisms, and deficient auditory memory span for verbal sequences, which leads to trouble with encoding and decoding.

Other writers [6] emphasize linguistic rather than auditory factors. They point to the children's difficulties in organizing input into stable linguistic categories and the way in which their verbal output resembles their poorly patterned intake. The verbal performance of aphasoid children may be similar to that of much younger children, as exemplified by their limited vocabularies and their difficulty in employing the basic rules of the language.

Young aphasoid children frequently exhibit a delay in symbolic play, but intensive language stimulation beginning at twenty-four to thirty months can bring about marked improvement. They often exhibit severe anxiety, which may be due in part to biological dysfunction as well as to the confusion and bewilderment they experience in being unable to express themselves effectively or to organize their cognitive and affective experiences.

Such children usually have severe difficulties in school, both academically and behaviorally. Their cognitive disability may cause problems with numerical and verbal learning. In addition, they frequently exhibit poor impulse control and difficulty in postponing gratification, characteristics which may interfere with learning and cause interpersonal and behavioral problems.

There is a controversy whether the problems of a language-disordered child represent a maturational defect or a maturational lag. Proponents of the defect theory point out that these children are different from normal children of any age, that they use constructions that normal children would not use. Proponents of the maturational lag theory hold that children with linguistic disorders are simply delayed in their language development, that they use immature constructions that are part of the repertoire of younger, normal children [6].

Delayed Language Development

Delayed language development frequently appears in families in which one member or another exhibits some kind of language disability. It may also be found in children with other signs of central nervous system dysfunction. When it is severe, delayed language development may be equivalent to a mild developmental aphasia. Early defects in language comprehension in two- and three-year olds are frequently overlooked; however, they are significant in terms of their implications for subsequent learning disabilities. Information handling processes are sensitive to dysfunctions

in other areas — genetic, neurophysiological, affective, and environmental. A child who has a weakness in this area may need special
stimulation.

Usually, a normal child will employ markers to indicate plurality,
past tense, and possessiveness before the age of three. Linguistic laggards
neither understand nor use such markers until much later. Even when the
third birthday brings a spurt in language development, phonemic, syntac-
tic, and semantic aspects do not reach normal levels of achievement. It
may be only when the child enters kindergarten that the teacher discovers
the youngster can comprehend only the simplest directions. [5] Children
who are poor listeners may have difficulty in processing input.

Early intervention is important. The most rapid growth in language
occurs between twenty and forty months of age. Language stimulation
that starts at twenty-eight months has been found to be far more effective
than stimulation that does not start until forty-six months. The pediatrician should be alert to the possibility of such difficulties and should
do a careful evaluation of a child's language development, not just his
articulation [11].

Disorders of Articulation

Articulatory disorders consist of difficulties with phonology. They include
developmental dysarthria, developmental articulatory apraxia, and
dyslalia.

Developmental dysarthria refers to difficulty in executing the movement patterns necessary for expressive speech. Although motor factors are
usually emphasized, sensory deficits, e.g., difficulty in processing proprioceptive input, may contribute to the condition. The nerve pathways
innervating the peripheral speech mechanism may be interfered with
even when there is no neuromuscular pathology. Developmental dysarthria may be confused with developmental articulatory apraxia.

Developmental articulatory apraxia refers to problems in performing
the highly integrated movements required to produce and combine
speech sounds. Nonarticulatory movements are normal, as are both receptive and inner speech. Developmental articulatory apraxia may be confused with some kinds of expressive aphasia.

A large majority of articulatory disorders fall into the third
category — *dyslalia*. Dyslalia is immature speech in children having normal neuromusculature. In one study of normal four-year-olds, the speech
of 17 percent of the children was not intelligible to close relatives. The
basis for articulatory difficulties is thought to be a maturational delay in
the neurological processes underlying speech. The immaturity may be

familial. Frequently children improve rapidly and spontaneously after the age of four. The acquisition of speech sounds proceeds in a developmental sequence. *S* may not be produced correctly until age seven or eight. If a child is adjusting socially, can express himself and communicate so that he can be understood, and has mastered the basic rules of language, maturation may do the rest. However, the doctor should check to make sure that the child does not have a defect in language processing. [5]

Clinical manifestations of different kinds of articulatory deficits overlap. A child may substitute, omit, or telescope words, simplify clusters, or make phonetic errors. Such problems may be related to inferior auditory discrimination, short auditory-memory span, defective feedback mechanisms, dyspraxic tendencies, or difficulties in sequencing. In addition to making phonetic errors, other children also make phonemic errors which reflect an inadequate grasp of the phonological system of the language. For example, a child may be able to make the appropriate sounds when saying words in isolation, e.g., half, halves, demonstrating that he has no motor difficulty, but he may make a mistake in forming the plural, saying *halfs* instead of *halves*, revealing that he has failed to master certain linguistic rules. Many functional articulatory disorders are of this type [6].

Disorders of Rhythm

Cluttering is a disorder of linguistic organization which has both expressive and receptive features. Clutterers can repeat words easily, but they have difficulty with spontaneous sequencing. They transpose syllables in words and words in sentences. Their speech is dysrhythmic and monotonous. They have severe word-finding difficulties and spell poorly. Their written language has the same disorganized quality as their speech. Receptive deficiencies include a short auditory-memory span and weak auditory discrimination. Frequently, clutterers do not seem to be aware that they have a problem, consequently they do not feel anxious about it and do not respond well to remediation.

Stuttering [6] is a controversial topic. Theories of etiology fall into three categories: (1) genogenic — stuttering is due to a biological defect; (2) psychogenic — stuttering is due to psychological mechanisms (obsessive-compulsive defenses) and to psychosocial factors, particularly family interactions; and (3) semantogenic — stuttering is a "learned pathological response" that occurs when the normal repetitions of syllables and words by the young child are labeled as stuttering.

Stuttering in young children illustrates the complex interaction of neurophysiological and affective factors that is typical of all language dysfunctions. The stuttering usually appears between the ages of 2 and 4, when the child is struggling with complex syntactical forms. From 1.5 to 3 years, the child progresses from using primitive language to exhibiting high level linguistic organization. During this period the child's neurophysiological maturation is not equal to his emotional and intellectual needs to express himself. At the same time, the child has to meet many psychological demands: He has to give up early instinctive gratification, inhibit aggressive impulses, and, quite possibly, cope with the appearance of a new sibling. Stuttering can be triggered by any severe psychological stress that occurs during this period, when the neurophysically immature child is struggling to master complex linguistic constructions.

Primary stuttering, the effortless repetition of syllables and words by young children, usually disappears as maturation enables the child to meet linguistic demands more easily unless psychological factors cause the stuttering to persist.

Some children are particularly vulnerable in the language area and hence more susceptible to stuttering. Vulnerable children include those with a family history of language disorders, children with delayed language development, children with severe word-finding difficulties, and clutterers. In such children, stress may cause the repetitions normally made by young children to become pathologically habitual. If this happens early intervention is usually effective. "In older children, stuttering with its severe blocking and its tonic manifestations and avoidance rituals, may occasionally mask psychopathology. More often, it is part of the ego's defensive mechanism and not remediable by a speech therapist" [6:2112]. Cases such as this would not fall into the category of developmental deviations.

COGNITIVE FUNCTIONS

Deviations in cognitive functions include (1) lags in development or deviations in the capacity for symbolic or abstract thinking, which may be reflected in learning disabilities in reading, writing, and arithmetic; (2) precocious or accelerated functioning in these areas; and (3) deviations in cerebral integration that are not due to brain damage as reflected in disturbances in thinking and awareness or memory. The thought processes of such children may still be dominated by prelogical associations or primitive fantasies. Both the so-called pseudoretarded and the functional mildly retarded whose poor functioning is not due to brain damage or to inborn inherent deficits would be included here [4].

Johnson and Myklebust [7] define a psychoneurological learning disability as a condition in which children have generalized integrity, i.e., "adequate motor ability, average to high intelligence, adequate hearing and vision and adequate emotional adjustment" but "cannot learn in the usual or normal way" [7:9]. Such children frequently have minor motor incoordinations, which affect the acquisition of such skills as hopping, skipping, bicycle riding, buttoning, and tying shoe laces, as well as a degree of emotional disturbance, but these factors are not physically or emotionally crippling.

Disabilities in *verbal learning* include deficits in the learning of arithmetic and deficiencies in acquiring spoken, read, and written language. Deficiencies in *nonverbal learning* include disturbances in learning to tell time, directions (east and west) and body orientation (left and right), and music and rhythm; disturbances in social perception and in learning the meaning of facial expressions (sadness, happiness) and the behavior of others, as well as meaning as expressed in art.

Children having a deficit in social perception may be unable to comprehend their world or to relate with others despite good verbal skills and no signs of emotional disturbance. Children who have a disturbed sense of time may experience difficulty in following routines, in keeping to a schedule. Those who have a disturbance in regard to spatial directions or bodily orientation may have difficulty in judging how far away an approaching car is or how to hang a coat on a hanger.

Disabilities in verbal learning may be due to disturbances in input processes, output processes, or integrative processes. The verbal systems are primarily auditory or visual. Much school learning is auditory, visual, or both. "The spoken word comprises auditory receptive capacities (comprehension-input) and an auditory expressive function (speech-output). Reading and writing entail visual receptive and visual expressive processes, reading being a receptive (input) and writing an expressive (output) function" [7:20]. Auditory and visual modalities are involved in most learning. Deficiencies might be auditory, visual, or both. Disabilities often occurring because of such involvements include the aphasias, dyslexias, spelling disorders, and dysgraphias.

As mentioned, the deficit in learning may be primarily in input (receptive), in output (expressive) processes, or both. However input and output functions may be intact and a child may still have a serious learning disability due to a *disturbance in integration or inner language*. Inner language is when experiences are integrated and transformed into symbols (verbal and nonverbal) for purposes of awareness, thinking, and adjustment. Examples of children with disturbances in integrative learning are the *echolalic child* who repeats what is said without grasping the meaning of the words and the *word caller* who identifies or calls out the words he sees in print without knowing the meaning of them. Although the words are received and expressed, they have no symbolic significance. The defect is in the ability to grasp meaning. There is a wide range within which such deficits appear. They are the most difficult to identify and many go undetected. However, when a defect in receptive functions is identified, one can expect that inner language (meaning) is also affected.

In order to evaluate integrative learning functions, the examiner may ask the child to demonstrate verbally or nonverbally that he has grasped the significance of the problem presented to him, or a "word test" might be used in which a child is given toy furniture and other common objects that he is to organize in a meaningful way. The examiner may also ascertain how well the child understands the concepts of time, size, direction, speed, length, and height and may use a test of social perception such as picture arrangement from the Wechsler Intelligence Scale for Children — Revised (WISC-R). Another measure of integration is to see how well a child grasps the meaning of a short story from reading it or hearing it.

Verbal receptive functioning may be evaluated by asking a child to follow directions or instructions which are spoken to him (auditory) or given to him to read (visual). Verbal expressive functioning may be evaluated by having the child write a story or describe a picture orally. Nonverbally, the child may be asked to identify various sounds and pictures by pointing (receptive) or to convey certain ideas through drawing, gesticulating, or pantomiming (expressive).

Psychoneurologically there are three types of learning: (1) intraneurosensory, which requires only one neurosensory system in the brain, e.g., auditory; (2) interneurosensory, which involves more than one; and (3) integrative, which requires that the systems function simultaneously.

There may be no learning that involves only one system in the strict sense; however, there are problems of auditory discrimination, comprehension, and memory that do not have comparable involvements in the visual system. Thus the learning disability may hinder the receiving, storing, recalling, and categorizing of auditory information without directly disturbing other types of learning. Similarly, disturbances of visual, tactile, and proprioceptive learning are relatively independent.

Much learning seems to require the functional interrelatedness of two systems. There are inner processes by which one type of neurosensory information is transduced into another within the brain. For example, a person may understand a word he hears spoken and be able to integrate and recall it but be unable to say it. The person cannot speak because he cannot convert the sounds he heard into their motor-kinesthetic equivalents. This is an *expressive aphasia*, a type of apraxia. Apraxias are commonly observed in children with neurogenic learning disabilities. At times apraxias involve nonverbal functions, but expressive aphasia and dysgraphia are the most common apraxias.

Dyslexia, or difficulty in reading, is another interneurosensory learning disability. When a child learns to read, he converts the words he sees into their auditory equivalents. In *auditory dyslexia* the child learns what the letters look like but cannot make the cross modal connection so as to associate the images with the way the words sound. In *visual dyslexia* the child learns what letters sound like but cannot connect the auditory image with the visual image of the word.

Many children with learning disabilities have another form of interneurosensory disturbance — *agnosias*. A child with agnosia receives information through the senses (auditory, visual, or tactual) but cannot comprehend or interpret what he sees, hears, or touches.

Although the most obvious deficits in auditorizing and visualizing are those related to verbal behavior, some children are seriously limited in their ability to recall *visual images* of obvious nonverbal aspects of their daily lives, e.g., the kind of furniture in their living room or whether there are streetlights on the street where they live. Others experience difficulty with *auditory images* and cannot learn or recall the sounds made by birds or animals, e.g., cats, dogs, cows, or frogs, or the sounds associated with cars, lawnmowers, airplanes, typewriters, or running water [7].

SOCIAL DEVELOPMENT

Deviations in social development include precocious, delayed, or uneven patterns of social capacities or relationships, such as aggressive behavior that is directed externally or internally, antisocial behavior, oppositional behavior, isolating behavior, problems in dominance-submission, and problems in dependence-independence which are not so severe or crystallized as to be considered a personality disorder [4].

Aggressive behavior that is directed externally includes antagonistic behavior, destructive behavior, fighting, hitting, kicking, scratching, biting, and verbal aggression such as threats. An example would be the child who immaturely acts out aggressive impulses. As previously pointed out, this may occur in children who have delayed language development and have not learned to express themselves in words. It may also occur in children with good language development who have been poorly socialized.

Oppositional behavior includes disobedience, extreme carelessness, negativism, dawdling, quarrelsomeness, teasing, and provocative behavior. Internally directed aggressive behavior includes self-blame, self-criticism, "putting oneself down," inhibited behavior, and depressed behavior. Isolating behavior includes withdrawal, excessive fantasy and daydreaming, excessive shyness, inhibited behavior, hoarding behavior, and narcissistic behavior. Problems in dominance-submission include boasting; active or passive controlling behavior; manipulative behavior; overly conforming, overly dominating, or overly submissive behavior;

and rebellious or rivalrous behavior. Problems in dependence-independence include overly dependent behavior as exemplified by clinging, whining, or overly demanding behavior; and overly independent behavior as exemplified by overly generous, responsible, or compensatory behavior [4:290].

PSYCHOSEXUAL DEVELOPMENT

Deviations in psychosexual development include (1) the precocious or delayed appearance of sexual curiosity, (2) the continuation of infantile autoerotic patterns, (3) the very early or very late development of heterosexual interests, and (4) deviations in heterosexual identifications as exemplified by markedly passive "feminine" boys or very "masculine" girls who do not display characteristics of actual sexual inversion or perversion. Such children may experience some internalized conflict but do not have a neurosis or a personality disorder [4].

During the period from about age four to the beginning of school, children are curious about everything, including sex. Children of both sexes may masturbate or may disrobe to play doctor or nurse. Little boys may compete to see who can urinate farthest. If a child is living in crowded quarters that allow little privacy or if he sleeps in his parents' bedroom, he may be exposed to adult sexual behavior that stimulates his curiosity at an even younger age. In addition to asking questions, he may try to imitate the behavior he has observed.

When children start asking questions, some parents may feel embarrassed and may make the child feel guilty or ashamed about his questions or about behaviors such as exposure of his body, masturbating, and "playing doctor." Under such circumstances, the child may become very inhibited and stifle his curiosity so that it is delayed until a much later age.

All infants engage in some autoerotic behavior. If the child's adult caretaker is slow in meeting his needs, the infant may become very dependent on autoerotic stimulation to relieve tension. Such activity may become so pleasurable and gratifying that the child is not inclined to give it up, consequently it may persist long after most children have relinquished such patterns of behavior.

In Western culture, most youngsters exhibit little interest in the opposite sex during the latency or elementary school years, seeming to prefer companions of their own gender. With the beginning of adolescence, interest in members of the opposite sex increases. Since there are wide variations in the onset of puberty, in the acquisition of social skills, and in community expectations, what is normal covers a wide range. In general it seems that if children exhibit a strong interest in the opposite sex during latency, they might be considered to be precocious in this regard; whereas if they exhibit little interest until late adolescence, they are delayed.

Green [3] has studied the atypical sex role behavior of fifty preadolescent boys who prefer the dress, activities, toys, and companionship of girls, comparing them and their families with a control group. He has identified certain early experiences which seem to characterize the lives of the feminine boys. They include:

1   Parental encouragement or unconcern for feminine behavior in the boy during his first years.
2   Lack of psychological separation of the boy from his mother, resulting from factors that include such things as excessive holding of a cuddly baby.
3   Maternal overprotection of the young boy, with marked inhibition of rough and tumble play and male peer group interaction.
4   Lack of availability of male playmates during the earliest years of socialization, coupled with the accessibility of female companions.
5   Absence of an older male to serve as an identity model during the boy's first years.
6   Gross rejection of the boy by his father.
7   Unusual physical beauty in the boy which influences adults to treat him as though he were a girl [6:1409].

Of the above experiences, the first is the one that seems to be necessary for a boy to develop a strong feminine identity, i.e, during the first two to four years of life the parents view the boy's feminine behavior as being cute or a passing phase and do nothing to discourage it. Green [3] does not hold that a boy's behavior depends entirely upon such experiences exclusive of innate or constitutional factors. He acknowledges that individual differences in temperament, neonatal cuddliness, activity level, and level of aggressivity may play a role. The mothers of Green's feminine boys typically described their sons as having been the cuddliest of their children. The boys themselves avoided rough-and-tumble play and sought the companionship and activities of girls and women.

There is some evidence that neuroendocrine factors contribute to such individual differences. Preadolescent girls who have been exposed to large amounts of androgenic hormones prenatally have been found to exhibit unusually rough-and-tumble behavior and culturally unfeminine behavior.

Although such neuroendocrine data are impressive, studies by Money, Hampson, and Hampson [9,10] indicate that socialization experiences are even more powerful. Children develop a sexual identity consistent with the sex assigned to them and the pattern of rearing even when the sex assigned is not consonant with such anatomical criteria for sex, as chromosomal configuration and internal reproductive structures. Two cases dramatically illustrate this point [1]. Both patients were chromosomal females with the adrenogenital syndrome who were born with ambiguous external genitalia. At birth, one was designated male, one was designated female. Each patient developed a gender identity congruent with the sex designation.

Many preschool boys dress up as girls or women occasionally, sometimes play with dolls or play the role of mother or teacher. When they start grade school such behavior usually drops out. However, from the first years of life a small group of anatomically normal boys exhibit a persistent and overriding interest in the clothes, activities, and toys of girls [3]. They assume feminine roles in their play, prefer girls as playmates, choose a Barbie doll as their favorite toy, and express a desire to be a girl. They are interested in feminine fashions and make drawings replete with females. Reviewing the few studies that have been done following such strongly feminine boys into adulthood, Green concludes that "boys who show a considerable degree of cross-gender behavior appear to have a greater than average probability of later manifesting one of three patterns of atypical sexuality — homosexuality, transvestism, and transsexualism" [3:1411].

It must be emphasized that the data currently available are limited, and that even in the extreme population discussed above, a significant number of feminine boys became heterosexual. It seems likely that there is a spectrum of feminine boys with the outcome being dependent upon the intensity and the interaction of the various factors involved—neuroendocrinological, psychological, and social-environmental.

Culturally masculine behavior or tomboyishness in preadolescent girls is much more common than feminine behavior in boys. However, such behavior in girls is more socially acceptable, frequently even being prized, whereas feminine behavior in boys is ridiculed. For the most part, parental statements to the effect that "she'll outgrow it" tend to be true. However, some girls do not relinquish their masculine orientation as they reach adolescence. At present, there is insufficient evidence to predict which girls will grow out of their tomboyishness and which ones will not. The critical variable may be found by differentiating two components of gender identity — one's basic sense of being male or female and a preference for masculine or feminine gender role behavior. [3]. Most tomboys like being girls and do not wish to be boys. They just perceive the social system as granting more rewards for boyish behavior. When they reach adolescence and the social system provides more rewards for acting in a culturally feminine way, they change their role behavior. It is the girls whose basic identity is male — the ones who want to be boys — who do not respond to the change in social rewards but continue to exhibit masculine behaviors.

AFFECTIVE DEVELOPMENT

Deviations in affective development consist of continuing tendencies to exhibit greater or lesser affect or more unstable affect than is typical in the average child in the absence of structured psychoneurotic reactions or personality disorders. They include moderate anxiety, less mature emotional lability than expected for one's age, marked overcontrol of feelings, mild depression or apathy, and cyclic patterns of euphoria and hypomanic activity alternating with depression and diminished activity. Such children may exhibit apprehensive behavior, multiple fears or a specific fear or panic states, separation anxiety or stranger anxiety past the usual age, uncontrollable screaming or crying, or other manifestations of anxiety. If elated, they may behave in a manic way, act silly, or have spells of uncontrollable laughing or giggling. They may be very moody, overly sensitive, have strong feelings of inadequacy or inferiority, or be easily angered or shamed [4].

The tendency of a child to overreact with fear is often related to the sensitivity of his autonomic nervous system. Thus, highly sensitive children [2] might be expected to have more than the average number of fears. Less sensitive children may be conditioned by early experiences of a very frightening kind so that they subsequently feel acute apprehension in similar situations. Other children may have excessive fears because of the outward projection of their own hostile impulses. This may occur in children with unresolved oedipal feelings or in children who have been rejected, neglected, or abused.

Children described as being difficult and ones labeled slow-to-warm-up tend to exhibit more extreme and prolonged negative reactions to strangers. This is in keeping with their general tendency to exhibit predominantly negative responses to new situations and to adapt slowly [14].

Whether or not a behavior is viewed as being a deviation also depends to a large extent on the goals and values of the parents and the socioeconomic class to which they belong. The apprehensive behavior or moderate anxiety of a slow-to-warm-up child or the moodiness or uncontrollable crying of a difficult child might be viewed as a problem by a middle-class parent who stresses early self-care and social adaptability. It would be overlooked by a lower-class parent, who does not consider these issues important and expects the child to "outgrow" disturbing behavior [14].

DEVIATIONS IN INTEGRATIVE DEVELOPMENT

This category includes moderate deviations in the development of impulse controls and anxiety or frustration tolerance; the inability to play or overly dramatic play; disorganized behavior; uneven or overactive use of certain defense mechanisms, such as identification with the aggressor, projection, denial, and rationalization without the presence of personality disorder or psychosis [4].

As already mentioned, children with language disorders frequently exhibit disorientation in space and time. Mastery of the concept of time is important to a child's integrative development. The pleasure principle, the demand for immediate gratification, operates in the here-and-now. In contrast, the reality principle requires consideration of time. A child's capacity to wait grows as he comes to understand linguistic forms representing the future. The ability to verbalize feelings helps the child to establish control and reduces acting-out. By expressing magical and omnipotent fantasies in words, a child externalizes them, thus rendering them less powerful. This process aids reality testing. When a child's language development is delayed, he has less opportunities to test fantasies against reality and may be slower to relinquish magical thinking [6].

Some premature children seem to exhibit a loose and fragmented ego organization, displaying variability in attention, level of performance, management of stimulus input, and frame of reference [5]. Children who have not been born prematurely but who are immature in their development may exhibit similar characteristics. Even though they may be very bright, they may not be ready for school at age six, lacking the necessary ego development and drive control necessary for the ability to work. A delay in physiological maturation and a lag in ego development often go together. Such children may have reflex behavior, tonus, and posture characteristics of a chronologically young child. They behave impulsively and are inclined to express aggression through action rather than words. They may be preoccupied with conflicts usually associated with an earlier psychosexual phase. Their fantasies tend to be rather primitive, being characterized by longings for early instinctual gratifications, wish fulfillment, and magic solutions.

Some children may exhibit simplified organizational schemata. In talking about the prematurely born and educationally unready children of her study, de Hirsch [5] states: "Starting with early sensorimotor experiences and continuing all the way up to higher psychic functions, our children appear to have difficulties responding to and integrating gestalts—a difficulty which may be reflected in delayed development of the integrative function of the ego. Evidence of problems with gestalts is seen clearly in the lack of flow in the children's handwriting, in the absence of sentence melody when they read aloud" [5:115].

Ross [12] has described what he calls the unorganized child. Such children exhibit high distractability, short attention span, and low persistence. These characteristics interact with parental disorganization and overpermissiveness to yield an unorganized child. Unorganized children who have a high activity level may have problems in school due to restlessness or a tendency to chatter disruptively. Less active, unorganized children may daydream or be slowpokes. Those given to intense reactions may have temper tantrums.

REFERENCES

1   Ehrhardt, A. A., Epstein, R., and Money, J. Fetal androgens and female gender identity in the early-treated adrenogenital syndrome. *Johns Hopkins Med. J.* 122:160, 1968.

2   Escalona, S. K. "The differential impact of environmental conditions as a function of different reaction patterns in infancy." In *Individual differences in children,* ed. J. C. Westman, pp. 145–157. New York: Wiley, 1973.

3   Green, R. "Atypical sex role behavior during childhood." *Comprehensive textbook of psychiatry,* vol. 2, 2nd ed., eds. A. M. Freedman, H. I. Kaplan, and B. J. Sadock, pp. 1408–1414. Baltimore: Williams and Wilkins, 1976.

4   Group for the Advancement of Psychiatry, *Psychopathological disorders in childhood: Theoretical considerations and a proposed classification,* Report no. 62, pp. 226–229. New York: Group for the Advancement of Psychiatry, 1976.

5   de Hirsch, K. Language deficits in children with developmental lags. *Psychoanal. Study Child.* 30:95–125, 1975.

6   de Hirsch, K. "Language disabilities." In *Comprehensive textbook of psychiatry,* vol. 2, 2nd ed., eds. A. M. Freedman, H. I. Kaplan, and B. J. Sadock, pp. 2108–2116. Baltimore: Williams and Wilkins, 1976.

7   Johnson, D. J., and Myklebust, H. R. *Learning disabilities: Educational principles and practices.* New York: Grune and Stratton, 1967.

8   Mahler, M. "A study of the separation-individuation process and its possible application to borderline phenomena in the psychoanalytic situation." In *The psychoanalytic study of the child,* vol. 26, pp. 403–424. New York: Quadrangle, 1971.

9   Money, J., Hampson, J. G., and Hampson, J. L. An examination of some basic sexual concepts: The evidence of human hermaphroditism. *Bull. Johns Hopkins Hosp.* 97:301, 1955.

10   Money, J., Hampson, J. G., and Hampson, J. L. Imprinting and the establishment of gender role. *Arch. Gen. Psychiatry* 77, 333, 1957.

11   Peters, J. E., Davis, J. S., Goolsby, C. M., Clements, S. D., and Hicks, T. J. *Physician's handbook: Screening for MBD.* New York: CIBA Medical Horizons, 1973.

12   Ross, D. C. Poor school adjustment: A psychiatric study and classification. *Clin. Pediatr.* 5:109, 1966.

13   Thomas, A. "Impact of interest in early individual differences." In *Perspectives in child psychopathology,* ed. H. E. Rie, pp. 267–292. Chicago: Aldine Atherton, 1971.

14   Thomas, A., and Chess, S. *Temperament and development.* New York: Brunner/Mazel, 1977.

24

Adjustment Reactions and Behavior Disorders of Childhood

Robert Goshen, M.D.

The second edition of the *Diagnostic and Statistical Manual Disorders of Mental Disorders* (DSM-II) separates the categories of transient situational disturbances and behavior disorders of childhood and adolescence. Transient situational disturbances are *adjustment reactions*, which occur without underlying mental disorder as responses to some external stress. The symptoms diminish when the stress is removed. If symptoms don't diminish, then another diagnosis must be made. The adjustment reactions are subclassified by the developmental stages of infancy, childhood, and adolescence. Adjustment reactions may also occur in adults.

Behavior disorders, on the other hand, are less transient and more internalized than transient situational disturbances; but due to the fluidity of behavior in childhood, they are not so stable or fixed as to be labeled personality disorders or neuroses. The behavior disorders are subclassified by the various types of behaviors which are seen as the presenting symptoms, such as hyperkinetic reaction or withdrawing reaction.

In the proposed classification by the *Group for the Advancement of Psychiatry* (GAP) the term reactive disorders corresponds to the DSM-II transient situational reactions. Behavior disorders, however, are included within this category rather than named separately.

ADJUSTMENT REACTIONS

Reactive disorders (adjustment reactions) occur as reactions to external events or situations. Unlike healthy responses to similar environmental stresses, there is a pathological degree of disturbance. The symptoms result from conflicts between the child's aggressive and/or sexual drives and the expectations of his family and social environment. These conflicts are conscious, rather than internalized and unconscious conflicts as in neurosis. Underlying the child's conscious conflict with his environment there may be family disruptions which lessen the child's ability to cope with his normal anxieties. In some cases the parents unknowingly are reinforcing the child's negative behavior by providing a greater reward through their attention when the child is involved in negative behavior than they normally provide him when he is "good." The expectations of significant adults such as parents and school personnel may be out of step with the child's current level of development, resulting in frustration and increased anxiety on the part of the child. Or the adults may convey to the child their own anxieties, as is frequently observed in cases of children who appear to have a great deal of separation anxiety when in fact they are reflecting the separation anxiety of their mothers.

Because the conflict with the child's social environment is such a critical factor when diagnosing the reactive disorder, the precipitating situation must be demonstrated and it must also be shown that the situation is causally related to the reactive disorder. Such a precipitating situation may include illness, accident, or physical trauma suffered by the child; loss of a parent or sibling; birth of a sibling; or stresses resulting from the attitudes or behaviors of significant adults such as parents or school personnel. Not all children respond in the same way to the same stress. In showing a reactive disorder the child's dynamic state, including his past experiences, his developmental level, and the particular meaning a certain precipitating stress has for that child, should be determined. For example, the birth of a sibling may have a much more traumatic effect on a two-year-old child who has not yet completed the process of separating from his mother and developing his own individuality than on a six-year-old child who has already begun developing relationships outside of the family.

Adjustment reactions may present themselves with any of a number of symptoms. It is not the specific symptom but rather the fact that the symptom results from the child's reaction to an environmental situation that makes the condition a reactive disorder. In infants, presenting symptoms may include eating or sleeping disturbances, failure to thrive, and apathy. The older child may present a variety of psychological or behavioral symptoms. He may show other- or self-directed aggression or antisocial behavior, such as fire setting, lying, stealing, truancy, or vandalism. There may be oppositional behavior, such as disobedience, negativism, and passive-aggression; or isolating behavior, such as excessive shyness, inhibition, suspiciousness, or withdrawal into a fantasy world of daydreams and imaginary playmates. The older child may also respond with regressive behavior, such as loss of bladder or bowel control; psychophysiological disorders, such as urticaria, headaches, diarrhea, and vomiting; or habit disorders, such as thumb sucking and nail biting.

In making a diagnosis of adjustment reaction the specific presenting symptom and the developmental level (infancy, early childhood, later childhood, or adolescence) should be indicated. As an example, a child might be described as having a reactive disorder of early childhood manifested by enuresis and precipitated by the family moving to a different city. If the child had a preexisting disorder upon which the reactive disorder was superimposed this other diagnosis would also be given. It should be shown that there has been normal adjustment prior to the onset of the child's reactive disorder, that the reactive disorder resulted from some severe environmental stress, and that the child's symptoms respond quickly to the alleviation of the environmental stress.

Reactive disorders may be transient in nature as are the transient situational reactions of DSM-II but the course may be prolonged by various forces, such as the child remaining in a continually traumatic situation (for example, the prolonged physical or mental illness of a parent), or by the responses and attitudes of the social environment to his symptoms. For example, in the case noted above of the enuretic child whose family just moved to a new city, if the parents took a punitive attitude towards his enuresis this could possibly prolong the enuresis. The prolongation of the problem may lead to the development of a more chronic condition, such as neurosis, when the original conscious conflict becomes internalized through the action of defense mechanisms such as repression.

BEHAVIOR DISORDERS

As noted, the DSM-II classifies the behavior disorders into six different "reactions." Although each category is labeled with a characteristic behavior, such as hyperkinetic or withdrawing, many of the symptoms within each category are shared between the various categories. It is thus often difficult to limit a description of a child's behavior to only one category. With the exception of the hyperkinetic reaction, which appears to have a strong organic or developmental component, behavior disorders are most often seen as resulting from a chronic problem in parental attitudes or methods of discipline.

The six reactions subclassified by the DSM-II are hyperkinetic reaction, withdrawing reaction, overanxious reaction, runaway reaction, unsocialized aggressive reaction, and group delinquent reaction.

Hyperkinetic Reaction

The four primary characteristic features of hyperkinetic reaction, all of which may or may not be present in a particular child, are hyperactivity, short attention span, distractibility, and aggressiveness. There are a number of other symptoms which may also be present with this condition, including specific learning disability, enuresis, poor fine-motor coordination (example: poor handwriting), slow development of speech, or continuing speech impediment. The DSM-II describes hyperkinetic reaction as follows:

"This disorder is characterized by overactivity, restlessness, distractibility, and short attention span, especially in younger children; the behavior usually diminishes in adolescence.

"If this behavior is caused by organic brain damage, it should be diagnosed under the appropriate non-psychotic organic brain syndrome."

Although the DSM-II description excludes organic brain damage, the hyperkinetic reaction is frequently associated with "minimal" evidence of neurological impairment or immaturity. It appears that those children in whom there is a greater indication of organic brain damage may respond more readily to medication, whereas those children in whom there is less evidence of organic brain damage more frequently have some form of family pathology and may respond less readily to medication.

The hyperkinetic reaction may not be evident until after the child enters school and begins facing increasing demands for his attentiveness. The symptoms are more obvious when the child is functioning in a group, such as in the classroom, rather than when the child is relating one-to-one as when being evaluated by a physician. It is therefore imperative that a physician making a diagnosis of minimal brain dysfunction obtain reports on the child's characteristic behaviors both at home and in the school. The physician should also keep in mind the possibility of treatable organic causes, such as central nervous system trauma, infection, toxicity (there have been reports of higher body levels of lead in children with hyperactivity than controls), degenerative neurological conditions, or neoplasms. Treatment of this condition should involve parents and teachers as well as the child. Teachers can be advised to expect work from the child only within the limits of his attention span and to cut down on distracting stimuli in the classroom when the child is attempting to study. The parents often must be given support in providing consistent firm discipline, as these children appear to be unusually resistant to learning through normal discipline. Medication, particularly with central nervous system stimulants such as methylphenidate (Ritalin), has been found to be very effective in a large number of cases, particularly in decreasing the hyperactivity and increasing the attention span. The children are often helped by individual or group psychotherapy aimed at limit setting and dealing with the poor self-esteem that the child often develops through poor peer relationships and poor academic achievement despite normal potential.

Withdrawing Reaction

The DSM-II describes withdrawing reaction as follows: "This disorder is characterized by seclusiveness, detachment, sensitivity, shyness, timidity, and general inability to form close interpersonal relationships. This diagnosis should be reserved for those who cannot be classified as having schizophrenia and whose tendencies towards withdrawal have not yet stabilized enough to justify the diagnosis of schizoid personality."

This condition frequently first presents itself in early latency when the condition may be precipitated by such events as beginning school, the loss of an important family member, or the loss of familiar surroundings when the family moves. These children often have previously been somewhat slow in venturing from the home to meet peers and strange adults. The parents may encourage this through overprotectiveness or overrestrictiveness, or they may try to push the child outside when he feels unprepared for such a venture. The child may, on the other hand, wish to stay at home to protect a parent (usually the mother) who finds it difficult to move out of the house and who may convey to the child a sense of anxiety related to leaving the protection of the home.

Therapy with these children involves dealing with the parents' anxieties and helping them to provide support for the child as well as to increase opportunities for the child to have pleasant experiences outside the home. Psychotherapy with these children may be beneficial in providing an accepting atmosphere outside of the home where they can explore their fears of the outside world. A later stage in psychotherapy may involve the child in a group therapy situation with his age mates.

Overanxious Reaction

The DSM-II says that "this disorder is characterized by anxiety, excessive and unrealistic fears, sleeplessness, nightmares, and exaggerated autonomic responses. The patient tends to be immature, self-conscious, grossly lacking in self-confidence, conforming, inhibited, dutiful, approval seeking, and apprehensive in new situations and unfamiliar surroundings. It is to be distinguished from neurosis."

The presenting symptoms may be such things as sleeping or eating disturbances, specific phobias, and school avoidance. These children often rely on others to make decisions for them and may tend to have passive and dependent relationships with adults to whom they relate with fearful compliance. Because such children are often highly obedient, the parents may not be concerned with this behavior until their child's clinging dependency or sleeplessness become problems to them. These parents often have high expectations which the children are constantly striving to attain.

Parental counseling must encourage the parents to permit the child greater freedom of expression, whereas individual psychotherapy provides a special environment in which the child can experiment with his own spontaneous impulses. The child will frequently begin experimenting with some cautious "mischievous" behavior at home which the parents should be forewarned of so that they may show tolerance for this child's attempts to express himself. If the family does not seem prepared to accept such behavior it may be best to help them deal with it through family therapy.

Runaway Reaction

These are children who, according to DSM-II "characteristically escape from threatening situations by running away from home for a day or more without permission. Typically they are immature and timid, and feel rejected at home, inadequate, and friendless. They often steal furtively." Runaway reaction and the unsocialized aggressive reaction are the two "predelinquent" categories of the behavior disorders. The essential difference between these two is that the runaway child reacts by fleeing, whereas the unsocialized aggressive child reacts by standing his place and fighting. Temperamentally and physically the runaway child is often less aggressive and less adept. He may have poor relationships with peers and has received little experience in dealing with direct expression of aggression. The home environment is often quite poor, with neglect, rejection, and frequently even cruelty. The child thus feels helpless, has poor self-esteem, and sees no one within his environment to whom he can turn for help. The specific running episodes may occur when the child is fearful that he will be punished for some misdemeanor at home or at school or that he will retaliate against the parents after being punished.

Treatment of these cases often must start with radical changes within the home environment, even to the point of removing the child if it doesn't appear that the home environment will be able to provide enough support. In addition to changes in the home, these children can find support and an improved self-image by interaction with peers through activities in which they are able to succeed, such as well-programmed camp or club activities.

Unsocialized Aggressive Reaction

The DSM-II describes this as being: "Characterized by overt or covert hostile disobedience, quarrelsomeness, physical and verbal aggressiveness, vengefulness, and destructiveness. Temper tantrums, voluntary stealing, lying and hostile teasing of other children are common. These patients usually have no consistent parental acceptance and discipline. This diagnosis should be distinguished from antisocial personality, runaway reaction of childhood, and group delinquent reaction of childhood." The family situation in these cases resembles the families of the runaway child, but the unsocialized aggressive child is more temperamentally able to stand up for himself. In some cases the parents overtly or covertly protect the child from the consequences of his antisocial and destructive behavior. In other cases, harsh discipline meted out by the parents may lead to further anger and frustration with increased problem behaviors. The child may reenact the cruel and harsh treatment from his parents onto other children, becoming a domineering bully among his peers. The family situation is often very unstable with a great deal of disagreement between the parents on handling the child, resulting in an inconsistent approach to the child's behavior. The child's behavior, particularly in younger children, often seems to be a pointless rageful assault on everyone within his environment. He may have a long history of demandingness and impulsive behavior. There is frequently a violent reaction to any attempts on the part of the parents to restrict his behavior.

In treating these children both the child and his parents must learn that his behavior can be controlled. It is therefore important to start with these children at as early an age as possible when their behavior can in fact be controlled by parental discipline. The parents should be counseled on providing consistent, firm discipline as well as rewarding positive behavior on the part of the child. Siblings who must deal with the child's behavior may also be involved in treatment.

Often the parents will attempt to place the child into foster care when they feel they can no longer tolerate his behavior. The same type of behavior is likely to continue in the foster care situation. It is the unfortunate experience of many of these children that they are moved from one foster home to another, and at each stage their impression is confirmed that their behavior indeed can't be controlled by anyone. Although a brief separation from the family may at times help the family to "regroup" in order to better deal with the child, this should be done in a carefully planned way with continuing parental exposure so that the child can eventually be led to believe that at least some adults, and hopefully his parents, are able to control his behavior. The use of stimulant medications, as with hyperkinetic reaction, has proven to be helpful in a certain number of these children. When these children's behavior has not been successfully dealt with at an early age, their behavior can lead into delinquency upon reaching adolescence.

Group Delinquent Reaction

The DSM-II describes these children as having "acquired the values, behavior, and skills of a delinquent peer group or gang to whom they are loyal and with whom they characteristically steal, skip school, and stay out late at night. The condition is more common in boys than in girls. When group delinquency occurs with girls it usually involves sexual delinquency, although shoplifting is also common." The behavior of these children is sometimes described as being socialized, as opposed to the often solitary behavior of the runaway or unsocialized aggressive child. Although the group delinquent reaction is most often described as occurring among adolescents, young children may be found engaging in similar behaviors apparently in emulation of local gang "heroes." The emergence of delinquent gangs is seen within the context of wide ranging social and cultural changes and disruptions. It seems to be particularly characteristic of densely populated and highly industrialized areas or during times of social and cultural upheaval, such as when there is a large influx of newly immigrating people or with the disturbances of war. Delinquency also seems to be highly correlated with the impoverished social conditions of big city slums where the excitement and status of gang membership may be a relief from an otherwise depressing and nonrewarding living situation. Often in the above social conditions there is a lack of adequate "healthy" adult role models within the family or within the community. Children may see their parents as being beaten down by the "system," while the gang in turn offers them a way around. In some communities, where delinquent gang structures are well entrenched, it may be a necessary and protective part of a child's growing up to belong to a gang rather than try to make it on his own as an isolated individual. Although there is often inadequate parenting and family disruption these family problems may themselves be results of the same sociocultural factors. Family disruption is frequently an accepted fact of life within the slum communities. Compared to the previous categories of runaway reaction and un-socialized aggressive reaction the group delinquent child often shows much greater ability to relate to his peers and even to adults.

Although the group delinquent child may occasionally become in-volved in individual problem behaviors, such as shoplifting, lying, and stealing, the child's delinquent acts are usually done together with or under the direction of the gang in which he participates. The gang may at times assign specific delinquent tasks to its various members to be done on their own but with at least the "moral" encouragement of the gang. As-sociated with these behaviors the child may demonstrate poor school per-formance or school truancy, or both.

Because the child's underlying personality structure is often fairly healthy the prognosis is frequently good for these children. This is espe-cially so if the child is able to relate to some favorable adult model whom he may find among local civic leaders, recreational counselors, probation officers, or even through the staff of training or reformatory schools.

Many children do wind up in institutions such as training or refor-matory schools which may act to dissuade them from further delinquent acts and may provide them with important growing experiences which can turn them to more constructive behaviors. Unfortunately, on the other hand, these institutions may give them an opportunity to become more involved in gangs, learn more delinquent behavior, and continue the de-linquent life-style. This latter turn of events is probably much more likely to occur in a rigidly authoritarian type of institution which duplicates the same sort of circumstances from which the child has just come. Because these children are often so dependent on their peer groups for role models, some programs have been successful by making use of reformed former gang members as counselors.

RECOMMENDED READINGS

*   American Psychiatric Association. *Diagnostic and statistical manual of mental disorders*, DSM-II, Washington, D.C.: American Psychiatric Association, 1968.
*   Arieti, S., ed. *American handbook of psychiatry*, vol. 2. New York: Basic Books, 1959.
*   Freedman, A. M., and Kaplan, H. I. *The child: His psychological and cultural development*. Vol. 2, *The major psychological disorders and their treatment*. New York: Atheneum, 1972.
*   Group for the Advancement of Psychiatry. Psychopathological disorders in childhood: Theoretical considerations: A proposed classification. New York: Jason Aronson, 1974.

25

Learning Disorders in Children

Eleanore M. Jantz, Ph.D.

One of the most frequent and subtle medical problems confronting the physician is that of a child with a primary learning disorder. It has been estimated in various studies that between 5 and 20 percent of children have some type of learning disability. Boys are from three to eight times more frequently affected than girls. Often in the past the basic problem went unrecognized in an underachiever, the common complaint of teachers and parents being that the child was undisciplined or unmotivated. Year after year report cards would be sent home with the message, "Johnny needs to pay better attention in class and concentrate on finishing his work. He could do better if he really tried." This engendered a good deal of frustration and guilt in the child as well as anxious exasperation in the parents, to the detriment of both. Rejection by his peer group further aggravated the child's unhappiness.

Usually some crisis, such as failing a grade, the development of school phobia, or serious emotional disturbance brought such a child to the attention of the physician. All too often, on finding nothing physically wrong, the physician would reassure the anxious parents that Johnny would "grow out of it."

Just what Johnny was supposed to grow out of has until recent years been obscure. If a child had been found to be in good health and of normal intelligence, it had generally been assumed that poor scholastic achievement was due to an emotional block to learning. Only the gradual recognition that psychodynamic and psychotherapeutic approaches were ineffective in correcting or lessening the incidence of academic failure forced further investigation.

The current belief of most educators and child health-care professionals is that, although some cases of school failure and dropout doubtless occur for social and psychological reasons, the vast majority of academic underachievers, particularly in the early school years, suffers from a learning disorder.

DEFINITION

The term *specific learning disorder* refers to the inability of a child to acquire particular intellectual skills in the usual manner and at the expected rate, based on the average progress of normal children in the regular school system. In other respects a child so affected may be functioning adequately or even brilliantly. What distinguishes him from the retarded child is the specific nature of his handicap, whereas in mental retardation the deficit is a markedly lowered ability to function in all spheres of activity, intellectual and social.

Not infrequently a learning-disabled child will have an above-average score on a standardized intelligence test. Just as often he may have a score that is somewhat below average because of a severe handicap in one or more items that lowers his total IQ. In any case, his test profile will be an uneven one, with high scores in some areas and deficiencies in others. He may, for example, do well in verbal tasks and poorly in tasks requiring motor coordination, or vice versa. For this reason the term specific learning disability has come into usage.

In this chapter the concept of a primary learning disorder excludes gross mental retardation and *primary* emotional disturbance. Emotional maladjustment as a secondary or reactive feature of the learning disorder is, of course, almost invariant; a fact that has often resulted in diagnosticians putting the cart before the horse in their assessment of the problem. Also to be eliminated from consideration are secondary learning difficulties associated with cerebral palsy, deafness, blindness, or cultural deprivation; and temporary learning problems due to medical conditions such as illness or allergy. Epilepsy, on the other hand, when not accompanied by mental retardation, may be associated with a learning disability. Many learning-disabled children have a history of seizures.

Learning disability is most often present in the general area of language development, manifested by *dyslexia,* the impairment of the ability to acquire skill in reading, spelling and written communication. Some children, on the other hand, find their greatest difficulty in the area of number ability or arithmetic calculation, manifested by *dyscalculia.* Sometimes both areas are compromised. The two symptoms, dyslexia and dyscalculia, thus affect the most basic academic skills required in the educational and social setting. The child who fails in one or both of these subjects may be disadvantaged for his entire life, both in the occupational choices open to him and in the level of attainment possible. The damage to his self-concept and personality is equally serious and long-lasting, particularly since such high value is placed on these attainments in modern culture.

Because of the high incidence of learning disorders in the population, the long-lasting and widespread effect on the individual, and the fact that learning disability is a remediable symptom, the importance of early diagnosis and appropriate management on the part of the physician, the family, and the educator cannot be too strongly emphasized.

ETIOLOGY

The above definition of a learning disorder embraces a syndrome of cognitive and behavioral symptoms associated with low levels of performance in specific areas, the causes of which are still incompletely understood. Strauss and Lethinen [17] were the first to present a comprehensive study of the learning problems of brain-injured children. From the work of these and other investigators came the impetus for the study of learning disabilities in children who had no history of brain injury, yet who displayed many of the same kinds of learning difficulties and behavioral symptoms seen in children with known brain damage. It came to be assumed that the similarity between brain-injured and learning-disabled children could be explained as due to some degree of brain damage in both instances. Because the symptoms were more mild and clear neurological signs were absent in the learning-disabled child, his condition was termed *minimal brain damage.* Subsequently the term *minimal cerebral dysfunction* came into use in order to signify that the primary learning disability is a symptom of cerebral impairment of function dissociated from structural brain damage. Another term in use is *hyperkinetic child* in recognition of the hyperactivity often seen in children with learning disorders. All these terms refer to learning disability of presumed neurological origin. This diagnosis was for many years highly controversial, and today there are still physicians who deny its existence. Rourke [14] published a paper reporting a program of carefully planned and systematically thought out research that for the first time established the diagnosis on more than a presumptive basis.

He concluded that "the nature, patterning, and extent of some (perhaps not all) of these deficits appear to be entirely consistent with the view that at least one crucial factor limiting the satisfactory adaptation of children with learning disabilities is cerebral dysfunction" [14:918].

An interesting finding of Rourke was that learning-disabled children aged nine to fourteen years performed on psychological tests similarly to what would be predicted for cerebral dysfunction when compared to adults with known cerebral lesions. That is to say, they made the same types of errors and demonstrated similar patterns of deficits. Younger children, on the other hand, did not present such clear-cut patterns of abilities and deficits. This points out the fact that learning disability is a developmental phenomenon and perhaps explains why the learning-disabled child may (but usually does not) appear to be quite normal until he enters school and is required to learn to read and write. A careful history of such children, however, often reveals signs of slowness in learning to talk, motor clumsiness, or overactivity that were overlooked or assumed to be due to immaturity. It is not difficult to recognize a very young child who displays signs associated with cerebral dysfunction, but the difficulty lies in predicting which ones will prove to have a learning disability when they reach school age.

The etiology of learning disabilities is seldom clear in individual cases. Some of the causes which have been suggested in various studies are heredity, possible prenatal or perinatal brain injuries associated with the health of the mother or conditions at birth, prematurity, biochemical irregularities in the brain, certain childhood diseases such as measles or epilepsy, head trauma, and nutritional deficiency. The use of drugs, alcohol, and tobacco by the mother during pregnancy has also been implicated. Emotional maladjustment and cultural deprivation were long thought to be the chief factors.

The present state of knowledge concerning the etiology of learning disabilities is admittedly inconclusive. This will inevitably be the case as long as the basic structures and brain mechanisms involved are unknown. Until the necessary basic research has been done, clinicians will continue to be dependent upon descriptive and correlative data in their approach to diagnosis and treatment of this complex problem.

DIAGNOSIS

One of the difficulties in making a diagnosis of primary learning disability, or minimal cerebral dysfunction, is that the pathognomonic signs are common in more than a single disorder. For example, the behavioral indicators such as hyperactivity, short attention span, distractibility, emotional lability, temper trantrums, aggressive acting-out, and school phobia are seen in brain-injured and emotionally disturbed children as well as in learning-disabled children. Furthermore, such signs vary from child to child and sometimes within a given child, depending on the age or situation. Not all children display all these signs. Then, too, the child with a primary learning disorder will often display emotional disturbance or antisocial behavior as a reaction to pressure, frustration, failure, and rejection.

Another complicating factor in the early diagnosis of the preschool child is the developmental variability in children. Some of the characteristics of a learning disorder are normally seen in young children and disappear with maturation. It is the persistence of these early signs beyond the age when they should have disappeared that is pathological. One of the most common adjectives used to describe learning-disabled children is immature, by which it is meant that, both physically and behaviorally, they give the impression of being younger than their chronological age. It is for this reason that physicians often adopt a wait-and-see attitude toward mild developmental deviations in young children, on the premise that further maturation will correct the problem.

In making the diagnosis of learning disorder, the first step is a very careful and detailed history, including the family history. It is not unusual to find evidence of a familial trait in learning disorders. There may be more than one affected sibling in a family or first cousins who had similar problems. Sometimes one or both parents may be affected or have had siblings who had difficulty in school.

Following the family history, one proceeds through the pregnancy, birth, neonatal and later postnatal, and early childhood periods. If one concurs with the view that learning disorders have a neurogenic basis, it should not be surprising to find frequent histories in which there is some possibility of insult to the nervous system. For example, bleeding during the pregnancy (especially in the first trimester) is often reported. The mother may report previous interrupted pregnancies or difficulty in carrying a child to term. The birth history may be of a long, hard labor with difficult delivery. The sudden, spontaneous delivery is very frequently reported and seems to be especially hard on the infant. Information about the birth is often noncontributory because the mother was sedated and does not know or remember the circumstances. Prematurity with a birth weight less than five pounds has been found to be associated with learning disorders in several studies. Denhoff and Tarnopol [5] reported a study of forty-eight children with learning disorders in which the incidence of perinatal complications and accidents or infections before the third year was found to be overwhelmingly greater than socioenvironmental factors such as emotional instability, parental divorce, or adoption.

The developmental history of the learning-disabled child frequently includes slowness in one or more of the developmental landmarks. Most often, language is the disturbed area, although motor retardation or motor clumsiness is often a feature. Hyperactivity and temper tantrums are common complaints from infancy on. The kind of hyperactivity that is meant is an impulsive, purposeless kind of restlessness that has no direction or constructive goal. The young child wanders from one object or place to another, touching and often breaking things, leaving things in disorder without seeming to be aware of, or even looking at, what he is doing. He seems constantly in motion, with only fleeting interest in any activity. Teachers will often complain that a child wanders about the classroom, being a distraction to the other children. Restraint or reprimand will bring on a tantrum or crying.

Sometimes a child is said to be accident prone, and there may be a history of head trauma from a fall. There may be, but often is not, a history of seizures, occasionally associated with high fevers. Severe illnesses are reported. Toilet training may have been slow and difficult in such children. Bed-wetting can be the first symptom that is called to the physician's attention. By the time he is in school, distractibility and short attention span are frequently mentioned.

Usually it is the pediatrician or the family physician to whom parents first bring a child who is in trouble. A routine physical examination will reveal nothing to account for the child's problems. The neurological examination, while lacking evidence of clinical abnormalities, is likely to reveal soft neurological signs. These soft signs are so called because they are minimal or inconsistent and not clinically significant of a definite syndrome, such as nonspecific motor awkwardness, twitches of the face or body, or impulsivity. Beyond the age of eight years, one can be concerned about a child's inability to carry out diadochokinetic movements smoothly, to skip, or to hop on one foot, or to catch a ball. Touching fingers to thumb may be executed inadequately or not at all, and there may be adventitious movements of the mouth or resting hand during the effort. The physician may find that the child cannot copy a square or a diamond. It has been found consistently on standardized tests that children should be able to draw a square with four right-angle corners by the age of five and an elongated diamond by the age of seven. This provides a simple and reliable test of perceptual-motor development.

Since reading retardation is by far the most frequently seen learning disability, the physician should include some sample of reading and writing in his examination of the child. Characteristics of dyslexia that he should look for include omissions of words in oral reading or the transposition of letters within words, such as reading *saw* for *was*. In writing and spelling it is common to find reversals or rotations of letters such as *p, b,* and *d*. Also there may be confusion among similar appearing letters such as *n*, *m*, and *w*. Reversals and rotations occur normally in preschool children; however, their occurrence in the reading, writing, or drawing of children eight years or older is pathological. Although visual problems seldom play a role in dyslexia, an ophthalmological examination should be given to rule out possible visual defects.

The literature abounds with conflicting views about the usefulness of the electroencephalogram (EEG) in the diagnosis of learning disorders. It is a limitation of the EEG that a negative (normal) record does not rule out the presence of pathology. However, positive or abnormal records are a different matter. It is important to obtain both a waking and sleeping record, as a very common finding in learning and behavior disorders is the 6–14 per second positive spike in the sleep phase. The high incidence of this pattern in the population has caused many investigators to question its clinical significance. Nevertheless, the consensus is that it is an abnormal pattern. A frequent complaint of children with this pattern is severe headaches and/or abdominal pains. Migraine headaches are also mentioned. Another common EEG finding is a pattern of paroxysmal sharp waves. The usefulness of the EEG to the physician often lies not as much in its diagnostic reliability as in its role in determining which medication to prescribe in a particular instance.

Innovative uses of the EEG are being experimented with which show promise of elucidating relationships between brain and behavior. The cortical evoked potential is being used to study differences in latencies between children and adults. Evoked responses are being used to compare dyslexic children with children who have other types of learning problems. Discrepancies between the hemispheres are also under investigation. Rourke [14] reported using the EEG to study lateralized and nonlateralized abnormalities. He also mentions an investigation by MacDonald and Rourke in which it was found that children with learning disabilities who differ in EEG habituation of the cortical arousal response also perform differently in motor, perceptual, language, and cognitive abilities. Thus the clinical significance of the EEG can be enhanced by measuring the rate of habituation to a complex auditory stimulus.

In making a difficult differential diagnosis, it is usual for the physician to refer his patient to a psychologist for an evaluation of cognitive and emotional factors. Standardized psychological tests which provide quantitative measures of cognitive function have been the most useful techniques in discriminating the child with a learning disorder. The most widely used test battery in clinical practice consists of the Wide Range Achievement Test (WRAT), the Wechsler Intelligence Scale for Children (WISC), the Bender Gestalt Test, human figure drawings, and a variety of projective tests, such as the Rorschach, the Thematic Apperception Test

(TAT), or the Kinetic Family Drawing, depending on the age of the child or the individual circumstances. Koppitz [9] has provided an extremely useful standardized scoring method for the Bender test that contains signs for brain-damaged children. The kinds of errors observed in her sample are frequently found in learning disorders as well. These tests form a core battery on which the clinical psychologist can build, adding other tests as needed. Other psychological techniques for examining specific functions in detail are particularly useful, both in research and in guiding remediation methods to be utilized by the teacher. In clinical practice, however, the standard battery has proven to be efficient and time-saving for diagnostic purposes. As it is, the psychological evaluation takes from three to five hours of patient contact to administer. The physician may also refer a child to a language pathologist for diagnosis and treatment when a speech abnormality or aphasia is suspected.

Psychological tests yield a quantitative measure of the level of performance on a variety of perceptual and motor tasks which can be compared to standardized norms for the population at large. They indicate what can be expected of the normal person at given ages and how far below or above that norm an individual performs. More importantly, they offer a profile of relative strengths and weaknesses in an individual, together with insights into his attitudes and personal problems.

In learning disabilities one usually finds marked discrepancies in performance among the subscales of the WISC. A bright child who obtains a high score in general information yet cannot recall more than three digits backwards and is seriously deficient in reading and arithmetic may be utilizing other means of acquiring knowledge than through written symbols. For this reason it is wise to counsel parents to give their children every opportunity to learn through the use of television, movies, trips, museums, phonograph records, or lectures. In this way it is possible to counteract the general constriction of interest and intellectual development that is attendant upon holding a child back a grade in school or placing him in special classes that are programmed for the level of his handicap at the cost of his potential in other respects.

Discrepancies among test scores are particularly significant in the diagnosis of specific learning handicaps, since they pinpoint both the strengths and the weaknesses of the individual child. Differences of ten or more points between the verbal IQ and the performance IQ *in either direction* should alert the physician to consider the possibility of a primary learning disorder. This is especially valid in that Reitan [13] demonstrated that the WISC verbal IQ and the performance IQ were among the most powerful measures differentiating brain-damaged and normal children in the early school years. Rourke and associates [15] found WISC verbal-performance discrepancies to be correlated with performance on a variety of tasks in children with learning disabilities. Belmont and Birch [2] found retarded readers to have lower verbal than performance IQs.

Learning is a matter of attention and information processing in the brain, sensory input, integration with previous experience, storage, and retrieval. The psychological evaluation can sometimes give a behavioral description suggesting which phase of learning seems most affected in a person. Attempts to specify brain localization of specific test behavior have been largely unsuccessful, although there is some evidence to point to lateralization: The verbal scale is thought to represent left hemisphere activity, whereas the performance scale represents the right hemisphere. Reitan [12] found the two scales to differentiate right and left cerebral lesions in adults. The more recent work of Sperry [16] supported the theory that the two hemispheres have specialized cognitive functions; the left processing verbal, abstract symbolic information and the right more concrete, nonverbal operations.

Orton [10] first proposed that dyslexic children had mixed dominance which somehow interfered with learning, an idea which has been enthusiastically endorsed by educators without sufficient evidence. A person presumably may demonstrate mixed dominance by picking up a hollow tube in one hand (the dominant hand) and sighting through it with the eye on the opposite side. However, the theory of mixed dominance implies that contralateral hand-eye preference refers to the two hemispheres, whereas recent research suggests that the action of carrying hand to eye may be a spatial function governed by the right hemisphere alone. Benton and Sahs [3] reported the incidence of left-handedness and ambidexterity to be two to three times greater in dyslexic children than in the normative population, which they interpreted as mixed cerebral dominance for language. However, in an excellent brief review of the status of dyslexia, Graff and associates [7] pointed out that in at least three studies 85 percent to 90 percent of dyslexic children were right-handed with no evidence of mixed cerebral dominance. Two recent articles by Galin [6] and Kinsbourne [8] contained extremely interesting accounts of work bearing on the general area of hemispheric specialization and dominance.

Attempts to isolate predictive patterns of psychological test scores that would correlate with clinical findings, such as the conventional EEG, have so far failed. This is probably explained "because the relationship between a behavioral deficit and the area of brain damage that gives rise to the deficit is not direct" [8:52]. In other words, a complex skill is not localized at one specific point in the brain. The fact that the psychologist's use of the differential test score approach has not uncovered any WISC subtest patterns that were uniformly predictive of an undifferentiated class of children with learning disorders is not surprising when one considers the complexity of brain function. Nevertheless, individual patterning of test scores can yield information that is both clinically significant and useful to the remedial teacher. For example, it is possible to determine whether an individual child is differentially handicapped in retention of auditory or visual material or whether difficulty in spelling and writing is related to perceptual or motor factors. Such an assessment is necessarily inferential at this stage of understanding of brain-behavior relationships.

TREATMENT

Children with learning and behavior disorders often find their way to the neurologist and the psychiatrist, depending on the orientation and bias of the referring individual. The former is especially helpful in ruling out neurological disease or abnormality and in prescribing medication, whereas the latter plays an important role in the rehabilitation of the emotionally disturbed handicapped child, as well as in counseling the family concerning management of the child. The impact of such a child on the family in all spheres — emotional, social, and financial — is a topic unto itself. Much attention has been devoted to the influence of parenting on the child, whereas relatively little attention has been paid to the child's effect on the family. The physician needs to be alert to parental distress and to know enough about community resources to be helpful to parents who are faced with the task of finding (and financially supporting) appropriate educational facilities for their learning-disabled but otherwise normal child. The public educational system provides special classes for the retarded, the physically handicapped, the emotionally disturbed, and the child with specific learning disability (SLD). All too often the learning-disabled child cuts across these arbitrary boundaries and fits into none.

The important thing to remember is that when one speaks of a learning disability one is referring to a *difficulty* (rather than an impossibility) that in most instances can be overcome, i.e., compensated for, by appropriate teaching techniques and sympathetic support.

Just as in diagnosis, the management of children with learning disorders calls for a multidisciplinary approach: medical, educational, and psychological. Only the educational aspect is outside the province of the physician. Beyond monitoring the general health of the child, the physician must consider what role medication should play in the treatment of a child with a learning or behavior problem. The array of available drugs is considerable, and the responses of children to them are highly variable. It therefore often requires time and a number of trials to find the right drug and the right dosage for an individual. Moreover, drug therapy in the management of behavior demands close watching, as many drugs have undesirable side effects. An interesting finding is the paradoxical effect of many drugs on children, i.e., they have opposite effects from that observed in adults. Dextroamphetamine, for example, is a stimulant for adults, yet has an apparent calming effect on hyperactive children. Conners [4] related this to the individual child's basic level of the arousal mechanism, suggesting that stimulation of the arousal mechanisms enhances the cortical inhibitory capacity, thereby reducing hyperactivity in children who demonstrate low central-arousal levels. Kinsbourne [8] used the concept of arousal to describe the manner in which individuals respond to cues in the environment. In a fascinating discussion of attention he linked cognitive and personality variables. He described people who attend to a wide range of stimuli (high arousal level), as extraverts, who are stimulus seekers, in contrast to introverts (low arousal level), who tend to narrow their focus of attention so as to avoid stimuli. According to this view, hyperactivity is the extreme of extraversion, in that the child has difficulty in focusing attention and is constantly distracted. Stimulant drugs such as amphetamine, which affect arousal mechanisms, increase the ability to focus attention by enhancing cortical inhibitory capacity. Kinsbourne [18] conjectured that hyperactivity in children may be due to underdevelopment of frontal-lobe control over cue utilization and avoidance tendencies.

The chemical composition and characteristic effects of the major classes of drugs has been outlined by Whitsell [18]. Of the many drugs available, those most commonly prescribed in learning disorders are dextroamphetamine (Dexedrine), thioridazine (Mellaril), methylphenidate (Ritalin), diphenylhydantoin (Dilantin), and diphenhydramine (Benadryl). In cases where the EEG showed the 6–14 per second positive spike, Dilantin has often been the drug of choice. Most of these drugs have been prescribed separately or in combination.

From the educational standpoint, a number of remedial teaching programs have been proposed by educators, most of them aimed at correcting or overcoming neurological deficits presumed to relate to reading disability. Balow [1] reviewed the literature and concluded that no adequately designed or controlled studies have been found that demonstrate the effectiveness of such programs in correcting reading disability. Perhaps this is because investigators have not been looking at the proper basic elements or processes involved in reading or spelling. Some children do improve in remedial programs, but it is not clear why or how they do so. No doubt many factors unrelated to reading, such as small size of the classes, individual attention, conditions of reinforcement, or isolation from distracting stimuli, play a role. Behavioral modification techniques offer promise of controlling behavior and shaping learning in the classroom. The experimental use of teaching machines has given encouraging results for a variety of reasons. Rourke [14] has reported finding the use of positive reinforcement to be successful in shaping attention in the investigation of younger children who exhibited deficits in reaction time to visual and auditory stimuli. He concluded that simple visual reaction-time deficit was a reliable indicator of central nervous system dysfunction in young children, but that it was age dependent. Older children, whether brain-injured or learning-disabled, did not differ from their normal age mates. In the absence of longitudinal studies, it is not known whether children with attention deficits adapt to or overcome this symptom of slower reaction time.

EMOTIONAL DISTURBANCE AND LEARNING

It would not be accurate to leave the impression that emotional factors are unrelated to learning. One may, it is true, observe school failure in the emotionally disturbed child, but for different reasons from those noted in children with a primary learning disability. Extreme anxiety, hostile negativism, or passive withdrawal can influence a child's willingness or ability to attend to or profit from instruction. Usually, however, the history of the child with a primary emotional disturbance reveals a definite time of onset that can be related to an event or situation or person. There is often evidence of disturbance in the home. The medical examination is usually negative, with no suggestion of neurological involvement. Physical development, motor coordination, and ability to control activity are usually normal. Generally speaking, performance on psychological tests of intelligence is higher for the emotionally disturbed children as a group than it is for the learning-disabled children. There is usually not very much verbal-performance discrepancy. On the other hand, the projective material is likely to reveal anxiety and intrapsychic conflict. The attitude of the child is often a leading clue. In such cases, psychotherapy, rather than remedial education, is essential. The use of drugs in the treatment would be limited to extreme cases.

I began this chapter with the statement that psychotherapy was ineffective in correcting a primary learning disorder, but it is often necessary in order to help the child to cope with frustration or anxiety. In the case of a learning disorder that is secondary to emotional disturbance, psychotherapy often is the only means of freeing a child's energies in order that he can apply them constructively in the learning situation. Rabinovitch [11] provided an admirably balanced view of the multiplicity of factors involved in learning disorder, discussing the role of emotional problems in the impairment of academic achievement.

REFERENCES

1   Balow, B. Perceptual-motor activities in the treatment of severe reading disability. *Reading Teacher*, 24:513–525, 1971.

2   Belmont, L., and Birch, H. G. The intellectual profile of retarded readers. *Percept. Mot. Skills* 22:787–816, 1966.

3   Benton, A. L., and Sahs, A. L. Aspects of developmental dyslexia. *Iowa Med. Soc. J.* 58:377–383, 1968.

4   Conners, C. K. "Drugs in the management of children with learning disabilities." In *Learning disorders in children*, ed. L. Tarnopol, pp. 253–301. Boston: Little, Brown, 1971.

5   Denhoff, E., and Tarnopol, L. "Medical responsibilities in learning disorders." In *Learning disorders in children*, ed. L. Tarnopol, pp. 65–118. Boston: Little, Brown, 1971.

6   Galin, D. "Hemispheric specializations: Implications for psychiatry." In *Biological foundations of psychiatry*, vol. 1, eds. R. G. Grenell and S. Gabay, pp. 145–176. New York: Raven Press, 1976.

7   Graff, M., Scott, W. E., and Stehbens, J. A. The physician and reading problems. *Am. J. Dis. Child.* 128:516–520, 1974.

8   Kinsbourne, M. The neuropsychological analysis of cognitive deficit. In *Biological foundations of psychiatry*, vol. 1, eds. R. S. Grenell and S. Gabay, pp. 527–589. New York: Raven Press, 1976.

9   Koppitz, E. M. *The Bender Gestalt Test for young children*. New York: Grune and Stratton, 1964.

10   Orton, S. T. *Reading, writing, and speech problems in children*. New York: Norton, 1937.

11   Rabinovitch, R. D. "Reading and learning disabilities." In *American handbook of psychiatry*, vol. 1, ed. S. Arieti. New York: Basic Books, 1959.

12   Reitan, R. M. Certain differential effects of left and right cerebral lesions in human adults. *J. Comp. Physiol. Psychol.* 48:474–477, 1955.

13   Reitan, R. M. "Psychological effects of cerebral lesions in children of early school age." In *Clinical neuropsychology: Current status and applications*, eds. R. M. Reitan and L. A. Davison. Washington, D.C.: Winston, 1974.

14   Rourke, B. P. Brain-behavior relationships in children with learning disabilities: A research program. *Am. Psychol.* 30:911–920, 1975.

15   Rourke, B. P., Young, G. C., and Flewelling, R. W. The relationships between WISC verbal-performance discrepancies and selected verbal, auditory-perceptual, visual-perceptual, and problem-solving abilities in children with learning disorders. *J. Clin. Psychol.* 27:475–479, 1971.

16   Sperry, R. W. "Lateral specialization of cerebral function in surgically separated hemispheres." In *The psychophysiology of thinking*, eds. F. J. McGuigan and R. A. Schoonover. New York: Academic Press, 1973.

17   Strauss, A. A., and Lethinen, L. E. *Psychopathology and education of the brain-injured child*. New York: Grune and Stratton, 1947.

18   Whitsell, L. J. "Clinical pharmacology of psychotropic drugs: With special reference to children." In *Learning disorders in children*, ed. L. Tarnopol, pp. 331–359. Boston: Little, Brown, 1971.

26

Psychosomatic or Psychophysiological Disorders of Childhood

Lloyd O. Eckhardt, M.D., and
Dane G. Prugh, M.D.*

The basic approach to the understanding of the psychosomatic (psycho-physiological) disorders of childhood should be founded upon an adequate diagnostic evaluation and the subsequent weighing of the degree of operation of somatic and psychological factors. In biologically predisposed individuals, psychophysiological disorders may be precipitated, exacerbated, or perpetuated by a variety of stressful stimuli. These triggers can be of a physical, psychological, or social nature. From whatever source derived, they impinge on the child to bring about a derangement of his adaptive equilibrium and the appearance of a disorder at the physiological level. Such disorders ordinarily involve those organ systems that are innervated by the autonomic or involuntary portion of the central nervous system. The symptoms of disturbed functioning at the vegetative

* Part of this work was carried out with the assistance of a training grant (MH 07740–13) from the National Institute of Mental Health.

level are regarded as having physiological rather than psychological symbolic significance. It is important to distinguish these illnesses from conversion disorders which involve those organ systems innervated by the voluntary portion of the central nervous system; overall, these symptoms tend to have symbolic rather than physiological significance. In certain disorders, some measure of overlap can occur. Structural changes can occur in psychophysiological disorders and may continue to a point that is irreversible, and, in some cases, life threatening.

Mirsky [30] and others have stressed the fact that psychophysiological disorders have multiple etiological contributants: (1) *biological predisposing factors* of genetic or inborn nature, probably involving latent biochemical deviations; (2) *developmental psychosocial determinants*, with a limited kind of specificity; and (3) *current precipitating* factors of an individually stressful significance. Conflict situations of particular types together with fairly consistent psychosocial patterns may frequently be involved in the predisposition towards and precipitation of these disorders. However, no type-specific personality profile, parent-child relationship, or family pattern has as yet emerged which can be consistently associated with individual psychophysiological disorders. Many similar psychological or psychosocial characteristics may be found in children having other disorders without psychophysiological disturbances, and similar psychophysiological disorders may be seen in children with very different psychological or psychosocial characteristics.

THERAPEUTIC CONSIDERATIONS

In the potentially serious and life-threatening disorders, such as ulcerative colitis or diabetes, psychotherapeutic measures must never be undertaken without concomitant medical treatment and follow-up. A supportive psychological approach should be undertaken at the beginning in order to avoid stirring up intense feelings which may lead to exacerbations or additional medical complications. Later a more intensive and insight-promoting approach may be employed.

In such disorders as asthma and other allergic problems, ulcerative colitis, anorexia nervosa, migraine, and skin disorders, formal psychotherapy in conjunction with the appropriate medical measures have been reported effective. The effects of psychotherapy in other disorders, such as peptic ulcer, appear to be variable. In hypertension, rheumatoid arthritis, and hyperthyroidism the results are more difficult to evaluate [9]. Nevertheless, as part of a comprehensive therapeutic approach for all children with such disorders, a supportive psychotherapeutic approach focused on the child and his or her parents should be considered. Different modalities of psychotherapy (individual, family, or group; hypnosis; behavior modification techniques; and biofeedback) may be used alone or in combination to ensure the maximum therapeutic benefit.

SPECIFIC PSYCHOPHYSIOLOGICAL DISORDERS

The following list of disorders is divided by organ systems, according to the classification offered in 1966 by the Group for the Advancement of Psychiatry (GAP) [20]. Only the major disorders will be considered in this chapter.

Skin Disorders

Atopic eczema is a disorder which may be seen as an infantile condition or in a later, more chronic form. It usually occurs in the children of families with an allergic diathesis. Children affected by the chronic form are generally rigid, tense, and sometimes compulsive. They have a tendency to repress strong emotions, particularly resentment toward their father or mother. The resented parent is frequently overly controlling and may have offered inadequate contact comforts during the child's infancy. Exacerbations during adolescence are usually related to increased conflicts over independence and sexuality. Many of these children become overly inhibited individuals with strong underlying narcissistic bodily concerns, and they receive a great deal of gratification, often self-punitive, from their persistent and self-injurious scratching.

Recurrent urticaria appears to be closely related to dermatographia. The skin reactivity is often constitutionally derived and is frequently associated with positive scratch tests. The clinical manifestations may be brought out by emotionally traumatic experiences or intensified by conflicts over sexuality and independence. Patients are often shy and easily embarrassed, with ready blushing. They are frequently passive, immature, withdrawn or inhibited children, with feelings of inadequacy, unconscious exhibitionistic trends, and overdependence on the mother. In younger children, urticaria may be brought on by overexertion or overexcitement.

Musculoskeletal Disorders

Juvenile rheumatoid arthritis is seen in children who often exhibit conflicts over the expression of aggression and dependence; intense closeness to and dependence upon the mother are characteristically present. The arthritis itself may represent types of autoimmune responses and psychophysiological interrelationships that are as yet unclear. Exacerbations of this disorder may be clinically related to shifts in the family's interpersonal balance that often involve situations in which the child fears loss of a key relationship and at the same time experiences angry feelings that he is afraid to express. Muscle tension, related to these inner conflicts, may help to intensify the inflammation around the involved joints. Psychotherapeutic measures designed to help the child deal with these feelings and to help the parents understand the child's conflicts, as well as their own, may add to the effectiveness of medical treatment.

Tension headaches involve a tightening of the scalp and neck muscles. These occur in tense, often compulsive, individuals in association with emotional conflicts. Psychotherapeutic intervention can be most effective. New techniques in the field of biofeedback have been symptomatically helpful.

Respiratory Disorders

This category includes certain cases of bronchial asthma, allergic rhinitis, and chronic sinusitis. It does not encompass breath-holding spells, which begin with a voluntary action.

Bronchial asthma is seen twice as frequently in boys as in girls. In families with an allergic diathesis, asthmatic attacks may be triggered by fears of separation from the parent, open conflict between child and parent, marital battles, and other situational conflicts. The involuntary psychophysiological mechanisms may involve conditioned vagal responses producing reflex bronchoconstriction and increased bronchial mucus. These involuntary mechanisms overlap with symbolic or voluntary components, such as hyperventilation, in triggering asthmatic attacks. These trigger mechanisms may combine and vary with the intensity of the allergic stimuli.

During an asthmatic attack the parent may fear that the child will die from suffocation. This frequently results in overanxious and overprotective parental behavior leading in turn to overdependent child behavior. Certain parents will show resentment or ambivalence toward the child, and the child may then feel rejected. The child may respond to such parental feelings with denial of his illness or with oppositional or manipulative behavior. Struggles for control can occur with the child manipulating the parent by hyperventilating and developing an attack of asthma.

In a study by Block and her colleagues [5] children scoring low on an allergic potential scale (APS) showed greater psychopathology, with more conflict in family and parent-child relationships than did those with higher allergic potential. Similar differences in psychopathology between "rapidly remitting" and "steroid-dependent" groups of children have also been demonstrated by Purcell [34], the "rapidly remitting" group showing the greater psychopathology.

The major psychological issues to be dealt with are separation anxiety, guilt, and anger towards the parents. Psychological support must be offered to the parents, especially the mother, to help them with their feelings of guilt, resentment, and inadequacy in aiding their child. Intensive psychotherapy for the child and parents may be necessary. This is most effective if serious pulmonary structural change has not occurred. Hypnosis has allowed certain patients to abort attacks and has helped them to realize that they have some control over the onset, as well as the degree of severity of an attack. Behavior modification programs have also seemed helpful [31]. Group therapy for parents of asthmatic children has been effective in reducing parental guilt and anxiety. Self-care clubs and recreational group programs in summer camps have a similar goal.

The dangers of overmedication, the possibility of steroid side effects (including depression and toxic psychosis), and the possibility of psychological dependence on nebulizers and steroids are all important considerations in the medical management of this disorder. Incipient changes in body image and growth lag secondary to prolonged steroid use must also be considered.

Cardiovascular Disorders

Some children show intense autonomic responses to emotional conflicts or stressful situations which may precipitate episodes of *paroxysmal supraventricular tachycardia* followed by syncopal attacks [14,35]. Supportive psychotherapy may be of value in reducing such conflicts.

Children with *essential hypertension* have not been extensively studied from a psychophysiological basis. It is recognized, however, that the disorder does occur fairly commonly in childhood and adolescence.

Studies [27,32] have shown that in both normotensive and hypertensive subjects, discussion of conflictual topics is accompanied by an increase in blood pressure. Along with this, increased catecholamines, peripheral resistance, and renal artery constriction, occurs. Hypertensive patients, however, show a much more intense and prolonged response.

Since parental hypertension is significantly more common in the families of hypertensive children, a biological predisposition to the development of hypertension is probably involved. Some infants show hyperresponsivity to cold pressor tests which continues into adolescence. Young adults who later develop hypertension often have a premorbid tendency to marked fluctuation in blood pressure.

Supportive psychotherapeutic measures should be combined with the appropriate medical treatment. It is hoped that such an approach in childhood may prevent serious hypertension and complications of hypertensive disease in adult life. Biofeedback techniques also seem promising in helping to control hypertension [38].

Children with chronic or recurrent *orthostatic hypotension* appear to be tense, anxious, and emotionally restricted. Constitutionally labile autonomic responses also appear to be involved in this disorder. A supportive psychotherapeutic approach combined with parent counseling can be helpful. At times, referral for intensive psychotherapy may be necessary.

Migraine begins to appear during school age. Attacks are paroxysmal, sometimes periodic, and often hemicranial; they may be associated with focal electroencephalogram (EEG) changes. Other localized reflex neurological disturbances which relate to initial vasoconstriction and later vasodilation of the cerebral blood vessels, mediated through the autonomic nervous system, are often present.

Migraine patients tend to be overcompliant, rigid, and perfectionistic individuals, with difficulties in handling feelings of anger. The parents are often tense and overcontrolling, and the patient may have a special conflict-producing role in the family [29]. Emotional crises combined with fatigue often precipitate attacks. The presence of an aura may be difficult to determine in children, and nausea and vomiting may occur more frequently than headaches.

Medical measures and supportive psychotherapy with parental counseling can be of help. Intensive psychotherapy is often necessary. Ergotamine tartrate should be used cautiously in children because the side effects, such as numbness of the extremities, are quite distressing, and the drug may produce nausea and vomiting. With adults, biofeedback techniques [37], hypnosis, and other relaxation approaches have been shown to be symptomatically helpful.

Hemic and Lymphatic Disorders

Numerous physiological concomitants of anxiety or responses to stress are encountered in relation to this system. These include variations in the blood level of leukocytes, lymphocytes, eosinophils, glutathione values, relative blood viscosity, clotting time, hematocrit, and sedimentation rates. Ordinarily, these are reversible, and they are important principally because they present diagnostic problems. Chronic or recurrent states of leukocytosis may occur, however, as may "stress" or "benign" polycythemia [28] (this involves a decrease in plasma volume with a normal red cell volume) which may lead to stroke or heart attack (in adulthood). Evidence exists that "spontaneous" bleeding, unrelated to injury, may occur in response to emotional stress in children with hemophilia; the exact mechanisms are as yet unclear [25]. In addition, transient rash and hematuria have been reported in relation to exercise and emotion.

Gastrointestinal Disorders

The gastrointestinal tract is extraordinarily responsive to emotional stimuli and this category, therefore, includes a wide variety of disorders. Among the major disorders are nonaganglionic megacolon, peptic ulcer, ulcerative colitis, the irritable bowel syndrome, certain types of recurrent abdominal pain, and anorexia nervosa.

Nonaganglionic megacolon of psychophysiological nature has its origin in the infant's withholding of the stool during coercive toilet training. Autonomic imbalance seems to contribute to the enlargement of the colon, and some constitutional factor may be involved in the predispositions to this disorder. In its treatment, initial cleaning out of the bowel with oil retention or other enemas, with an attempt to regularize bowel evacuation, may be helpful, but as a rule psychotherapeutic measures are also necessary.

Peptic ulcer and ulcerative colitis begin to appear with some frequency in the school-age period; both have been reported at birth and in the neonatal period. These early cases, however, probably represent a response by pituitary-adrenal mechanisms to stress or medication. This may be related to the higher gastric acidity and higher level of adrenocortical steroids which occur during the first few hours and days of life. Both disorders may, of course, occur later as complications of adrenal steroid or adrenocorticotropic hormone (ACTH) administration. Acute "stress" ulcers with massive bleeding may occur in response to intense physical exertion associated with emotional tension.

In school-age children and adolescents, the symptoms of peptic ulcer are different from those in adults. A preponderance of duodenal ulcers is seen, and boys are predominantly affected. Abdominal pain is not well localized and symptoms are not clearly related to meals. Nausea and vomiting are common, and anorexia, headaches, and early morning pain are often seen.

Children and adults who develop peptic ulcers have difficulty in handling feelings of anger. They are generally tense, overcompliant, passive, and dependent. However, they often demand affection. The mother is usually dominant and overprotective. The father frequently is distant and passive, although occasionally rigid and punitive. The ulcer often develops in a situation involving actual, threatened, or symbolic loss. This may take the form of divorce, death of a loved one, intensified marital conflict, or other sources of threatened separation.

Children with peptic ulcer often respond readily to bland diets, antacids, and antispasmodics. Such a medical regimen should be combined with a supportive psychotherapeutic approach. Intensive psychotherapy for the child and his parents may be necessary. Surgery is rarely indicated, but for occasional complications, such as perforation or massive bleeding, it may be life saving.

Ulcerative colitis is a potentially severe, life-threatening disorder. Children with ulcerative colitis are generally overdependent, passive, inhibited, and show compulsive behaviors. Often a core of depression exists. The family constellation often reveals a mother who is the dominant figure and a passive and retiring father. Characteristically, these families exhibit problems in communication especially concerning negative feelings. Within broad limits, the more serious the psychological problems are, the more stormy and difficult is the course of the illness.

The initial onset in childhood involves bleeding more frequently than it does diarrhea. The precipitation of a fulminating type of colitis usually takes place in a situation involving actual or threatened loss of emotional support from a key figure, usually a parent. On the other hand, the insidious type of onset is more likely to be associated with stressful forces which gradually build up to significant levels. An acute mild onset may also occur, with bleeding for only a few days or weeks. In children with the more mild forms of the illness, an apparently permanent remission will often occur. Exacerbations of ulcerative colitis are frequently related to family crises or to other intensifications of emotional conflict.

The nonspecific inflammatory response usually, though not always, begins in the lower colon. It may progress upward and in very rare cases even into the terminal ilium. Predisposing factors probably include familial patterns of autonomic response to stress. In "bowel-oriented" families, this tends to involve the lower gastrointestinal tract. It is possible that the frequently coercive toilet training leads to conditioning of the defecation reflex to emotional conflict. Maternal overprotection and overdomination in early childhood leads to a combination of overdependence and resentment as the child begins to strive for autonomy. Some as yet unidentified biological predisposing factor, however, seems to produce the abnormal mucosal response of bleeding in patients who develop ulcerative colitis. This may possibly be related to an abnormality in the inflammatory process or to an autoimmunization process. Such findings reinforce the impression that this is often a systemic process rather than one limited to the bowel.

Treatment of this potentially life-threatening illness should always include both medical and psychotherapeutic measures. Several studies

[21,33] have demonstrated the contribution of psychotherapy to physio-logical improvement. However, there are other studies [2] which suggest that only the patient's psychological adjustment is helped. In any case, the early phases of the psychotherapeutic approach should ordinarily be limited to supportive measures. Premature emotional insights can pro-duce exacerbations in the more fragile, overly dependent patient. At a later phase in treatment, more insight-producing psychotherapeutic approaches can be valuable; Sperling [41] has successfully employed psychoanalysis.

In the case of the child who is depressed or hopeless and who is not responding to steroids but who is too ill for surgery, psychotherapy may be life saving. Children with milder physical and psychological problems will often respond readily to a supportive approach. Dependence upon the pediatrician may develop rather rapidly and prompt cessation of symp-toms may then follow. The more seriously disturbed overdependent or manipulative personalities require more intensive psychotherapy. This includes extensive work with parents who tend to respond overanxiously to the child's fears or demands. Marital conflicts may also be precipitated or exacerbated and will require appropriate counseling. Teamwork among the medical, nursing, psychiatric, social work, and surgical staff is espe-cially important [26]. The pediatrician should be the captain of this team.

Careful follow-up is necessary. The course of ulcerative colitis may be of a remitting, a chronic intermittent, or a chronic continuous type. A significant percentage of children with early onset and with a chronic con-tinuous course may later develop bowel carcinoma. This may occur even after many years of remission. However, if the symptoms are under con-trol, surgery to prevent carcinoma does not seem warranted. If significant response to combined medical and psychological measures does not ap-pear within at least two years or if "silent" progression of structural bowel changes occurs in spite of psychological improvement, surgery should be considered.

Older children and adolescents with *chronic nonspecific diarrhea* (spastic colitis, mucous colitis, irritable bowel syndrome) have family backgrounds that exhibit many of the same psychosocial conflicts found in patients with ulcerative colitis. However, they generally show less psy-chological disturbance. In these patients, bowel response to vagal stimula-tion (as a result of intensified emotional conflict) seems to be very active; indeed, the bowel response is even stronger than in patients with ulcera-tive colitis. Strong family predispositions exist for this illness, and there is frequently a history of coercive bowel training. The biological predisposi-tion toward abnormal tissue response and mucosal bleeding, however, seems to be absent. The most effective treatment approach seems to be a combined medical and supportive psychotherapeutic program. This can often be provided by the pediatrician in conjunction with the social worker and consulting psychiatrist.

Recurrent abdominal pain is a frequent symptom, occurring in about 10 percent of boys and 13 percent of girls [1]. Over 90 percent of children with recurrent abdominal pain show no physical basis for the pain. The ability to localize pain is still poor in school-age children, and the majority of symptoms are located in the epigastric or periumbilical areas. The recurrent episodes of pain are usually related to some emotional crisis; they are likely to appear in tense, timid, apprehensive, inhibited, and often overly conscientious children who have usually experienced parental overprotection. Abdominal pain, headaches, or nervous tension are frequently present in one of the parents or another close family member. A supportive approach by the pediatrician is helpful along with reassurance to the parents and the patient regarding the absence of serious physical causes.

Anorexia nervosa is a syndrome that is observed most frequently during adolescence or postadolescence. It may, however, appear during the late school-age or prepubertal phases. It should be differentiated from anorexia as a symptomatic response in depression or other disorders. In the true syndrome, the conflict over eating becomes internalized and chronic. Loss of psychological appetite; denial of physical hunger; aversion to food; severe weight loss; hypoproteinemia, with edema at times; emaciation and pallor; amenorrhea; lowered body temperature, pulse rate, and blood pressure; flat or occasionally diabetic blood sugar curves; dryness of the skin and brittleness of the nails; and intolerance to cold may be encountered in part or together and with variable severity. Even in the face of marked loss of body weight (denial of emaciation), activity is often strikingly maintained. Indeed, some patients may exercise unrealistically in order to lose weight. Patients often appear preoccupied or irritable and have difficulty talking about their feelings. Some of the symptoms appear to be the result of a psychophysiological disturbance involving the pituitary-adrenal-cortical axis. Others, such as amenorrhea, may be the result of starvation. Although "pituitary cachexia" or hypopituitarism must not be ruled out, its occurrence is rare.

Anorexia nervosa occurs predominantly in girls but may occasionally be seen in boys. The mother or occasionally the father has usually been strongly overcontrolling toward the patient, and an ambivalent, hostile-dependent relationship develops between the mother and the daughter. There is often a history of early feeding problems. The parents may value slimness and physical attractiveness, and the relationship of the girl with her father may have an overtly seductive quality. Not infrequently the parents, as well as some late adolescent patients, are engaged in occupations related to food preparation. This may provide a compensatory sublimination for a few early or mild chronic cases.

During preadolescence, the patients are often overconscientious, energetic, and highly achieving persons. They remain strongly dependent upon their parents; unconsciously, however, they resent the parental control. Problems in emancipation from the parents are also usually involved; these reflect underlying difficulties in separation-individuation [8]. Food intake then becomes the area in which patients can assert their control. Many girls have previously been chubby or obese or have had fears of becoming fat. The onset of the syndrome occurs in relation to a strenuous attempt at dieting. The diet is continued until it cannot be controlled. These patients may also go through periods of alternating obesity and anorexia as well as periods of bulimia followed by self-induced vomiting. During puberty, these patients show significant difficulties in heterosexual relationships and often avoid dates or other social interaction by their many activities, athletic preoccupations, or social isolation.

Three main diagnostic groups of patients may be distinguished [22]:

1   Those patients with a psychoneurotic disorder who show mixed hysterical and phobic trends. For these patients, eating appears to have strong sexual implications which are derived from earlier unresolved conflicts. Highly symbolic meanings are attached to bodily weight and contours and are often associated with unconscious pregnancy fantasies or fears.

2   Those patients who have obsessive-compulsive personality disorders. They manifest rigid, overconscientious, driving, and sometimes secretive personality trends, and often develop fears of contamination or dirt in food.

3   Those patients with schizophrenic or borderline psychotic states. The thought disorder and massive projection that these patients experience may produce fears that their food is poisoned.

In all three of the above groups, self-destructive or unconscious suicidal implications of the failure to eat may be associated with their anorexia. Bruch [8] has described an additional small group of patients who have a severe reactive disorder with strong depressive trends superimposed on an overly dependent personality disorder. Underlying the personality disturbance there is often a distorted self-concept. These patients fail to be in touch with their body sensations or functions.

For the first and second group of patients the symptoms begin in relation to puberty. These adolescents are often involved in developmental crises. Those exhibiting an hysterical or phobic psychoneurotic picture are usually less disturbed and have a better prognosis for response to treatment. Those showing obsessive-compulsive personality disorders are more rigid and are difficult to treat. In the third group this syndrome develops in late adolescence or during postadolescence, and the patients tend more frequently to be of the schizophrenic or borderline psychotic type. For these patients, the prognosis is much more guarded.

The less disturbed psychoneurotic group can benefit from a supportive psychotherapeutic approach by the pediatrician. This can include the judicious use of psychiatric consultation and help for the parents in order to avoid battles over food and can often be done on an outpatient basis. Intensive psychotherapy for patients and parents may be necessary, however, and family therapy may be especially effective in this group. Behavior therapy, with positive rewards for weight gain, has been of value to some of these patients; if behavioral methods are used, follow-up is important, and work with parents is essential [4]. For those patients who have a more rigid, obsessive-compulsive personality disorder a psychiatrist or psychologist, working closely with the pediatrician, can often be effective. Individual outpatient psychotherapy can be combined with family therapy [24]. If necessary, a pediatric adolescent inpatient ward can serve as a temporary adjunct to outpatient treatment [17].

Seriously disturbed patients with schizophrenic, borderline, and severe reactive disorders can be handled most successfully with psychiatric hospitalization or residential treatment [39]. This is particularly indicated for those patients who are extremely manipulative and controlling toward their parents. In such a setting, patients can be permitted to prepare their own food on the ward. This may help to deal with fears or suspicions about the food. Pressure should not be put on the patient to eat. However, the seriousness of the problem should be pointed out to the patient and parents. Bruch [7] has stated that the primary psychotherapeutic problem is to aid patients in what is a desperate struggle for a separate and self-respecting identity. The rigid regulation of food intake and low body weight is made necessary by their need to achieve and maintain some type of control and identity, however shaky, uncertain, and unhealthy. A more healthy identity can permit patients to give up this pattern.

If the body weight falls toward half its original level, combined medical and psychiatric treatment, using tube feeding if necessary, should be employed. Patients can be helped to accept the tube feeding if they are told this is being done to protect them from doing themselves harm from their diet. Patients usually respond favorably when the doctor "takes over" responsibility for their welfare during this critical time.

Endocrine Disorders

Diabetes is known to involve a hereditary predisposition and is also significantly influenced by psychophysiological mechanisms. Metabolic changes undoubtedly antedate the onset of the manifest clinical disorder. This is shown by the high percentage of women, particularly obese ones, who give birth to babies over eleven pounds and later develop diabetes. Prediabetic individuals often show elevated oral glucose tolerance curves without other signs or symptoms. A controlled study revealed that adolescent diabetics had a significantly higher incidence of parental loss and severe family disturbance prior to the onset of the disorder than did a comparable group of adolescents with blood dyscrasias [43]. Other observations indicate that diabetes is often precipitated in a setting of increased conflict, most often involving a real or threatened loss of a key figure or relationship. Exacerbations, including diabetic coma in children and adolescents, are frequently precipitated by family crises or by other stressful stimuli [42].

In childhood diabetes, the onset is often more abrupt and the course more stormy than in the adult form. This is particularly true during adolescence [13]. In contrast to some of the other psychophysiological disorders, diabetes becomes a permanent handicap, and children and parents must be able to mourn effectively the loss of certain expectations. This is necessary even though there are no visible signs of disability and the resultant changes in life-style may not be great.

Adolescents may feel socially isolated because of their diabetes and may worry about marriage and the effect of their illness on their children [44]. As a result of the impact of the disorder, different coping styles emerge involving varying responses [45]. Some young persons may try to control their diet rigidly and carefully regulate their insulin. Others may deny the disorder and refuse to take their insulin, precipitating hyperglycemia and acidosis. Insulin reactions, if severe and often repeated, can produce brain damage and deleterious effects upon academic and social functioning. Some younger children may misinterpret the illness and its treatment as punishment. Parents may show reactions ranging from overprotective and overanxious to rigid and occasionally rejecting. Struggles for control between parents and child may result in stealing food or overeating. In a number of families, however, the parents encounter no serious difficulty in accepting the illness and no significant personality disturbance appears in the child.

The use of a "flexible" diet can include appropriate snacks, covered by adequate insulin, with limitations only on concentrated sweets and second helpings of some desserts. This seems to help make life more normal for those children and adolescents with diabetes [16]. Such an approach does not seem to significantly increase the incidence of diabetic complications in adult life and may also help to avoid the daily battles over dietary control, stealing and hoarding of food, and related problems. A few adolescents, however, seem to want some external controls and may do better with the structure offered by a basic diet, with permission for some deviations on special occasions.

For many children and parents, counseling within a supportive relationship with the pediatrician will often suffice to handle most problems. Group discussions have been helpful with older children and adolescents, and special summer camp programs for such young people have aided the development of their capacity for self-regulation [46]. Disturbed adolescents, who often use their diabetes to control or rebel against their parents or who exhibit unconscious self-destructive behavior by overeating or refusing to take insulin, require a more intensive psychotherapeutic approach, involving close cooperation among psychiatrist, social worker, and pediatrician. Inpatient pediatric or psychiatric settings may be necessary for this more acting-out disturbed group. Family therapy is a useful adjunct in such settings.

Children and adolescents who develop *thyrotoxicosis* often experience the onset of this disorder in the context of gradually intensifying stressful circumstances or under conditions of real or threatened loss of an important emotional relationship. They appear to have particular difficulty in handling dependency needs. Some show openly dependent tendencies, whereas others attempt to deny and cover up such needs with an overly pseudoindependent facade. Some are chronically depressed. Unplanned pregnancies, marital conflicts, overcontrolling parents, maternal deprivation, and broken homes are frequent events in the histories of these children [6].

The effectiveness and ease of medical treatment of thyrotoxicosis in childhood usually makes formal psychotherapy unnecessary for the disorder itself. However, problems around dependence ordinarily continue, and psychotherapy may be indicated for such problems. Lability of mood with occasional intense projection may be seen in children with a thyroid disorder and may require at least brief psychotherapeutic intervention.

Nervous System Disorders

Children with *idiopathic epilepsy* often experience feelings of inferiority. They are troubled by shyness and a sense of being different from others. Many epileptic children show inhibition of their aggression associated with an increase in seizure activity [19]. However, some may show irritability, temper outbursts, or aggressive behavior, particularly before a seizure. Children tend to experience fears of death just before a seizure; afterwards, during the amnesic period, they may fear they have said or done something "bad." They are often afraid to ask what happened. However, there is no type-specific epileptic personality. Most of the disturbances in behavior are the result of the reaction of the children and their parents to the illness.

Experimental studies in adolescents and adults have investigated their response to the experiencing of different emotional states. They have demonstrated that such states can give rise to paroxysmal changes in electroencephalographic activity and the triggering of actual seizures [3]. Such emotional factors involve hypothalamic-cortical interconnections; they are regarded by some as the most frequent precipitating factors. Fatigue, low blood sugar, head trauma, and other stresses may also precipitate seizures in individuals with a lowered convulsive threshold.

Children with *petit mal seizures* are often inhibited emotionally, and they often show considerable guilt and conflict over handling feelings of anger. Scolding, anxiety, upsetting sights, or unacceptable anger may all precipitate petit mal attacks [40], or the child may have attacks only in the presence of a particular parent with whom some conflict exists. Various types of sensory stimulation, often associated originally with a disturbing experience, may also serve to precipitate attacks (auditory or musicogenic and televisionlike photosensitivity or "flicker fusion" effects). Some disturbed children, when confronted by conflictual situations, may even precipitate such attacks themselves by moving their fingers rapidly in front of their eyes.

Psychomotor equivalents are encountered in the school-age group [36]. These may involve episodes of bizarre, automatic, or stereotyped movements, associated with autonomic disturbances emanating from a temporal lobe focus. Some clouding of consciousness combined with partial or complete amnesia may occur. Chewing and smacking movements, incoherent or irrelevant speech, outbursts of rage, and confused or somnabulisticlike states may suddenly appear, and may last for a few minutes or for several hours. Such episodes often appear in relation to some emotional crisis. At times the content of such seizures may have meaningful psychodynamic significance [12].

Other symptoms such as headache, abdominal pain, and bursts of destructive behavior have been said to represent "latent epilepsy" or "seizure equivalents." Attacks of paroxysmal pain, usually periumbilical in location and colicky in nature, have been described, associated with ictal discharge on the electroencephalogram and often followed by sleep; these have been referred to as "abdominal epilepsy" [11] or by some as "abdominal migraine." Such attacks are quite rare, however, and are to be differentiated from the recurrent abdominal pain mentioned earlier. The tendency to make a diagnosis of epileptic equivalent on the basis of exaggerated fears, repeated tantrums, aggressive behavior, marked withdrawal, running away from home, or sleepwalking, combined with poorly defined abnormalities on the EEG, is far too widespread. Most of the children suspected of such equivalents show disturbances in behavior related to conflicts within the family, and "treatment" of the EEG with anticonvulsant medication is not indicated.

In the treatment of these disorders through counseling and support, the pediatrician can help parents to see the child's illness more realistically. The physician can thus deal with parental guilt as well as their fears of death, mental illness, or retardation. He can help them to keep their anxiety from overrestricting the child (beyond such limits as those of climbing high trees, swimming alone, and so forth) and from blocking the child's every step toward independence. Of equal importance, he can help the parents and child avoid oppositional struggles over drug therapy or other control issues. Group discussions have been helpful, both with parents and with children [10]. Through a supportive relationship, the physician or health associate can be of help to the child in dealing with his fears or social difficulties and can also offer greater understanding of the child's problems to parents, teachers, or other adult figures. The prognosis for response to treatment is good, as is the child's chance to live a relatively unrestricted, independent, and constructive life.

A few parents openly reject or stigmatize the child with epilepsy because of guilt or other feelings. In such a situation, early referral for psychiatric help is indicated. For the more seriously disturbed children, psychotherapy for the child and his parents can help deal with the underlying emotional conflicts [19,40]. This can reduce the component of anxiety involved in emotional trigger mechanisms and can render drug therapy more effective. Family therapy has been reported to be beneficial [23]. A few seriously disturbed children may require psychiatric hospitalization or residential treatment. In some children with petit mal, hypnosis has been reported to be effective [18]. Conditioning techniques using desensitization have been tried with some success on patients where photosensitivity components have played a role in their seizures [23].

If at all possible, the goal of therapy should be complete control of seizures. The threat of another seizure can be devastating to certain children and their parents. Nevertheless, care should be taken to avoid using too much or too many antiepileptic drugs. This may result in children becoming "dopey" or even mildly delirious. In addition, the use of phenobarbital can result in paradoxical stimulation with resultant hyperactivity. This paradoxical effect is seen more frequently in preschool children. As with other psychophysiological disorders or any chronic illness, there are families where the child's invalidism has become a significant feature in the family's balance of interpersonal forces [15]. Complete relief from symptoms may then pose a problem in readaptation for the children and indeed for everyone concerned, and individual psychotherapy or family therapy may be very helpful in such situations.

Fever of psychophysiological origin may occur in certain children who show excitement, or continued emotional tension, in the absence of physical overactivity. In infants with "hospitalism" or in school-age children who are chronically anxious, such fever may be encountered on a chronic low-grade basis. In the latter instance, the parents, especially the mother, are often overanxious, and continue to take the child's temperature daily long after the subsidence of a mild respiratory or other infection. The fever (generally under 101°) usually disappears upon discontinuance of the daily measurements. The physician should discuss the parents' apprehensions related to guilt or other feelings rather than offer blanket reassurance. When an infant with such fever has no other signs of physical illness, his discharge from the hospital after such a discussion usually brings the temperature down to normal [47].

REFERENCES

1   Apley J. The Child with recurrent abdominal pain. *Pediatr. Clin. North Am.* 14:63–72, 1967.

2   Arajarvi, T., Pentti, R., and Aukee, M. Ulcerative colitis in children: A clinical, psychological, and social follow-up study. *Ann. Paediatr. Fenn.* 7:259, 1961; 8:1–16, 1962.

3   Berlin, I. N., and Yaeger, C. L. Correlation of epileptic seizures, electroencephalograms, and emotional state. *Amer. J. Dis. Child.* 81:664–670, 1951.

4   Blinder, B. J., Freeman, D. M. A., and Stunkard, A. J. Behavior therapy of anorexia nervosa. *Am. J. Psychiatry* 126:1093–1098, 1970.

5   Block, J. Jennings, P. H., Harvey, E., and Simpson, E. Interaction between allergic potential and psychopathology in childhood asthma. *Psychosom. Med.* 26:307–320, 1964.

6   Boswell, J. J., Lewis, C. P., Freeman, D. F., and Clark, K. M. Hyperthyroid children: Individual and family dynamics: A study of twelve cases. *J. Am. Acad. Child Psychiatry* 6:64–85, 1967.

7   Bruch, H. Psychotherapy in primary anorexia nervosa. *J. Nerv. Ment. Dis.* 150:51–67, 1970.

8   Bruch, H. *Eating disorders: Obesity, anorexia nervosa, and the person within.* New York: Basic Books, 1973.

9   Chalke, F. C. R. Effect of psychotherapy for psychosomatic disorders. *Psychosomatics* 6:125–131, 1965.

10   DeFries, Z., and Browder, S. Group therapy with epileptic children and their mothers. *Bull. N.Y. Acad. Med.* 38:235–240, 1952.

11   Douglas, E. F., and White, P. T. Abdominal epilepsy: A reappraisal. *J. Pediatr.* 78:59–67, 1971.

12   Epstein, A. W., and Ervin, F. Psychodynamic significance of seizure content in psychomotor epilepsy. *Psychosom. Med.* 18:43–55, 1956.

13   Falstein, E. I., and Judas, I. Juvenile diabetes and its psychiatric implications. *Am. J. Orthopsychiatry* 25:330–342, 1955.

14   Falstein, E. J., and Rosenblum, A. H. Juvenile paroxysmal supraventricular tachycardia: Psychosomatic and psychodynamic aspects. *J. Am. Acad. Child Psychiatry* 1:246–264, 1962.

15   Ferguson, S. M., and Rayport, M. The adjustment to living without epilepsy. *J. Nerv. Ment. Dis.* 140:26, 1965.

16   Forsyth, C. C., and Payne, W. W. Free diets in the treatment of diabetic children. *Arch. Dis. Child.* 31:245–253, 1956.

17   Gladston, R. Mind over matter: Observations on fifty patients hospitalized with anorexia nervosa. *J. Am. Acad. Child Psychiatry* 13:246–263, 1974.

18   Gardner, G. G. Use of hypnosis for psychogenic epilepsy in a child. *Am. J. Clin. Hypn.* 15:166–169, 1973.

19   Gottschalk, L. A. Effects of intensive psychotherapy on epileptic children. *Arch. Neurol. Psychiatry* 70:361–384, 1953.

20   Group for the Advancement of Psychiatry. *Psychopathological disorders in childhood: Theoretical considerations and proposed classification,* vol. 6, report no. 62. New York: Group for the Advancement of Psychiatry, 1966.

21   Langford, W. S. The psychological aspects of ulcerative colitis. *Clin. Proc. Child. Hosp. Wash., D.C.* 20:89–97, 1964.

22   Lesser, L. J., Ashenden, J. F., Debuskey, M., and Eisenberg, L. Anorexia nervosa in children. *Am. J. Orthopsychiatry* 30:572–580, 1960.

23   Libo, S. S., Palmer, C., and Archibald, D. Family group therapy for children with self-induced seizures. *Am. J. Orthopsychiatry* 41:506–509, 1971.

24   Liebman, R., Minuchin, S., and Baker, L. The role of the family in the treatment of anorexia nervosa. *J. Am. Acad. Child Psychiatry* 13:264–273, 1974.

25   Mattsson, A., Gross, S., and Hall, T. W. Psychoendocrine study of adaptation in young hemophiliacs. *Psychosom. Med.* 33:215–225, 1971.

26   McDermott, J. F., and Finch, S. M. Ulcerative colitis in children: Reassessment of a dilemma. *J. Am. Acad. Child Psychiatry* 6:512–525, 1967.

27   McKegney, F. O., and Williams, R. B. Psychological aspects of hypertension. II. The differential influence of interview variables on blood pressure. *Am. J. Psychiatry* 123:1539–1545, 1967.

28   Mendels, J. Stress polycythemia. *Am. J. Psychiatry* 123:1570–1572, 1967.

29   Menkes, M. M. Personality characteristics and family roles of children with migraine. *Pediatrics* 53:560–564, 1974.

30   Mirsky, I. A. The psychosomatic approach to the etiology of clinical disorders. *Psychosom. Med.* 19:424–430, 1957.

31   Moore, N. Behavior therapy in bronchial asthma: A controlled study. *J. Psychosom. Res.* 9:257–276, 1965.

32   Ostfeld, N. M., and Lebowits, B. Z. Personality factors and pressor mechanisms in renal and essential hypertension. *Arch. Int. Med.* 104:43–52, 1959.

33   Prugh, D. G., and Jordan, K. "The management of ulcerative colitis in childhood." In *Modern perspectives in international child psychiatry,* ed. J. G. Howells, pp. 494–524. London: Oliver and Boyd, 1969.

34   Purcell, K. Critical appraisal of psychosomatic studies of asthma. *N.Y. State J. Med.* 65:2103–2109, 1965.

35   Rahe, R. H., and Christ, A. E. An unusual cardiac (ventricular) arrythmia in a child: Psychiatric and psychophysiologic aspects. *Psychosom. Med.* 28:181–188, 1966.

36   Robertiello, R. C. Psychomotor epilepsy in children. *Dis. Nerv. Syst.* 14:337–339, 1953.

37   Sargent, J. D., Green, E. E., and Walters, E. D. Preliminary report on the use of autogenic feedback training in the treatment of migraine and tension headaches. *Psychosom. Med.* 35:129–135, 1973.

38   Shapiro, D., Tursky, B., Gershon, E., and Stern, M. Effects of feedback and reinforcement on the control of human systolic blood pressure. *Science* 163:588–590, 1969.

39   Sours, J. A. Clinical studies of the anorexia nervosa syndrome. *N.Y. State J. Med.* 68:1363–1369, 1968.

40   Sperling, M. Psychodynamics and treatment of petit mal in children. *Int. J. Psychoanal.* 34:248–252, 1953.

41   Sperling, M. Ulcerative colitis in children: Current views and therapies. *J. Amer. Child Psychiatry* 8:336–351, 1969.

42   Starr, P. H. Psychosomatic consideration of diabetes in childhood. *J. Nerv. Ment. Dis.* 121:493–504, 1955.

43   Stein, S. P., and Charles, E. Emotional factors in juvenile diabetes mellitus: A study of early life experiences of adolescent diabetics. *Amer. J. Psychiatry* 128:56–57, 1971.

44   Sterky, G. Family background and state of mental health in a group of diabetic schoolchildren. *Acta. Pediatr. Scand.* 52:377–390, 1963.

45   Tietz, W., and Vidman, T. The impact of coping styles on the control of juvenile diabetes. *Psychiatry Med.* 3:67–74, 1972.

46   Weil, W. B., et al. Social patterns and diabetic glycosuria. *Am. J. Dis. Child* 113:464–469, 1967.

47   White, K. L., and Long, W. N., Jr. The incidence of "psychogenic" fever in a university hospital. *J. Chronic Dis.* 8:567–586, 1958.

27

Psychoneurotic Disorders of Childhood

Jon A. Shaw, M.D.

The psychiatric disorders of childhood are presently conceptualized within the framework of a developmental psychology. Initially, the child is dependent upon the external environment for the satisfaction of his needs. Reality dictates that these needs will at times come into conflict with the external world. Such external conflicts are usually momentary and transient. With increasing differentiation of the personality, there is a tendency for conflicts to be internalized, i.e., experienced as existing between the child's needs and his internal representations of the external world.

Nagera [10] has proposed a scheme in which the emerging manifest symptomatology and disturbances in childhood proceed through stages of increasing internalization of conflict which finally culminates in the infantile neurosis. It is his assumption that a combination of developmental interferences, developmental conflicts, and isolated neurotic conflicts in different proportions are the components which may lead to the development of specific forms of childhood neuroses. In this model *developmental interferences* are defined as factors which disturb the unfolding of the developmental processes. This usually involves parental and environmental interferences with certain developmental needs of the child. A child hospitalized for an emergency medical procedure during the second year of life may experience exaggerated phase-specific conflicts associated with the separation-individuation process and manifest increased clinging and dependency. *Developmental conflicts* arise when the child's specific phases of development and maturation may come into conflict with environmental demands. A child might experience conflict around the issue of toilet training when the external demand is for excessive cleanliness and restriction of motility, and he may manifest symptoms such as temper tantrums, oppositional behavior, and misbehavior. Developmental conflicts are generally characterized by their disappearance when the next higher stage of development is achieved. *Neurotic conflicts* occur when there is a continuation of a developmental conflict which has failed to be resolved within the appropriate developmental sequence. These symptoms usually represent a conflict between a component instinct (oral, anal, or phallic derivatives) striving for gratification and another aspect of the personality which stands in opposition to the gratification. In this sense the external demand has been gradually internalized and the developmental conflict is replaced by what is predominantly an internal conflict. A young child's preoccupation with order and cleanliness may represent an internal prohibition and defense against the wish to be messy. *Infantile neuroses* represent the organization of all the earlier neurotic conflicts and developmental disturbances integrated with all the conflicts of the phallic-oedipal phase (three to six years) of development into a structuralized nuclear complex. Since conflicts of this nature depend for their existence on established boundaries between the id and the ego, the conscious and the unconscious, neurotic symptoms are not found in the preoedipal phases of development, the unstructured personality of early infancy.

The oedipal phase is seen as a critical point in the development of the immature psychic apparatus. There is an increasing sense of gender identity with the wish to implement an exclusive relationship with the parent of the opposite sex while experiencing rivalry with the parent of the same sex. Insofar as the oedipus complex is the culmination of the differentiation of the id and the ego and the structuralization of the superego, it is the nuclear complex of every neurosis. Through the process of repression of sexual and aggressive impulses, identification, internalization, and the use of other unconscious defense mechanisms, the external conflicts are replaced by internalized conflicts existing between the wishes to express various impulses and the inner representatives of the external order. While the complex is usually partly conscious during childhood, it is mostly unconscious in later life. The extent of its resolution, however, is observable in adult behavior, attitudes, object choice, character structure, the nature of object relationships, sexual identity, fantasy formation, and sexual patterns and activities. "It has been found to be characteristic of a normal individual that he learns to master his oedipus complex, whereas the neurotic subject remains involved in it" [4:245–246].

Present understanding of psychoneurosis was derived from Freud's [5] psychoanalysis of adults suffering from hysteria, phobias, obsessions, and compulsions. He noted that specific sexual and aggressive drive derivatives threatening to enter into conscious awareness produced anxiety. This anxiety results from the dangers of instinctual expression associated with the successive phases of the child's early psychosexual development. The specific dangers experienced in early childhood are: (1) loss or separation from the significant object, usually the mothering one; (2) loss of the love of the loved object; (3) loss or damage to the genitals (castration complex); and (4) guilt predicated on the disapproval of one's self relative to one's own internalized moral standards. The ego reacts with anxiety to the possible emergence into awareness of these instinctual drives (id) and their attendant dangers. This anxiety alerts and stimulates repression and the other ego defenses to control and limit the expression of those drives, producing neurotic symptom formation. Invariably, these symptoms represent compromise formations that are symbolic in nature and provide defense against the expression of the impulse while allowing disguised gratifications of the instinctual drive. The neurotic symptom represents the ego's efforts to integrate the opposing demands of the id and superego with the demands of external reality. The psychoneuroses are characterized by inner conflicts in which the structures of the mind — id, ego, and superego — stand in opposition to each other.

It has been estimated that approximately 10 percent of the emotional and mental disorders of children can be categorized as representing a psychoneurotic disorder [9]. The proposed classification of the psychoneuroses of childhood reported by the Group for the Advancement of Psychiatry (GAP) has been generally accepted and is congruent with psychoanalytic theory [8]. In this context, the psychoneuroses are reserved for those disorders based upon unconscious conflicts over the handling of sexual and aggressive impulses. Although these conflicts and the associated unacceptable impulses are removed from awareness by repression, they remain unresolved and active in exerting an influence on the individual's behavior. The neurotic symptom is the product of the ego acting as an intermediary between the drive derivatives and the rational and productive moral claims of the individual.

CLASSIFICATION

The child in the early school years may exhibit various neurotic symptom complexes, such as conversion reactions, dissociations, obsessions, compulsions, and phobias which are relatively self-perpetuating and symbolic of an internalized conflict. The GAP [8] report recognized essentially seven subdivisions of the psychoneurotic disorders based on the nature of the presenting symptoms: anxiety type, phobic type, conversion type, obsessive-compulsive type, depressive type, dissociative type, and other. Anxiety is the cardinal feature of the neuroses. It is precipitated by the unconscious conflict over the handling of sexual and aggressive impulses and its threatened emergence into awareness. This anxiety may be experienced and expressed directly, or it may be controlled unconsciously by the mechanisms of defense which provide the various neuroses with their particular configuration and manifest symptomatology. The child experiences the neurotic symptom complex as painful and distressful and seeks relief.

Anxiety Type

The anxiety neuroses are characterized by the flooding of consciousness with free-floating anxiety arising from the threatened emergence into awareness of some aspect of the internalized conflict. There is a subjective sensation of panic, apprehension, and impending disaster. This is in contrast to the apprehension or fear associated with a realistic and objective source of danger. This anxiety is frequently associated with psychological symptoms of distress under the control of the autonomic nervous system, such as palpitations, rapid respirations, gastrointestinal upset, sweating, lightheadedness, and paresthesias. These physiological symptoms are not associated with any structural changes in the organ systems involved. In contrast to the other psychoneurotic disorders, anxiety neuroses have no predictable configurations or patterns of psychological defense by which the anxiety is modulated and controlled. Ordinarily the anxiety neurosis in children progresses to one of the more focalized symptom neuroses, such as a phobic neurosis. In some instances the anxiety may abate with further maturation and development of the ego's capacities for mastery and the increasing sophistication and differentiation of the psychological mechanisms of defense.

Phobic Type

Phobia (meaning dread or fear) indicates that an object, condition, or situation is feared. The phobia refers to an unreasonable and irrational fear not warranted by the degree of realistic danger posed by the situation. The more commonly experienced phobias are zoophobia — the fear of animals, acrophobia — the fear of heights, claustrophobia — the fear of enclosed spaces, and agoraphobia — the fear of open spaces.

In phobias the various ego defenses operate in such ways that an inner danger becomes an external danger. The phobic neuroses are characterized by the unconscious projection and displacement of one of the aspects of the internalized conflict onto a symbolically significant object or situation in the external environment which is then avoided as if it were the source of danger. Freud's [3] analysis of Little Hans revealed that his phobia of a horse biting him had its origin in Hans' aggressive wish to remove the father in his affectionate relationship to his mother so that he might have mother to himself. Hans projected his aggression onto the father with subsequent fears of retaliation from him. The ambivalently loved father would have been experienced by Hans as the source of anxiety were it not for his displacement of the source of danger to horses which realistically could be avoided. Thus, through a process of projection, displacement, and avoidance, it was possible for Hans to deal with his internalized conflict over the wish to possess his mother exclusively and to do away with his father. It is to be noted that the very nature of Hans' phobia resulted in him having to spend more time indoors and consequently in the company of the object of his affections — his mother. Neurotic solutions represent a compromise between the prohibition and the gratification of the instinctual wish.

The phobic neuroses have to be differentiated from those mild fears associated with developmental phases. Fears of separation from the mother and fears of animals, thunder, and the dark are common in childhood between two and four years of age. These as well as fears associated with realistic events, such as hospitals, doctors, or needles, and those reactive fears associated with a traumatic event are usually of short duration.

Conversion Type

Conversion reactions represent a complex process by which intrapsychic conflicts are expressed in somatic symptomatology. They are characterized by the partial failure of repression of the internalized conflict with subsequent anxiety and the conversion of the anxiety and the content of the conflict into a somatic symptom. The somatic symptoms involve the special sensory systems and/or those bodily structures which come under voluntary control of the central nervous system. These symptoms express, in symbolic body language, a compromise between the forbidden sexual and aggressive impulses and the defensive processes. The symbolic nature of the symptom may reveal an unconscious need for punishment, a memory of a traumatic event, or an identification with a lost object. An eight-year-old boy developed enuresis following the death of his father who was enuretic in his last days as he was dying from carcinoma of the bladder [6]. The anxiety associated with the internalized conflict is bound to the somatic symptom, resulting in the child experiencing little subjective sense of anxiety or even what might be expected to be a normal degree of concern associated with loss of a bodily function.

A four-year-old boy developed a bilateral blinking eye tic which was preceded by a sudden widening of the palpebral fissure. This symptom had its onset after the boy, experiencing a nightmare, entered his father's bedroom and observed his father's amputated leg, which was always kept hidden. The next day the eye blink was noted whenever the father was present. The blinking represented the conflict over the wish to see and the wish not to see. Analysis of the symptom revealed that the widening of the palpebral fissure represented the partial gratification of the wish to see more — the blinking a visual denial of the traumatic sight and its implications [7].

Conversion reactions have to be differentiated from physical illness and psychophysiological illness. The disturbance in function conforms to the child's naive view of bodily function rather than following anatomical lines of distribution. Conversion reaction, not infrequently, may be observed in hysterical, passive-dependent, and immature personality disorders.

Dissociative Type

The dissociative reactions are characterized by a transient disorganization of the personality occurring when the anxiety associated with internal conflicts over sexual and aggressive impulses threatens to enter into awareness. In this reaction, there occurs a defensive pattern of aimless or "freezing" behavior such as sleepwalking (somnambulism), fugue states, catalepsy, cataplexy, transient catatonic states, twilight states, pseudodelirious and stuporous behavior, depersonalization, or pseudopsychotic states. These disorders are associated with disturbances in consciousness and may be characterized by disturbances in self-representation as manifested in a personality dissociation or multiple personality formation. The dissociative states, while often frightening in their psychotic-appearing unpredictability, are relatively well-structured entities within which the anxiety and the content of the conflict are modulated under a curtain of amnesia.

Twilight states and somnambulism are particularly frequent in childhood, occurring more commonly in girls. An eight-year-old girl began experiencing episodes of sleepwalking after her father left the home as a result of prolonged marital discord. Her tendency to express her conflicts and wishes in activity rather than words resulted in her motorically attempting to effect conflict resolution through seemingly searching behavior. In other instances, sleepwalking may represent an attempt to escape rather than approach a situation of gratification. Sleepwalking seems to be a response to the latent or manifest content of a dream. Children inclined to experience dissociations are often shy and unsophisticated in their adaptive capacities. These disturbances, like conversion reactions, often occur in immature, emotionally labile, and relatively dependent individuals. They must be differentiated from epileptic conditions, other neurological diseases, and psychotic conditions.

Depressive Type

Depression in children and adolescents tends to be manifested in three relatively distant ways [1]. First and most common are the masked depressive reactions. They are manifested by a variety of symptoms not usually associated with depression, such as aggressive behavior, hyperactivity, delinquency, hypochondriasis, and sleep disturbances. Second is acute depression which is more clearly identifiable and is associated with loss of self-esteem, sad affect, self-depreciation, guilt, or feelings of hopelessness and helplessness with little evidence of psychomotor retardation. The acute depressions are associated in all instances with a severe trauma related to object loss, although this loss may be actual, threatened, or symbolic. The death of a loved one or the loss of the love of a loved object through divorce, personal difficulties, or geographical mobility may result in diminution of the love and care received. Third are the chronic depressions which occur in children with a history of marginal social adjustment and repeated separations from important adults. Their early life is replete with chaotic and traumatic events which result in the loss of consistent and predictable maternal care.

Neurotic depressive disorders of a more traditional nature involving internalized conflicts associated with ambivalent feelings toward a lost love object are infrequently seen in children. A nine-year-old boy visiting his divorced father became significantly depressed after being injured by his angry father for inadvertently hurting his three-year-old stepsister. In the following weeks he experienced tearfulness, loss of appetite, sleep disturbances, feelings of self-depreciation, fantasies of being hurt and knocked down in the gutter, and threats of suicide. Suicidal threats, while rare before adolescence, may occur in significantly depressed children. Neurotic depression has to be distinguished from reactive disorders relative to developmental or situational crises, psychotic depression, cyclical mood swings, and schizoaffective disorders. The masked depression has to be differentiated from impulse disorders and physical illness.

Obessive-Compulsive Type

These disorders are characterized by the counteracting of the anxiety associated with the unconscious internal conflict with thoughts (obsessions), acts or impulses to act (compulsions), or mixtures of both which serve the purpose of preventing conscious awareness of the unacceptable impulse. The child may experience persistent and repetitive intrusion of unwanted thoughts, trains of thoughts, words, ruminations, or urges to carry out sequences of motoric behavior which are known by the individual to be nonsensical. The compulsive acts may vary from simple movements, such as touching, to complex rituals, such as hand washing. Frequently the external behavior will represent the opposite of the unconscious and unacceptable impulse, such as when the child is preoccupied with excessive cleanliness, orderliness, and neatness, which stands in contradistinction to his wish to soil or mess. Counting and touching ceremonials may be present as a substitute for threatened intrusions of unacceptable sexual and aggressive drive derivatives. The interruption of a compulsive ritual or of obsessional trains of thought frequently precipitates anxiety which may approach paniclike proportions.

The clinical picture of the obsessional neurosis results from regression to the anal phase of development because of severe conflicts associated with the sexual and aggressive wishes of the oedipal phase. The return to the anal phase is characterized by a posture of being either defiant, controlling, sadistic, degrading, or passively complying and conforming in their object relations. The predominant defense mechanisms include reaction formation, isolation and undoing — with excessive use of intellectualization, rationalization, denial, magical thinking, ambivalence, indecision, and a rigid and intrapunitive superego.

A nine-year-old boy was referred who had a number of rituals. He had developed a preoccupation with orderliness and cleanliness. Books had to be arranged in a particular manner, clothes had to be separated from each other in his chest of drawers, the pillow had to be placed centrally on his bed. The bed could be entered only from the left side, and shoes were put on left before right. He also had a specific counting ceremony. This occurred in a boy who was overly courteous, compliant, and regulated in his relationship with a very controlling mother. He was inhibited and lacked age-appropriate methods and patterns for discharging aggressive and competitive impulses.

These disorders need to be differentiated from the age-appropriate compulsivelike mannerisms or ritualistic behaviors occasionally associated with bedtime activities, from involvement in various games and from transient developmental characteristics of a child entering school or latency-age activities. They must also be distinguished from repetitive behaviors in children with significant ego defects, such as autistic children, who demonstrate a global need for sameness, with little capacity to tolerate change.

Other Types

Within this category should be subsumed those neurotic disorders that do not fit specifically within the previous categories. Ideally, mixed neurosis should be incorporated under the predominant psychoneurotic disorder. *Traumatic neurosis* may be included in this category. This reflects a neurosis in which overwhelming tension and painful affects, such as anxiety and guilt resulting from a traumatic experience, cannot be mastered by the usual defensive operations of the ego. Symptoms may include emotional lability, anxiety, fear, rage, sleep disturbances, and typical dreams in which the trauma is painfully reexperienced. Reliving of the traumatic experience commonly occurs in the waking state in the form of fantasies, thoughts, and feelings. With increasing mastery there is recession of the overt memory experience of the traumatic elements and increasing development of a psychoneurotic constellation. It is possible for a traumatic event, such as a child being bitten by a dog, to be used symbolically with subsequent development of an internalized and structured neurosis.

CHILDHOOD NEUROSIS AND ADULT DISTURBANCE

Mental health in children is evaluated relative to the child's capacity to maintain progressive development. Normally, the traversing of the various phases of development is associated with a certain fluidity which allows for flexible coping and adaptation to internal and external conflicts. The infantile neurosis may persist for a period of time and cause considerable distress, but more frequently it runs a latent course with the defense organization gaining the upper hand during the period of latency (six to twelve years) with the development of a stronger ego organization. Yet not infrequently the earlier neurosis is the kernel for the adult neurosis.

The childhood neurosis which has persisted through latency may be modified by adolescent sexual maturation which alters the intrapsychic balance and mitigates internal conflicts. This is particularly noted in children who previously were somewhat passive and had experienced significant bisexual problems. Although adolescence may mitigate earlier conflicts, it likewise may be associated with reactivation of earlier conflicts and with transient symptom formation that may eventually lead to an adult neurosis. The psychoanalysis of an adult neurosis often leads to a symbolic reconstruction of an earlier neurosis associated with its particular defense constellations. It is generally accepted that adult neuroses almost invariably have their origins in earlier childhood disturbances validating the poetic truth that "the child is father of the man." It is Freud's [3:147] conclusion that psychoneurosis in the adult is preceded by an infantile neurosis, although they are not necessarily continuous nor need they have the same manifest symptomatology. A phobic neurosis of childhood may take the form of an obsessive-compulsive neurosis in adulthood [2].

TREATMENT

The psychoneuroses are thought to have a good prognosis and may resolve spontaneously within the vicissitudes of the maturational and developmental processes. Although the psychoneuroses may be mitigated spontaneously in the process of development, they are often reexperienced and reenacted throughout the various stages of development. Intensive psychotherapy is the treatment of choice for these disorders. The task of the therapy is to promote integration of what was before disconnected: the unconscious and the conscious, the past and the present, affects and ideas, the unacceptable and the acceptable. With psychotherapy, the unacceptable impulses and their derivatives are increasingly allowed awareness into the child's conscious mind through the interpretation of the defense mechanisms. It is important for the child to become aware of his internal compromises and how these have resulted in a restrictive pattern of living, curtailing his spontaneity and culturally acceptable patterns of satisfying his impulse life. Psychotherapy should be directed toward uncovering the underlying conflict rather than toward the symptom itself. Repression is replaced by conscious evaluation and consideration of consequences. The impulses come under the influence of conscious control with variable outcomes of expression, rejection, or compromise. While tranquilizers and antidepressants may be used as adjuncts where appropriate, the therapeutic aim should be insight and increasing ego maturation. Psychotherapy should not proceed without a careful physical examination being undertaken when there is a consideration of organic illness.

Psychotherapy of the child is usually coupled with parental counseling. The parents have unwittingly perpetuated the child's conflicts in many instances by various misunderstandings and actions which are often the product of their own intrapsychic conflicts. The parents are able to provide collateral information regarding the child's ongoing life experiences during the course of his therapy. In some instances, it may be necessary for the parents to be seen either individually or conjointly in psychotherapy in order to facilitate an understanding of their own contributions to the child's neurosis.

REFERENCES

1   Cytryn, L., and McKnew, D. Proposed classification of childhood depression. *Am. J. Psychiatry* 129:149–155, 1972.
2   Freud, A. Obsessional neurosis: A Summary. *Internat. Journ. Psycho-Analysis* 47:116–122, 1966.
3   Freud S. "Analysis of a phobia in a five-year-old boy," 1909. In *Standard edition*, vol. 10, ed. J. Strachey. London: Hogarth Press, 1955.
4   Freud S. "Two encyclopaedia articles," 1923. In *Standard edition*, vol. 18, ed. J. Strachey. London: Hogarth Press, 1955.
5   Freud, S. "Inhibitions, symptoms and anxiety," 1926. In *Standard edition*, vol. 20, ed. J. Strachey. London: Hogarth Press, 1955.
6   Gerard, M. W. Enuresis: A study in etiology. *Am. J. Orthopsychiatry* 9:48–58, 1939.
7   Gerard, M. The psychogenic tic in ego development. *Psychoanal. Study Child.* Vol. 2, pp. 133–162, 1946.
8   Group for the Advancement of Psychiatry. Theoretical considerations and a proposed classification, rep. 62, vol. 6. New York: Group for the Advancement of Psychiatry, 1966.
9   Joint Commission on Mental Health of Children. *Crisis in child mental health: Challenge for the 1970s.* New York: Harper and Row, 1969.
10 Nagera, H. *Early childhood disturbances, the infantile neurosis, and the adulthood disturbances.* Psychoanalytic Study of the Child, Monograph no. 2. New York: International Universities Press, 1966.

28

Psychotic Disorders
in Childhood

Ülkü Ülgür, M.D.

Disorders subsumed in the category of childhood psychosis are extremely heterogenous. Different authors use many different names for children with various types of psychotic disturbances. Childhood schizophrenia, infantile autism, atypical child and borderline psychosis are among the most commonly used labels, which may apply to the same or overlapping clinical entities. Ever since Kanner [7] and Bender [1] offered their unique descriptions of early infantile autism and childhood schizophrenia, clinicians have attempted to delineate relevant subcategories that are related to psychological structure, genetic, developmental hypotheses and prognosis. In this chapter, in order to minimize the nosological problems and confusion which stems from the disparities among nomenclatural terms, I followed the guidelines and diagnostic standards set forth by the Committee on Child Psychiatry of the Group for the Advancement of Psychiatry (GAP) [5]. This committee saw as its first task the "formulation of a conceptual framework that would encompass the characteristics of personality formation and development in childhood in sufficiently comprehensive fashion to permit professional people from differing schools of thought to agree at least upon a point of departure to a classification of disturbances and deviations. The influence of hereditary factors, the impact of familial and other environmental influences, the significance of developmental capacities and vulnerabilities, the fluidity of the young child's personality characteristics, and other considerations had to be taken into account" [5:6].

Symptoms of psychosis manifested in childhood and adolescence do not necessarily carry the same significance as they do in adult life. Many authors have pointed out that in contrast to later stages of development, it is more difficult to draw a line of demarcation between mental health and mental illness in childhood and adolescence. During the early years of life the relative strands of the id and the ego are in a constant state of flux. The transition from one developmental level to the next constitutes a potential psychological hazard, for, at this point, major and minor stress is more likely to produce arrest in development, malfunction, fixation, or regression. Therefore the assessment of child psychopathology hinges on one crucial variable — the child's capacity to move forward in progressive stages until maturation has been achieved.

DEFINITION

As it has been proposed by GAP's Committee on Child Psychiatry

> in childhood, psychotic disorders are characterized by marked pervasive deviations from the behavior that is expected for the child's age. Psychotic disorder is often revealed by severe and continued impairment of emotional relationships with persons, associated with an aloofness and a tendency toward preoccupation with inanimate objects, loss of speech or failure in its development, disturbances in sensory perception, bizarre or stereotyped behavior and motility patterns, marked resistance to change in environment or routine, outbursts of intense and unpredictable panic, absence of a sense of personal identity, and blunted, uneven or fragmented intellectual development. In some cases, intellectual performance may be adequate or better, with the psychotic disorder confining itself to other areas of personality functioning [5:79].

It is now generally agreed that functional psychoses of childhood are seen as a basic disorder in ego functioning in which the emerging process of ego development shows extreme distortion. This distortion is revealed in disturbances of those ego functions subserving thought, affect, perception, motility, language, and sense of self, or identity. Associated disorders in object relationships and reality testing are also importantly present. Some manifestations of psychotic behavior appear to represent the individual's efforts at restitution or compensation for the psychotic process.

ETIOLOGY

Although during the past two decades, worldwide investigations into the etiology of childhood psychosis have yielded significant amounts of knowledge, there is still no definite agreement concerning the fundamental causes of childhood psychosis. The disappointing truth is the investigators do not have adequate answers and no specific etiological factors have been isolated. Theories of etiology range from a psychogenic determinant based upon defective intrafamilial relationships to genetic, neurological, and biochemical factors.

The question of the genetic contribution to childhood psychosis is presently under active debate and more research in this area is needed. Chief investigators in the field of genetics — Kallman [6], Book [2], and Slater [9] — tried to prove the role of genetic determinants, but their findings were inconclusive and conflicting. Bender [1] and her associates and co-workers in their clinical and research work also focused on genetic and neurophysiological aspects of childhood psychosis. Bender believes that a prenatal or perinatal defect, trauma, or damage or a "physiological crisis" is the stress that decompensates the genetically vulnerable child and produces a clinically recognizable picture of childhood psychosis.

Genetic studies presently underway reflect a shift from concentration on the dilemma of genetics versus environment to more productive attempts to define the specific ways in which a genetic predisposition interacts with the environment to produce childhood and adult schizophrenia. Many important questions remain to be answered. For example, can an individual child develop a functional psychosis without a genetic predisposition? Which environmental influences are most schizophrenogenic when interacting with a genetic predisposition? The high risk and family studies, in particular, offer logical extensions to the geneticists' vulnerability determinations in seeking answers to these questions.

Parents of psychotic children have been the focus of investigation since Kanner [7] originally characterized them as "refrigerator parents." An appreciable number of influential investigators have taken the position that familial or parent-child relationships are major determiners of schizophrenia among offspring. They have each singled out various aspects of the relationships as most culpable: familial, chaotic, climate, parental irrationality, familial pseudomutuality, parent-child symbiosis, schizophrenogenic mother, strong mother–weak father, overprotective mother, cold rejecting mother, double binding, relating to the child in terms of the parent's own unresolved childhood conflicts, and fragmenting the child's attention. It should be pointed out that some of these conclusions are based on subjective generalizations and inadequate data and, as such, are subject to possible distortion.

The current research in child development and some of the animal experiments point to the need for adequate sensory stimulation, coupled with responsive nurturance during the critical first few days and months of the infant's life, as crucial in determining learning capacities and developing social and adaptive functions. From this new exciting research today we clearly know that the affective and cognitive development of a child can be seriously affected by interpersonal and neurobiochemical influences early in life. Although most of the etiological theories may be conceptually distinct, in the main one would expect failures to occur in more than one type of function for any given individual child. In fact, one could almost define a psychotic child as an individual who has substantial difficulty in socialization and cognitive integration and who is overwhelmed by anxiety under even a minor stress.

DIAGNOSIS

There are no objective criteria for diagnosis of childhood psychosis. Although far less prevalent than schizophrenia of adolescence and adulthood, the severe functional disorders of childhood are equally perplexing.

One of the cardinal features of a psychotic child is his inability to experience a clear-cut perception of himself and his body. As a result of this deficiency, there are always marked deviations from age-related behavioral expectations. Functions related to thought, affect, perception, speech, motility, and object relationship are usually severely affected. Withdrawal from people, tendency to retreat into a world of fantasy, marked distortion of reality, bizarre and exaggerated emotional reactions to even a minor stress, stereotyped behavior patterns, and poorly developed speech are among the common symptoms. But controversy still exists over more specific characteristics: Which and how many signs and symptoms within these broad functional categories are necessary or sufficient to make a diagnosis? It is possible, nevertheless, to consider diagnosis as a process and intervention in itself, as actually the beginning of treatment. A clinical evaluation for the purpose of establishing a diagnosis of childhood psychosis should take into account a number of parameters: (1) the age of onset, (2) the typicality and severity of psychotic symptoms, (3) prenatal and postnatal sociomedical history, (4) the nature of intrafamilial relationships, (5) intelligence, and (6) prognosis.

A variety of conditions may stimulate the childhood psychosis. Children who come from very deprived homes that provide inadequate stimulation may manifest somewhat similar symptomatology, but their intellectual deficit and developmental retardation and perceptual problems are more reversible than the psychopathology of typically psychotic children.

Differential diagnosis between functional psychosis, brain dysfunction, and mental retardation are considered to be one of the most complicated. The confusion stems from the fact that details of early history are often unavailable or unreliable, and by the time they reach the clinicians, many children with these conditions exhibit similar bizarre, stereotyped behavior and severe communication problems, such as mutism and echolalia. Their overall intellectual functioning is often at a retarded level.

It is also important to differentiate primary functional childhood psychosis from emotional problems secondary to language deficits. Severely limited speech output, distortion of perception, and defects in body image and concept are common characteristics of both psychotic children and children with severe communicative disorders. However, in childhood psychosis, the psychopathology involves the total personality organization and the absence of communicative intent is more apparent. The failure of psychotic children to establish stable object relationships is reflected in their echolalic speech, but its mechanical, birdlike quality is markedly different from the echolalic utterances of children with severe communication disorders [4]. The latter may echo words with the intent and purpose of communication and clarification. Pitch and inflection are also usually normal. On the other hand, in psychotic children, sentence melody and pitch are inappropriate. According to Kanner [7], the utterances of autistic children, which seem to have no meaningful connection with the situation in which they are voiced, sometimes may be traced to earlier experiences of the child; but in general, language in psychotic children more often expresses primary process and is not in the service of ego and reality.

SPECIAL CATEGORIES OF CHILDHOOD PSYCHOSIS

Psychosis of Infancy and Early Childhood

Two syndromes of early infantile psychoses seem rather clearly distinguishable. One is early infantile autism and the other is symbiotic psychotic syndrome, or interactional psychotic disorder. These syndromes are related to each other and often overlap, and they have at least two basic features in common. One is alienation, or withdrawal from reality; the other is severe disturbance of the individual child's feelings of self-identity. If these two cardinal features are not present, the clinician should not designate the child's disturbance as psychotic. A third group of childhood psychosis is the more benign group in which autistic, symbiotic, and neurotic mechanisms are used simultaneously or alternately by the ego. For each of these major pictures of childhood psychosis it is possible to predict from early forms the diseased process that moves along developmental lines to severe pathology. Because distinctions among these categories remain blurred, prevalence rates vary widely (estimates range from 2 to 6 per 10,000 population), and disagreement among clinicians diagnosing the same child is common.

Kanner [7], who first described the syndrome of *early infantile autism* in 1943, recently suggested that it should be seen as a total psychobiological disorder and stressed the need for a comprehensive study of this dysfunction at each level of integration — biological, psychological, and social. From a sociological point of view, early infantile autism represents fixation at, or regression to, the first most primitive phase of extrauterine life which is described as the normal autistic phase. At this stage the self, even the bodily self, seems not to be distinguished from the inanimate objects of the environment. The mother, as the representative of the outside world, seems not to be perceived at all by the child. This inability to engage the surrounding world results in the inability to develop the necessary internal word in conjunction with the differentiation of ego functions. The autistic personality remains empty. Autism is a clinically and behaviorally defined specific syndrome that is manifested at birth or shortly thereafter and remains throughout the patient's life. These children's symptoms are expressive of underlying neuropathophysiologic process that affects developmental rate, sensorimotor integration, language, cognitive and intellectual development, and ability to relate. Their histories contain descriptions of earliest behavior which reveal that there was no anticipatory postulate to nursing, no reaching-out gestures, and no specific smiling response. The mothers describe their infants' behavior in the following ways: "I never could reach my baby." "He never smiled at me." "The minute she could walk, she ran away from me." The entire symptomatology and behavior patterns of the infantile autistic syndrome is developed around the fact that the autistic child is unable to utilize the auxiliary executive ego functions of the symbiotic partner—the mother— to orient himself in the outside or inner world. His cardinal symptoms and characteristic behavior patterns are the classical features described by Kanner [7]: (1) obsessive desire for the preservation of sameness, (2) a stereotyped preoccupation with few inanimate objects, (3) lack of tolerance of any change in his inanimate surroundings, (4) complete muteness or language that is not used for functional communication, and (5) behavior that seems as if the child has heard nothing. This lack of response is one of his most conspicuous symptoms and could be described as a hallucinatory denial of perception rather than real deafness. They may also exhibit autoaggressive activities such as head knocking, self-biting, or other self-hurting, mutilating activities which seem to help these children feel their bodies in order to attain a sense of identity. Stereotyped motor patterns, often bizarre or primitive in nature, are frequent. Intellectual development may be normal or advanced, or it may be restricted and uneven in areas. In any case, the lack of capacity to perceive reality correctly and to communicate through speech may render most intellectual functions ineffective. In order to establish the diagnosis it must be demonstrated that before age three the patient had specific disturbances in developmental rate, perceptions, relatedness, and language. Many but not all patients demonstrate typical motility disturbances.

Margaret Mahler's [8] concept of symbiotic psychosis syndrome, which is related to a critical period of ego development, and Bowlby's [3] studies on maternal deprivation and separation anxiety have helped to clarify the role of early mother-infant attachment in normal personality development and its deviations. The category of *interactional psychotic disorder* covers children with symbiotic psychosis, which represents fixation at, or regression to, a more differentiated stage of development than in autism. Here the child's primitive ego, unlike that of the autistic child, seems to have progressed in development to the symbiotic phase and frequently shows the beginning of differentiation in terms of separation-individuation. Many of these children seem to have developed reasonably adequately for the first year or two of life, with awareness of, or attachment to the mother figure appearing during the first year. Subsequently, the child may show unusual dependence upon the mother in the form of intensification and prolongation of the attachment, apparently failing to master successfully the step of separation and individuation. The clinical picture is dominated by agitated catatonialike temper tantrums and panic-stricken behavior. These frequent violent temper tantrums seem to be attempts to restore and to perpetuate the delusional omnipotent phase of the mother-infant fusion of the first year. The stereotyped speech productions show a predominance of hallucinatory talk with the introjected object. Clinical symptoms may and often do become manifest between the ages of two and five, with the peak in the fourth year. The onset occurs usually in relation to some real or fantasied threat to the mother-child relationship. In addition to childhood psychosis, an inability to deal with separation and individuation can also be clearly established in borderline conditions of childhood.

Psychoses of later childhood

Schizophreniform disorder. This reaction ordinarily is not seen until the age period between six and twelve or thirteen years. The onset may be gradual with neurotic symptoms appearing first, followed by marked and primitive denial and projection. In this form of childhood psychosis, severely impaired reality testing; thought disorders of primary nature; language systems in which there is often no clear separation between thought, act and impulse; constant returns to fusion states; and temporary but complete autistic withdrawals; low frustration tolerance; and hypochondriacal tendencies are prominent features. In these children, regression is ordinarily not as marked as in adults. True hallucinations are not commonly recognized until the later school period. Some children show sudden and wild outbursts of either aggressive or self-mutilating behavior, inappropriate mood swings, and suicidal threats and attempts. Paranoid thinking and other manifestations seen in adults may also occur. Although these childhood and adolescent disorders frequently resemble adult conditions, the prognosis for recovery from the initial episode is generally good. Many children with this picture exhibit a maturation lag or marked unevenness in motor or cognitive performance. Children in this category have been also frequently designated as having childhood schizophrenia. However, the term schizophreniform is preferred by the Committee on Child Psychiatry of the Group for the Advancement of Psychiatry [5]. School reports describe these children as being dependent and clinging with teachers, especially in early grades. Peer relations are often poor. By the third or fourth school year, they begin to withdraw into fantasy and exhibit inappropriate behavior. Some may have violent temper tantrums in school and disrupt classroom activities by making noises or laughing or talking to themselves. Despite their severe difficulties in school, however, these children usually retain some of their ability to relate to adults.

    Psychotic conditions of adolescents are much nearer those of adulthood and seem to permit classificatory systems resembling those used in the diagnosis of adults. These conditions include problems of hysterical psychosis, schizophrenia, paranoid states, catatonic states, severe psychoticlike psychopathology, psychotic acting-out, and the many borderline conditions of childhood and adolescence. Most of the current clinical studies describe a functionally psychotic adolescent as any individual who is destined to develop adult schizophrenia. His birth process is likely to have been disturbed, and as an infant, he may have shown neurological abnormalities and possibly some unusual stimulus responsivity. By several years of age, he probably was rather withdrawn and inattentive, and his feelings had begun to seem overly inhibited or poorly controlled. He was not likely to have been a serious behavior problem in school but may have been somewhat aggressive (or if a girl, inhibited) and guarded in his interaction with peers. In adolescence his difficulties with peers may have grown more severe. Until this sketchy picture of the preschizophrenic is more clearly and conclusively drawn, clinicians should make a determined effort to avoid prematurely labeling children who may manifest some of these characteristics.

MANAGEMENT

Although different workers in the field have described their special approaches in working with psychotic children, at the present there is no therapy which will cure the disordered thinking, which is the basic dysfunction of childhood psychosis. The treatment of functional psychosis of childhood remains as perplexing as its etiology. For the most part, the psychoactive drugs, so useful with adult patients, have failed to produce similar results with these children. In view of the difficulties described earlier, the prognosis in most cases must be guarded. Psychotic children usually are brought to psychotherapy by desperate parents as emergencies; the parents and frequently the children are driven by a sense of panic and hopelessness.

Psychiatrists are not in full agreement about treatment methods for childhood psychosis. Most of the workers tend to emphasize their special approaches, and the results achieved seem to be dictated more by the original degree of severity of illness than by the specifics of the therapeutic procedure employed. Various nonsomatic treatments are currently employed, including behavior therapy, psychotherapy, and psychoeducational therapy. Although supportive individual psychotherapy is widely utilized in the treatment of psychotic children, in the case of autistic children the problem of making nonthreatening and helpful contact is a particularly difficult one. Only certain selective cases can be treated in office practice. Therefore, psychotherapy itself is not often the dominant treatment method of choice. Residential and milieu therapy, group psychotherapy, behavior therapy, and behavior modification are all well-known modalities in the treatment of psychotic children.

REFERENCES

1   Bender, L. "The nature of childhood psychosis." In *Modern perspectives international psychiatry*, vol. 3, ed. J. G. Howells, pp. 649–678. Edinburgh: Oliver and Boyd, 1969.
2   Book, J. A. "Genetic aspects of schizophrenic psychoses." In *The etiology of schizophrenia*, ed. D. D. Jackson, pp. 346–372. New York: Basic Books, 1960.
3   Bowlby, J. *Attachment and loss*, vols. 1–2. New York: Basic Books, 1969–1973.
4   DeHirsch, K. "Language disturbances." In *Comprehensive textbook of psychiatry*, eds. A. M. Freedman and H. I. Kaplan, pp. 1376–1380. Baltimore: Williams and Wilkins, 1975.

5   Group for the Advancement of Psychiatry. *Psychopathological disorders in childhood*, vol. 6. New York: Group for the Advancement of Psychiatry, 1974.

6   Kallman, F. J. *Heredity in health and mental disorders*. New York: Norton, 1953.

7   Kanner, L. *Childhood psychosis, initial studies, and new insights*. Washington, D.C.: Winston, 1973.

8   Mahler, M. S. "The symbiosis theory of infantile psychosis." In *On human symbiosis and the vicissitudes of individuation*, vol. 1, pp. 32–65. New York: International Universities Press, 1968.

9   Slater, E. The monogenic theory of schizophrenia. *Acta Genet.* 8:50–56, 1958.

29

Psychiatric Disorders
of Adolescence

Ghislaine D. Godenne, M.D.

There seems to be no adequate classification for the disorders of childhood and adolescence. The second edition of the *Diagnostic and Statistical Manual of Mental Disorders* (DSM-II), published by the American Psychiatric Association (APA) is frequently of little use when one has to fit a specific adolescent emotional disorder within its nomenclature [1]. In 1974, to partially remedy the situation, the Group for the Advancement of Psychiatry (GAP) published *Proposed Classification of the Psychopathological Disorders in Childhood* [2]. Once more, unfortunately, adolescent disorders were not considered as separate and distinct entities. This lack of specific nomenclature for adolescent disturbances can be understood by the fact that adolescent psychiatry is a fairly new field in psychiatry. It is still in the process of fighting its way out of the gray zone between child and adult psychiatry and asserting its existence as a stage of development which requires a nosology of its own.

Be that as it may, this chapter follows, as closely as possible, the classification suggested by GAP [2], which includes the following major categories: (1) healthy responses, (2) reactive disorders, (3) developmental deviations, (4) psychoneurotic disorders, (5) personality disorders, (6) psychotic disorders, (7) psychophysiological disorders, (8) brain syndromes, (9) mental retardation, and (10) other disorders.

EVALUATION

Hereditary, biological, developmental, and environmental factors play a greater or lesser part in the etiology of all disturbances. It is therefore imperative that the interviewer obtain a careful and detailed history not only of the presenting symptom for which the adolescent is referred but also of the adolescent's early development, of the family in which he grew up, of the peer group he associated with, and of the particular social group he belongs to. It is only after such information is obtained that one is able not only to diagnose the present condition but also to formulate the psychodynamic aspects of the disorder. The following excerpts of Paula's history, obtained during her initial interview, will help to clarify what should be included in the psychiatric evaluation of an adolescent in order to make the correct diagnosis, to understand the disturbance and, finally, to be in a position to establish appropriate treatment plans.

Paula is a fifteen-year-old girl whom I first met as she was waiting outside my office with both her parents. She is an attractive girl, quite verbal and cooperative. She was wearing bluejeans, a sweat shirt, and a windbreaker. Her longish hair was somewhat disheveled. She was wearing no makeup. She told me that she was seeing me because she was doing poorly in school as she recently lacked any motivation to do any work. She has had many minor health problems this year which have kept her home, and she blames her absences from school on her disinterest in school work because "it's so hard to catch up once you missed several days." She had always made As and Bs but this year, in the tenth grade, she is making a C average.

I asked Paula with whom she lives. She said her mother and father. When I asked her if she had any siblings she answered, "a sister, three years older who is in her first year of college; a brother one year younger in the ninth grade; and two brothers, six and seven years old." Her father is an executive in an important industrial firm. Her mother is a housewife. She feels her parents have a happy marriage; her father is both the boss and the main disciplinarian. She does not feel that her parents are too strict. She is closer to her mother and feels her father doesn't like her as she was told that he wanted a boy as a second child and was disappointed when she was born. Her brother Peter, the fourteen-year-old sibling, does very well in school and is on the football team. Her father pays attention only to him.

When I asked Paula about friends, she said she used to have many friends, but she doesn't anymore. She said she doesn't care about that situation as she can amuse herself alone. She dated a boy earlier in the year but broke up with him. She has done some necking and petting but never had intercourse.

I asked Paula about her interests outside of school. She loves to play hockey and soccer and is on the school hockey team. She proudly added that her school has been undefeated this year. She loves to read and watch television. She likes to take long walks alone; she enjoys writing poetry. If need be she enjoys cooking. I heard then that her mother often goes out of town to visit her grandmother, and she is then in charge of the household. She enjoys fixing meals for the family, and when I inquired if her family liked her cooking she said, "Father never makes any comments about it, and my brother says it stinks."

I asked Paula if she ever left home for summer camp, and she said she did four years ago but was so homesick that she had to come back.

In the future Paula would like to be a banker. When I wondered where she got this idea, she said her father had mentioned that this was a good profession and advised her brother to go into that field.

I came back then to Paula's presenting problems. She told me that for the last two years she and her brother had been in the same junior high school. She was doing A-B work and her brother was a straight A student. Her parents reacted to her report cards by commenting on the Bs that should become As and gave her no credit for her As. This upset her as she did the best she could. She also told me that her sister was a very good student. She was very close to her and misses her this year, as she left for college. She feels her father only cares about her brother now, attends all his football games but never comes to one of her hockey games.

She explained that she works hard but takes so long to do any assignment that she often goes to school without having done all her homework. Her homework has to be perfect and she checks it over and over again before deciding if it is good enough to turn in. She is so frightened of what the teacher might say or do about her unfinished work that she can't sleep. Since this September she has not been feeling well and often at night develops bad stomach cramps and diarrhea which keeps her home for half a day.

After seeing Paula I saw her parents. Her father is a tall, well-built, handsome man in his early forties. Her mother is petite, attractive, and has bleached blond hair. Her father talked first, and when her mother talked he often stepped in to correct what she was saying.

I heard that Paula was not doing well in school and that the teachers said she was not working to her potential. Her sister had been valedictorian of her class and is now in college. Her brother makes straight As and is a born athlete. Paula is neither one. At home Paula is alternately very clinging to her mother, who cannot stand her dependence, or very rude and rebellious. Paula had dated a boy she met at Catholic Youth Organization dances; however, he stopped calling her after a few months. The parents wonder what happened.

The mother said that she was often out of town to visit her ailing mother, and Paula was given charge of the household. Father interjected that she did all right but would do crazy things like insist that they eat dinner by candlelight, especially when he was having dinner alone with her.

When I inquired about the past history, I was told that Paula was the product of a normal pregnancy. When she was born the family was disappointed to have a second girl. They had planned to have a boy and call him Paul, so they immediately tried again for a boy and Peter was born eleven months later. When Paula was two years old the parents separated for six months. The mother took Peter with her. The two girls remained with father and a housekeeper. When they returned together Paula could not stand her mother going out of the house, and she would put up a tremendous fuss when first taken to kindergarten. In school she always got above average grades and was well liked. Lately she has placed a great emphasis on excelling in sports, although she is not especially athletic and she has always been rather afraid of physical contact sports.

Last year the parents started noticing a change in their daughter. She became interested in boys and mother found much mention of boys in her diary. Paula was reprimanded for that and told she would not be allowed on dates for a while if she was that boy-crazy. At about the same time Paula had become quite rebellious at home, insisting, for example, that she be allowed an 11 P.M. curfew on weekends. However shortly after Paula's mother found and read her diary, Paula became more withdrawn and cries often at night. She has lost weight and her grades have fallen. Paula's parents have tried punishing her for her poor report cards by taking away her allowance, but nothing seems to touch her. Because of her physical complaints Paula saw Dr. X, her pediatrician, who advised her to see a psychiatrist. Mr. Z, however, does not believe in psychiatry. He feels that all Paula really needs is "a little will power."

Father comes from a very poor family. He made his way through college by excelling in football. He was an only child.

Mother was father's first secretary. She came from a family of low socioeconomic level and has a younger sister whom she feels was her parents' favorite and whom she still resents because of her special position in the family.

These vignettes from Paula's history show clearly that she is depressed and confused. What are the psychodynamics behind her present emotional distress? Her depression might come from her frustrated efforts to live up to her siblings' academic success. She is envious of them and tries to deny their existence by omitting mentioning them. It might also be a reaction to her sister's departure for college and a disappointment in her father, for whom she has strong oedipal feelings, but he seems to pay little attention to her. Her physical symptoms appear to be conversion symptoms masking her depression and her anxiety about school. Her rebelliousness and her interest in boys are phase specific.

In her early history, by learning that her parents were disappointed not to have had a boy when she was born, one can hypothesize that Paula tries very hard through engaging in masculine activities to be the boy they had wished for. The early separation from her mother might explain her separation anxiety. Finally her parents' history is significant: Father was a sports fan, so in order to please him she tries to excel in sports. Mother was envious of the attention her parents gave her sister and thus she might displace her resentment for her sister on to her daughter.

It is important to note that all symptoms are multidetermined, and through the patient's work in psychotherapy she will undoubtedly discover other determinants for her behavior.

Since the importance of a carefully obtained history has been demonstrated, it is appropriate to discuss the most frequent emotional disorders of adolescence or those which are relevant to the adolescent period.

HEALTHY RESPONSES

This category, which includes healthy responses to developmental crises and situational crises as well as other responses, is of utmost importance in the evaluation of an adolescent, since only too frequently the clinician is tempted to consider as pathological behavior which is characteristic of the adolescent period. Although the distinction between what is developmental and what is situational is often hard to make, internal forces predominate in developmental crises, whereas external events trigger situational crises. In order for a specific behavior to be labeled a healthy response, one has to take in consideration not only the past functioning of the adolescent but the amount of interference his behavior presents to his normal development.

In *developmental* crises one might include, for instance, behavior which can be understood in the light of the adolescent's search for an identity, his fight for independence, his need to test out his newly acquired skills, or his healthy move towards peer relationship concomitant with his relinquishment of an intense attachment to his parents.

A healthy response to a *situational* crisis might be best illustrated through a case history of a young man who was referred with the explicit instruction to consider him for immediate hospitalization.

Alex had an argument with his mother, locked himself in the bathroom, jumped out of the bathroom window, and, after being found wandering the streets by his father, was mute and unresponsive. When first seen, Alex was sullen and uncooperative until he was convinced that the therapist was not about to hospitalize him without getting a clear idea of the events that led to his referral. He then said that he indeed had an argument with his mother and had wanted to get away from her to "cool off." He had gone to his room where she followed him and had then retreated to the bathroom, the only room with a lock! His mother, fearing he might hurt himself, tore the bathroom door down with a hammer and Alex, reasonably frightened, had jumped out of the window. When his father found him he was in no mood to talk with his parents, so he remained mute. In the light of this history, confirmed later by the parents, it was clear that Alex's behavior was healthy. He wanted to retreat to his room, fearing his own aggression, but his mother insisted on pursuing their argument. He had found a safe refuge in the bathroom, but his mother's aggressive behavior aroused in him fears of body harm (including unconscious castration fears), and once more as a defense against both his and his mother's aggression, he fled through the window, the only exit still available to him. Alex (like so many adolescents) could not, at the height of his emotional turmoil, share with his parents his intense feelings. This explains why once found by his father he remained mute. Alex and his parents were by no means emotionally disturbed. Alex was struggling with his drives, his needs for independence, privacy, and so on, and since he was the oldest child in his family, his parents had difficulties understanding the behavior of their first adolescent and thus erred in its management. After two visits with Alex and his parents he was discharged with a clean bill of health.

The work of mourning, not only for the biological loss of a parent, a friend, or a pet but also for the psychological loss of a dear one, can also be seen as a situational crisis. It is important to allow children, adolescents, and adults alike to mourn their loved one by progressively decathecting every object or situation which reminds them of the lost person or pet. The decathexis, although a slow process, is limited in time, and the mourning becomes pathological only if it extends over many months or years. For example, a young adolescent patient, while in treatment, lost his dog. His parents in the face of his profound grief immediately purchased another dog. My patient, although appreciative of his parents' thoughtfulness, told the therapist, with tears in his eyes, "I wished they had waited before buying Rex. I can't love him now because I still miss Duke. Everything reminds me of Duke, and I don't want my new dog to use what still in my mind belongs to Duke."

REACTIVE DISORDERS

This category, to quote GAP, "should be used for those disorders in which the behavior and/or symptoms shown by the child are judged to be primarily a reaction to an event, a set of events, or a situation. Such disturbances must be considered to be of pathological degree, thus distinguishing them from situational crises in the category of healthy responses" [2:50]. Reactive disorders result from a conscious conflict between the adolescent's drives and feelings and his or her social environment. Adolescence is a time of intense feelings. Before acquiring the capability of internalizing their emotions, adolescents often express them in a variety of behavior disorders. For instance, an adolescent boy who is late maturing might, in order to compensate for the absence of his physical signs of masculinity, attempt to convince himself of his manhood by fighting, daring his parents or the police by antisocial exploits, and so forth.

> Joe, for instance, although fourteen, has not as yet reached puberty. His classmates are all taller than he is and tease him by nicknaming him "the dwarf." To assert himself among his peers he smokes in the school and gets himself suspended. He later is dared into placing a firecracker in the principal's letter box. He is caught and expelled from school. Later he is accused of shop-lifting and referred for help. When interviewed he readily admits that his behavior is unacceptable but says, "They would call me chicken if I did not do it. I was with five of my friends. We decided to see if each of us could steal $3 worth of things from the 5 & 10¢ store. I managed without getting caught to take $8 worth. I had made it. They no longer called me 'the

dwarf,' but when my parents found the stolen goods, they had me return them to the store and sent me here to see you."

Some adolescents when placed in a class far above their intellectual capacity respond to their continual frustration by dropping out of school, clowning, withdrawing from their peers, and so forth. A young girl, upset by her mother's constant state of inebriety, started stealing from her home as a revenge. Another adolescent girl in order to defend herself against her stepfather's sexual advances frequently ran away from home.

It should be clear that once the situation to which the adolescent is reacting is remedied or accepted, the reactive disorder, commonly called adolescent situational reaction, with time, will disappear.

DEVELOPMENTAL DEVIATIONS

This category refers to behavior which is anachronistic to the adolescent period. It includes deviations in maturational patterns and deviations in specific dimensions of development.

When the disturbance is the result of a *deviation in maturational patterns* the adolescent displays childlike behavior. This may be due to *regression*, in which a type of behavior appropriate to an earlier phase of development reappears. It can be the consequence of a *fixation*, in which a specific type of behavior has persisted since childhood. Bed-wetting, which persists after five years of age, might be the result of a fixation. Reappearance of destructiveness, thumb sucking, and bed-wetting can be signs of regressive behaviors. Fixations to the oral or anal phase of development may be the result of deprivation or overindulgence during those periods, faulty child-mother relationships, or severe psychological stress in the family during that period. Regression, which incidentally can be adaptive in that it walls off dangerous impulses, occurs when an adolescent is faced with a stressful situation for which he is ill prepared. He regresses then to a period of his life which he had learned to master. For instance, a fourteen-year-old boy after losing his leg in a car accident could not fall asleep without his mother reading him a bedtime story.

Deviations in specific dimensions of development can be categorized as deviations in motor development, sensory development, speech development, cognitive functions, social development, psychosexual development, affective development, and finally integrative development.

It is important before making the diagnosis of developmental deviation to establish clearly the fact that the adolescent is not mentally retarded or brain damaged, both conditions having a nomenclature of their own.

However, one could entertain the diagnosis of deviation in a specific dimension of development, for example, in a thirteen-year-old girl who still frequently uses baby talk or sucks her thumb, or a high school senior who prefers playing after school with his younger neighbors rather than participating in peer group activities or who has no interest in reading books discussed in his English class but devours comics, a late adolescent who is still so poorly coordinated that he shys away from competitive sports, or one who still prefers to be driven places than to drive himself.

PSYCHONEUROTIC DISORDERS

Psychoneurotic disorders originate from unconscious conflicts between the drives (the id) and the ego. It seems relevant to mention special forms which these disorders frequently take in adolescence.

Even though the very essence of adolescence is fertile ground for a *psychoneurotic disorder of anxiety or depressive type* to occur, both affects (depression and anxiety) are intolerable for the adolescent. In order to avoid experiencing them the teenager frequently acts them out; consequently one has to guard against misdiagnosing him or her as having a behavior disorder. Depressive or anxiety equivalents can cover a wide variety of behavior, such as use of drugs and alcohol, promiscuous behavior, frantic search for new activities, delinquency, defiance, aggression, and running away. At times it is through the use of psychosomatic symptoms, excessive fatigue, obsessive-compulsive behavior, maniclike states, regression, or even depersonalization that the adolescent attempts to cover up his feelings. It is through a keen awareness of the frequent use of depressive or anxiety equivalents in adolescence that the psychotherapist will not only avoid making an erroneous diagnosis but will be guided in his treatment strategies. When the acting-out behavior is seen as a defensive maneuver against experiencing depressive or anxious feelings, it should be dealt with accordingly. One should remember, for instance, that one does not attempt to uncover what is behind a defense before some preliminary psychiatric work has been done in order for the patient to be ready and able to look at what he or she is defending against. A thirteen-year-old boy seen in consultation had stolen from the foster home he had just left various items which belonged to his foster parents and foster siblings. When discovered, he first vehemently stated that they were given to him as farewell presents "because they love me." Later he tearfully admitted that he took them "to make myself believe they love me."

As in adult patients, suicidal threats should be taken seriously. Suicidal gestures are often the adolescent's final attempt to be heard. Many depressed adolescents are seen who have asked for help only to be told

"You will grow out of it." Only when their parents are faced with an aborted suicide do they receive the attention they so badly needed. Wrist or arm slashing is not uncommon especially in depressed and/or masochistic adolescent girls. "I had to feel pain, to feel alive."

Phobic reaction is another psychoneurotic disorder, and in adolescence it most frequently takes the form of school phobia, which should not be confused with separation anxiety. The latter usually occurs in adolescents who have an early history of separation anxiety that manifested upon first starting school. Often through a carefully obtained history one learns that it is not only going to school that is dreaded but leaving home for any reason. School phobia, on the other hand, is, properly speaking, a phobic reaction to some unconscious threat inherent in going to school. In both cases it is rarely useful to allow the teenager to be tutored at home, as not only does it prolong the symptom by not dealing with its dynamics, but, to use an analogy, it is difficult to teach someone how to swim out of water!

The conversion type of psychoneurotic disorder differs little from what is seen in children or adults. A clue to differentiating between a conversion reaction and an organic illness lies in the patient's reaction to being referred to a psychiatrist. When a patient deals with an unconscious conflict through the defensive use of a conversion reaction, he will resist the idea that his problem might be psychosomatic and instead clings tenaciously to his defense mechanism by insisting that his symptoms are organic. On the other hand, if the patient is immediately amenable to the idea that his difficulties are of emotional origin, more likely than not he suffers from some organic illness.

Conversion reactions are not only defensive but provide to their sufferers secondary gains which increase their resistance to abandoning them. A patient with a conversion type of leg paralysis, for instance, enjoyed the fact that her entire family was at her beck and call. To abandon her symptom was once more to "just be one of the seven children."

One patient had spent six months in two prestigious pediatric departments in order to diagnose his recurrent "pseudo stupors." As his extensive workup failed to show any organic pathology it was finally felt that his disorder might be functional. Not only the patient but his parents tried frantically to convince the therapist that his problems were not emotional even though the pediatrician had clearly stated that the workup for organicity was negative. Psychotherapy was thus met with great resistance. Finally, however, after a rather clear homosexual dream it became clear to the patient and to the therapist that his stupors were primarily a defense to ward off threatening impulses. Soon after this newly acquired insight he was relieved of his symptom.

The *obsessive-compulsive* type of psychoneurotic disorder serves frequently in adolescence as a last defense against psychosis. This does not mean, however, that clearly limited rituals such as counting, touching, and hand washing are ominous signs of more severe emotional illness. Although the adolescent sees them as unreasonable, their interference provokes great anxiety. It is when the obsessive-compulsive behavior is such that it interferes with the adolescent's daily life that one should consider it as masking a severe emotional disturbance. One patient had obsessive thoughts which involved a fantasy of having smeared feces on pictures of Jesus. To avoid his sacrilegious fantasies he had to pray constantly in order to keep those thoughts out of his mind. His strenuous and compulsive physical exercises, along with his constricted dietary habit, served as an atonement for his guilt. He was hospitalized when his obsessive-compulsive behavior became so crippling that he could not function at home or in school. Soon after his admission to the hospital he became clearly psychotic.

PERSONALITY DISORDERS

"These disorders are characterized by chronic or fixed pathological trends, representing traits which have become ingrained in the personality structure," according to GAP [2:65]. In psychoneurosis the symptoms are unacceptable to the ego, (ego dystonic), and the patient seeks psychiatric help because he hurts. In personality disorders the behavior is not alien to the ego but is egosyntonic, and psychiatric help is sought, not because the patient suffers intrapsychically, but because of difficulties in interpersonal relationships. Although personality disorders undoubtedly exist in children and adolescents, one has to keep in mind that their personalities are in a state of flux and thus the fixity characteristic of adult personality disorders might not be as relevant in adolescence.

Adolescents with a *compulsive personality* "show chronic and excessive concern with orderliness, cleanliness, and conformity" [2:68]. This disorder has its origin in the anal phase and is considered a reaction formation against the enjoyment of being dirty, of smearing feces, and the like. These adolescents are rarely referred to psychiatrists because their personality disorder is often most appreciated by parents and teachers. Many mothers, when they observe the utter chaos of their children's bedrooms, would enjoy having teenagers who fall into this group. In school these adolescents usually perform well academically and are reliable. It is in peer relationships that they have trouble because of their rigidity, lack of spontaneity, inability to "let loose," and so forth. In general they are thrown off balance when they encounter unexpected situations.

Hysterical personalities were, in the past, almost exclusively seen in girls but are now present in both sexes. They are characterized by exaggerated, dramatic, affective, suggestible, and labile behavior. Hysterical adolescents are often seductive and manipulative, and their behavior is flamboyant. Socially such adolescents appear well adjusted; however, they are overly dependent on the environment for ego supplies and a sense of identity. Seductive behavior has the quality of "a tease." The teenager, although seemingly comfortable in heterosexual relations, becomes suddenly disinterested and frigid when the sexual act appears imminent.

The *anxious personality* depicts an adolescent who perceives any new situation as threatening. In such disorders the adolescent conjures up catastrophies that might possibly occur. Anxiety thus interferes with enjoyment of planned ventures.

The *overly dependent personality* describes an adolescent who requires constant help and support in order to function adequately. The disorder is often the result of overly protective parents who have not allowed their growing child any initiative and have denied them any responsibility by constantly hovering over them.

The *oppositional personality* is a new name for an old disorder, previously known as the passive-aggressive personality. The adolescent with this type of personality disorder is prone to engender much anger in those around him. Although overtly he does nothing wrong, his behavior, in its negativism, is most frustrating. Sally, an eleven-year-old girl, would go for months without talking to her foster mother aside from greeting her in the morning and wishing her a good night as she was about to retire. All attempts by her foster mother to get her to talk were met with complete silence. Sally enjoyed the frustration she provoked and the fact that she could not be punished because, "I did nothing bad." Her behavior is reminiscent of the struggle parent and child occasionally get caught in during the toilet training period. An adult patient recalled that in her childhood she had several fecal impactions due to her constant refusal to go to the toilet when her mother placed her on the "potty." As she grew older she always did her own thing, her own way. She would pay "lip service" to her husband's request. When angry with the therapist she would "forget appointments" or misplace her checkbook when her bill was due. On the other hand, she was always pleasant, and her behavior was never overtly aggressive. Stubbornness is a feature of this disorder.

The *overly inhibited personality* describes adolescents who shy away from contacts with people, be it their peers, adults, or children. They are often also severely restricted in their motor action and initiative. Their behavior appears as a reaction formation against their aggressive and sexual drives. They fear losing control if they allow their drives free reign.

Saul, a sixteen-year-old boy, was referred when his excessive shyness became of concern to his mother. The incident, which precipitated his referral, was the following: Saul wanted a summer part-time job, but in order to get it had to obtain a reference. After many weeks of procrastination he called his swimming instructor to ask him for a recommendation. As soon as his instructor answered the phone, he burst into tears and ran to his mother saying, "Ask him, I can't." Saul had no friends in school because he shied away from any contacts with his peers. However, he functioned well academically, and in solo activities he performed adequately. When, after a few months of psychotherapy, he became more socially aggressive and engaged in activities with his peers, his mother called to complain that she had lost her "sweet little boy." Previously having washed his clothes once a week because he "never messed them up," she now had to launder them daily. As soon as he ended high school he left home and chose a vocation in which he could, in a socially acceptable way, sublimate his aggression.

In marked contrast to the above disorder, one encounters adolescents belonging to the *overly independent personality* category. These adolescents think and act in a pseudoadult way. They are active, full of initiative, appear independent, and resent limits set by adults. However, at heart, they are still children longing to be taken care of and nurtured. Judy sought help after, to her mother's utter surprise, she confided in her that she felt like killing herself. She had always been an active, independent adolescent who had many friends and was well liked by teachers. Her mother stated that she had always been very independent and seemingly not in need of her parents' support. Judy, however, felt cheated and excluded from her family. She felt that all her parents' attention was focused on her two older siblings who did better than she academically and were leaders in their respective schools. Although she resented her parents' interference in her activities, she longed for it. Her pseudoindependence was achieved in order to act like her older siblings, whom she felt had gained full parental approval.

The *isolated personality* can be distinguished from the inhibited personality in that its serious limitations are not confined to the expression of feelings but extend to the very experience of emotions. When interviewed, these teenagers display a fairly flat affect and relate to the interviewer with a great deal of reserve as a result not only of shyness but mainly of "uninvolvement." They are withdrawn and appear detached from their environment. Their behavior is usually unobtrusive and compliant; however they occasionally show outbursts of aggression seemingly unrelated to external stimuli. In the past isolated personalities were included under the terminology of schizoid personality. However, they do not necessarily represent latent schizophrenia.

Mistrustful personality is a diagnosis given to adolescents who are overly suspicious of others, are rigid in their thinking, and make extensive use of projection. They rarely progress to an actual paranoid state. It seems appropriate in this context to advise against the frequent misuse of the term paranoid. If an adolescent feels, for instance, that no one likes him, the feeling might be due to his low self-esteem or his general feeling of depression. It is only when he admits to a feeling that people are out to get him that one can talk of mistrust or paranoia. For example, an adolescent patient was convinced that the therapist shared with his parents the content of his sessions despite efforts to reassure him of their confidentiality, or a teenage girl had to check the tape recorder before a session to make sure that it was not turned on before she entered the office. Frequently, in the past, these adolescents have been deceived by parents, educators, or friends and thus "transfer" their suspicion onto the therapist.

In *tension discharge* disorders, the GAP nomenclature includes such disorders as "antisocial personality, psychopathic personality, impulsive character, sociopathic personality, dyssocial personality, affectionless character, acting out personality, neurotic character disorder, primary behavior disorder, neurotic behavior disorder and conduct disorder" [2:73]. Basically all such disorders refer to adolescents who exhibit chronic ego-syntonic behavioral patterns of emotional expression. These patterns which, although acceptable to their ego, are unacceptable to society at large. These behaviors are maladaptive or even destructive and are usually in response to intrapsychic or external stress. Chronic running away from home or recurrent destructive behavior would fall in this category. In the former, the disorder is a form of repetitive avoidance and, in the latter, a misuse of aggression. Antisocial behavior performed alone is prognostically less favorable than group delinquent behavior, which might be viewed as a means to an end, i.e., an attempt to be accepted by one's peers to "belong" in the gang.

GAP breaks these tension discharge disorders into two subgroups: impulse ridden personality and neurotic personality disorders. They both have in common a tendency to "discharge rather than to delay or to inhibit, impulses unacceptable to the larger society" [2:75]. The neurotic group includes adolescents who have reached a higher level of personality development than those of the impulse ridden group and whose repetitive behavior has an unconscious symbolic significance rather than a predominant need for impulse discharge. Joel, a fourteen-year-old boy, illustrates a neurotic personality disorder. When his older sister turned sixteen and got her driver's license, he felt more convinced than ever before that he was inferior to her. He had an urge to "prove himself" by driving for a period of about four months an average of two or three stolen cars a week. Ralph, on the other hand, suffers from an impulse ridden personality. As soon as he is frustrated or angry he disappears from home. He has been turned over to juvenile authorities for breaking and entering and stealing property.

It is obvious that without a careful evaluation the distinction between both subgroups is hard to ascertain. What is immediately apparent in interviewing adolescents with tension discharge disorders is that they are unable to explain their actions and feel little guilt over their antisocial behavior. They might state that they feel badly because they were caught, but the guilt resulting from superego disapproval is absent. Most adolescents in this group have a history of early extreme deprivation and to quote an adolescent boy, "I have had a rotten life, now I'm getting my revenge." Adolescents who have been transferred from one foster home to another since their early childhood often belong in this classification of personality disorders. They seem "affectionless," as they do not allow themselves to form meaningful relationships. In order to avoid the pain of losing, once more, the object of their attachment, they remain distant and aloof.

As earlier stated, one should be careful not to confuse the antisocial behavior used as a defense against depression or anxiety with this type of personality disorder.

In the *sociosyntonic personality* disorder the adolescent's behavior, although considered deviant in the society at large, is acceptable in the adolescent's milieu. For instance in the ghetto population physical aggression is almost a way of life, a means of survival. Promiscuity and pregnancy in unwed mothers is more acceptable in some societal groups than in others.

Finally *sexual deviation,* although included in the classification of personality disorders, should be used with considerable discretion to characterize adolescent psychopathology. Fleeting homosexual behavior or other sporadic sexually deviant behaviors are not sufficient evidence for a diagnosis of sexual deviation. The adolescent, through his teens, before he has achieved a sexual identity, experiments with a variety of behaviors in order to discharge his sexual drives. It is only when his behavior has become ego syntonic and fixed that one should label him a sexual deviant.

It seems in order at this point to briefly comment on masochism or sadism, exhibitionism or voyeurism, which only become perversions after the establishment of the genital primacy. They are called component or partial instincts and, through satisfying them, the child experiences sexual satisfaction. For instance, a little boy might respond with sexual excitation to his pulling off the wings of flies. However, once the genital primacy is established, these instincts should only play a secondary role in obtaining genital satisfaction. They are signs of perversion if they are sought independently. To look and to be seen, to act aggressively and to endure passively, are part of the sexual act which culminates in intercourse. It is when the Peeping Tom obtains full sexual satisfaction by looking that his action is considered perverse.

It seems appropriate to mention here the *borderline personality* structure, although it is not included in the GAP nomenclature. Borderline adolescents characteristically show a maturational lag. They are narcissistically orally fixated; they use maladaptive defenses (such as splitting, denial, projection, acting-out); they form poor object relationships and almost always, diagnostically, have a history of oral deprivation and fixation. Some authors place borderline disorders on the boundary between neurotic disorders and psychotic disorders. Others consider that they fall in the category of personality disorders.

PSYCHOTIC DISORDERS

It should not be surprising that the adolescent's ego, struggling to control the drives and engaged in improving its functions and in dealing with issues such as identity and independence, might break down when faced with an additional burden. This explains why psychotic episodes are not uncommon in adolescence and belong mainly to the two following groups:

1   *Acute confusional states* are transient mental disorders too often confused with schizophrenia. They characteristically have an abrupt onset and occur in adolescents whose premorbid personalities were unremarkable. Although the disorder often shows the gamut of schizophrenic symptoms, the psychotic adolescent in this group usually maintains a capacity for meaningful relationships. The prognosis is usually regarded as good.

2   *Schizophrenia* in adolescence resembles adult schizophrenia and thus will not be discussed in this chapter. It is important, however, to keep in mind that normal adolescents can often display schizophrenic features which are evident through psychological testing. Adults who show test results similar to those obtained in adolescents are highly suspect of schizophrenia.

PSYCHOPHYSIOLOGICAL DISORDERS

Psychophysiological disorders "refers to those disorders in which there is a significant interaction between somatic and psychological components, with varying degrees of weighing of each component" [2:86]. A variety of organ systems may participate in psychophysiological disorders, such as the skin, the musculoskeletal system, the respiratory and cardiovascular system, the hemic and lymphatic system, the gastrointestinal and genitourinary system, the endocrine and nervous system, and finally the organs of sense. In adolescence the systems most frequently involved include the skin, which may be afflicted with eczema, psoriasis, alopecia, acne, and other conditions. It is of note that adolescents are especially sensitive about skin disorders, not only because of the great cathexis they place on their body image but because skin disorders are hard to conceal. Some adolescents, for instance, withdraw completely from their peers because of facial acne. Respiratory disorders such as asthma, musculoskeletal disorders such as tension headaches or other types of myalgia, genitourinary disorders such as polyuria, dysuria, or — in females — dysmenorrhea, amenorrhea, and premenstrual tension are not uncommon systemic disorders in this age group. Among the nervous system disorders, idiopathic epilepsy, narcolepsy, sleep disturbances, dizziness, and certain types of hyperactivity are worth mentioning.

Finally among the gastrointestinal psychophysiological disorders which are occasionally seen in the practice of adolescent medicine, one might list peptic ulcer, gastritis, ulcerative colitis, mucous colitis, spastic colon, regional enteritis, heartburn or gastric hyperactivity, constipation, diarrhea, and recurrent vomiting. Obesity of reactive origin is by far the most common symptom in this group.

Lately anorexia nervosa has become a fashionable disease and is predominantly seen in adolescent girls from the upper socioeconomic strata. Although many diagnostic formulations have been suggested to explain this crippling and life-threatening syndrome, it appears that the core of the disorder stems from a faulty parent (mainly mother)-child relationship. By refusing themselves all nourishment despite hunger, anorexia nervosa patients gain a feeling of great mastery and superiority over their surroundings. Depression, withdrawal, delusions about body image and body functions, and regression are all part of the anorectic syndrome. Frequently overeating sprees or marked bulimic episodes are interspersed with the starvation periods. The erratic food intake, the frequent use of induced vomiting, the excessive consumption of laxatives, all contribute to disturbance in body electrolytes with its resulting side effects.

BRAIN SYNDROMES

Brain syndromes, acute or chronic, differ little from what one sees in children or adults. However the minimal brain-damaged adolescent is often ostracized by his peers because of his "oddities" and as a result withdraws into himself and feels lonely and depressed. Diagnostically, an adolescent who states he has no friends but starves for meaningful friendships should be highly suspect of suffering from a chronic brain syndrome. The schizophrenic adolescent differs by being friendless but wishes to remain so. The depressed adolescent admits that once he had friends but has lost them all.

MENTAL RETARDATION

Mental retardation poses an unusual array of problems in adolescence. As with his normal counterpart, the retarded adolescent's drives increase at puberty; however, his ego, unlike the ego of the normal adolescent, is limited in its functions and thus is less capable of keeping his drives in check. The retarded adolescent wants also to belong to a peer group but often, if only mildly retarded, he lives among normal teenagers who ridicule him and force him to withdraw into himself. He too has dreams for the future, but as they are often unrealistic he constantly faces defeat.

It should be clear that only in rare instances can one diagnostically fit a troubled adolescent into a single category of the preceding nomenclature. More often than not one will encounter patients who fall into several categories and for whom multiple diagnoses are required with the predominant pattern given primary listing. For instance, asthma might occur in an overly dependent adolescent or an impulsive behavior disorder in a mentally retarded teenager. In order to further clarify the diagnosis it is important to state if the disease is acute or chronic; if it is severe, moderate, or mild; and, finally, to specify the manifest nature of individual symptoms. For this purpose a very comprehensive symptom list has been drawn up by the GAP [2:98–120]. The symptoms are divided into eight main categories, each of which contain subcategories that are, in turn, further broken down. The grouping is made along the lines of symptoms as follows:

1   Related to bodily functions — eating, sleeping, bowel function, bladder function, speech, motoric patterns, rhythmic patterns, habit patterns, sensory disturbances, and finally other disturbances
2   Related to cognitive functions — precocity, learning failure, disturbance in thinking, disturbance in memory, disturbance in awareness, and others

3 Related to affective behavior disturbances — manifestly fearful behavior, manifest anxiety, depressive symptoms, euphoric behavior, hypochondriacal behavior, and other affective states
4 Related to disturbances in development — physical growth, maturational patterns
5 Related to disturbances in social behavior — aggressive behavior, antisocial behavior, oppositional behavior, isolating behavior, problem of dominance-submission, problem of dependence-independence, problem in sexual adjustment
6 Related to disturbances in integrative behavior — impulsive behavior, incapacity to play, low anxiety tolerance, low frustration tolerance, overuse of adaptative mechanisms, disorganized behavior, folie à deux, other disturbances
7 Related to other behavioral disturbances — such as stereotyped behavior, tantrum behavior, hallucinations, delusions, malingering behavior, and finally addictive behavior
8 Related to other disturbances not elsewhere listed

Using the above nomenclature, and the history obtained so far, a provisional diagnosis can be formulated for the initial case history of Paula: developmental crisis and reactive disorder in an adolescent with compulsive personality. Psychoneurotic depression, separation anxiety, conversion reaction (gastrointestinal type) are present; all symptoms are chronic and moderate.

REFERENCES

1 American Psychiatric Association. *Diagnostic and statistical manual*-II. Washington, D.C.: APA, 1968.
2 Group for the Advancement of Psychiatry. *Psychopathological disorders in childhood: Theoretical considerations and a proposed classification.* New York: Jason Aronson, 1974.

RECOMMENDED READINGS

• Bruch, H. "The enigma of anorexia nervosa." In *The Golden Cage.* Cambridge: Harvard University Press, 1978.
• Crow, A., and Crow, L. D. *Adolescent development and adjustment.* New York: McGraw-Hill, 1956.
• Federn, P. *Ego psychology and the psychosis.* New York: Basic Books, 1952.
• Godenne, G. D. Adolescent crises today. *Clin. Proc. Children's Hosp.* 26(10):317–322, 1970.

- Godenne, G. D. "Sex and today's youth." In *Adolescence*. 9(33):67–72, 1974.
- Godenne, G. D. Outpatient management of the borderline adolescent. Paper presented at Eastern Seaboard Conference, American Society for Adolescent Psychiatry, Washington, D.C., 1976.
- Godenne, G. D. "Depressive and schizophrenic reactions in adolescence." *Medical care of the adolescent*, 3rd ed., eds. J. R. Gallagher, F. P. Heald, and D. C. Garell, pp. 231–240. New York: Appleton-Century-Crofts, 1976.
- Godenne, G. D. "Unwed mothers." *International Encyclopedia of Psychiatry, Psychology, Psychoanalysis and Neurology*, vol. II, ed. B. B. Wolman, pp. 344–347. Boston: Van Nostrum, Reinhold, Aesculapius, 1977.
- Goldman, A. E. A comparative-developmental approach to schizophrenia. *Psychol. Bull.* 59:57–69, 1962.
- Josselyn, I. M. *Adolescence*. New York: Harper and Row, 1971.
- Kanner, L. *Child psychiatry*, 2nd ed. Springfield, Ill.: Thomas, 1955.
- Masterson, J. The borderline adolescent. *Adolesc. Psychiatry* 2:240–268, 1973.
- Sandler, J., Joffee, W. G. Notes on childhood depression, *Internat. J. Psychoanal.* 46:88–96, 1965.
- Toolan, J. M. "Depression in adolescence." In *Modern Perspectives in Adolescent Psychiatry*, vol. 4, ed. J. G. Howells, pp. 358–380. New York: Brunner/Mazel, 1971.
- Van Krevelen, D. A. Psychosis in adolescence. *Mod. Perspect. Adolesc. Psychiatry* 4:381–403, 1971.
- Wolman, B. B., ed. *Manual of child Psychopathology*. New York: McGraw-Hill, 1972.

Index